BRIAN MI

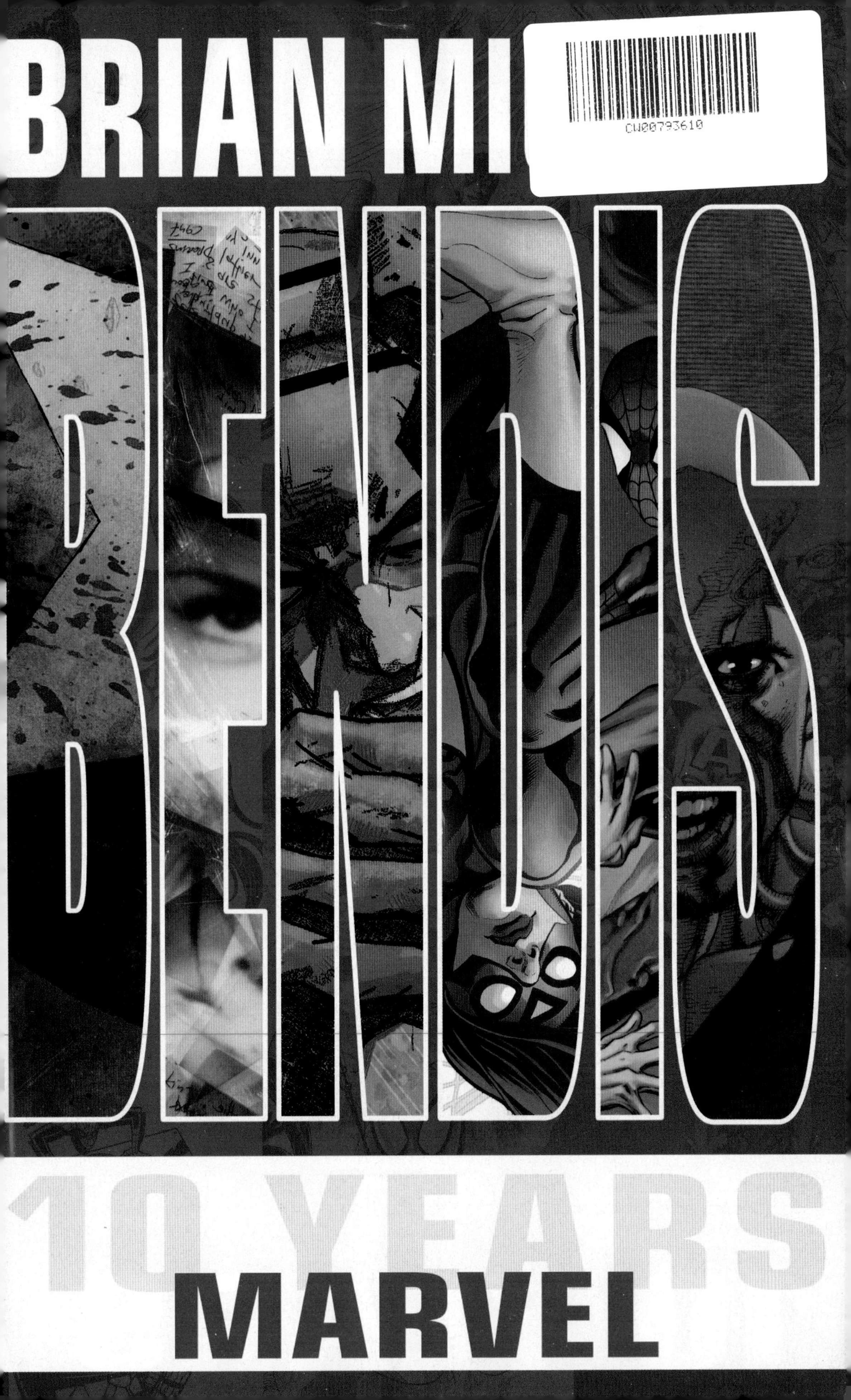
BENDIS

10 YEARS

MARVEL

BRIAN

BEN

Writer
BRIAN MICHAEL BENDIS

ULTIMATE SPIDER-MAN #13
Penciler: **Mark Bagley**
Inker: **Art Thibert**
Colorist: **Transparency Digital**
Letterers: **RS & Comicraft**
Cover Art: **Mark Bagley**
Assistant Editor: **Brian Smith**
Editor: **Ralph Macchio**

NEW AVENGERS #22
Artist: **Leinil Yu**
Colorist: **Dave McCaig**
Letterers: **RS & Comicraft's
Albert Deschesne**
Cover Art: **Leinil Yu**
Assistant Editors: **Molly Lazer &
Aubrey Sitterson**
Editor: **Tom Brevoort**

ALIAS #10
Artist: **Michael Gaydos**
Letterers: **RS & Comicraft**
Cover Art: **David Mack**
Assistant Editor: **Nick Lowe**
Editors: **Stuart Moore & Joe Quesada**
Associate Managing Editor: **Kelly Lamy**
Managing Editor: **Nanci Dakesian**

ULTIMATE SPIDER-MAN ANNUAL #1
Penciler: **Mark Brooks**
Inker: **Jaime Mendoza**
Additional Finishes: **Scott Hanna**
Colorist: **Dave Stewart**
Letterer: **Chris Eliopoulos**
Cover Art: **Mark Brooks &
Richard Isanove**
Assistant Editors: **John Barber &
Nicole Boose**
Editor: **Ralph Macchio**

CIVIL WAR: THE CONFESSION
Artist: **Alex Maleev**
Color Artist (Pages 14-22): **Jose Villarrubia**
Letterer: **Chris Eliopoulos**
Cover Art: **Alex Maleev**
3-D Iron Man Design: **Josh Singh**
Assistant Editors: **Molly Lazer &
Aubrey Sitterson**
Editor: **Tom Brevoort**

ULTIMATE SPIDER-MAN SUPER SPECIAL
Art:
Spider-Man: **Alex Maleev**
Blade: **Dan Brereton**
Peter & Mary Jane: **John Romita Sr.
& Al Milgrom**
Elektra: **Frank Cho**

Peter & Mary Jane: **Jim Mahfood**
Daredevil: **Scott Morse**
At School: **Craig Thompson**
Captain America: **Michael Avon Oeming**
Fantastic Four: **Jason Pearson**
Human Torch: **Sean Phillips**
At School: **Mark Bagley
& Rodney Ramos**
Ultimates: **Bill Sienkiewicz**
Doctor Strange: **P. Craig Russell**
Iron Man: **Jacen Burrows
& Walden Wong**
Black Widow & S.H.I.E.L.D.:
Leonard Kirk & Terry Pallot
Fantastic Four: **Dave Gibbons**
X-Men: **Michael Gaydos**
Mutants: **James Kochalka**
Wolverine: **David Mack**
Daredevil & Punisher:
Brett Weldele
Elektra: **Ashley Wood**
Conclusion: **Mark Bagley & Art Thibert**
Colorists: **Transparency Digital &
Digital Chameleon**
Letterer: **Chris Eliopoulos**
Cover Art: **Michael Golden**
Associate Editors: **Brian Smith
& C.B. Cebulski**
Editor: **Ralph Macchio**

10 YEARS

ICHAEL

DIS

ULTIMATE X-MEN #41
Penciler: **David Finch**
Inker: **Art Thibert**
Colorist: **Frank D'Armata**
Letterer: **Chris Eliopoulos**
Assistant Editors: **MacKenzie Cadenhead & Nick Lowe**
Associate Editor: **C.B. Cebulski**
Editor: **Ralph Macchio**

"WHERE IS STAN THE MAN WHEN YOU NEED HIM?"
(From Stan Lee Meets Doctor Strange)
Penciler: **Mark Bagley**
Inker: **Drew Hennessy**
Colorist: **Studio F**
Letterer: **Dave Lanphear**
Cover Art: **Alan Davis**

DAREDEVIL #65
Art:
Michael Golden (pg. 2-6)
Greg Horn (pg. 7-12)
P. Craig Russell (pg. 13-17)
Phil Hester & Ande Parks (pg. 18-26)
Chris Bachalo & Tim Townsend (pg. 27-33)
Jae Lee (pg. 34)
David Finch (pg. 35)
Frank Quitely (pg. 36)
Alex Maleev (pg. 37-38)
Colorists:
Justin Ponsor with
Greg Horn (pg. 7-12)
Chris Bachalo (pg. 27-33)
June Chung (pg. 34)
Frank D'Armata (pg. 35)
Letterer: **Virtual Calligraphy's Randy Gentile**
Cover Art: **Greg Land & Matt Ryan**
Special thanks to **Jamie Grant**
Assistant Editor: **Cory Sedlmeier**
Editor: **Jennifer Lee**
Executive Editor: **Axel Alonso**

NEW AVENGERS #15
Artist: **Frank Cho**
Colorist: **Jason Keith**
Letterers: **RS & Comicraft's Albert Deschesne**
Cover Art: **Frank Cho**
Assistant Editors: **Molly Lazer & Aubrey Sitterson**
Associate Editor: **Andy Schmidt**
Editor: **Tom Brevoort**

ULTIMATE MARVEL TEAM-UP #9
Artist: **Jim Mahfood**
Letterer: **Dave Sharpe**
Colorist: **Transparency Digital**
Associate Editor: **Brian Smith**
Editor: **Ralph Macchio**

DARK AVENGERS #9
Artist: **Mike Deodato**
Colorist: **Rain Beredo**
Letterer: **Virtual Calligraphy's Cory Petit**
Cover Art: **Mike Deodato**
Associate Editor: **Lauren Sankovitch**
Editor: **Tom Brevoort**

WHA...HUH?
Artist: **Jim Mahfood**
Colorist: **Shaughn Struble**
Letterer: **Chris Eliopoulos**
Associate Editor: **MacKenzie Cadenhead**
Editor: **C.B. Cebulski**

Collection Editor
Jennifer Grünwald
Assistant Editors
Alex Starbuck & John Denning
Editor, Special Projects
Mark D. Beazley
Senior Editor, Special Projects
Jeff Youngquist
Senior Vice President of Sales
David Gabriel
Book Design
Jeff Powell

Editor in Chief: **Joe Quesada**
Publisher: **Dan Buckley**
Executive Producer: **Alan Fine**

T MARVEL

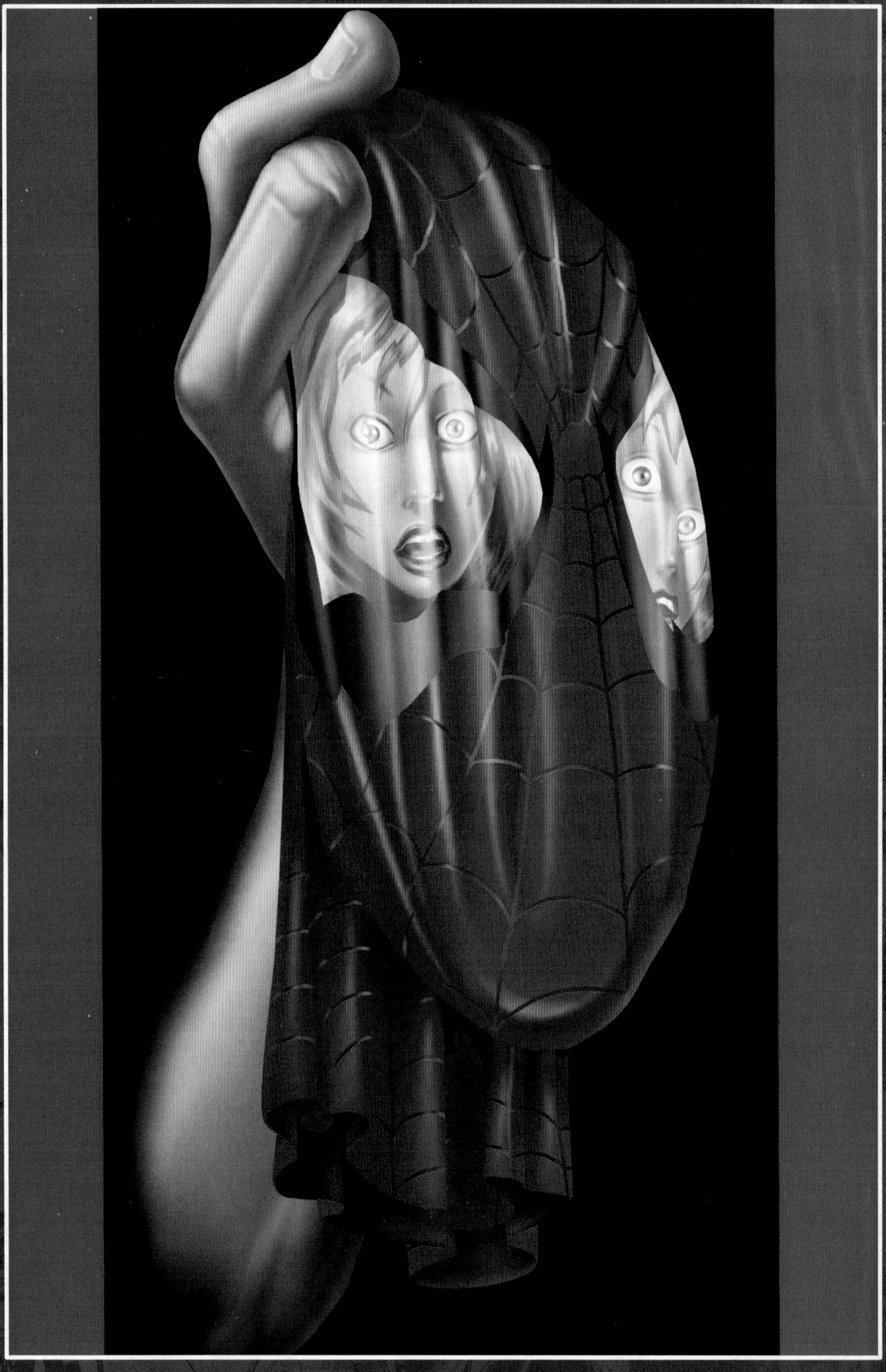

ULTIMATE SPIDER-MAN #13

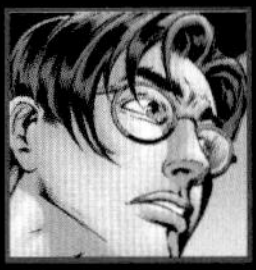
Peter Parker

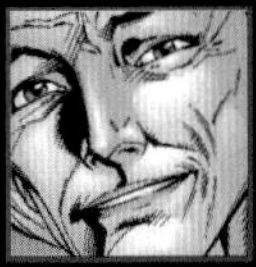
Aunt May

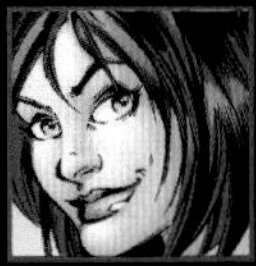
Mary Jane Watson

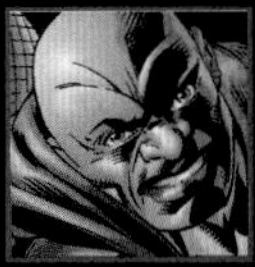
Ox

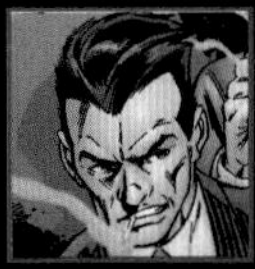
Fancy Dan

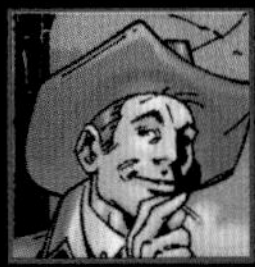
Montana

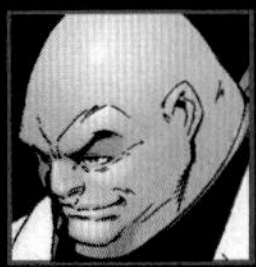
Kingpin

PREVIOUSLY IN ULTIMATE SPIDER-MAN...
Previously

FAN MAIL!
Fan Mail

Stan Lee PRESENTS:

ULTIMATE SPIDER-MAN

BRIAN MICHAEL BENDIS script
MARK BAGLEY pencils
ART THIBERT inks
JC colors
RS & COMICRAFT'S
ALBERT DESCHESNE letters
BRIAN SMITH assistant editor
RALPH MACCHIO editor
JOE QUESADA editor in chief
BILL JEMAS president and inspiration

PREVIOUSLY...

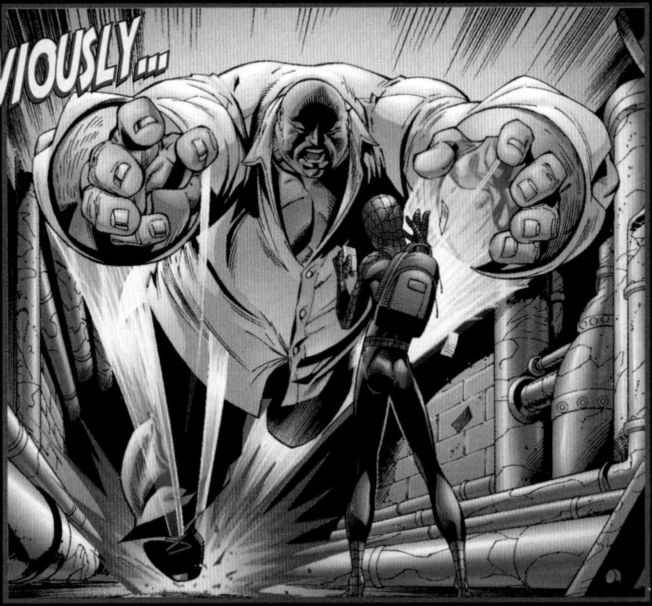

ACCIDENTALLY BITTEN BY A GENETICALLY ALTERED SPIDER, TEENAGER PETER PARKER NOW FINDS HE HAS THE PROPORTIONATE ABILITIES OF A SPIDER: STRENGTH, AGILITY, A SPIDER-LIKE SIXTH SENSE WARNING HIM OF PERSONAL DANGER AND – MOST AMAZING OF ALL – PETER CAN WALK ON WALLS! ARMED WITH HOMEMADE WEB-SHOOTERS AND A STRONG BELIEF THAT WITH GREAT POWER THERE MUST COME GREAT RESPONSIBILITY, HE FEARLESSLY DONS THE COSTUME OF:

SPIDER-MAN

PREVIOUSLY:

SPIDER-MAN HAS HIS FIRST TRUE VICTORY AS A SUPER HERO. THE KINGPIN OF CRIME AND ALL OF HIS MEN HAVE BEEN TAKEN DOWN BY SPIDEY'S MIX OF INGENUITY AND BRAVERY. BUT DURING THE COURSE OF THE BATTLE, PETER INADVERTANTLY DISSED ONE OF HIS ONLY FRIENDS, MARY JANE WATSON. WITH THE KINGPIN OUT OF THE COUNTRY IN HIDING, PETER ASKS MARY JANE TO COME OVER AFTER SCHOOL BECAUSE HE HAS SOMETHING IMPORTANT TO TELL HER.

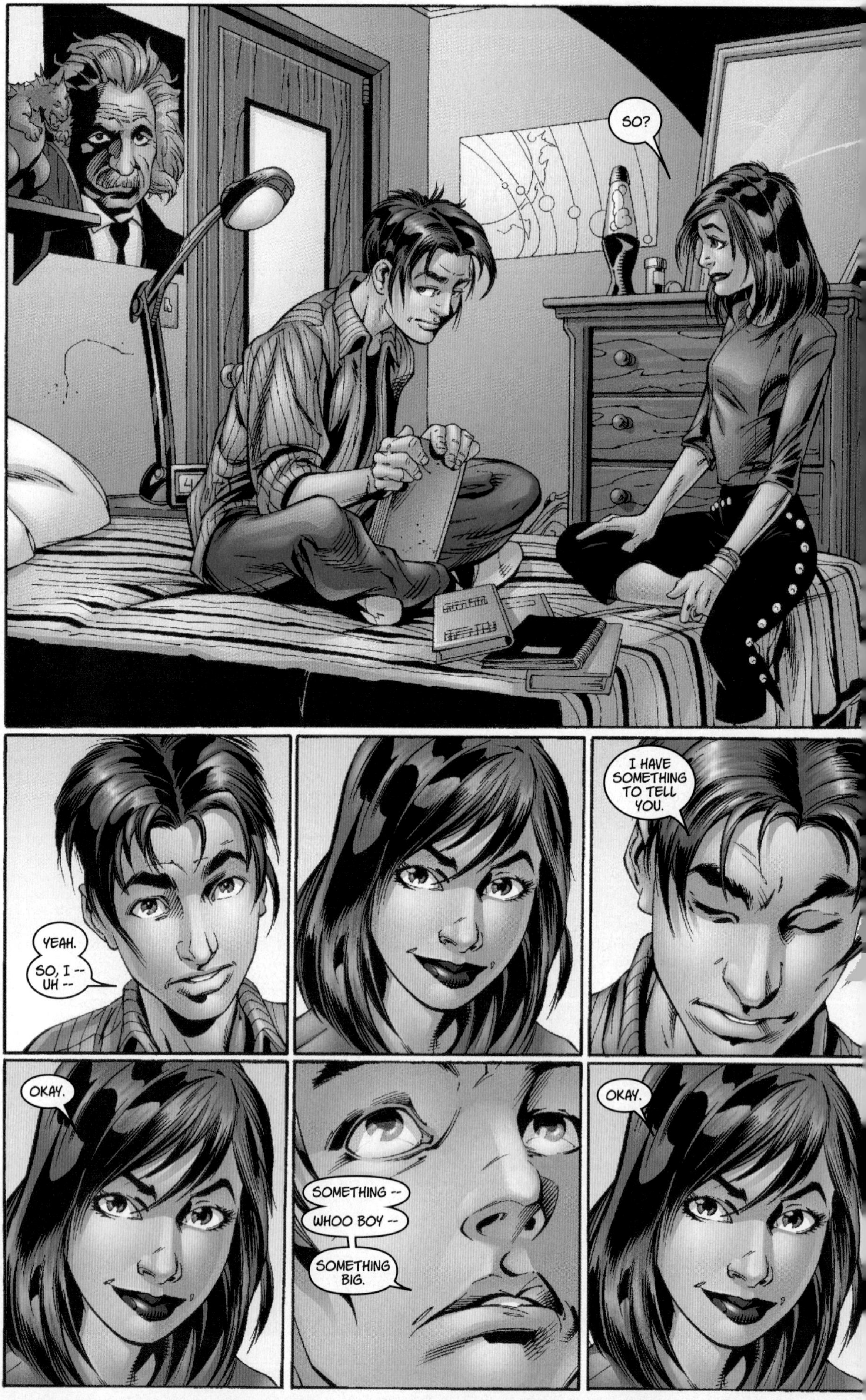
SO?
YEAH.
SO, I -- UH --
I HAVE SOMETHING TO TELL YOU.
OKAY.
SOMETHING --
WHOO BOY --
SOMETHING BIG.
OKAY.

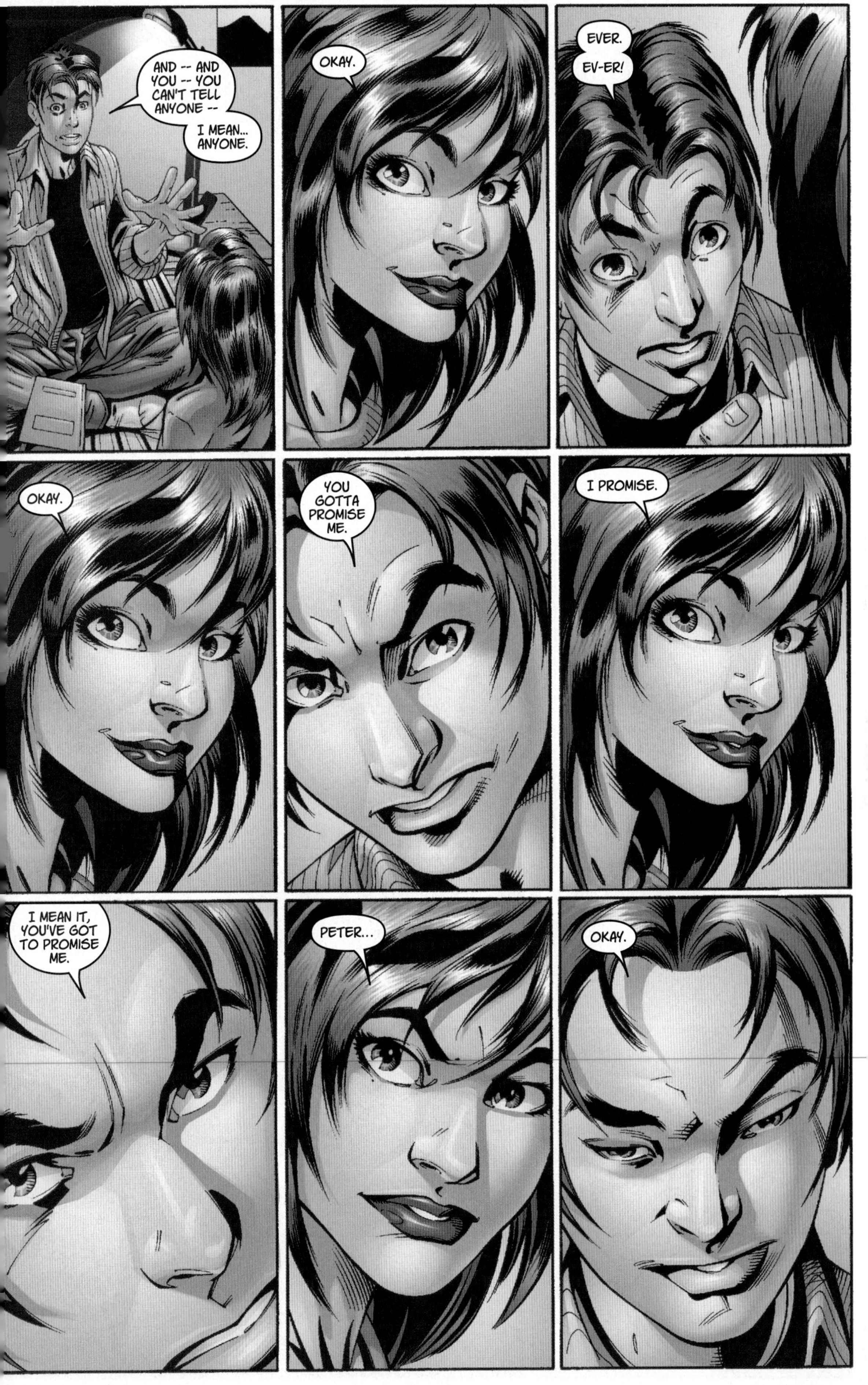
AND -- AND YOU -- YOU CAN'T TELL ANYONE --
I MEAN... ANYONE.
OKAY.
EVER.
EV-ER!
OKAY.
YOU GOTTA PROMISE ME.
I PROMISE.
I MEAN IT, YOU'VE GOT TO PROMISE ME.
PETER...
OKAY.

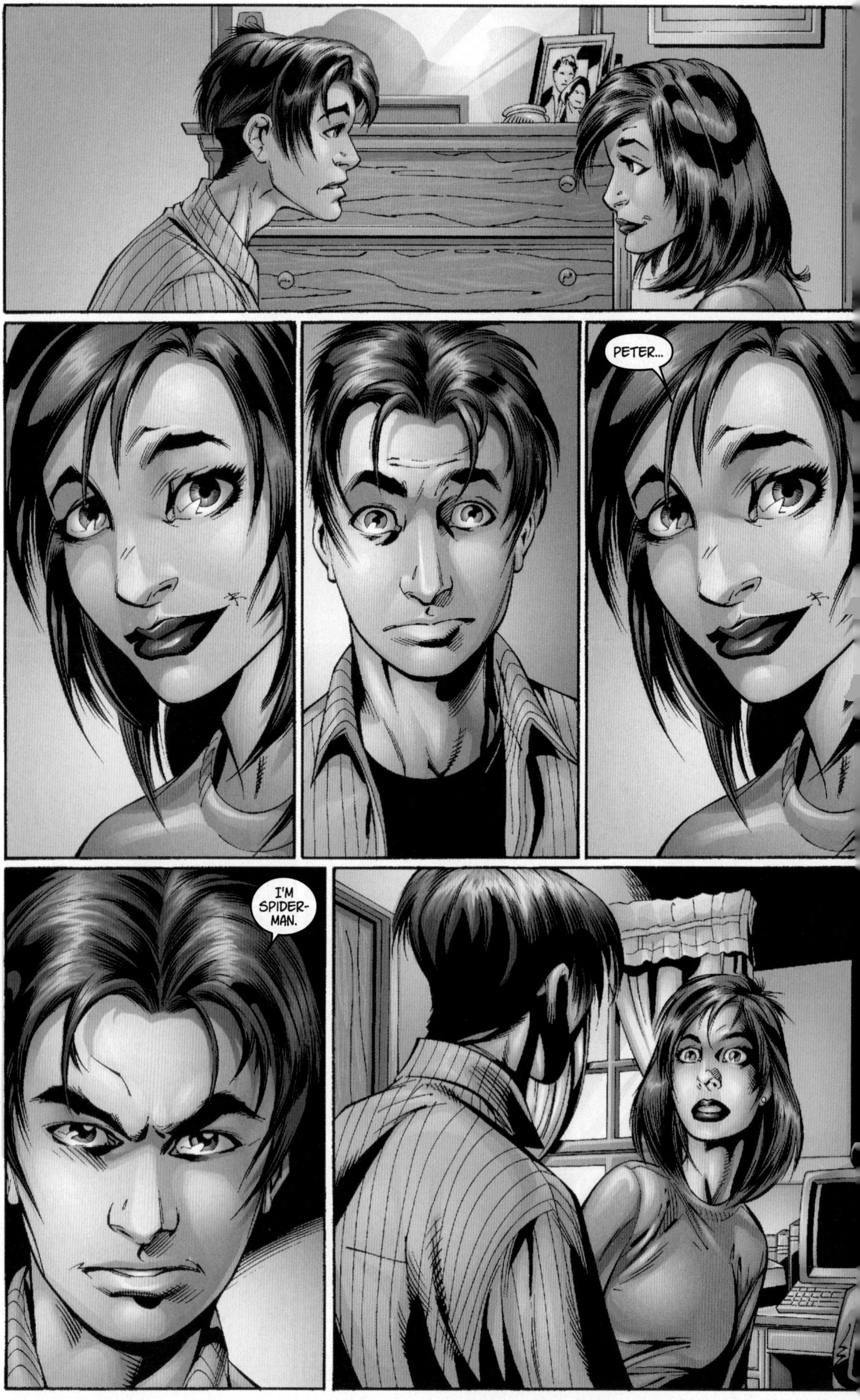

PETER...
I'M SPIDER-MAN.

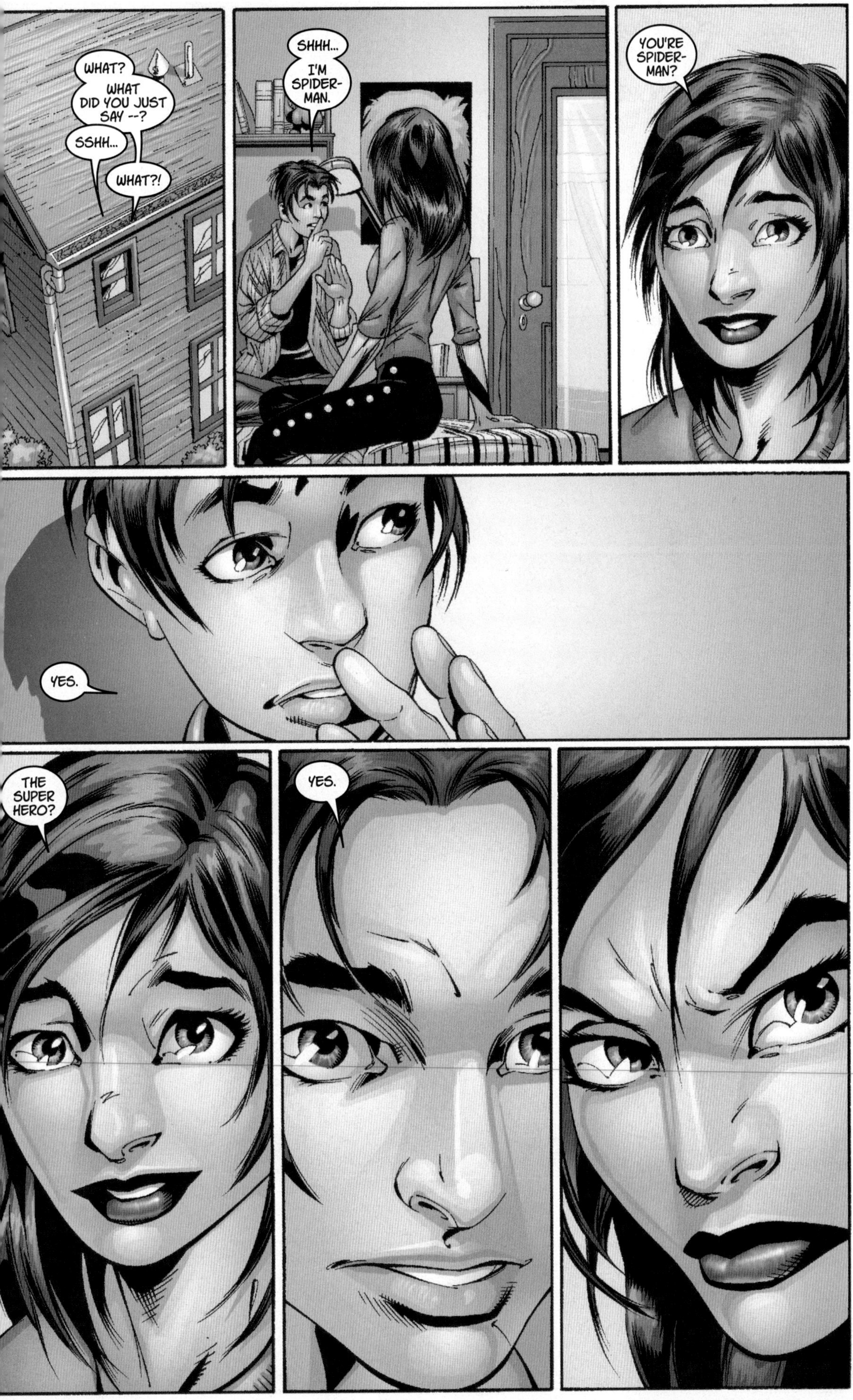

WHAT? WHAT DID YOU JUST SAY --?
SSHH...
WHAT?!
SHHH... I'M SPIDER-MAN.
YOU'RE SPIDER-MAN?
YES.
THE SUPER HERO?
YES.

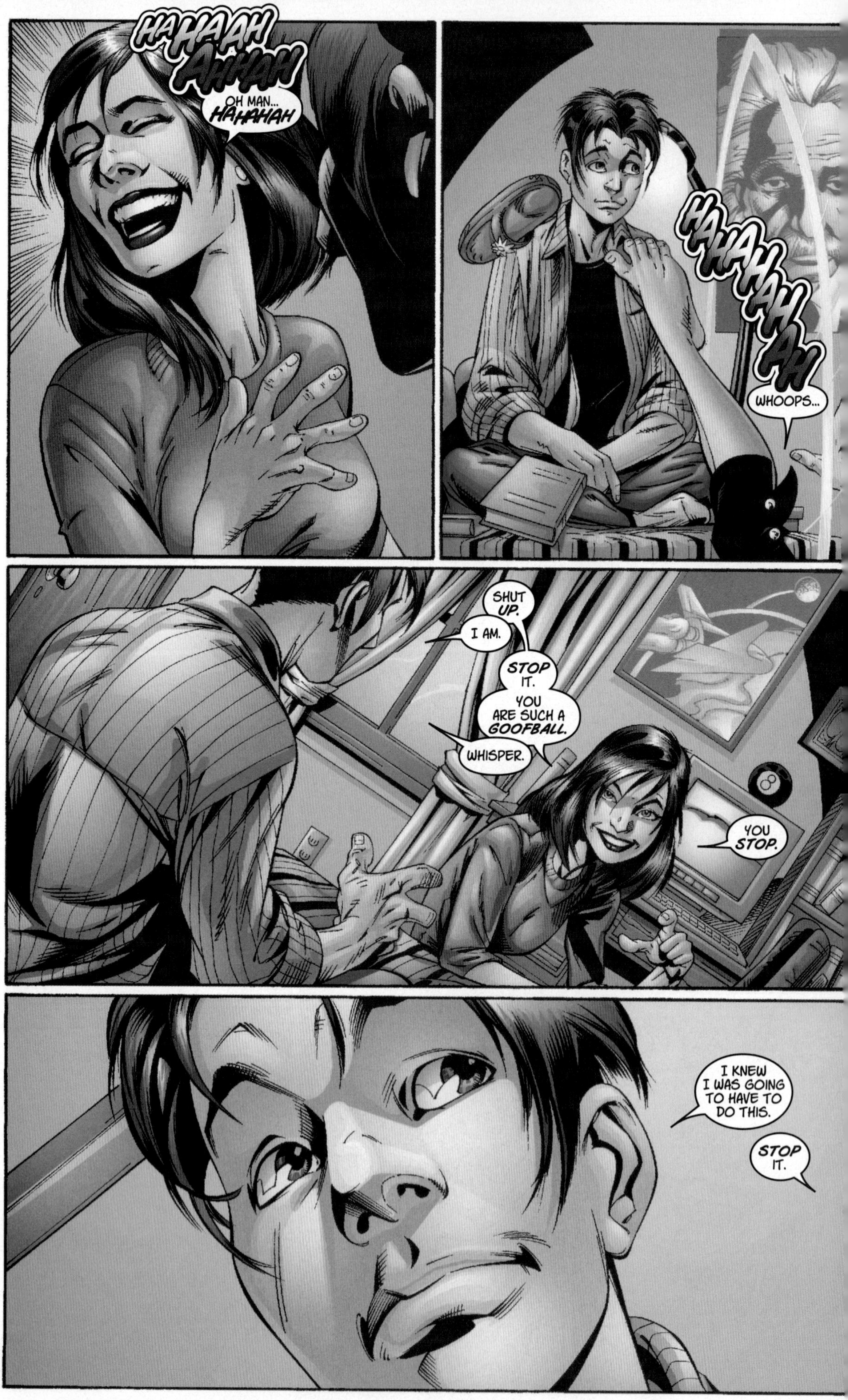
HAHAAAH AHHAH
OH MAN... HAHAHAH
HAHAHAHAHAH
WHOOPS...
SHUT UP.
I AM.
STOP IT.
YOU ARE SUCH A GOOFBALL.
WHISPER.
YOU STOP.
I KNEW I WAS GOING TO HAVE TO DO THIS.
STOP IT.

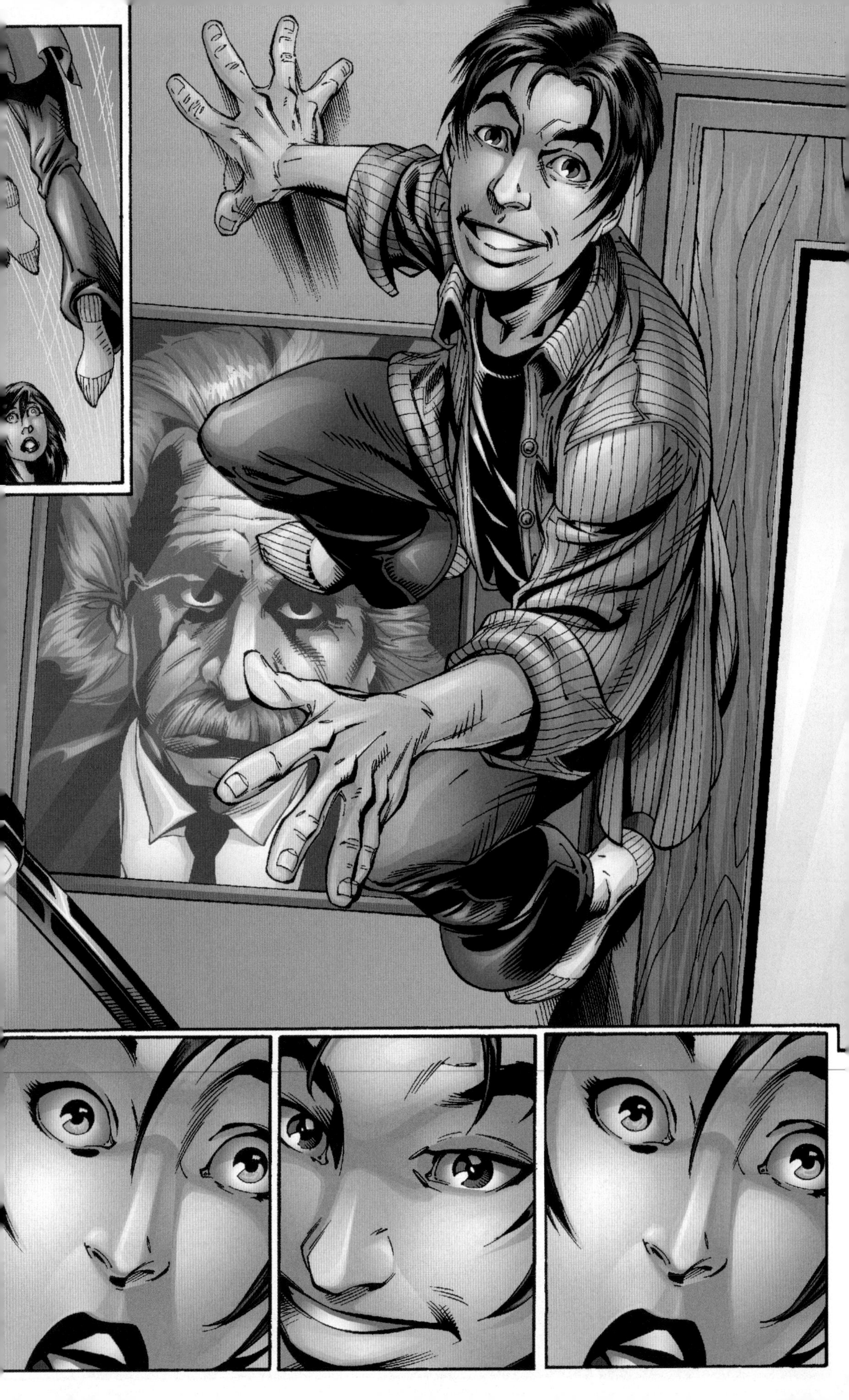

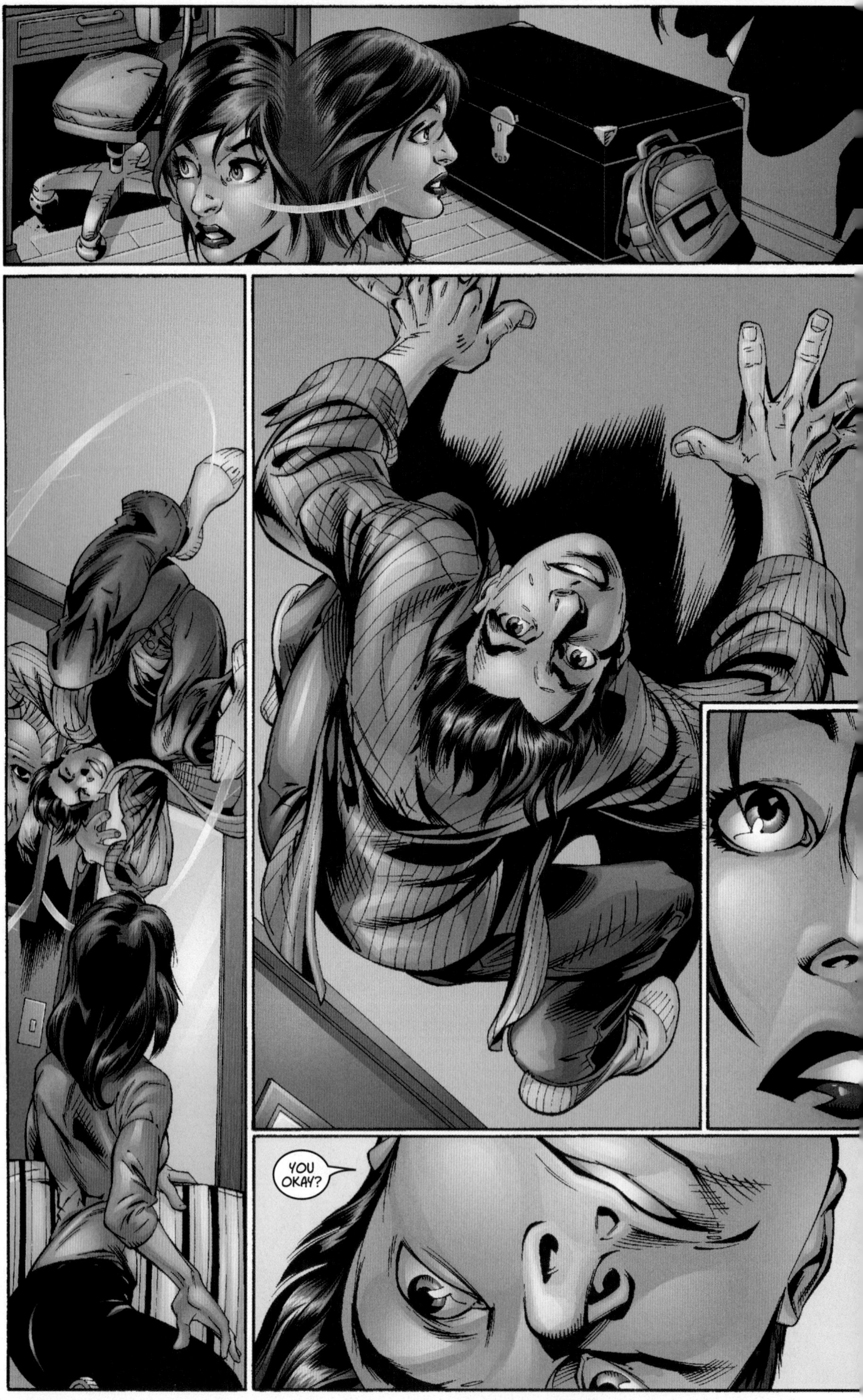
YOU OKAY?

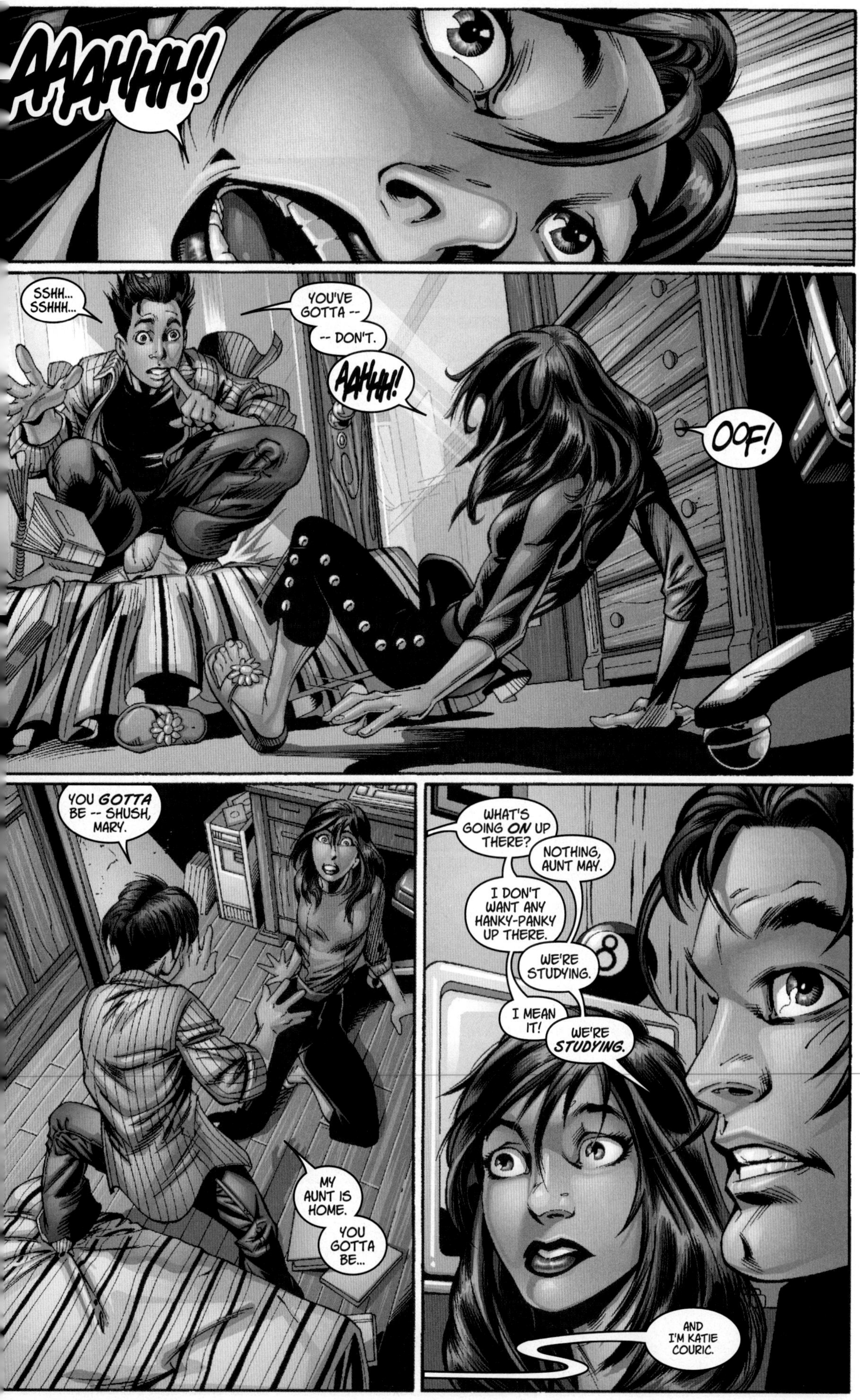

AAAHHH!
SSHH... SSHHH...
YOU'VE GOTTA --
-- DON'T.
AAHHH!
OOF!
YOU GOTTA BE -- SHUSH, MARY.
MY AUNT IS HOME.
YOU GOTTA BE...
WHAT'S GOING ON UP THERE?
NOTHING, AUNT MAY.
I DON'T WANT ANY HANKY-PANKY UP THERE.
WE'RE STUDYING.
I MEAN IT!
WE'RE STUDYING.
AND I'M KATIE COURIC.

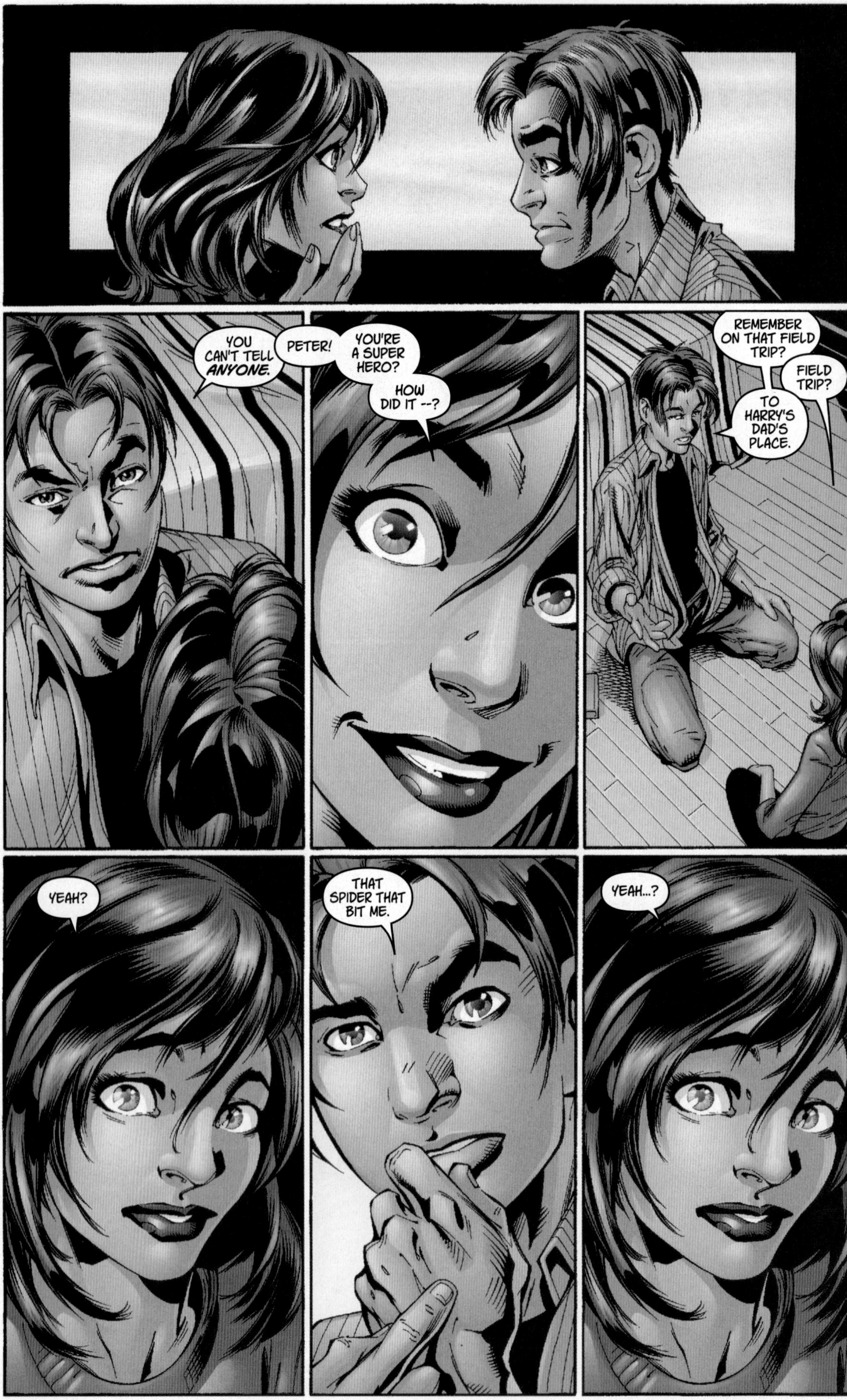
YOU CAN'T TELL *ANYONE*.
PETER!
YOU'RE A SUPER HERO?
HOW DID IT --?
REMEMBER ON THAT FIELD TRIP?
FIELD TRIP?
TO HARRY'S DAD'S PLACE.
YEAH?
THAT SPIDER THAT BIT ME.
YEAH...?

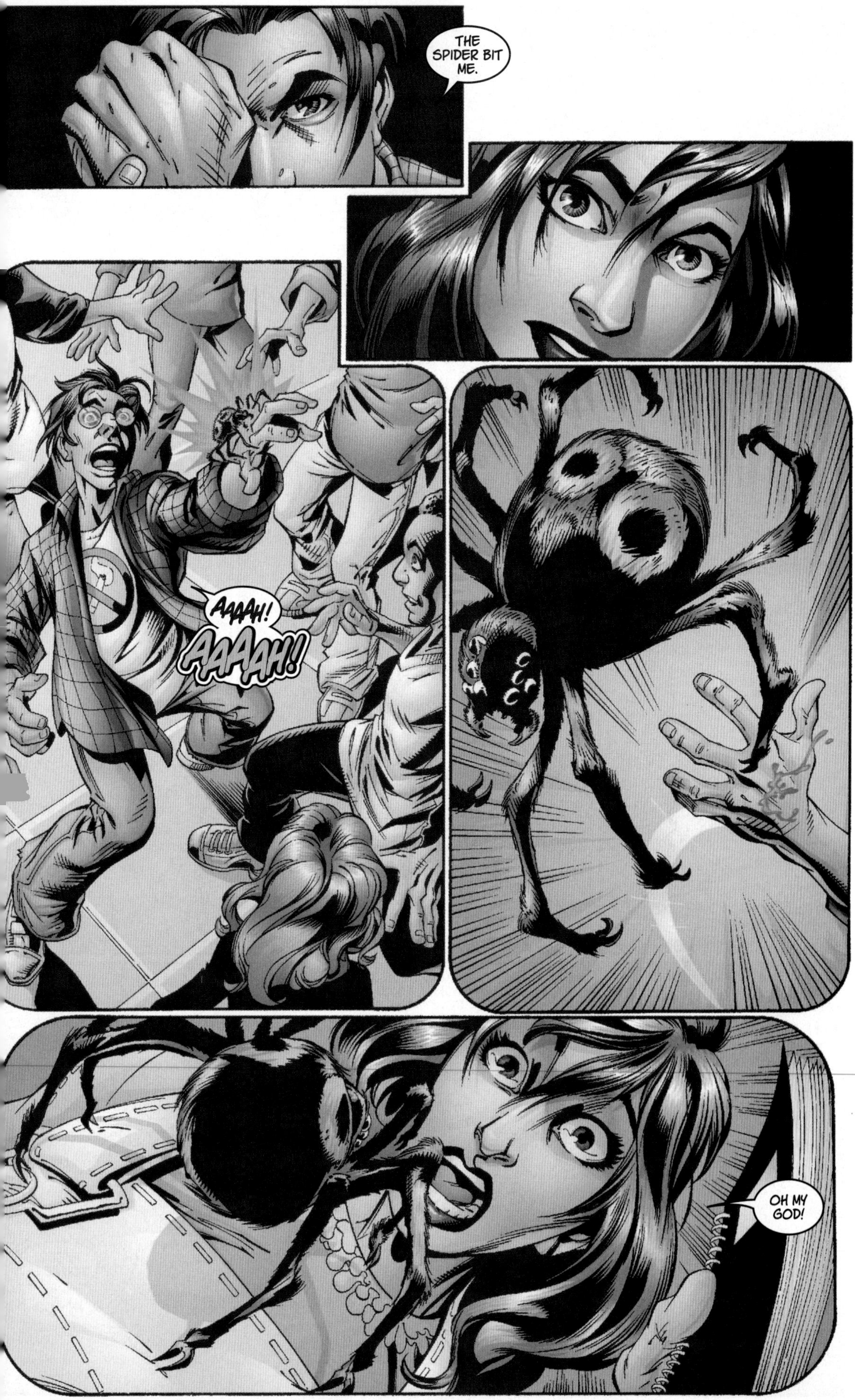
THE SPIDER BIT ME.
AAAAH!
AAAAH!
OH MY GOD!

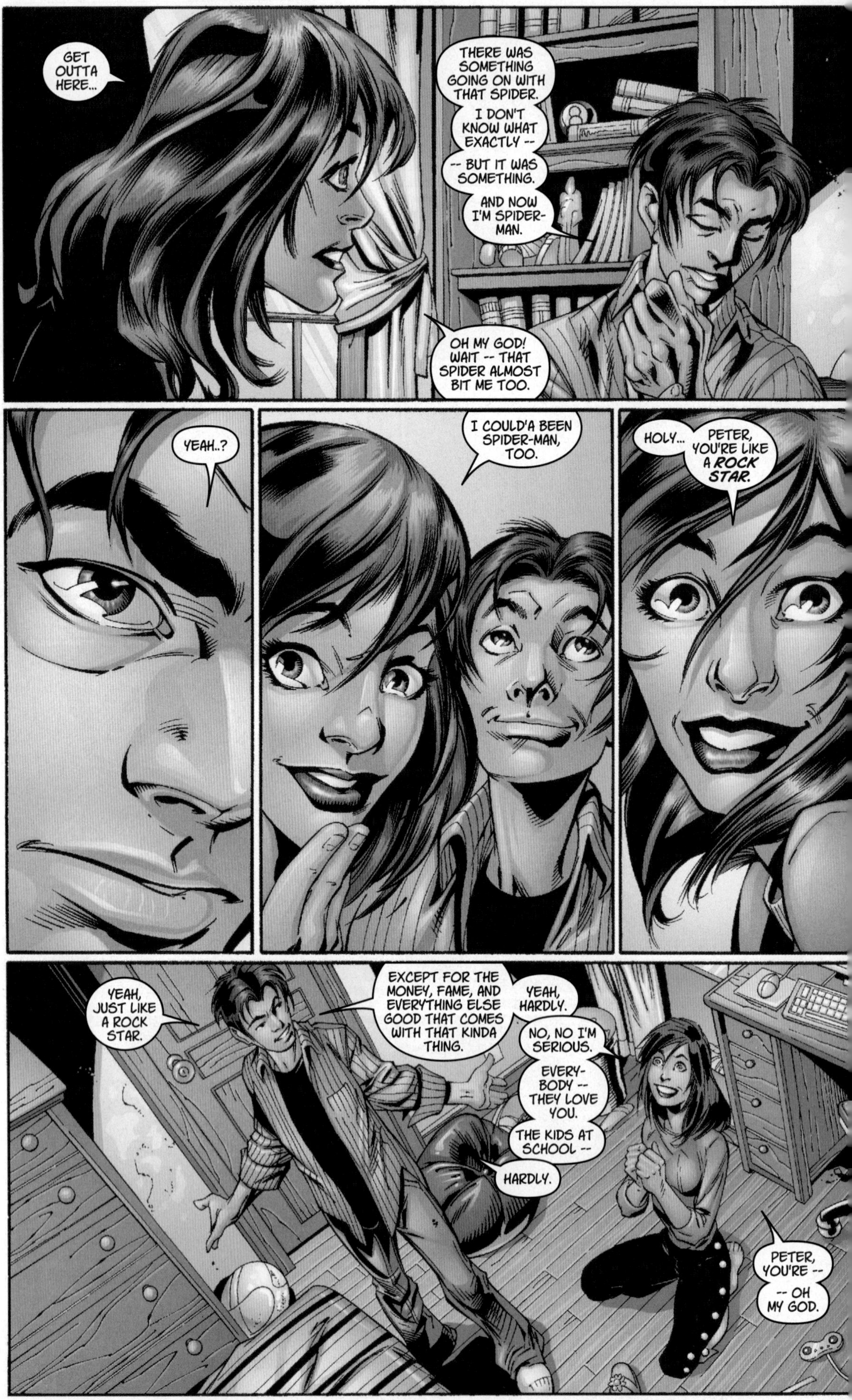

GET OUTTA HERE...
THERE WAS SOMETHING GOING ON WITH THAT SPIDER.
I DON'T KNOW WHAT EXACTLY --
-- BUT IT WAS SOMETHING.
AND NOW I'M SPIDER-MAN.
OH MY GOD! WAIT -- THAT SPIDER ALMOST BIT ME TOO.
YEAH..?
I COULD'A BEEN SPIDER-MAN, TOO.
HOLY...
PETER, YOU'RE LIKE A ROCK STAR.
YEAH, JUST LIKE A ROCK STAR.
EXCEPT FOR THE MONEY, FAME, AND EVERYTHING ELSE GOOD THAT COMES WITH THAT KINDA THING.
YEAH, HARDLY.
NO, NO I'M SERIOUS.
EVERY-BODY -- THEY LOVE YOU.
THE KIDS AT SCHOOL --
HARDLY.
PETER, YOU'RE --
-- OH MY GOD.

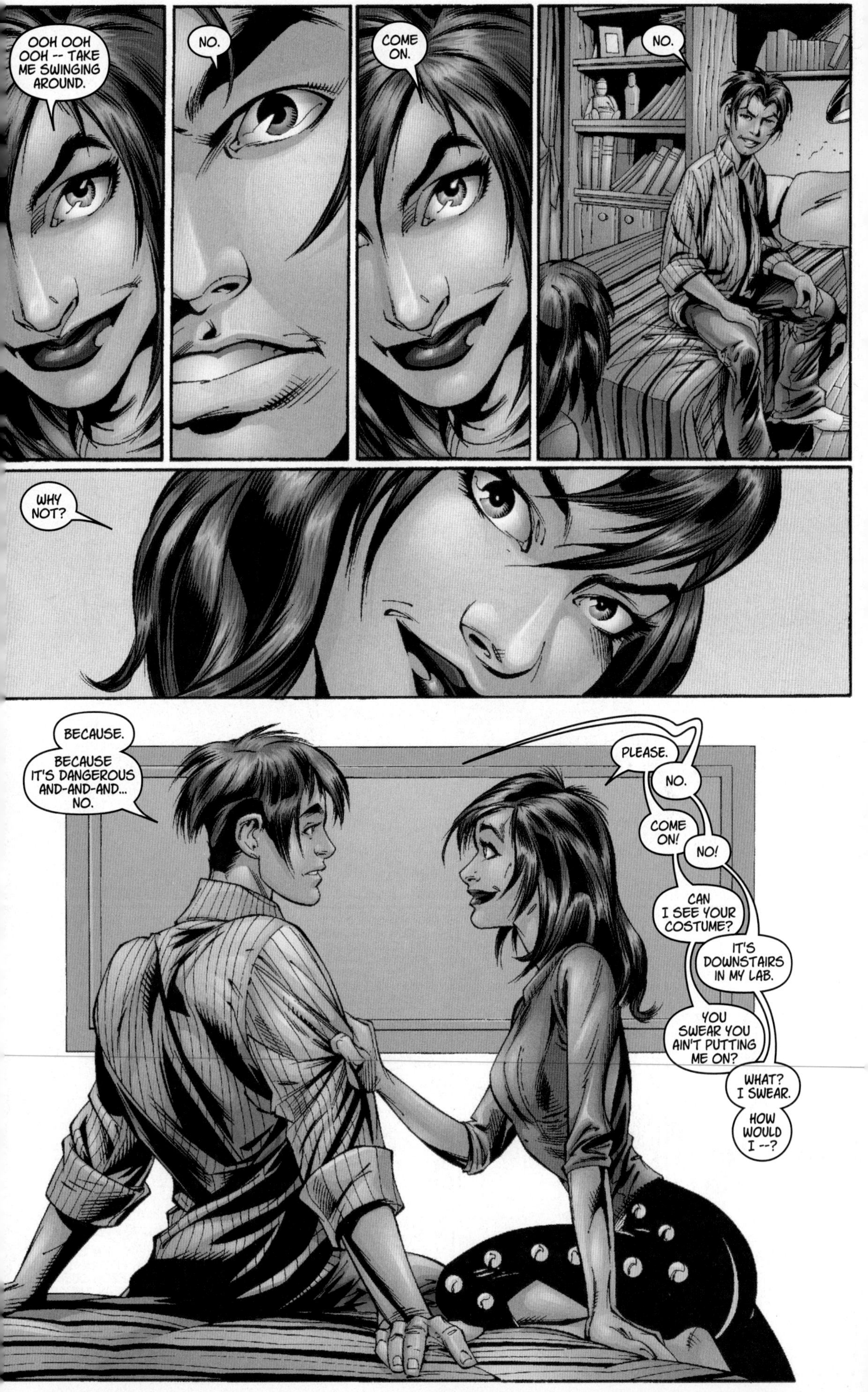
OOH OOH OOH -- TAKE ME SWINGING AROUND.
NO.
COME ON.
NO.
WHY NOT?
BECAUSE.
BECAUSE IT'S DANGEROUS AND-AND-AND... NO.
PLEASE.
NO.
COME ON!
NO!
CAN I SEE YOUR COSTUME?
IT'S DOWNSTAIRS IN MY LAB.
YOU SWEAR YOU AIN'T PUTTING ME ON?
WHAT? I SWEAR.
HOW WOULD I --?

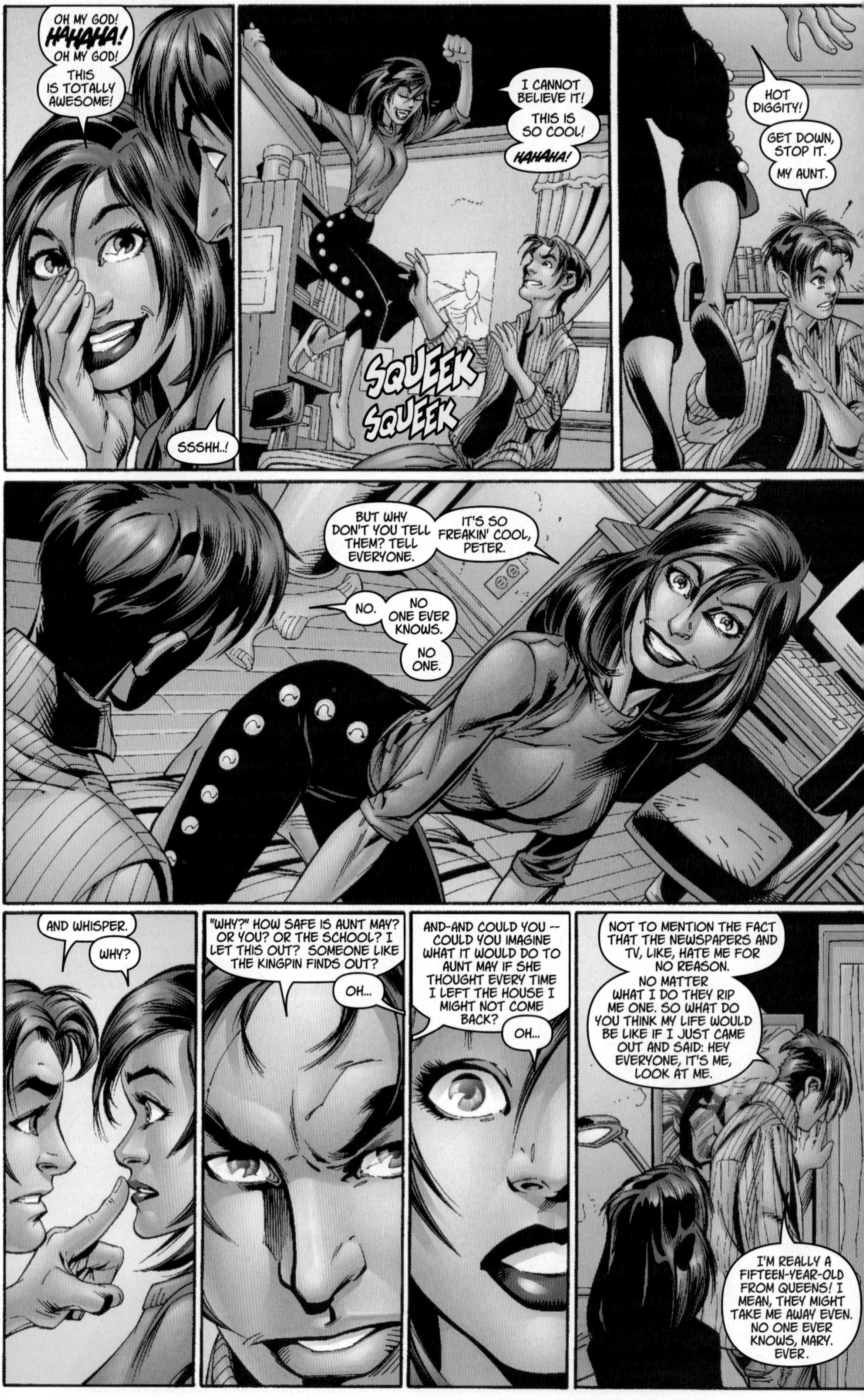
OH MY GOD! HAHAHA! OH MY GOD!
THIS IS TOTALLY AWESOME!
SSSHH..!
I CANNOT BELIEVE IT!
THIS IS SO COOL!
HAHAHA!
SQUEEK SQUEEK
HOT DIGGITY!
GET DOWN, STOP IT.
MY AUNT.
IT'S SO FREAKIN' COOL, PETER.
BUT WHY DON'T YOU TELL THEM? TELL EVERYONE.
NO.
NO ONE EVER KNOWS.
NO ONE.
AND WHISPER.
WHY?
"WHY?" HOW SAFE IS AUNT MAY? OR YOU? OR THE SCHOOL? I LET THIS OUT? SOMEONE LIKE THE KINGPIN FINDS OUT?
OH...
AND-AND COULD YOU -- COULD YOU IMAGINE WHAT IT WOULD DO TO AUNT MAY IF SHE THOUGHT EVERY TIME I LEFT THE HOUSE I MIGHT NOT COME BACK?
OH...
NOT TO MENTION THE FACT THAT THE NEWSPAPERS AND TV, LIKE, HATE ME FOR NO REASON.
NO MATTER WHAT I DO THEY RIP ME ONE. SO WHAT DO YOU THINK MY LIFE WOULD BE LIKE IF I JUST CAME OUT AND SAID: HEY EVERYONE, IT'S ME, LOOK AT ME.
I'M REALLY A FIFTEEN-YEAR-OLD FROM QUEENS! I MEAN, THEY MIGHT TAKE ME AWAY EVEN. NO ONE EVER KNOWS, MARY. EVER.

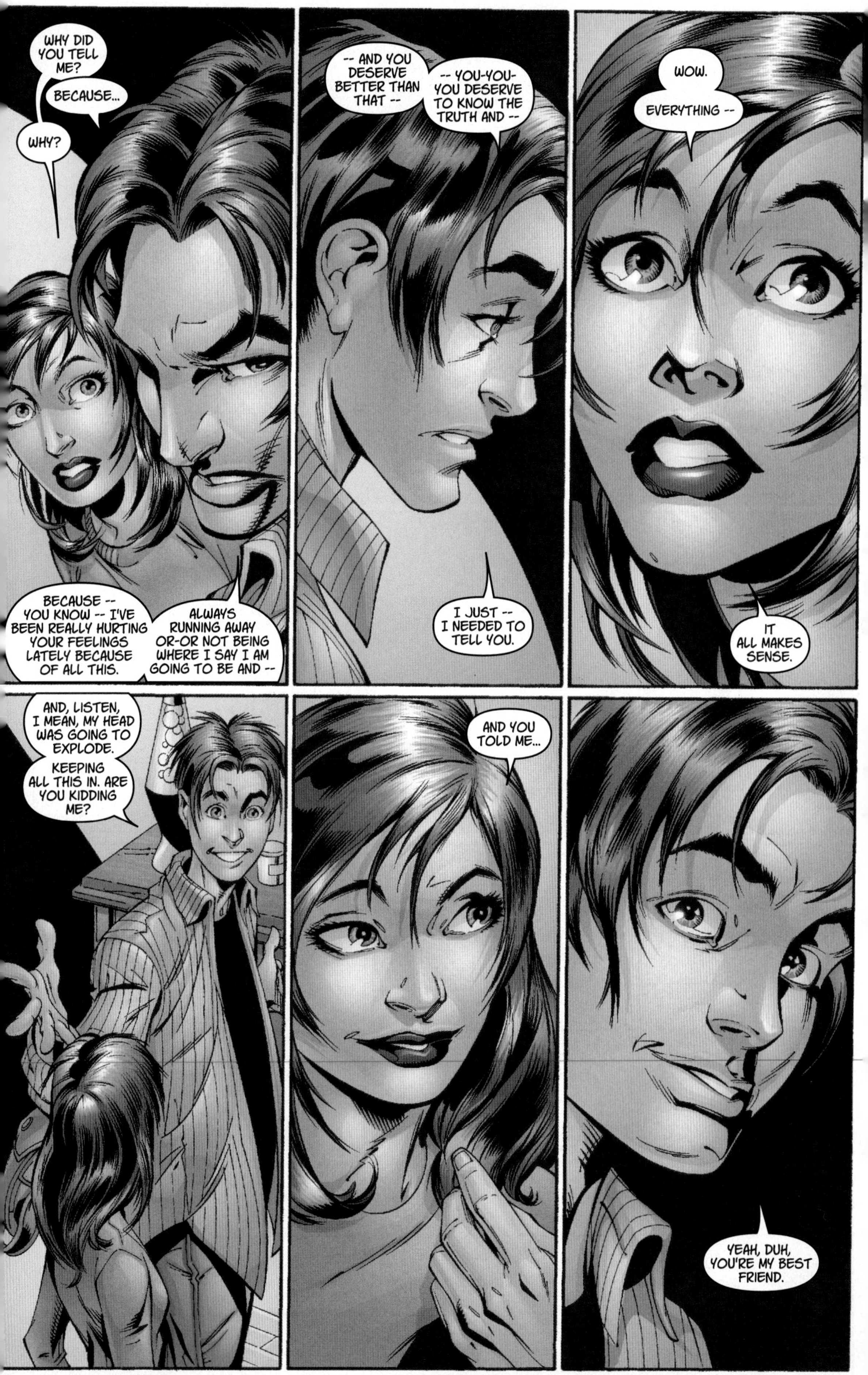
WHY DID YOU TELL ME?
BECAUSE...
WHY?
BECAUSE -- YOU KNOW -- I'VE BEEN REALLY HURTING YOUR FEELINGS LATELY BECAUSE OF ALL THIS.
ALWAYS RUNNING AWAY OR-OR NOT BEING WHERE I SAY I AM GOING TO BE AND --
-- AND YOU DESERVE BETTER THAN THAT --
-- YOU-YOU-YOU DESERVE TO KNOW THE TRUTH AND --
I JUST -- I NEEDED TO TELL YOU.
WOW.
EVERYTHING --
IT ALL MAKES SENSE.
AND, LISTEN, I MEAN, MY HEAD WAS GOING TO EXPLODE.
KEEPING ALL THIS IN. ARE YOU KIDDING ME?
AND YOU TOLD ME...
YEAH, DUH, YOU'RE MY BEST FRIEND.

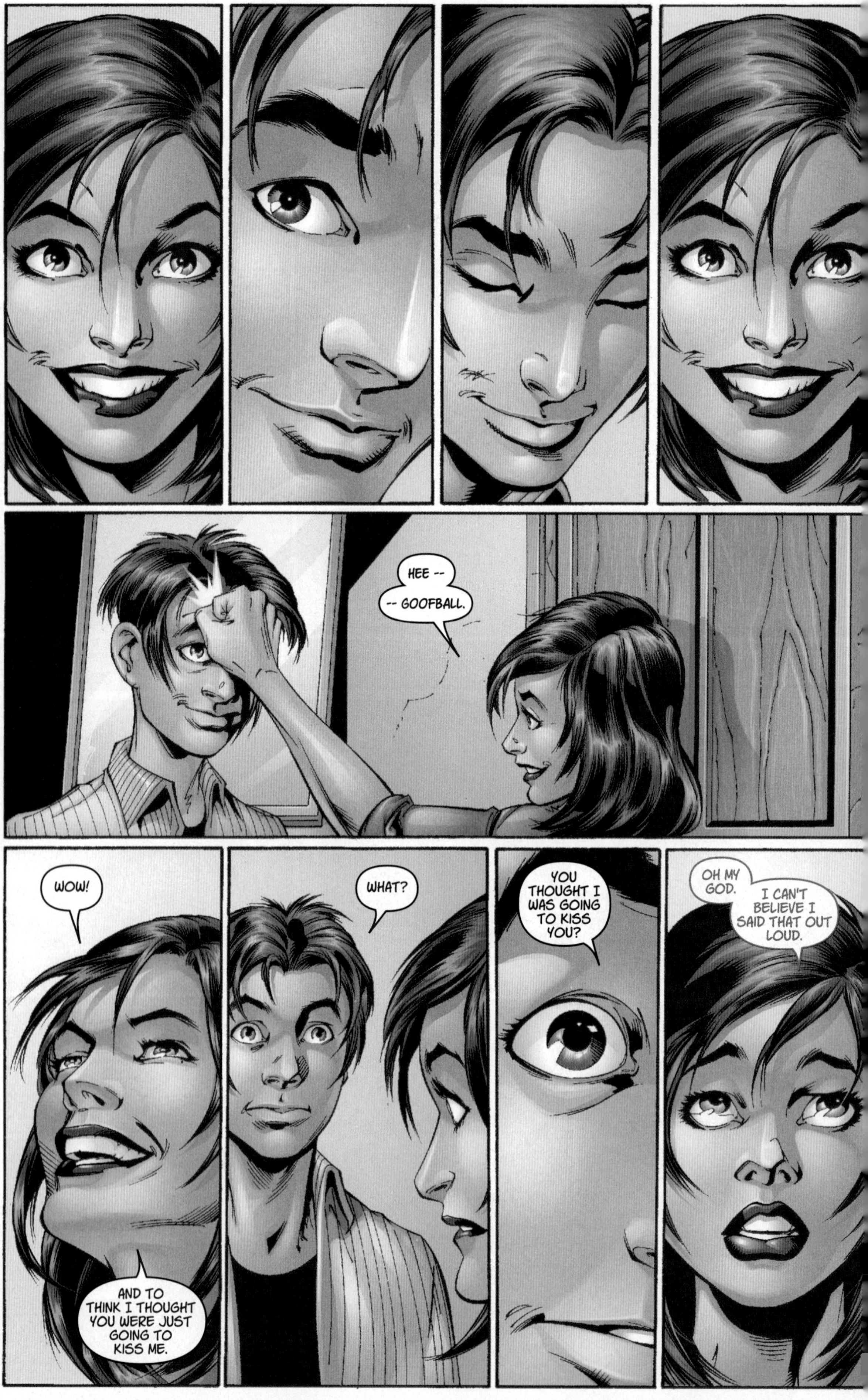
HEE --
-- GOOFBALL.
WOW!
AND TO THINK I THOUGHT YOU WERE JUST GOING TO KISS ME.
WHAT?
YOU THOUGHT I WAS GOING TO KISS YOU?
OH MY GOD.
I CAN'T BELIEVE I SAID THAT OUT LOUD.

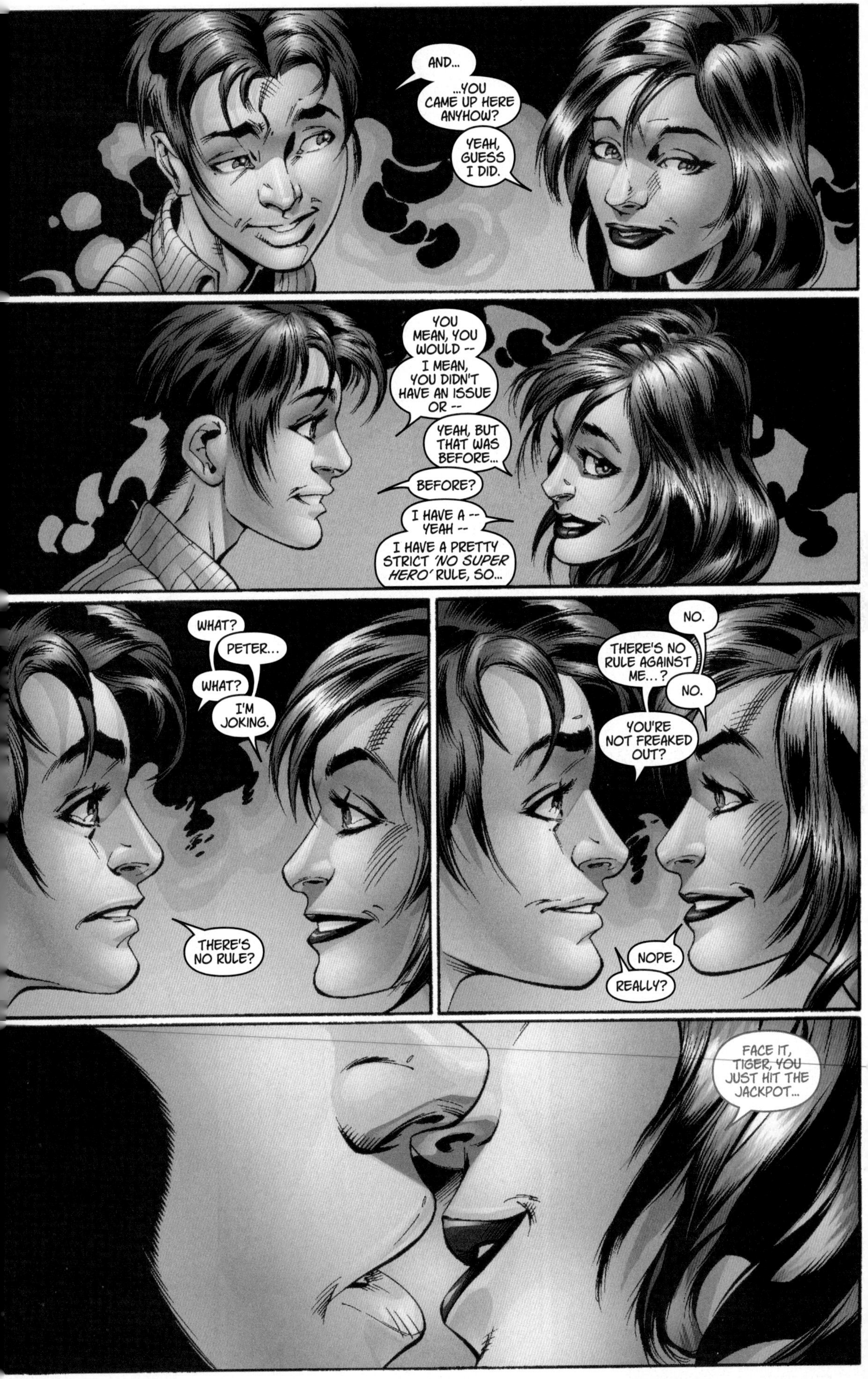
AND...
...YOU CAME UP HERE ANYHOW?
YEAH, GUESS I DID.
YOU MEAN, YOU WOULD -- I MEAN, YOU DIDN'T HAVE AN ISSUE OR --
YEAH, BUT THAT WAS BEFORE...
BEFORE?
I HAVE A -- YEAH -- I HAVE A PRETTY STRICT *'NO SUPER HERO'* RULE, SO...
WHAT?
PETER...
WHAT?
I'M JOKING.
THERE'S NO RULE?
NO.
THERE'S NO RULE AGAINST ME...?
NO.
YOU'RE NOT FREAKED OUT?
NOPE.
REALLY?
FACE IT, TIGER, YOU JUST HIT THE JACKPOT...

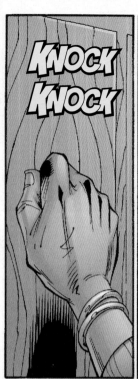

KNOCK KNOCK

PHONE!

WHAT?

THE PHONE. IT'S MARY'S MOM.

I DIDN'T HEAR THE PHONE RING.

IT DIDN'T. I CALLED HER.

HELLO? MOM?

WE -- WE WEREN'T.

WE WERE NOT.

NO -- NO!

WE WERE STUDYING.

GOD! WHAT?! WHY?

IT'S 4:30 IN THE AFTERNOON.

WHAT? OH, COME ON. WE'RE IN THE MIDDLE OF SOMETHING IMPORTANT!

UGGH!

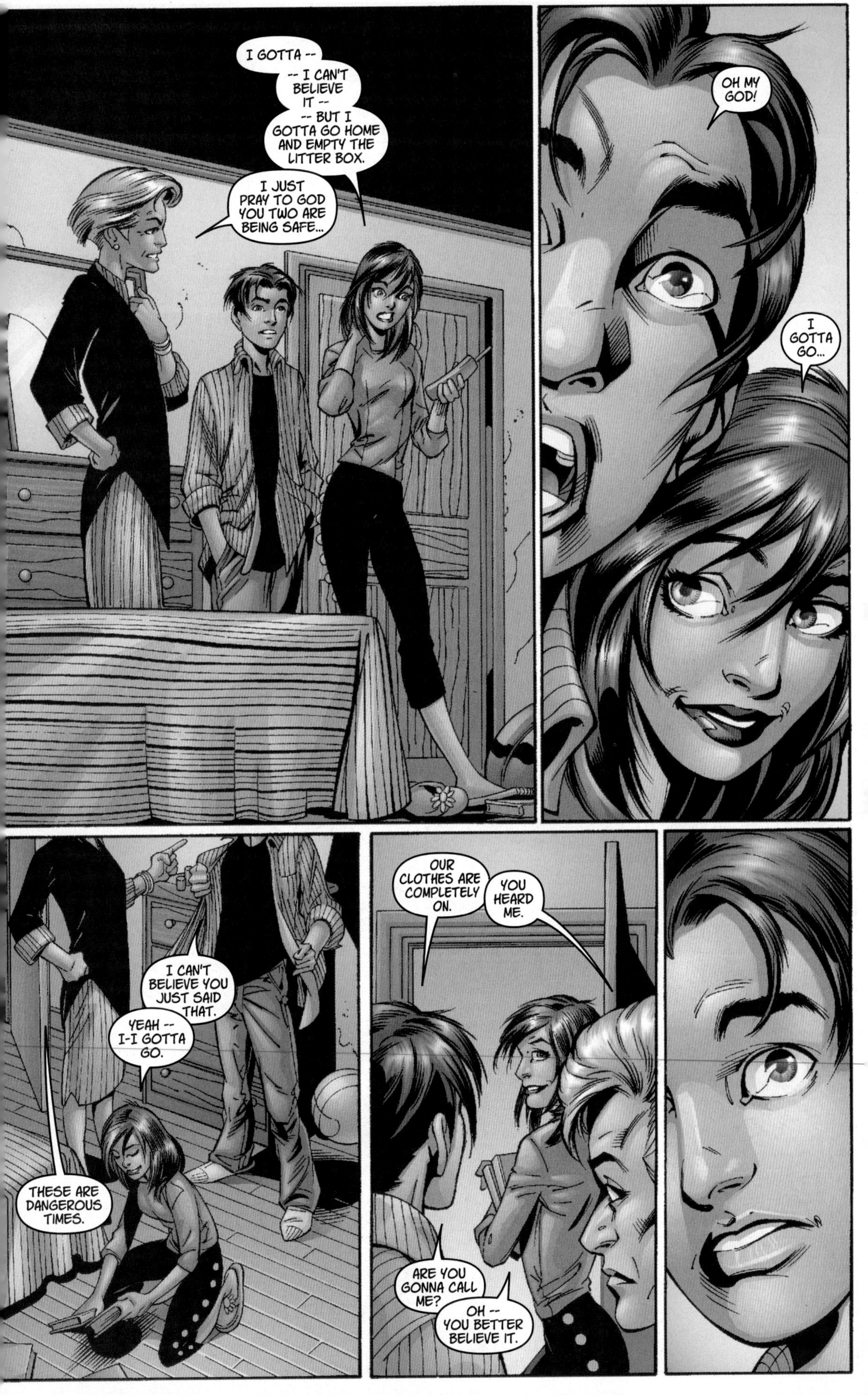

I GOTTA --
-- I CAN'T BELIEVE IT --
-- BUT I GOTTA GO HOME AND EMPTY THE LITTER BOX.
I JUST PRAY TO GOD YOU TWO ARE BEING SAFE...
OH MY GOD!
I GOTTA GO...
I CAN'T BELIEVE YOU JUST SAID THAT.
YEAH -- I-I GOTTA GO.
THESE ARE DANGEROUS TIMES.
OUR CLOTHES ARE COMPLETELY ON.
YOU HEARD ME.
ARE YOU GONNA CALL ME?
OH -- YOU BETTER BELIEVE IT.

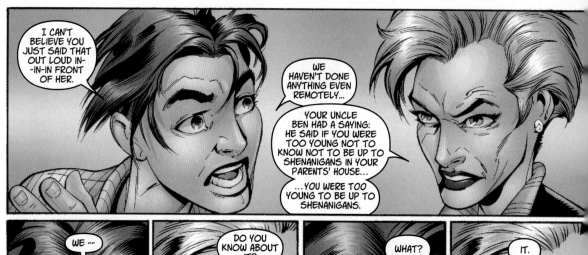

I CAN'T BELIEVE YOU JUST SAID THAT OUT LOUD IN--IN-IN FRONT OF HER.

WE HAVEN'T DONE ANYTHING EVEN REMOTELY...

YOUR UNCLE BEN HAD A SAYING: HE SAID IF YOU WERE TOO YOUNG NOT TO KNOW NOT TO BE UP TO SHENANIGANS IN YOUR PARENTS' HOUSE...

...YOU WERE TOO YOUNG TO BE UP TO SHENANIGANS.

WE -- WEREN'T -- DOING -- ANYTHING.

DO YOU KNOW ABOUT IT?

WHAT?

IT. DO YOU KNOW ABOUT --?

OH GOD! PLEASE STOP TALKING.

DO YOU?

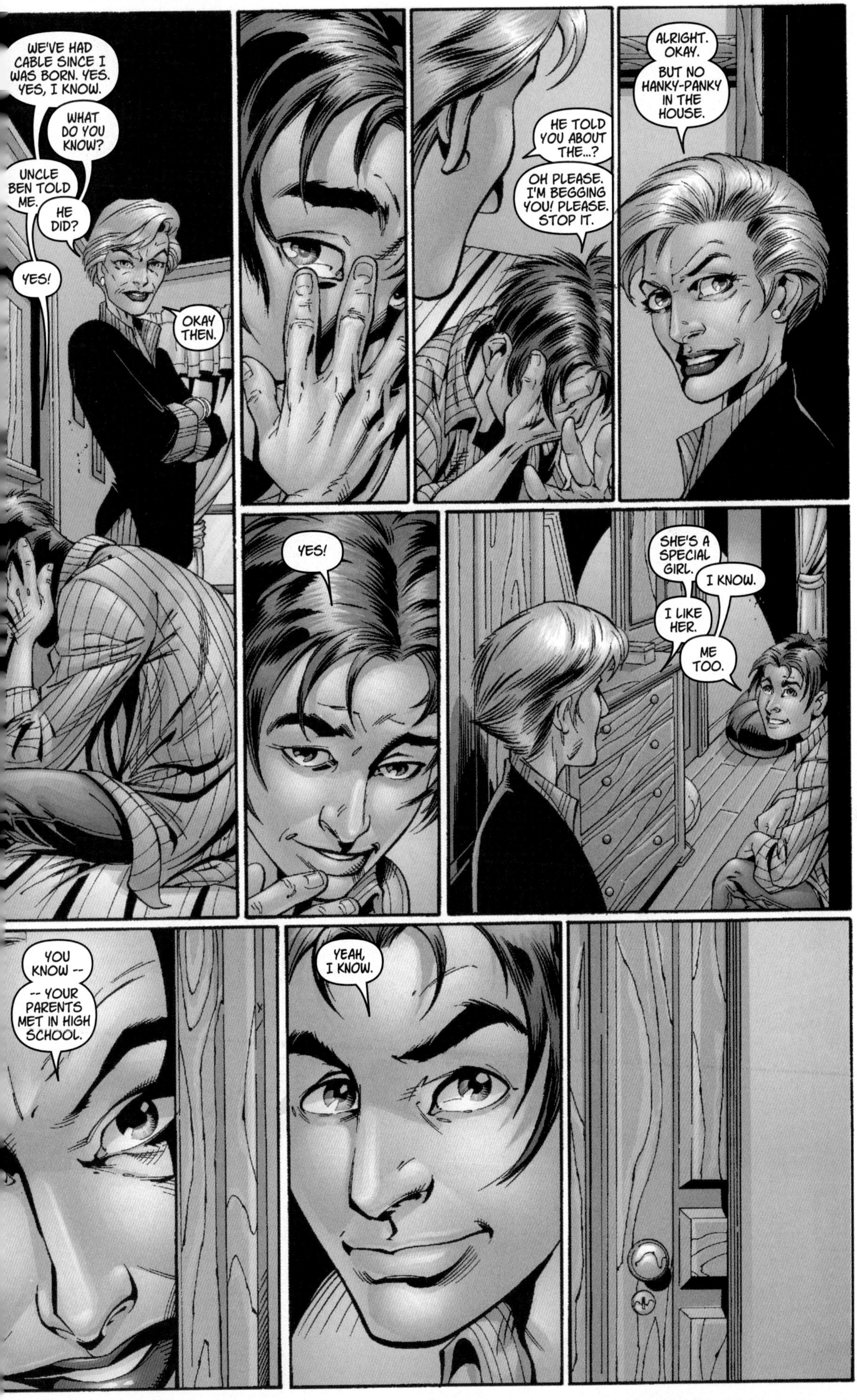
WE'VE HAD CABLE SINCE I WAS BORN. YES. YES, I KNOW.
WHAT DO YOU KNOW?
UNCLE BEN TOLD ME.
HE DID?
YES!
OKAY THEN.
HE TOLD YOU ABOUT THE...?
OH PLEASE. I'M BEGGING YOU! PLEASE. STOP IT.
ALRIGHT. OKAY.
BUT NO HANKY-PANKY IN THE HOUSE.
YES!
SHE'S A SPECIAL GIRL.
I KNOW.
I LIKE HER.
ME TOO.
YOU KNOW --
-- YOUR PARENTS MET IN HIGH SCHOOL.
YEAH, I KNOW.

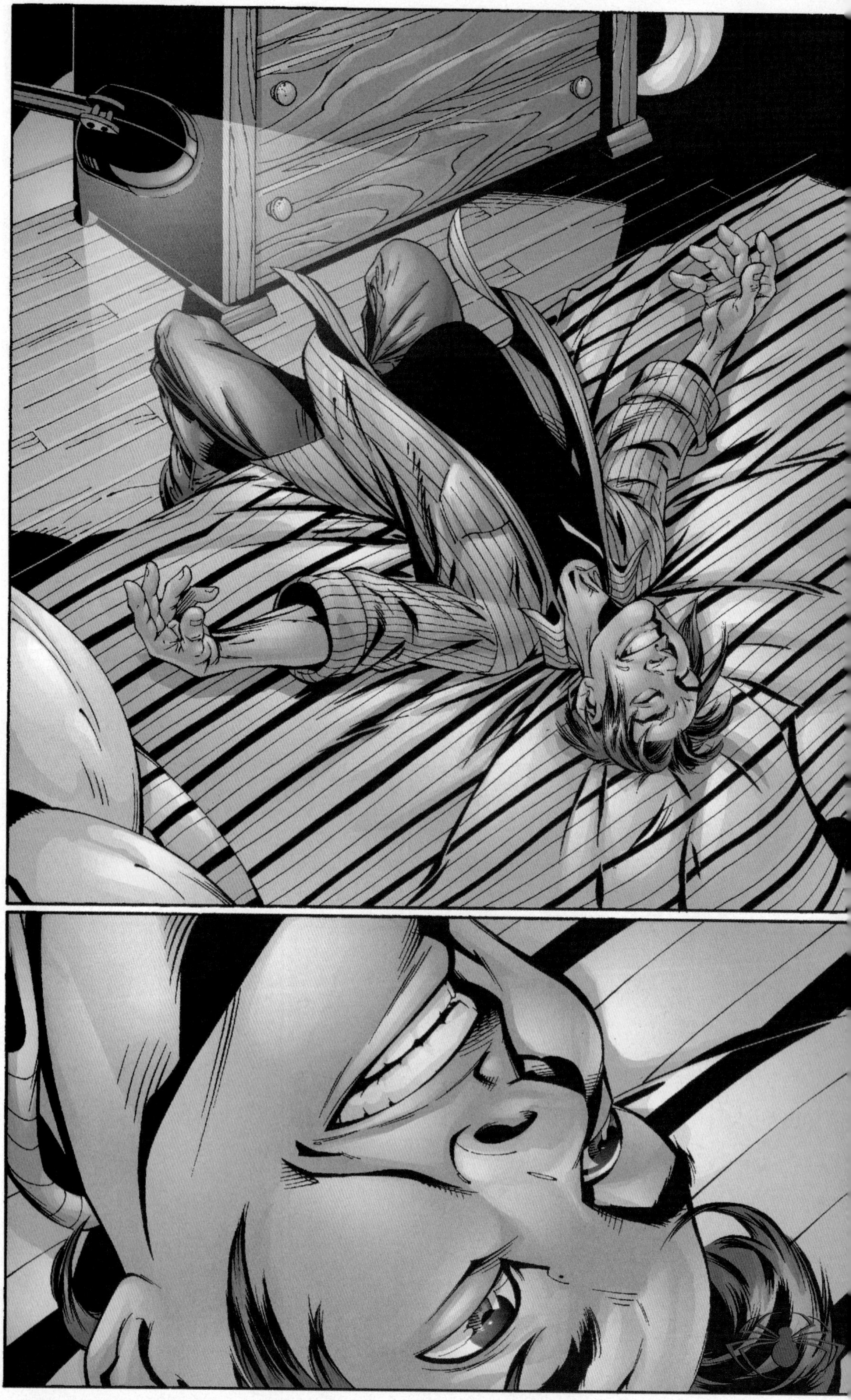

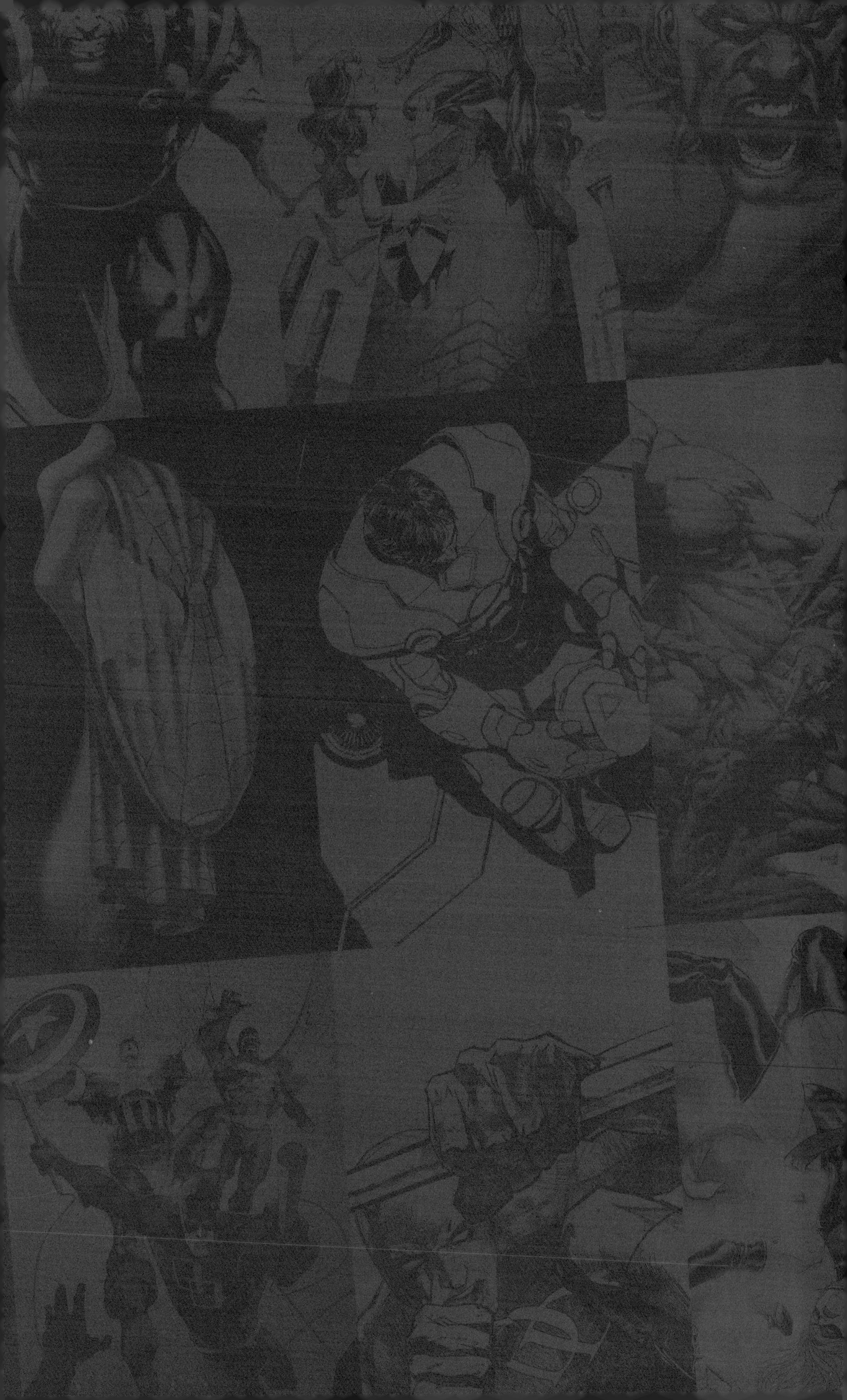

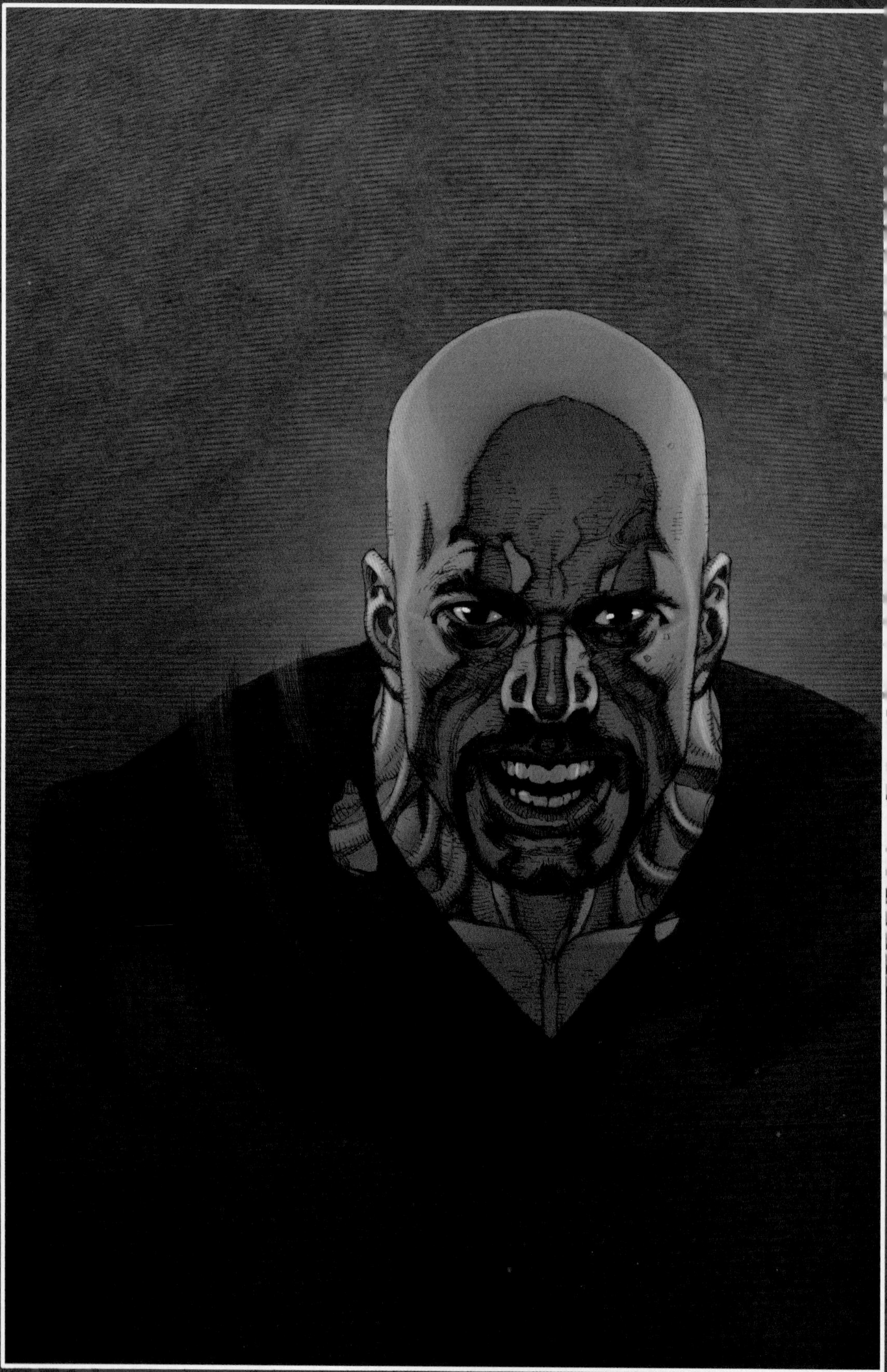

NEW AVENGERS #22

THE NEW AVENGERS

PREVIOUSLY IN CIVIL WAR...

After a fight between a quartet of dangerous villains and the New Warriors accidentally causes the destruction of Stamford, Connecticut and the deaths of hundreds of bystanders, public sentiment turns against super heroes. Advocates call for reform, and, as a result, a Superhuman Registration Act is debated, which would require all those possessing paranormal abilities to register with the government, divulging their true identities to the authorities and submitting to training and sanctioning in the manner of federal agents.

Some heroes, such as Iron Man, see this as a natural evolution of the role of superhumans in society, and a reasonable request. Others take umbrage at this assault on their civil liberties. After being called upon to hunt down his fellow heroes who are in defiance of the Registration Act, Captain America goes underground and, with the help of his former partner, the Falcon, begins to form a resistance movement.

MIDNIGHT:
REGISTRATION ACT BECOMES LAW
SONY
REGISTRATION ACT BECOMES LAW REGISTRATION

Today, the Act has been passed — the law goes into effect at midnight. Any person possessing superhuman powers who doesn't register will be considered a criminal.

Writer
Brian Michael Bendis

Artist
Leinil Yu

Color Art
Dave McCaig

Letterer
RS & Comicraft's
Albert Deschesne

Production
Rich Ginter

Assistant Editors
Molly Lazer &
Aubrey Sitterson

Editor
Tom Brevoort

Editor in Chief
Joe Quesada

Publisher
Dan Buckley

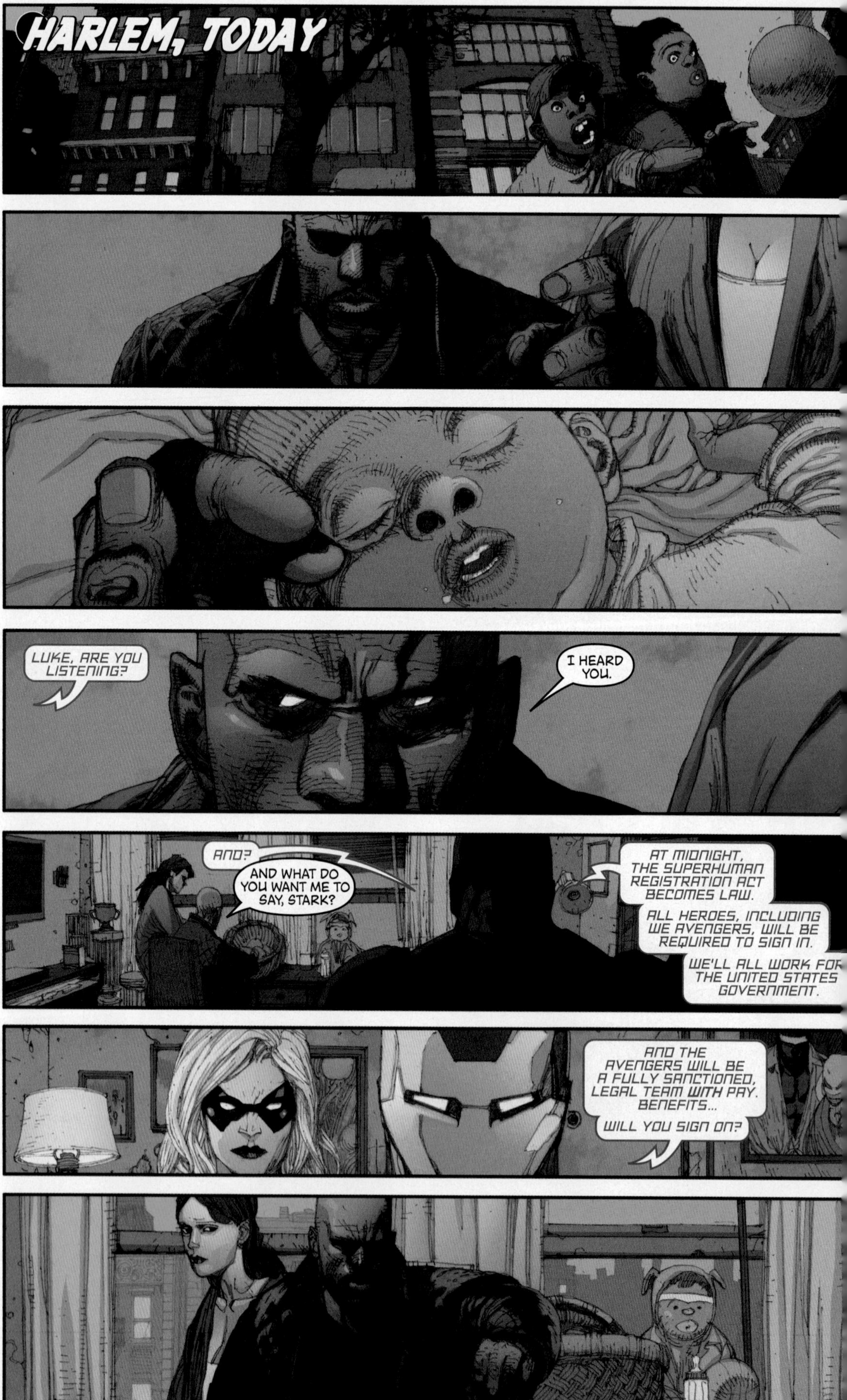
HARLEM, TODAY
LUKE, ARE YOU LISTENING?
I HEARD YOU.
AND?
AND WHAT DO YOU WANT ME TO SAY, STARK?
AT MIDNIGHT, THE SUPERHUMAN REGISTRATION ACT BECOMES LAW.
ALL HEROES, INCLUDING WE AVENGERS, WILL BE REQUIRED TO SIGN IN.
WE'LL ALL WORK FOR THE UNITED STATES GOVERNMENT.
AND THE AVENGERS WILL BE A FULLY SANCTIONED, LEGAL TEAM WITH PAY. BENEFITS...
WILL YOU SIGN ON?

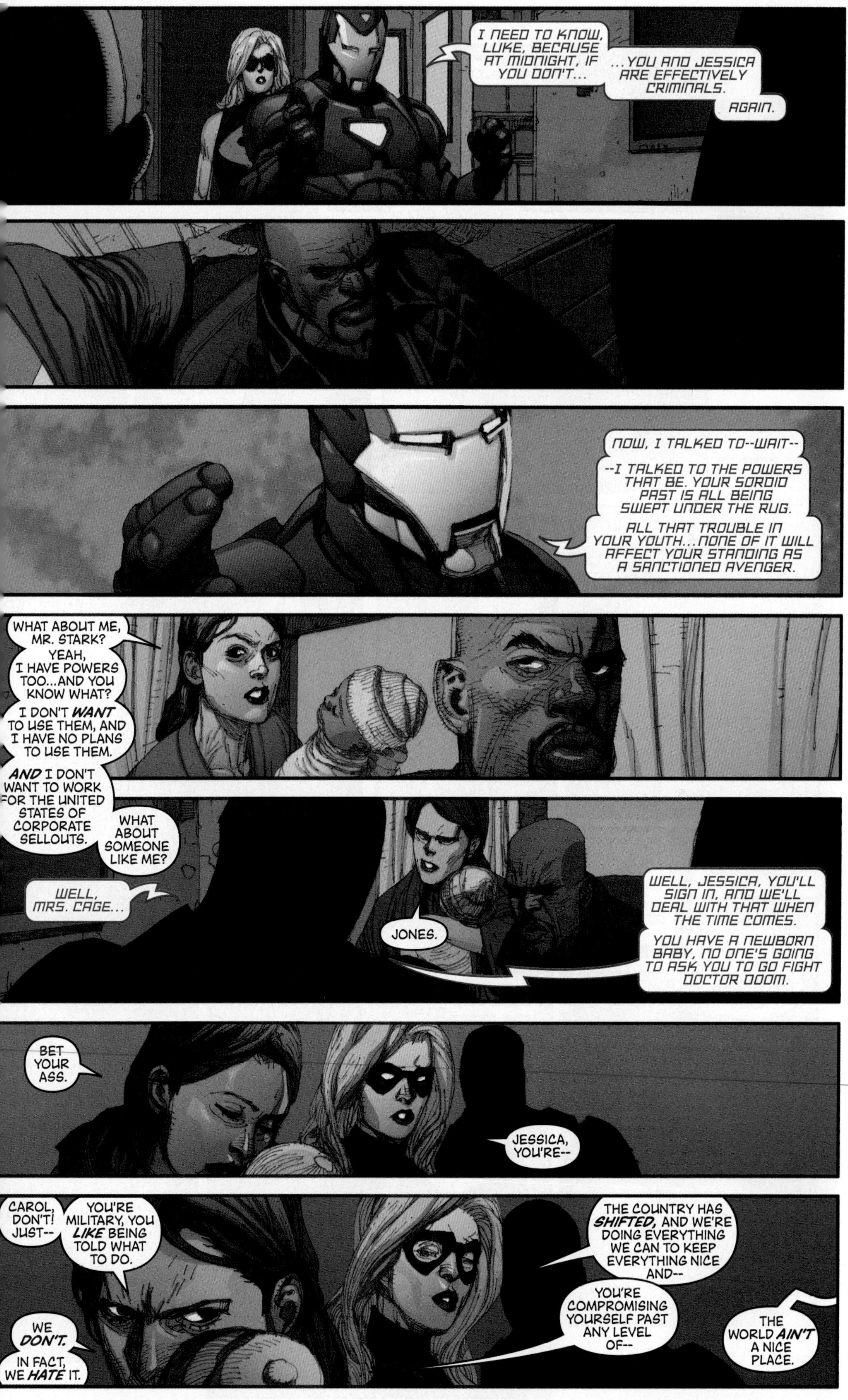
I NEED TO KNOW, LUKE, BECAUSE AT MIDNIGHT, IF YOU DON'T...
...YOU AND JESSICA ARE EFFECTIVELY CRIMINALS.
AGAIN.
NOW, I TALKED TO--WAIT--
--I TALKED TO THE POWERS THAT BE. YOUR SORDID PAST IS ALL BEING SWEPT UNDER THE RUG.
ALL THAT TROUBLE IN YOUR YOUTH...NONE OF IT WILL AFFECT YOUR STANDING AS A SANCTIONED AVENGER.
WHAT ABOUT ME, MR. STARK?
YEAH, I HAVE POWERS TOO...AND YOU KNOW WHAT?
I DON'T WANT TO USE THEM, AND I HAVE NO PLANS TO USE THEM.
AND I DON'T WANT TO WORK FOR THE UNITED STATES OF CORPORATE SELLOUTS.
WHAT ABOUT SOMEONE LIKE ME?
WELL, MRS. CAGE...
JONES.
WELL, JESSICA, YOU'LL SIGN IN, AND WE'LL DEAL WITH THAT WHEN THE TIME COMES.
YOU HAVE A NEWBORN BABY, NO ONE'S GOING TO ASK YOU TO GO FIGHT DOCTOR DOOM.
BET YOUR ASS.
JESSICA, YOU'RE--
CAROL, DON'T! JUST--
YOU'RE MILITARY, YOU LIKE BEING TOLD WHAT TO DO.
WE DON'T.
IN FACT, WE HATE IT.
THE COUNTRY HAS SHIFTED, AND WE'RE DOING EVERYTHING WE CAN TO KEEP EVERYTHING NICE AND--
YOU'RE COMPROMISING YOURSELF PAST ANY LEVEL OF--
THE WORLD AIN'T A NICE PLACE.

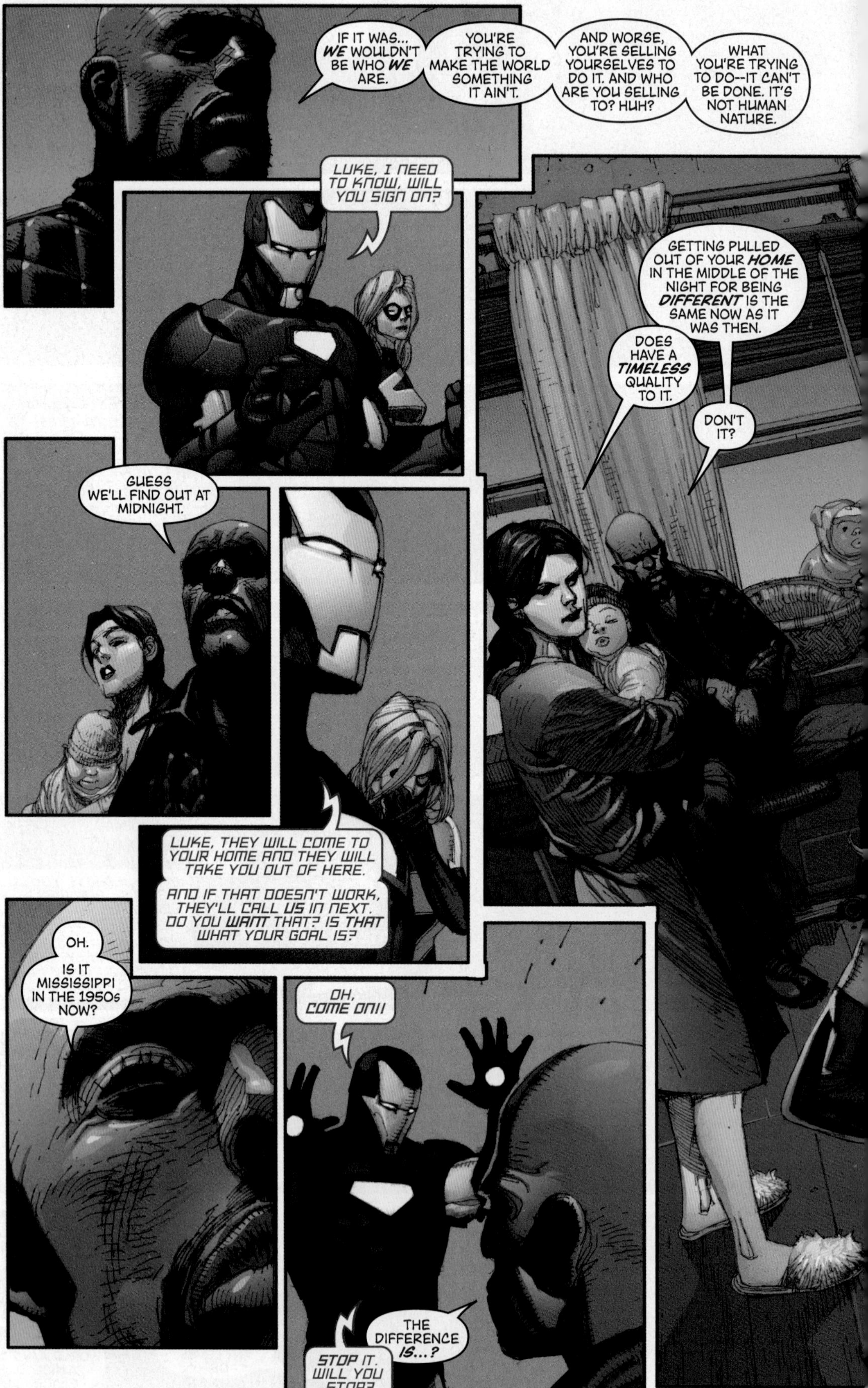
IF IT WAS... WE WOULDN'T BE WHO WE ARE.
YOU'RE TRYING TO MAKE THE WORLD SOMETHING IT AIN'T.
AND WORSE, YOU'RE SELLING YOURSELVES TO DO IT. AND WHO ARE YOU SELLING TO? HUH?
WHAT YOU'RE TRYING TO DO--IT CAN'T BE DONE. IT'S NOT HUMAN NATURE.
LUKE, I NEED TO KNOW, WILL YOU SIGN ON?
GUESS WE'LL FIND OUT AT MIDNIGHT.
LUKE, THEY WILL COME TO YOUR HOME AND THEY WILL TAKE YOU OUT OF HERE.
AND IF THAT DOESN'T WORK, THEY'LL CALL US IN NEXT. DO YOU WANT THAT? IS THAT WHAT YOUR GOAL IS?
OH.
IS IT MISSISSIPPI IN THE 1950s NOW?
OH, COME ON!!
THE DIFFERENCE IS...?
STOP IT. WILL YOU STOP?
GETTING PULLED OUT OF YOUR HOME IN THE MIDDLE OF THE NIGHT FOR BEING DIFFERENT IS THE SAME NOW AS IT WAS THEN.
DOES HAVE A TIMELESS QUALITY TO IT.
DON'T IT?

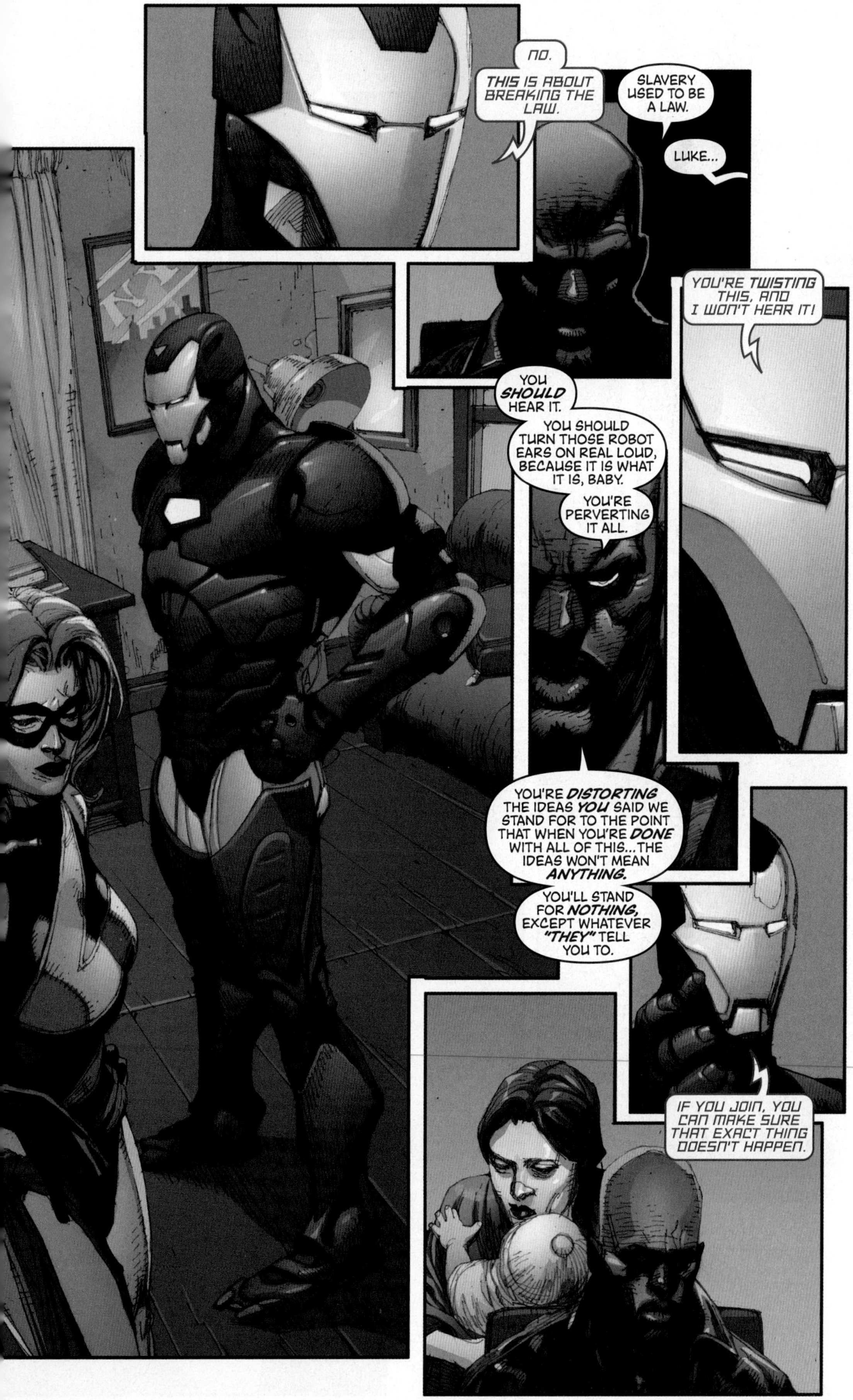
NO.
THIS IS ABOUT BREAKING THE LAW.
SLAVERY USED TO BE A LAW.
LUKE...
YOU'RE TWISTING THIS, AND I WON'T HEAR IT!
YOU SHOULD HEAR IT.
YOU SHOULD TURN THOSE ROBOT EARS ON REAL LOUD, BECAUSE IT IS WHAT IT IS, BABY.
YOU'RE PERVERTING IT ALL.
YOU'RE DISTORTING THE IDEAS YOU SAID WE STAND FOR TO THE POINT THAT WHEN YOU'RE DONE WITH ALL OF THIS... THE IDEAS WON'T MEAN ANYTHING.
YOU'LL STAND FOR NOTHING, EXCEPT WHATEVER "THEY" TELL YOU TO.
IF YOU JOIN, YOU CAN MAKE SURE THAT EXACT THING DOESN'T HAPPEN.

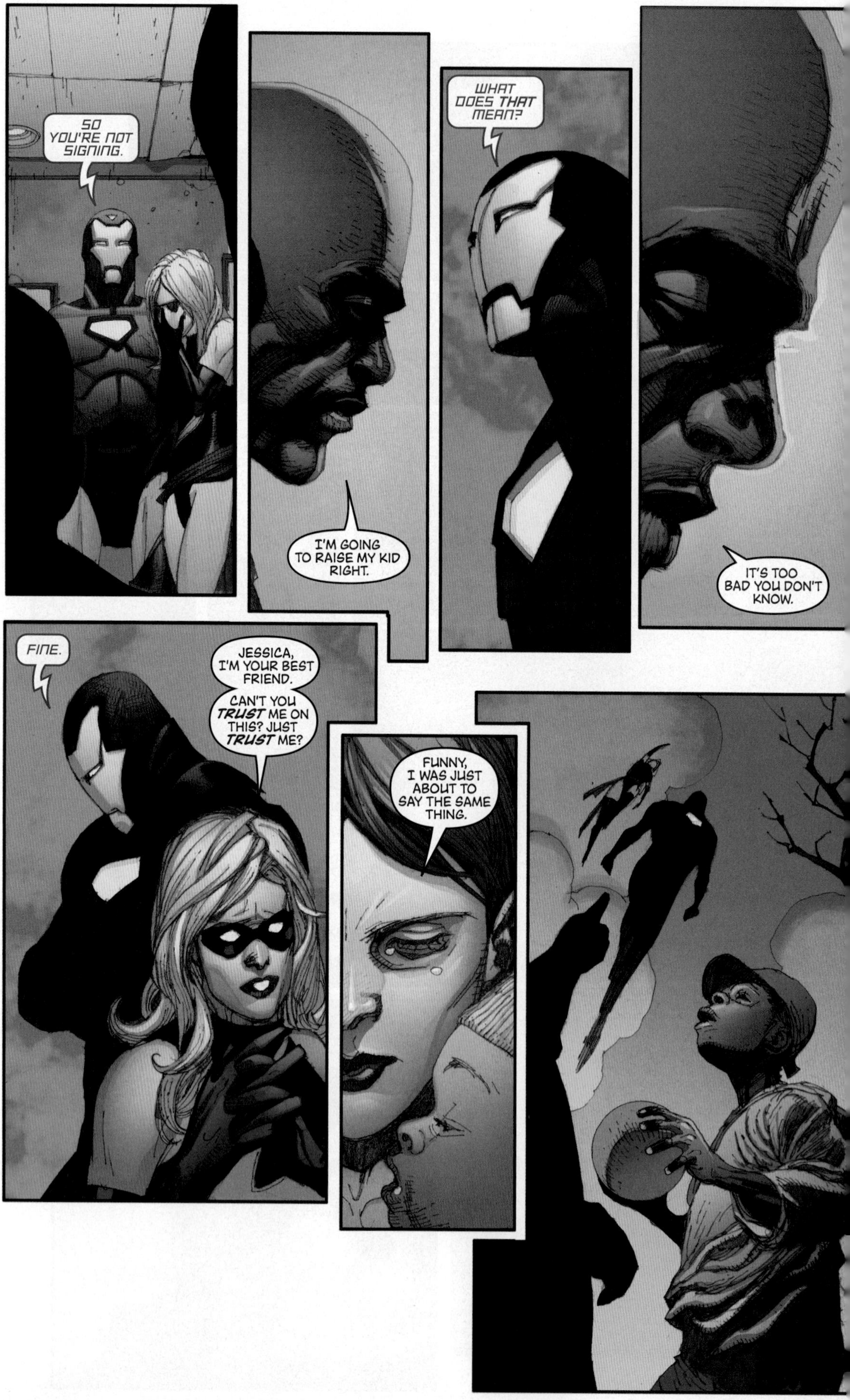
SO YOU'RE NOT SIGNING.
I'M GOING TO RAISE MY KID RIGHT.
WHAT DOES THAT MEAN?
IT'S TOO BAD YOU DON'T KNOW.
FINE.
JESSICA, I'M YOUR BEST FRIEND.
CAN'T YOU TRUST ME ON THIS? JUST TRUST ME?
FUNNY, I WAS JUST ABOUT TO SAY THE SAME THING.

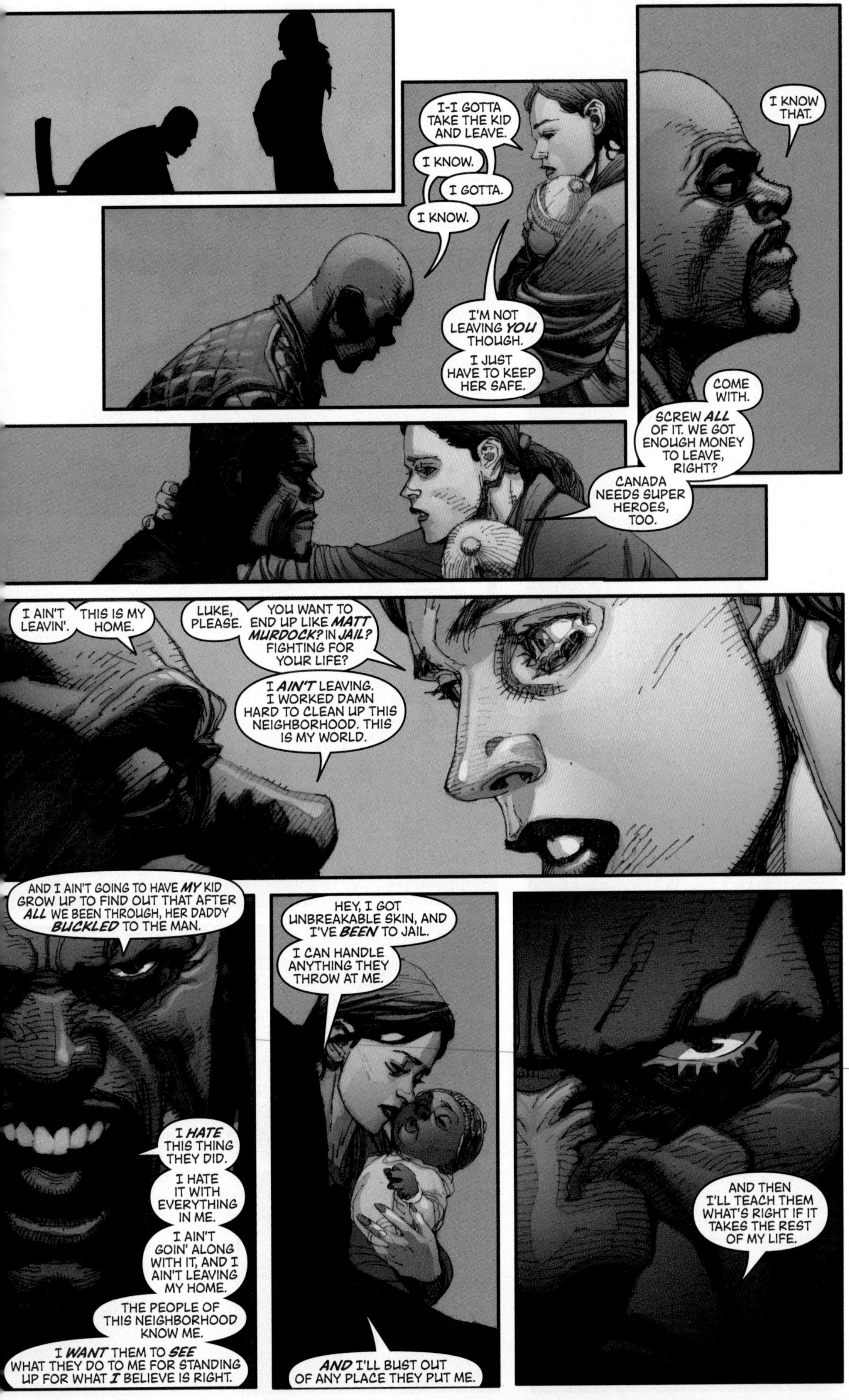
I-I GOTTA TAKE THE KID AND LEAVE.
I KNOW.
I GOTTA.
I KNOW.
I'M NOT LEAVING YOU THOUGH.
I JUST HAVE TO KEEP HER SAFE.
I KNOW THAT.
COME WITH.
SCREW ALL OF IT. WE GOT ENOUGH MONEY TO LEAVE, RIGHT?
CANADA NEEDS SUPER HEROES, TOO.
I AIN'T LEAVIN'.
THIS IS MY HOME.
LUKE, PLEASE.
YOU WANT TO END UP LIKE MATT MURDOCK? IN JAIL? FIGHTING FOR YOUR LIFE?
I AIN'T LEAVING. I WORKED DAMN HARD TO CLEAN UP THIS NEIGHBORHOOD. THIS IS MY WORLD.
AND I AIN'T GOING TO HAVE MY KID GROW UP TO FIND OUT THAT AFTER ALL WE BEEN THROUGH, HER DADDY BUCKLED TO THE MAN.
I HATE THIS THING THEY DID.
I HATE IT WITH EVERYTHING IN ME.
I AIN'T GOIN' ALONG WITH IT, AND I AIN'T LEAVING MY HOME.
THE PEOPLE OF THIS NEIGHBORHOOD KNOW ME.
I WANT THEM TO SEE WHAT THEY DO TO ME FOR STANDING UP FOR WHAT I BELIEVE IS RIGHT.
HEY, I GOT UNBREAKABLE SKIN, AND I'VE BEEN TO JAIL.
I CAN HANDLE ANYTHING THEY THROW AT ME.
AND I'LL BUST OUT OF ANY PLACE THEY PUT ME.
AND THEN I'LL TEACH THEM WHAT'S RIGHT IF IT TAKES THE REST OF MY LIFE.

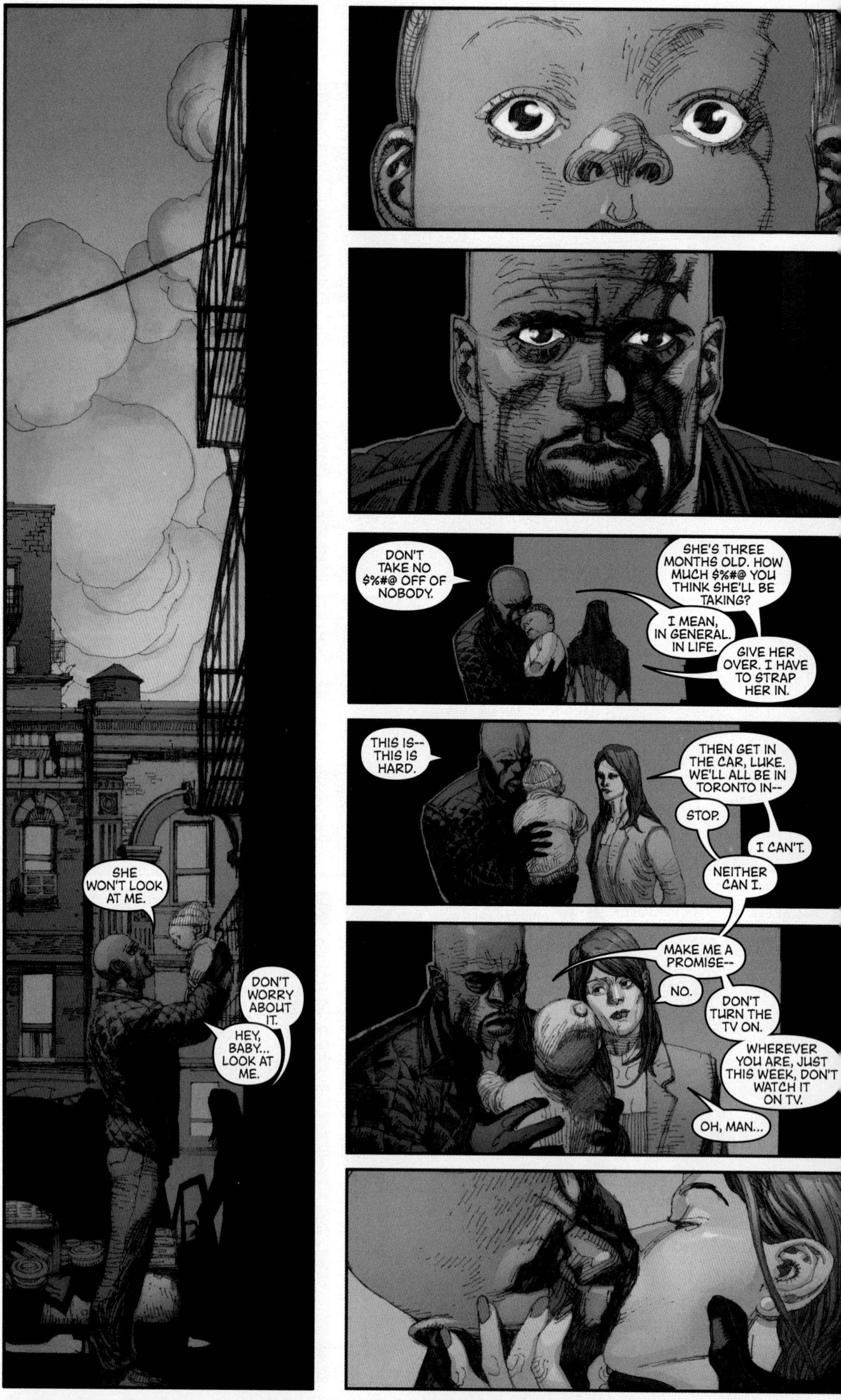
SHE WON'T LOOK AT ME.
DON'T WORRY ABOUT IT.
HEY, BABY... LOOK AT ME.
DON'T TAKE NO $%#@ OFF OF NOBODY.
SHE'S THREE MONTHS OLD. HOW MUCH $%#@ YOU THINK SHE'LL BE TAKING?
I MEAN, IN GENERAL. IN LIFE.
GIVE HER OVER. I HAVE TO STRAP HER IN.
THIS IS-- THIS IS HARD.
THEN GET IN THE CAR, LUKE. WE'LL ALL BE IN TORONTO IN--
STOP.
I CAN'T.
NEITHER CAN I.
MAKE ME A PROMISE--
NO.
DON'T TURN THE TV ON.
WHEREVER YOU ARE, JUST THIS WEEK, DON'T WATCH IT ON TV.
OH, MAN...

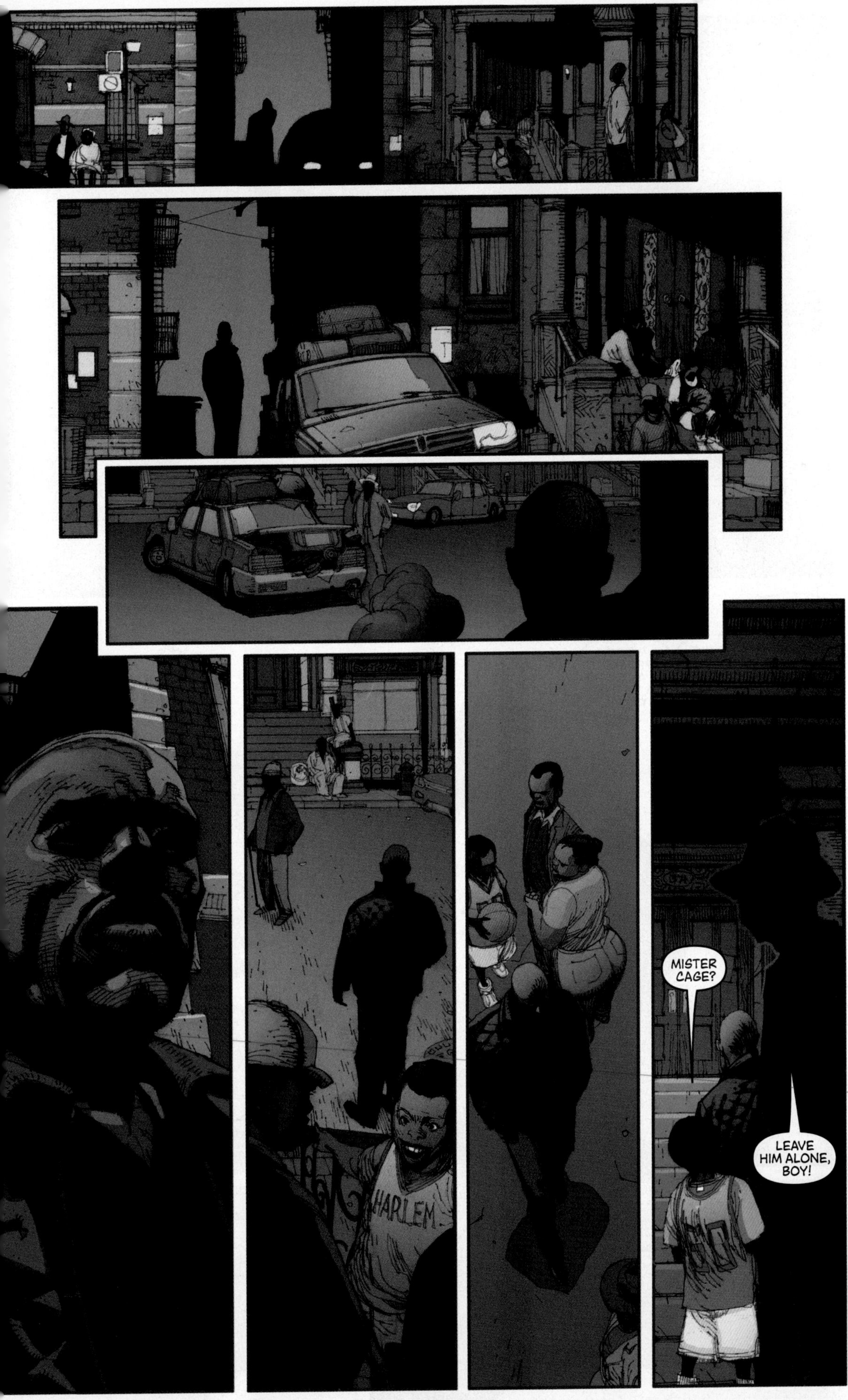
MISTER CAGE?
LEAVE HIM ALONE, BOY!

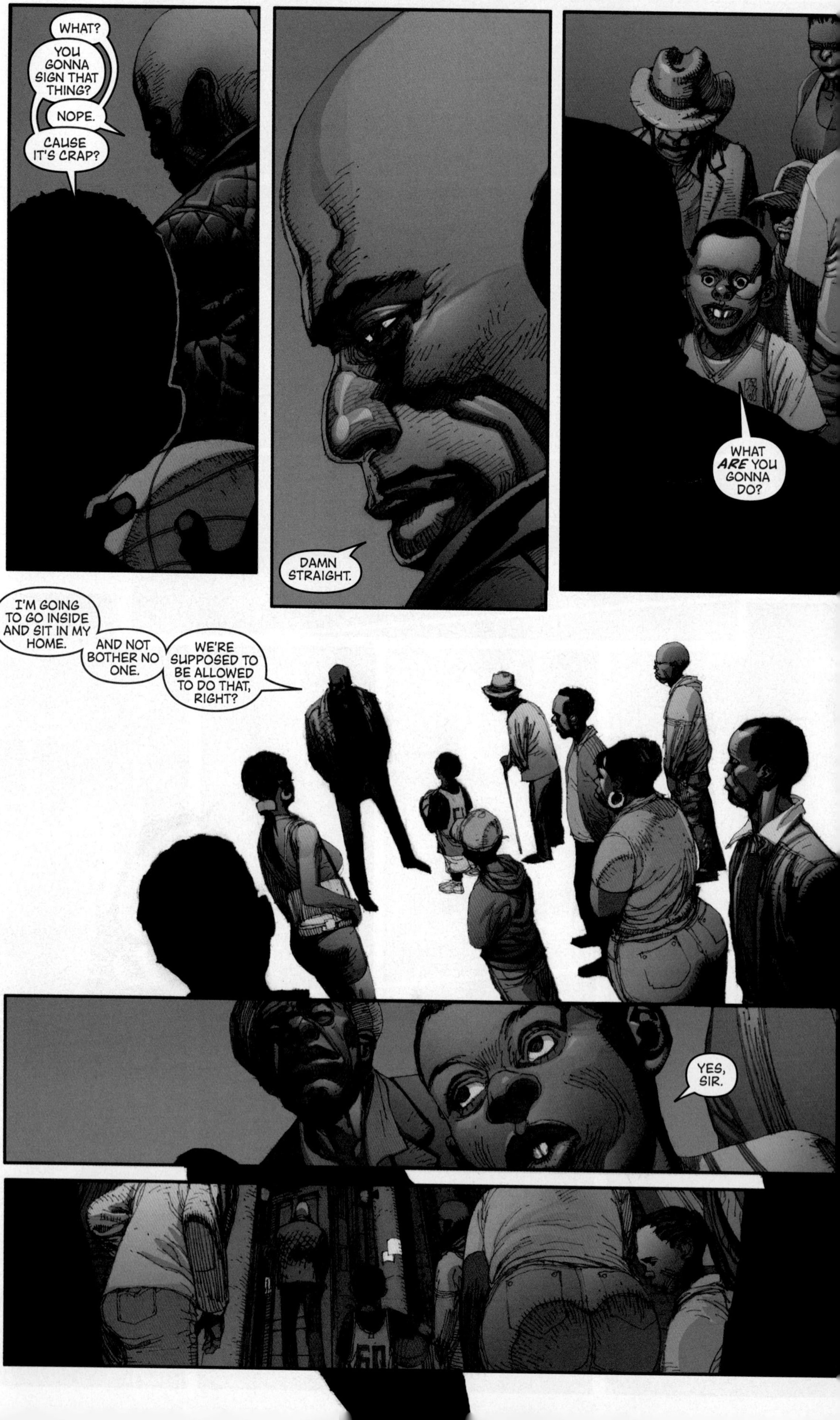
WHAT?
YOU GONNA SIGN THAT THING?
NOPE.
CAUSE IT'S CRAP?
DAMN STRAIGHT.
WHAT *ARE* YOU GONNA DO?
I'M GOING TO GO INSIDE AND SIT IN MY HOME.
AND NOT BOTHER NO ONE.
WE'RE SUPPOSED TO BE ALLOWED TO DO THAT, RIGHT?
YES, SIR.

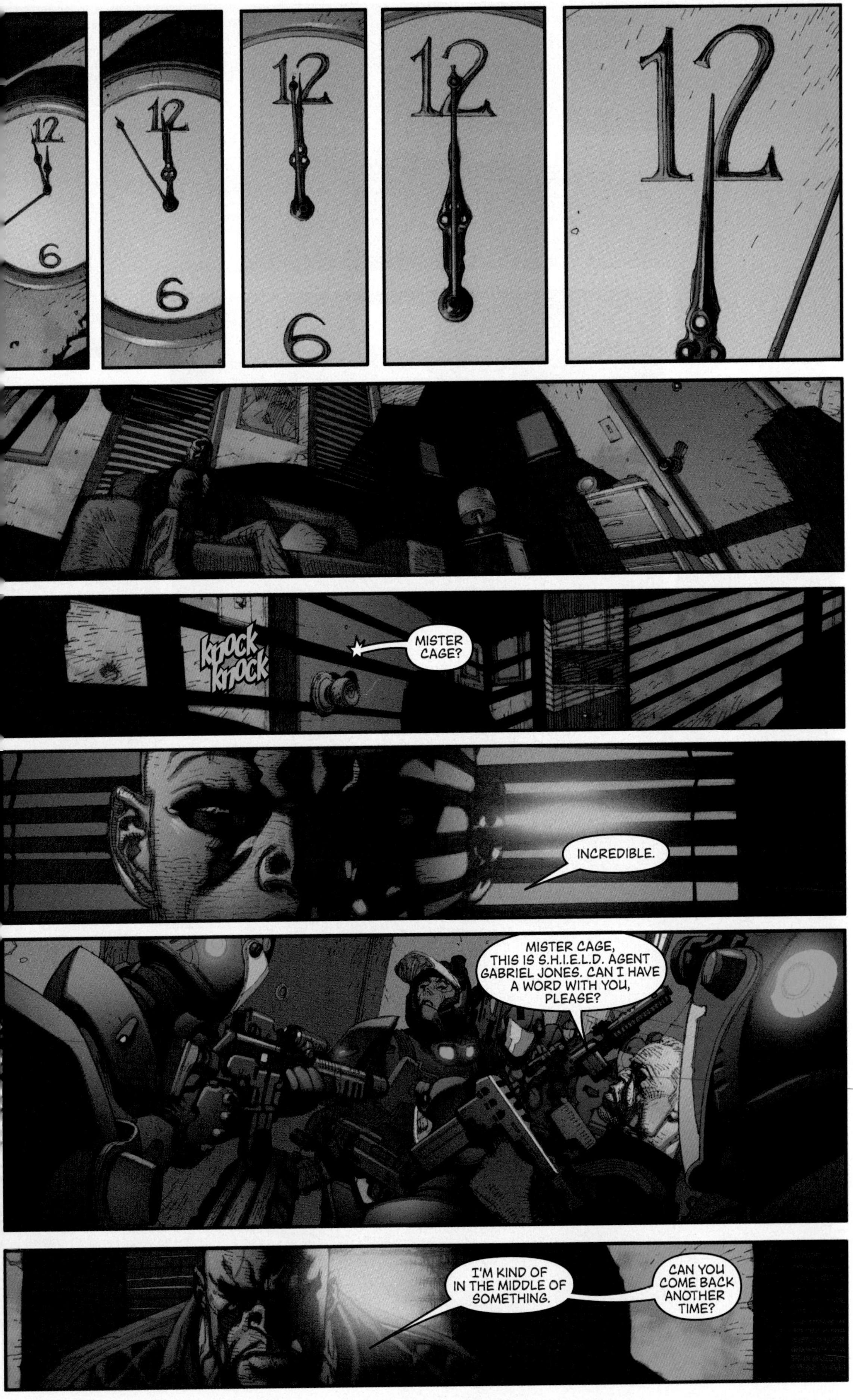
12
6
12
6
12
6
12
6
12
12
knock knock
MISTER CAGE?
INCREDIBLE.
MISTER CAGE, THIS IS S.H.I.E.L.D. AGENT GABRIEL JONES. CAN I HAVE A WORD WITH YOU, PLEASE?
I'M KIND OF IN THE MIDDLE OF SOMETHING.
CAN YOU COME BACK ANOTHER TIME?

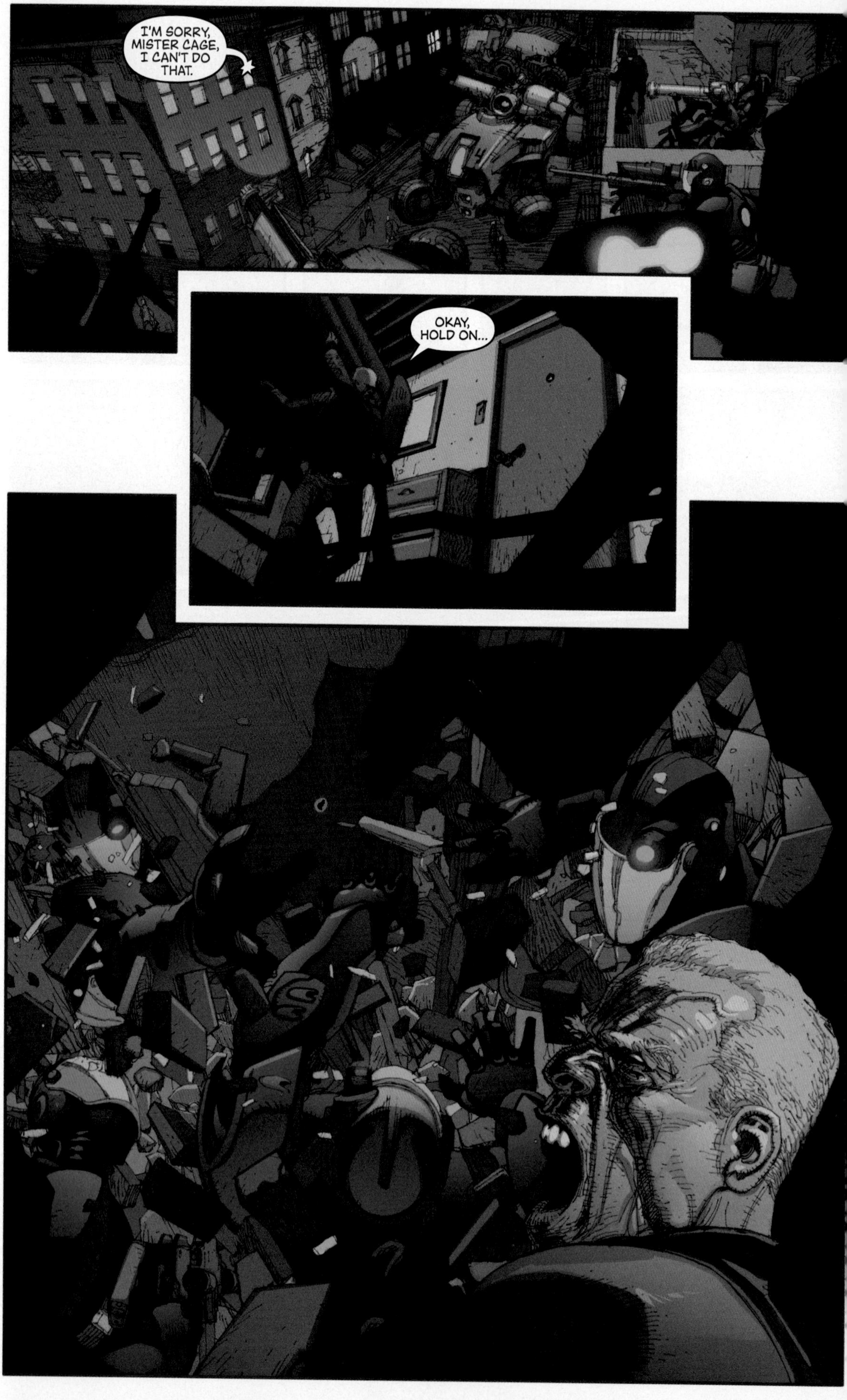
I'M SORRY, MISTER CAGE, I CAN'T DO THAT.
OKAY, HOLD ON...

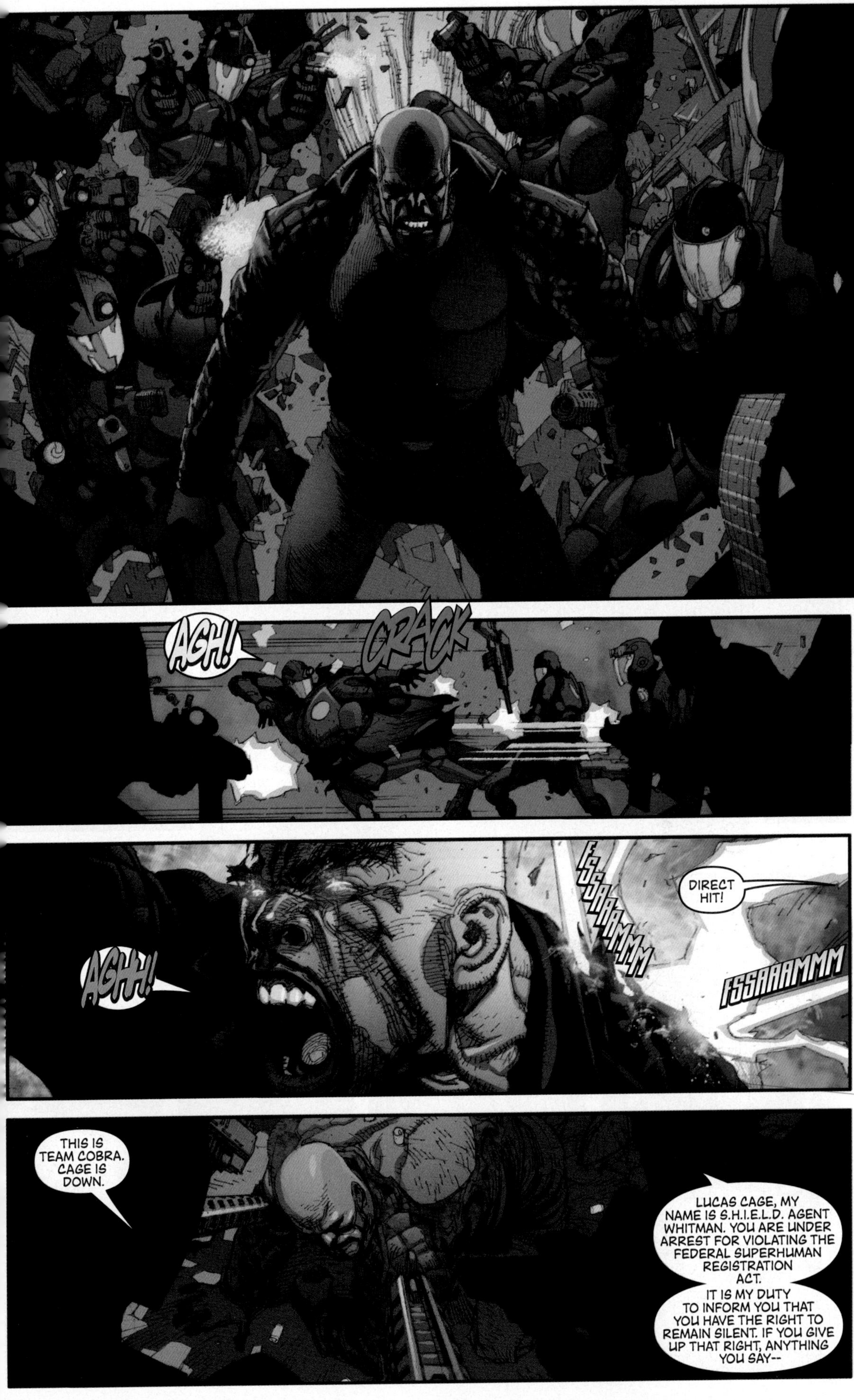
AGH!
CRACK
FSSAAAMMM
DIRECT HIT!
AGHH!
FSSAAAMMM
THIS IS TEAM COBRA. CAGE IS DOWN.
LUCAS CAGE, MY NAME IS S.H.I.E.L.D. AGENT WHITMAN. YOU ARE UNDER ARREST FOR VIOLATING THE FEDERAL SUPERHUMAN REGISTRATION ACT.
IT IS MY DUTY TO INFORM YOU THAT YOU HAVE THE RIGHT TO REMAIN SILENT. IF YOU GIVE UP THAT RIGHT, ANYTHING YOU SAY--

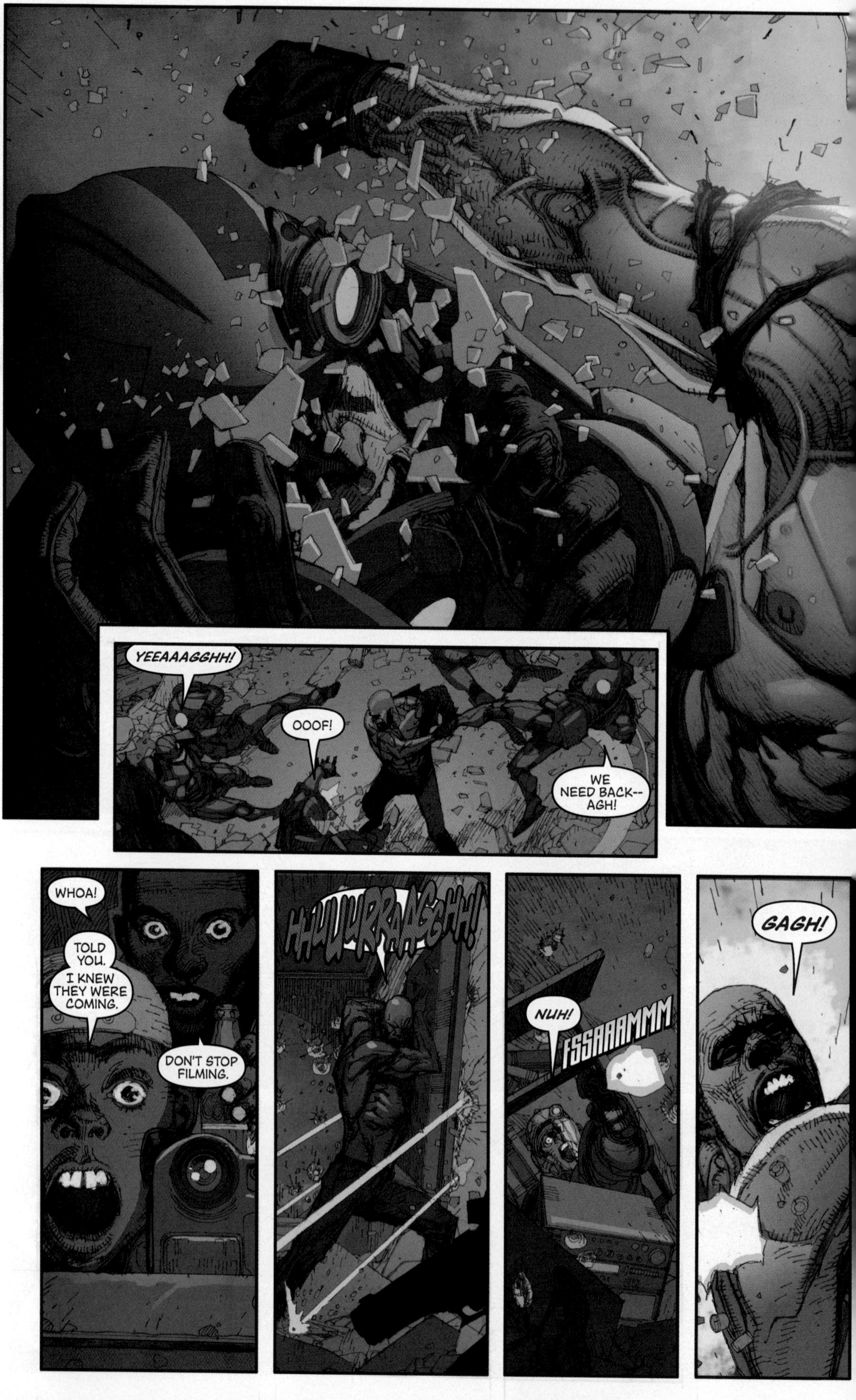
YEEAAAAGGHH!
OOOF!
WE NEED BACK-- AGH!
WHOA!
TOLD YOU. I KNEW THEY WERE COMING.
DON'T STOP FILMING.
HHUUURRAAGGHH!
NUH!
FSSAAAMMM
GAGH!

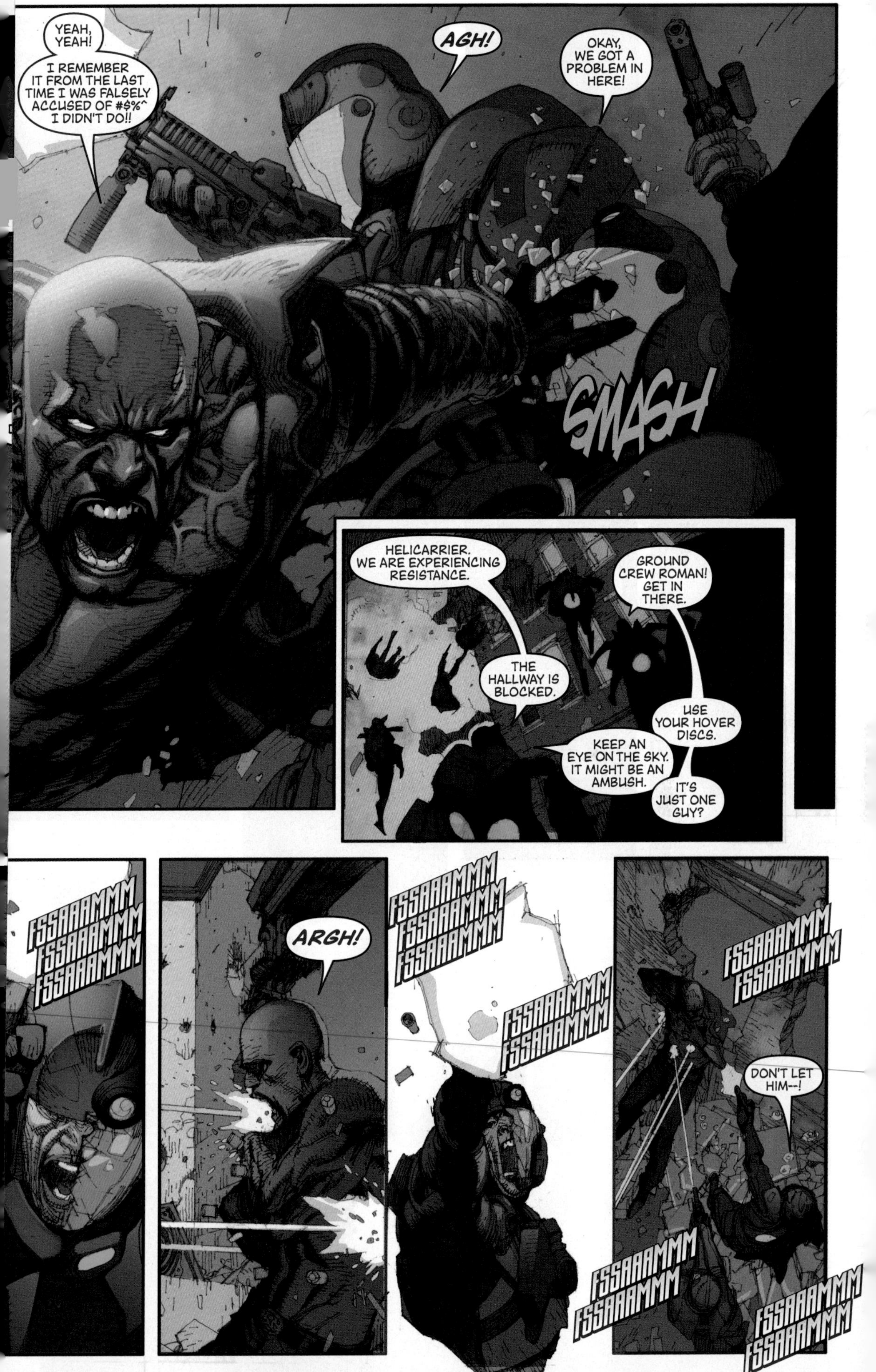
YEAH, YEAH!
I REMEMBER IT FROM THE LAST TIME I WAS FALSELY ACCUSED OF #$%^ I DIDN'T DO!!
AGH!
OKAY, WE GOT A PROBLEM IN HERE!
SMASH
HELICARRIER. WE ARE EXPERIENCING RESISTANCE.
GROUND CREW ROMAN! GET IN THERE.
THE HALLWAY IS BLOCKED.
USE YOUR HOVER DISCS.
KEEP AN EYE ON THE SKY. IT MIGHT BE AN AMBUSH.
IT'S JUST ONE GUY?
FSSAAAMMM FSSAAAMMM FSSAAAMMM
ARGH!
FSSAAAMMM FSSAAAMMM FSSAAAMMM
FSSAAAMMM FSSAAAMMM
FSSAAAMMM FSSAAAMMM
DON'T LET HIM--!
FSSAAAMMM FSSAAAMMM
FSSAAAMMM FSSAAAMMM

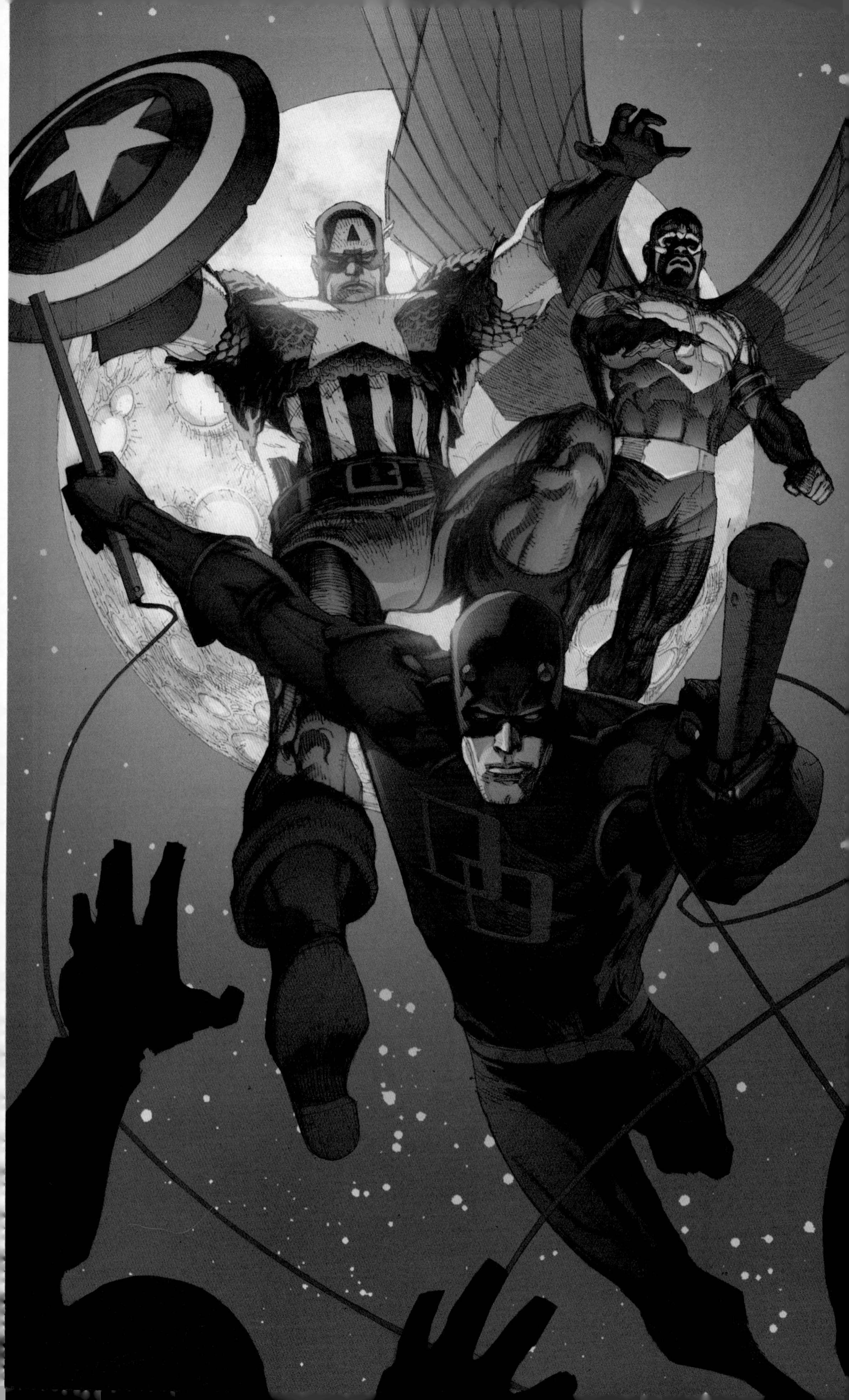

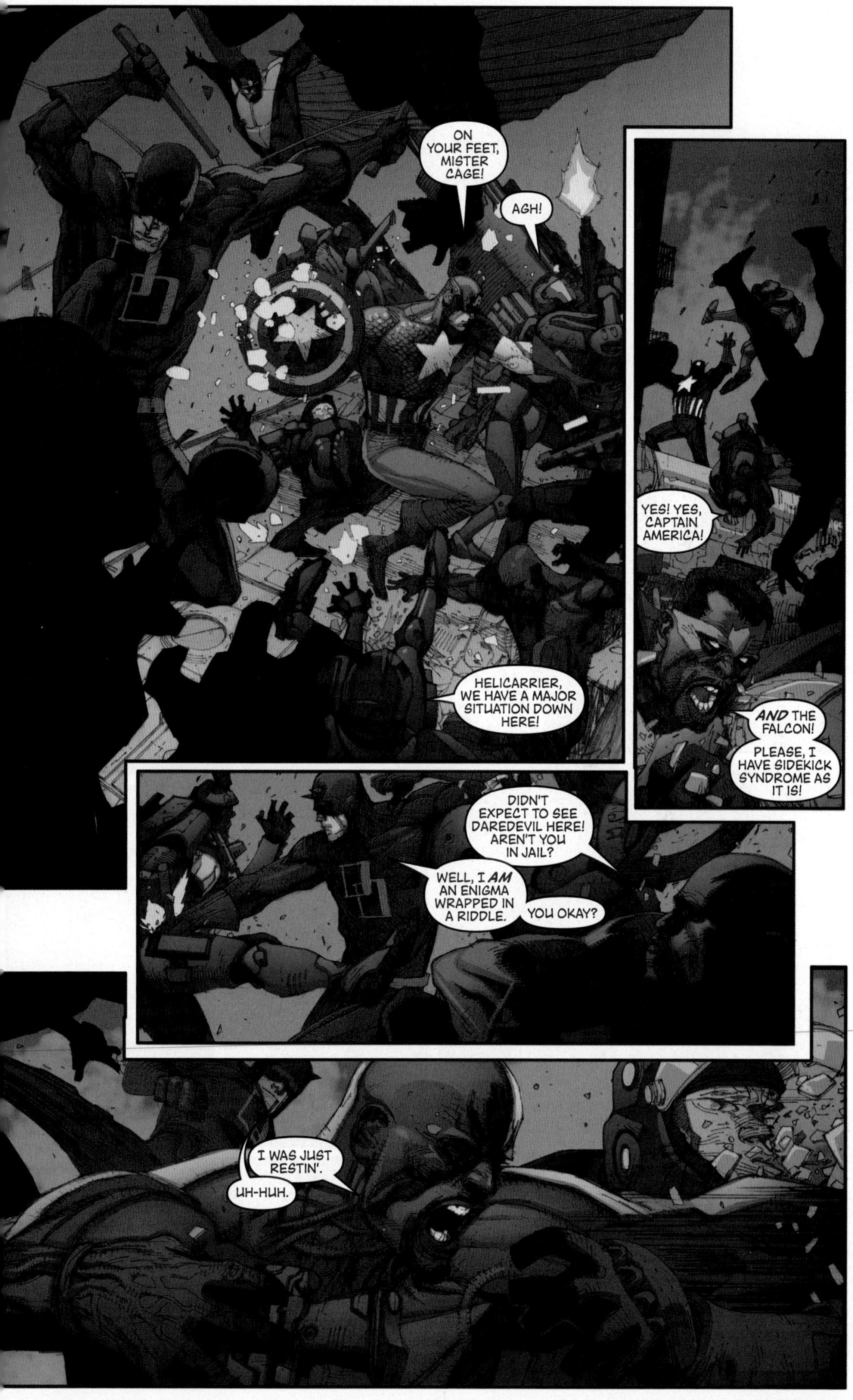
ON YOUR FEET, MISTER CAGE!
AGH!
HELICARRIER, WE HAVE A MAJOR SITUATION DOWN HERE!
YES! YES, CAPTAIN AMERICA!
AND THE FALCON!
PLEASE, I HAVE SIDEKICK SYNDROME AS IT IS!
DIDN'T EXPECT TO SEE DAREDEVIL HERE! AREN'T YOU IN JAIL?
WELL, I AM AN ENIGMA WRAPPED IN A RIDDLE.
YOU OKAY?
I WAS JUST RESTIN'.
UH-HUH.

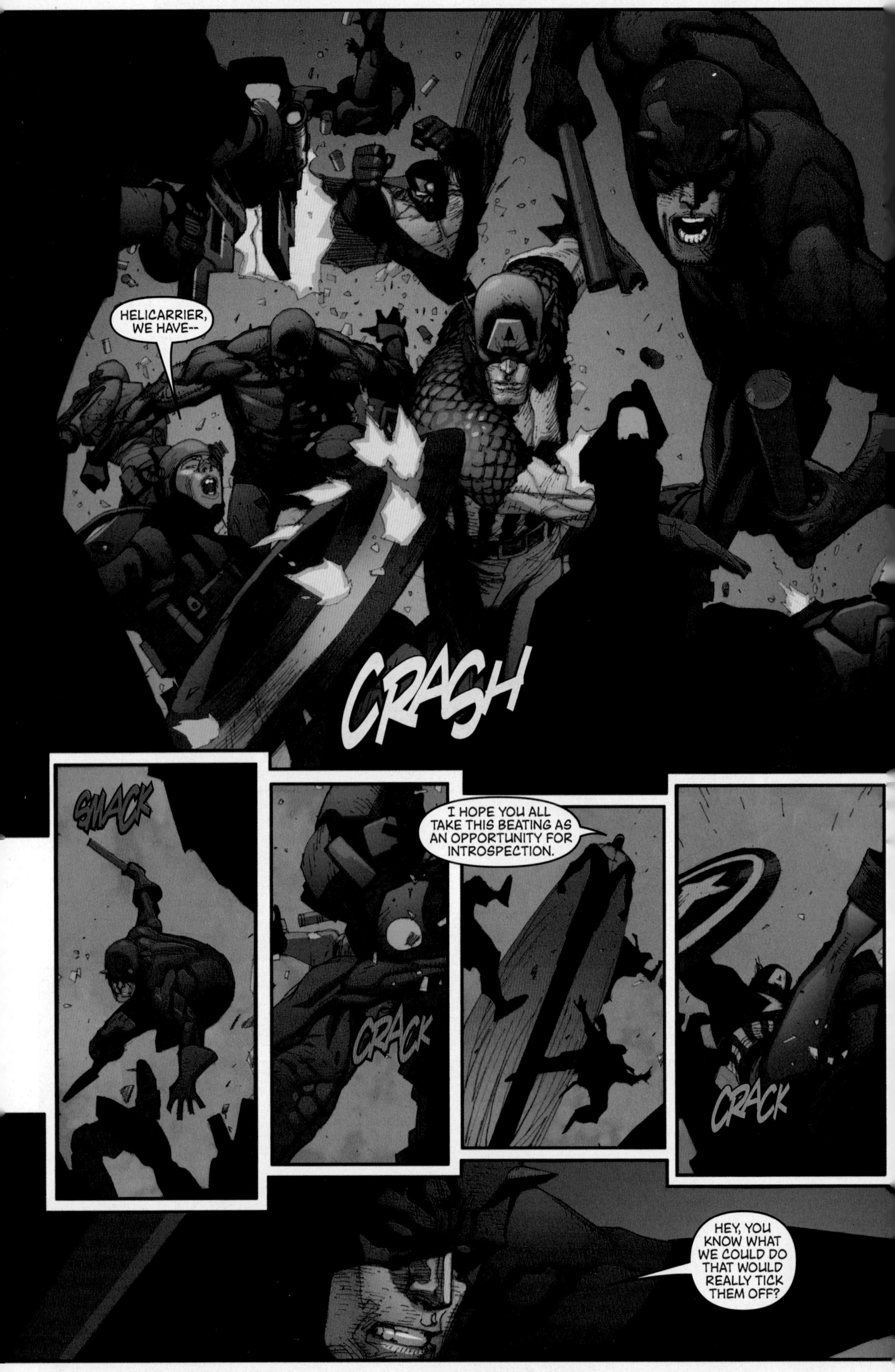
HELICARRIER, WE HAVE--
CRASH
SMACK
CRACK
I HOPE YOU ALL TAKE THIS BEATING AS AN OPPORTUNITY FOR INTROSPECTION.
CRACK
HEY, YOU KNOW WHAT WE COULD DO THAT WOULD REALLY TICK THEM OFF?

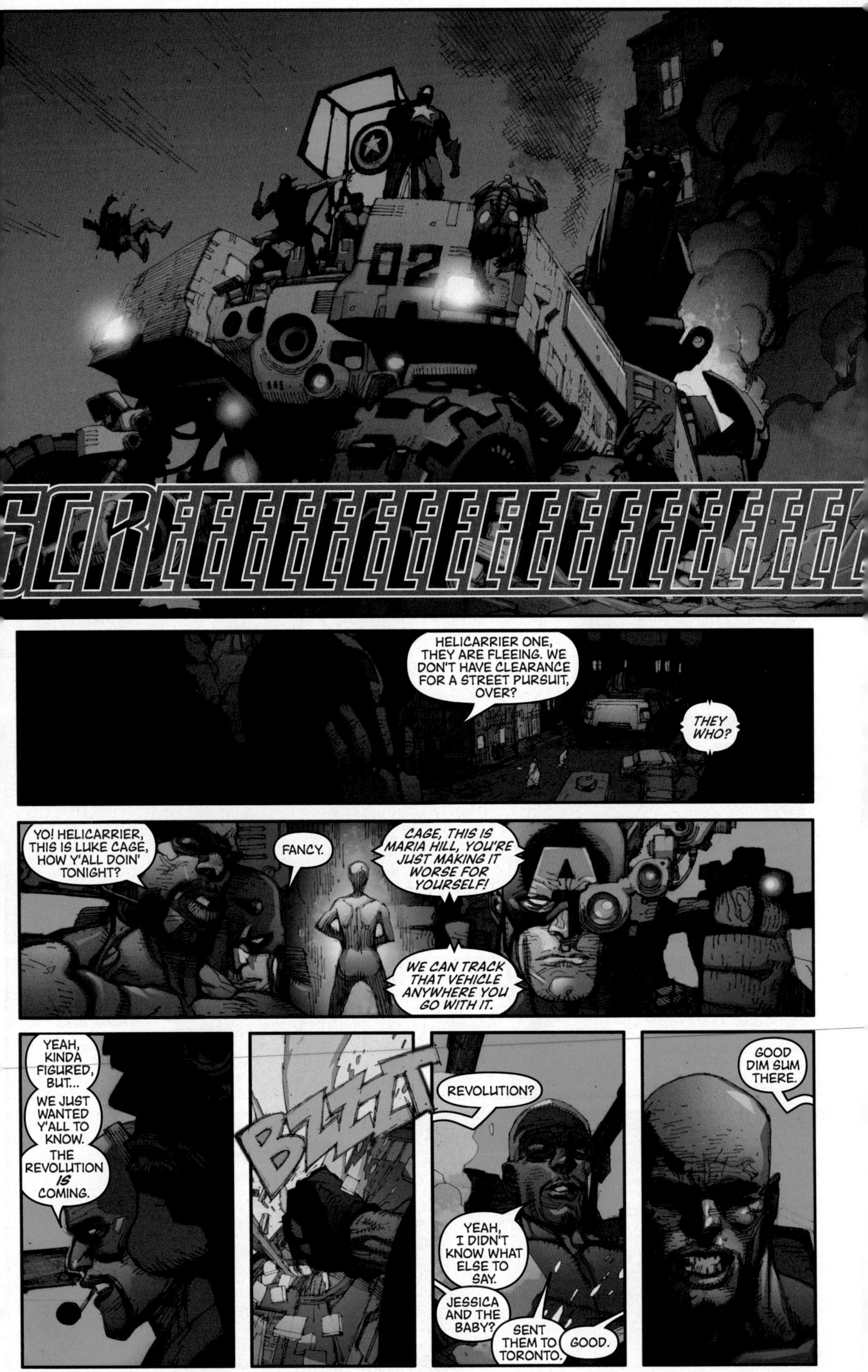
SCREEEEEEEEEEEEEEEEEEEEL
HELICARRIER ONE, THEY ARE FLEEING. WE DON'T HAVE CLEARANCE FOR A STREET PURSUIT, OVER?
THEY WHO?
YO! HELICARRIER, THIS IS LUKE CAGE, HOW Y'ALL DOIN' TONIGHT?
FANCY.
CAGE, THIS IS MARIA HILL, YOU'RE JUST MAKING IT WORSE FOR YOURSELF!
WE CAN TRACK THAT VEHICLE ANYWHERE YOU GO WITH IT.
YEAH, KINDA FIGURED, BUT...
WE JUST WANTED Y'ALL TO KNOW.
THE REVOLUTION IS COMING.
BZZZT
REVOLUTION?
YEAH, I DIDN'T KNOW WHAT ELSE TO SAY.
JESSICA AND THE BABY?
SENT THEM TO TORONTO.
GOOD.
GOOD DIM SUM THERE.

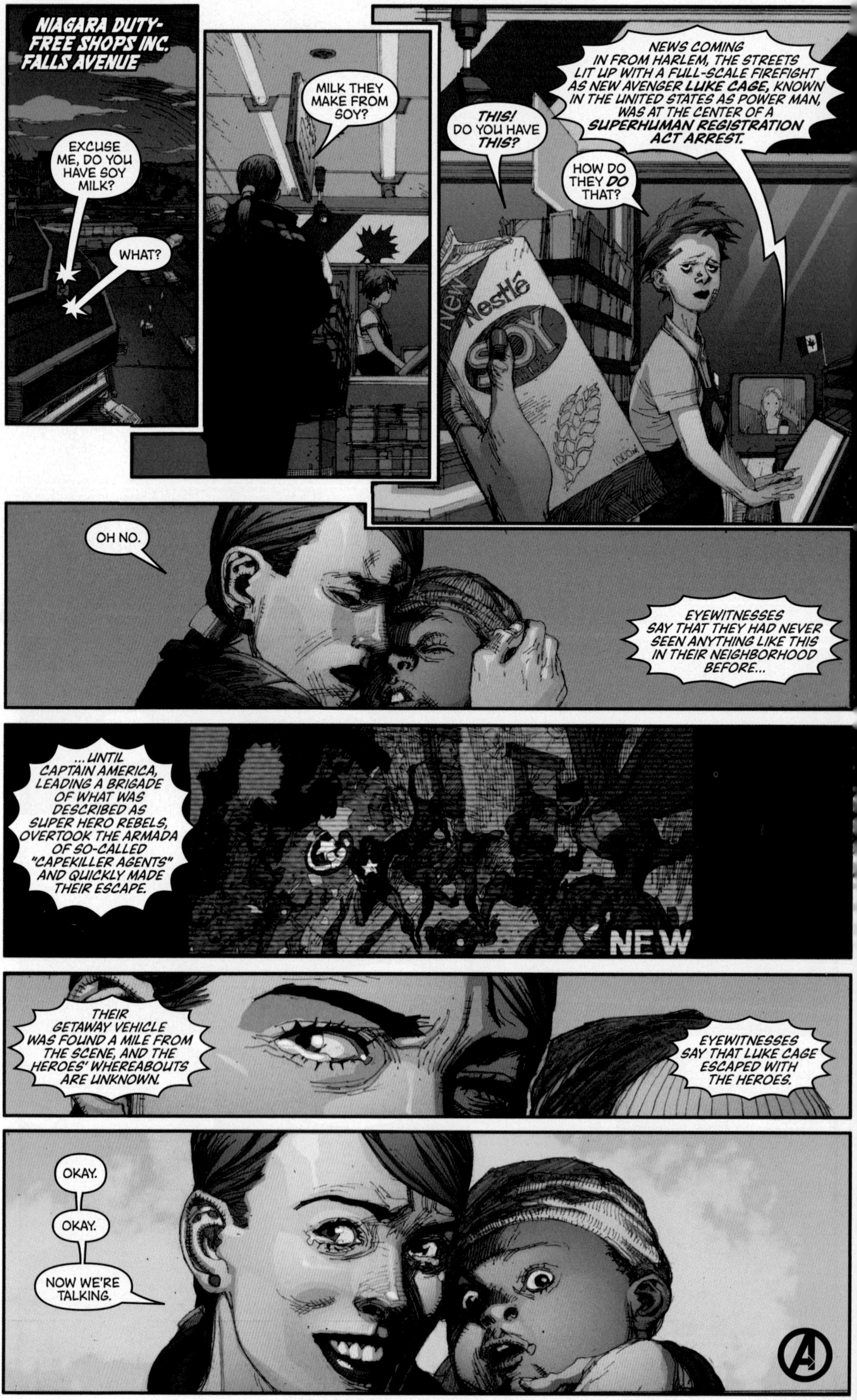
NIAGARA DUTY-FREE SHOPS INC. FALLS AVENUE
EXCUSE ME, DO YOU HAVE SOY MILK?
WHAT?
MILK THEY MAKE FROM SOY?
THIS! DO YOU HAVE THIS?
HOW DO THEY DO THAT?
NEWS COMING IN FROM HARLEM, THE STREETS LIT UP WITH A FULL-SCALE FIREFIGHT AS NEW AVENGER LUKE CAGE, KNOWN IN THE UNITED STATES AS POWER MAN, WAS AT THE CENTER OF A SUPERHUMAN REGISTRATION ACT ARREST.
Nestlé SOY
OH NO.
EYEWITNESSES SAY THAT THEY HAD NEVER SEEN ANYTHING LIKE THIS IN THEIR NEIGHBORHOOD BEFORE...
...UNTIL CAPTAIN AMERICA, LEADING A BRIGADE OF WHAT WAS DESCRIBED AS SUPER HERO REBELS, OVERTOOK THE ARMADA OF SO-CALLED "CAPEKILLER AGENTS" AND QUICKLY MADE THEIR ESCAPE.
NEW
THEIR GETAWAY VEHICLE WAS FOUND A MILE FROM THE SCENE, AND THE HEROES' WHEREABOUTS ARE UNKNOWN.
EYEWITNESSES SAY THAT LUKE CAGE ESCAPED WITH THE HEROES.
OKAY.
OKAY.
NOW WE'RE TALKING.

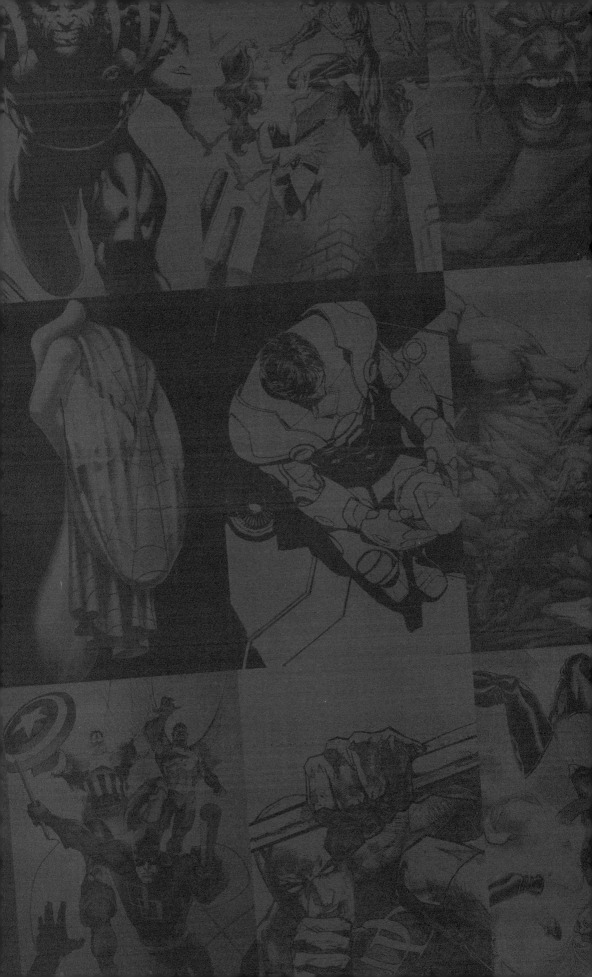

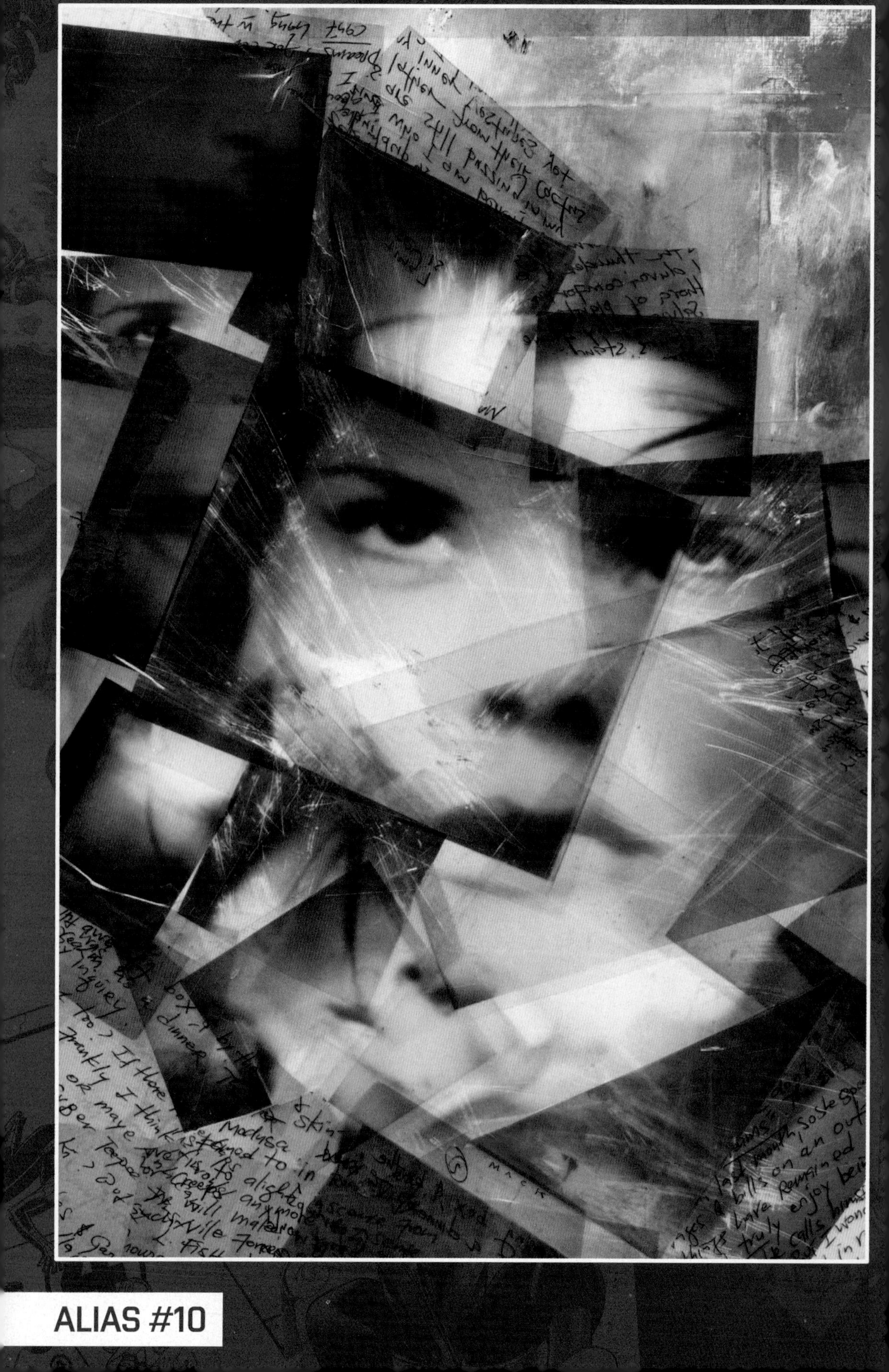

ALIAS #10

Previously in

BRIaN MICHaEL BENDIS
story

MICHaEL GaYDOS
art

MaTT HOLLINGSWORTH
colors

RICHaRD STaRKINGS aND
RS & COMICRaFT'S WES aBBOTT
letters

created by
BRIaN MICHaEL BENDIS

STUaRT MOORE
editor

KELLY LaMY
associate managing editor

NaNCI DaKESIaN
managing editor

JOE QUESaDa
editor in chief

BILL JEMaS
president

Jessica Jones, a former costumed super hero, is now
the owner and sole employee of Alias Investigations
— a small private investigative firm.

RECEPTIONIST
Ms. Jones, can I get you anything?

JESSICA JONES
When is this article from?

RECEPTIONIST
Um -- I'm not sure. There might be a date on it.

JESSICA JONES
Jameson wrote this himself?

RECEPTIONIST
Yes, ma'am, I guess he did.

JESSICA JONES
Didn't realize he'd been in newspapers for so long.

RECEPTIONIST
He's what he likes to call a "lifer." Can I get you anything to drink? Water? Coffee?

JESSICA JONES
No. No, I'm fine.

RECEPTIONIST
Mr. Jameson will be in shortly. He's on a call.

JESSICA JONES
Do you know why he asked me here?

RECEPTIONIST
No. Sorry, I don't. I'm not his personal assistant. I'm just the --

JESSICA JONES
Okay.

RECEPTIONIST
Sorry.

JESSICA JONES
No, it's okay.

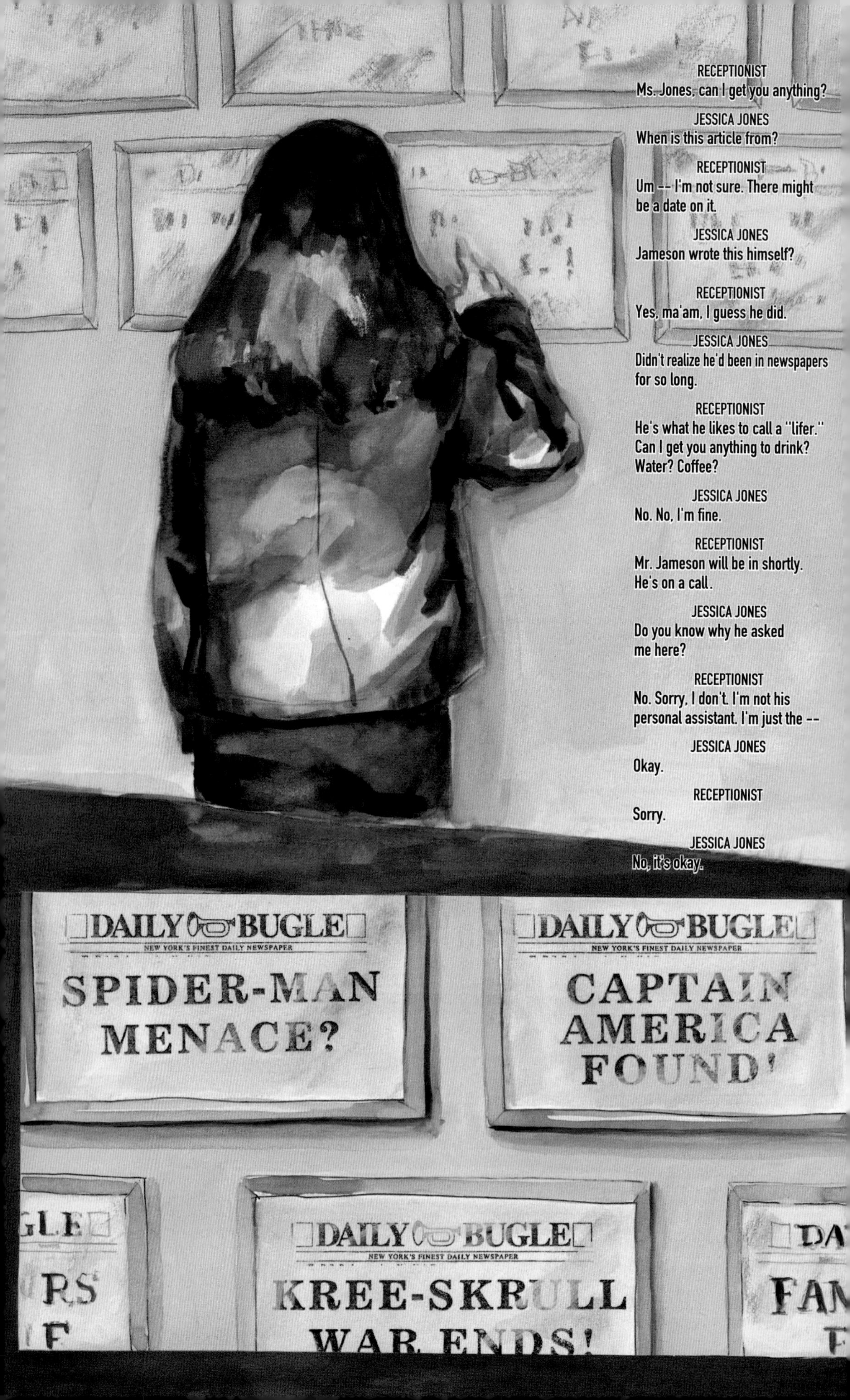
DAILY BUGLE
NEW YORK'S FINEST DAILY NEWSPAPER
SPIDER-MAN MENACE?
DAILY BUGLE
NEW YORK'S FINEST DAILY NEWSPAPER
CAPTAIN AMERICA FOUND!
DAILY BUGLE
NEW YORK'S FINEST DAILY NEWSPAPER
KREE-SKRULL WAR ENDS!

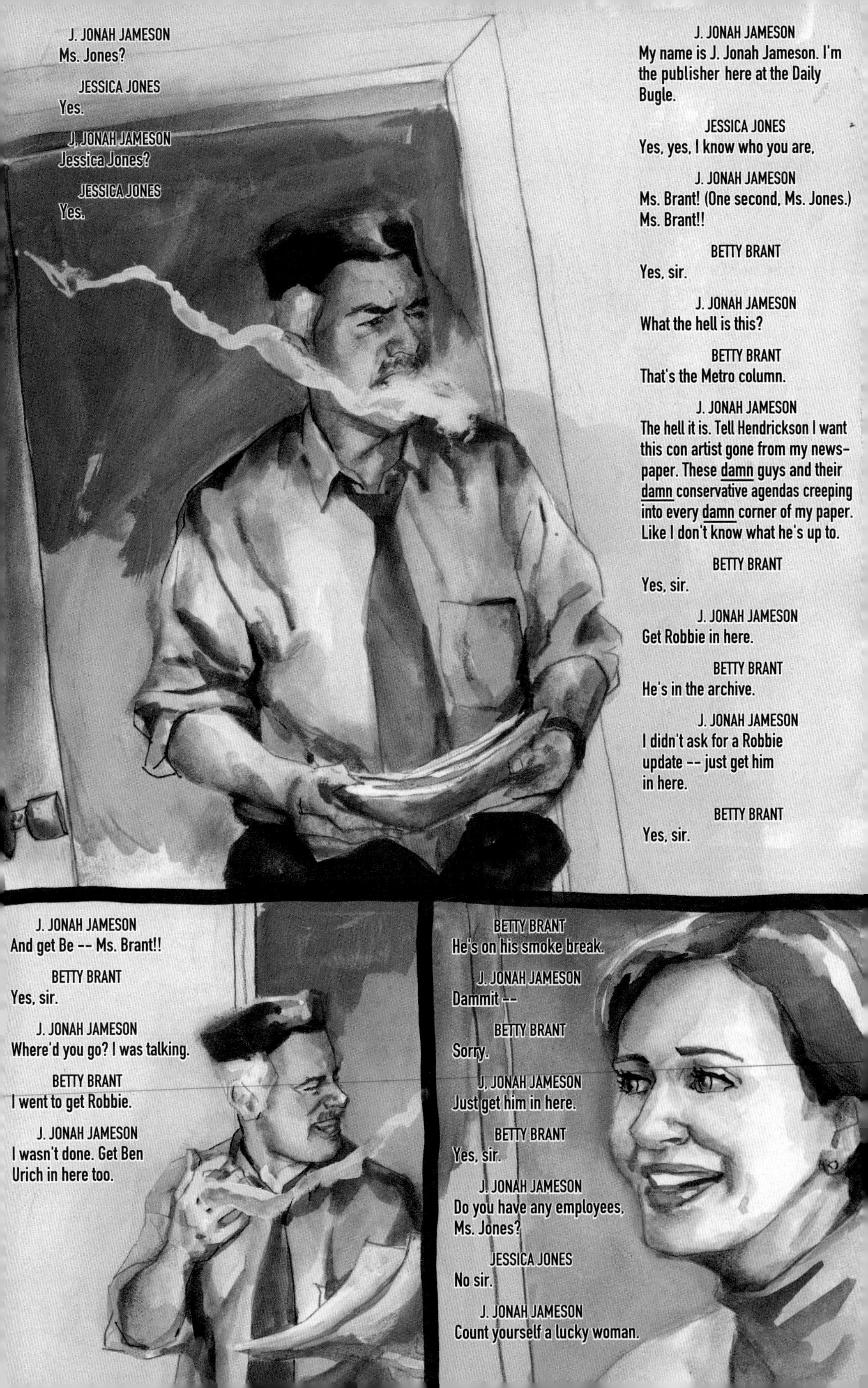
J. JONAH JAMESON
Ms. Jones?
JESSICA JONES
Yes.
J. JONAH JAMESON
Jessica Jones?
JESSICA JONES
Yes.
J. JONAH JAMESON
My name is J. Jonah Jameson. I'm the publisher here at the Daily Bugle.
JESSICA JONES
Yes, yes, I know who you are,
J. JONAH JAMESON
Ms. Brant! (One second, Ms. Jones.) Ms. Brant!!
BETTY BRANT
Yes, sir.
J. JONAH JAMESON
What the hell is this?
BETTY BRANT
That's the Metro column.
J. JONAH JAMESON
The hell it is. Tell Hendrickson I want this con artist gone from my news-paper. These damn guys and their damn conservative agendas creeping into every damn corner of my paper. Like I don't know what he's up to.
BETTY BRANT
Yes, sir.
J. JONAH JAMESON
Get Robbie in here.
BETTY BRANT
He's in the archive.
J. JONAH JAMESON
I didn't ask for a Robbie update -- just get him in here.
BETTY BRANT
Yes, sir.
J. JONAH JAMESON
And get Be -- Ms. Brant!!
BETTY BRANT
Yes, sir.
J. JONAH JAMESON
Where'd you go? I was talking.
BETTY BRANT
I went to get Robbie.
J. JONAH JAMESON
I wasn't done. Get Ben Urich in here too.
BETTY BRANT
He's on his smoke break.
J. JONAH JAMESON
Dammit --
BETTY BRANT
Sorry.
J. JONAH JAMESON
Just get him in here.
BETTY BRANT
Yes, sir.
J. JONAH JAMESON
Do you have any employees, Ms. Jones?
JESSICA JONES
No sir.
J. JONAH JAMESON
Count yourself a lucky woman.

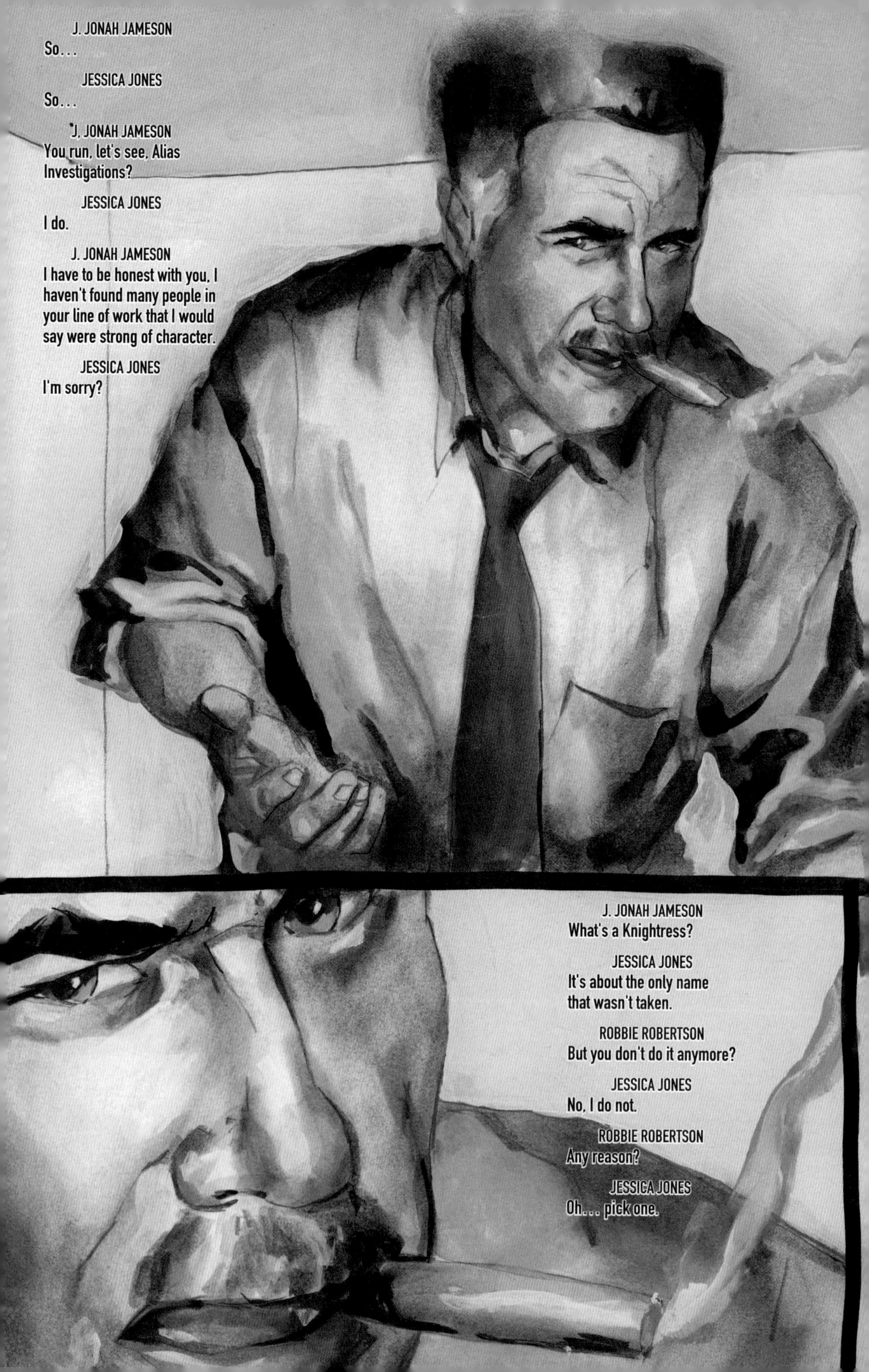
J. JONAH JAMESON
So...
JESSICA JONES
So...
J. JONAH JAMESON
You run, let's see, Alias Investigations?
JESSICA JONES
I do.
J. JONAH JAMESON
I have to be honest with you, I haven't found many people in your line of work that I would say were strong of character.
JESSICA JONES
I'm sorry?
J. JONAH JAMESON
What's a Knightress?
JESSICA JONES
It's about the only name that wasn't taken.
ROBBIE ROBERTSON
But you don't do it anymore?
JESSICA JONES
No, I do not.
ROBBIE ROBERTSON
Any reason?
JESSICA JONES
Oh... pick one.

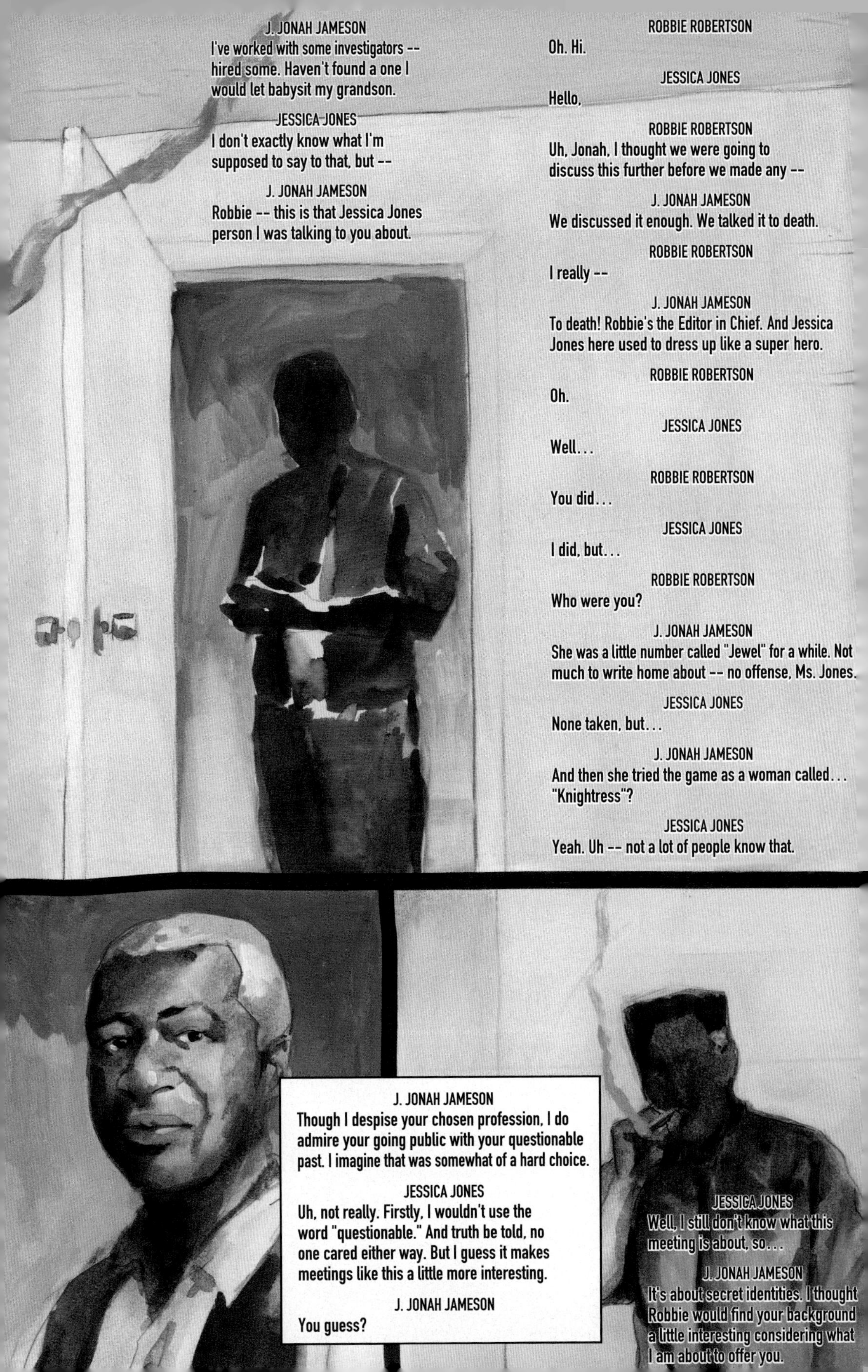
J. JONAH JAMESON
I've worked with some investigators -- hired some. Haven't found a one I would let babysit my grandson.
JESSICA JONES
I don't exactly know what I'm supposed to say to that, but --
J. JONAH JAMESON
Robbie -- this is that Jessica Jones person I was talking to you about.
ROBBIE ROBERTSON
Oh. Hi.
JESSICA JONES
Hello.
ROBBIE ROBERTSON
Uh, Jonah, I thought we were going to discuss this further before we made any --
J. JONAH JAMESON
We discussed it enough. We talked it to death.
ROBBIE ROBERTSON
I really --
J. JONAH JAMESON
To death! Robbie's the Editor in Chief. And Jessica Jones here used to dress up like a super hero.
ROBBIE ROBERTSON
Oh.
JESSICA JONES
Well...
ROBBIE ROBERTSON
You did...
JESSICA JONES
I did, but...
ROBBIE ROBERTSON
Who were you?
J. JONAH JAMESON
She was a little number called "Jewel" for a while. Not much to write home about -- no offense, Ms. Jones.
JESSICA JONES
None taken, but...
J. JONAH JAMESON
And then she tried the game as a woman called... "Knightress"?
JESSICA JONES
Yeah. Uh -- not a lot of people know that.
J. JONAH JAMESON
Though I despise your chosen profession, I do admire your going public with your questionable past. I imagine that was somewhat of a hard choice.
JESSICA JONES
Uh, not really. Firstly, I wouldn't use the word "questionable." And truth be told, no one cared either way. But I guess it makes meetings like this a little more interesting.
J. JONAH JAMESON
You guess?
JESSICA JONES
Well, I still don't know what this meeting is about, so...
J. JONAH JAMESON
It's about secret identities. I thought Robbie would find your background a little interesting considering what I am about to offer you.

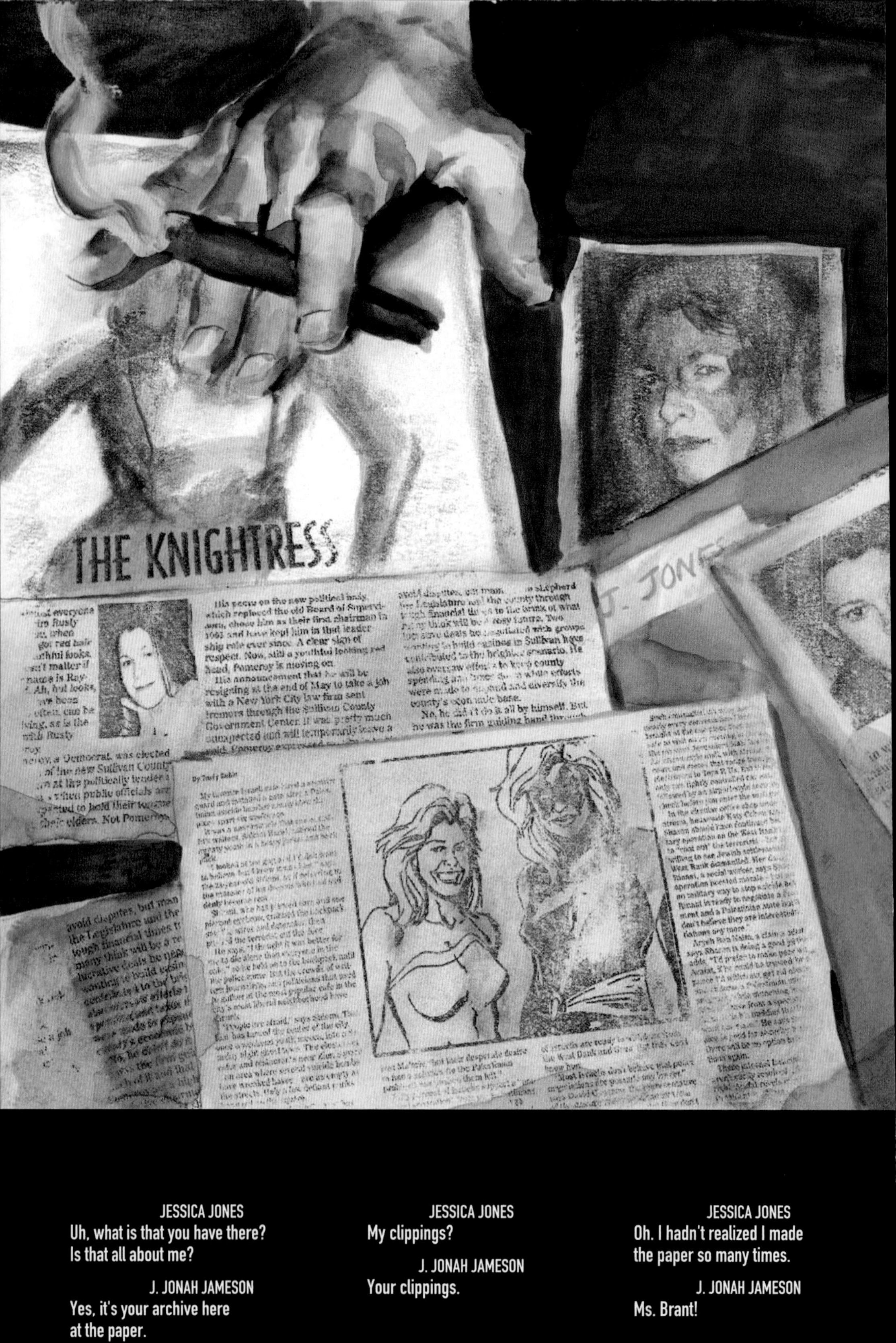
THE KNIGHTRESS
J. JONES

JESSICA JONES
Uh, what is that you have there?
Is that all about me?

J. JONAH JAMESON
Yes, it's your archive here
at the paper.

JESSICA JONES
My clippings?

J. JONAH JAMESON
Your clippings.

JESSICA JONES
Oh. I hadn't realized I made
the paper so many times.

J. JONAH JAMESON
Ms. Brant!

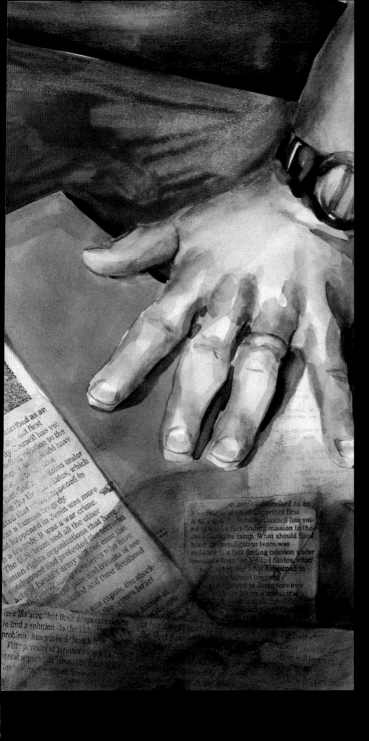

J. JONAH JAMESON
Make yourself a little scrapbook. So, Ms. Jones, are the numbers on your web site correct?

JESSICA JONES
You mean my fees?

J. JONAH JAMESON
Yes.

JESSICA JONES
You want to hire me?

J. JONAH JAMESON.
Yes. I -- Ms. Brant!!

ROBBIE ROBERTSON
You just sent her to make copies.

J. JONAH JAMESON
Dammit! Where's Urich?

ROBBIE ROBERTSON
He's coming. Jonah, can we discuss this a little before --?

J. JONAH JAMESON
What we'd like to do, Ms. Jones, is hire you -- pay you your full wage and have one of my reporters follow you.

JESSICA JONES
Follow me where?

J. JONAH JAMESON
Ben, where were you?

BEN URICH
I didn't know you were --

J. JONAH JAMESON
Sit down. Say hi to Jessica Jones.

BEN URICH
Why is that name familiar?

J. JONAH JAMESON
You can do the niceys later. Jessica is a private investigator. The Daily Bugle is hiring her to find out who Spider-Man really is.

JESSICA JONES
Uh -- what?

J. JONAH JAMESON
Jessica here is going to crack his world in half and you are going to follow her while she does it.

JESSICA JONES
Well, I . . .

J. JONAH JAMESON
What we're hoping for is a series of articles. A real conversation piece to spread over days -- but hey! If all it is is a big red headline -- then all it is is a big red headline.

BETTY BRANT
Yes, sir.

J. JONAH JAMESON
Take this to Xerox and make a copy of it for Ms. Jones. Every paper.

BETTY BRANT
Yes, sir.

JESSICA JONES
Oh, uh, thanks.

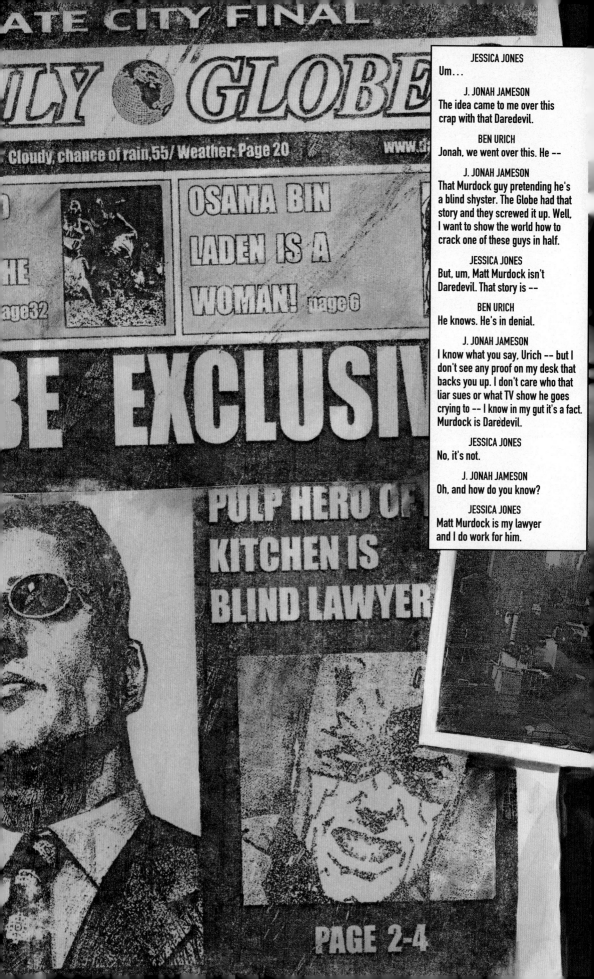

ATE CITY FINAL

ILY GLOBE

Cloudy, chance of rain,55/ Weather: Page 20   www.d

OSAMA BIN
LADEN IS A
WOMAN! page 6

BE EXCLUSI

PULP HERO OF
KITCHEN IS
BLIND LAWYER

PAGE 2-4

JESSICA JONES
Um...

J. JONAH JAMESON
The idea came to me over this crap with that Daredevil.

BEN URICH
Jonah, we went over this. He --

J. JONAH JAMESON
That Murdock guy pretending he's a blind shyster. The Globe had that story and they screwed it up. Well, I want to show the world how to crack one of these guys in half.

JESSICA JONES
But, um, Matt Murdock isn't Daredevil. That story is --

BEN URICH
He knows. He's in denial.

J. JONAH JAMESON
I know what you say, Urich -- but I don't see any proof on my desk that backs you up. I don't care who that liar sues or what TV show he goes crying to -- I know in my gut it's a fact. Murdock is Daredevil.

JESSICA JONES
No, it's not.

J. JONAH JAMESON
Oh, and how do you know?

JESSICA JONES
Matt Murdock is my lawyer and I do work for him.

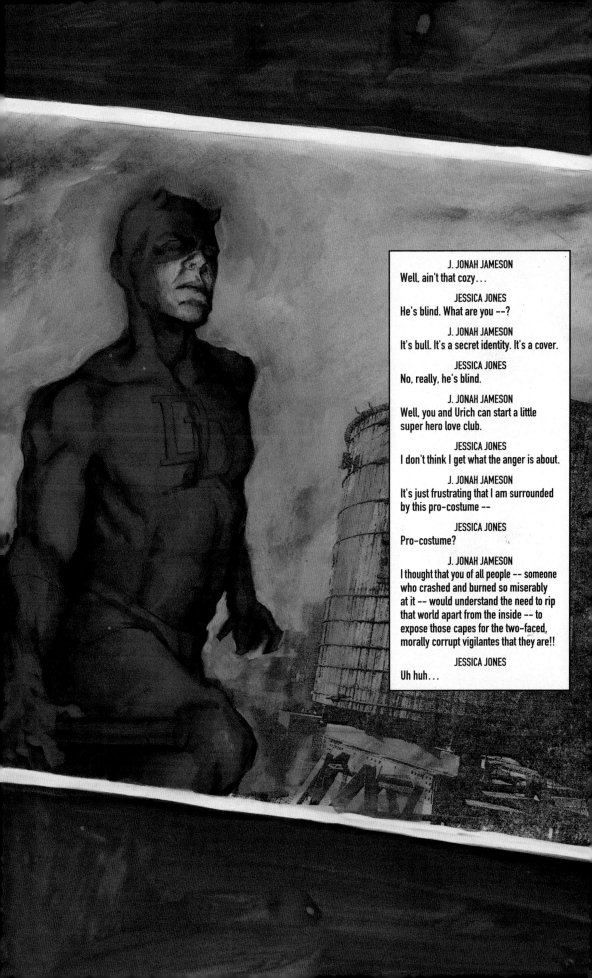

J. JONAH JAMESON
Well, ain't that cozy...

JESSICA JONES
He's blind. What are you --?

J. JONAH JAMESON
It's bull. It's a secret identity. It's a cover.

JESSICA JONES
No, really, he's blind.

J. JONAH JAMESON
Well, you and Urich can start a little super hero love club.

JESSICA JONES
I don't think I get what the anger is about.

J. JONAH JAMESON
It's just frustrating that I am surrounded by this pro-costume --

JESSICA JONES
Pro-costume?

J. JONAH JAMESON
I thought that you of all people -- someone who crashed and burned so miserably at it -- would understand the need to rip that world apart from the inside -- to expose those capes for the two-faced, morally corrupt vigilantes that they are!!

JESSICA JONES
Uh huh...

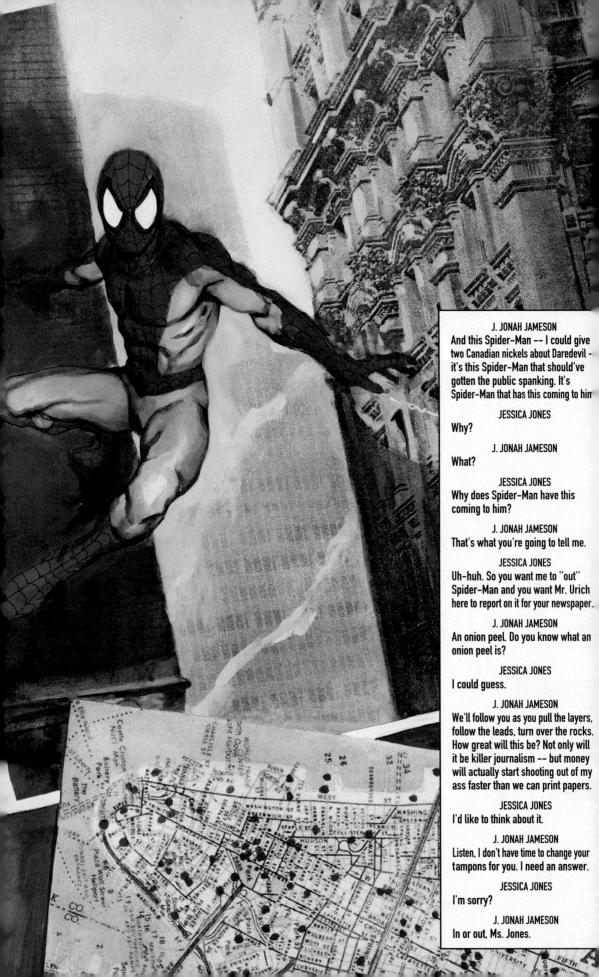

J. JONAH JAMESON
And this Spider-Man -- I could give two Canadian nickels about Daredevil - it's this Spider-Man that should've gotten the public spanking. It's Spider-Man that has this coming to him

JESSICA JONES
Why?

J. JONAH JAMESON
What?

JESSICA JONES
Why does Spider-Man have this coming to him?

J. JONAH JAMESON
That's what you're going to tell me.

JESSICA JONES
Uh-huh. So you want me to ''out'' Spider-Man and you want Mr. Urich here to report on it for your newspaper.

J. JONAH JAMESON
An onion peel. Do you know what an onion peel is?

JESSICA JONES
I could guess.

J. JONAH JAMESON
We'll follow you as you pull the layers, follow the leads, turn over the rocks. How great will this be? Not only will it be killer journalism -- but money will actually start shooting out of my ass faster than we can print papers.

JESSICA JONES
I'd like to think about it.

J. JONAH JAMESON
Listen, I don't have time to change your tampons for you. I need an answer.

JESSICA JONES
I'm sorry?

J. JONAH JAMESON
In or out, Ms. Jones.

JESSICA JONES
Well, these kinds of investigations are rather unique.

J. JONAH JAMESON
Don't toss my salad -- how much are we talking?

JESSICA JONES
Hard to say. I don't even know where I am going to begin.

J. JONAH JAMESON
Ms. Brant!!

BETTY BRANT
Here -- here -- I was making the copies.

J. JONAH JAMESON
Where's the Spider-Man map?

BETTY BRANT
It's right there.

J. JONAH JAMESON
Right where?

BETTY BRANT
Right under your elbow.

J. JONAH JAMESON
Oh...

JESSICA JONES
Map? Map?

J. JONAH JAMESON
We've taken the liberty of compiling a list and a chart of frequent Spider-Man sightings. Places where he is repeatedly seen. See? Empire State University, Queens...

JESSICA JONES
So, I'm not the first investigator you've had on this.

J. JONAH JAMESON
It's a pet project -- as I said -- renewed by this Daredevil news. Here are some pictures that Parker kid took a couple of years back. You can see -- see? You can see some of the same buildings in the background. I think it's Soho.

JESSICA JONES
What happened the last time you tried this?

J. JONAH JAMESON
I'll be blunt with you, Jones. I'm offering you fame and fortune. The kind you weren't able to put together on your own -- even in any of your silly little "identities." One would imagine that off the fumes of a story like this you'll be up to your elbows in "sneaky work" till the cows come home. So, last time, are you in or --?

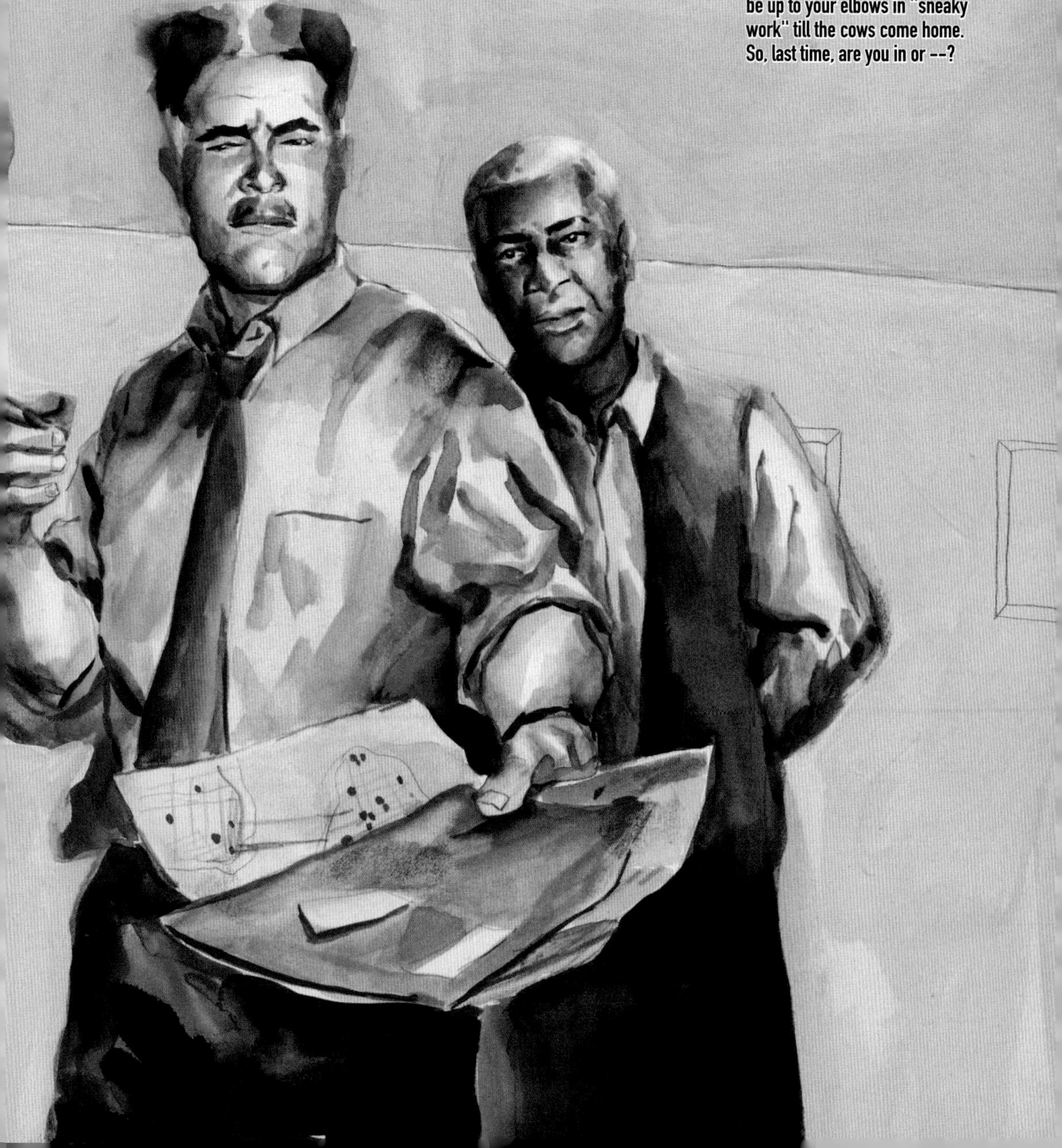

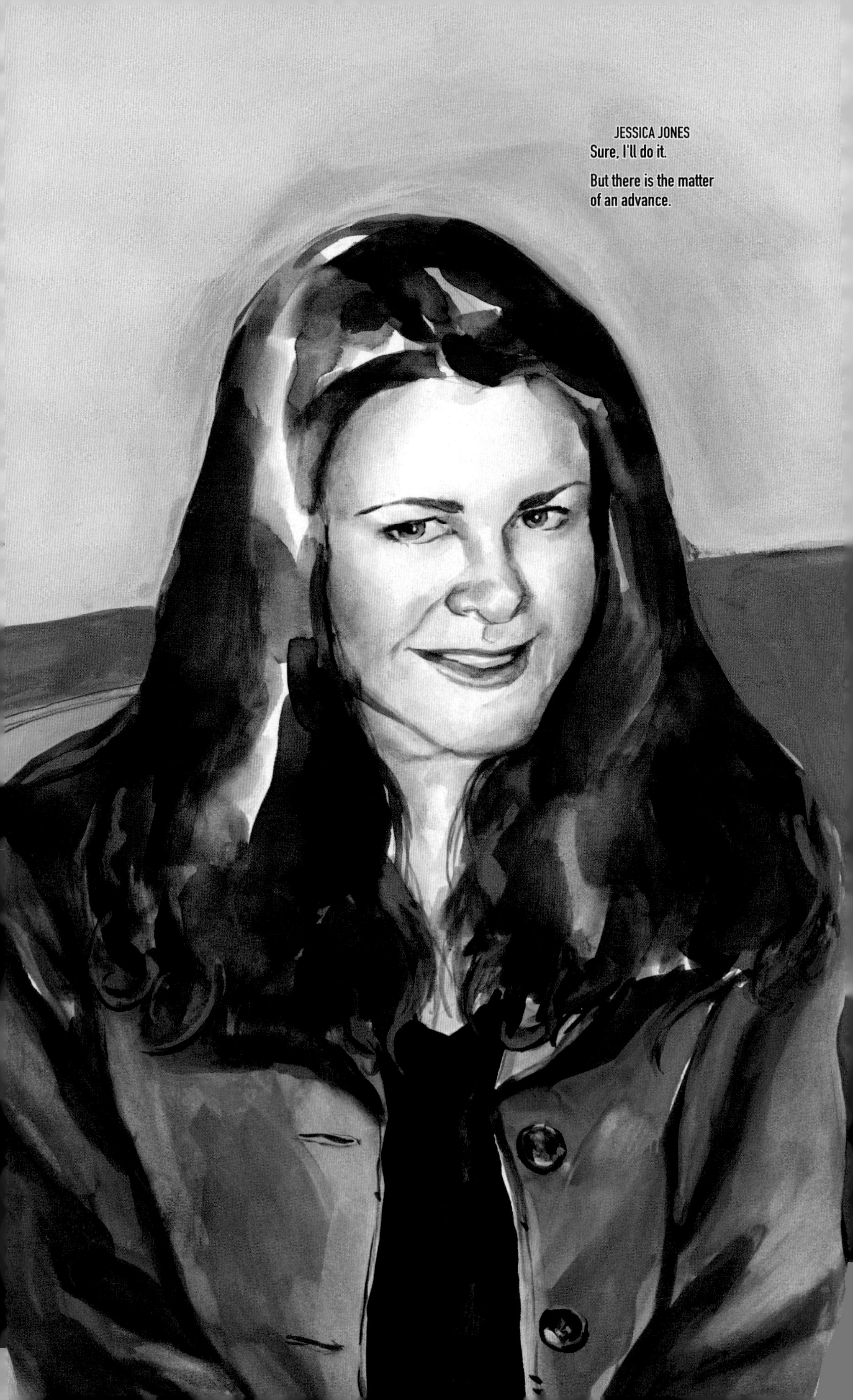
JESSICA JONES
Sure, I'll do it.
But there is the matter of an advance.

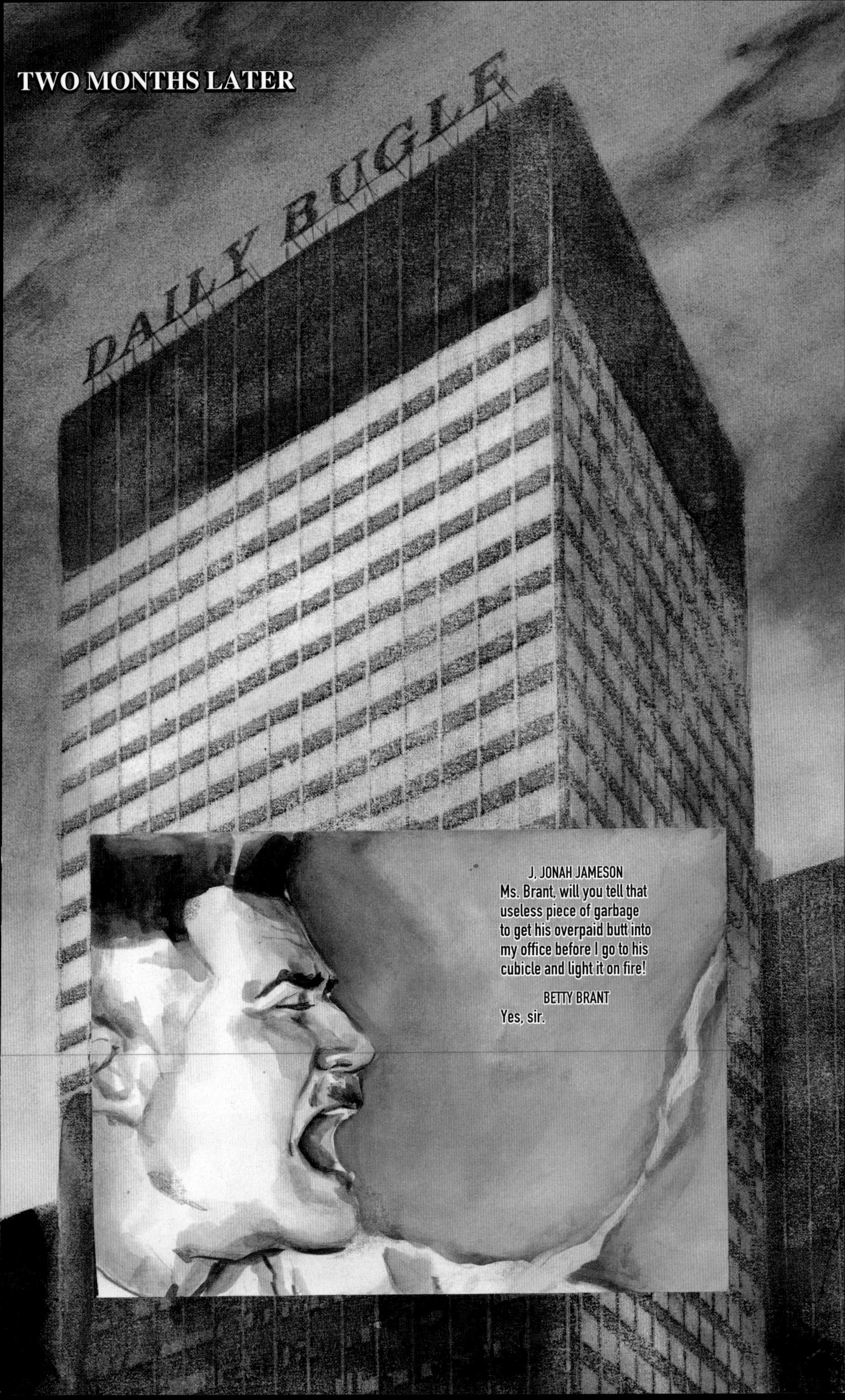
TWO MONTHS LATER
DAILY BUGLE
J. JONAH JAMESON
Ms. Brant, will you tell that useless piece of garbage to get his overpaid butt into my office before I go to his cubicle and light it on fire!
BETTY BRANT
Yes, sir.

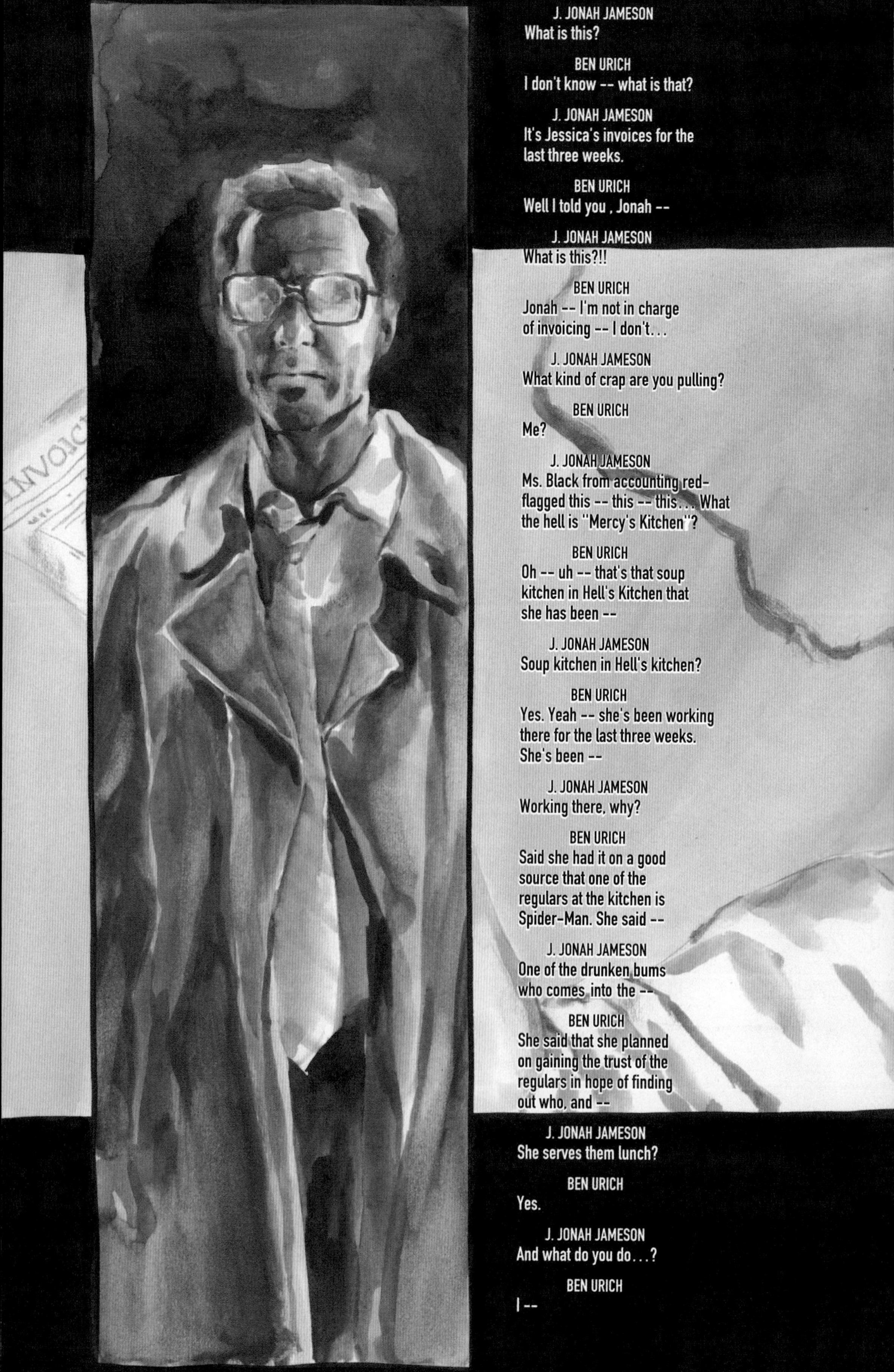
J. JONAH JAMESON
What is this?
BEN URICH
I don't know -- what is that?
J. JONAH JAMESON
It's Jessica's invoices for the last three weeks.
BEN URICH
Well I told you , Jonah --
J. JONAH JAMESON
What is this?!!
BEN URICH
Jonah -- I'm not in charge of invoicing -- I don't. . .
J. JONAH JAMESON
What kind of crap are you pulling?
BEN URICH
Me?
J. JONAH JAMESON
Ms. Black from accounting red-flagged this -- this -- this. . . What the hell is "Mercy's Kitchen"?
BEN URICH
Oh -- uh -- that's that soup kitchen in Hell's Kitchen that she has been --
J. JONAH JAMESON
Soup kitchen in Hell's kitchen?
BEN URICH
Yes. Yeah -- she's been working there for the last three weeks. She's been --
J. JONAH JAMESON
Working there, why?
BEN URICH
Said she had it on a good source that one of the regulars at the kitchen is Spider-Man. She said --
J. JONAH JAMESON
One of the drunken bums who comes into the --
BEN URICH
She said that she planned on gaining the trust of the regulars in hope of finding out who, and --
J. JONAH JAMESON
She serves them lunch?
BEN URICH
Yes.
J. JONAH JAMESON
And what do you do. . .?
BEN URICH
I --

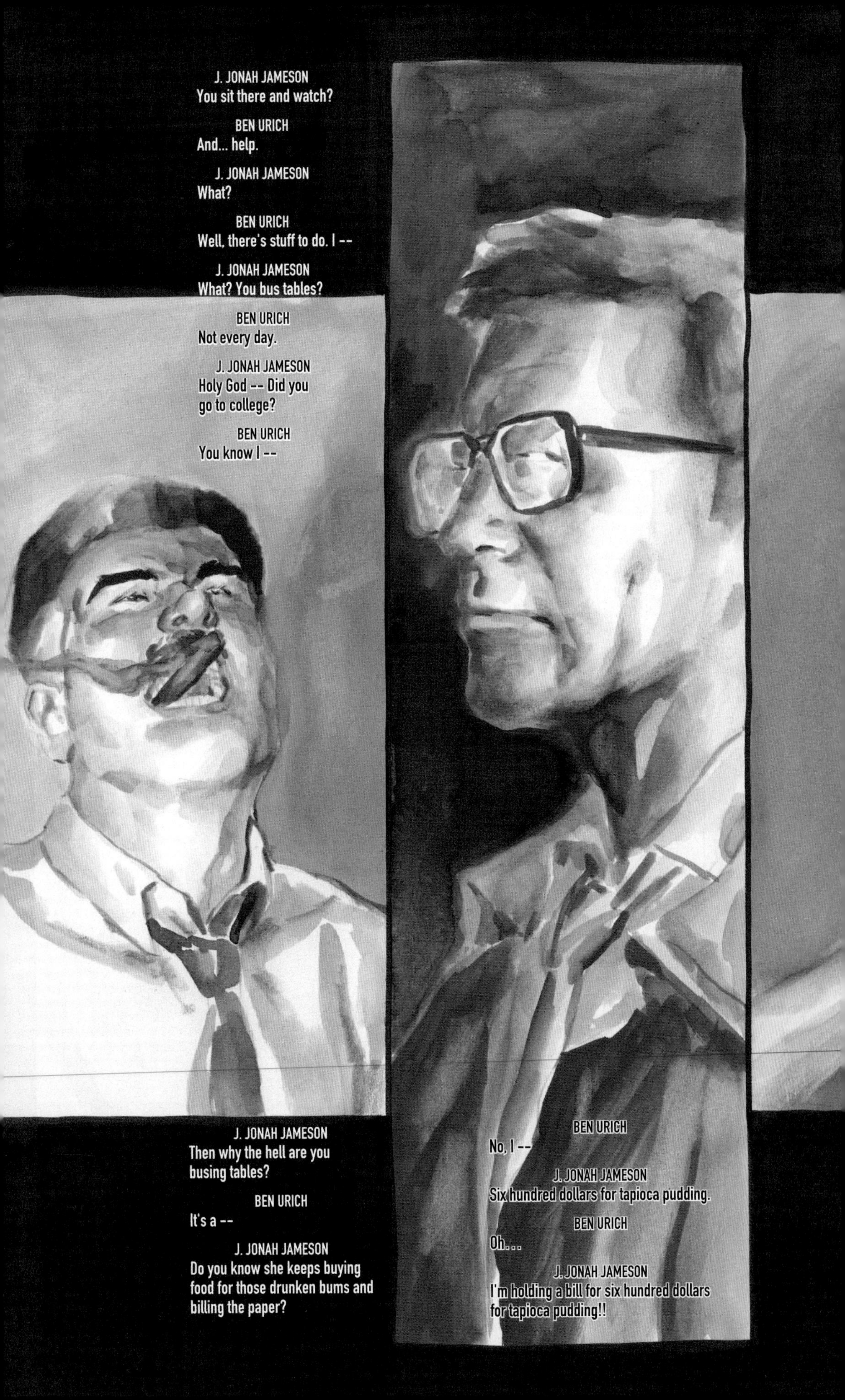
J. JONAH JAMESON
You sit there and watch?
BEN URICH
And... help.
J. JONAH JAMESON
What?
BEN URICH
Well, there's stuff to do. I --
J. JONAH JAMESON
What? You bus tables?
BEN URICH
Not every day.
J. JONAH JAMESON
Holy God -- Did you go to college?
BEN URICH
You know I --
J. JONAH JAMESON
Then why the hell are you busing tables?
BEN URICH
It's a --
J. JONAH JAMESON
Do you know she keeps buying food for those drunken bums and billing the paper?
BEN URICH
No, I --
J. JONAH JAMESON
Six hundred dollars for tapioca pudding.
BEN URICH
Oh...
J. JONAH JAMESON
I'm holding a bill for six hundred dollars for tapioca pudding!!

J. JONAH JAMESON
For the first time in my decades-long career as a -- She's buying pudding for drunks and trying to get me to pay for it --

BEN URICH
Well, she did say expenses.

J. JONAH JAMESON
Phone calls and paperclips are expenses!!! This is pudding!!

BEN URICH
I didn't know she was billing it to you.

J. JONAH JAMESON
Well, she is!! Two hundred dollars an hour, all day every day!! For her to serve pudding to meth addicts -- and one of my best reporters bussing tables!

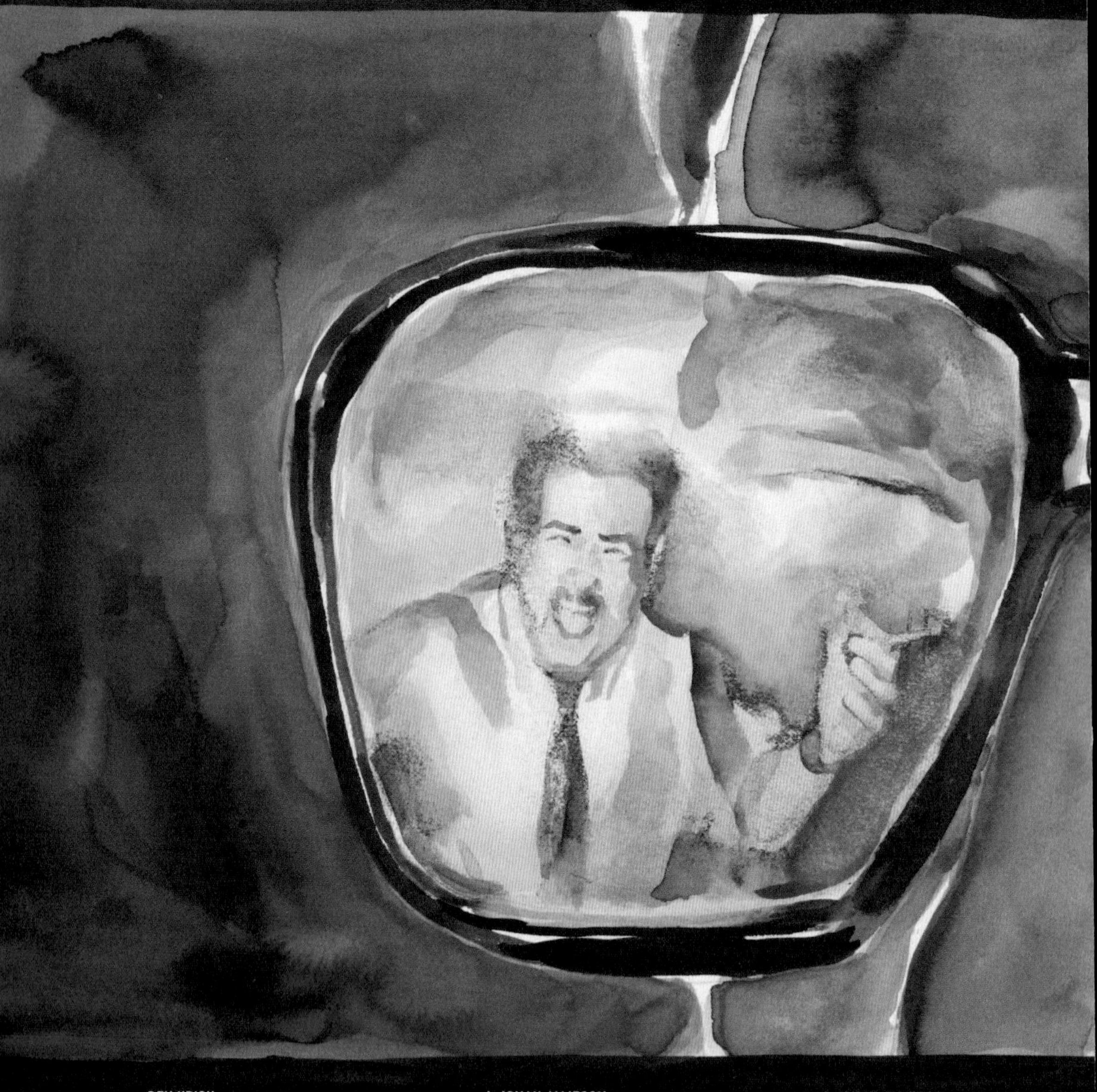

BEN URICH
Okay. Jessica told me that she asked around the quote superhero community and word was that Spider-Man has said he was an orphan. At these orphanages -- Jessica volunteered. helping out. Reading some books to the children.

J. JONAH JAMESON
How does reading books to a bunch of unwanted brats help her find out about Spider-Man?

BEN URICH
Well , I asked her that. I asked her, and again she said that familiarity breeds trust and that making herself a face would help gain access and information.

J. JONAH JAMESON
Uh huh.

ROBBIE ROBERTSON
It's the same for us in our business.

BEN URICH
Yes, and that's why I had no reason to question her, Jonah.

BEN URICH
Thanks --

J. JONAH JAMESON
Shut up! Give me the report so far --

BEN URICH
Didn't she send some kind of --

J. JONAH JAMESON
Give me your notes, Urich!!

BEN URICH
Okay, Okay. Here -- uh -- well, soon after you hired her we made the rounds to a handful of orphanages. Three orphanages. St. Alexis' of 49th, The Tony Stark Foundation Home for Wayward --

J. JONAH JAMESON
Come on --

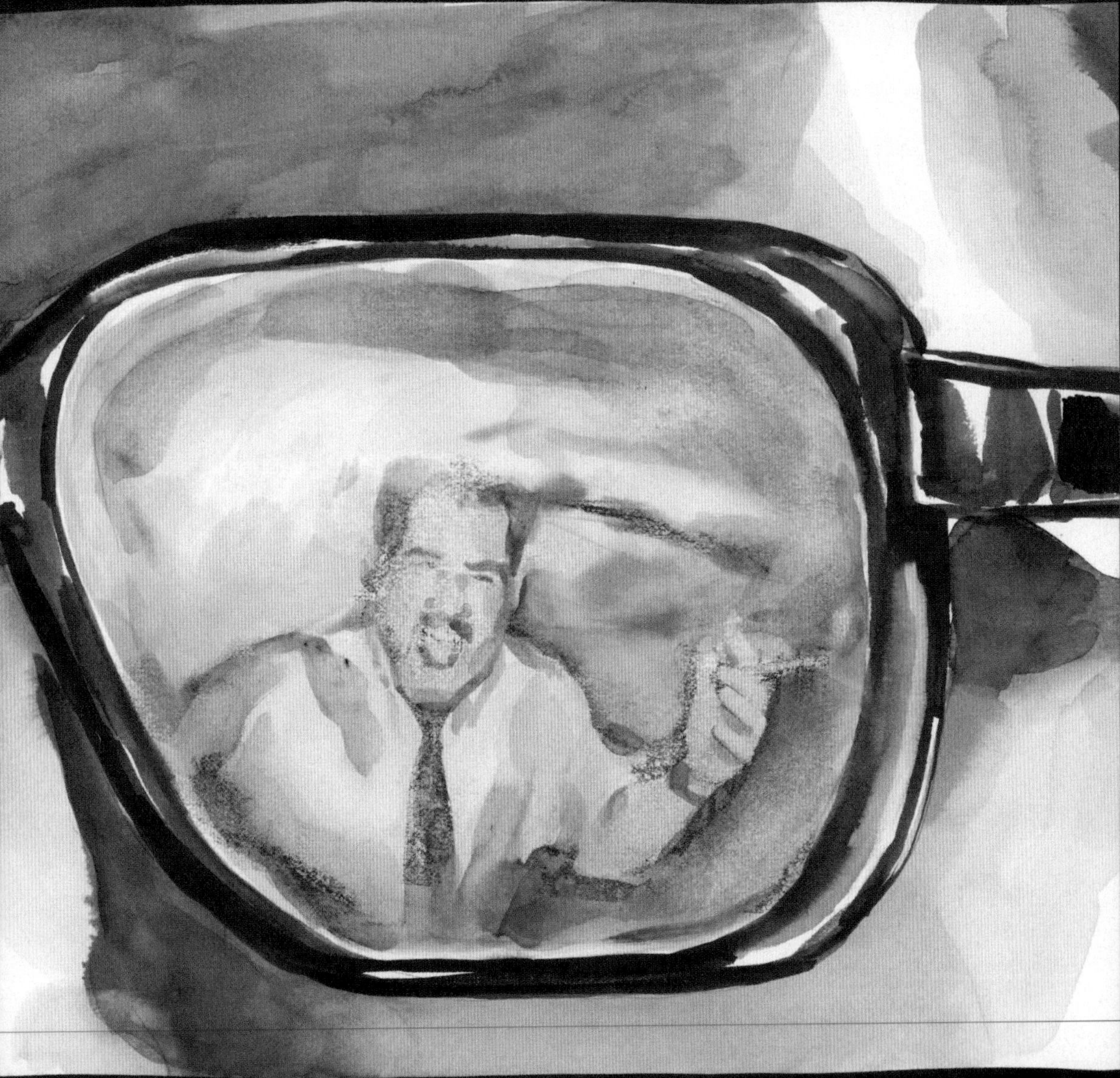

J. JONAH JAMESON
I have a bill here. She bought the kids cupcakes for a week at one of these --

BEN URICH
Then it was on to St. Catherine's Hospital where Jessica said she had a tip that one of the orderlies was Spider-Man. She said it was well known among her circle that he --

J. JONAH JAMESON
So she volunteered at the hospital.

BEN URICH
The AIDS ward.

J. JONAH JAMESON
Pssss...

BEN URICH
And for the last few weeks she's been at the soup kitchen...

J. JONAH JAMESON
Damn it, Urich!

BEN URICH
What?

J. JONAH JAMESON
She's scamming us!!
She's scamming me!!

BEN URICH
How is she --

J. JONAH JAMESON
AIDS patients, orphans, winos!!
Volunteering at two hundred
dollars an hour!

BEN URICH
I --

J. JONAH JAMESON
Were you ever there when she got
one of these little "tips" of hers?

BEN URICH
The actual tip? No. It was after --

J. JONAH JAMESON
Did you ever see any of her
so called super hero pals?

BEN URICH
Uh -- no.

J. JONAH JAMESON
No?

BEN URICH
No.

J. JONAH JAMESON
You stupid, WORTHLESS,
WASTE OF --

ROBBIE ROBERTSON
Jonah!

J. JONAH JAMESON
Dammit! She scammed us!
A damn scam artist!

ROBBIE ROBERTSON
Jonah --

BEN URICH
Well maybe if --

J. JONAH JAMESON
What??!!

BEN URICH
Nothing.

ROBBIE ROBERTSON
What Ben was going to say is --
that maybe when you hired her if
you hadn't insulted every single
facet of her life --

J. JONAH JAMESON
What?

ROBBIE ROBERTSON
Jonah. You. . .

J. JONAH JAMESON
What did I say?

ROBBIE ROBERTSON
You said that superheroes
deserve to be --

J. JONAH JAMESON
I say that in the paper
every freaking day.

ROBBIE ROBERTSON
You said that private investigators
are pieces of --

J. JONAH JAMESON
They are! She knows that.
Doesn't mean she can steal
from me --

ROBBIE ROBERTSON
Jonah --

J. JONAH JAMESON
Stole money out of me --

ROBBIE ROBERTSON
Jonah, you can't prove that.

J. JONAH JAMESON
What?

ROBBIE ROBERTSON
They are legitimate --

J. JONAH JAMESON
Shut up!

ROBBIE ROBERTSON
Legitimate claims --

J. JONAH JAMESON
Well, I'm not buying
this pudding.

ROBBIE ROBERTSON
You signed a contract with
the woman.

J. JONAH JAMESON
Ms. Brant!! Get in here!!

ROBBIE ROBERTSON
You signed a contract --

J. JONAH JAMESON
You know what, Ben? You write
your damn story -- you tell
the world what this lying --

ROBBIE ROBERTSON
That she what? Fed the homeless,
read to orphans, and cared for
AIDS patients?

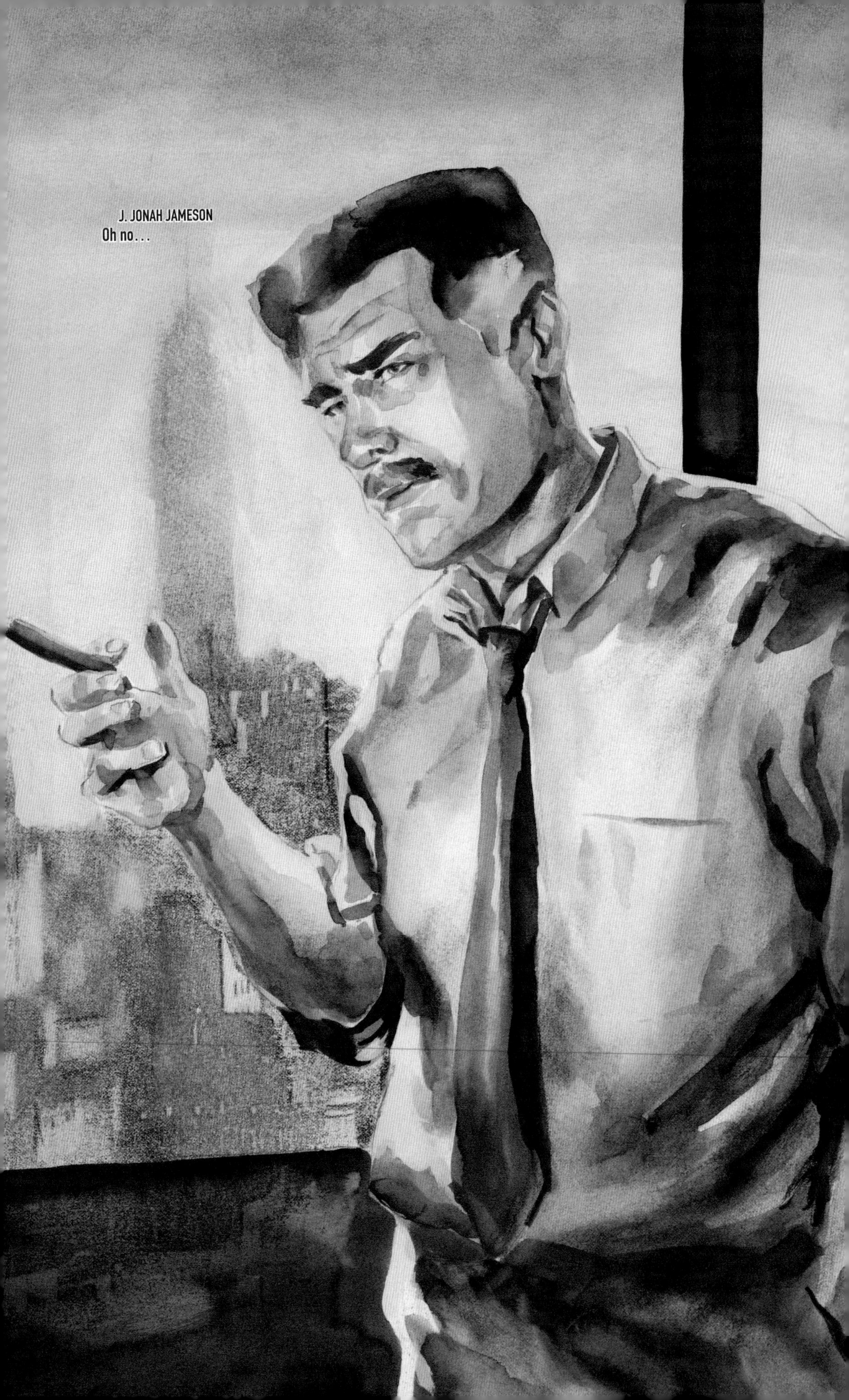
J. JONAH JAMESON
Oh no...

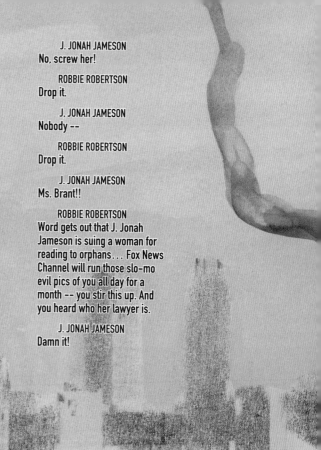

BEN URICH
Wow, you know -- I actually didn't see it -- it's a pretty decent scam.

J. JONAH JAMESON
You are the worst investigative reporter on the planet Earth.

BEN URICH
You just said I was the best --

J. JONAH JAMESON
I lied. You're the worst. You should have seen this coming --

BEN URICH
You didn't...

J. JONAH JAMESON
Get out! Ms. Brant, get my lawyer on the phone!

ROBBIE ROBERTSON
Drop it, Jonah.

J. JONAH JAMESON
No, screw her!

ROBBIE ROBERTSON
Drop it.

J. JONAH JAMESON
Nobody --

ROBBIE ROBERTSON
Drop it.

J. JONAH JAMESON
Ms. Brant!!

ROBBIE ROBERTSON
Word gets out that J. Jonah Jameson is suing a woman for reading to orphans... Fox News Channel will run those slo-mo evil pics of you all day for a month -- you stir this up. And you heard who her lawyer is.

J. JONAH JAMESON
Damn it!

ROBBIE ROBERTSON
Drop it.

J. JONAH JAMESON
Damn it!

ROBBIE ROBERTSON
Just chalk it up --

J. JONAH JAMESON
Damn super heroes --
every time.

ROBBIE ROBERTSON
All right, I'm going home.

J. JONAH JAMESON
Ms. Brant, get me that woman's
telephone number -- oh here
it is -- I got it! Never mind!

ROBBIE ROBERTSON
Jonah . . .

J. JONAH JAMESON
Oh no! Oh no! the least I get
to do -- the least I get to do
is let her know I know and
that the jig is up!

ROBBIE ROBERTSON
I don't think --

J. JONAH JAMESON
It's her machine. Doesn't
even have the guts to --
Ms. Jones, this is J. Jonah
Jameson, publisher of
the Daily Bugle.

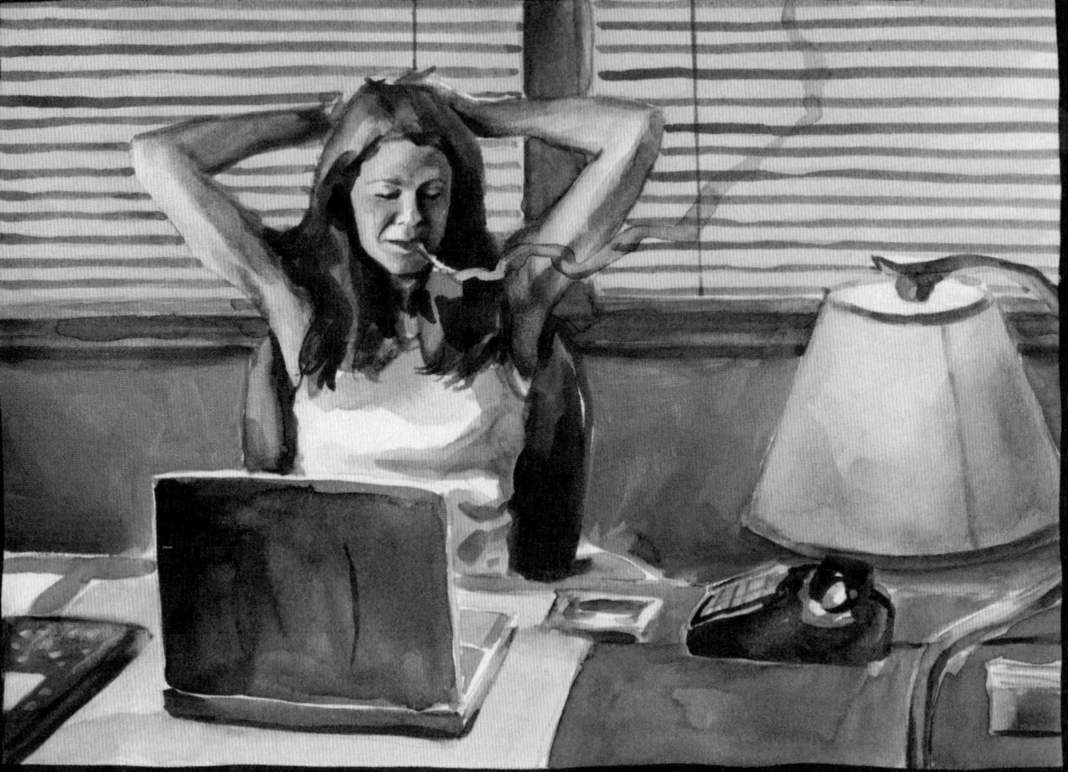

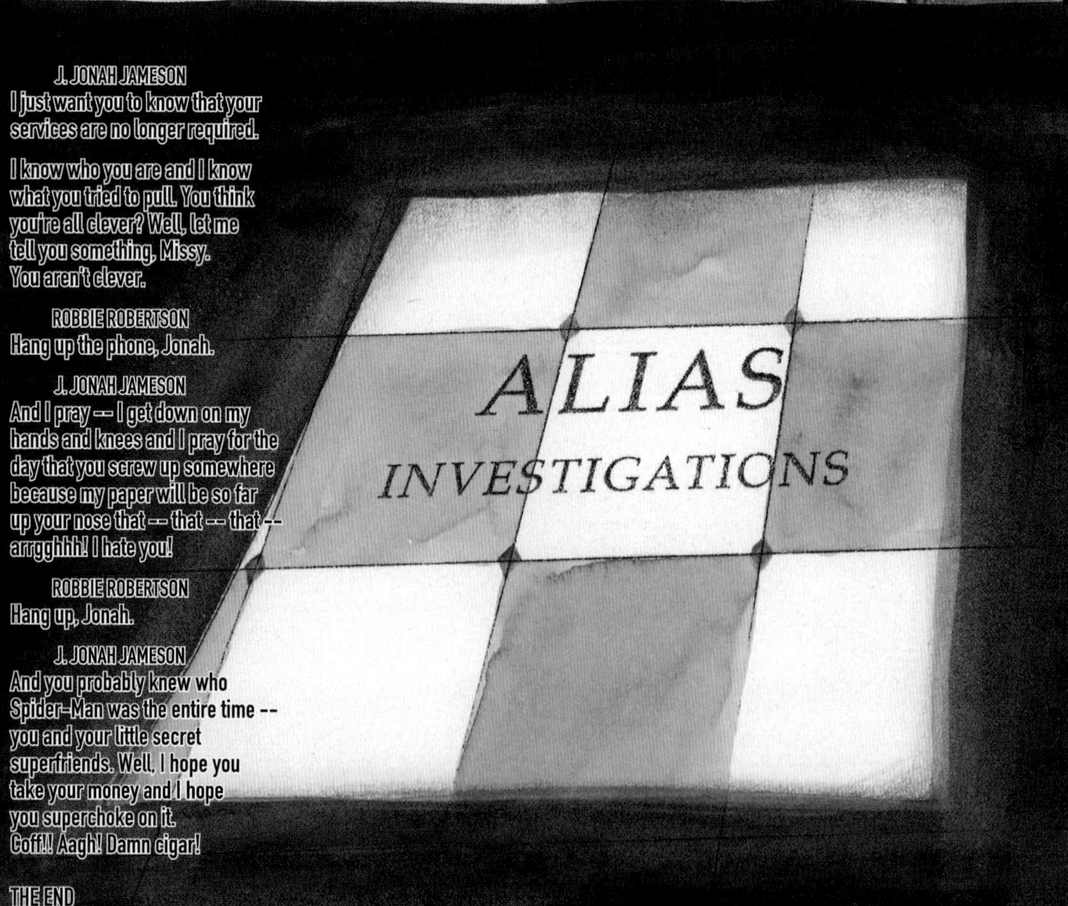
J. JONAH JAMESON
I just want you to know that your services are no longer required.
I know who you are and I know what you tried to pull. You think you're all clever? Well, let me tell you something, Missy. You aren't clever.
ROBBIE ROBERTSON
Hang up the phone, Jonah.
J. JONAH JAMESON
And I pray -- I get down on my hands and knees and I pray for the day that you screw up somewhere because my paper will be so far up your nose that -- that -- that -- arrgghhh! I hate you!
ROBBIE ROBERTSON
Hang up, Jonah.
J. JONAH JAMESON
And you probably knew who Spider-Man was the entire time -- you and your little secret superfriends. Well, I hope you take your money and I hope you superchoke on it. Coff!! Aagh! Damn cigar!
ALIAS
INVESTIGATIONS
THE END

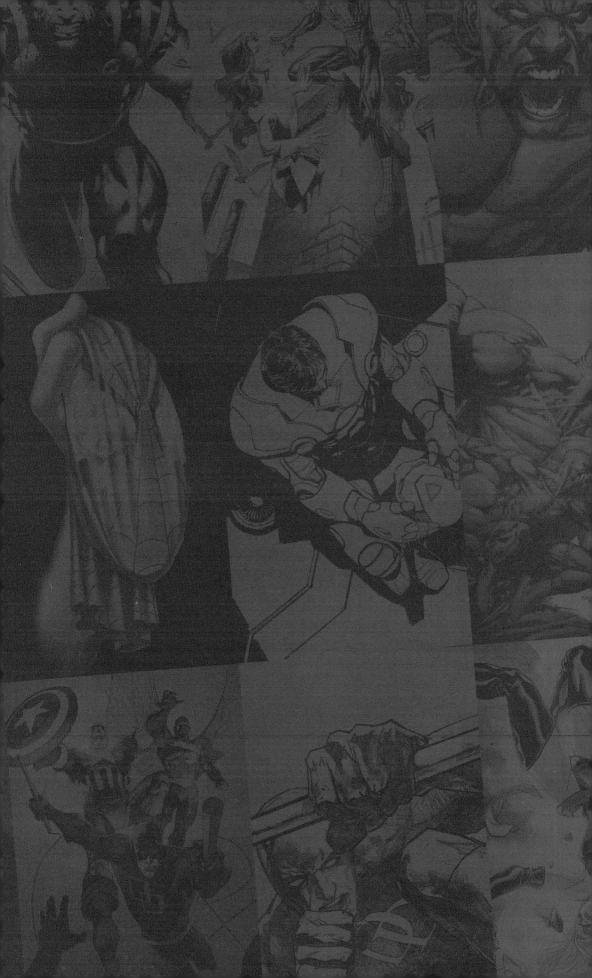

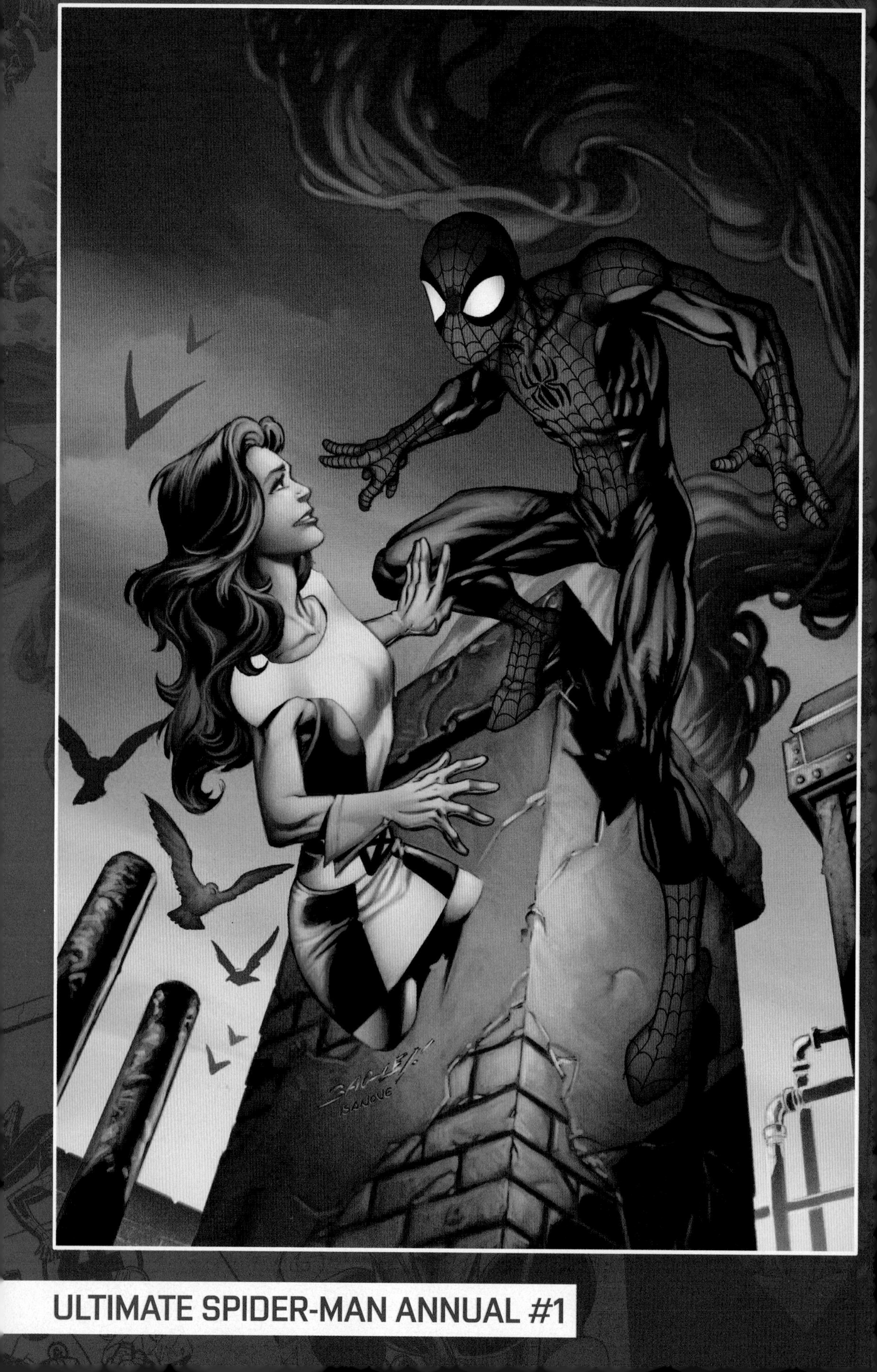

ULTIMATE SPIDER-MAN ANNUAL #1

ULTIMATE SPIDER-MAN

The bite of a genetically altered spider granted high school student Peter Parker incredible, arachnid-like powers! When a burglar killed his beloved Uncle Ben, a grief-stricken Peter vowed to use his amazing abilities to protect his fellow man. He learned the invaluable lesson that with great power there must also come great responsibility. Peter's life has been turned upside-down in recent months, thanks in no small part to his breakup with girlfriend Mary Jane Watson...

Born with strange and amazing abilities, the X-Men are young mutant heroes, sworn to protect a world that hates and fears them. Kitty Pride's ability to "phase" through solid objects has made her a valued member of the X-Men, even though she is the youngest person on the team. Kitty's also been having problems with her love life, and has just recently broken off her relationship with fellow teammate Bobby Drake (a.k.a Iceman)...

Writer	Penciler	Inker	Additional Finishes	Colorist	Letterer
Brian Michael Bendis	Mark Brooks	Jaime Mendoza	Scott Hanna	Dave Stewart	Chris Eliopoulos

Production	Assistant Editors	Editor	Editor in Chief	Publisher
Tom Valente	John Barber & Nicole Wiley	Ralph Macchio	Joe Quesada	Dan Buckley

Cover: Mark Bagley & Richard Isanove

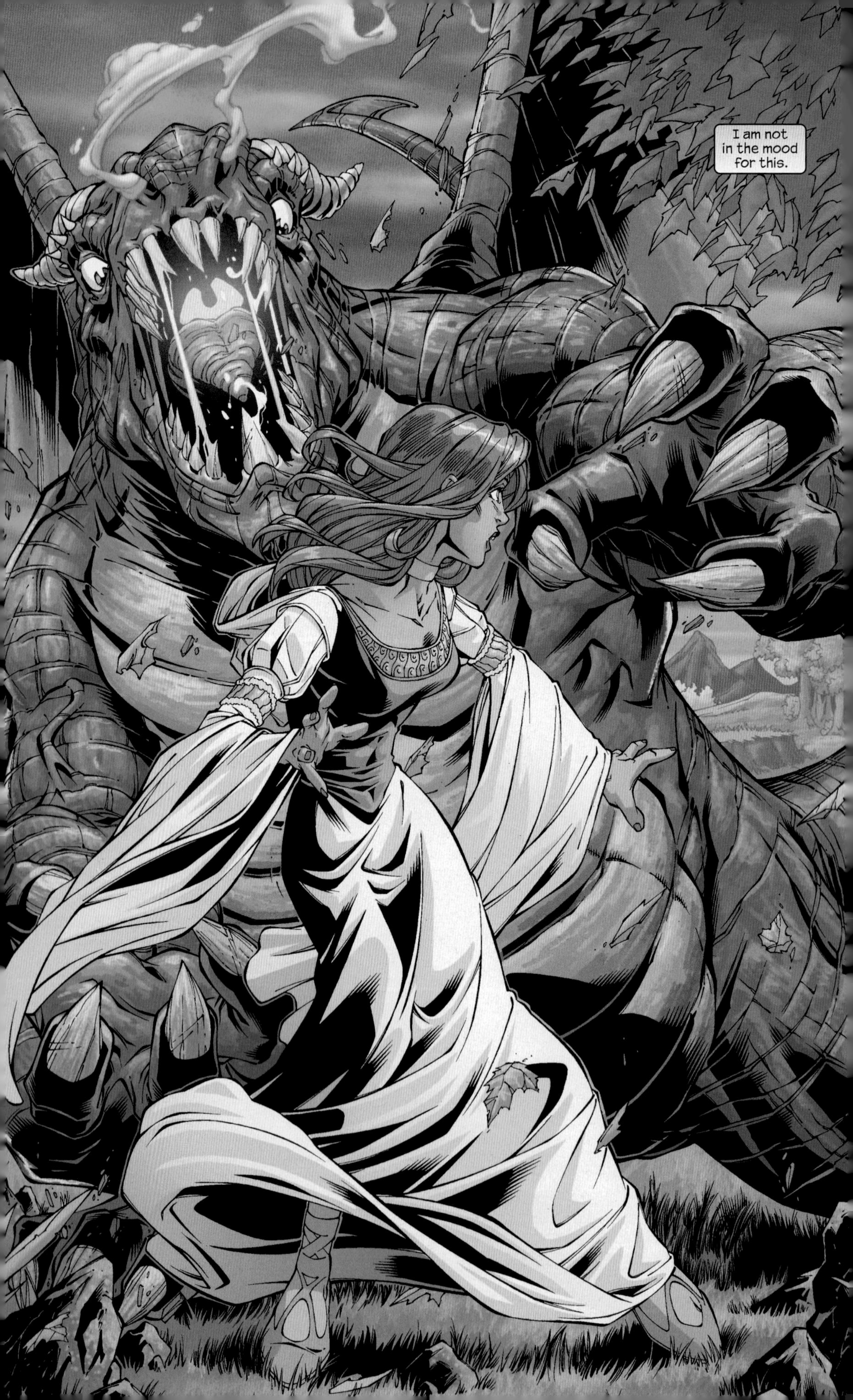
I am not in the mood for this.

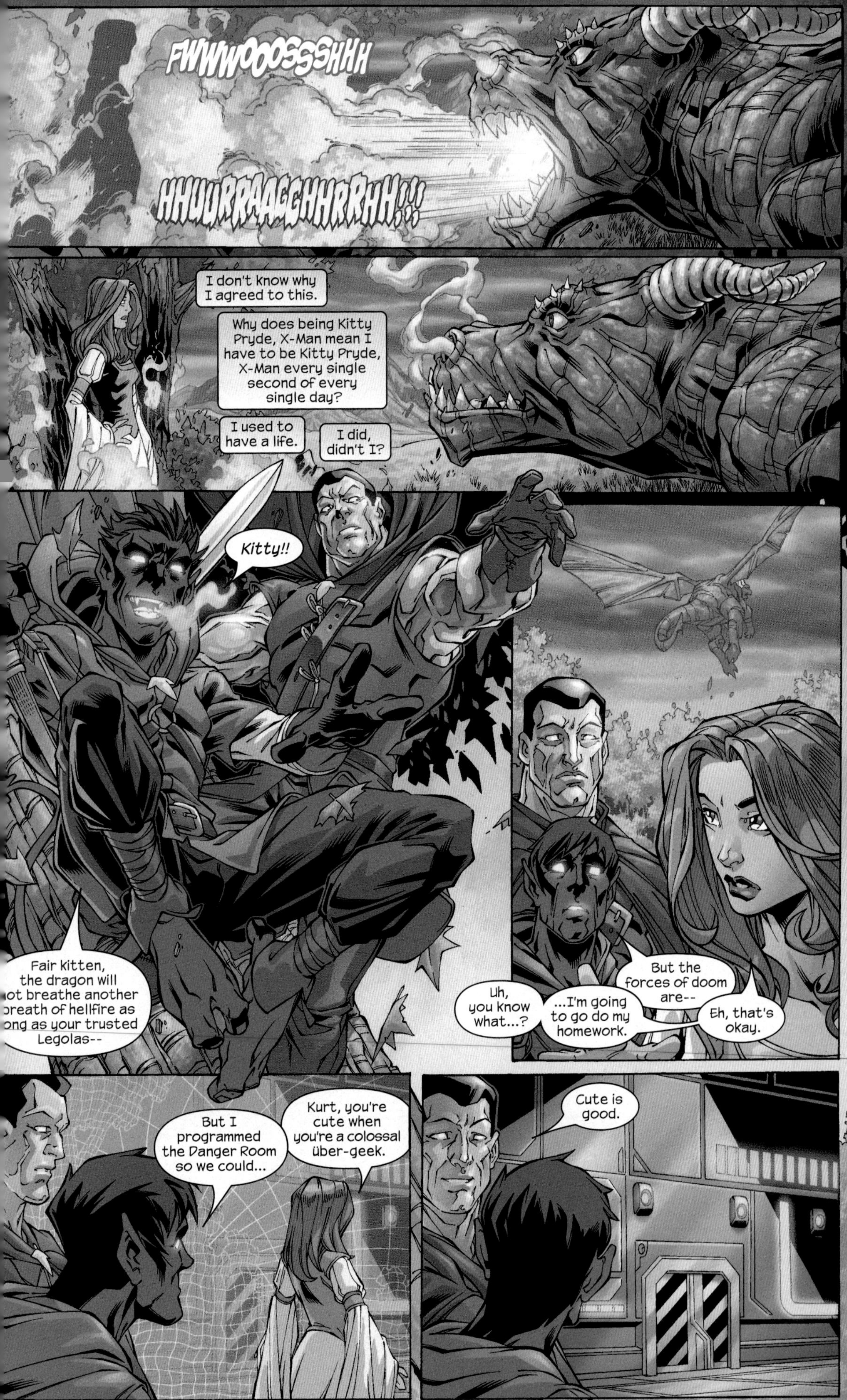
FWWWOOOSSSHHH
HHUURRAAGHHRRHH!!!
I don't know why I agreed to this.
Why does being Kitty Pryde, X-Man mean I have to be Kitty Pryde, X-Man every single second of every single day?
I used to have a life.
I did, didn't I?
Kitty!!
Fair kitten, the dragon will ot breathe another reath of hellfire as ong as your trusted Legolas--
Uh, you know what...?
But the forces of doom are--
...I'm going to go do my homework.
Eh, that's okay.
But I programmed the Danger Room so we could...
Kurt, you're cute when you're a colossal über-geek.
Cute is good.

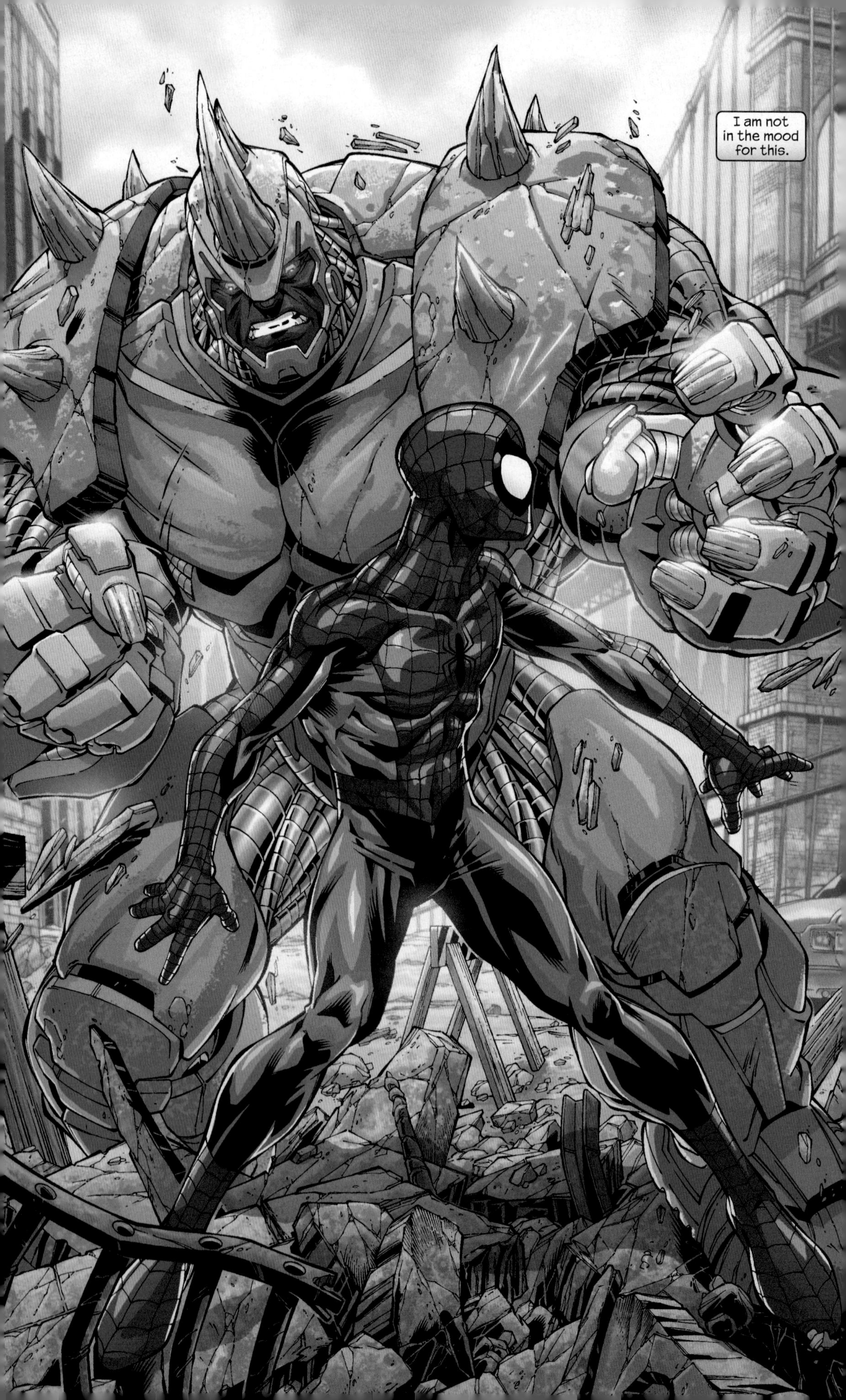
I am not in the mood for this.

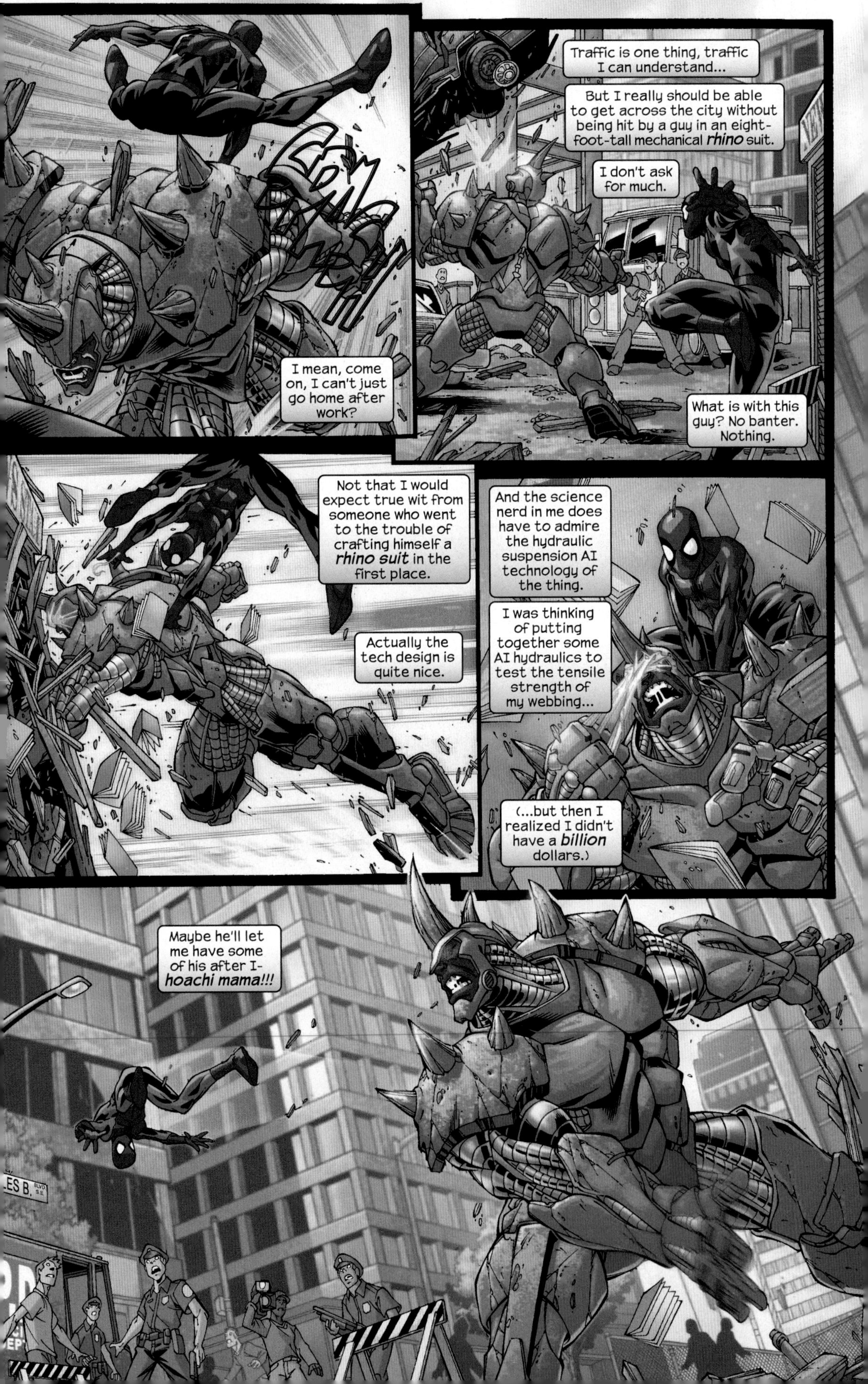
I mean, come on, I can't just go home after work?
Traffic is one thing, traffic I can understand...
But I really should be able to get across the city without being hit by a guy in an eight-foot-tall mechanical *rhino* suit.
I don't ask for much.
What is with this guy? No banter. Nothing.
Not that I would expect true wit from someone who went to the trouble of crafting himself a *rhino suit* in the first place.
Actually the tech design is quite nice.
And the science nerd in me does have to admire the hydraulic suspension AI technology of the thing.
I was thinking of putting together some AI hydraulics to test the tensile strength of my webbing...
(...but then I realized I didn't have a *billion* dollars.)
Maybe he'll let me have some of his after I- *hoachi mama!!!*

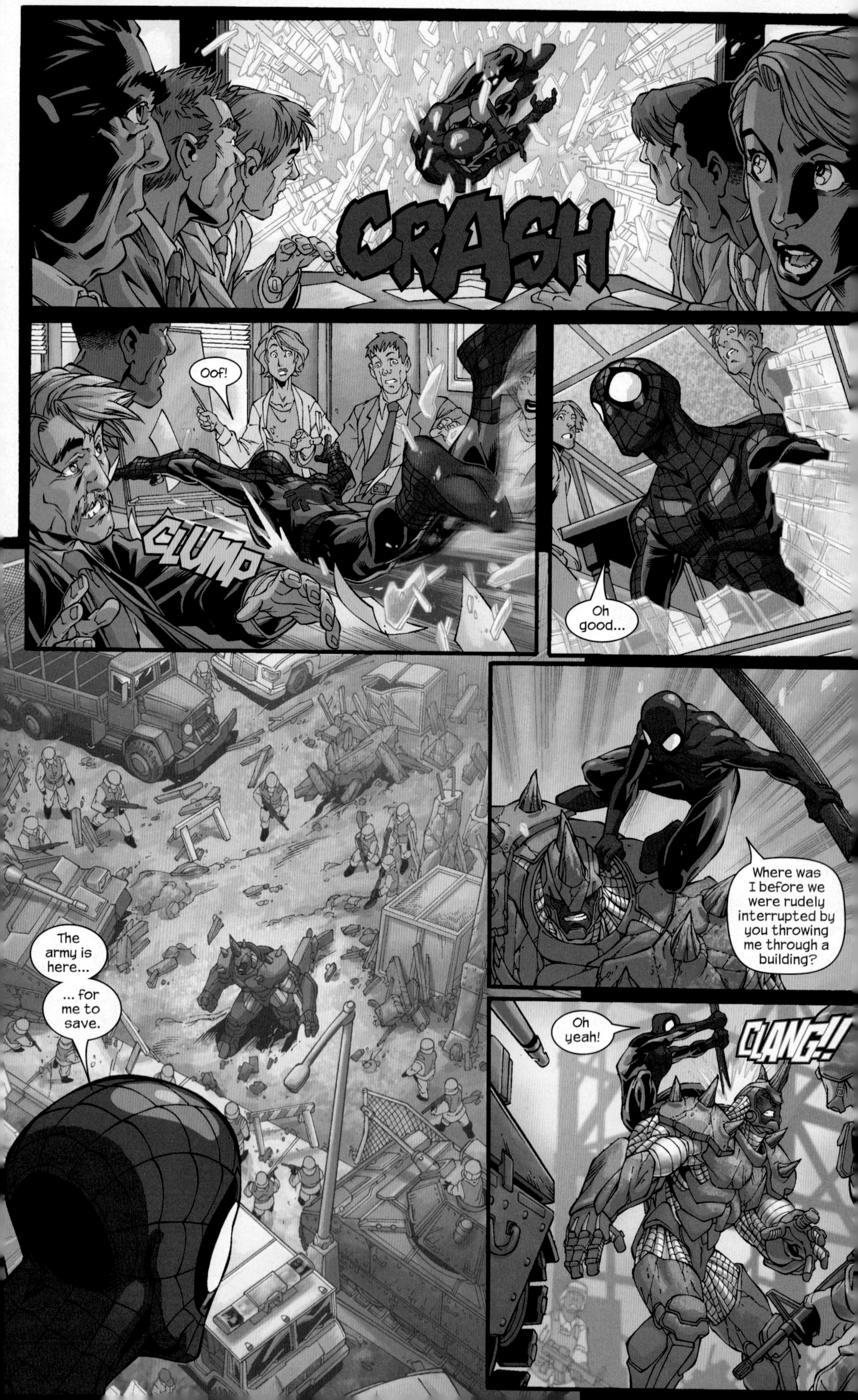
CRASH
Oof!
CLUMP
Oh good...
The army is here...
... for me to save.
Where was I before we were rudely interrupted by you throwing me through a building?
Oh yeah!
CLANG!!

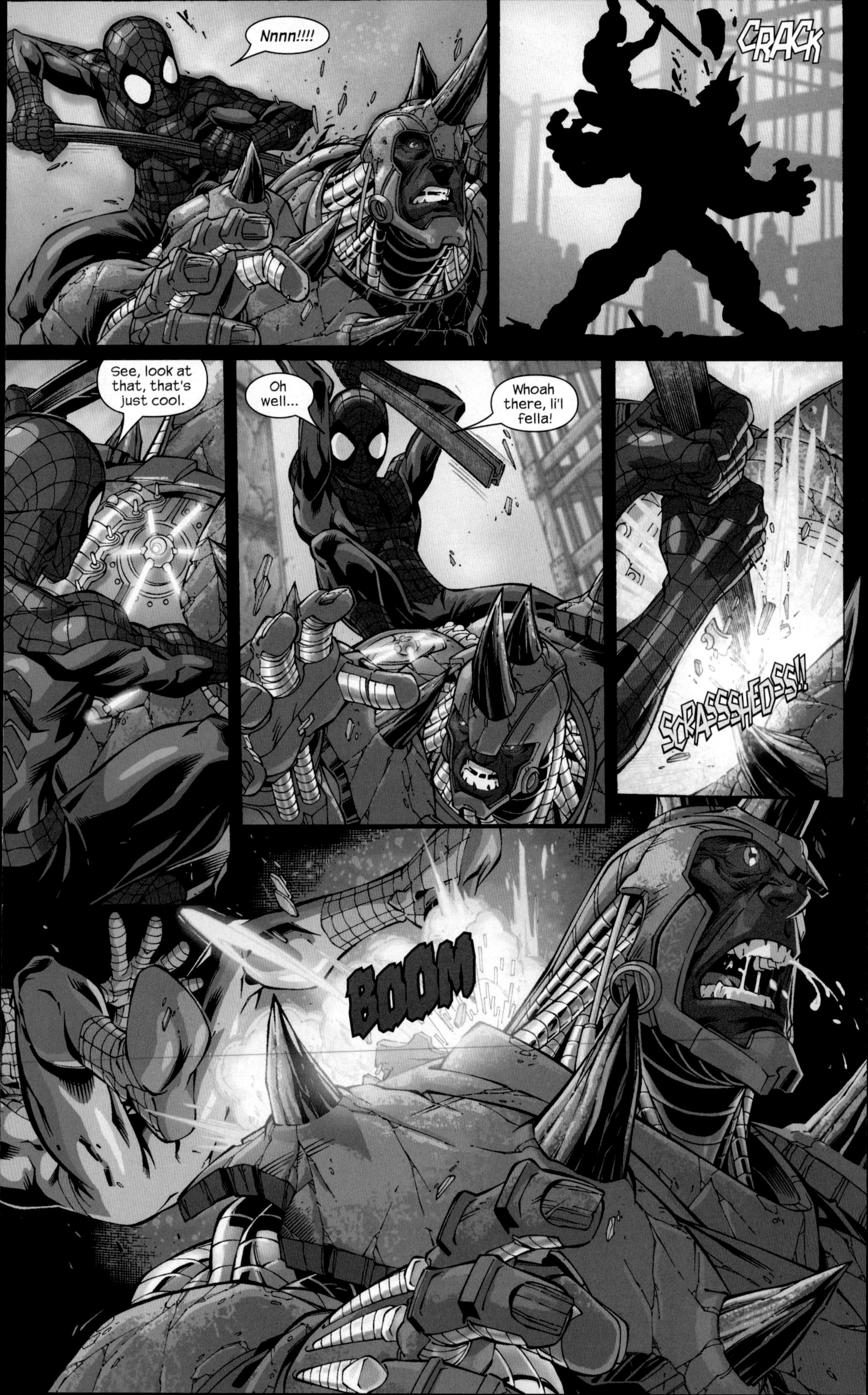
Nnnn!!!!
CRACK
See, look at that, that's just cool.
Oh well...
Whoah there, li'l fella!
SCRASSSHED-SS!!
BOOM

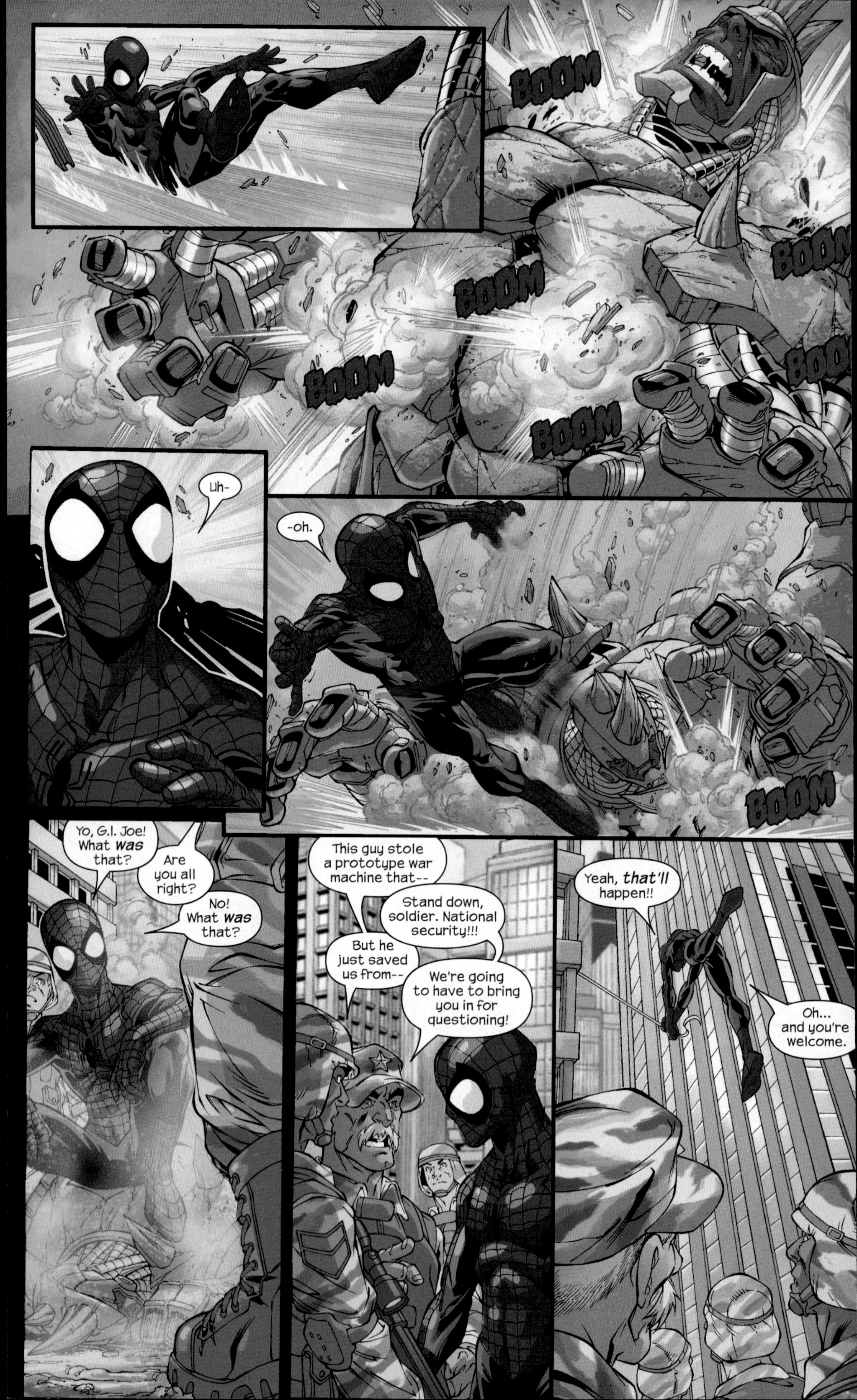
BOOM
BOOM
BOOM
BOOM
BOOM
BOOM
Uh-
-oh.
BOOM
Yo, G.I. Joe! What *was* that?
Are you all right?
No! What *was* that?
This guy stole a prototype war machine that--
Stand down, soldier. National security!!!
But he just saved us from--
We're going to have to bring you in for questioning!
Yeah, *that'll* happen!!
Oh... and you're welcome.

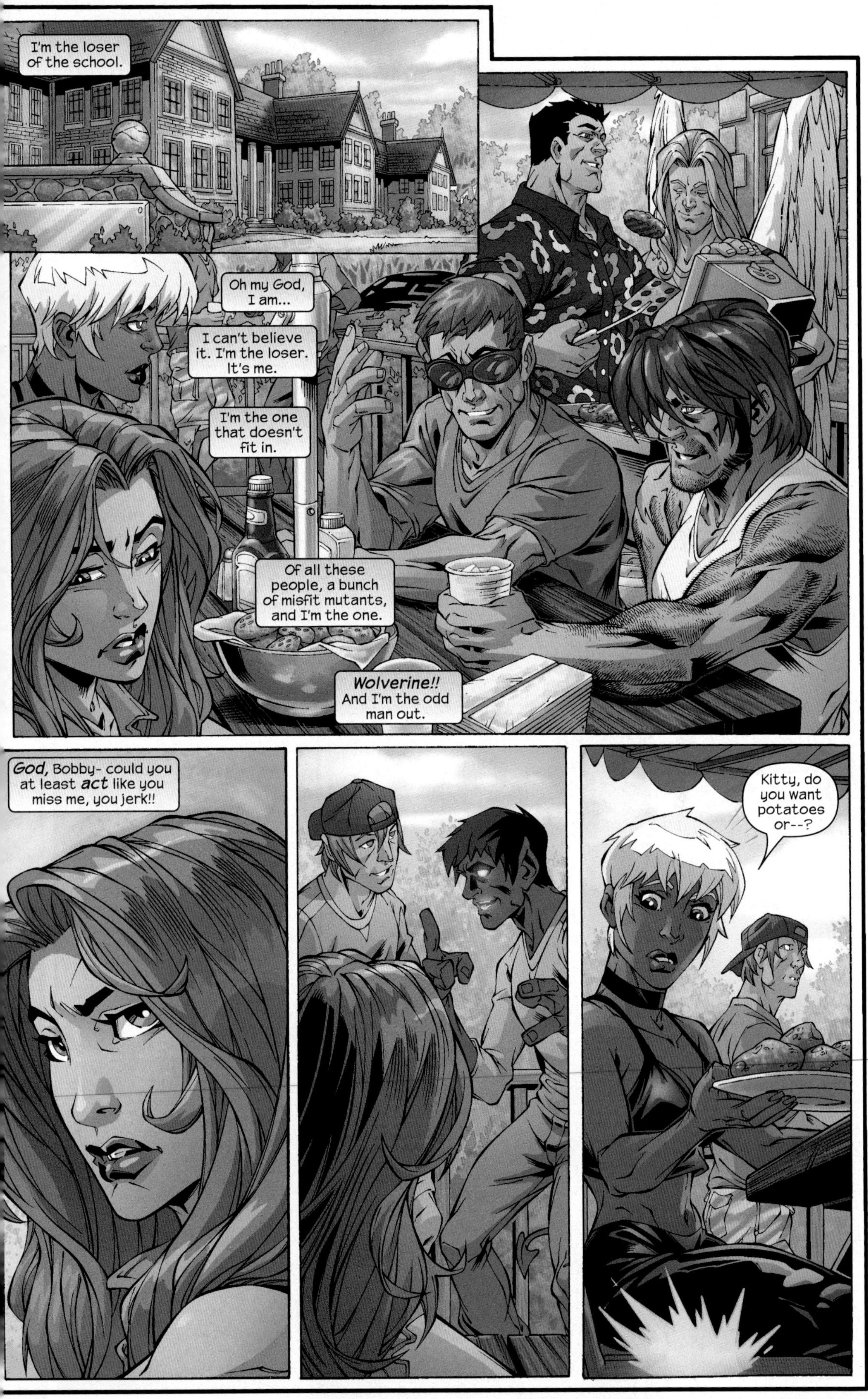
I'm the loser of the school.
Oh my God, I am...
I can't believe it. I'm the loser. It's me.
I'm the one that doesn't fit in.
Of all these people, a bunch of misfit mutants, and I'm the one.
Wolverine!! And I'm the odd man out.
God, Bobby- could you at least act like you miss me, you jerk!!
Kitty, do you want potatoes or--?

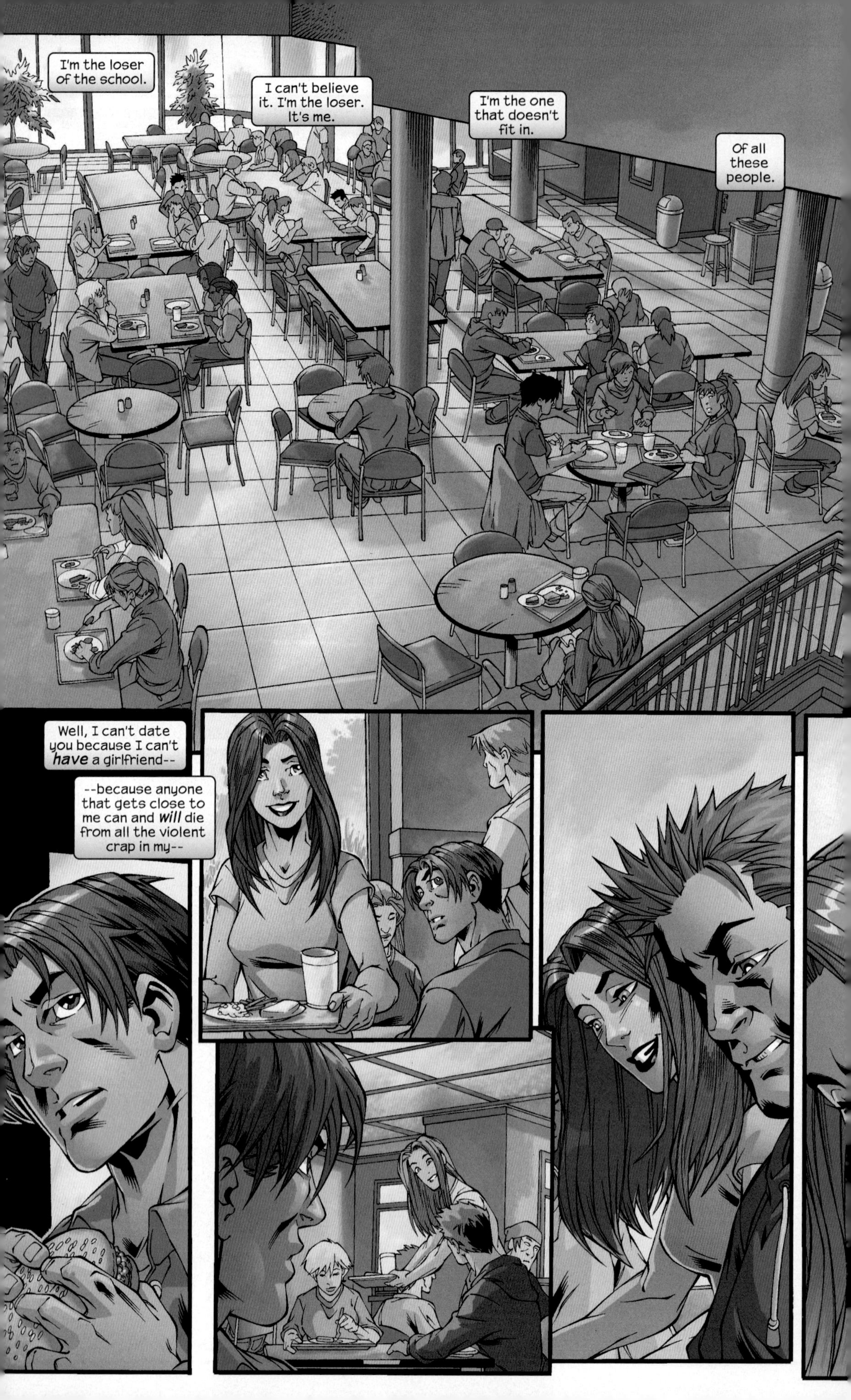
I'm the loser of the school.
I can't believe it. I'm the loser. It's me.
I'm the one that doesn't fit in.
Of all these people.
Well, I can't date you because I can't *have* a girlfriend--
--because anyone that gets close to me can and *will* die from all the violent crap in my--

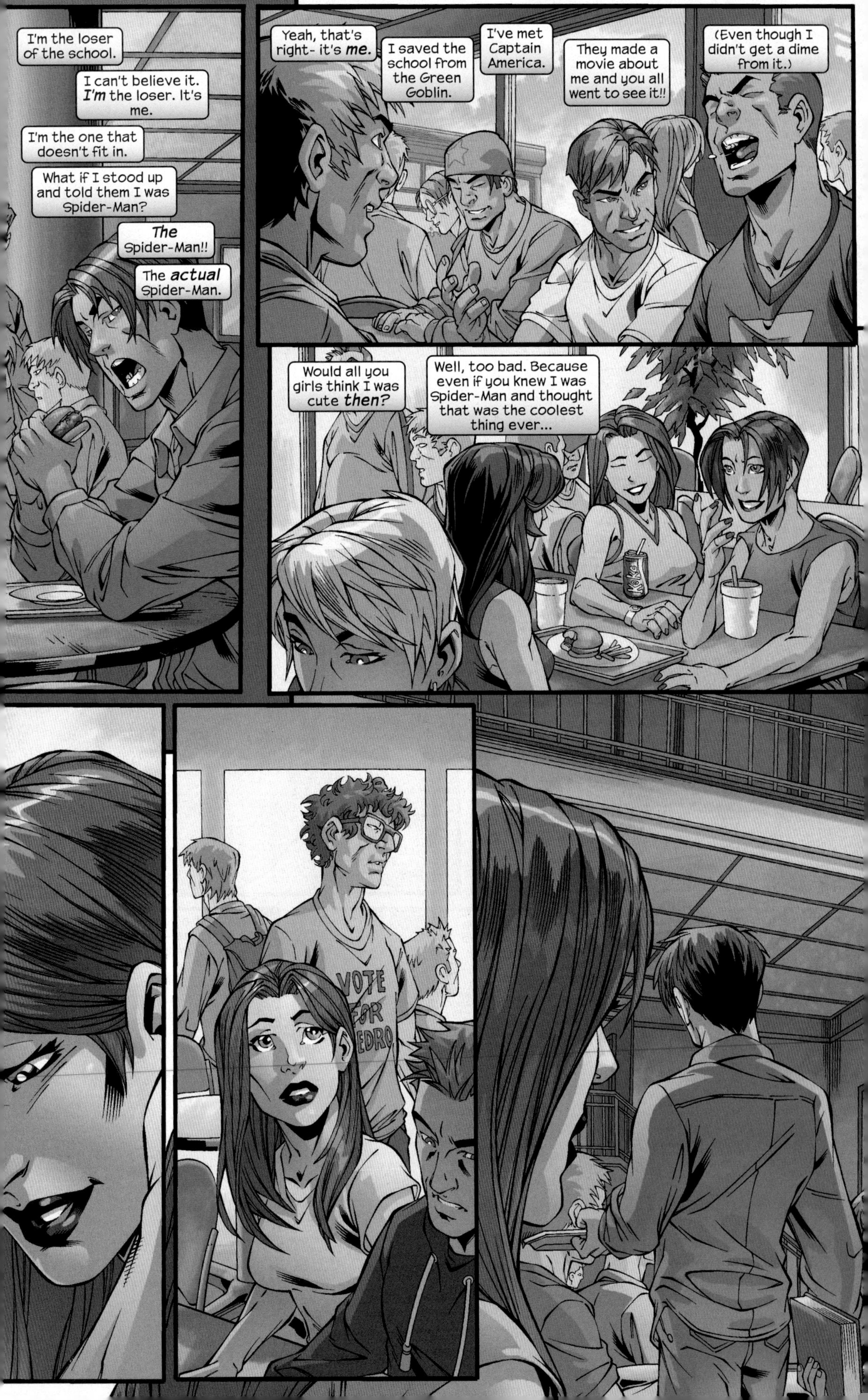

I'm the loser of the school.
I can't believe it. *I'm* the loser. It's me.
I'm the one that doesn't fit in.
What if I stood up and told them I was Spider-Man?
The Spider-Man!!
The *actual* Spider-Man.
Yeah, that's right- it's *me.*
I saved the school from the Green Goblin.
I've met Captain America.
They made a movie about me and you all went to see it!!
(Even though I didn't get a dime from it.)
Would all you girls think I was cute *then?*
Well, too bad. Because even if you knew I was Spider-Man and thought that was the coolest thing ever...
VOTE FOR PEDRO

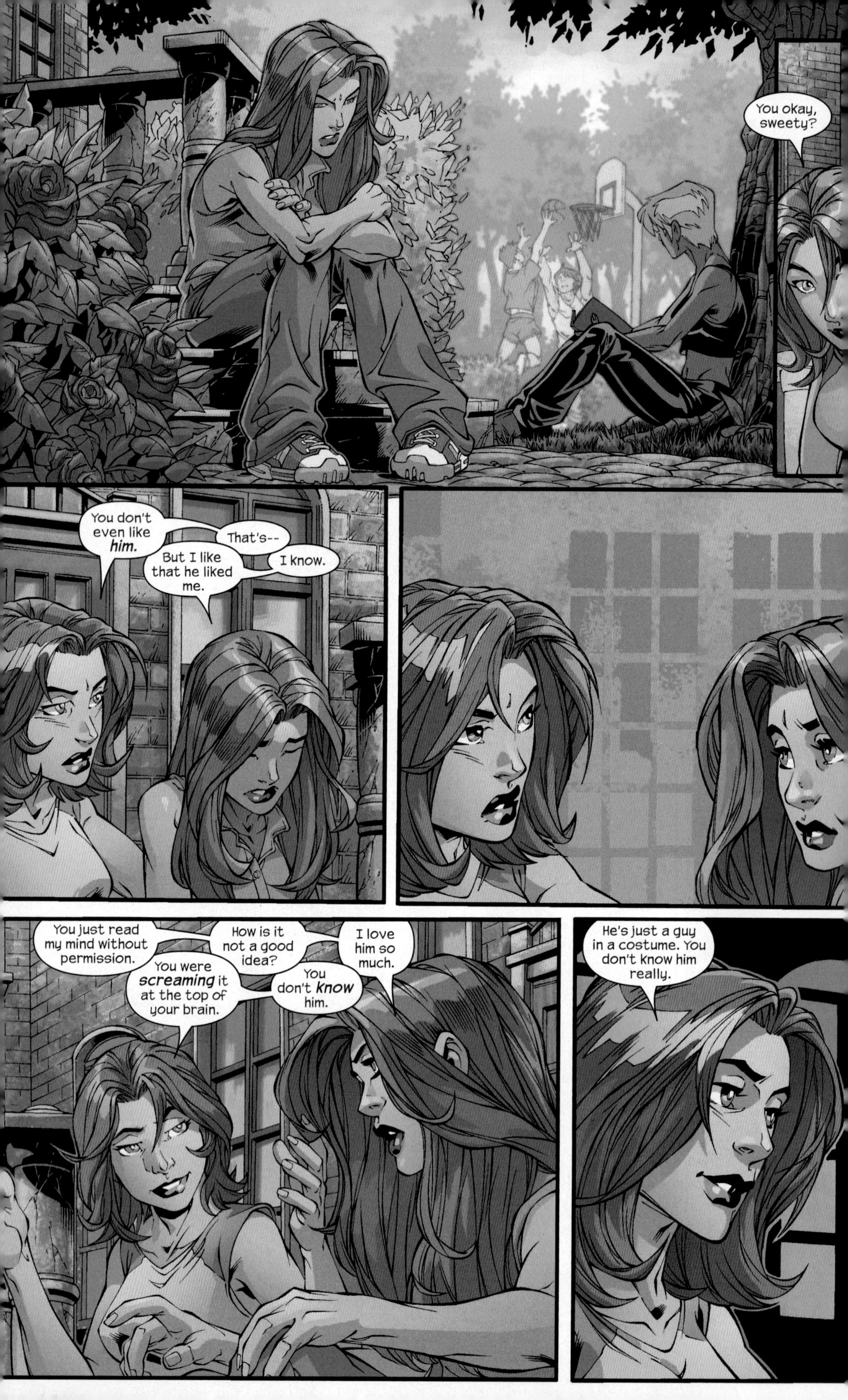
You okay, sweety?
You don't even like *him.*
That's--
But I like that he liked me.
I know.
You just read my mind without permission.
How is it not a good idea?
I love him so much.
You were *screaming* it at the top of your brain.
You don't *know* him.
He's just a guy in a costume. You don't know him really.

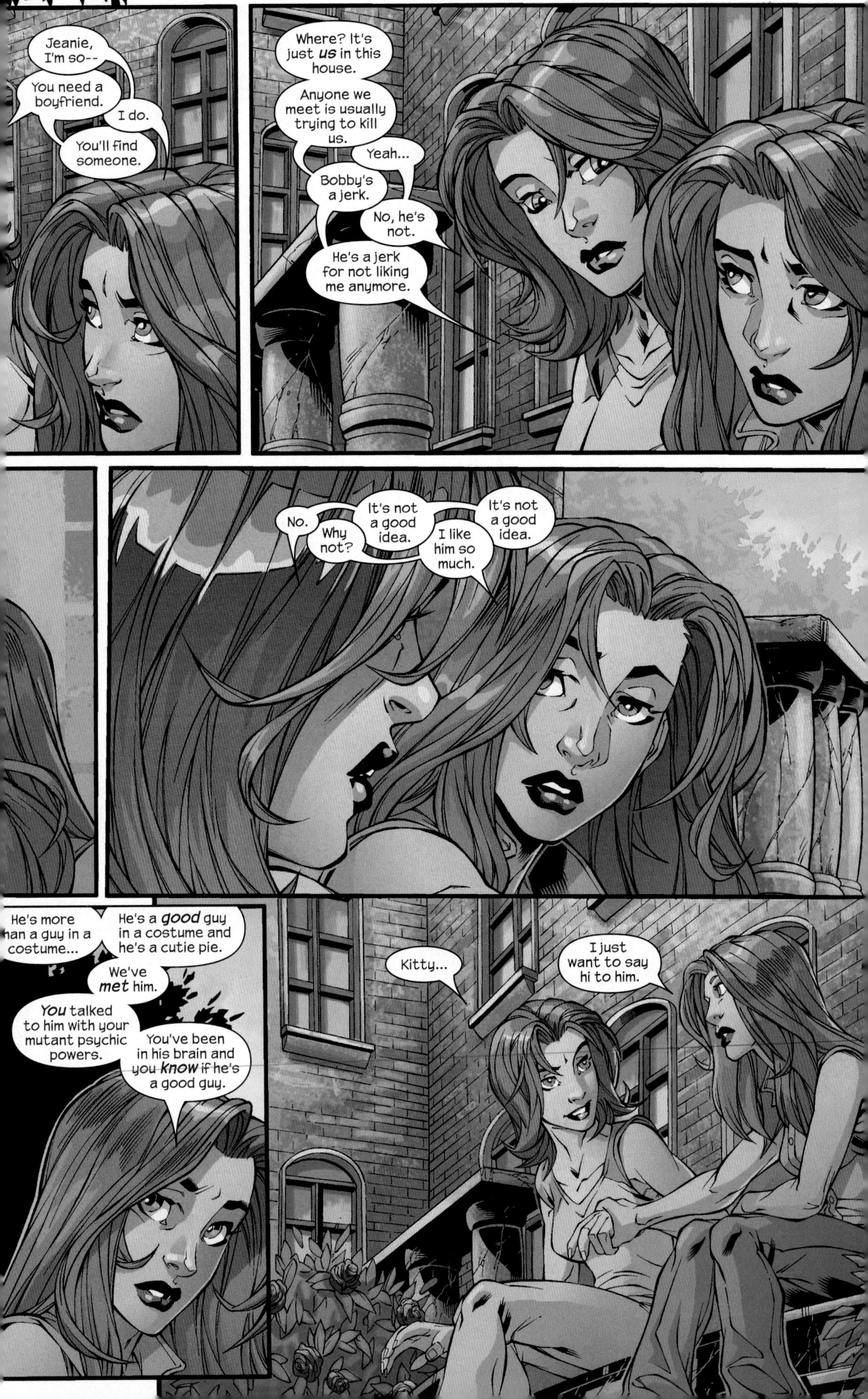
Jeanie, I'm so--
You need a boyfriend.
I do.
You'll find someone.
Where? It's just *us* in this house.
Anyone we meet is usually trying to kill us.
Yeah...
Bobby's a jerk.
No, he's not.
He's a jerk for not liking me anymore.
No.
Why not?
It's not a good idea.
I like him so much.
It's not a good idea.
He's more than a guy in a costume...
He's a *good* guy in a costume and he's a cutie pie.
We've *met* him.
You talked to him with your mutant psychic powers.
You've been in his brain and you *know* if he's a good guy.
Kitty...
I just want to say hi to him.

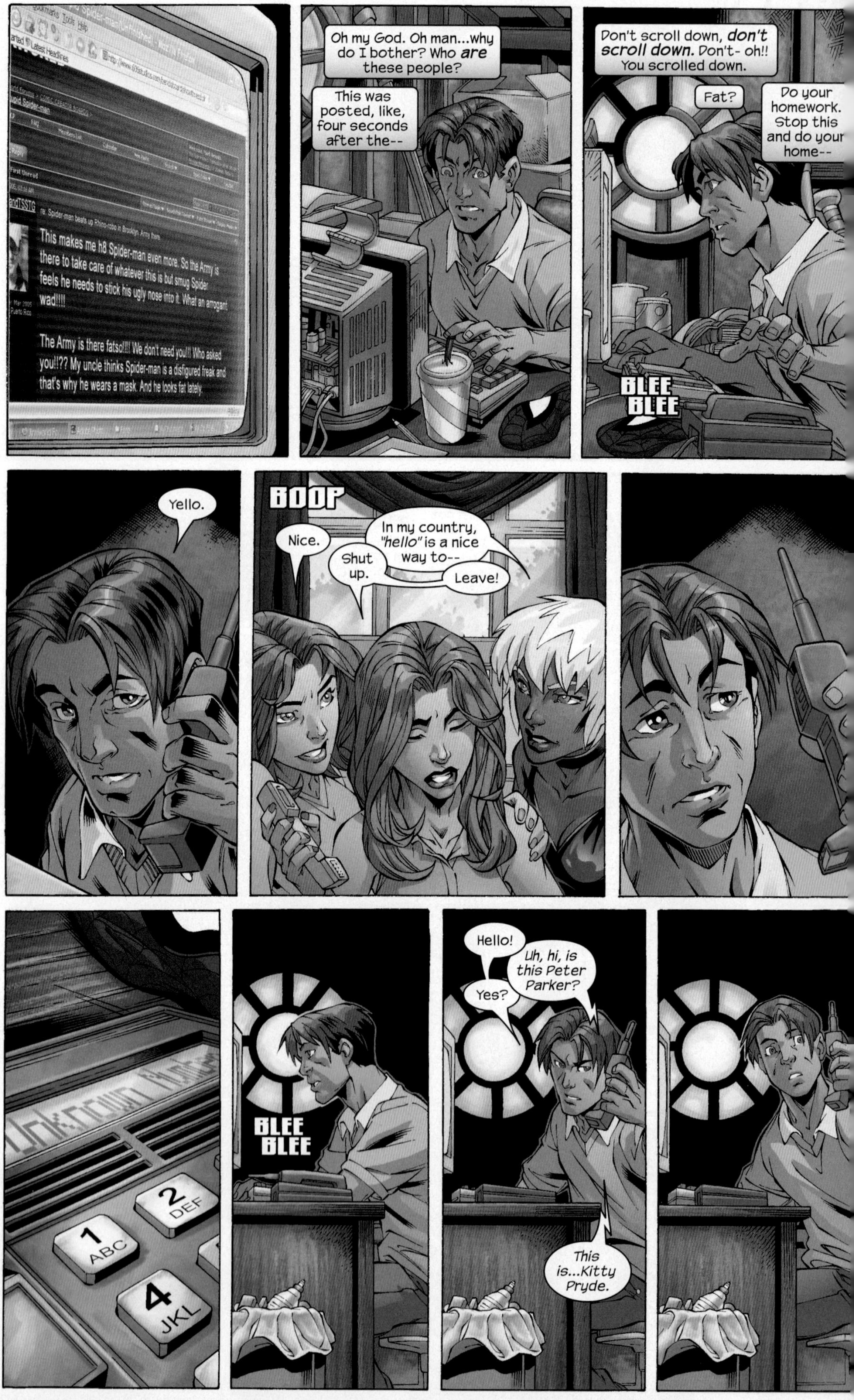

This makes me h8 Spider-man even more. So the Army is there to take care of whatever this is but smug Spider feels he needs to stick his ugly nose into it. What an arrogant wad!!!!
The Army is there fatso!!! We don't need you!!! Who asked you!!?? My uncle thinks Spider-man is a disfigured freak and that's why he wears a mask. And he looks fat lately.
Oh my God. Oh man...why do I bother? Who *are* these people?
This was posted, like, four seconds after the--
Don't scroll down, ***don't scroll down.*** Don't- oh!! You scrolled down.
Fat?
Do your homework. Stop this and do your home--
BLEE BLEE
Yello.
BOOP
Nice.
In my country, *"hello"* is a nice way to--
Shut up.
Leave!
1 ABC
2 DEF
4 JKL
BLEE BLEE
Hello!
Uh, hi, is this Peter Parker?
Yes?
This is...Kitty Pryde.

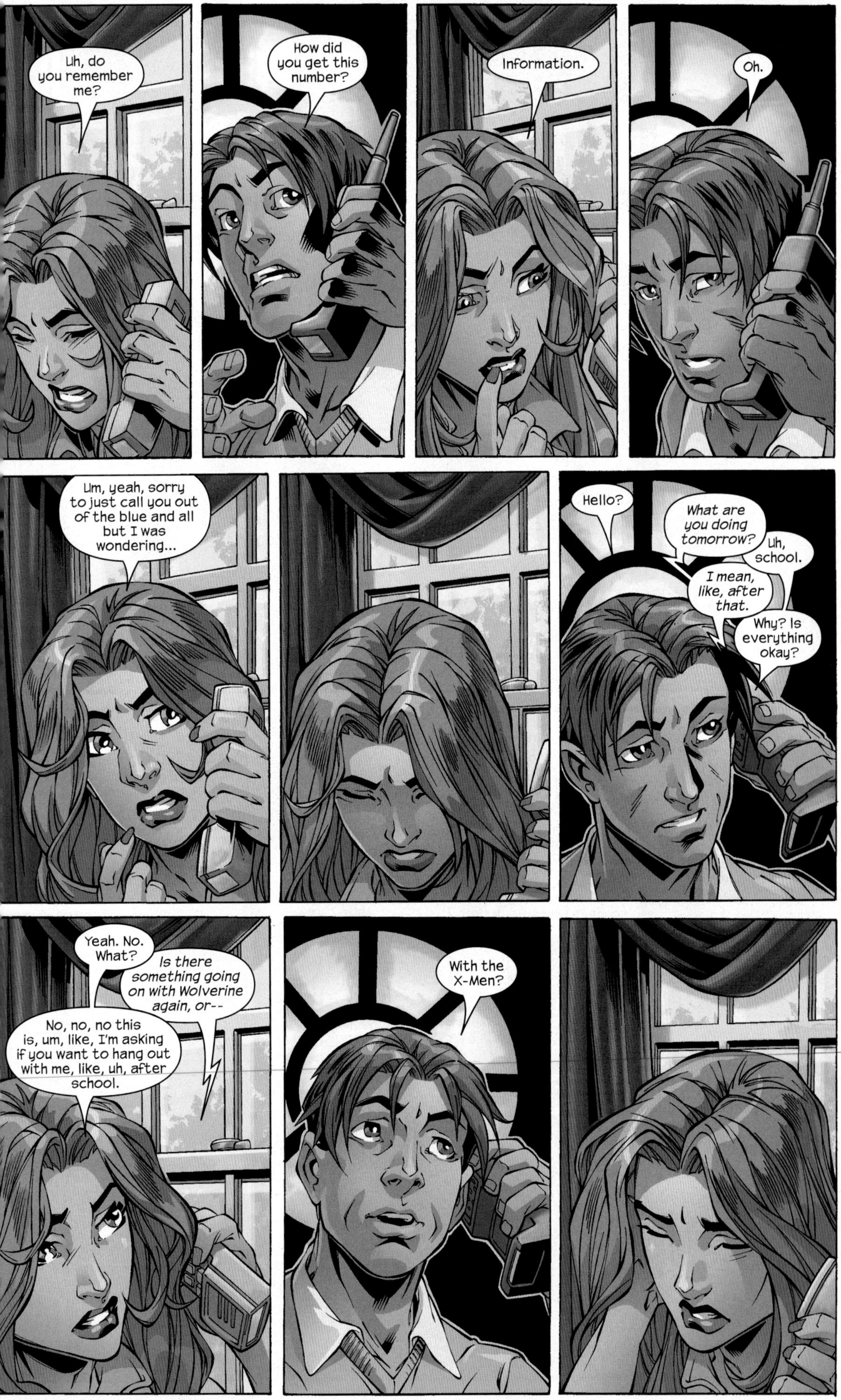
Uh, do you remember me?
How did you get this number?
Information.
Oh.
Um, yeah, sorry to just call you out of the blue and all but I was wondering...
Hello?
What are you doing tomorrow?
Uh, school.
I mean, like, after that.
Why? Is everything okay?
Yeah. No. What?
Is there something going on with Wolverine again, or--
No, no, no this is, um, like, I'm asking if you want to hang out with me, like, uh, after school.
With the X-Men?

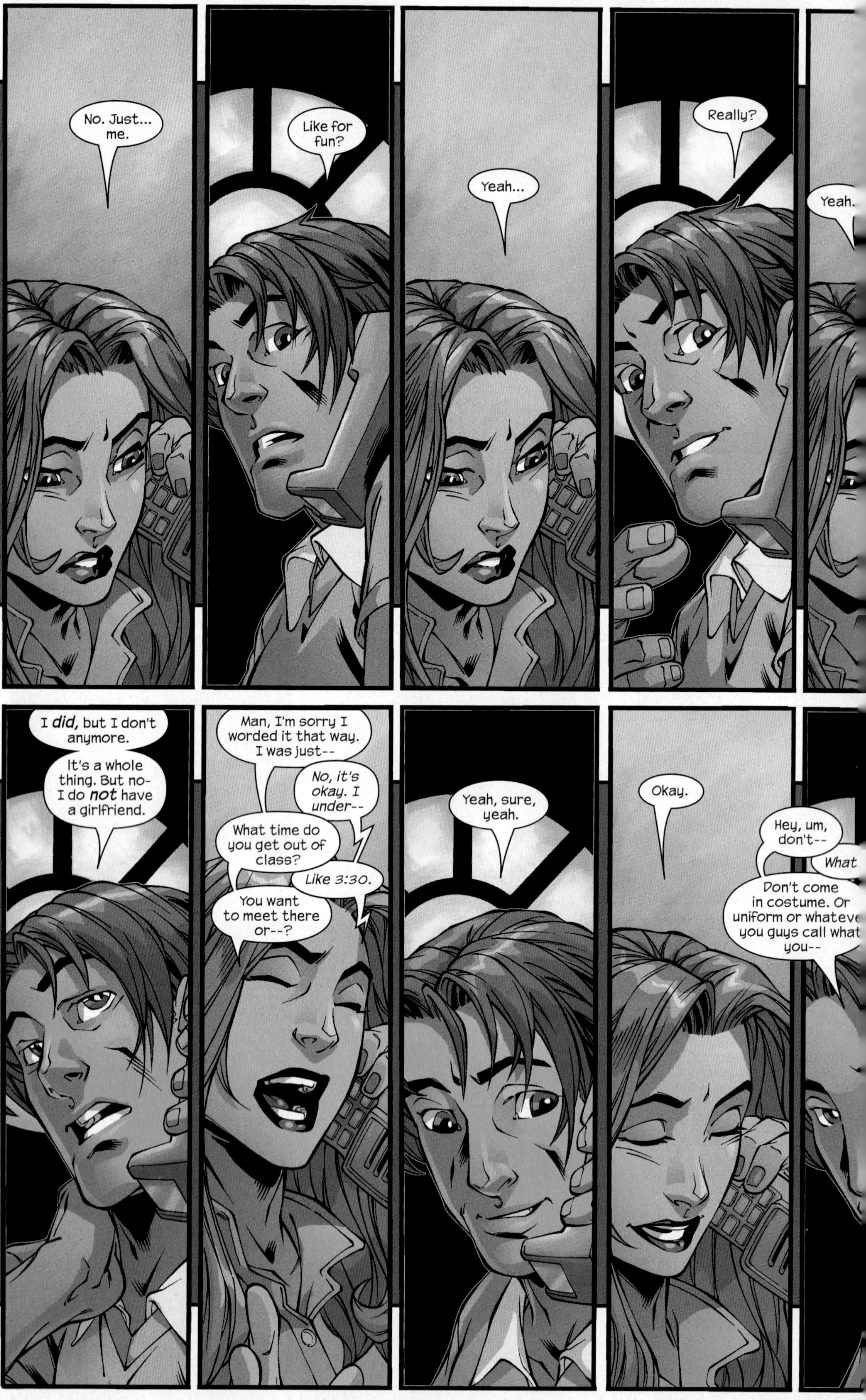
No. Just... me.
Like for fun?
Yeah...
Really?
Yeah.
I did, but I don't anymore.
It's a whole thing. But no- I do not have a girlfriend.
Man, I'm sorry I worded it that way. I was just--
No, it's okay. I under--
What time do you get out of class?
Like 3:30.
You want to meet there or--?
Yeah, sure, yeah.
Okay.
Hey, um, don't--
What
Don't come in costume. Or uniform or whateve you guys call what you--

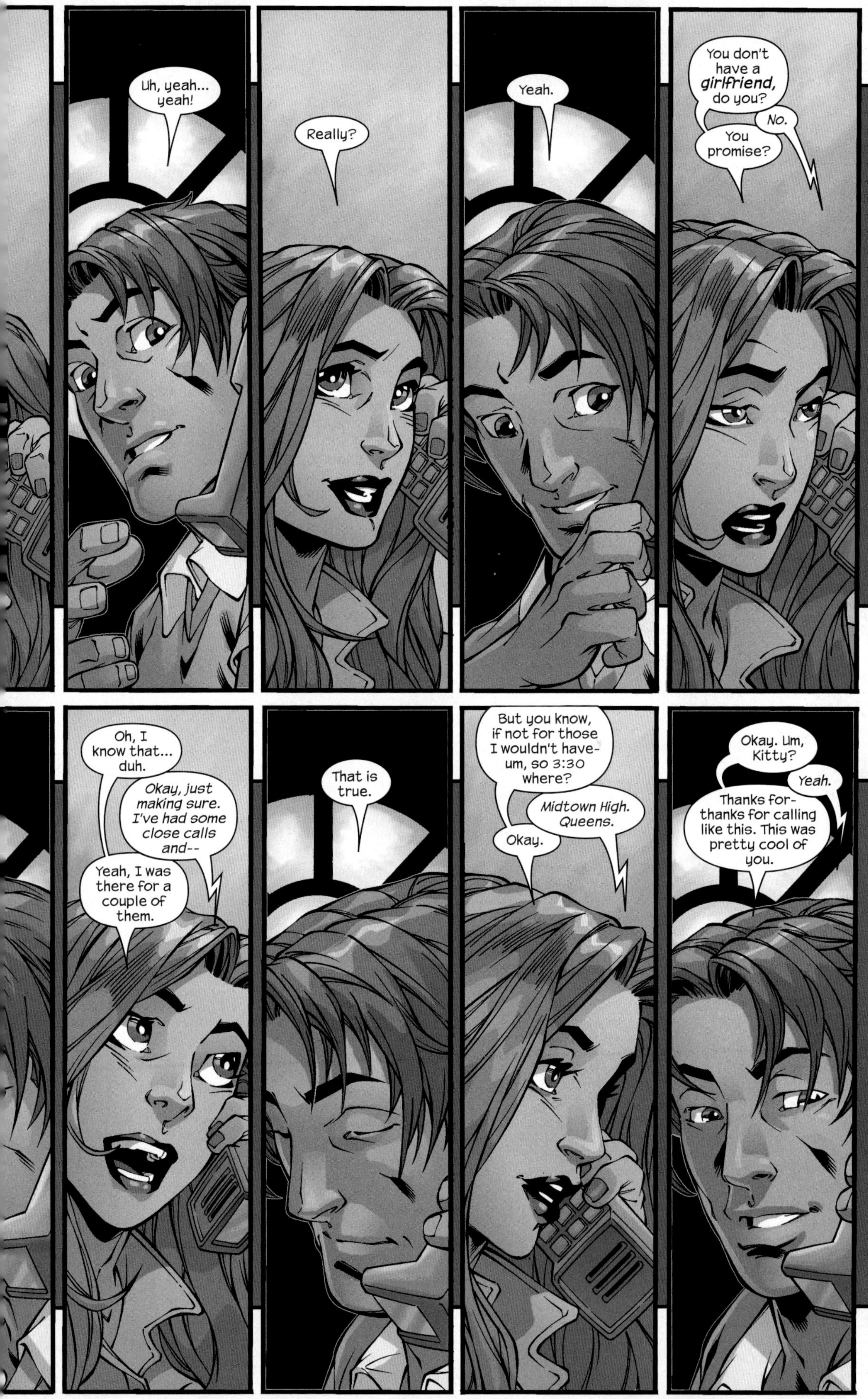

Uh, yeah... yeah!
Really?
Yeah.
You don't have a **girlfriend,** do you?
No.
You promise?
Oh, I know that... duh.
Okay, just making sure. I've had some close calls and--
Yeah, I was there for a couple of them.
That is true.
But you know, if not for those I wouldn't have-- um, so 3:30 where?
Midtown High. Queens.
Okay.
Okay. Um, Kitty?
Yeah.
Thanks for-- thanks for calling like this. This was pretty cool of you.

Goggle™

Web Images Groups News Froogle Local more »

X-MEN

Goggle Search   I'm Feeling Lucky

Advanced Search
Preferences
Language Tools

Advertising Programs

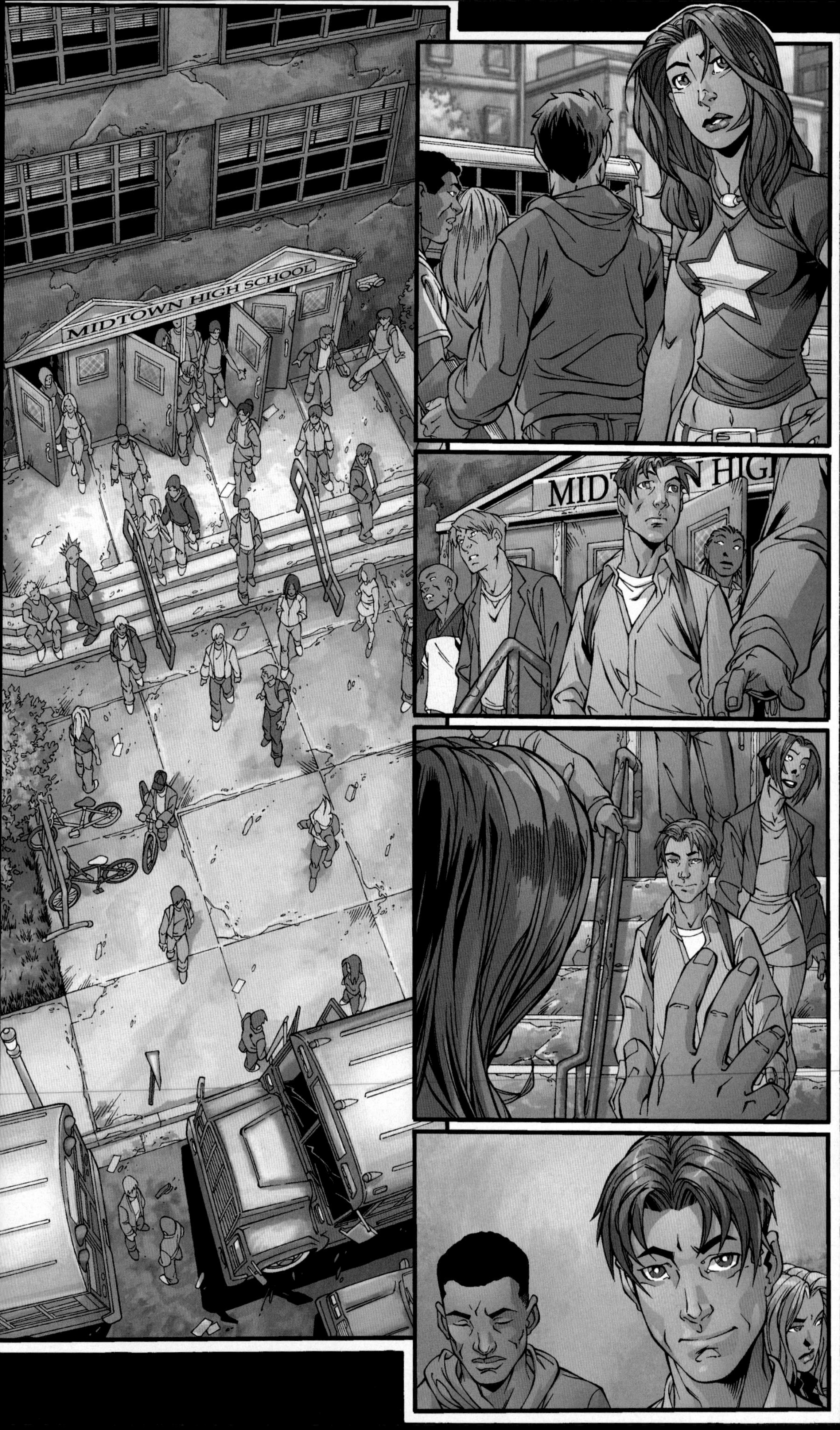
MIDTOWN HIGH SCHOOL

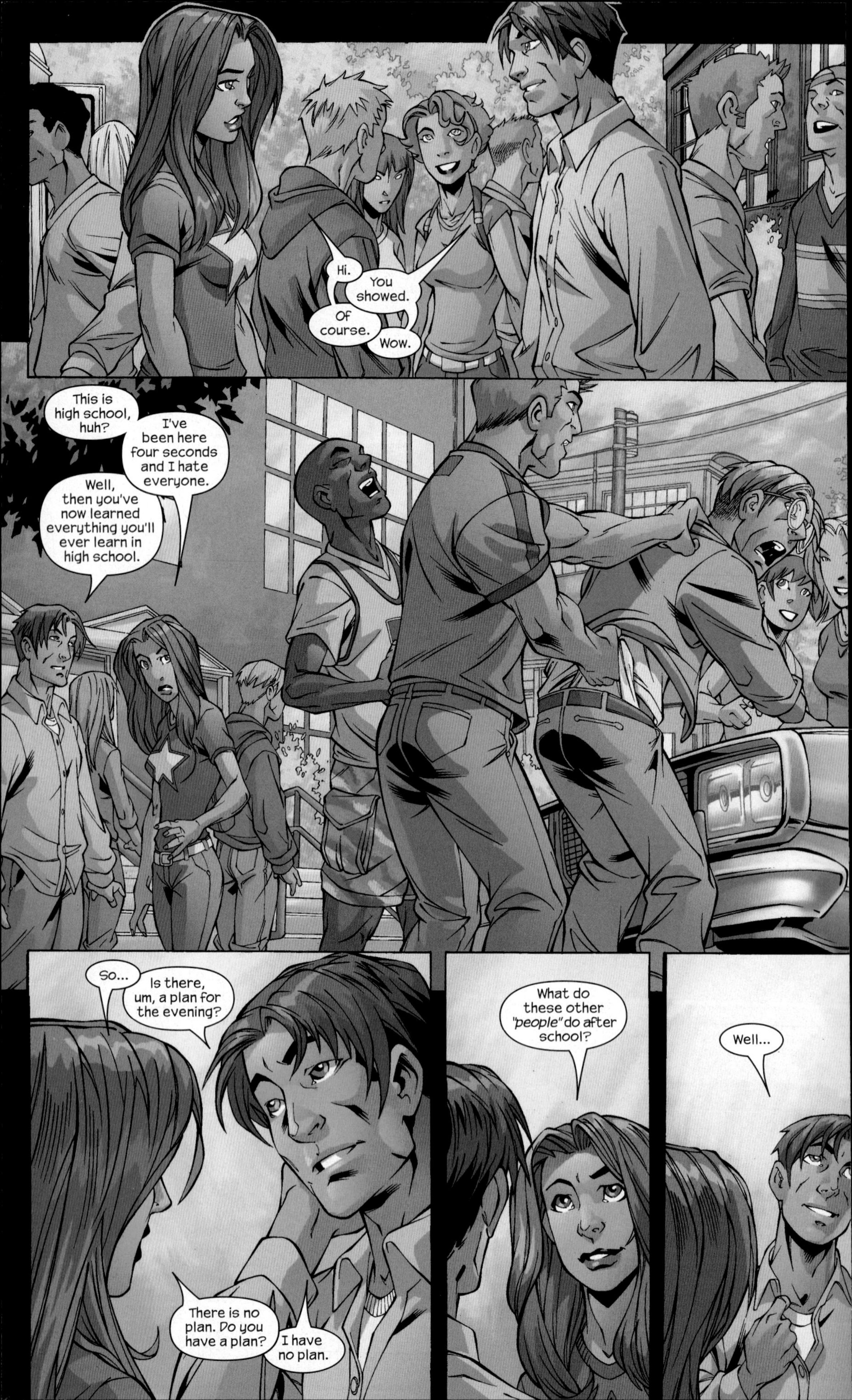
Hi.
You showed.
Of course.
Wow.
This is high school, huh?
I've been here four seconds and I hate everyone.
Well, then you've now learned everything you'll ever learn in high school.
So...
Is there, um, a plan for the evening?
There is no plan. Do you have a plan?
I have no plan.
What do these other *"people"* do after school?
Well...

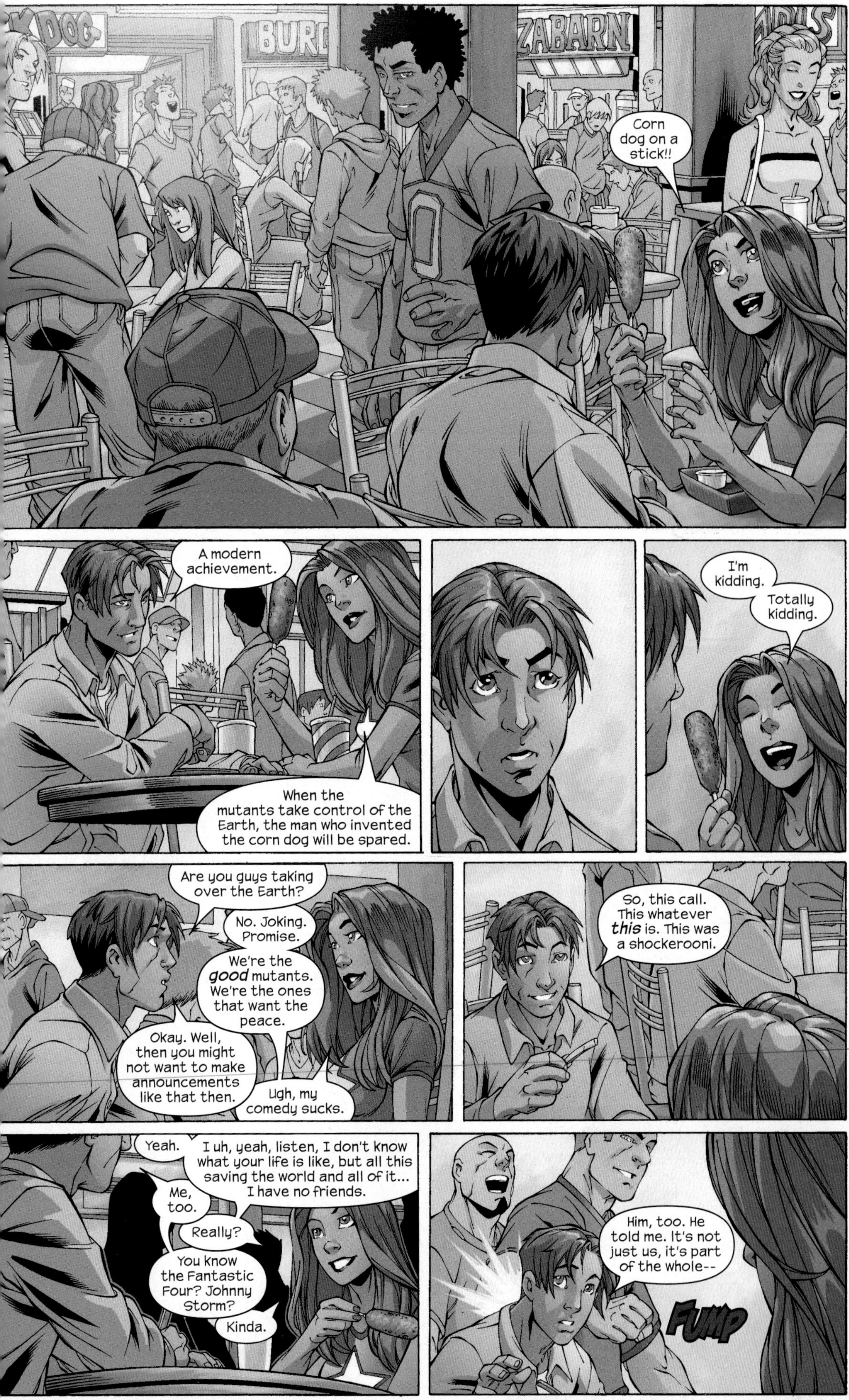
DOG
BUR
ZABARN
Corn dog on a stick!!
A modern achievement.
When the mutants take control of the Earth, the man who invented the corn dog will be spared.
I'm kidding.
Totally kidding.
Are you guys taking over the Earth?
No. Joking. Promise.
We're the *good* mutants. We're the ones that want the peace.
Okay. Well, then you might not want to make announcements like that then.
Ugh, my comedy sucks.
So, this call. This whatever *this* is. This was a shockerooni.
Yeah.
I uh, yeah, listen, I don't know what your life is like, but all this saving the world and all of it... I have no friends.
Me, too.
Really?
You know the Fantastic Four? Johnny Storm?
Kinda.
Him, too. He told me. It's not just us, it's part of the whole--
FUMP

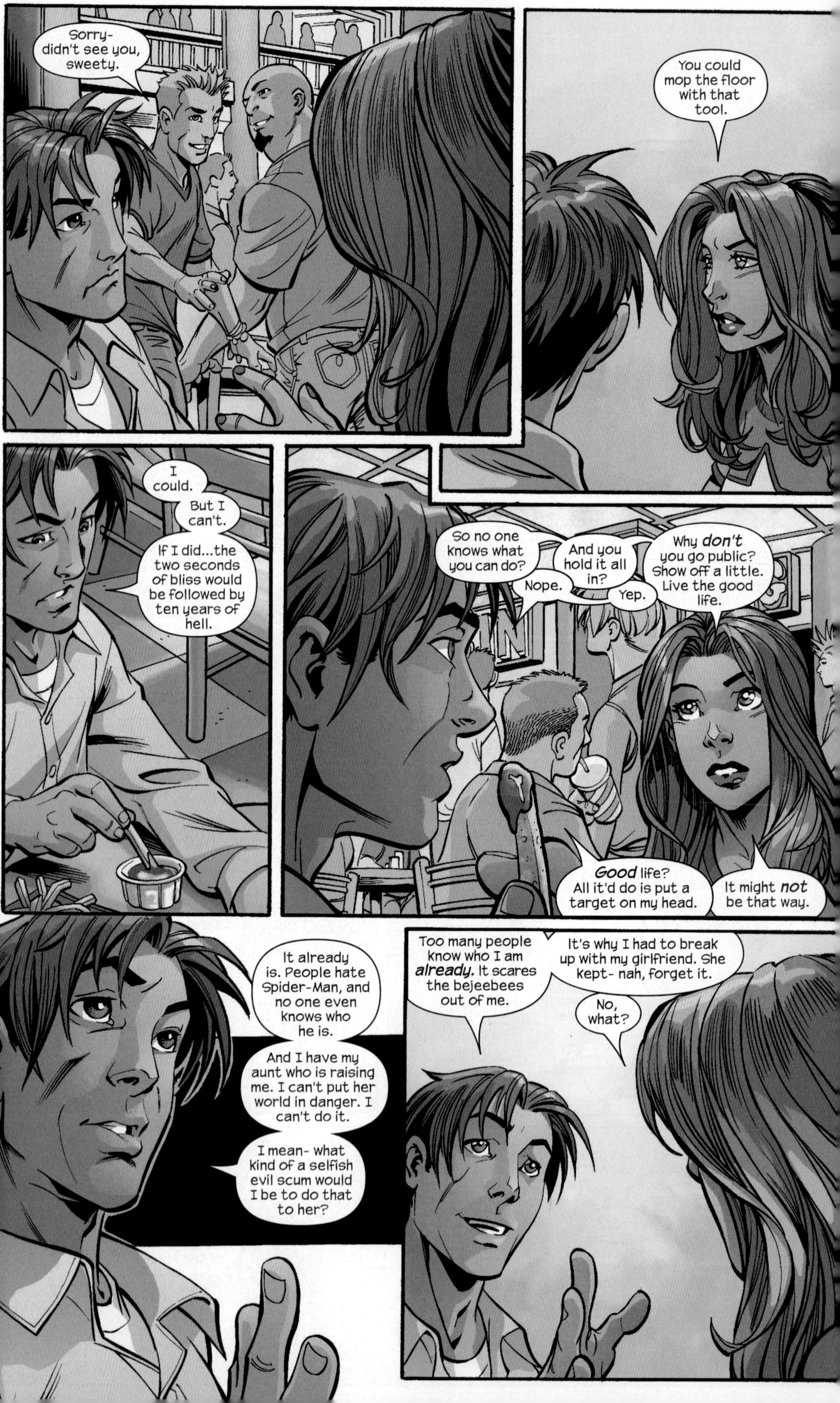
Sorry- didn't see you, sweety.
You could mop the floor with that tool.
I could.
But I can't.
If I did...the two seconds of bliss would be followed by ten years of hell.
So no one knows what you can do?
Nope.
And you hold it all in?
Yep.
Why don't you go public? Show off a little. Live the good life.
Good life? All it'd do is put a target on my head.
It might not be that way.
It already is. People hate Spider-Man, and no one even knows who he is.
And I have my aunt who is raising me. I can't put her world in danger. I can't do it.
I mean- what kind of a selfish evil scum would I be to do that to her?
Too many people know who I am already. It scares the bejeebees out of me.
It's why I had to break up with my girlfriend. She kept- nah, forget it.
No, what?

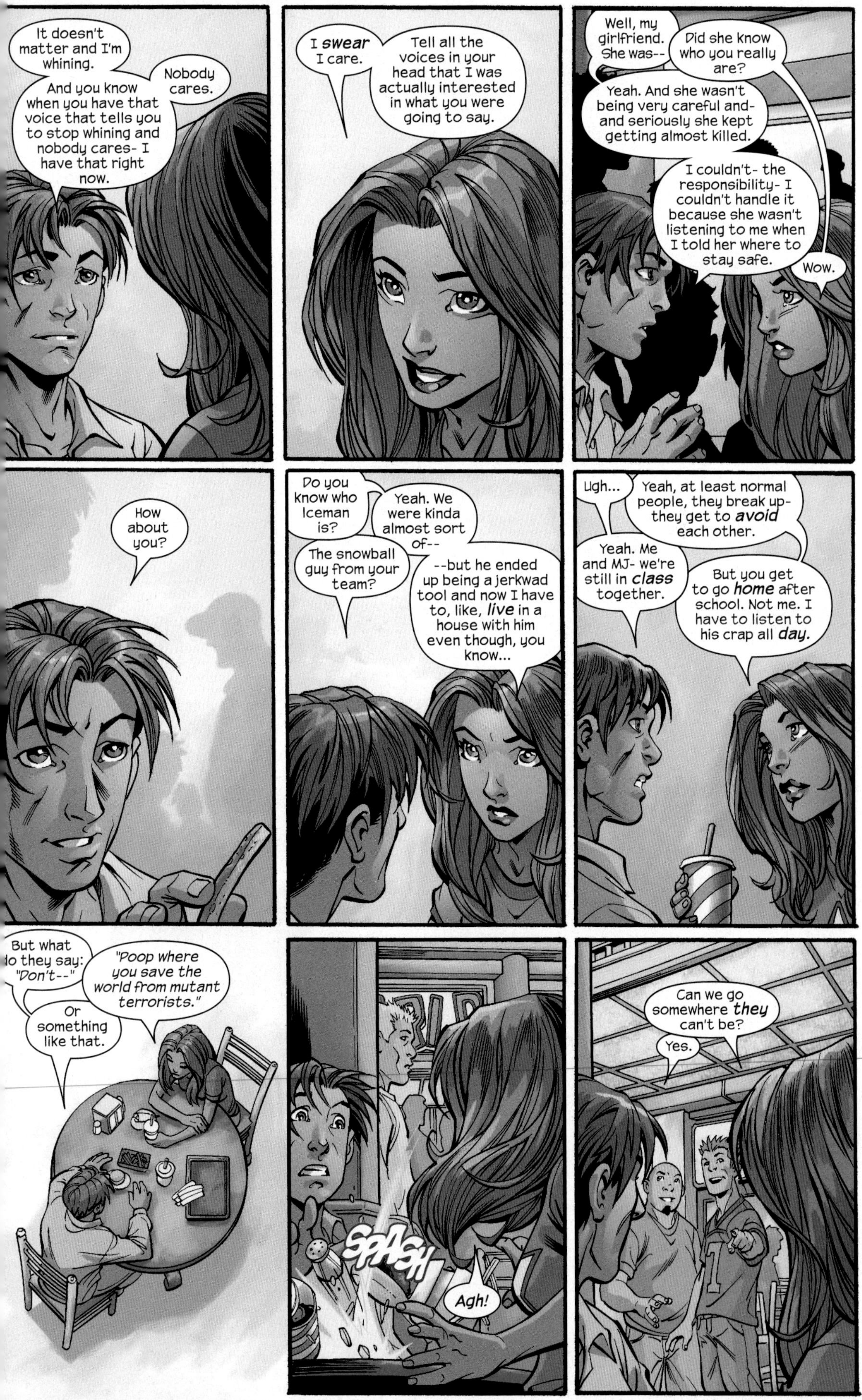

It doesn't matter and I'm whining.
Nobody cares.
And you know when you have that voice that tells you to stop whining and nobody cares- I have that right now.
I *swear* I care.
Tell all the voices in your head that I was actually interested in what you were going to say.
Well, my girlfriend. She was--
Did she know who you really are?
Yeah. And she wasn't being very careful and- and seriously she kept getting almost killed.
I couldn't- the responsibility- I couldn't handle it because she wasn't listening to me when I told her where to stay safe.
Wow.
How about you?
Do you know who Iceman is?
Yeah. We were kinda almost sort of--
The snowball guy from your team?
--but he ended up being a jerkwad tool and now I have to, like, *live* in a house with him even though, you know...
Ugh...
Yeah, at least normal people, they break up- they get to *avoid* each other.
Yeah. Me and MJ- we're still in *class* together.
But you get to go *home* after school. Not me. I have to listen to his crap all *day*.
But what do they say: "Don't--"
"Poop where you save the world from mutant terrorists."
Or something like that.
SPASH
Agh!
Can we go somewhere *they* can't be?
Yes.

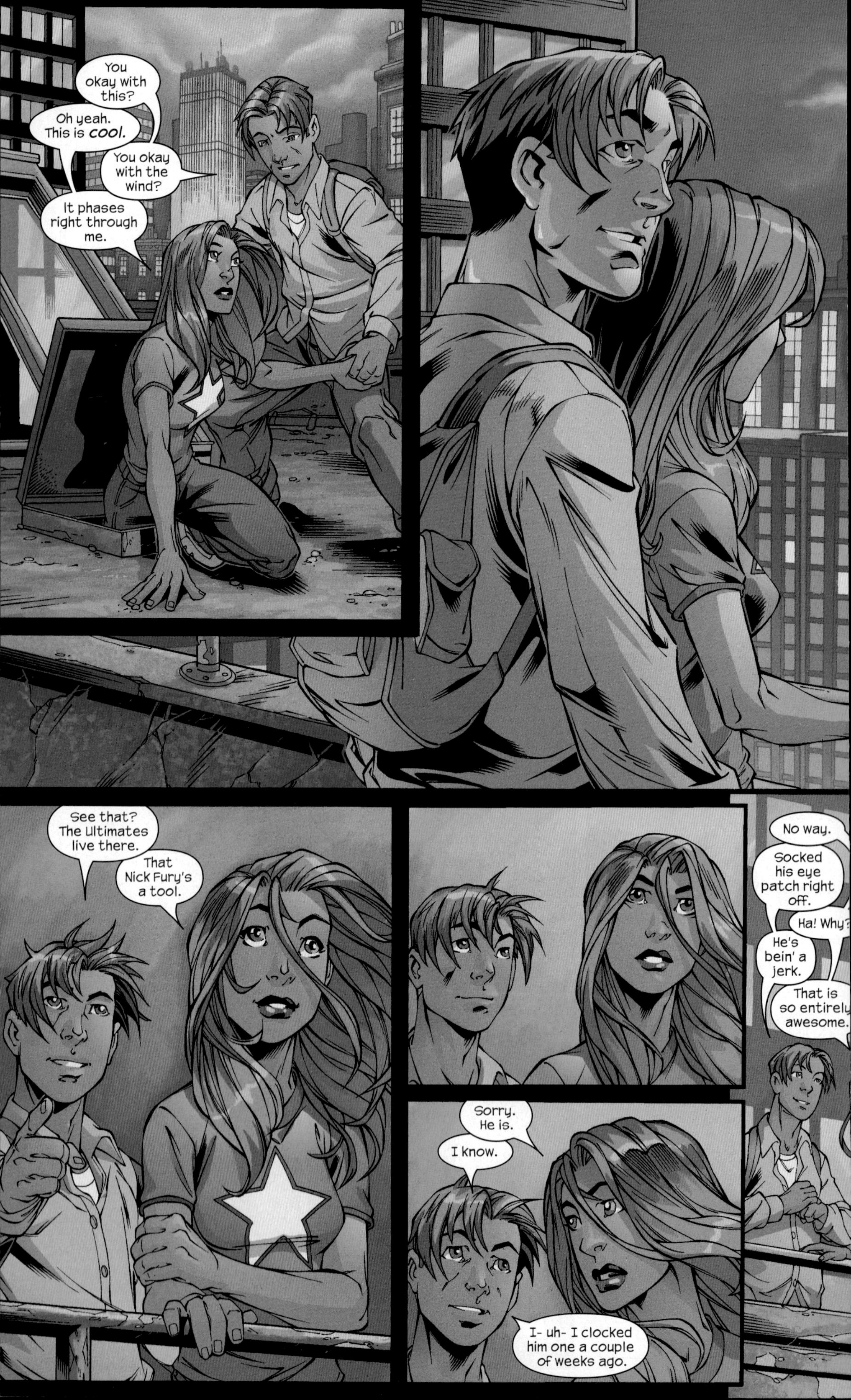
You okay with this?
Oh yeah. This is *cool.*
You okay with the wind?
It phases right through me.
See that? The Ultimates live there.
That Nick Fury's a tool.
No way.
Socked his eye patch right off.
Ha! Why?
He's bein' a jerk.
That is so entirely awesome.
Sorry. He is.
I know.
I- uh- I clocked him one a couple of weeks ago.

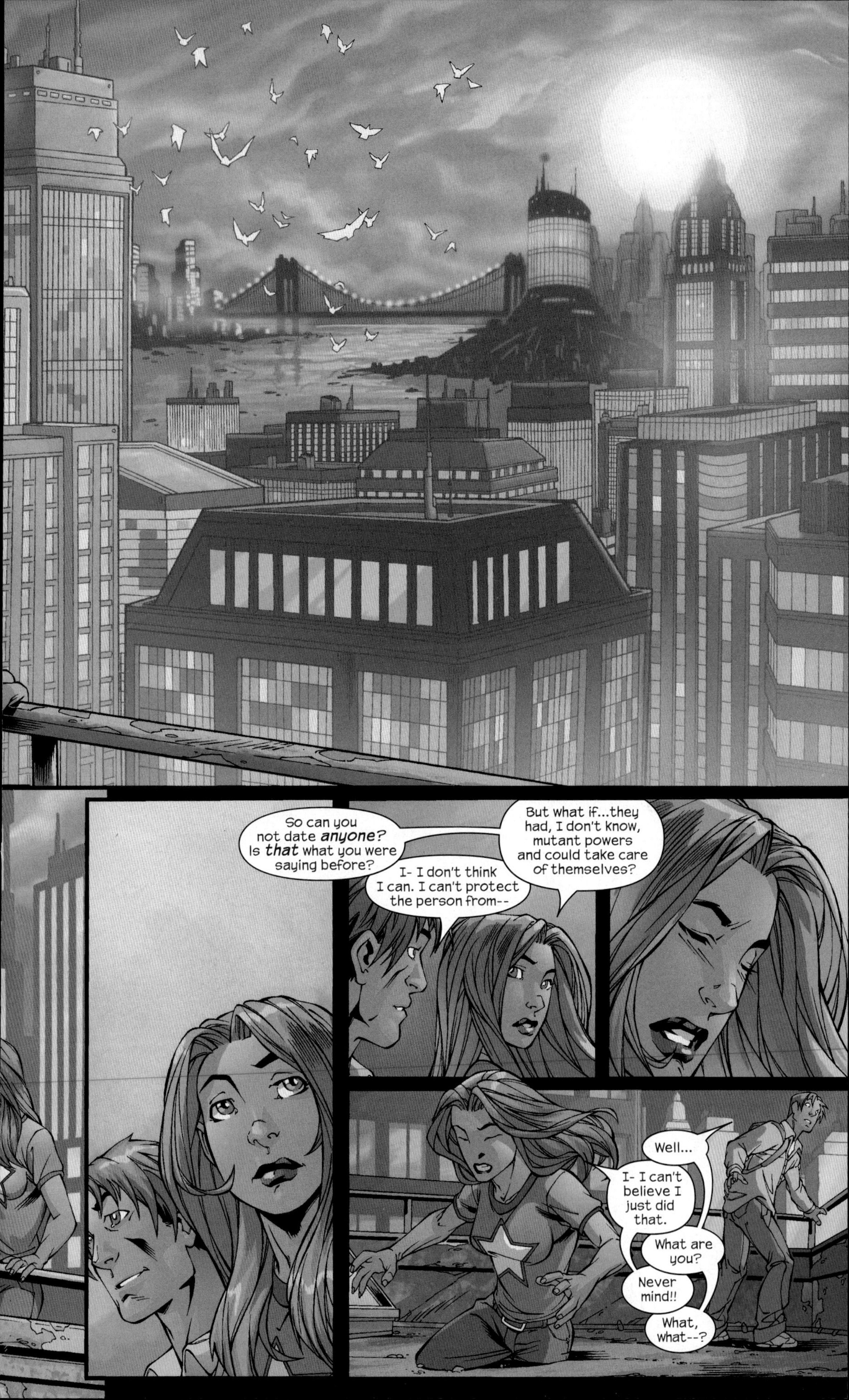

So can you not date *anyone*? Is *that* what you were saying before?
I- I don't think I can. I can't protect the person from--
But what if...they had, I don't know, mutant powers and could take care of themselves?
Well...
I- I can't believe I just did that.
What are you?
Never mind!!
What, what--?

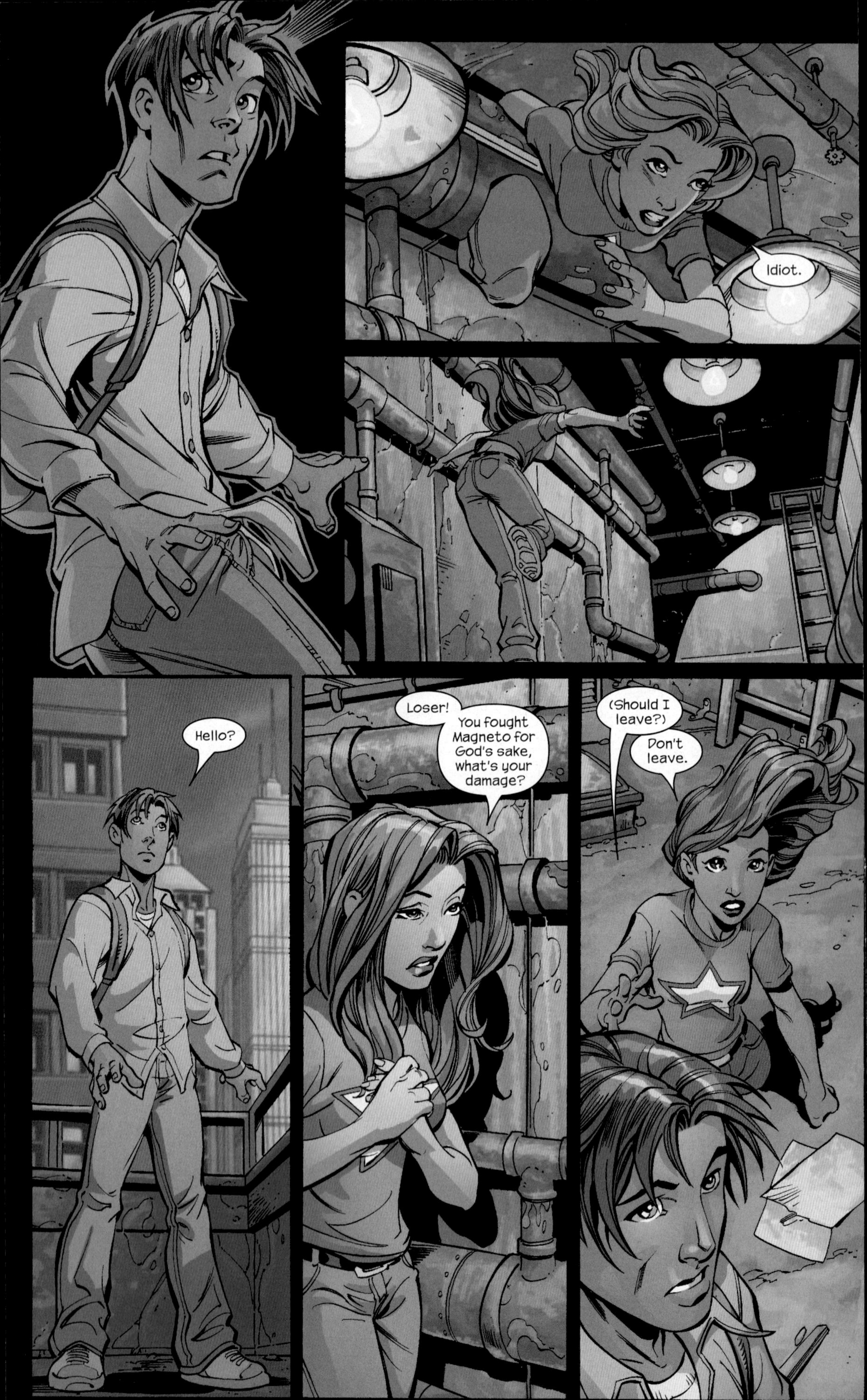
Idiot.
Hello?
Loser!
You fought Magneto for God's sake, what's your damage?
(Should I leave?)
Don't leave.

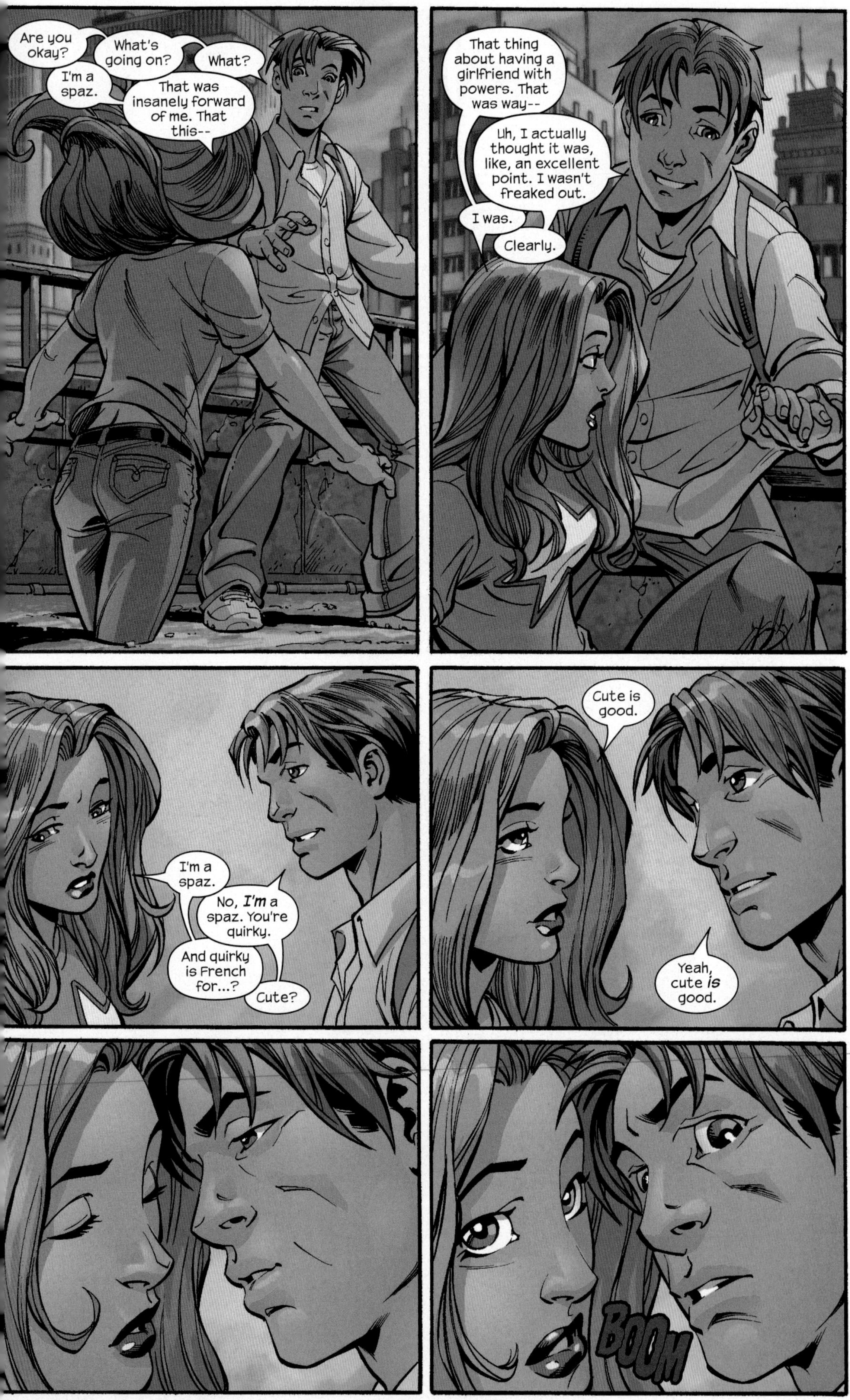
Are you okay?
What's going on?
What?
I'm a spaz.
That was insanely forward of me. That this--
That thing about having a girlfriend with powers. That was way--
Uh, I actually thought it was, like, an excellent point. I wasn't freaked out.
I was.
Clearly.
I'm a spaz.
No, *I'm* a spaz. You're quirky.
And quirky is French for...?
Cute?
Cute is good.
Yeah, cute *is* good.
BOOM

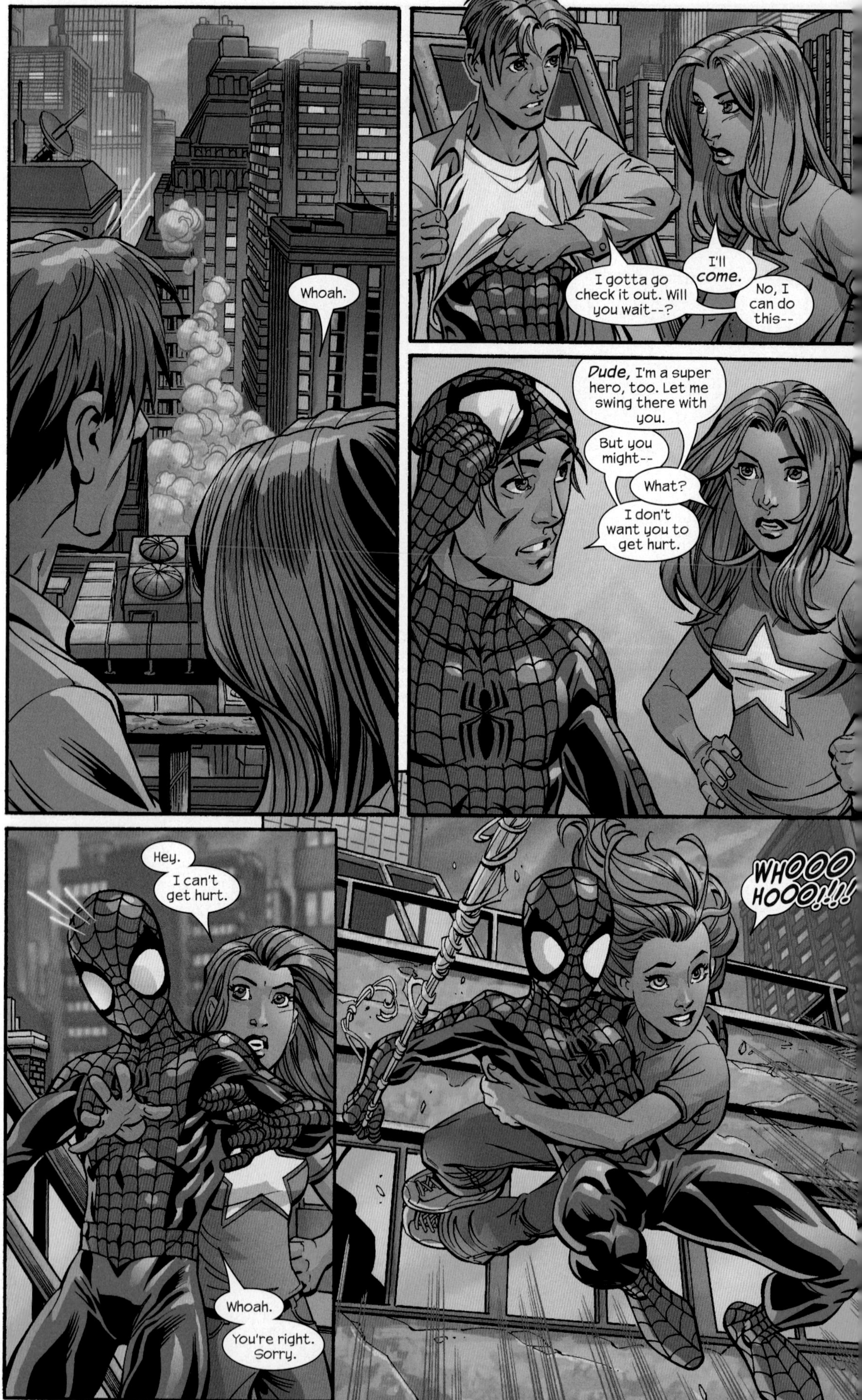
Whoah.
I gotta go check it out. Will you wait--?
I'll come.
No, I can do this--
Dude, I'm a super hero, too. Let me swing there with you.
But you might--
What?
I don't want you to get hurt.
Hey.
I can't get hurt.
Whoah.
You're right. Sorry.
WHOOO HOOO!!!

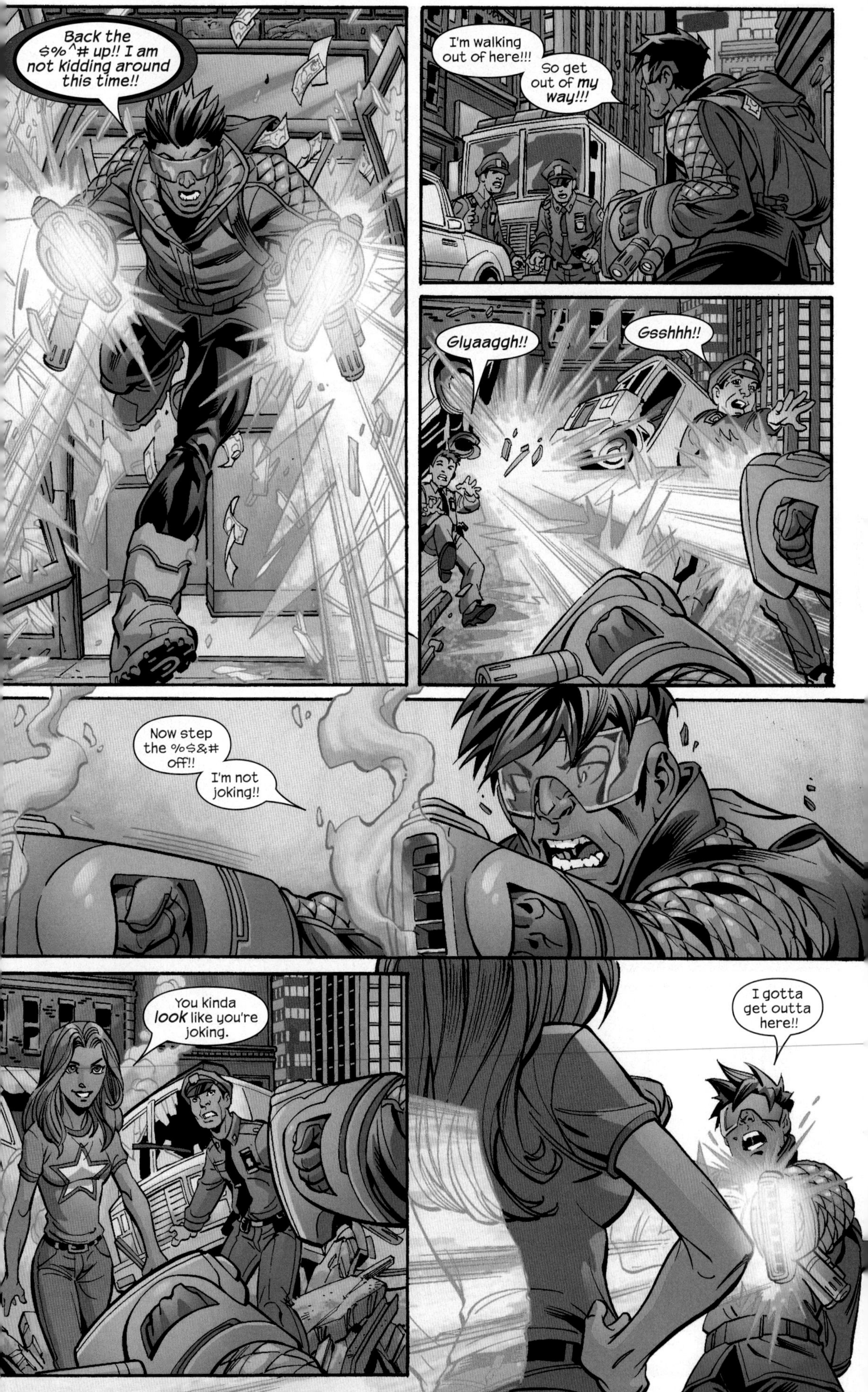
Back the $%^# up!! I am not kidding around this time!!
I'm walking out of here!!!
So get out of my way!!!
Glyaaggh!!
Gsshhh!!
Now step the %$&# off!!
I'm not joking!!
You kinda look like you're joking.
I gotta get outta here!!

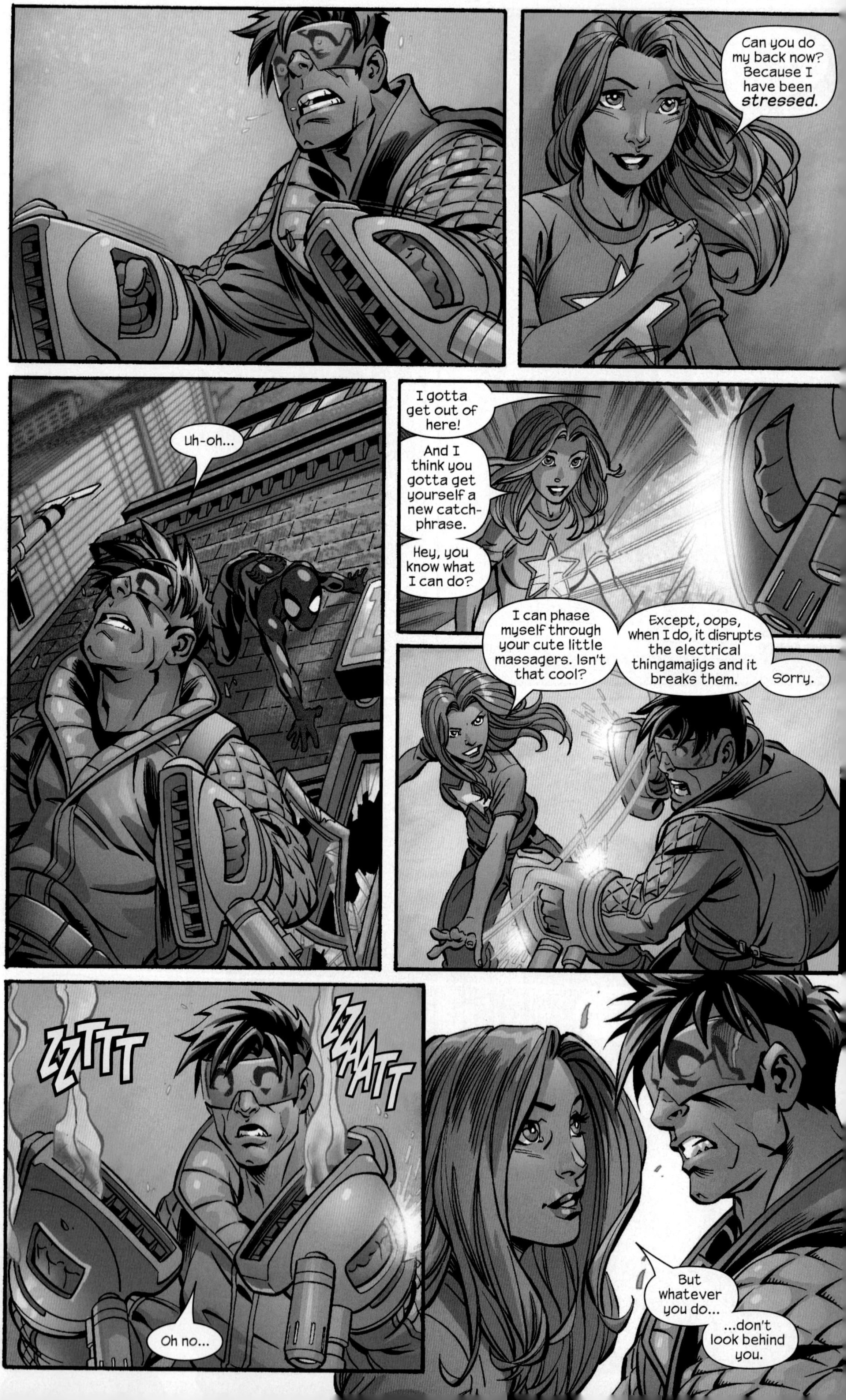
Can you do my back now? Because I have been *stressed.*
Uh-oh...
I gotta get out of here!
And I think you gotta get yourself a new catch-phrase.
Hey, you know what I can do?
I can phase myself through your cute little massagers. Isn't that cool?
Except, oops, when I do, it disrupts the electrical thingamajigs and it breaks them.
Sorry.
ZZTTTT
ZZAATT
Oh no...
But whatever you do...
...don't look behind you.

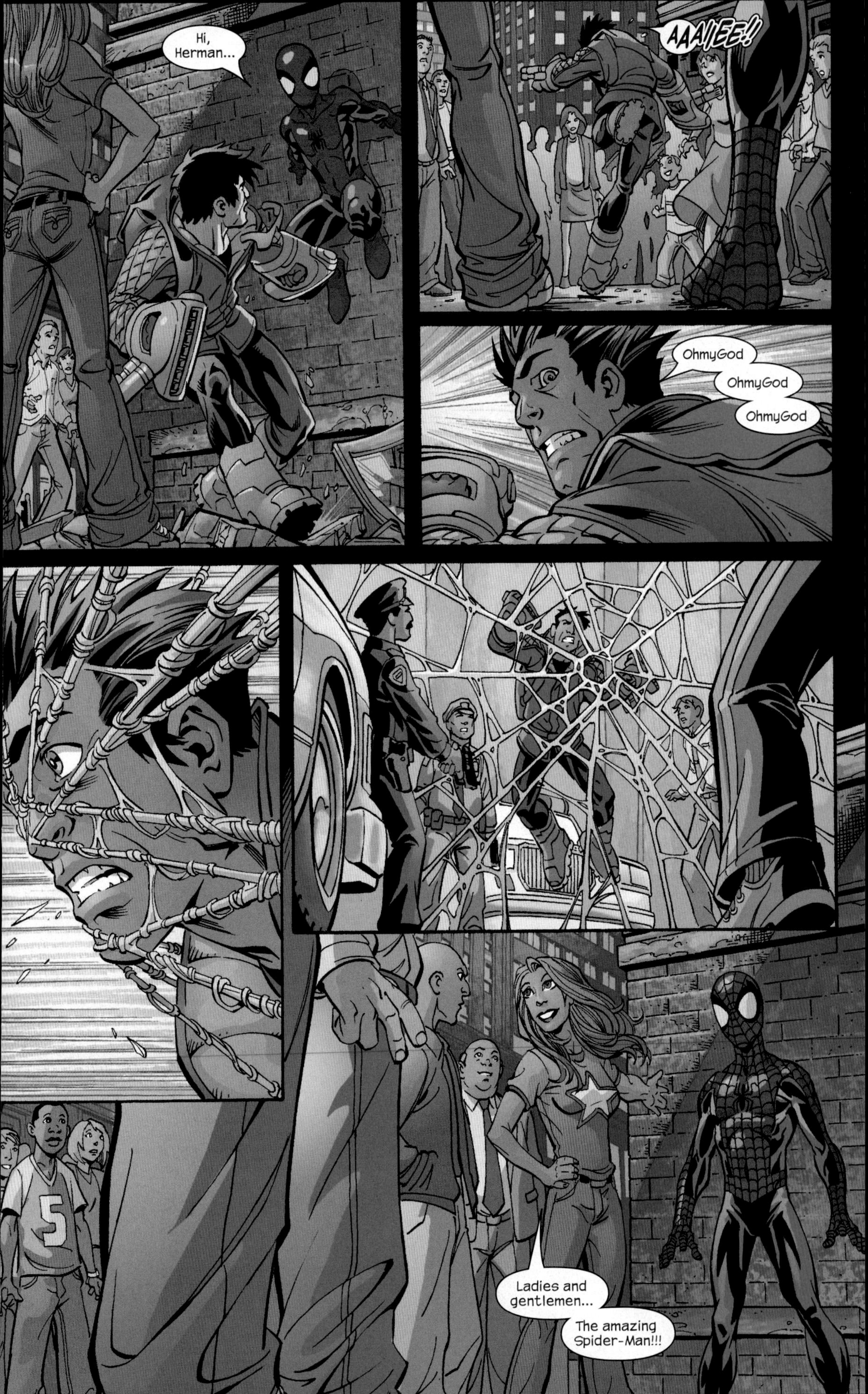

Hi, Herman...
AAAIIEE!!
OhmyGod
OhmyGod
OhmyGod
Ladies and gentlemen...
The amazing Spider-Man!!!

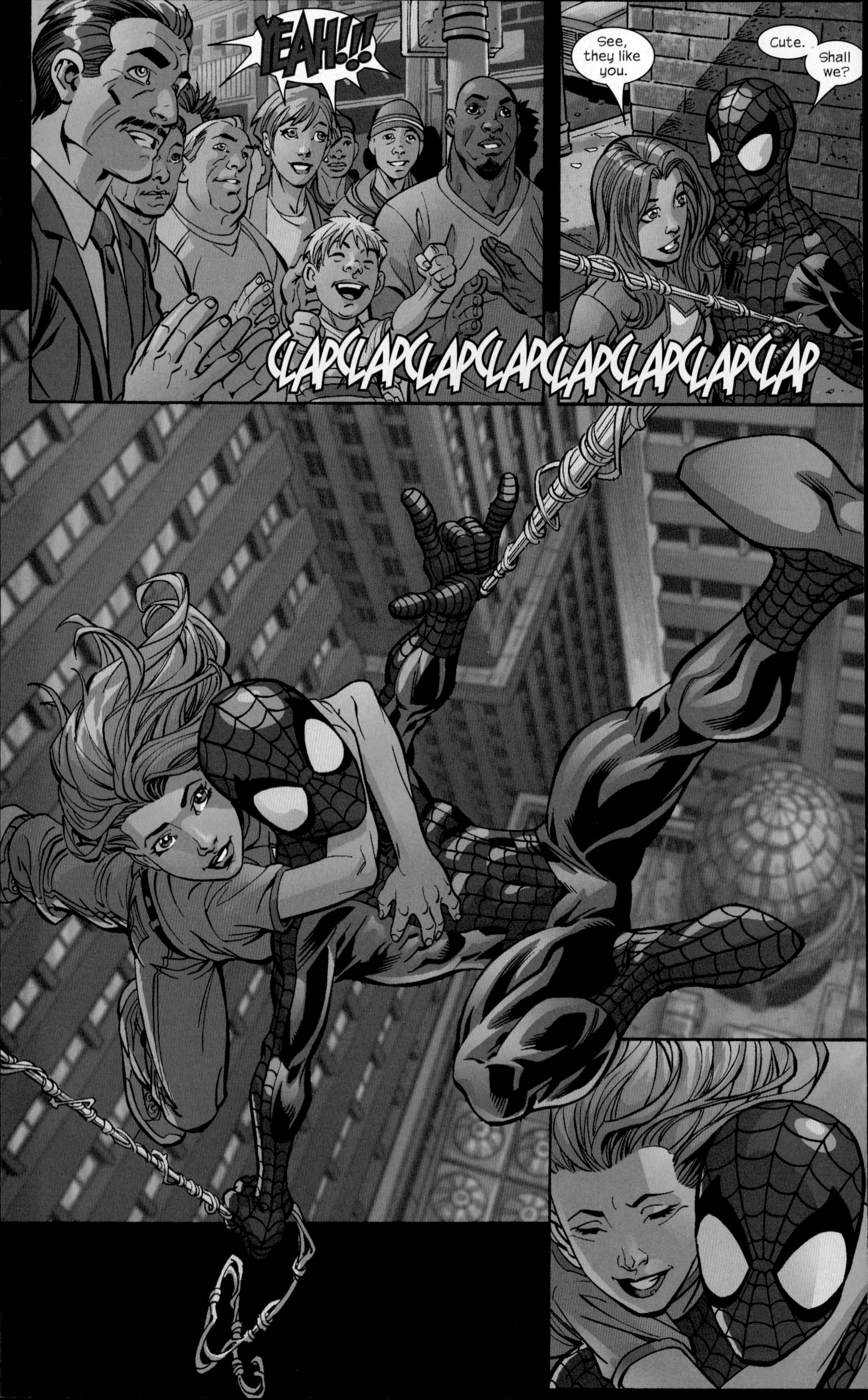
YEAH!!!
See, they like you.
Cute. Shall we?
CLAPCLAPCLAPCLAPCLAPCLAPCLAPCLAP

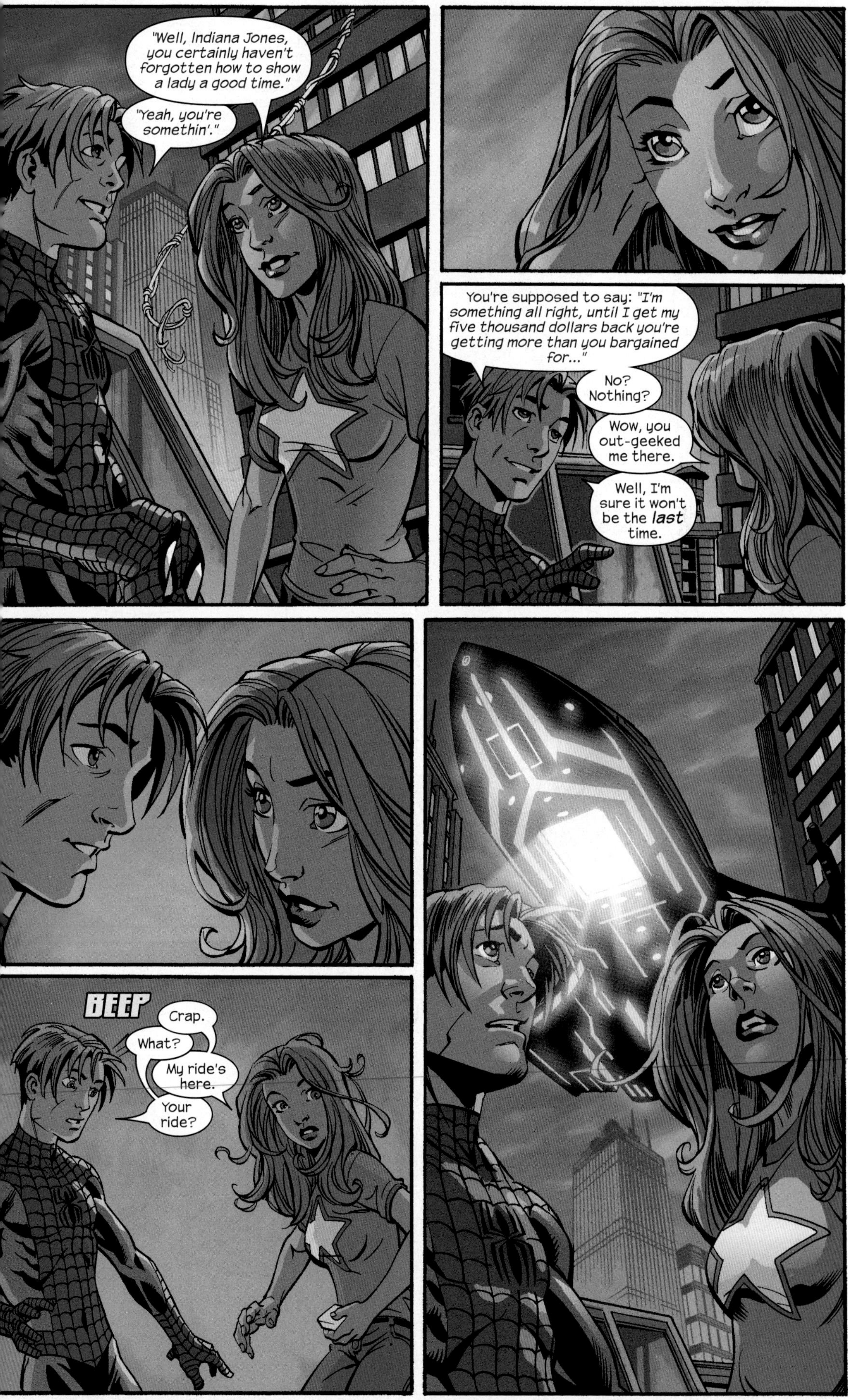
"Well, Indiana Jones, you certainly haven't forgotten how to show a lady a good time."
"Yeah, you're somethin'."
You're supposed to say: "I'm something all right, until I get my five thousand dollars back you're getting more than you bargained for..."
No? Nothing?
Wow, you out-geeked me there.
Well, I'm sure it won't be the last time.
BEEP
Crap.
What?
My ride's here.
Your ride?

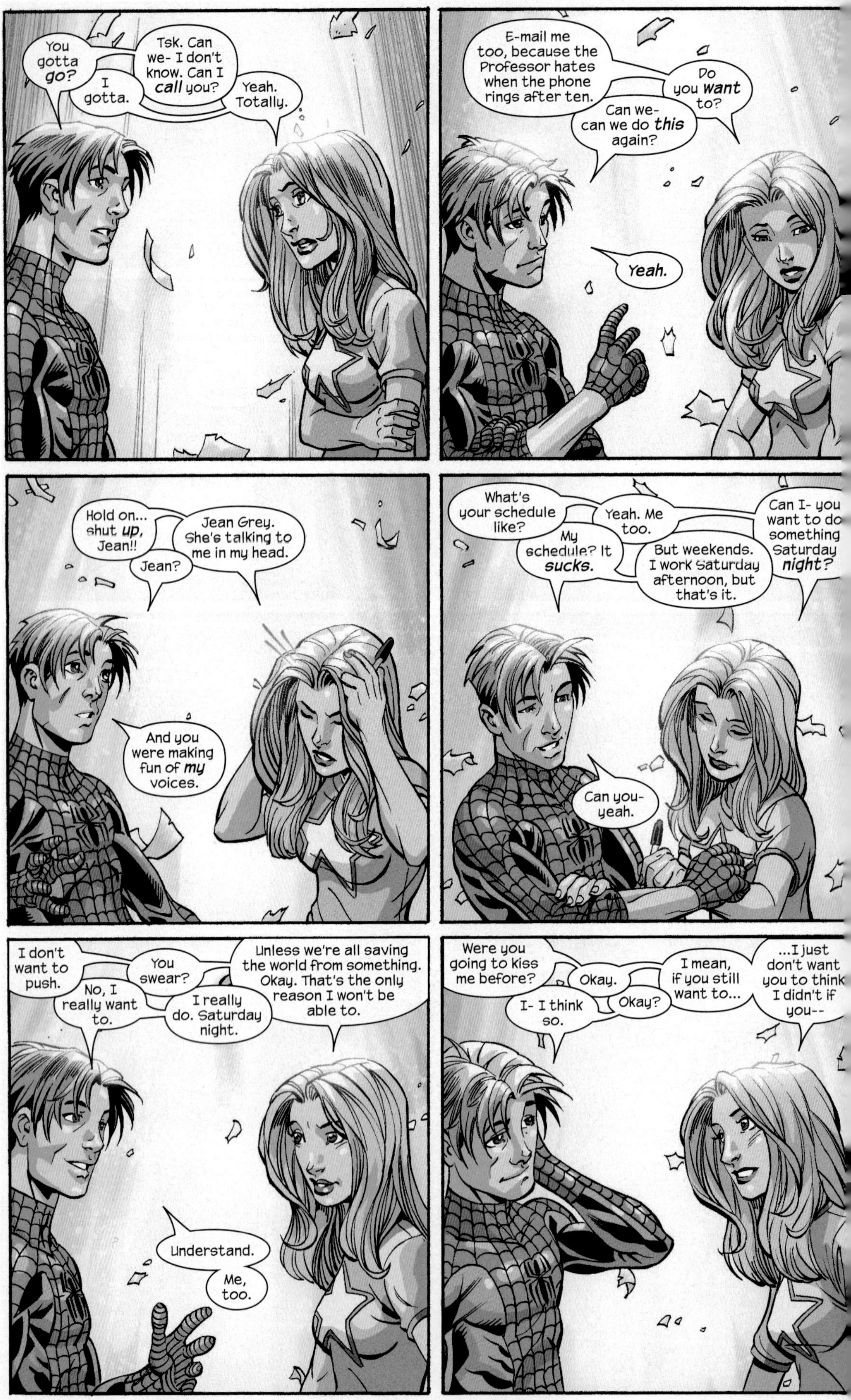
You gotta go?
I gotta.
Tsk. Can we- I don't know. Can I call you?
Yeah. Totally.
E-mail me too, because the Professor hates when the phone rings after ten.
Do you want to?
Can we- can we do this again?
Yeah.
Hold on... shut up, Jean!!
Jean?
Jean Grey. She's talking to me in my head.
And you were making fun of my voices.
What's your schedule like?
My schedule? It sucks.
Yeah. Me too.
But weekends. I work Saturday afternoon, but that's it.
Can I- you want to do something Saturday night?
Can you- yeah.
I don't want to push.
No, I really want to.
You swear?
I really do. Saturday night.
Unless we're all saving the world from something. Okay. That's the only reason I won't be able to.
Understand.
Me, too.
Were you going to kiss me before?
I- I think so.
Okay.
Okay?
I mean, if you still want to...
...I just don't want you to think I didn't if you--

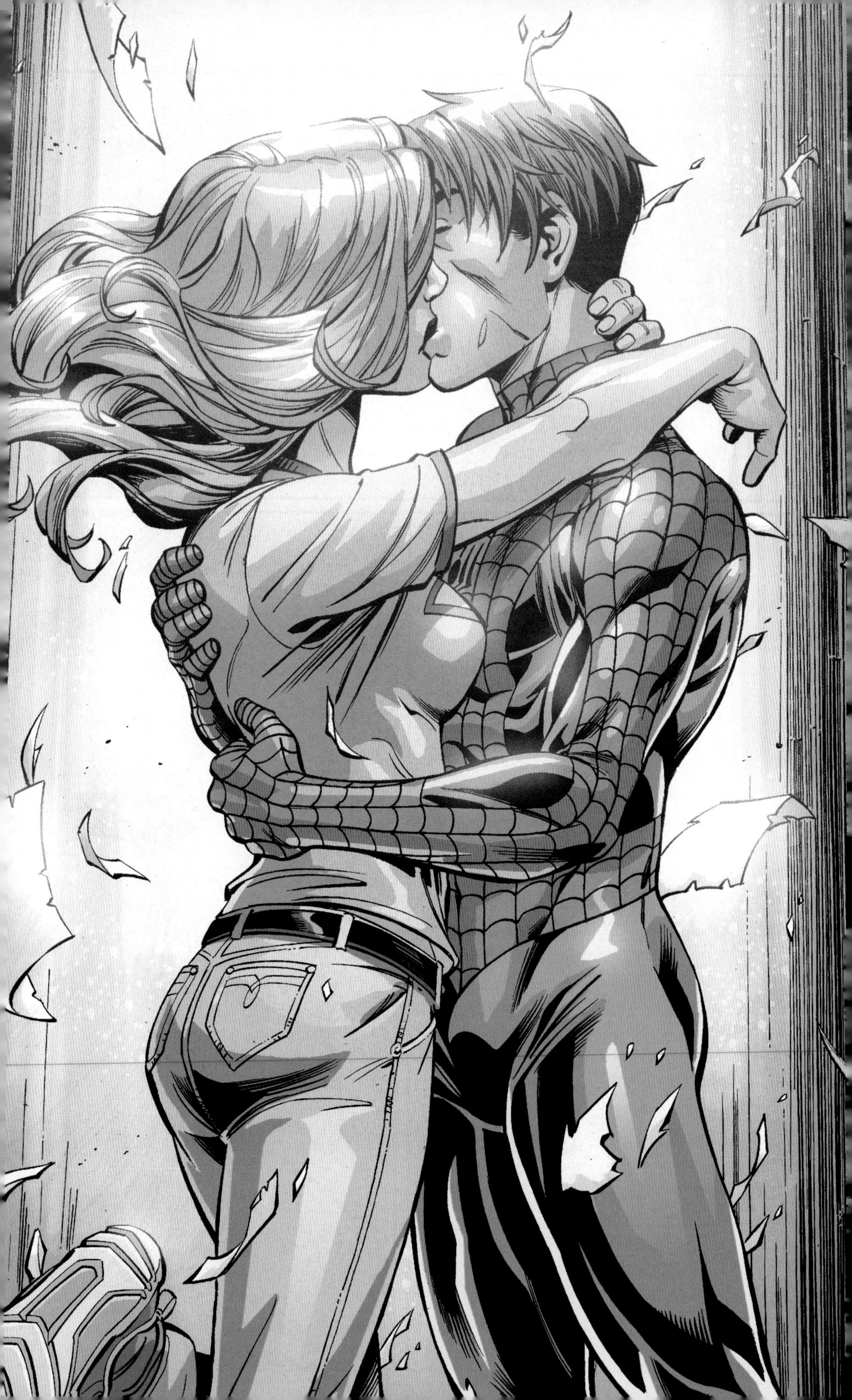

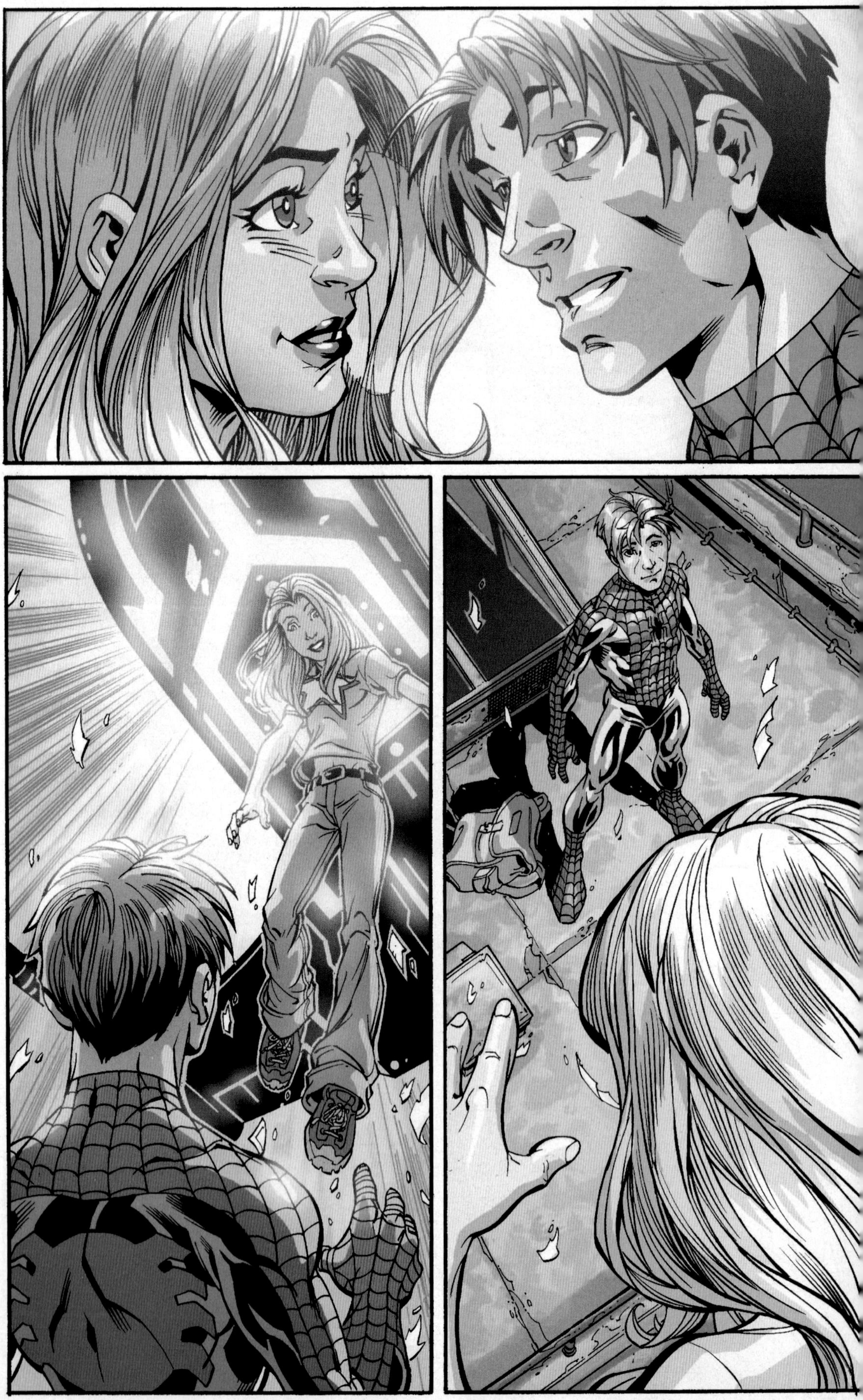

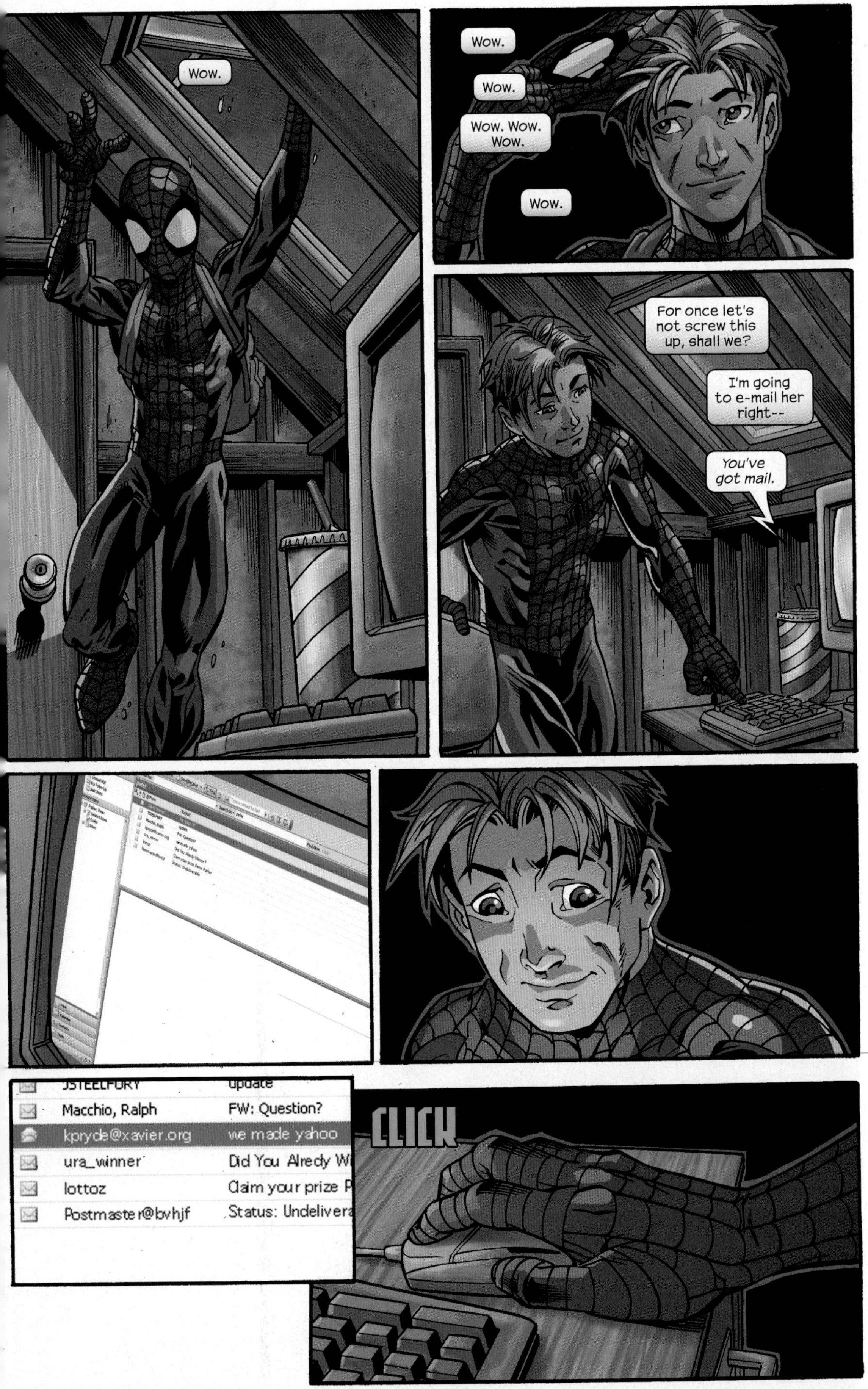
Wow.
Wow.
Wow.
Wow. Wow. Wow.
Wow.
For once let's not screw this up, shall we?
I'm going to e-mail her right--
You've got mail.
JSTEELFURY update
Macchio, Ralph FW: Question?
kpryde@xavier.org we made yahoo
ura_winner Did You Alredy W
lottoz Claim your prize P
Postmaster@bvhjf Status: Undelivera
CLICK

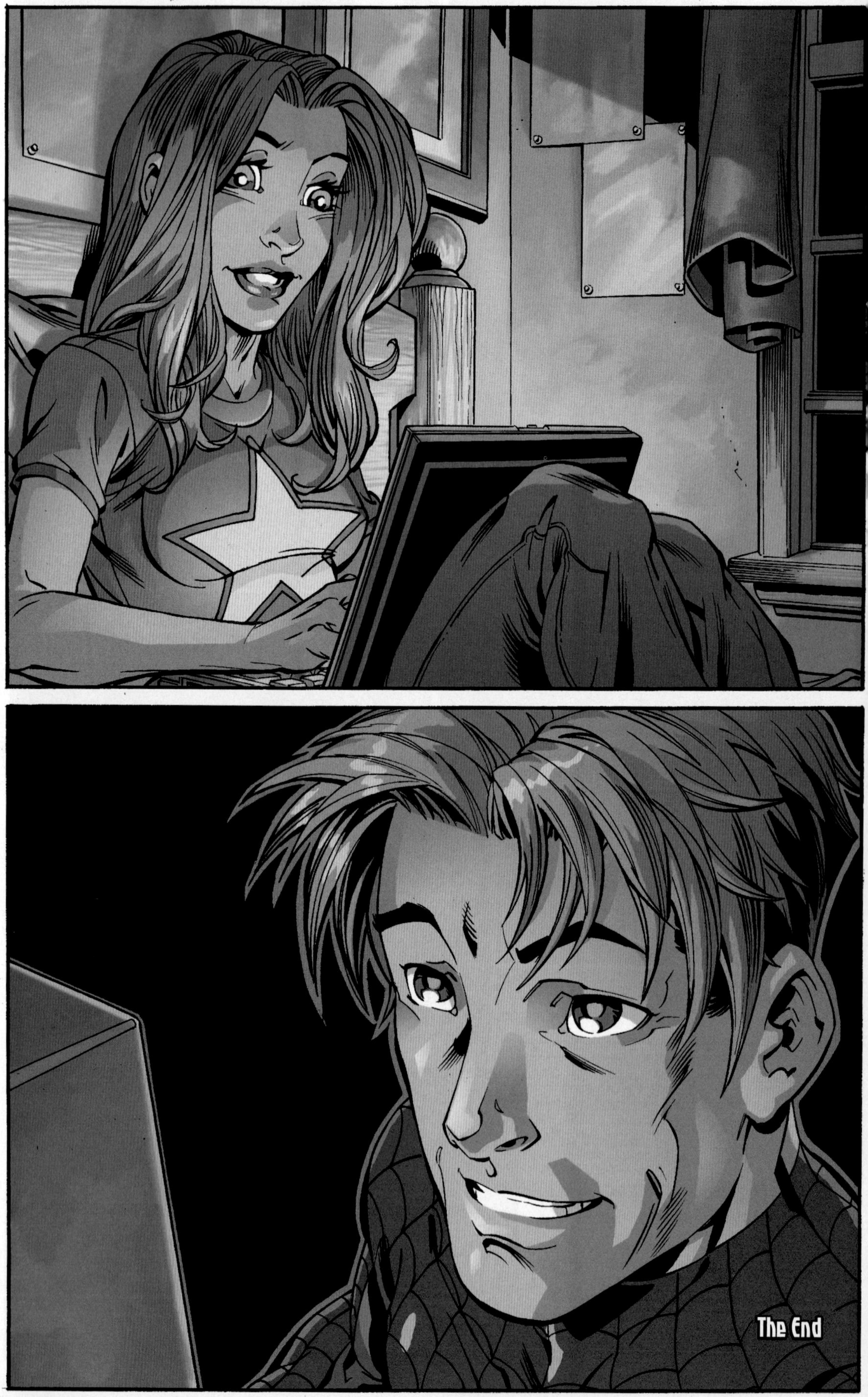
The End

THE CONFESSION
A MARVEL COMICS EVENT

CIVIL WAR™

CIVIL WAR
THE CONFESSION

A Superhuman Registration Act has been passed, requiring all individuals possessin
paranormal abilities to register their powers and identities with the governmen
Disagreement over the Act split the super hero community in two, with Tony Stark, Iro
Man, as the figurehead of the pro-registration faction, and Steve Rogers, Captain America
leading the anti-registration rebellion. The conflict erupted into violence, only endin
with the surrender and arrest—and eventual assassination—of Captain America.

Now, the Civil War is over, and Tony Stark has been named the Director of S.H.I.E.L.D., th
international peacekeeping force. He has set into motion THE INITIATIVE, a plan fo
training and policing super heroes in this brave new world.

BRIAN MICHAEL BENDIS
WRITER

ALEX MALEEV
ARTIST

JOSE VILLARRUBIA
(PAGES 14-22)
COLOR ARTIST

CHRIS ELIOPOULOS
LETTERS

JOSH SINGH
3-D IRON MAN DESIGN

RICH GINTER
PRODUCTION

MOLLY LAZER & AUBREY SITTERSON
ASSISTANT EDITORS

TOM BREVOORT
EDITOR

JOE QUESADA
EDITOR IN CHIEF

DAN BUCKLEY
PUBLISHER

MARVEL COMICS PRESENTS

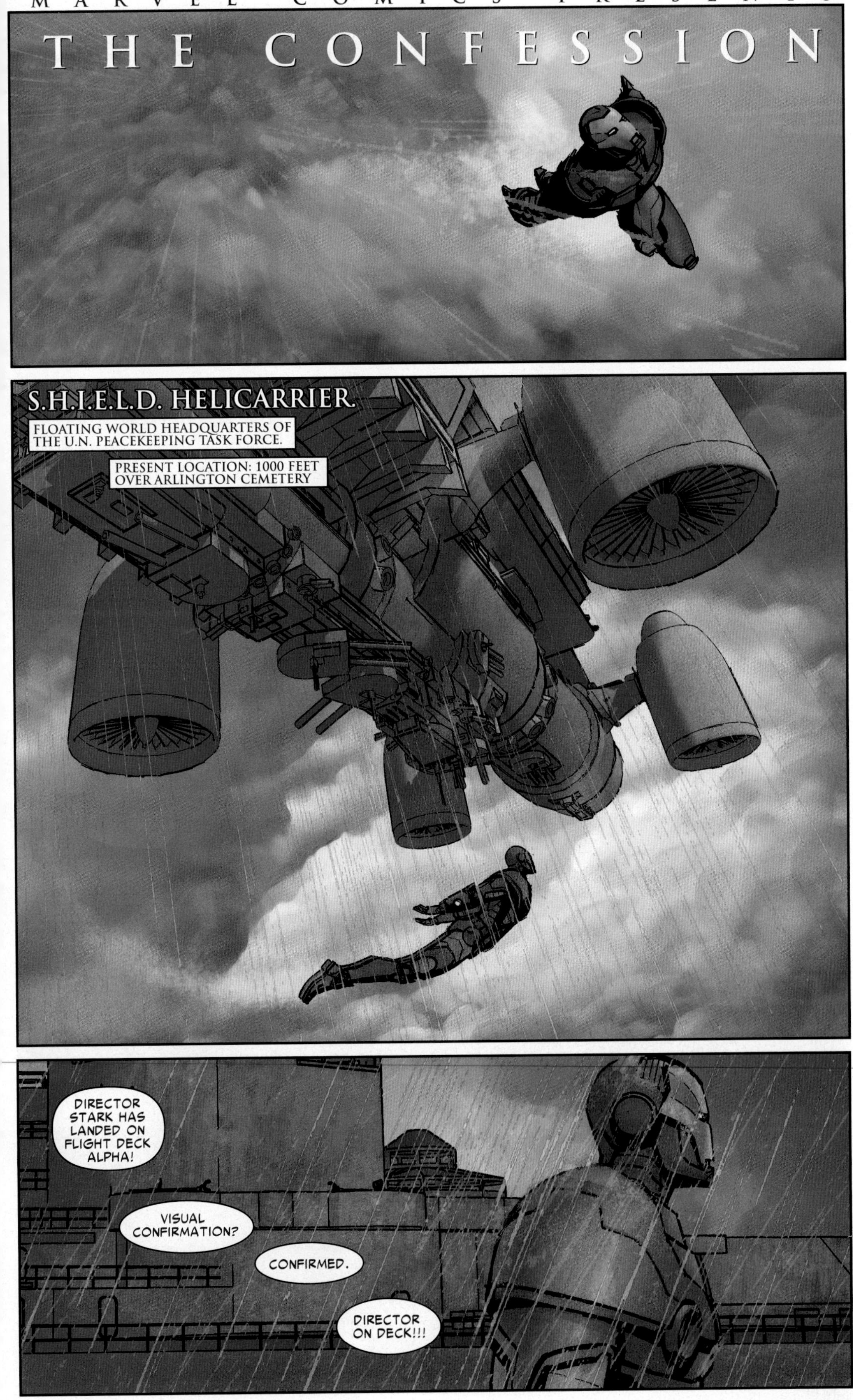
THE CONFESSION
S.H.I.E.L.D. HELICARRIER.
FLOATING WORLD HEADQUARTERS OF THE U.N. PEACEKEEPING TASK FORCE.
PRESENT LOCATION: 1000 FEET OVER ARLINGTON CEMETERY
DIRECTOR STARK HAS LANDED ON FLIGHT DECK ALPHA!
VISUAL CONFIRMATION?
CONFIRMED.
DIRECTOR ON DECK!!!

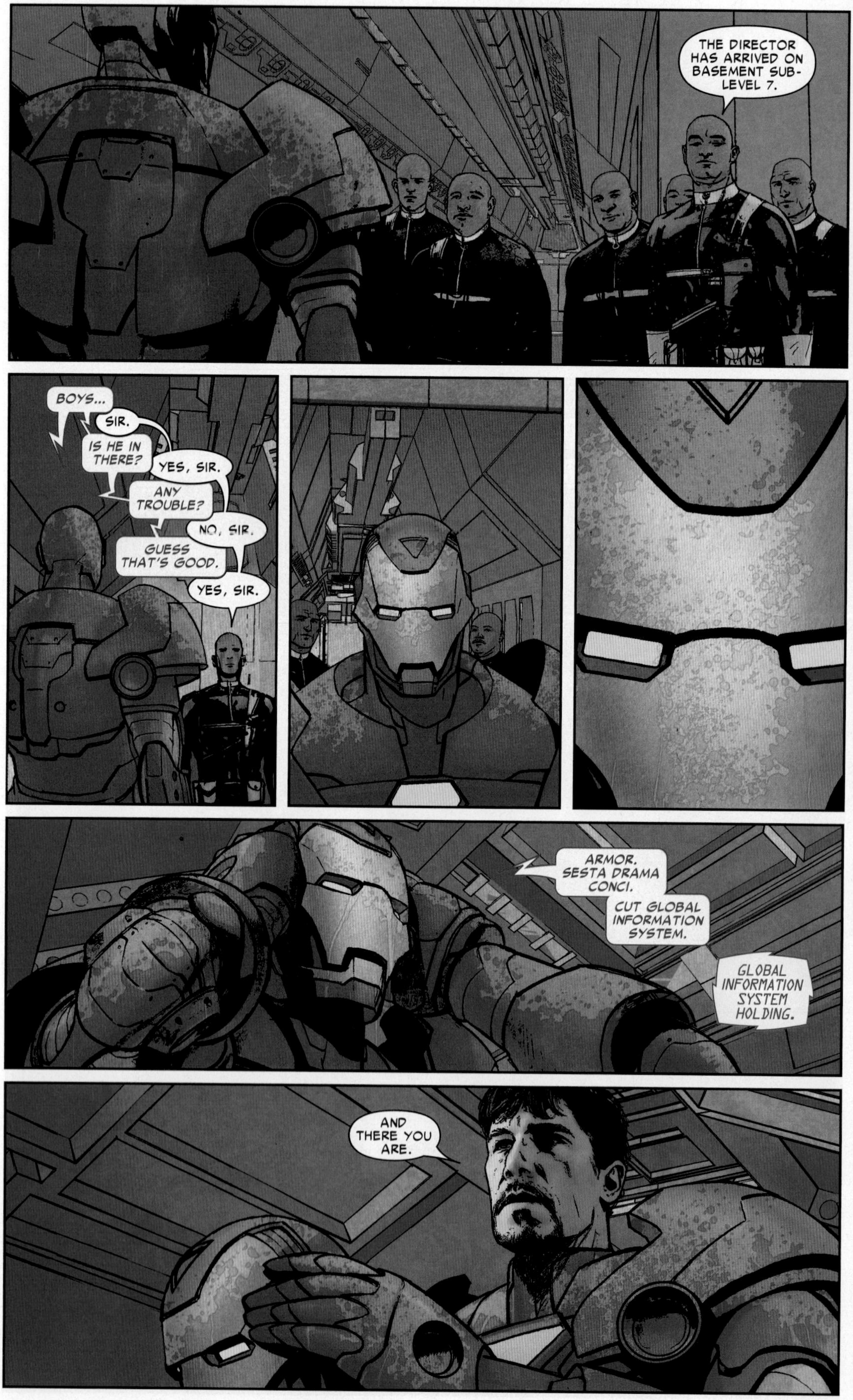
THE DIRECTOR HAS ARRIVED ON BASEMENT SUB-LEVEL 7.
BOYS...
SIR.
IS HE IN THERE?
YES, SIR.
ANY TROUBLE?
NO, SIR.
GUESS THAT'S GOOD.
YES, SIR.
ARMOR. SESTA DRAMA CONCI.
CUT GLOBAL INFORMATION SYSTEM.
GLOBAL INFORMATION SYSTEM HOLDING.
AND THERE YOU ARE.

CAN YOU FEEL IT OUT THERE?

THESE KIDS?

THEY'LL SALUTE AND FOLLOW ORDERS, BUT YOU CAN *FEEL* IT.

THEY'RE NICK FURY'S KIDS.

THEY DON'T *LIKE* ME HERE AND THEY DON'T *WANT* ME HERE.

THEY WANT THEIR DADDY BACK AND THAT'S THAT.

GUESS THEY'LL HAVE TO *LEARN* TO LOVE ME.

EH. IT'S *MY* FAULT, I MADE A TERRIBLE SPEECH TO THE COMMAND CREW.

YOU DID.

I WAS TRYING TO MAKE A *POINT* AND I--I TOLD THEM ABOUT KING PYRRHUS OF EPIRUS.

YOU KNOW WHO HE IS, RIGHT?

(YOU *PROBABLY* KNOW WHO HE IS.)

HE DEFEATED THE ROMANS DURING THE PYRRHIC WAR AT HERACLEA AND AGAIN AT THIS PLACE CALLED ASCULUM.

AND *THAT* WAR WENT ON FOREVER AND EVER AND THE CASUALTIES WERE *DEVASTATING*...

BODIES FROM BOTH SIDES LYING AS FAR AS THE EYE COULD SEE...

HIS *FRIENDS* WERE ALL DEAD, HIS *COMMANDERS* WERE ALL DEAD...

THOSE WHO WERE STILL ALIVE STARTED HIGH-FIVING EACH OTHER OVER THE *VICTORY*, BUT...

KING PYRRHUS JUST STOOD THERE AND SAID: "ONE MORE SUCH VICTORY WOULD UTTERLY UNDO ME."

MEANING THAT, WELL, *YOU* KNOW WHAT IT MEANS...

IT MEANS THERE'S WINNING AND THERE'S *WINNING* AND SOMETIMES WINNING DOESN'T FEEL LIKE WINNING.

IT FEELS LIKE ALMOST *LOSING*.

OR WE MIGHT *AS WELL* HAVE LOST IF *THIS* IS WHAT IT COSTS.

I *SAID* THIS TO MY NEW COMMAND BECAUSE I WANTED THEM TO KNOW HOW THIS FELT TO *ME*.

AND THEY LOOKED AT ME LIKE I DUMPED IN THEIR BREAKFAST BOWLS.

I WAS *TRYING* TO SAY--I WANTED THEM TO KNOW THAT I KNEW THE *REALITY* OF THIS. I KNEW HOW EVERYONE WAS FEELING.

BUT IT JUST CAME OFF LIKE I WAS CRITICIZING THEM FOR THEIR EFFORT.

THERE'S A WAY TO SPEAK TO SOLDIERS.

TO *RALLY* THEM, AND I--I DON'T HAVE IT.

I DON'T HAVE IT.

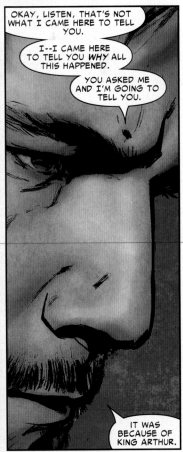

OKAY, LISTEN, THAT'S NOT WHAT I CAME HERE TO TELL YOU.

I--I CAME HERE TO TELL YOU *WHY* ALL THIS HAPPENED.

YOU ASKED ME AND I'M GOING TO TELL YOU.

IT WAS BECAUSE OF KING ARTHUR.

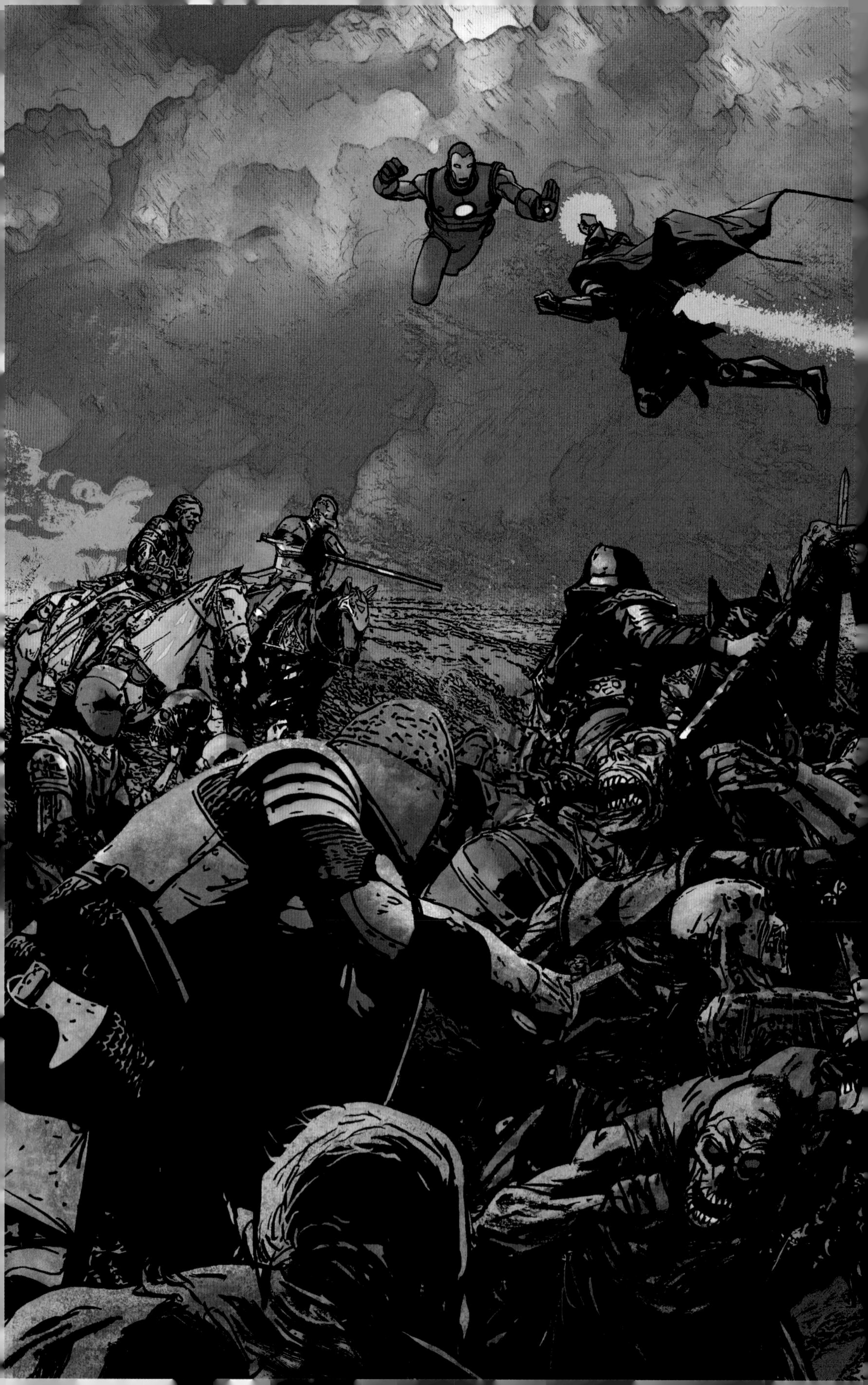

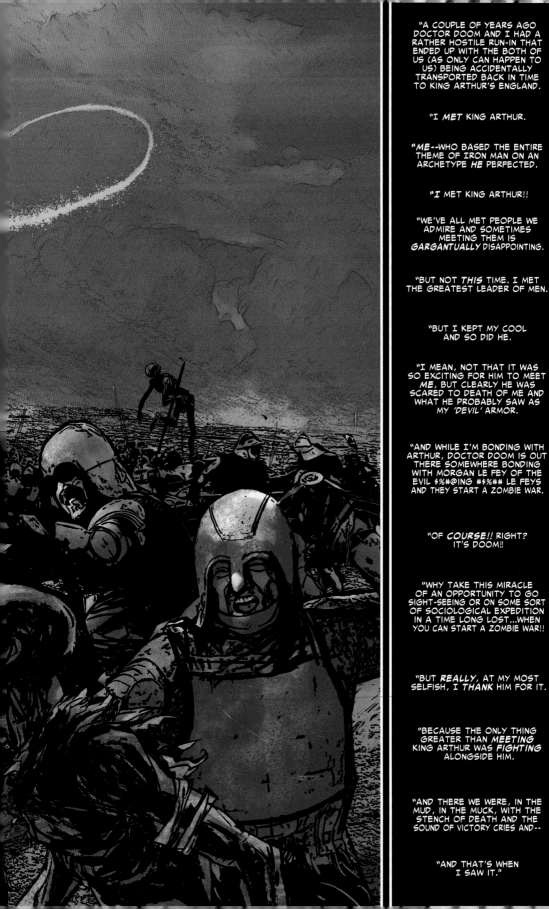

"A COUPLE OF YEARS AGO DOCTOR DOOM AND I HAD A RATHER HOSTILE RUN-IN THAT ENDED UP WITH THE BOTH OF US (AS ONLY CAN HAPPEN TO US) BEING ACCIDENTALLY TRANSPORTED BACK IN TIME TO KING ARTHUR'S ENGLAND.

"I *MET* KING ARTHUR.

"*ME*--WHO BASED THE ENTIRE THEME OF IRON MAN ON AN ARCHETYPE *HE* PERFECTED.

"*I* MET KING ARTHUR!!

"WE'VE ALL MET PEOPLE WE ADMIRE AND SOMETIMES MEETING THEM IS *GARGANTUALLY* DISAPPOINTING.

"BUT NOT *THIS* TIME. I MET THE GREATEST LEADER OF MEN.

"BUT I KEPT MY COOL AND SO DID HE.

"I MEAN, NOT THAT IT WAS SO EXCITING FOR HIM TO MEET *ME*, BUT CLEARLY HE WAS SCARED TO DEATH OF ME AND WHAT HE PROBABLY SAW AS MY 'DEVIL' ARMOR.

"AND WHILE I'M BONDING WITH ARTHUR, DOCTOR DOOM IS OUT THERE SOMEWHERE BONDING WITH MORGAN LE FEY OF THE EVIL $%#@ING #$%## LE FEYS AND THEY START A ZOMBIE WAR.

"OF *COURSE!!* RIGHT? IT'S DOOM!!

"WHY TAKE THIS MIRACLE OF AN OPPORTUNITY TO GO SIGHT-SEEING OR ON SOME SORT OF SOCIOLOGICAL EXPEDITION IN A TIME LONG LOST...WHEN YOU CAN START A ZOMBIE WAR!!

"BUT *REALLY*, AT MY MOST SELFISH, I *THANK* HIM FOR IT.

"BECAUSE THE ONLY THING GREATER THAN *MEETING* KING ARTHUR WAS *FIGHTING* ALONGSIDE HIM.

"AND THERE WE WERE, IN THE MUD, IN THE MUCK, WITH THE STENCH OF DEATH AND THE SOUND OF VICTORY CRIES AND--

"AND THAT'S WHEN I SAW IT."

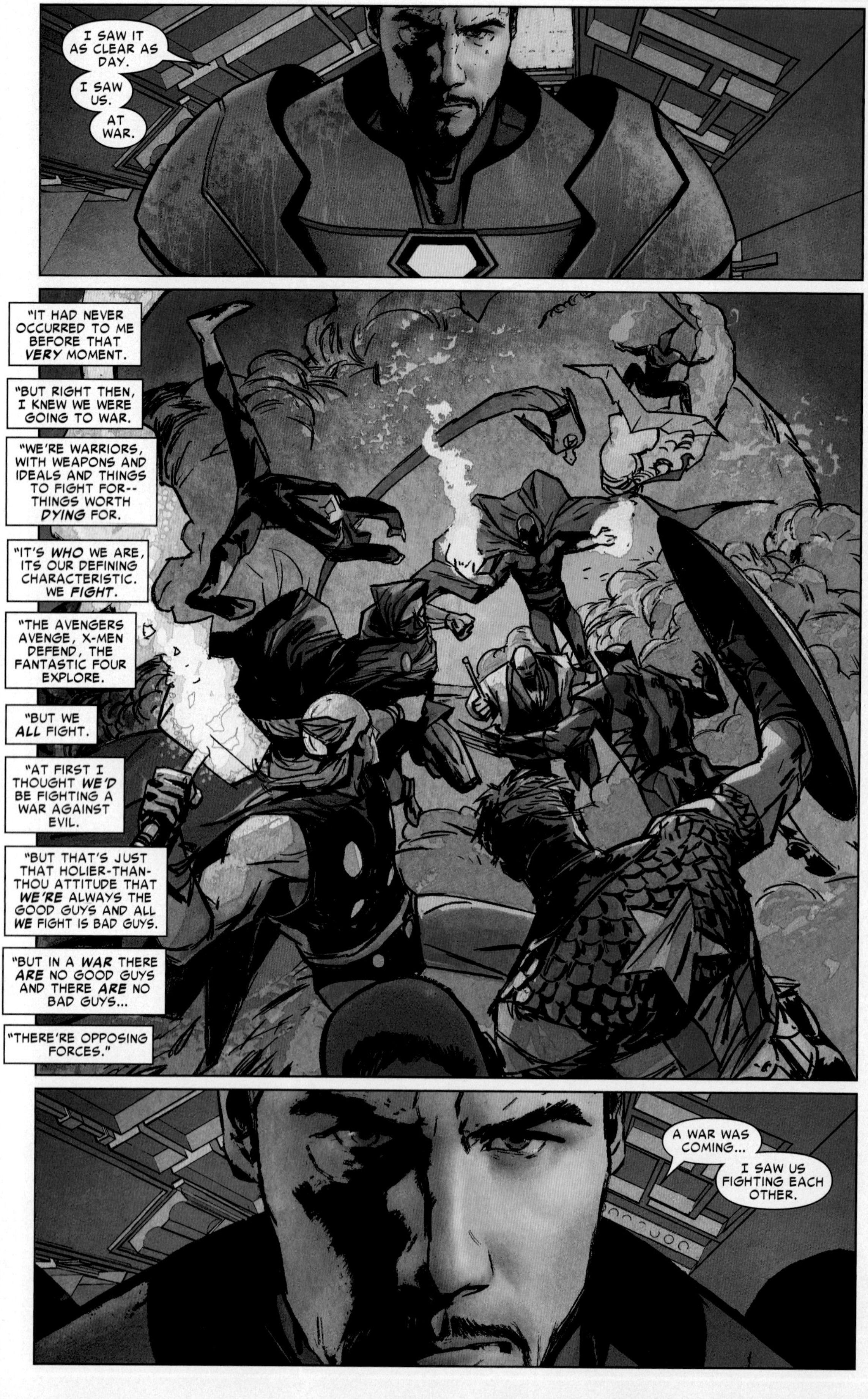
I SAW IT AS CLEAR AS DAY.
I SAW US.
AT WAR.
"IT HAD NEVER OCCURRED TO ME BEFORE THAT VERY MOMENT.
"BUT RIGHT THEN, I KNEW WE WERE GOING TO WAR.
"WE'RE WARRIORS, WITH WEAPONS AND IDEALS AND THINGS TO FIGHT FOR-- THINGS WORTH DYING FOR.
"IT'S WHO WE ARE, ITS OUR DEFINING CHARACTERISTIC. WE FIGHT.
"THE AVENGERS AVENGE, X-MEN DEFEND, THE FANTASTIC FOUR EXPLORE.
"BUT WE ALL FIGHT.
"AT FIRST I THOUGHT WE'D BE FIGHTING A WAR AGAINST EVIL.
"BUT THAT'S JUST THAT HOLIER-THAN-THOU ATTITUDE THAT WE'RE ALWAYS THE GOOD GUYS AND ALL WE FIGHT IS BAD GUYS.
"BUT IN A WAR THERE ARE NO GOOD GUYS AND THERE ARE NO BAD GUYS...
"THERE'RE OPPOSING FORCES."
A WAR WAS COMING...
I SAW US FIGHTING EACH OTHER.

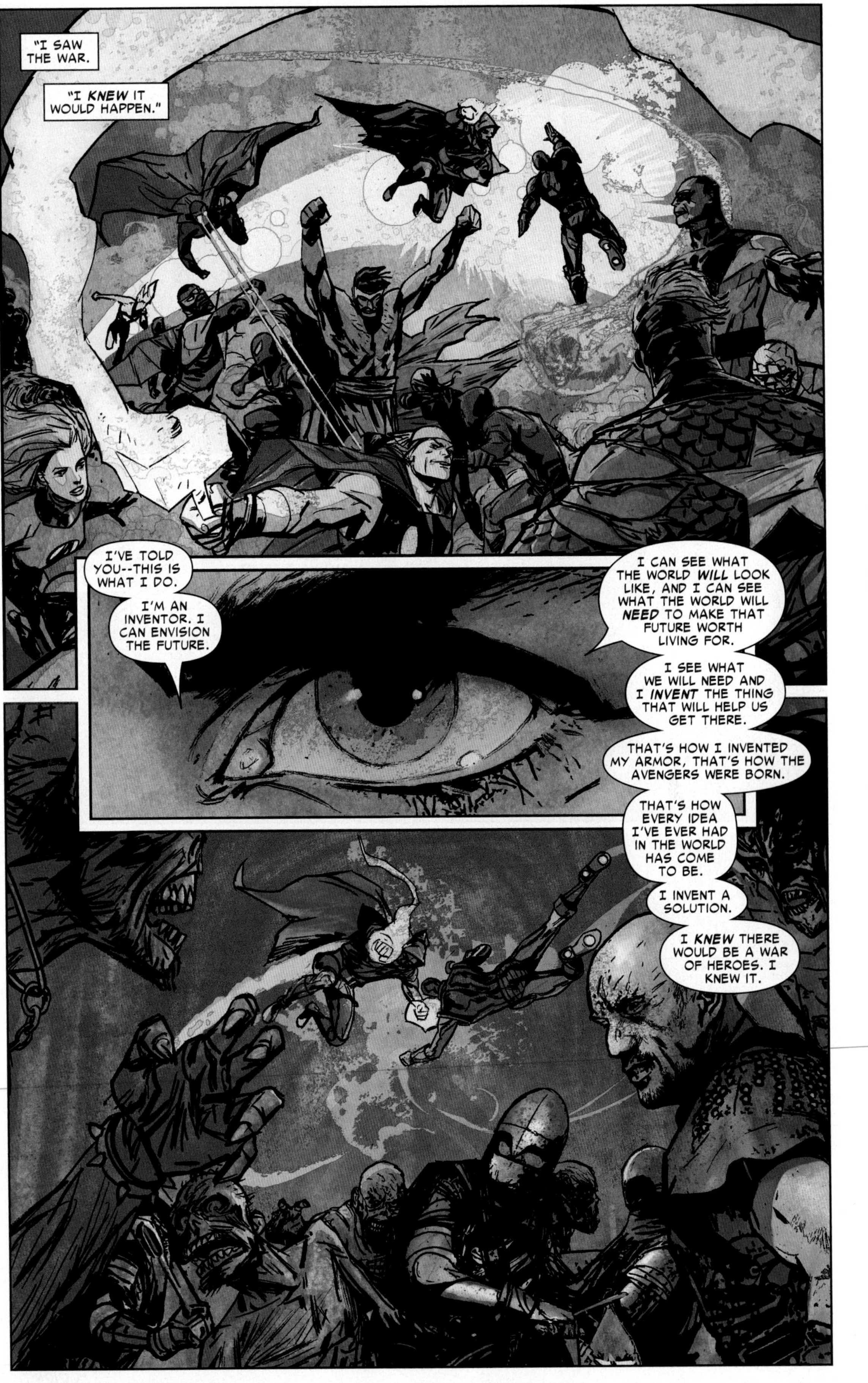
"I SAW THE WAR.
"I *KNEW* IT WOULD HAPPEN."
I'VE TOLD YOU--THIS IS WHAT I DO.
I'M AN INVENTOR. I CAN ENVISION THE FUTURE.
I CAN SEE WHAT THE WORLD *WILL* LOOK LIKE, AND I CAN SEE WHAT THE WORLD WILL *NEED* TO MAKE THAT FUTURE WORTH LIVING FOR.
I SEE WHAT WE WILL NEED AND I *INVENT* THE THING THAT WILL HELP US GET THERE.
THAT'S HOW I INVENTED MY ARMOR, THAT'S HOW THE AVENGERS WERE BORN.
THAT'S HOW EVERY IDEA I'VE EVER HAD IN THE WORLD HAS COME TO BE.
I INVENT A SOLUTION.
I *KNEW* THERE WOULD BE A WAR OF HEROES. I KNEW IT.

SO WHAT'S THE SOLUTION TO *THAT*?

I DIDN'T KNOW WHAT THE WAR WAS GOING TO BE *ABOUT* OR *WHEN* IT WAS COMING--

--BUT I KNEW I'D *KNOW* IT WHEN I *SAW* IT.

"I TRIED TO GET EVERYONE GATHERED. TO MAKE A PLACE WHERE WE COULD ALL GOVERN EACH OTHER.

"I TRIED TO STOP THIS WAR BEFORE IT EVEN GOT STARTED, BEFORE I EVEN KNEW IT WAS COMING.

"BUT I COULDN'T DO IT.

"ALL I GOT BACK WAS COMPROMISE AND HALF-TRUST.

"AND I *KNEW* MY FEARS WERE REAL EVEN THOUGH NO ONE WOULD BELIEVE ME.

"I KNOW HOW IT *SOUNDS*.

"I KNEW CONFESSING IT TO ANYONE, INCLUDING YOU, WOULD BE MET WITH A FRIENDLY LAUGH AND JUST...CONDESCENSION...

"SO I KEPT IT TO MYSELF."

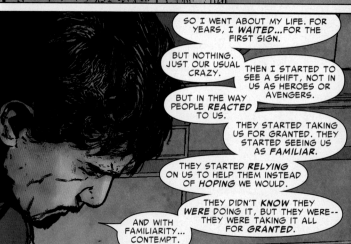

SO I WENT ABOUT MY LIFE. FOR YEARS, I *WAITED*...FOR THE FIRST SIGN.

BUT NOTHING. JUST OUR USUAL CRAZY.

THEN I STARTED TO SEE A SHIFT, NOT IN US AS HEROES OR AVENGERS.

BUT IN THE WAY PEOPLE *REACTED* TO US.

THEY STARTED TAKING US FOR GRANTED. THEY STARTED SEEING US AS *FAMILIAR*.

THEY STARTED *RELYING* ON US TO HELP THEM INSTEAD OF *HOPING* WE WOULD.

THEY DIDN'T *KNOW* THEY *WERE* DOING IT, BUT THEY WERE-- THEY WERE TAKING IT ALL FOR *GRANTED*.

AND WITH FAMILIARITY... CONTEMPT.

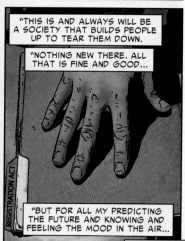

"THIS IS AND ALWAYS WILL BE A SOCIETY THAT BUILDS PEOPLE UP TO TEAR THEM DOWN.

"NOTHING NEW THERE. ALL THAT IS FINE AND GOOD...

"BUT FOR ALL MY PREDICTING THE FUTURE AND KNOWING AND FEELING THE MOOD IN THE AIR...

"I *DIDN'T* SEE THIS COMING.

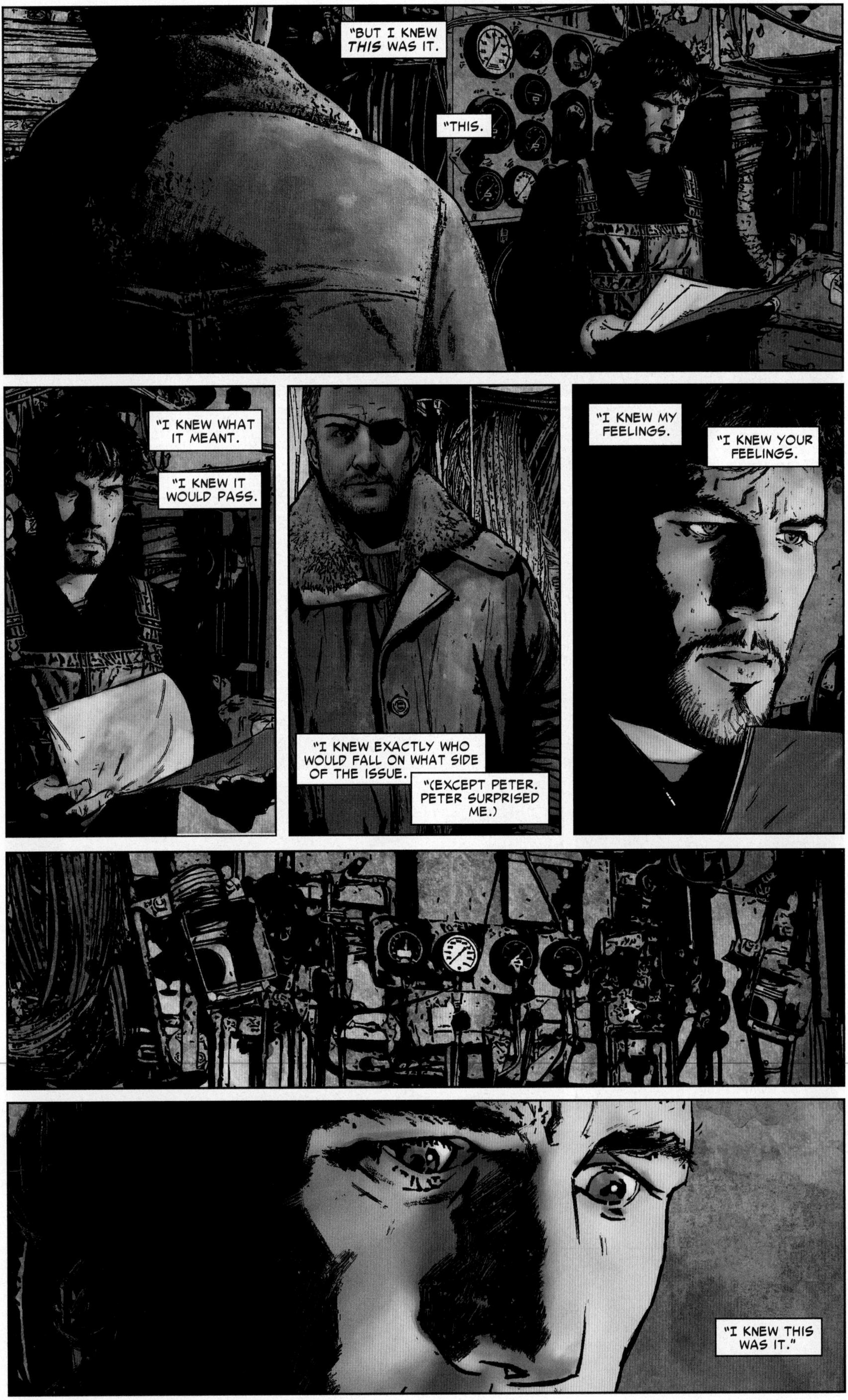
"BUT I KNEW THIS WAS IT.
"THIS.
"I KNEW WHAT IT MEANT.
"I KNEW IT WOULD PASS.
"I KNEW EXACTLY WHO WOULD FALL ON WHAT SIDE OF THE ISSUE.
"(EXCEPT PETER. PETER SURPRISED ME.)
"I KNEW MY FEELINGS.
"I KNEW YOUR FEELINGS.
"I KNEW THIS WAS IT."

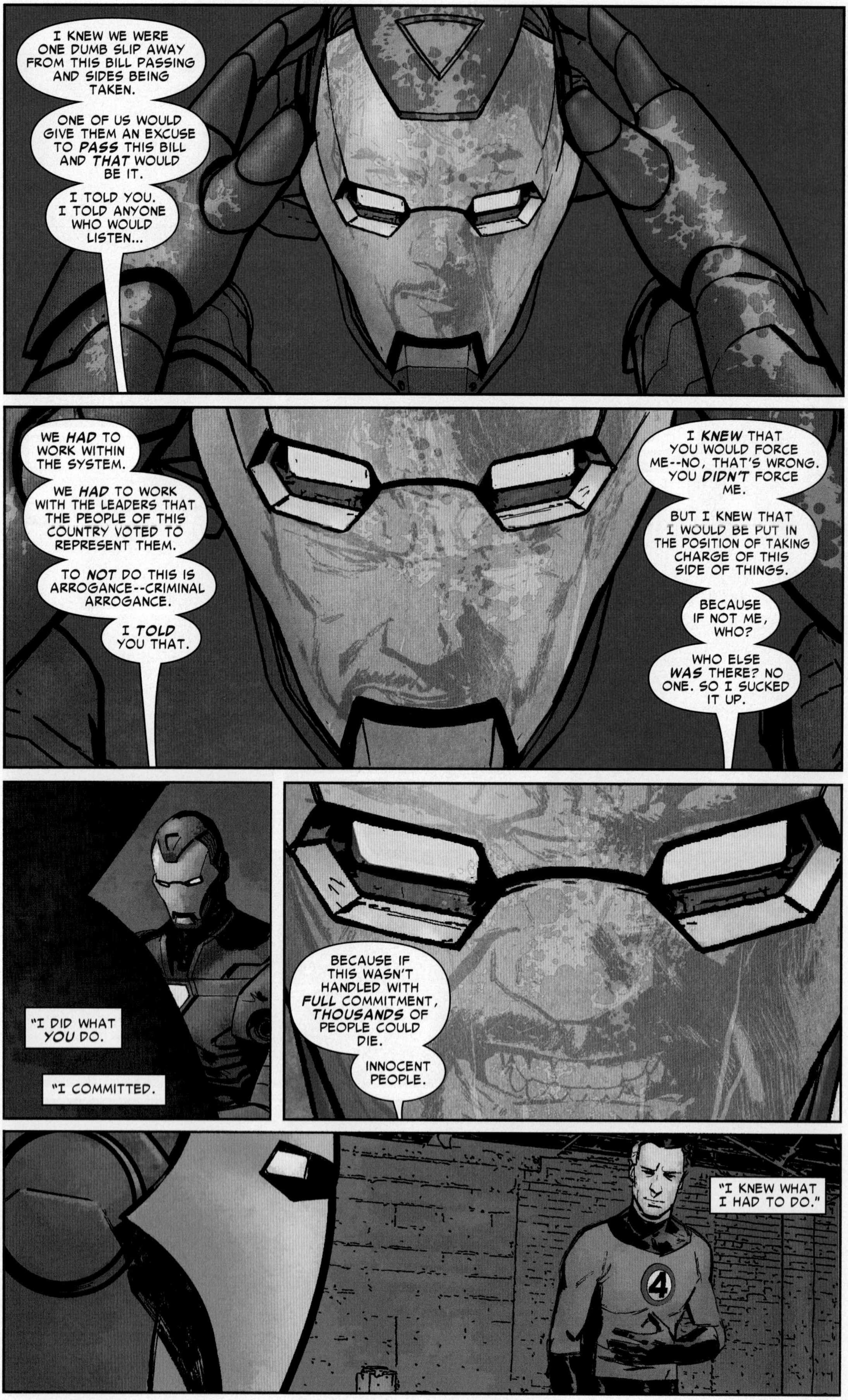

I KNEW WE WERE ONE DUMB SLIP AWAY FROM THIS BILL PASSING AND SIDES BEING TAKEN.
ONE OF US WOULD GIVE THEM AN EXCUSE TO *PASS* THIS BILL AND *THAT* WOULD BE IT.
I TOLD YOU. I TOLD ANYONE WHO WOULD LISTEN...
WE *HAD* TO WORK WITHIN THE SYSTEM.
WE *HAD* TO WORK WITH THE LEADERS THAT THE PEOPLE OF THIS COUNTRY VOTED TO REPRESENT THEM.
TO *NOT* DO THIS IS ARROGANCE--CRIMINAL ARROGANCE.
I *TOLD* YOU THAT.
I *KNEW* THAT YOU WOULD FORCE ME--NO, THAT'S WRONG. YOU *DIDN'T* FORCE ME.
BUT I KNEW THAT I WOULD BE PUT IN THE POSITION OF TAKING CHARGE OF THIS SIDE OF THINGS.
BECAUSE IF NOT ME, WHO?
WHO ELSE *WAS* THERE? NO ONE. SO I SUCKED IT UP.
"I DID WHAT *YOU* DO.
"I COMMITTED.
BECAUSE IF THIS WASN'T HANDLED WITH *FULL* COMMITMENT, *THOUSANDS* OF PEOPLE COULD DIE.
INNOCENT PEOPLE.
"I KNEW WHAT I HAD TO DO."

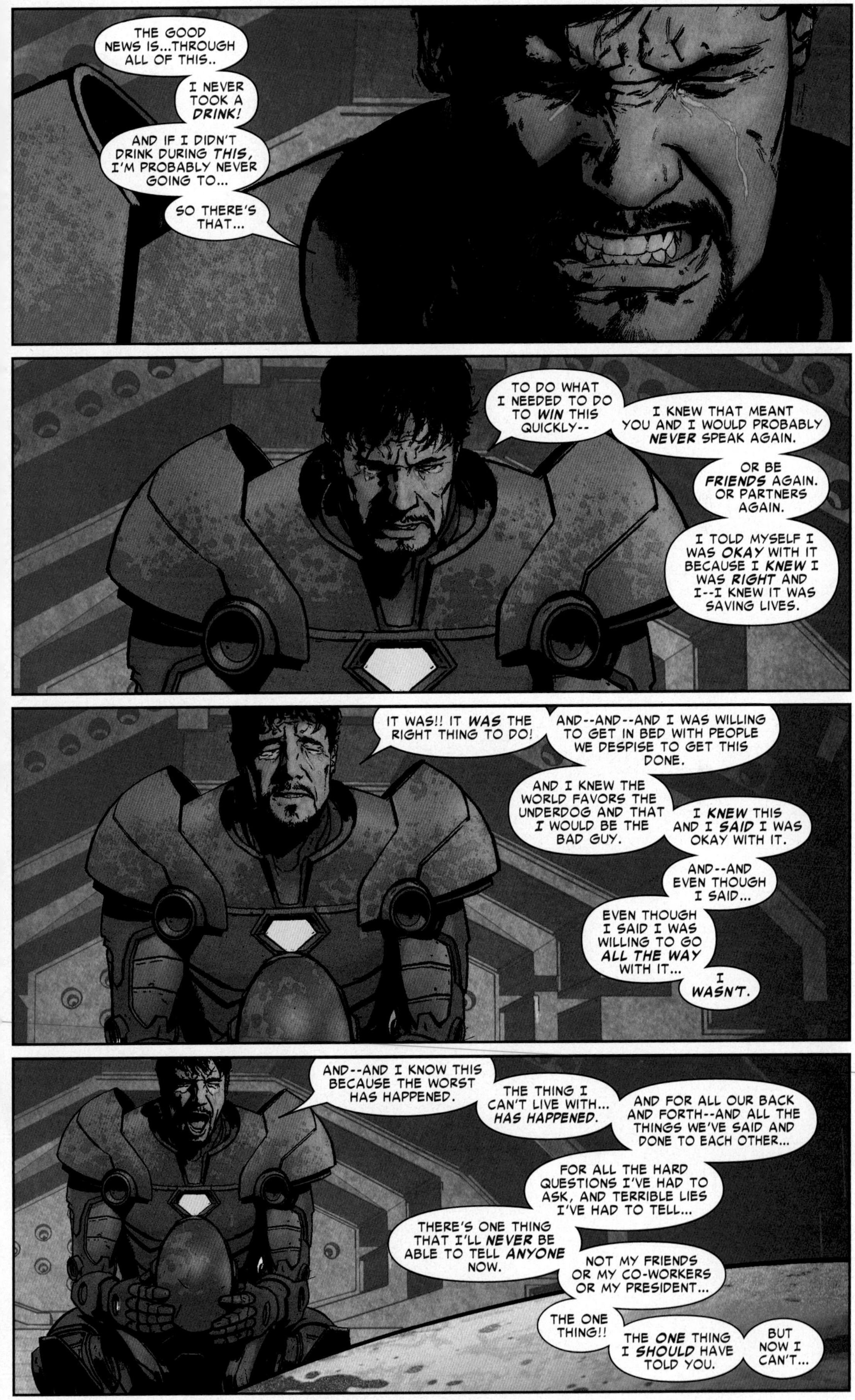

THE GOOD NEWS IS...THROUGH ALL OF THIS..
I NEVER TOOK A DRINK!
AND IF I DIDN'T DRINK DURING THIS, I'M PROBABLY NEVER GOING TO...
SO THERE'S THAT...
TO DO WHAT I NEEDED TO DO TO WIN THIS QUICKLY--
I KNEW THAT MEANT YOU AND I WOULD PROBABLY NEVER SPEAK AGAIN.
OR BE FRIENDS AGAIN. OR PARTNERS AGAIN.
I TOLD MYSELF I WAS OKAY WITH IT BECAUSE I KNEW I WAS RIGHT AND I--I KNEW IT WAS SAVING LIVES.
IT WAS!! IT WAS THE RIGHT THING TO DO!
AND--AND--AND I WAS WILLING TO GET IN BED WITH PEOPLE WE DESPISE TO GET THIS DONE.
AND I KNEW THE WORLD FAVORS THE UNDERDOG AND THAT I WOULD BE THE BAD GUY.
I KNEW THIS AND I SAID I WAS OKAY WITH IT.
AND--AND EVEN THOUGH I SAID...
EVEN THOUGH I SAID I WAS WILLING TO GO ALL THE WAY WITH IT...
I WASN'T.
AND--AND I KNOW THIS BECAUSE THE WORST HAS HAPPENED.
THE THING I CAN'T LIVE WITH... HAS HAPPENED.
AND FOR ALL OUR BACK AND FORTH--AND ALL THE THINGS WE'VE SAID AND DONE TO EACH OTHER...
FOR ALL THE HARD QUESTIONS I'VE HAD TO ASK, AND TERRIBLE LIES I'VE HAD TO TELL...
THERE'S ONE THING THAT I'LL NEVER BE ABLE TO TELL ANYONE NOW.
NOT MY FRIENDS OR MY CO-WORKERS OR MY PRESIDENT...
THE ONE THING!!
THE ONE THING I SHOULD HAVE TOLD YOU.
BUT NOW I CAN'T...

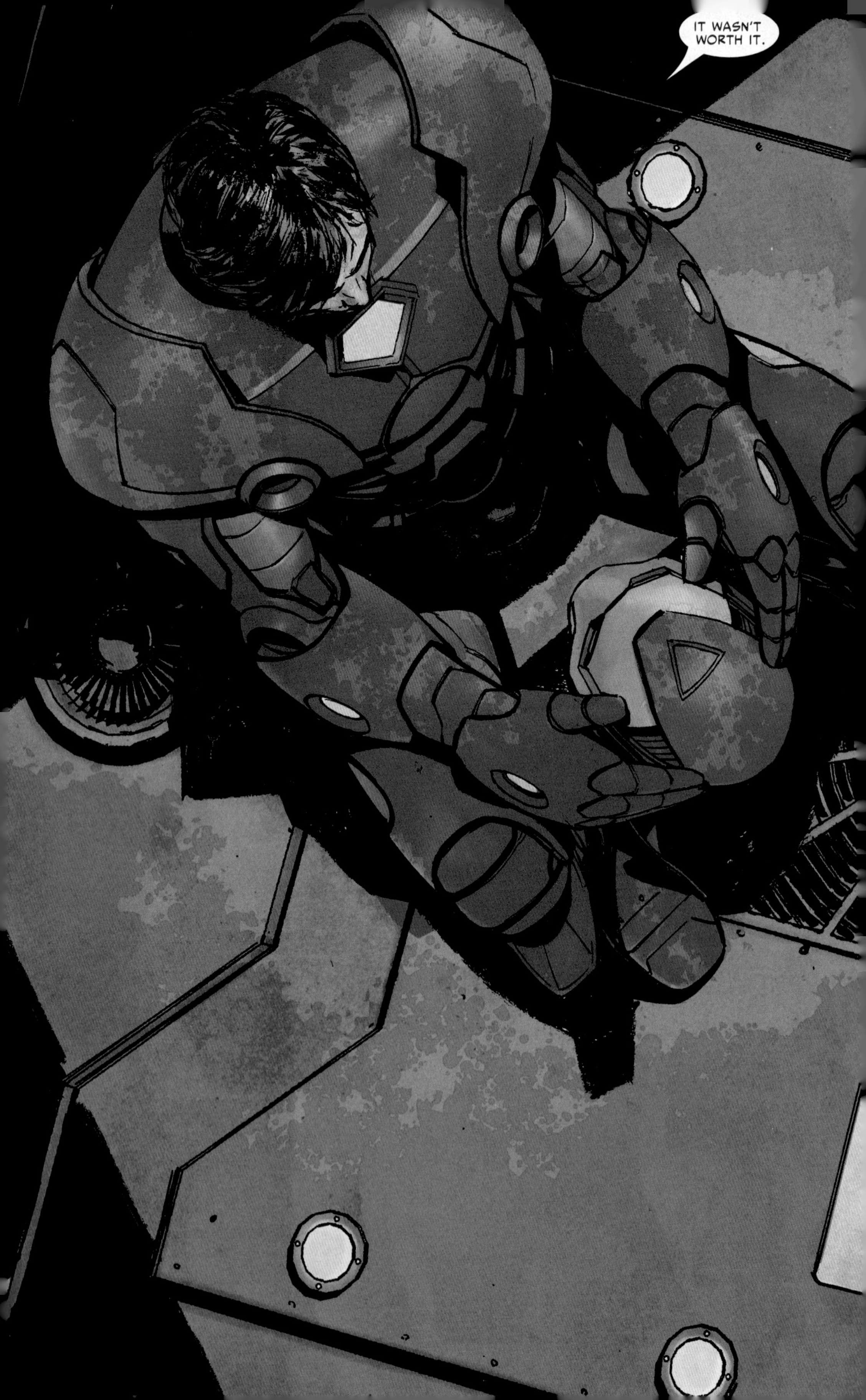
IT WASN'T WORTH IT.

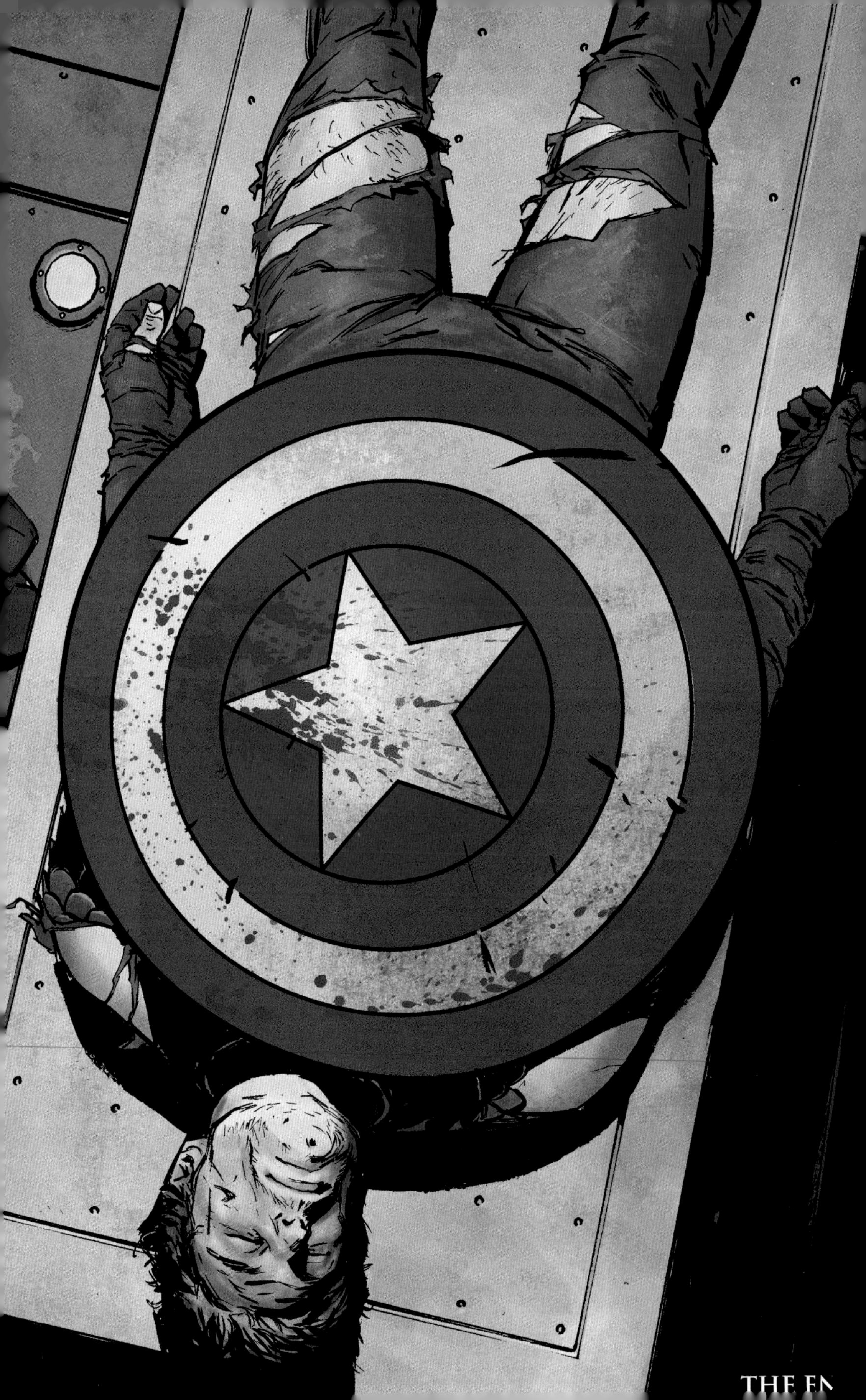
THE EN

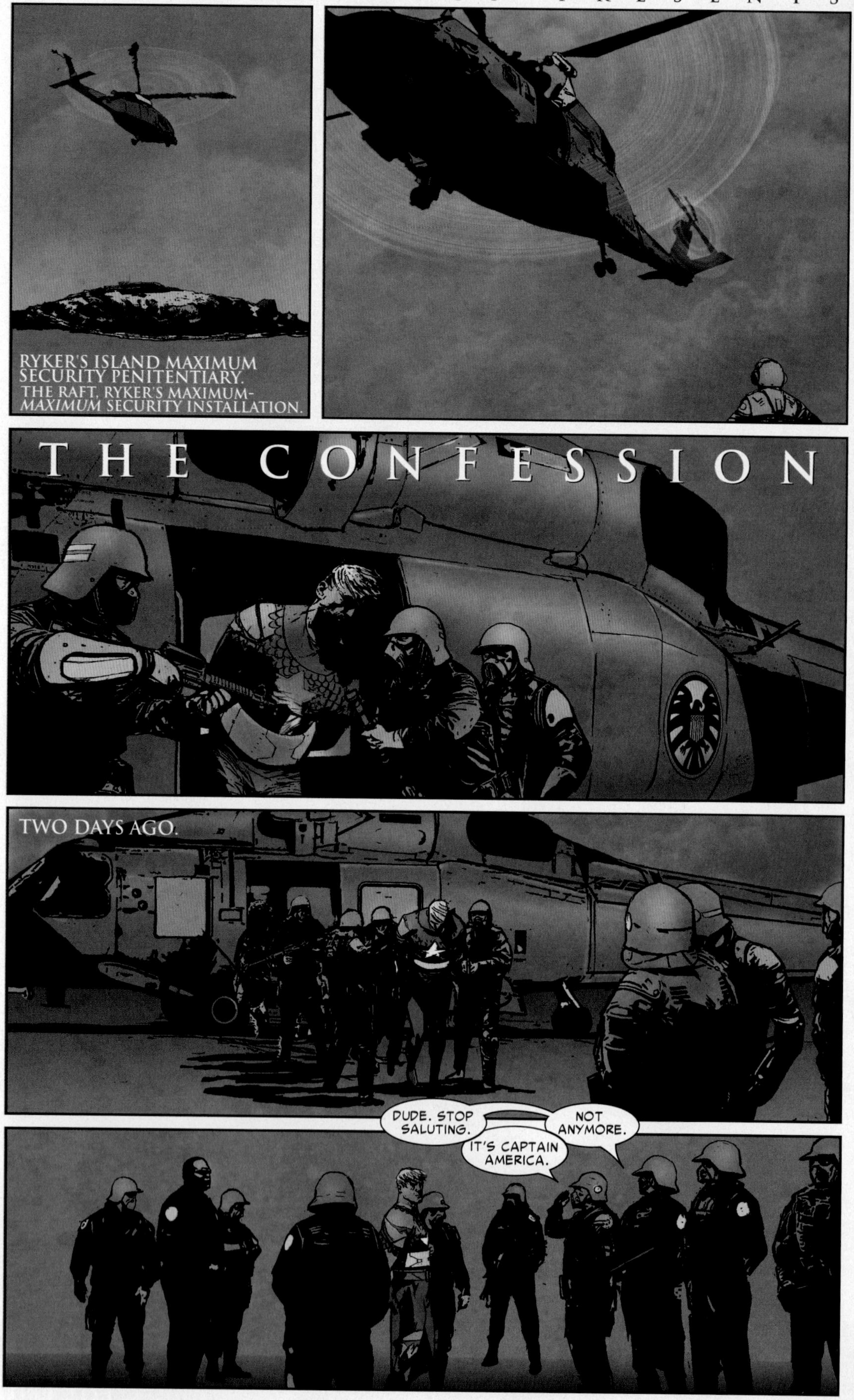
RYKER'S ISLAND MAXIMUM SECURITY PENITENTIARY.
THE RAFT, RYKER'S MAXIMUM-*MAXIMUM* SECURITY INSTALLATION.
THE CONFESSION
TWO DAYS AGO.
DUDE. STOP SALUTING.
IT'S CAPTAIN AMERICA.
NOT ANYMORE.

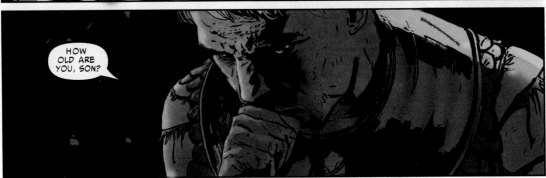

HOW OLD ARE YOU, SON?

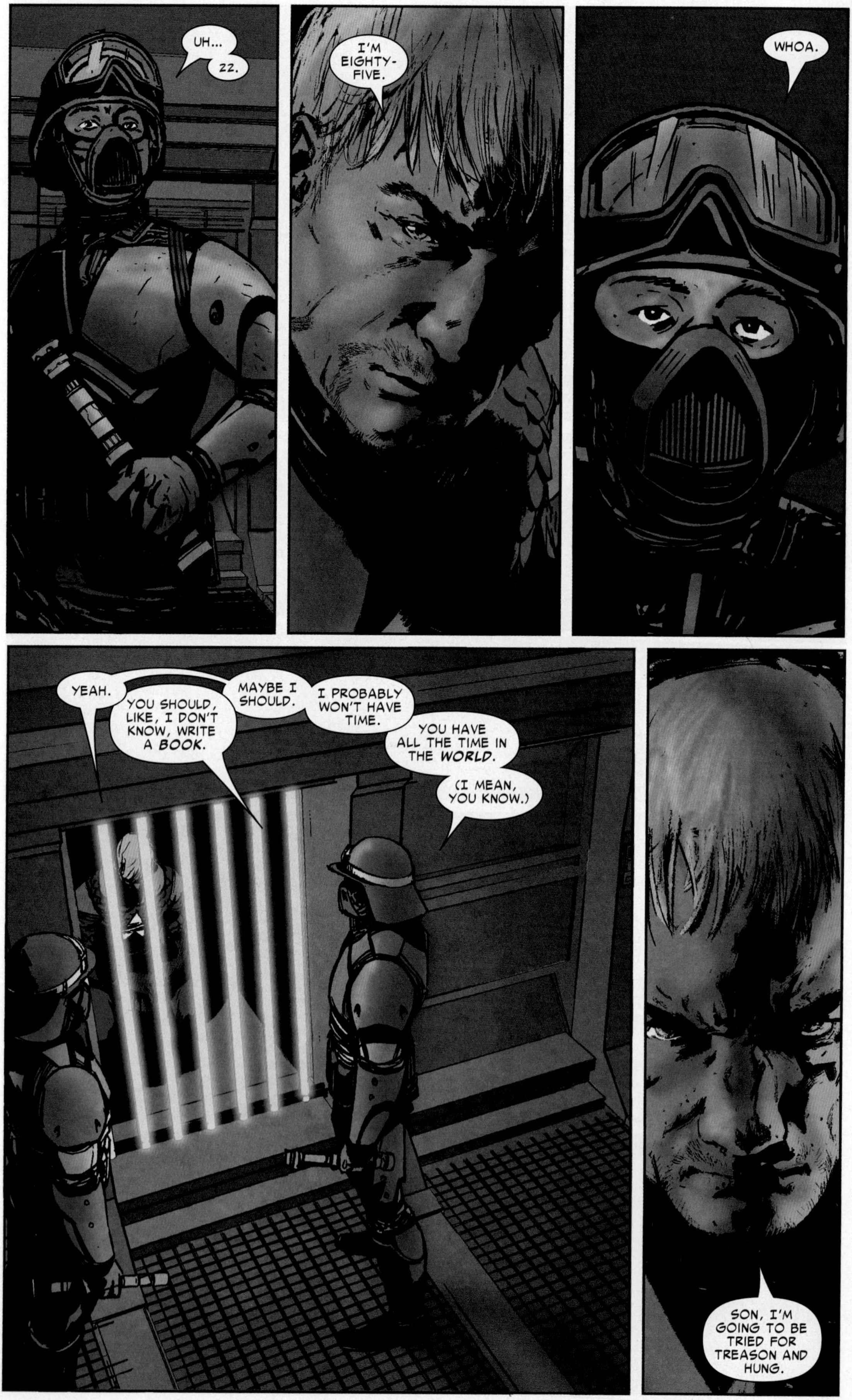
UH...
22.
I'M EIGHTY-FIVE.
WHOA.
YEAH.
YOU SHOULD, LIKE, I DON'T KNOW, WRITE A *BOOK*.
MAYBE I SHOULD.
I PROBABLY WON'T HAVE TIME.
YOU HAVE ALL THE TIME IN THE *WORLD*.
(I MEAN, YOU KNOW.)
SON, I'M GOING TO BE TRIED FOR TREASON AND HUNG.

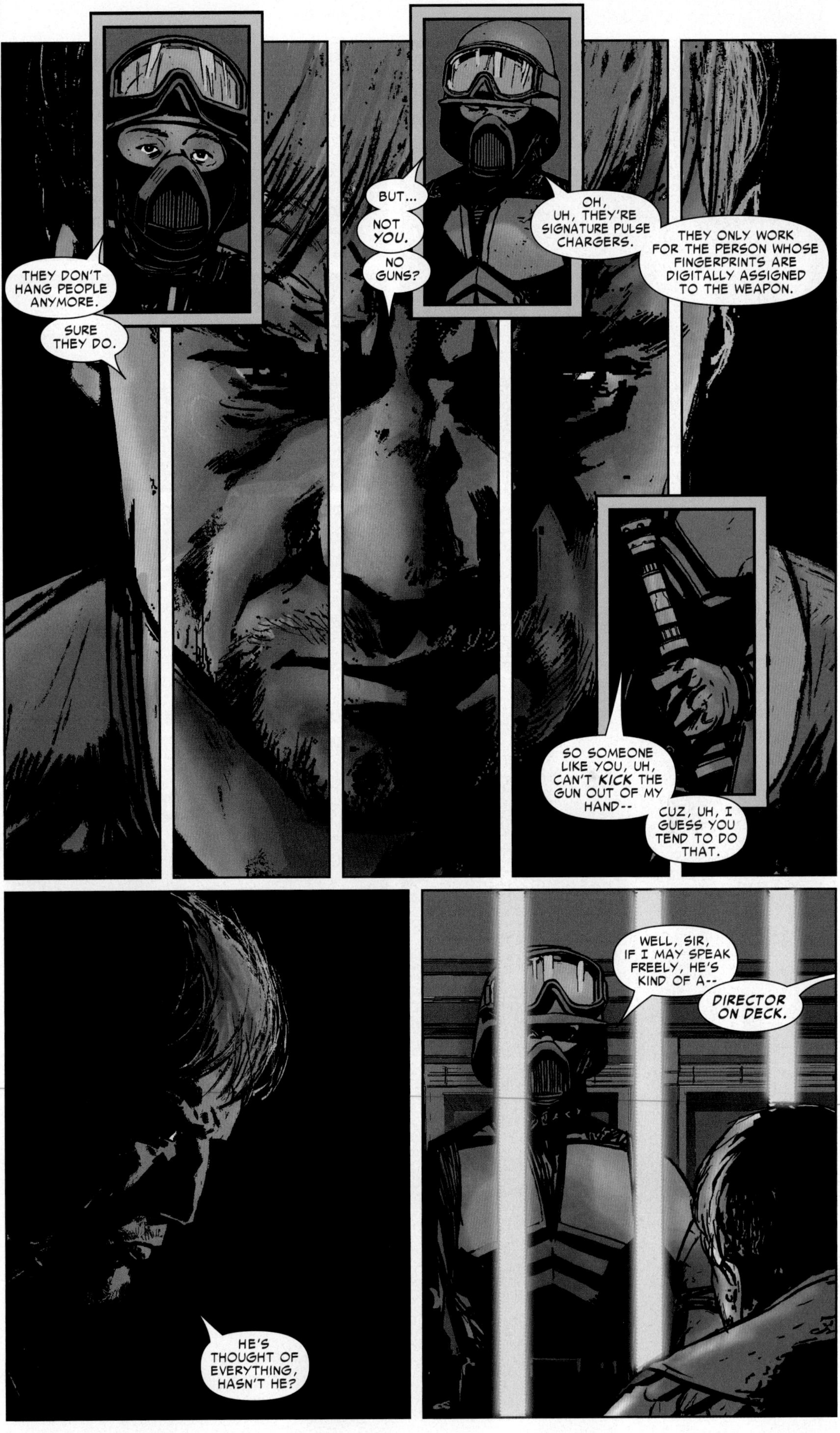

THEY DON'T HANG PEOPLE ANYMORE.
SURE THEY DO.
BUT...
NOT YOU.
NO GUNS?
OH, UH, THEY'RE SIGNATURE PULSE CHARGERS.
THEY ONLY WORK FOR THE PERSON WHOSE FINGERPRINTS ARE DIGITALLY ASSIGNED TO THE WEAPON.
SO SOMEONE LIKE YOU, UH, CAN'T KICK THE GUN OUT OF MY HAND--
CUZ, UH, I GUESS YOU TEND TO DO THAT.
HE'S THOUGHT OF EVERYTHING, HASN'T HE?
WELL, SIR, IF I MAY SPEAK FREELY, HE'S KIND OF A--
DIRECTOR ON DECK.

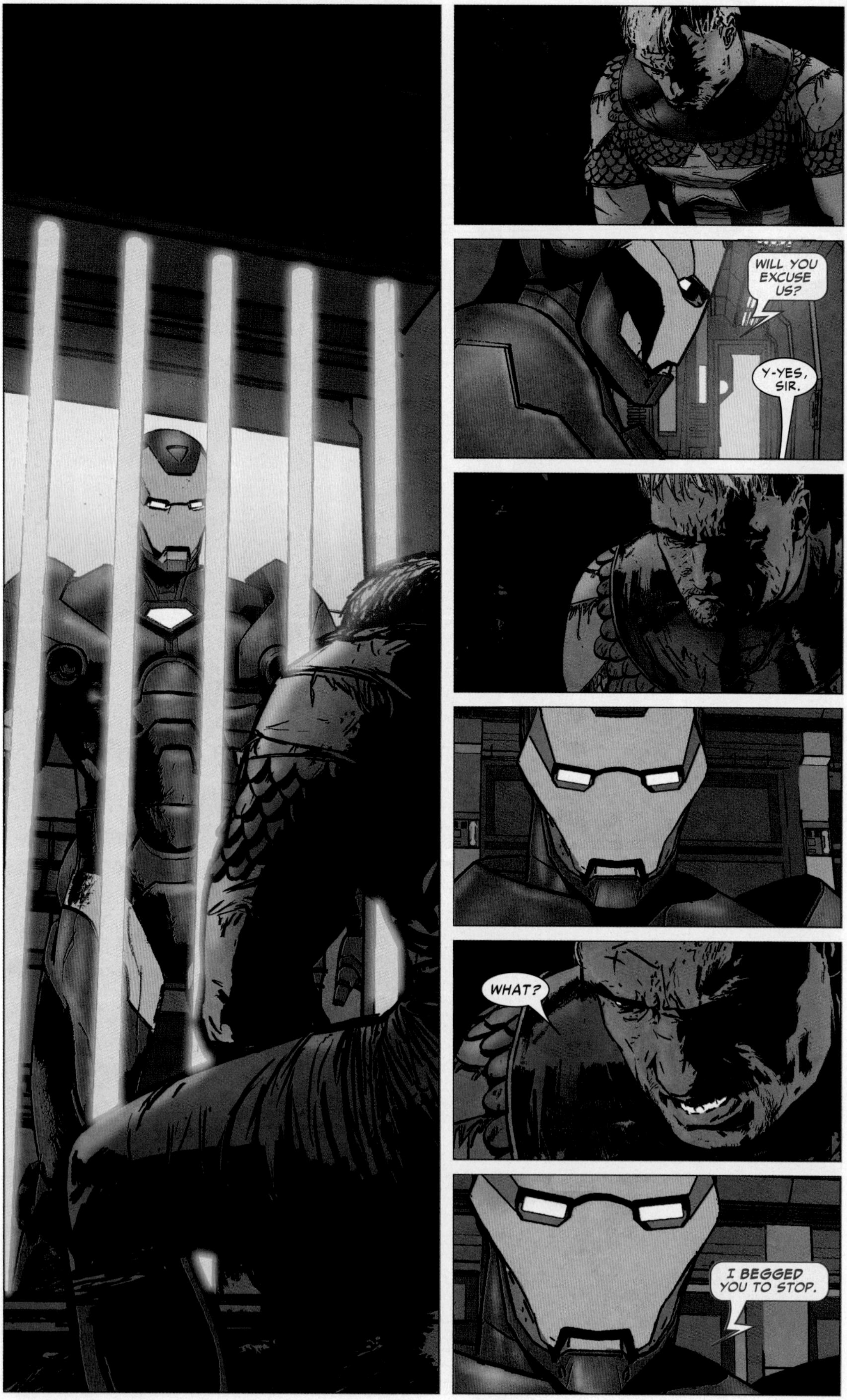
WILL YOU EXCUSE US?
Y-YES, SIR.
WHAT?
I BEGGED YOU TO STOP.

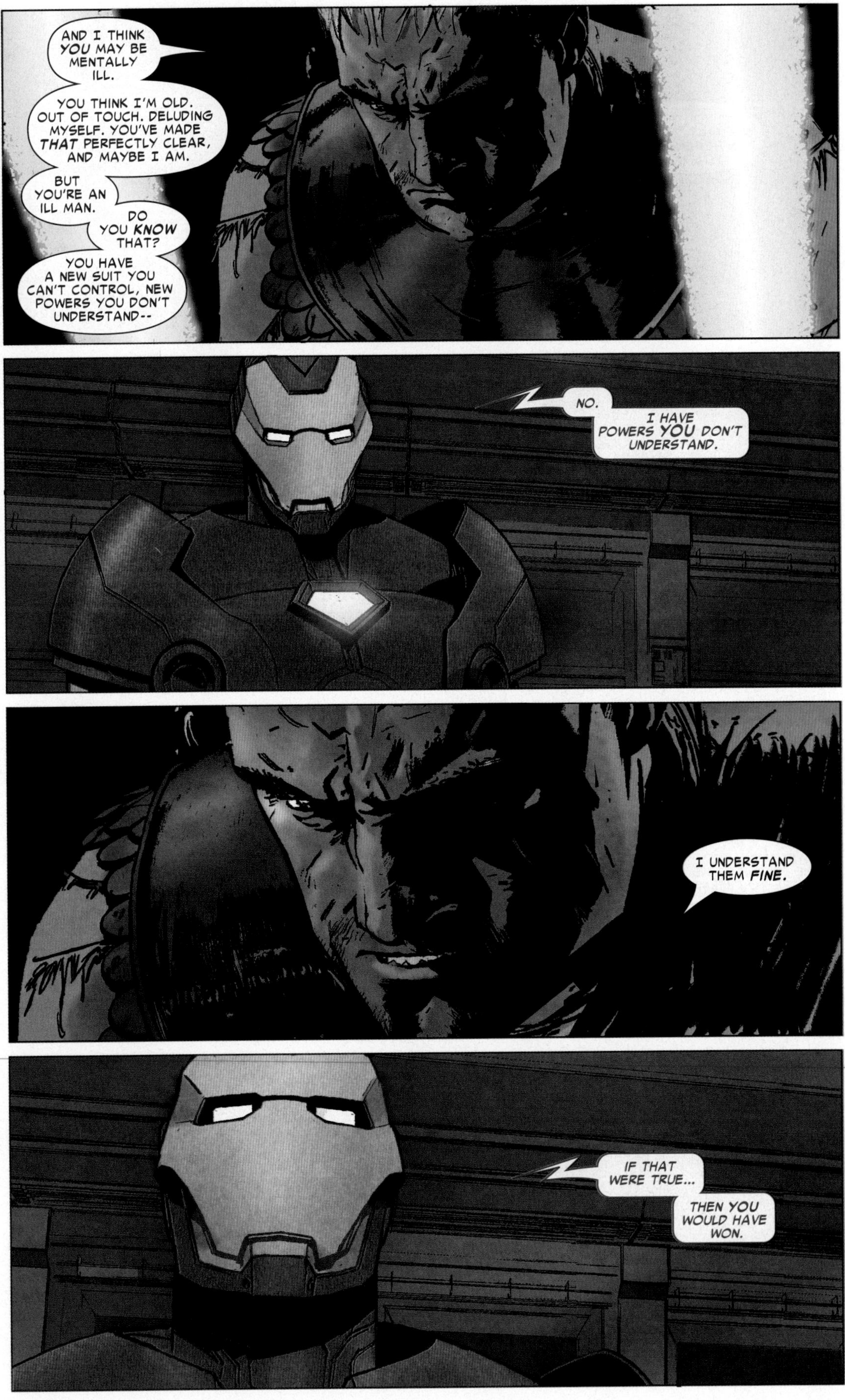
AND I THINK YOU MAY BE MENTALLY ILL.
YOU THINK I'M OLD. OUT OF TOUCH. DELUDING MYSELF. YOU'VE MADE THAT PERFECTLY CLEAR, AND MAYBE I AM.
BUT YOU'RE AN ILL MAN.
DO YOU KNOW THAT?
YOU HAVE A NEW SUIT YOU CAN'T CONTROL, NEW POWERS YOU DON'T UNDERSTAND--
NO.
I HAVE POWERS YOU DON'T UNDERSTAND.
I UNDERSTAND THEM FINE.
IF THAT WERE TRUE...
THEN YOU WOULD HAVE WON.

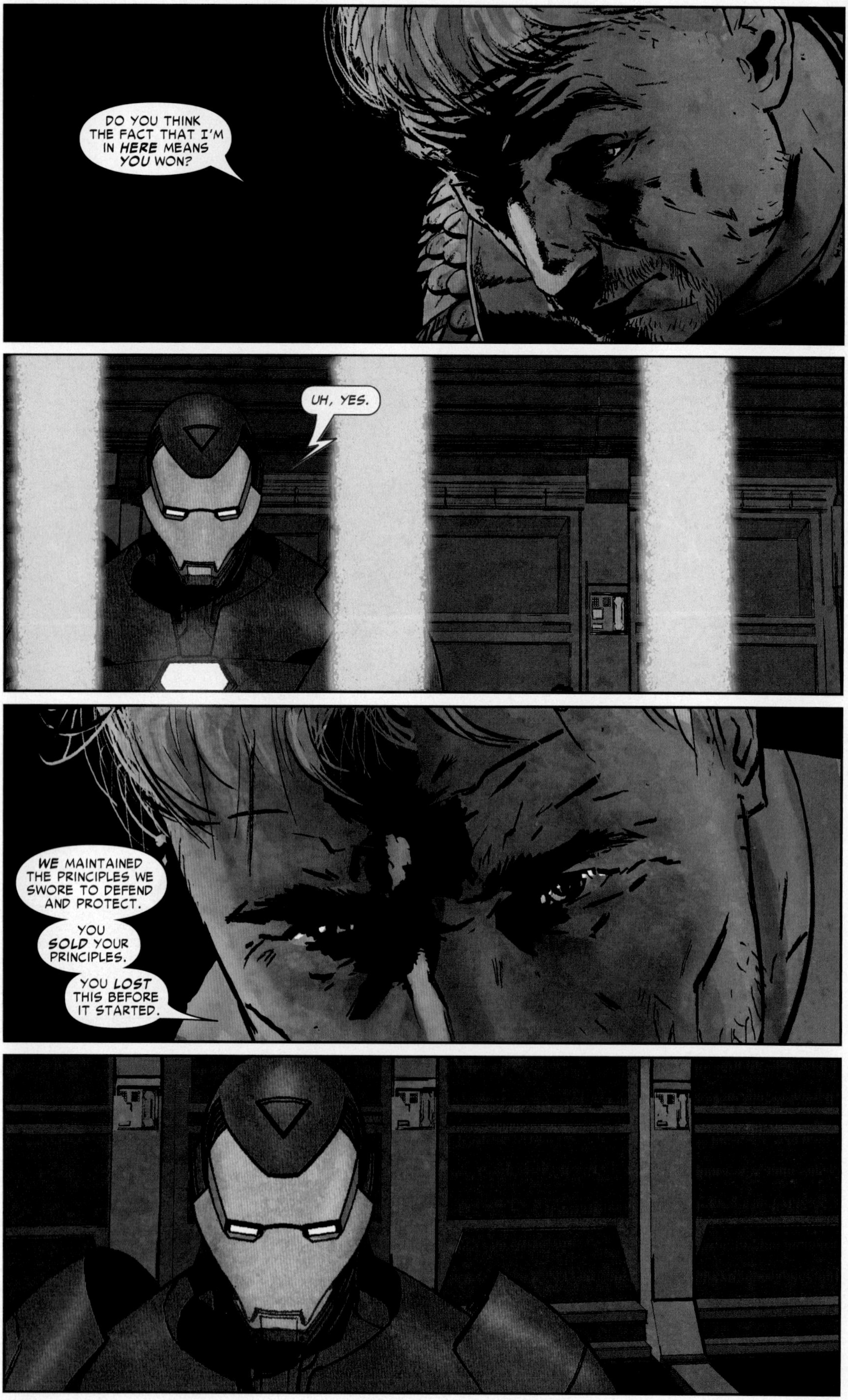
DO YOU THINK THE FACT THAT I'M IN HERE MEANS YOU WON?
UH, YES.
WE MAINTAINED THE PRINCIPLES WE SWORE TO DEFEND AND PROTECT.
YOU SOLD YOUR PRINCIPLES.
YOU LOST THIS BEFORE IT STARTED.

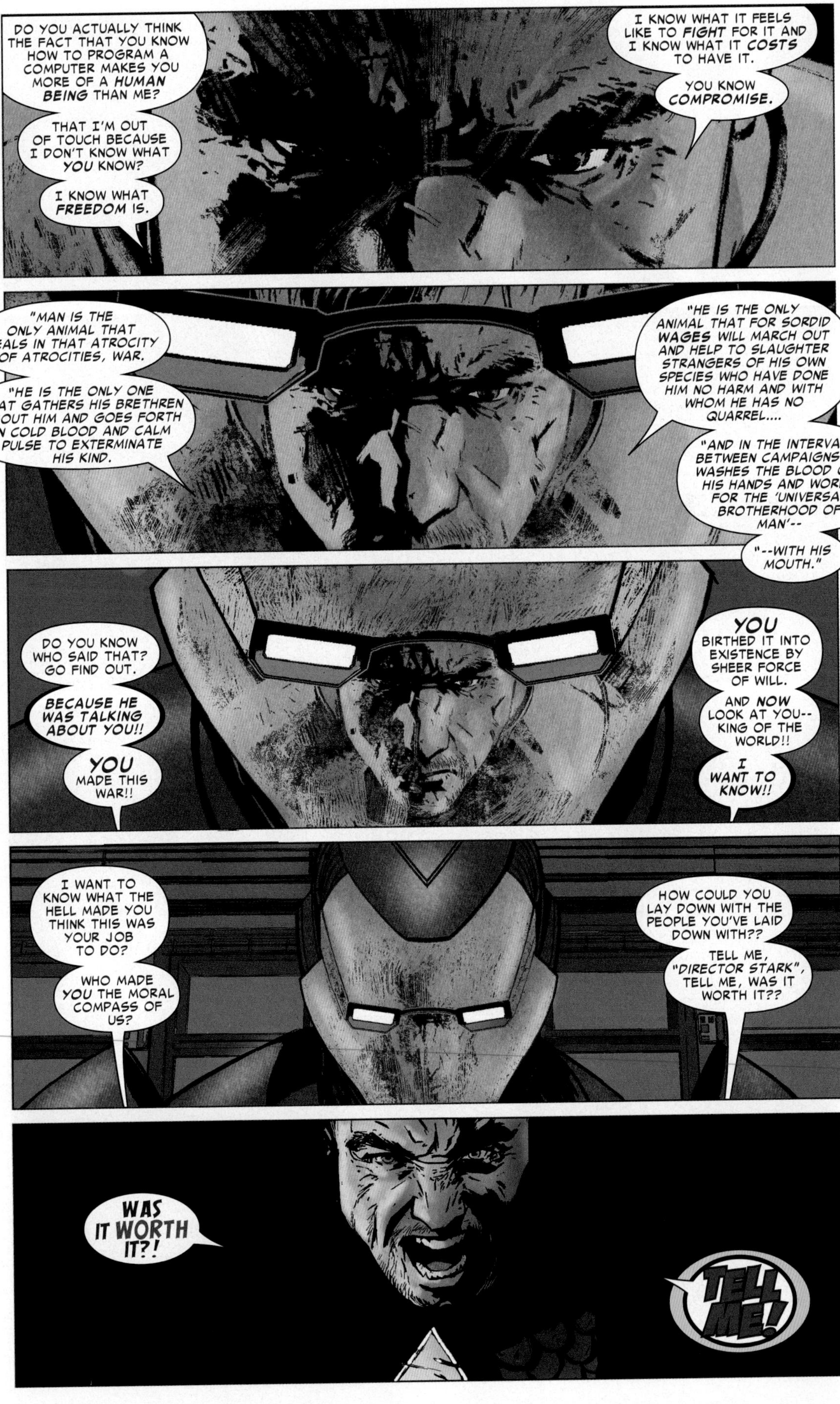
DO YOU ACTUALLY THINK THE FACT THAT YOU KNOW HOW TO PROGRAM A COMPUTER MAKES YOU MORE OF A HUMAN BEING THAN ME?
THAT I'M OUT OF TOUCH BECAUSE I DON'T KNOW WHAT YOU KNOW?
I KNOW WHAT FREEDOM IS.
I KNOW WHAT IT FEELS LIKE TO FIGHT FOR IT AND I KNOW WHAT IT COSTS TO HAVE IT.
YOU KNOW COMPROMISE.
"MAN IS THE ONLY ANIMAL THAT EALS IN THAT ATROCITY OF ATROCITIES, WAR.
"HE IS THE ONLY ONE HAT GATHERS HIS BRETHREN BOUT HIM AND GOES FORTH IN COLD BLOOD AND CALM PULSE TO EXTERMINATE HIS KIND.
"HE IS THE ONLY ANIMAL THAT FOR SORDID WAGES WILL MARCH OUT AND HELP TO SLAUGHTER STRANGERS OF HIS OWN SPECIES WHO HAVE DONE HIM NO HARM AND WITH WHOM HE HAS NO QUARREL....
"AND IN THE INTERVALS BETWEEN CAMPAIGNS HE WASHES THE BLOOD OFF HIS HANDS AND WORKS FOR THE 'UNIVERSAL BROTHERHOOD OF MAN'--
"--WITH HIS MOUTH."
DO YOU KNOW WHO SAID THAT? GO FIND OUT.
BECAUSE HE WAS TALKING ABOUT YOU!!
YOU MADE THIS WAR!!
YOU BIRTHED IT INTO EXISTENCE BY SHEER FORCE OF WILL.
AND NOW LOOK AT YOU-- KING OF THE WORLD!!
I WANT TO KNOW!!
I WANT TO KNOW WHAT THE HELL MADE YOU THINK THIS WAS YOUR JOB TO DO?
WHO MADE YOU THE MORAL COMPASS OF US?
HOW COULD YOU LAY DOWN WITH THE PEOPLE YOU'VE LAID DOWN WITH??
TELL ME, "DIRECTOR STARK", TELL ME, WAS IT WORTH IT??
WAS IT WORTH IT?!
TELL ME!

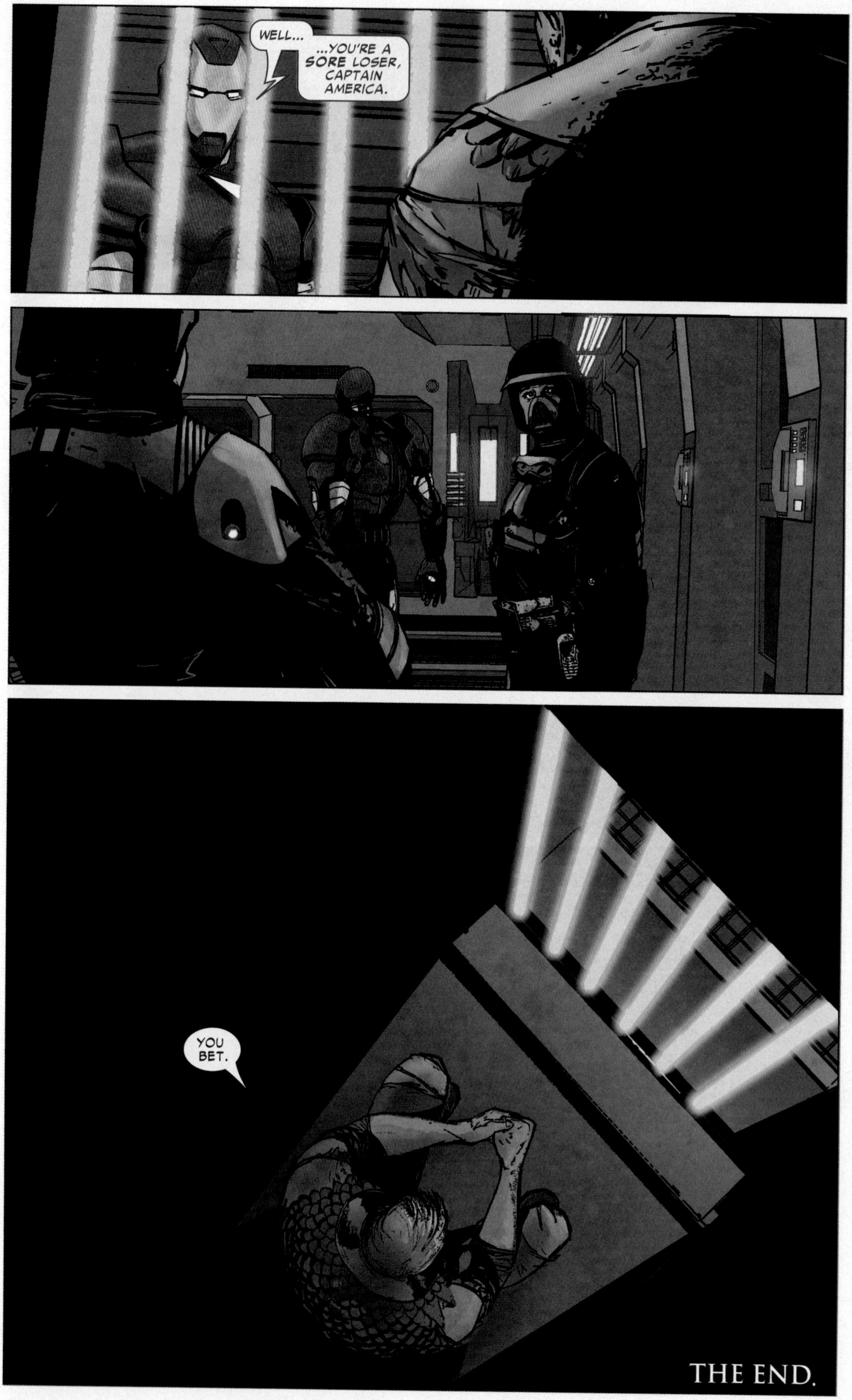
WELL...
...YOU'RE A SORE LOSER, CAPTAIN AMERICA.
YOU BET.
THE END.

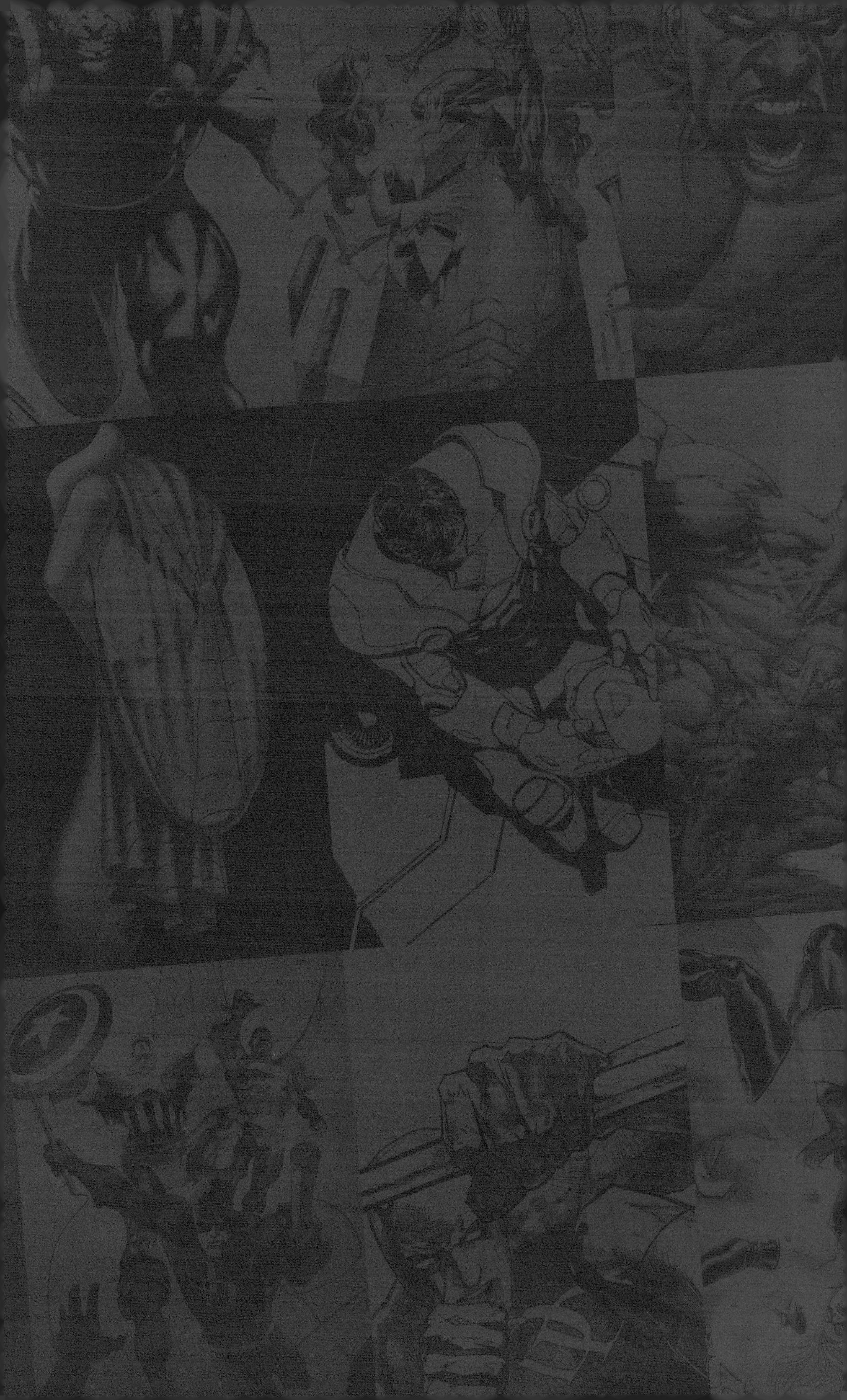

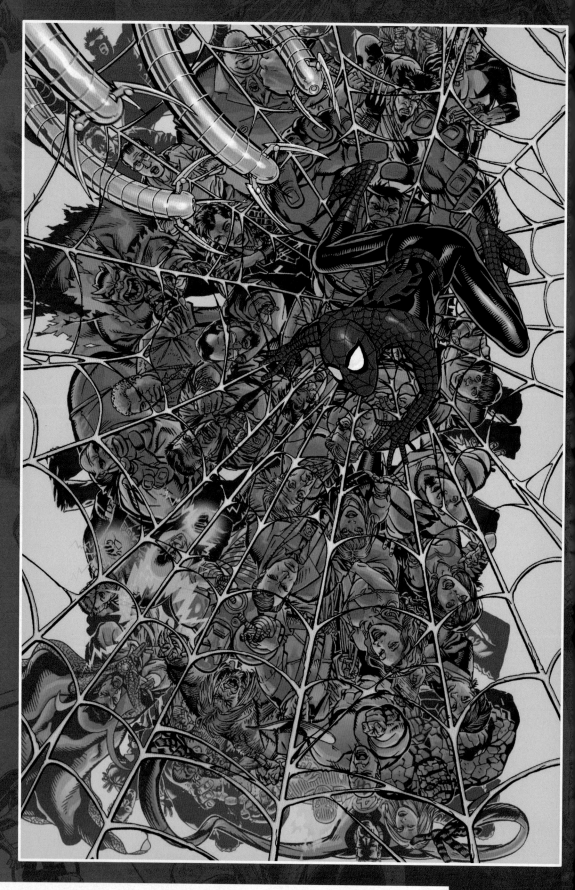

ULTIMATE SPIDER-MAN SUPER SPECIAL #1

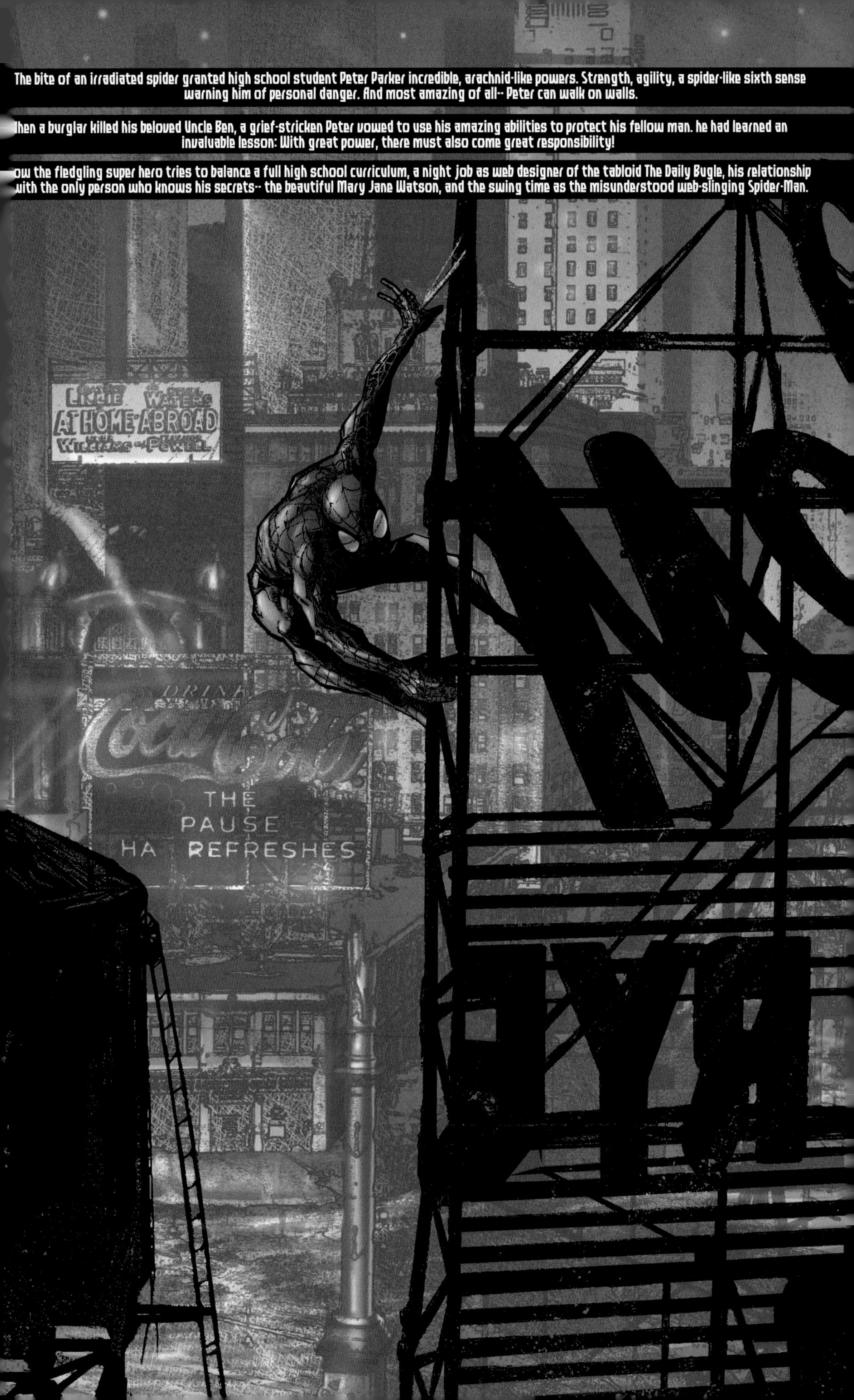
The bite of an irradiated spider granted high school student Peter Parker incredible, arachnid-like powers. Strength, agility, a spider-like sixth sense warning him of personal danger. And most amazing of all-- Peter can walk on walls.
hen a burglar killed his beloved Uncle Ben, a grief-stricken Peter vowed to use his amazing abilities to protect his fellow man. he had learned an invaluable lesson: With great power, there must also come great responsibility!
ow the fledgling super hero tries to balance a full high school curriculum, a night job as web designer of the tabloid The Daily Bugle, his relationship with the only person who knows his secrets-- the beautiful Mary Jane Watson, and the swing time as the misunderstood web-slinging Spider-Man.
AT HOME ABROAD
DRINK
THE PAUSE
HA REFRESHES

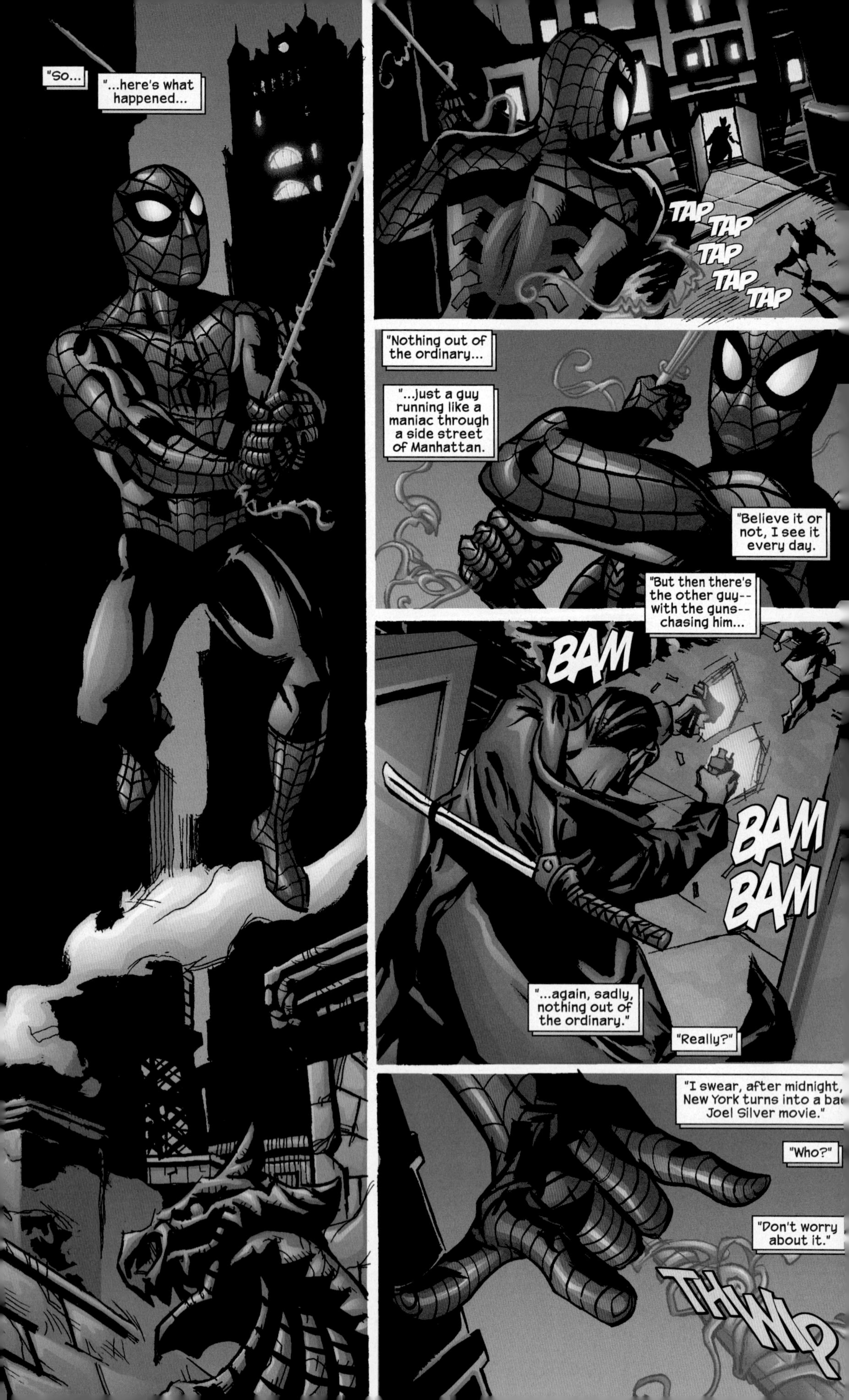

"So...
"...here's what happened...
TAP TAP TAP TAP TAP
"Nothing out of the ordinary...
"...just a guy running like a maniac through a side street of Manhattan.
"Believe it or not, I see it every day.
"But then there's the other guy--with the guns--chasing him...
BAM
BAM BAM
"...again, sadly, nothing out of the ordinary."
"Really?"
"I swear, after midnight, New York turns into a bad Joel Silver movie."
"Who?"
"Don't worry about it."
THWIP

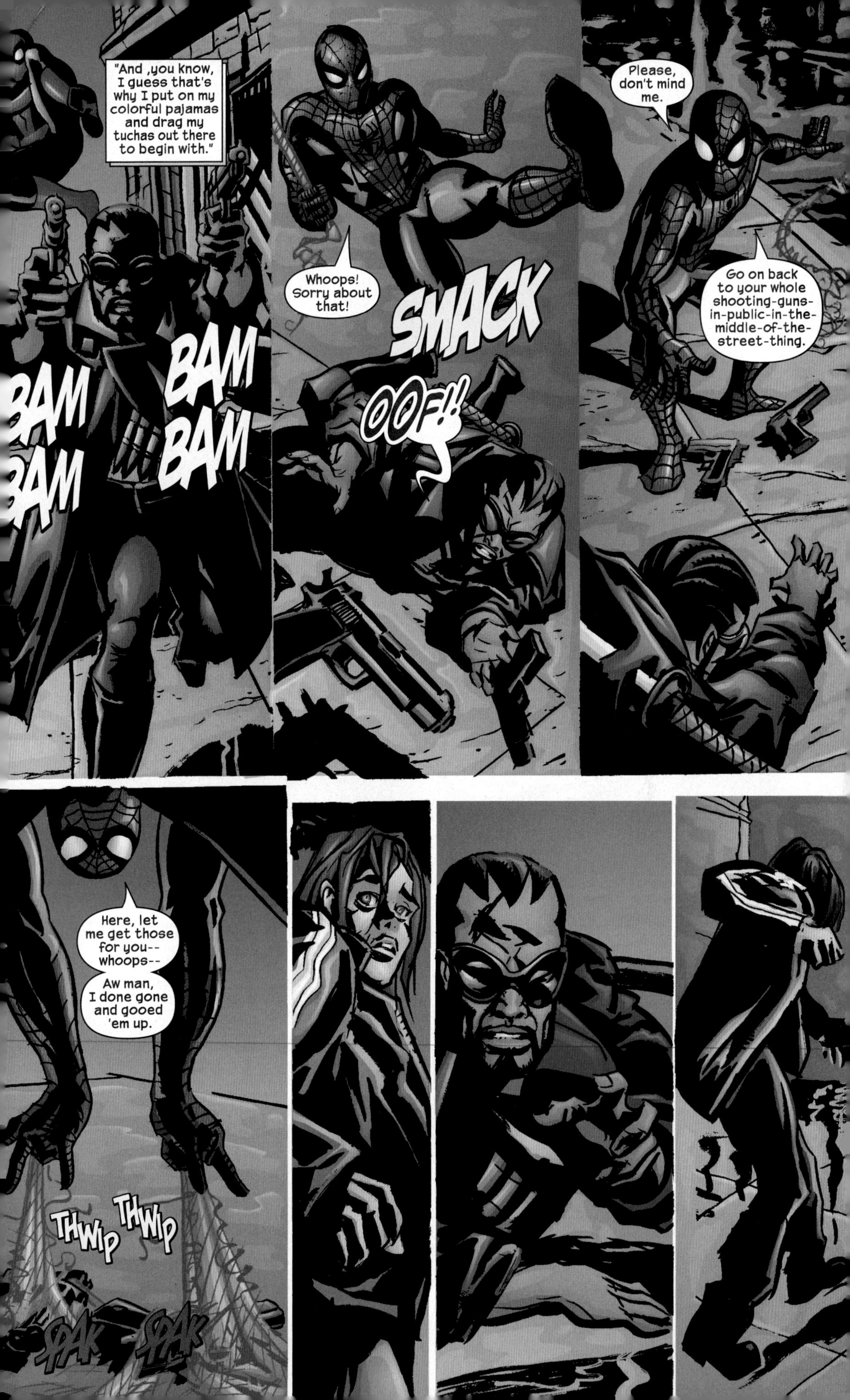

"And ,you know, I guess that's why I put on my colorful pajamas and drag my tuchas out there to begin with."
BAM BAM
BAM BAM
Whoops! Sorry about that!
SMACK
OOF!!
Please, don't mind me.
Go on back to your whole shooting-guns-in-public-in-the-middle-of-the-street-thing.
Here, let me get those for you-- whoops--
Aw man, I done gone and gooed 'em up.
THWIP THWIP
SPAK SPAK

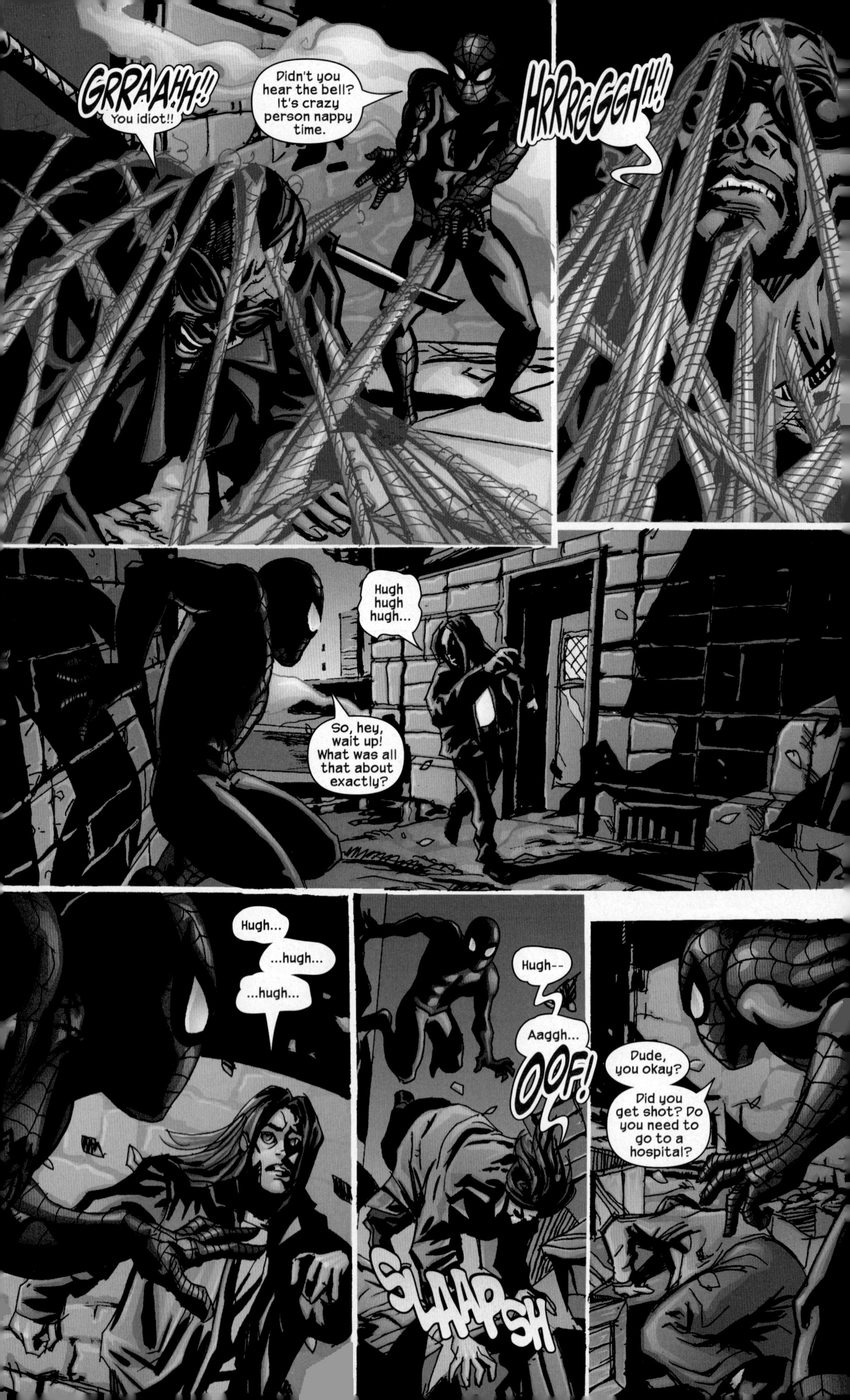
GRRAAHH!! You idiot!!
Didn't you hear the bell? It's crazy person nappy time.
HRRRGGGH!!
Hugh hugh hugh...
So, hey, wait up! What was all that about exactly?
Hugh...
...hugh...
...hugh...
Hugh--
Aaggh...
OOF!
SLAAPSH
Dude, you okay?
Did you get shot? Do you need to go to a hospital?

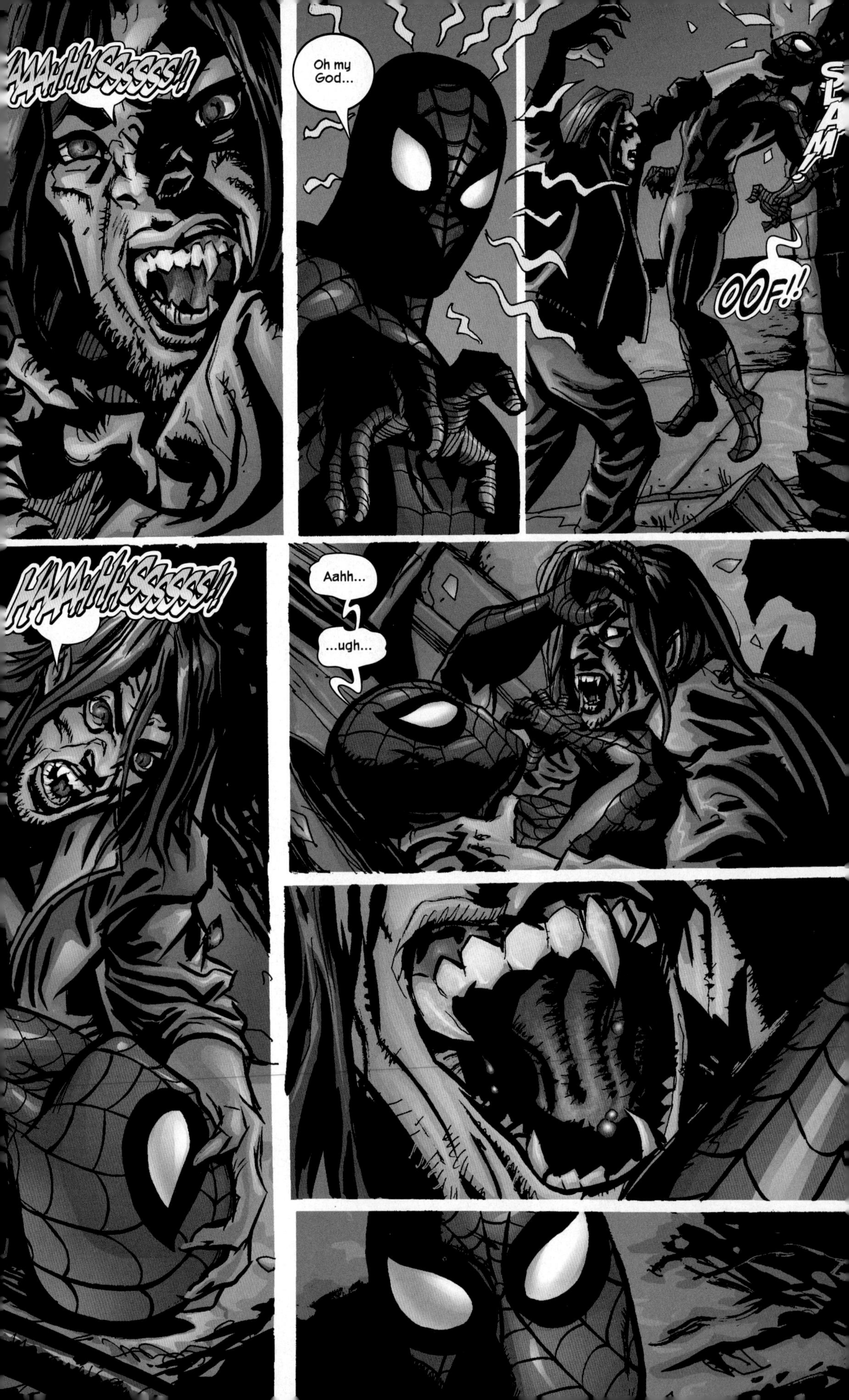
AAAAHHSSSSSS!!
Oh my God...
SLAM!
OOF!!
HAAAHHSSSSSS!!
Aahh...
...ugh...

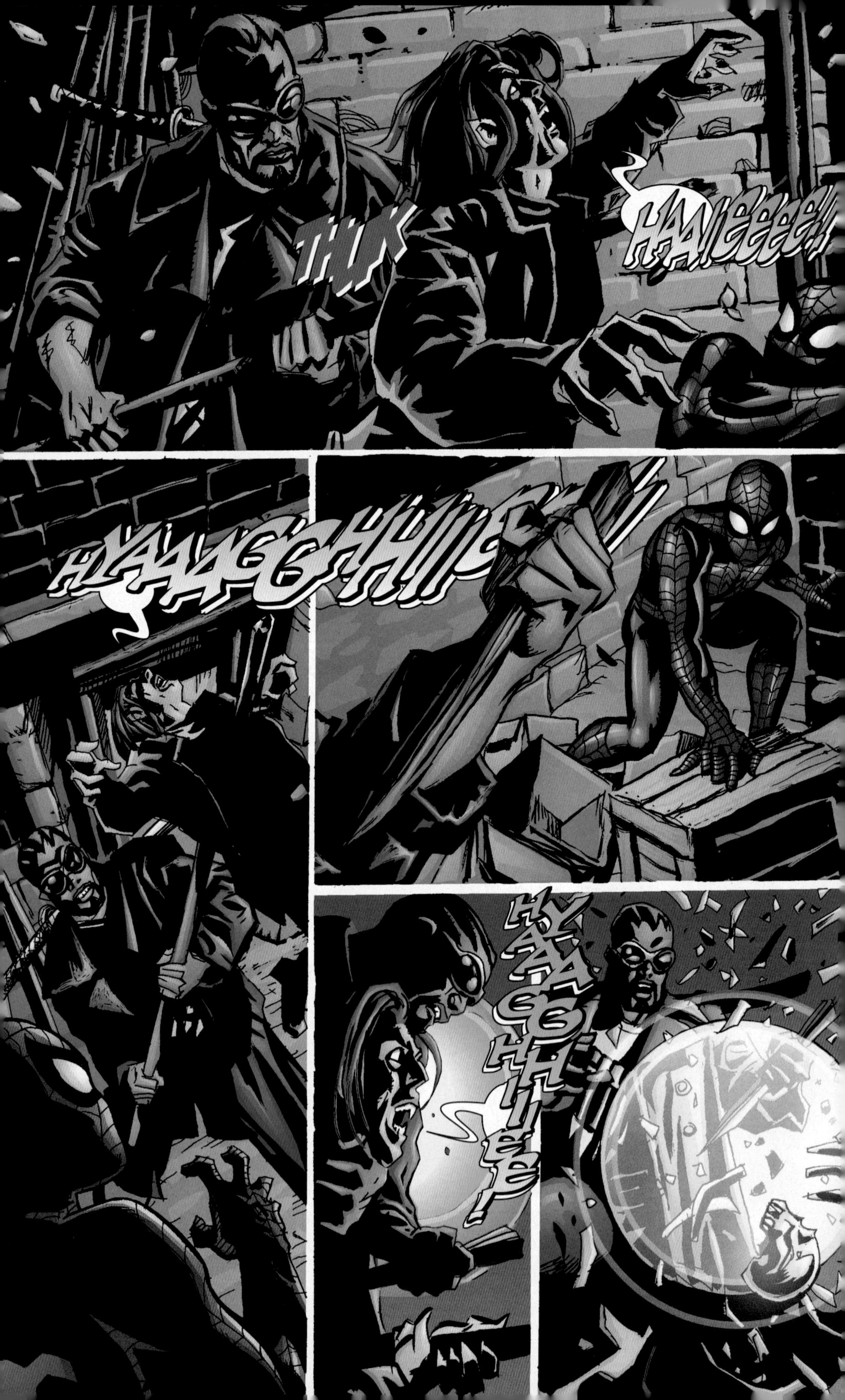
THUK
HAAIEEEE!!
HYAAAGHHIIEE
HYAAAGGHHIIEE!

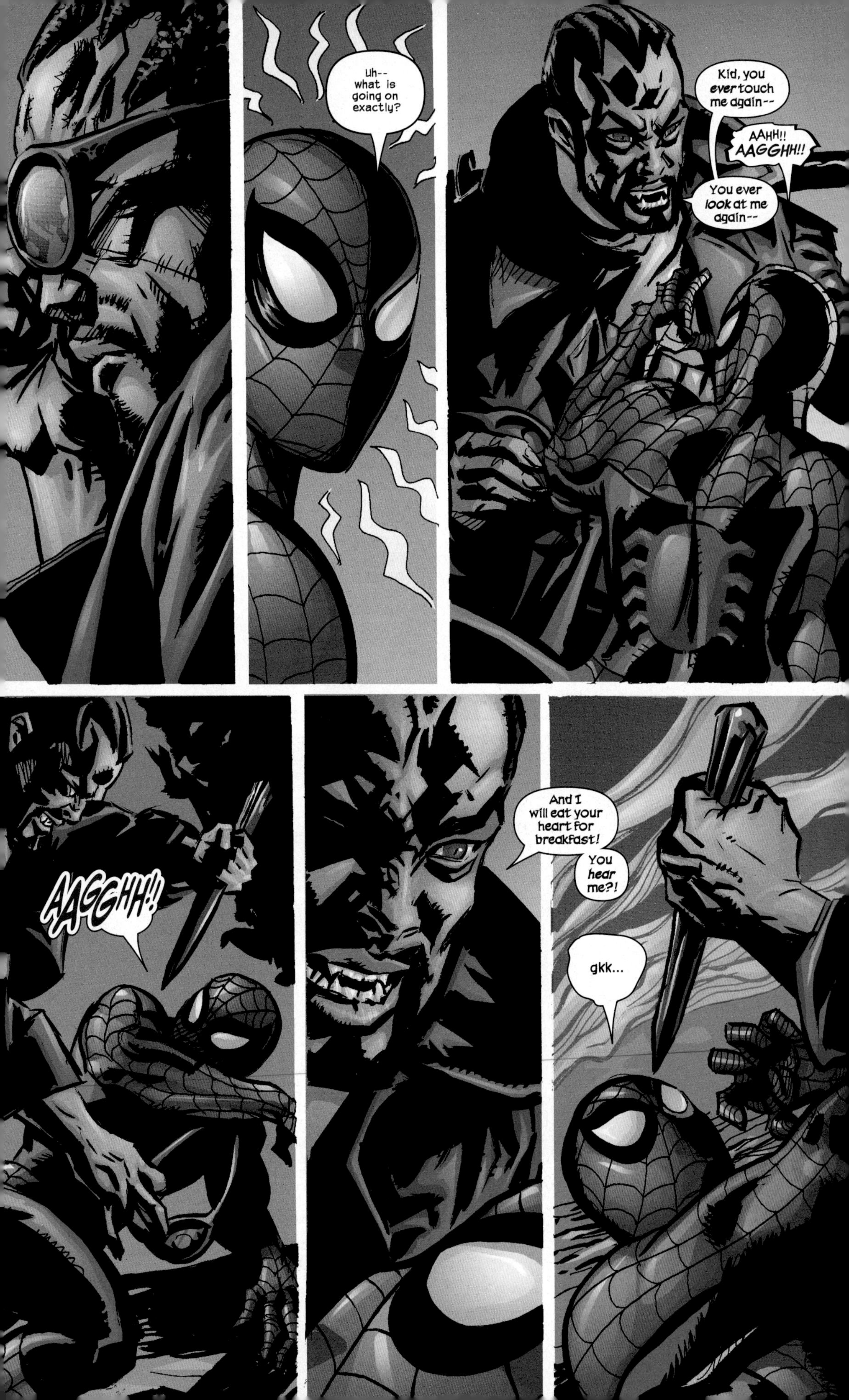
Uh-- what is going on exactly?
Kid, you ever touch me again--
AAHH!! AAGGHH!!
You ever look at me again--
AAGGHH!!
And I will eat your heart for breakfast!
You hear me?!
gkk...

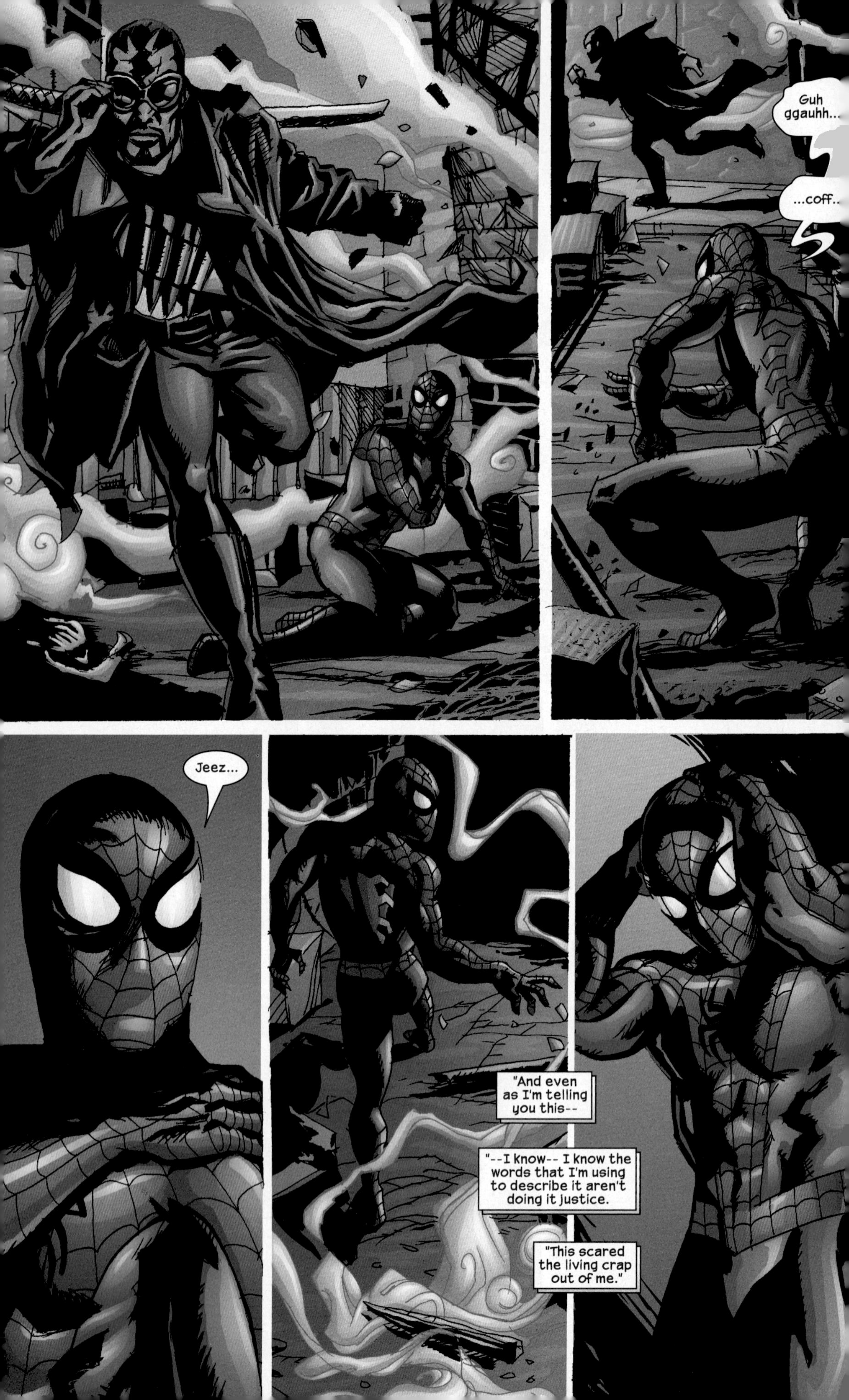
Guh ggauhh...
...coff...
Jeez...
"And even as I'm telling you this--
"--I know-- I know the words that I'm using to describe it aren't doing it justice.
"This scared the living crap out of me."

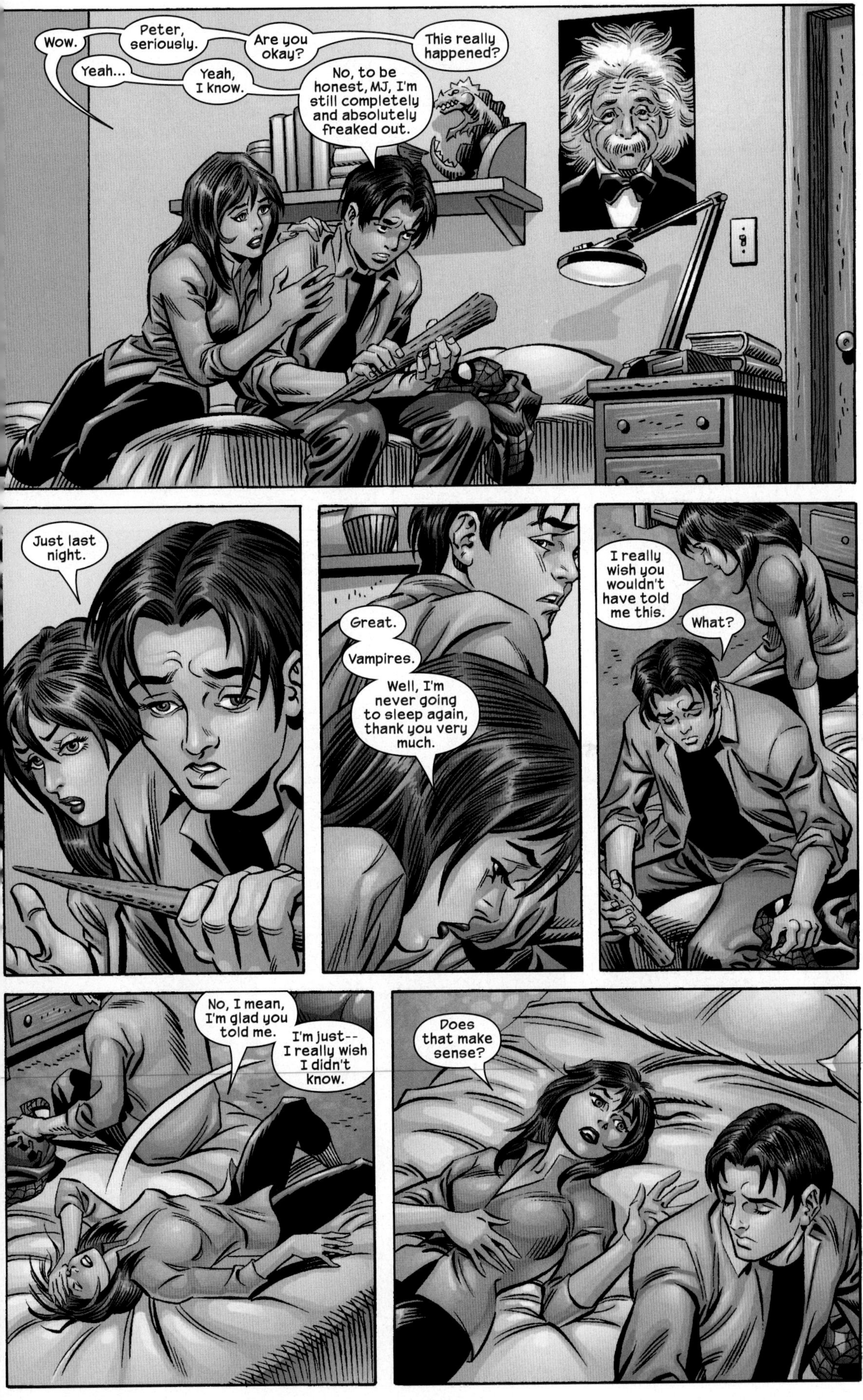
Wow.
Peter, seriously.
Are you okay?
This really happened?
Yeah...
Yeah, I know.
No, to be honest, MJ, I'm still completely and absolutely freaked out.
Just last night.
Great.
Vampires.
Well, I'm never going to sleep again, thank you very much.
I really wish you wouldn't have told me this.
What?
No, I mean, I'm glad you told me.
I'm just-- I really wish I didn't know.
Does that make sense?

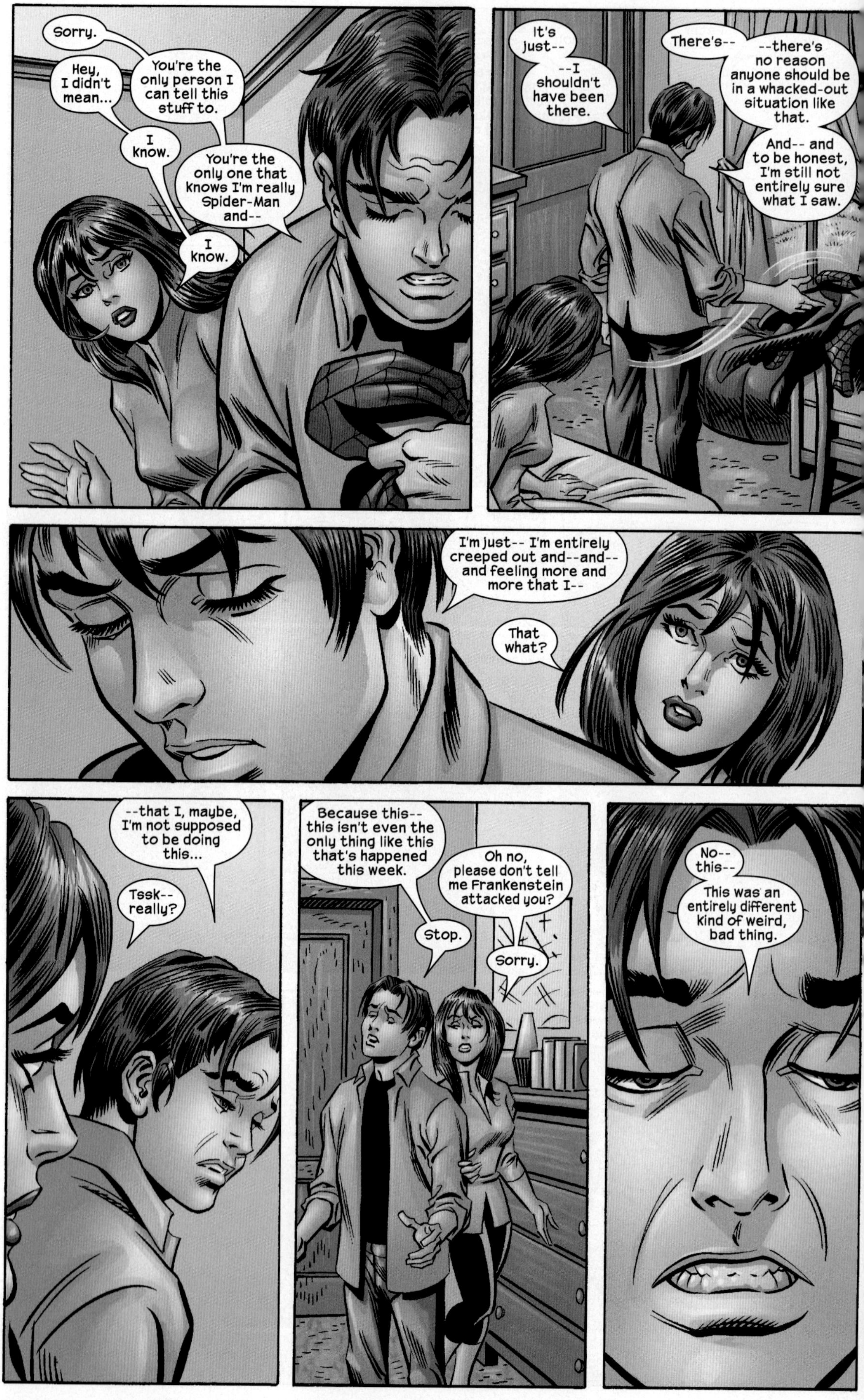
Sorry.
Hey, I didn't mean...
You're the only person I can tell this stuff to.
I know.
You're the only one that knows I'm really Spider-Man and--
I know.
It's just--
--I shouldn't have been there.
There's--
--there's no reason anyone should be in a whacked-out situation like that.
And-- and to be honest, I'm still not entirely sure what I saw.
I'm just-- I'm entirely creeped out and--and-- and feeling more and more that I--
That what?
--that I, maybe, I'm not supposed to be doing this...
Tssk-- really?
Because this-- this isn't even the only thing like this that's happened this week.
Oh no, please don't tell me Frankenstein attacked you?
Stop.
Sorry.
No-- this--
This was an entirely different kind of weird, bad thing.

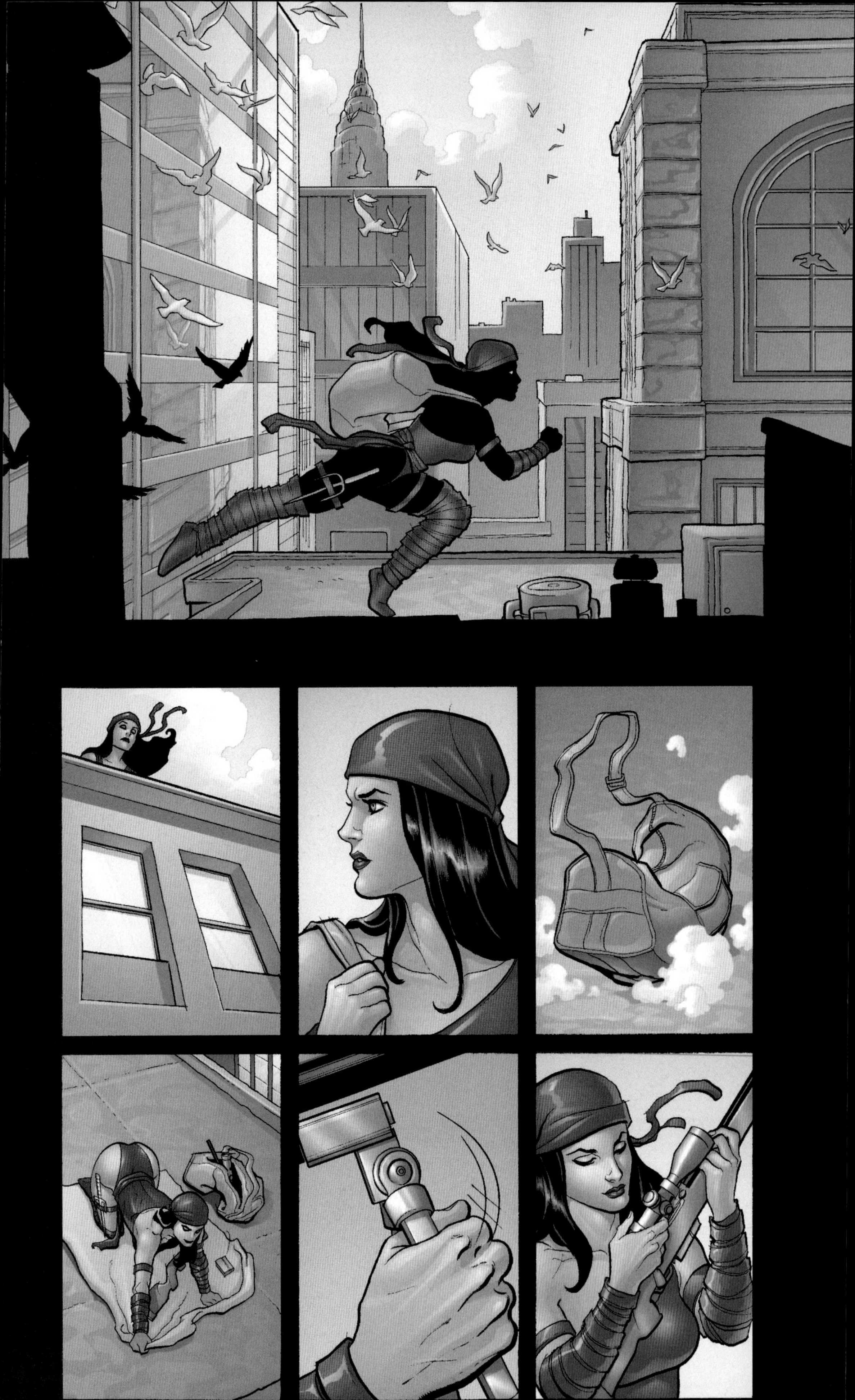

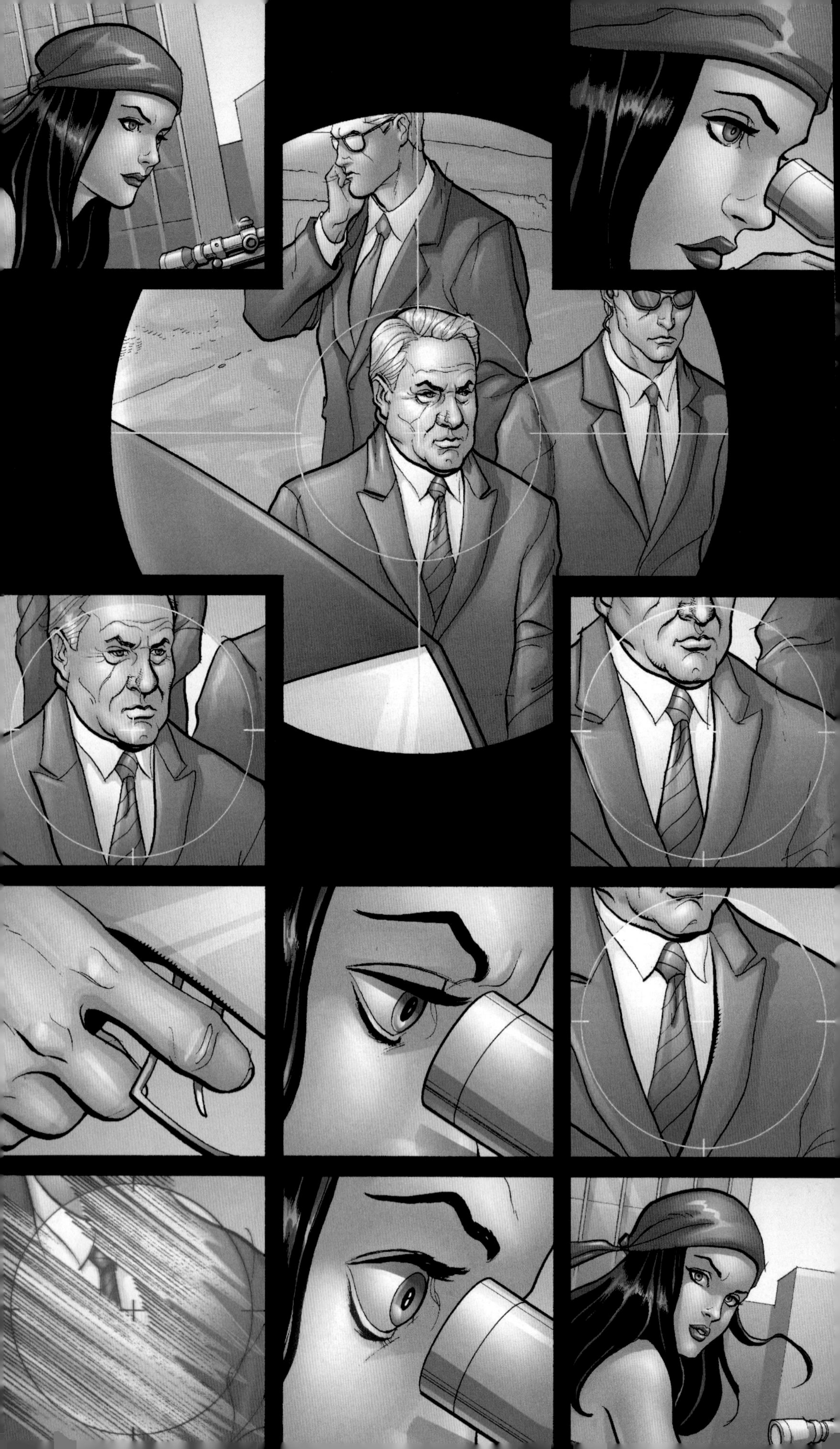

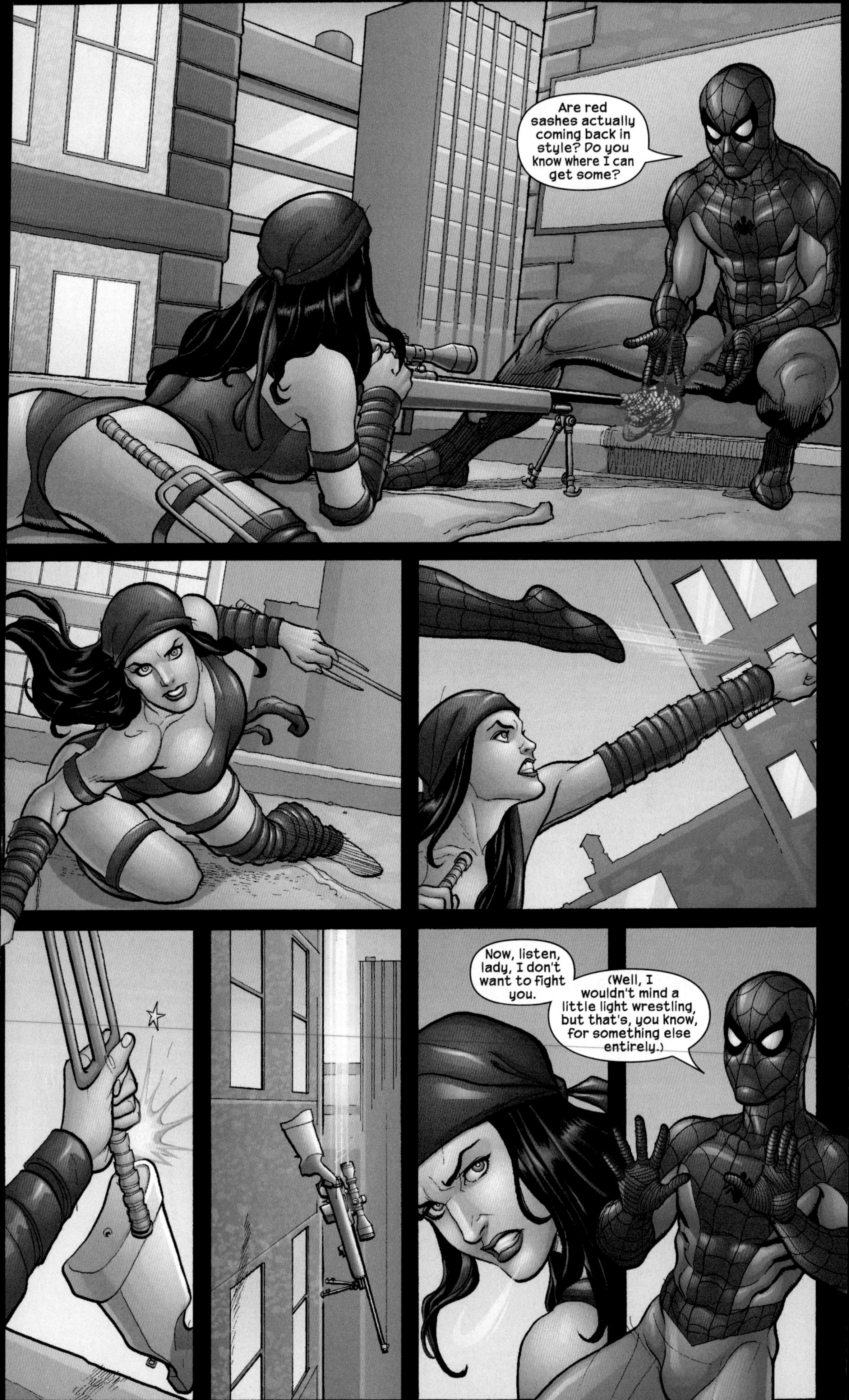
Are red sashes actually coming back in style? Do you know where I can get some?
Now, listen, lady, I don't want to fight you.
(Well, I wouldn't mind a little light wrestling, but that's, you know, for something else entirely.)

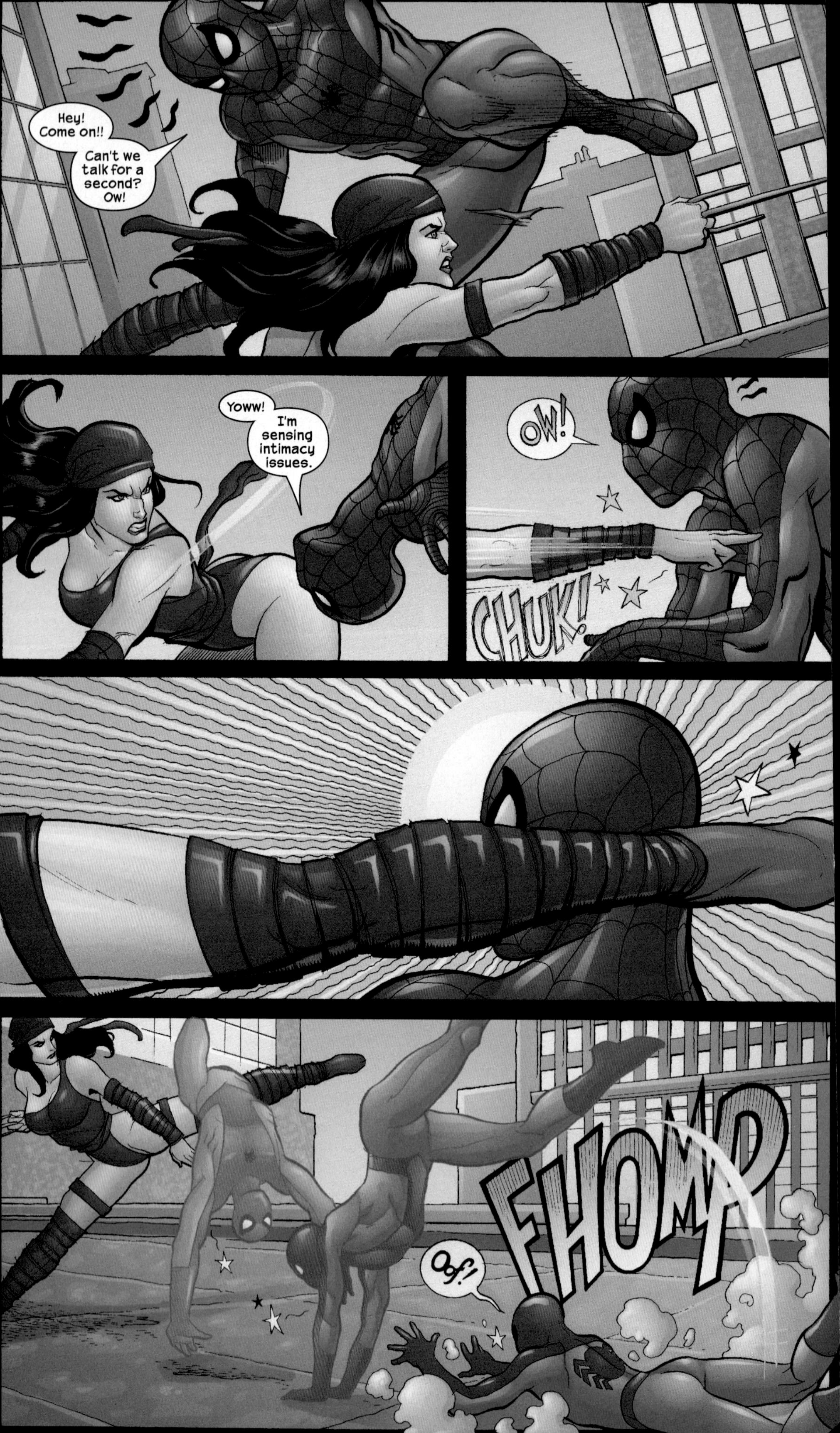
Hey! Come on!!
Can't we talk for a second? Ow!
YOWW! I'm sensing intimacy issues.
OW!
CHUK!
FHOMP
Oof!

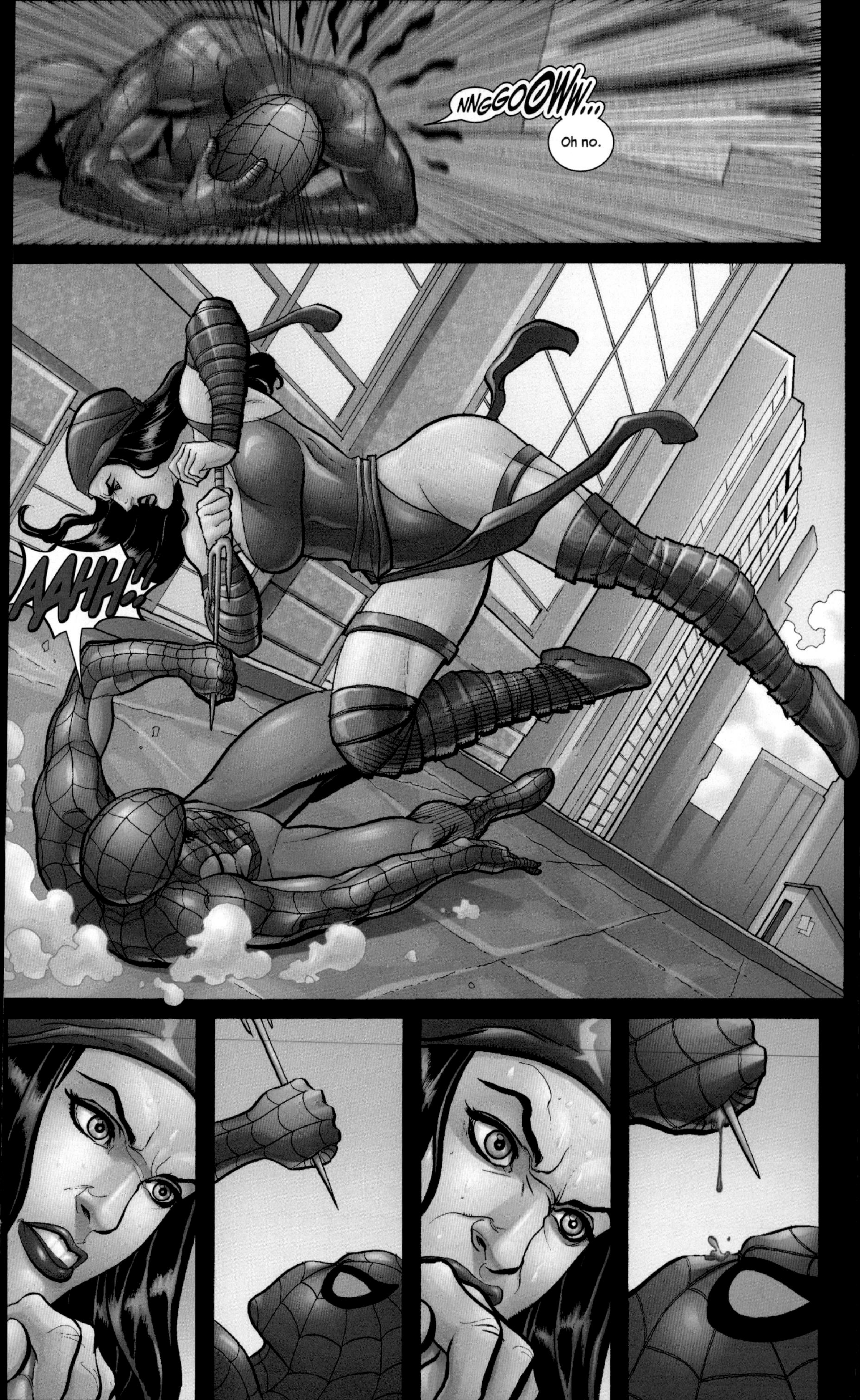
NNGGOOWW...
Oh no.
AAHH!!

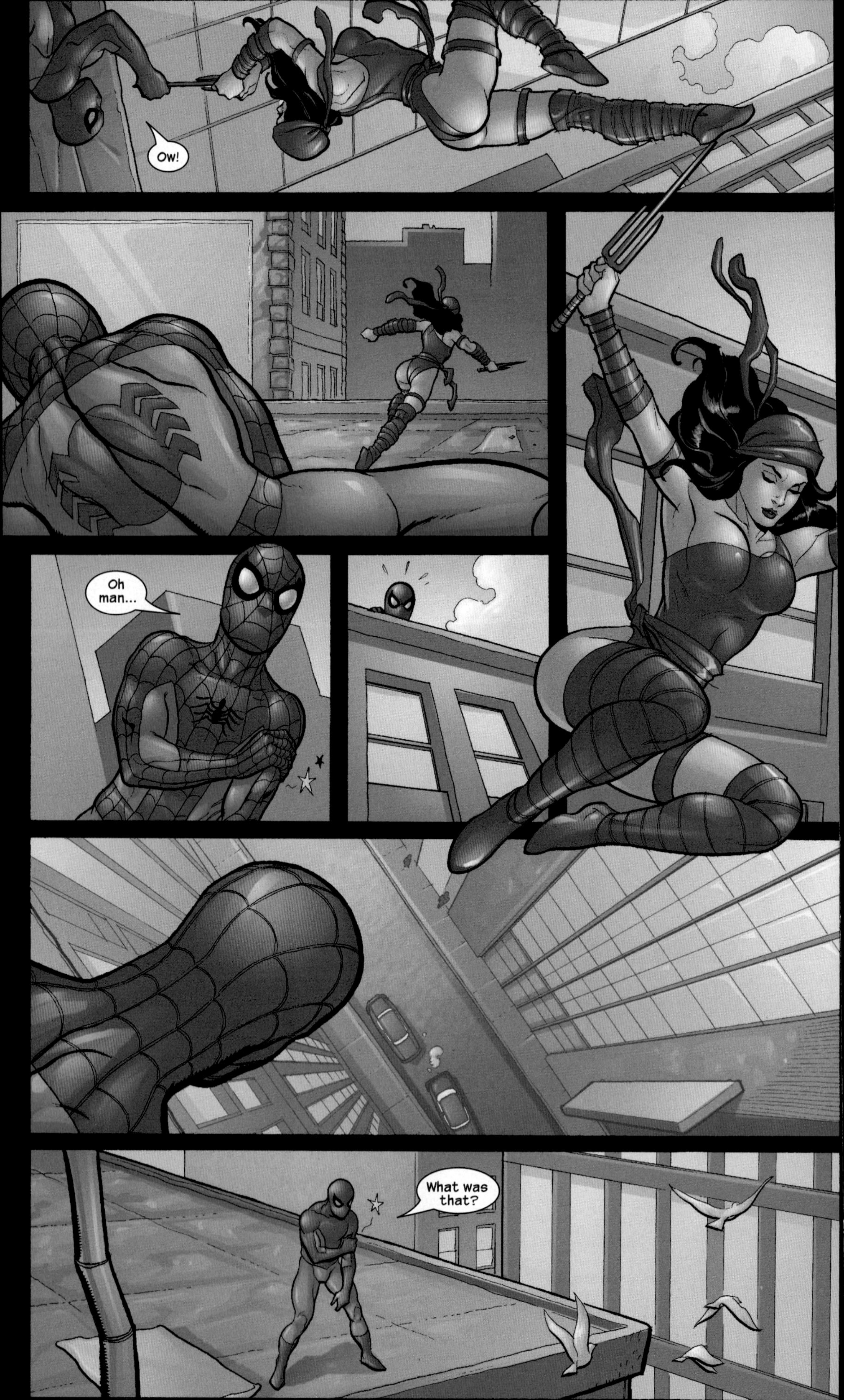
Ow!
Oh man...
What was that?

I know I just said this a second ago--

--but wow.

Okay, so check this then...

TAP

Real name:
Elektra Natchios
Occupation:
Assassin for hire
Base of operations:
Mobile
Rumored expertise:
Martial arts. Skills of the ancient Ninja of Japan.
Olympic-level athlete and gymnast.
Wields a pair of three-pronged daggers called
Sai -- though she also is proficient with a multitude
of martial arts weaponry.

What is this?

That's her?

What web site is this?

It's one of those cheesy web sites about serial killers and assassins.

And this is her?

Pretty sure. It's not a face you forget.

How did you find this?

I searched the web.

I can never find anything on the web.

You just need that extra bit of the obsessive compulsive, like me.

I guess.

"Elektra."

Real name:
Elektra Natch...
Occupation:
Assassin for hire
Base of op...
Mobile
Rumored e...
Martial ar... ...cient Ninja of Japan.
Olympic-level ...lete and gymnast.
Wields a pair o... ...ree-pronged daggers called
Sai -- though sh... ...also is proficient with a multitude
of martial arts w...aponry.

Elektra.

This is my life. People like this.

Thing is-- I still don't know what was going on.

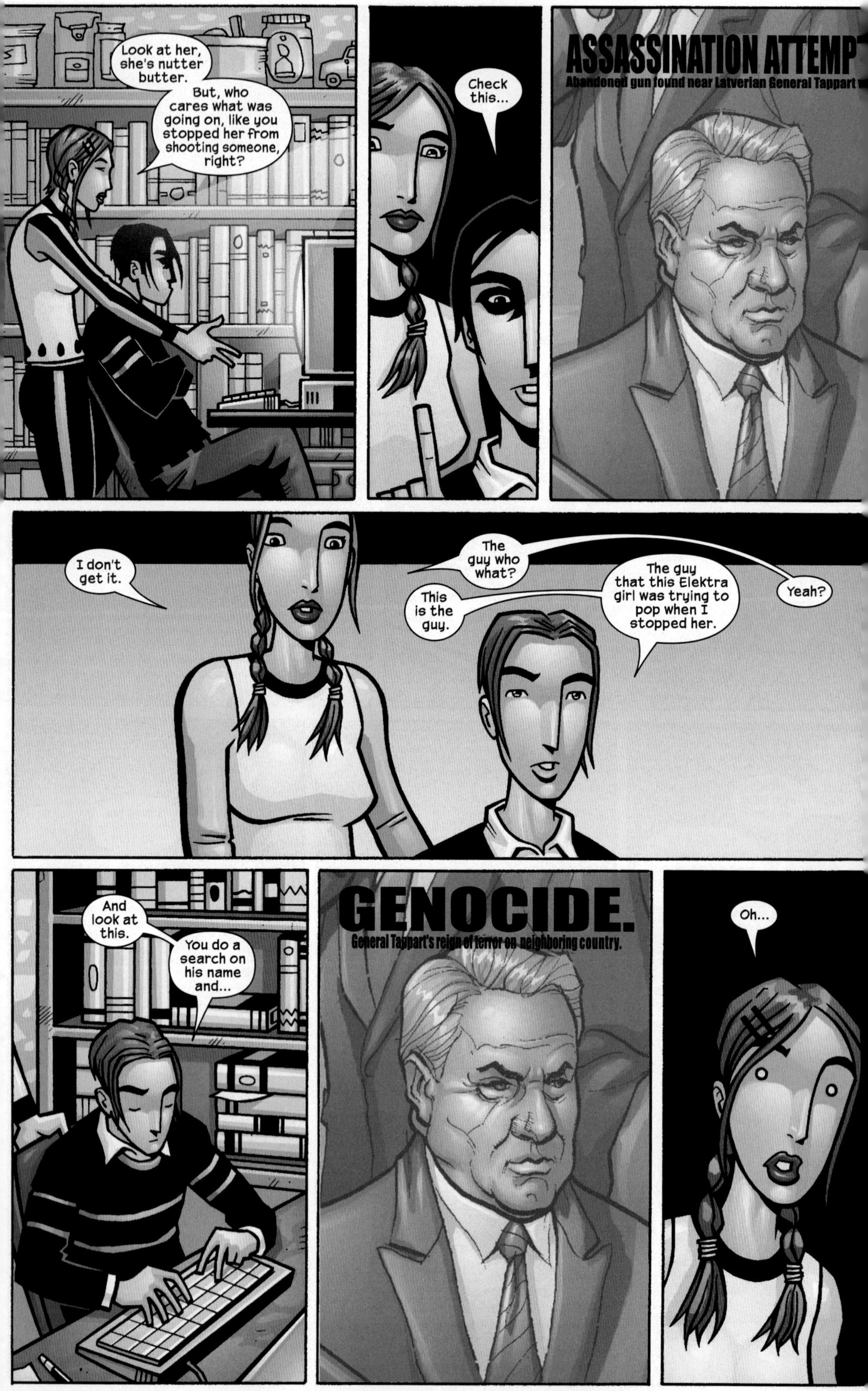
Look at her, she's nutter butter.
But, who cares what was going on, like you stopped her from shooting someone, right?
Check this...
ASSASSINATION ATTEMP
Abandoned gun found near Latverian General Tappart
I don't get it.
The guy who what?
This is the guy.
The guy that this Elektra girl was trying to pop when I stopped her.
Yeah?
And look at this.
You do a search on his name and...
GENOCIDE.
General Tappart's reign of terror on neighboring country.
Oh...

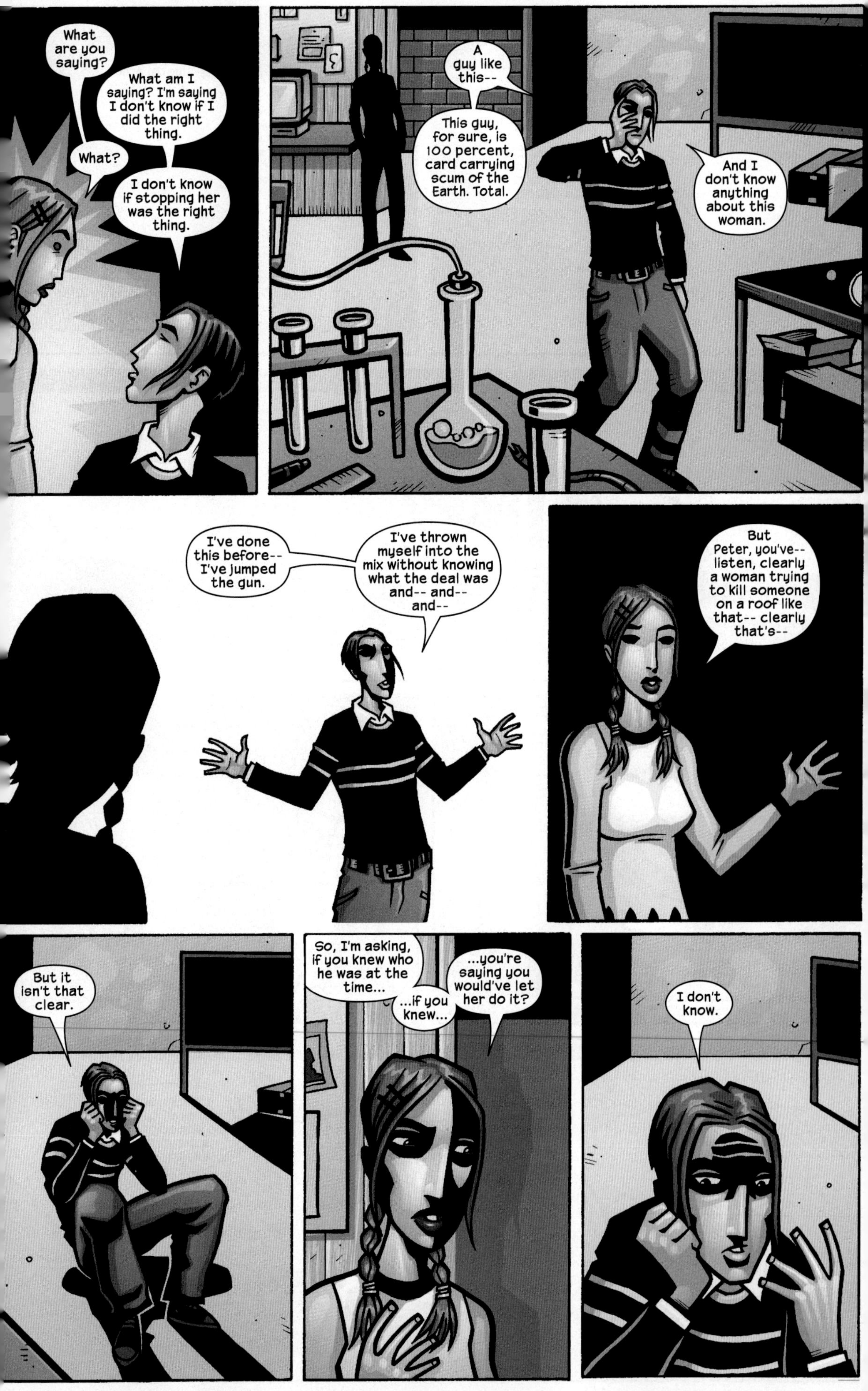
What are you saying?
What am I saying? I'm saying I don't know if I did the right thing.
What?
I don't know if stopping her was the right thing.
A guy like this--
This guy, for sure, is 100 percent, card carrying scum of the Earth. Total.
And I don't know anything about this woman.
I've done this before-- I've jumped the gun.
I've thrown myself into the mix without knowing what the deal was and-- and-- and--
But Peter, you've-- listen, clearly a woman trying to kill someone on a roof like that-- clearly that's--
But it isn't that clear.
So, I'm asking, if you knew who he was at the time...
...if you knew...
...you're saying you would've let her do it?
I don't know.

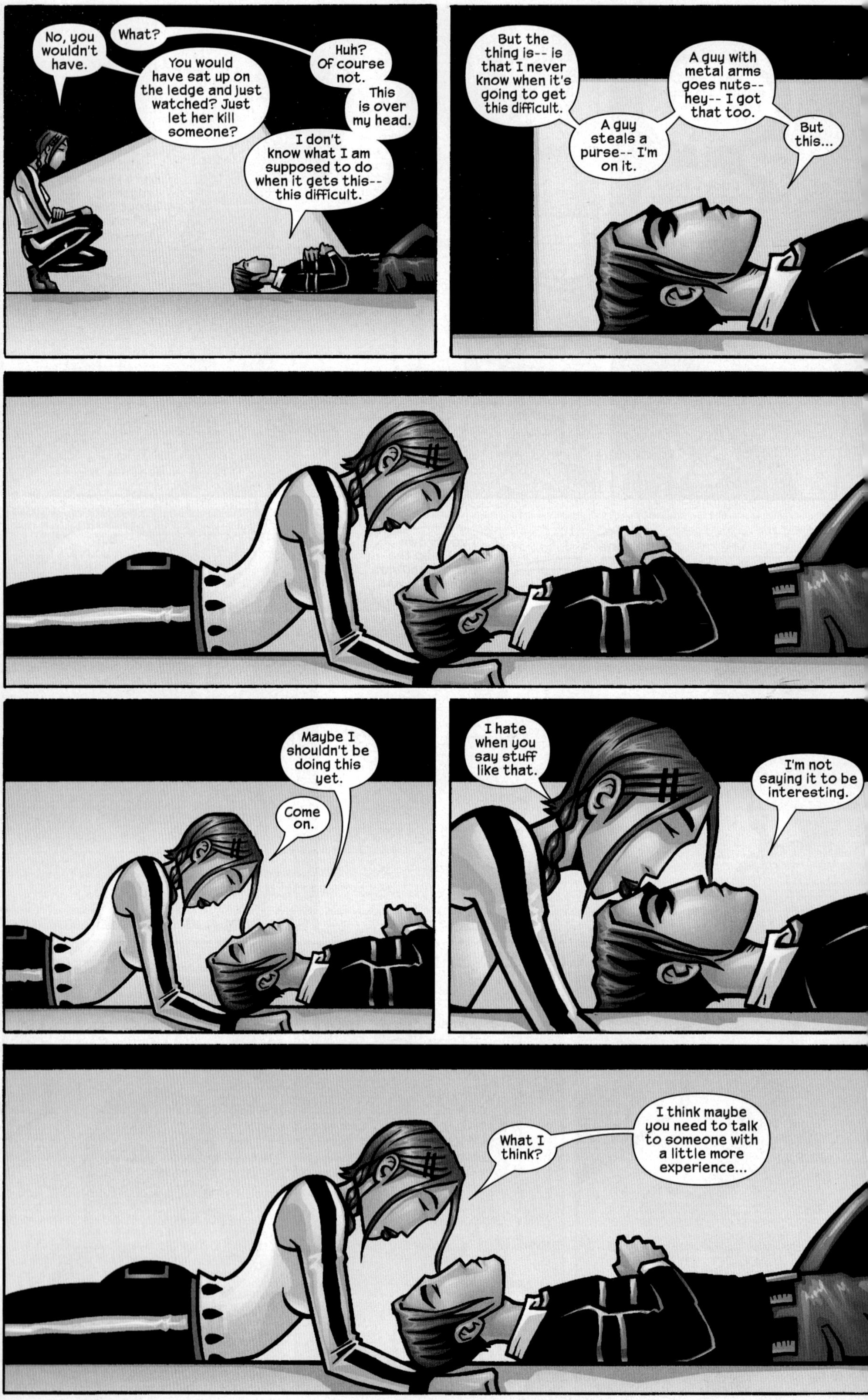
No, you wouldn't have.
What?
You would have sat up on the ledge and just watched? Just let her kill someone?
Huh? Of course not.
This is over my head.
I don't know what I am supposed to do when it gets this-- this difficult.
But the thing is-- is that I never know when it's going to get this difficult.
A guy steals a purse-- I'm on it.
A guy with metal arms goes nuts-- hey-- I got that too.
But this...
Maybe I shouldn't be doing this yet.
Come on.
I hate when you say stuff like that.
I'm not saying it to be interesting.
What I think?
I think maybe you need to talk to someone with a little more experience...

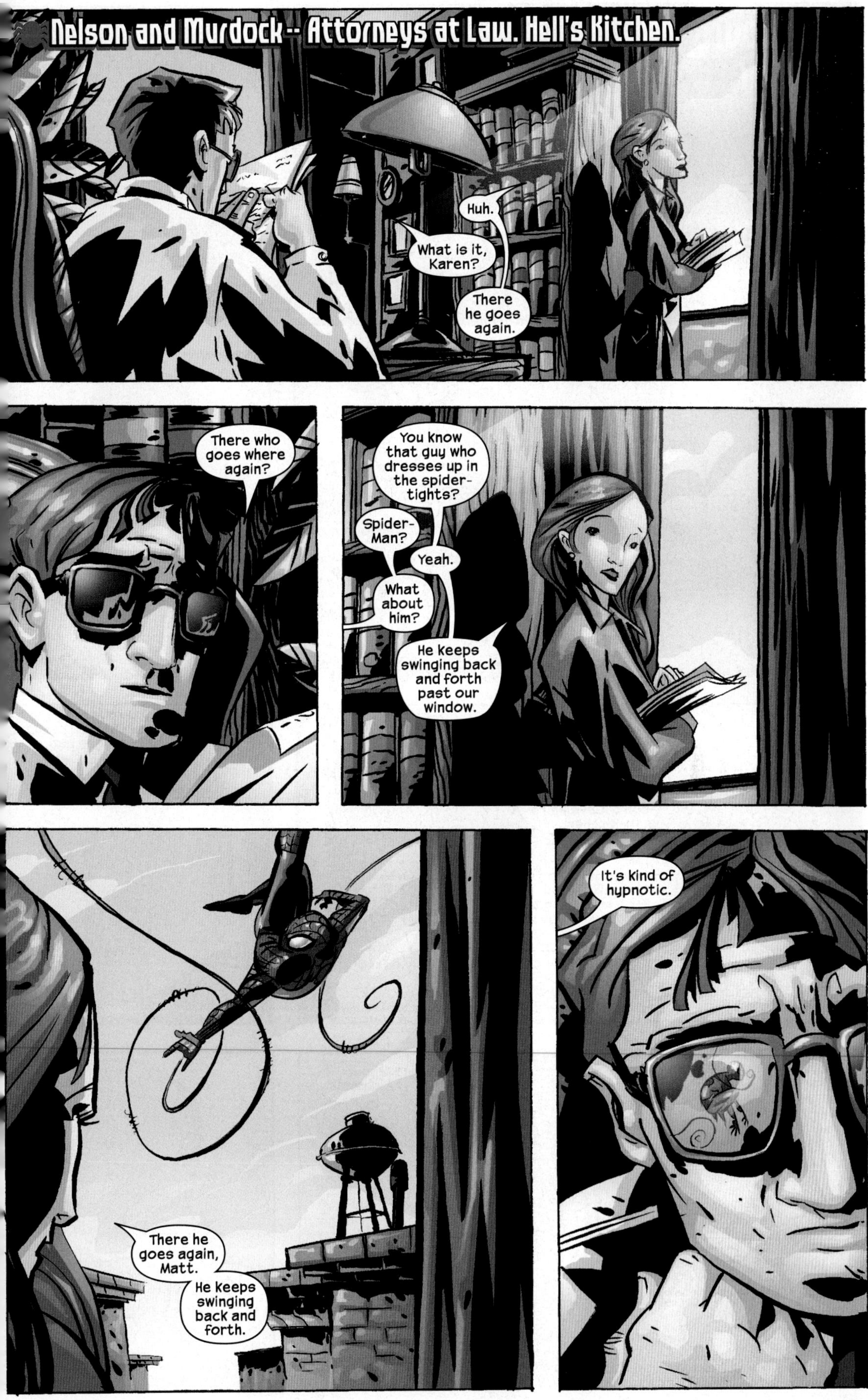

Nelson and Murdock -- Attorneys at Law. Hell's Kitchen.
Huh.
What is it, Karen?
There he goes again.
There who goes where again?
You know that guy who dresses up in the spider-tights?
Spider-Man?
Yeah.
What about him?
He keeps swinging back and forth past our window.
There he goes again, Matt.
He keeps swinging back and forth.
It's kind of hypnotic.

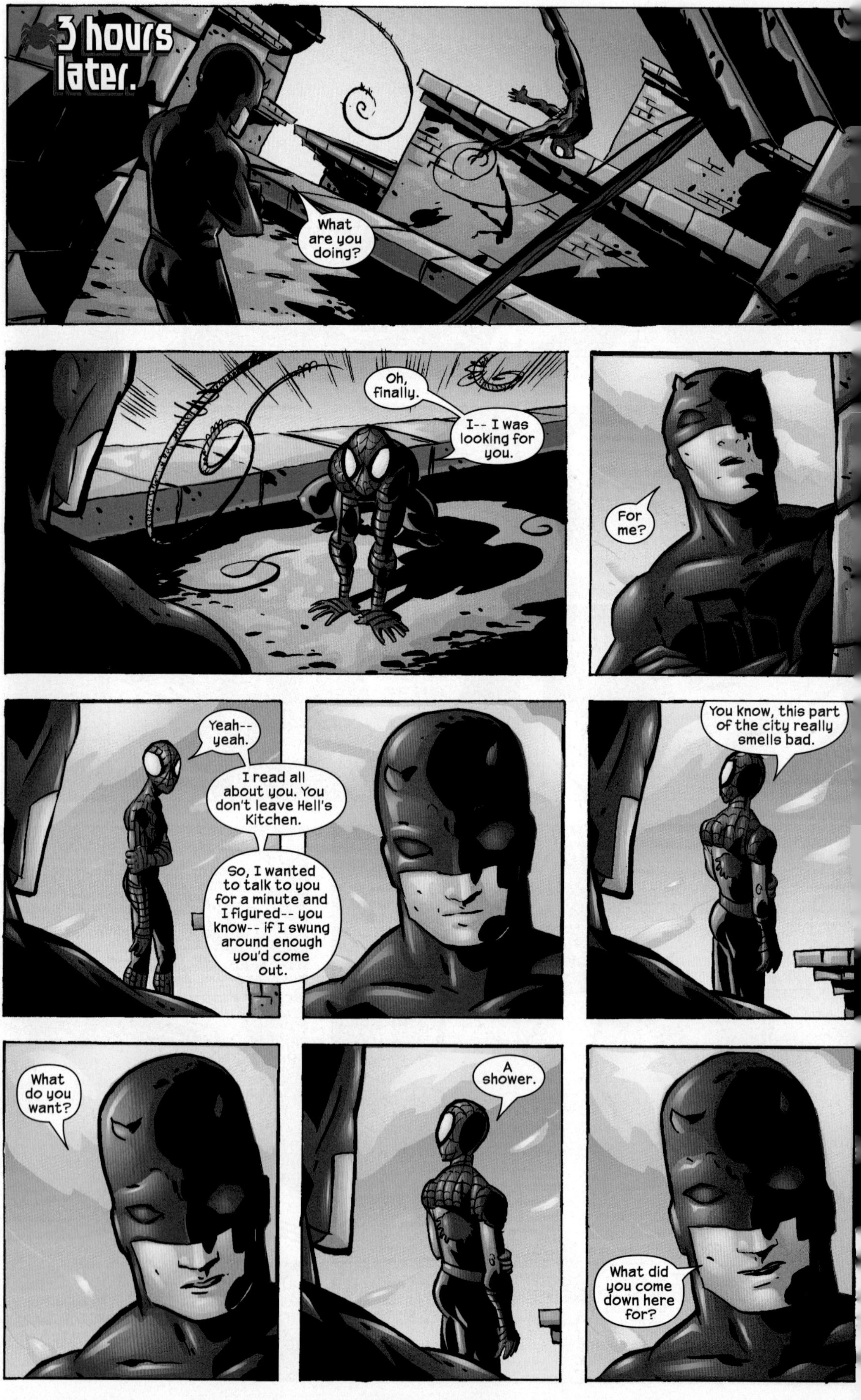
3 hours later.
What are you doing?
Oh, finally.
I-- I was looking for you.
For me?
Yeah-- yeah.
I read all about you. You don't leave Hell's Kitchen.
So, I wanted to talk to you for a minute and I figured-- you know-- if I swung around enough you'd come out.
You know, this part of the city really smells bad.
What do you want?
A shower.
What did you come down here for?

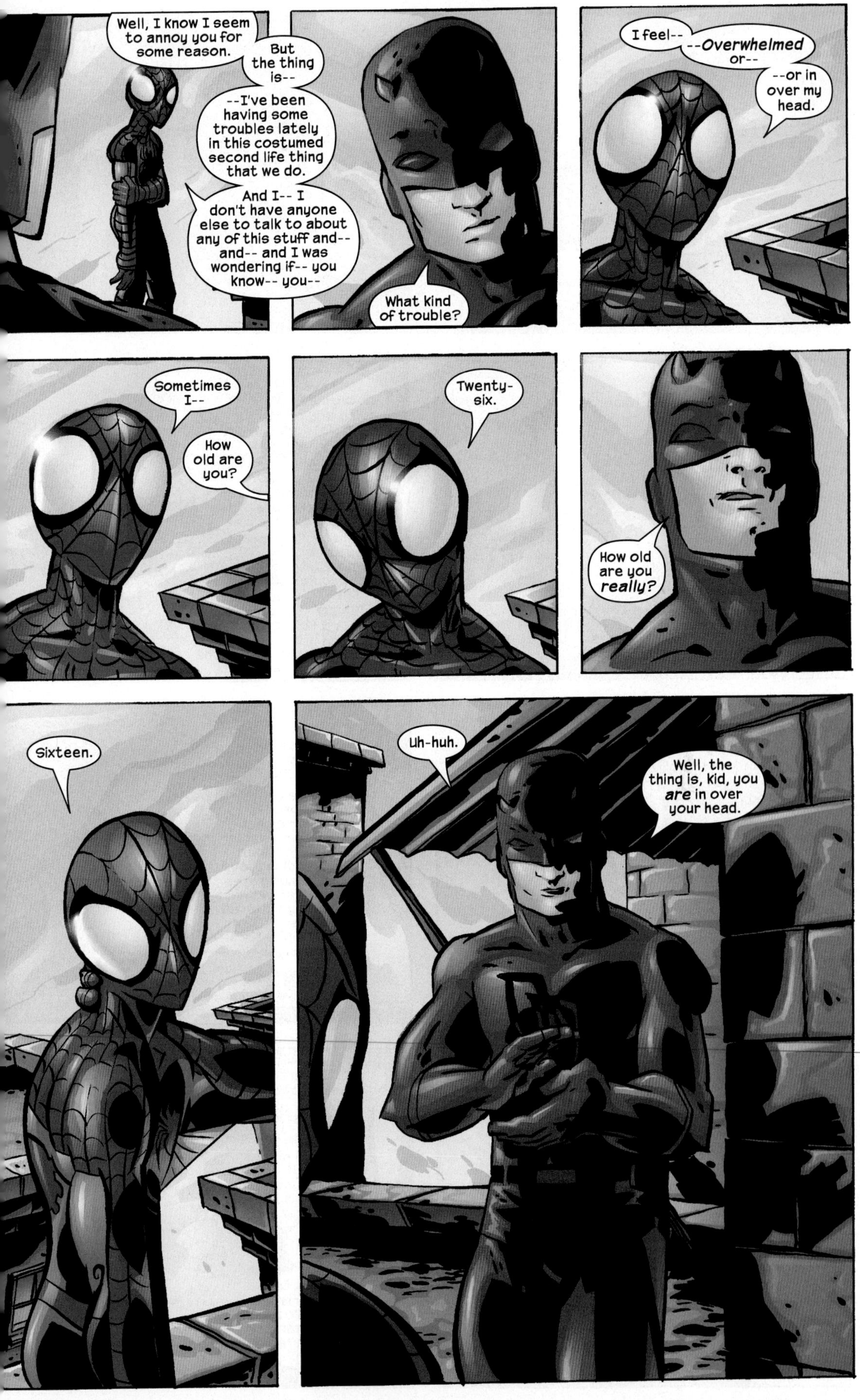
Well, I know I seem to annoy you for some reason.
But the thing is--
--I've been having some troubles lately in this costumed second life thing that we do.
And I-- I don't have anyone else to talk to about any of this stuff and-- and-- and I was wondering if-- you know-- you--
What kind of trouble?
I feel--
--Overwhelmed or--
--or in over my head.
Sometimes I--
How old are you?
Twenty-six.
How old are you really?
Sixteen.
Uh-huh.
Well, the thing is, kid, you are in over your head.

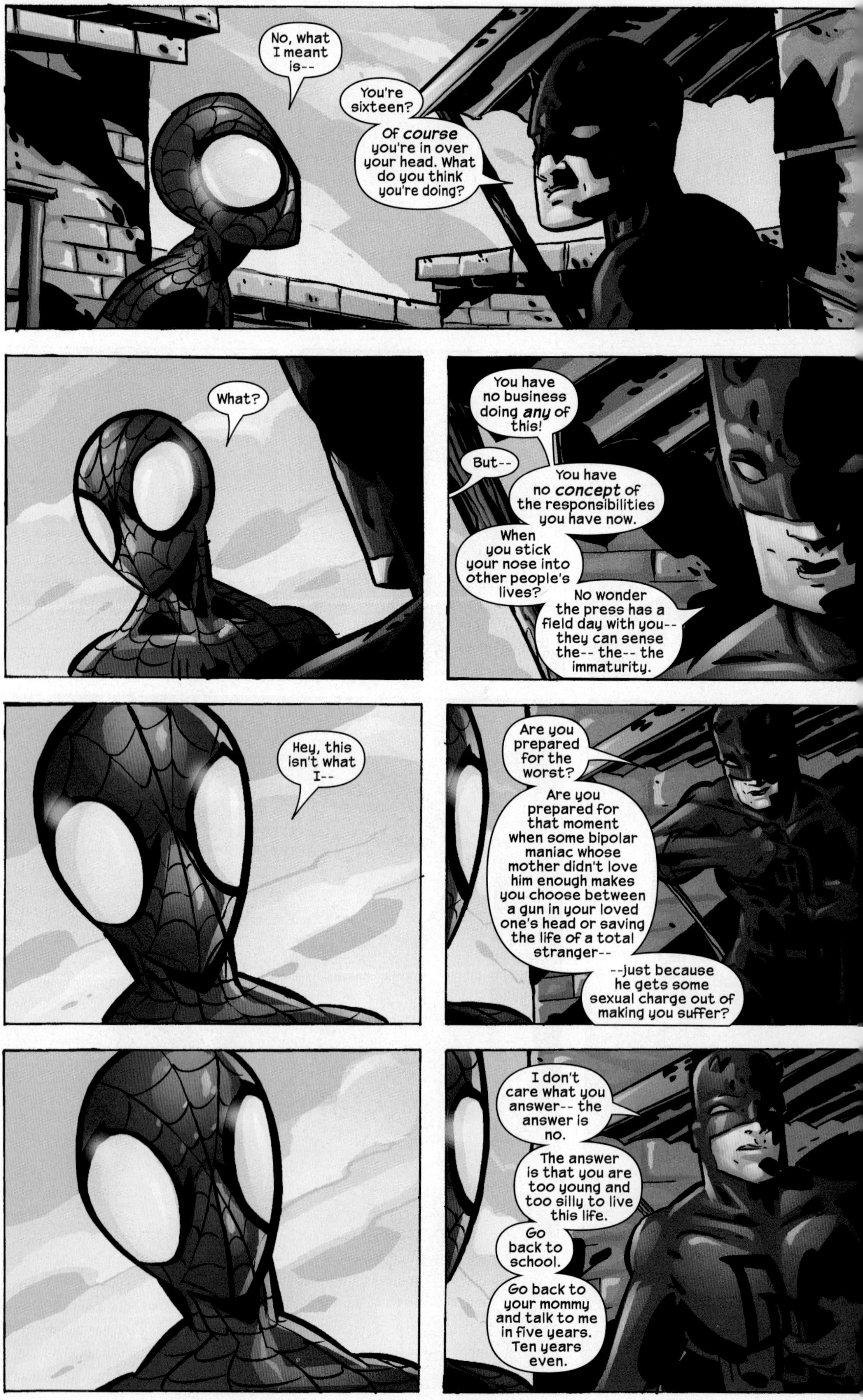
No, what I meant is--
You're sixteen?
Of *course* you're in over your head. What do you think you're doing?
What?
You have no business doing *any* of this!
But--
You have no *concept* of the responsibilities you have now.
When you stick your nose into other people's lives?
No wonder the press has a field day with you-- they can sense the-- the-- the immaturity.
Hey, this isn't what I--
Are you prepared for the worst?
Are you prepared for that moment when some bipolar maniac whose mother didn't love him enough makes you choose between a gun in your loved one's head or saving the life of a total stranger--
--just because he gets some sexual charge out of making you suffer?
I don't care what you answer-- the answer is no.
The answer is that you are too young and too silly to live this life.
Go back to school.
Go back to your mommy and talk to me in five years. Ten years even.

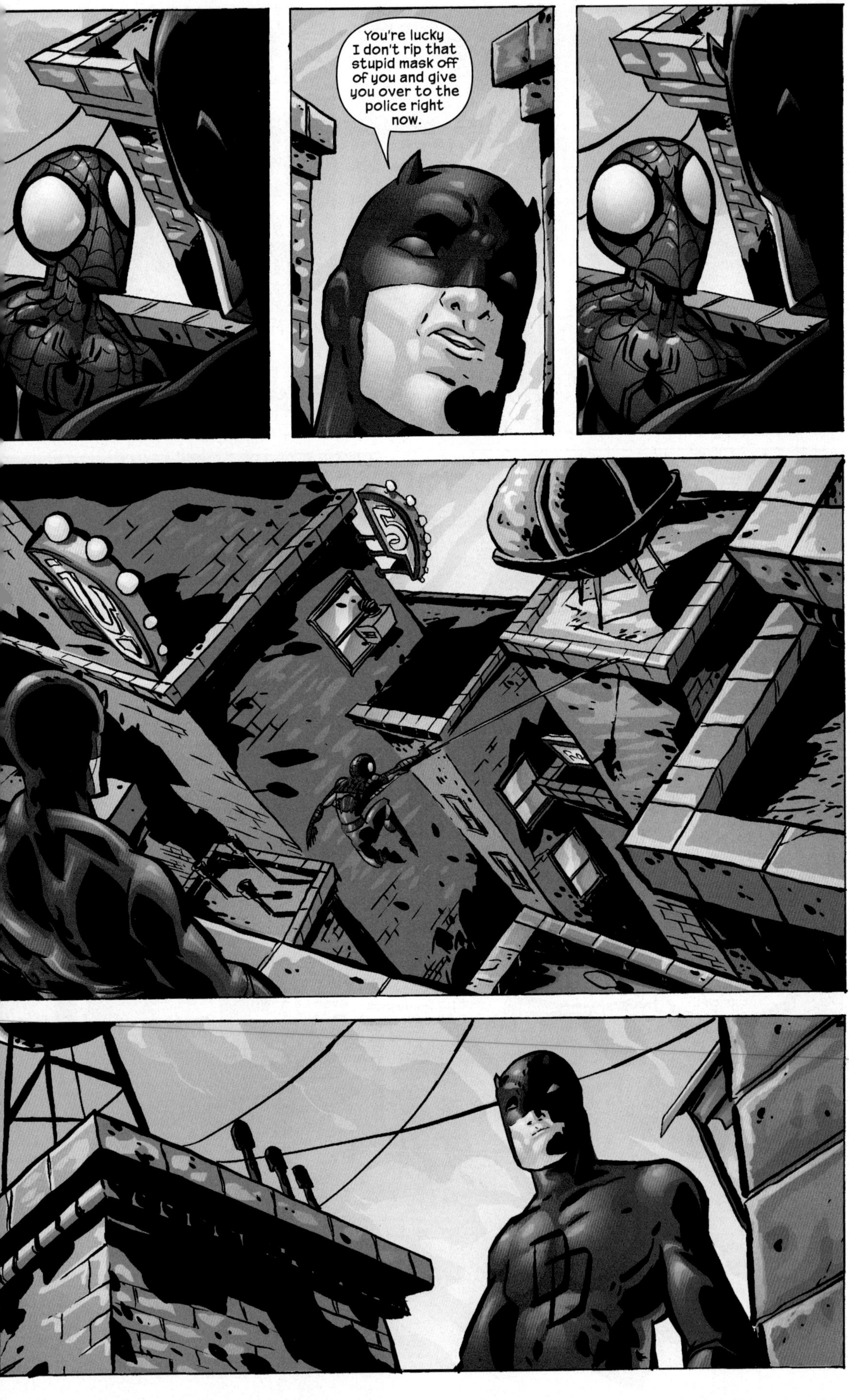
You're lucky I don't rip that stupid mask off of you and give you over to the police right now.

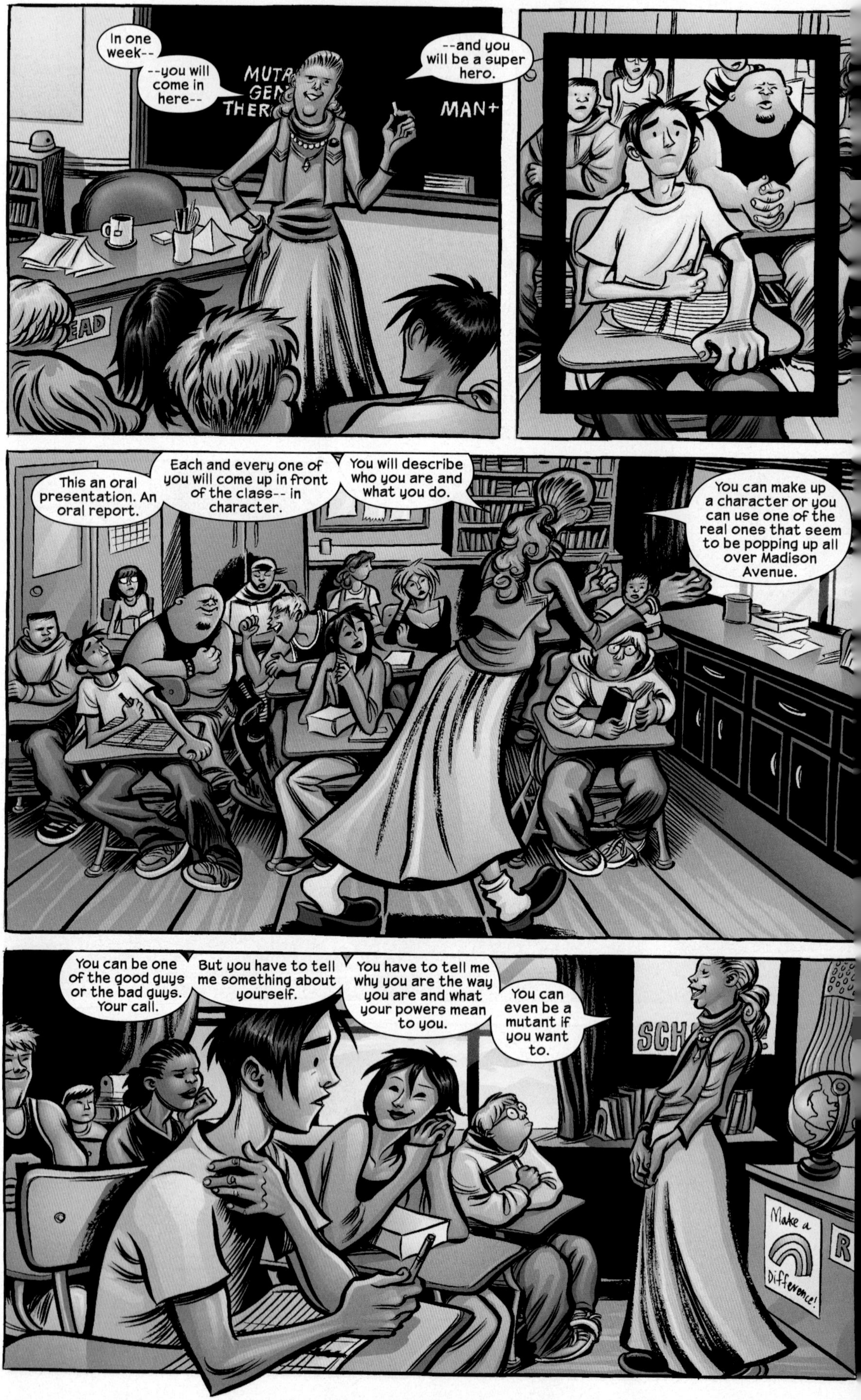
In one week--
--you will come in here--
MUTA
GEN
THER
MAN+
--and you will be a super hero.
This an oral presentation. An oral report.
Each and every one of you will come up in front of the class-- in character.
You will describe who you are and what you do.
You can make up a character or you can use one of the real ones that seem to be popping up all over Madison Avenue.
You can be one of the good guys or the bad guys. Your call.
But you have to tell me something about yourself.
You have to tell me why you are the way you are and what your powers mean to you.
You can even be a mutant if you want to.
Make a Difference!

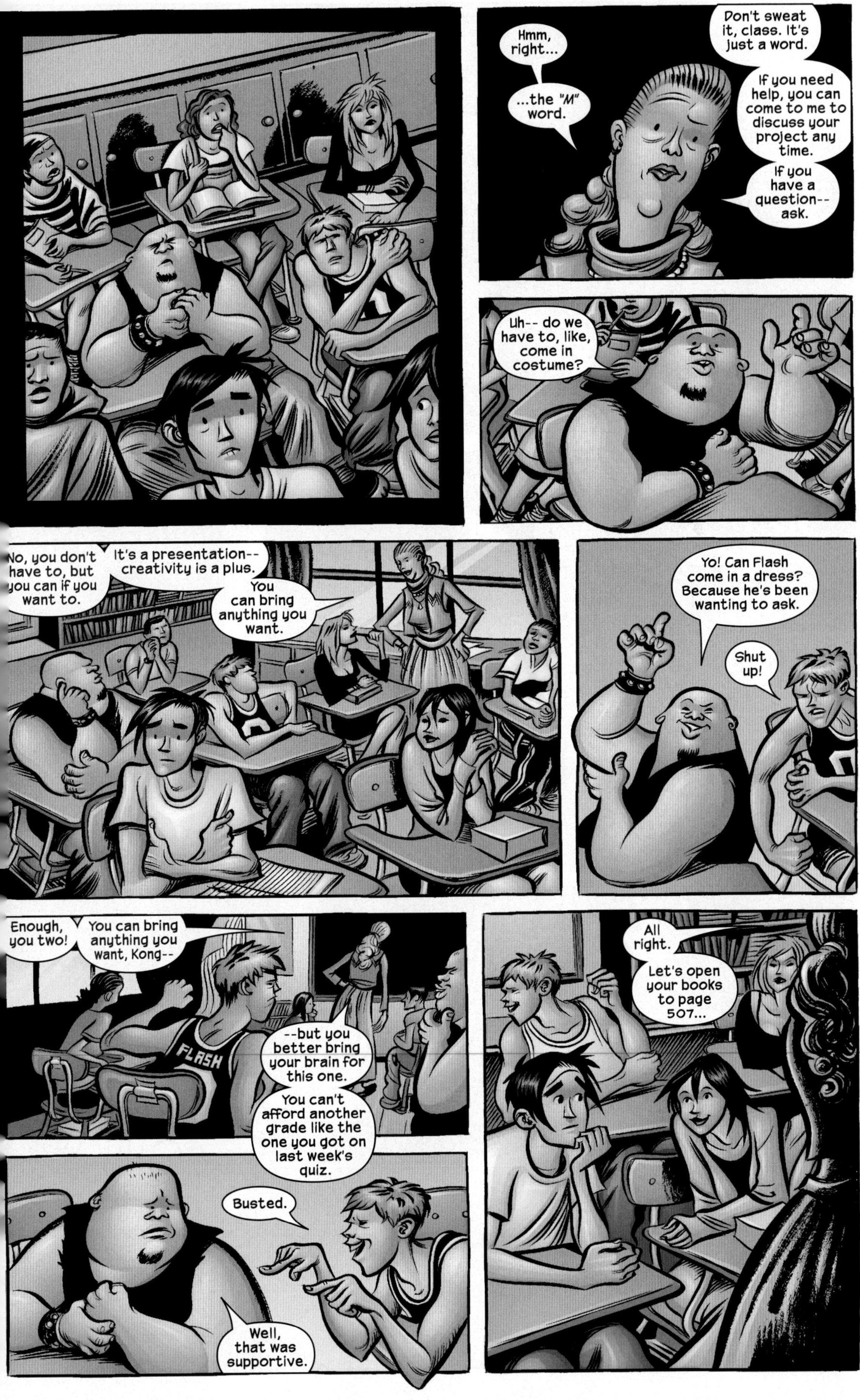
Hmm, right...
...the "M" word.
Don't sweat it, class. It's just a word.
If you need help, you can come to me to discuss your project any time.
If you have a question-- ask.
Uh-- do we have to, like, come in costume?
No, you don't have to, but you can if you want to.
It's a presentation-- creativity is a plus.
You can bring anything you want.
Yo! Can Flash come in a dress? Because he's been wanting to ask.
Shut up!
Enough, you two!
You can bring anything you want, Kong--
--but you better bring your brain for this one.
You can't afford another grade like the one you got on last week's quiz.
Busted.
Well, that was supportive.
All right.
Let's open your books to page 507...

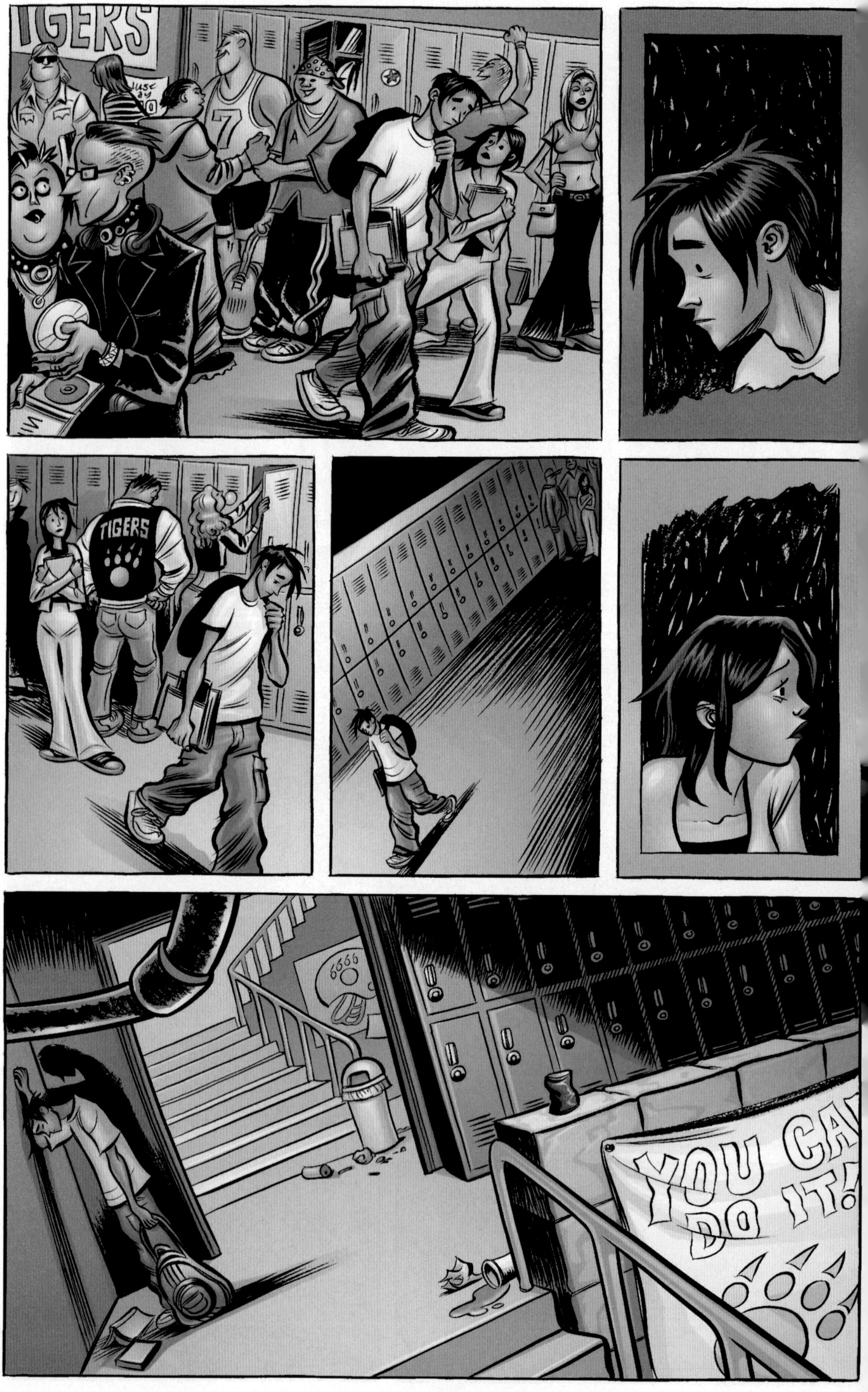
IGERS
TIGERS
YOU CA
DO IT!

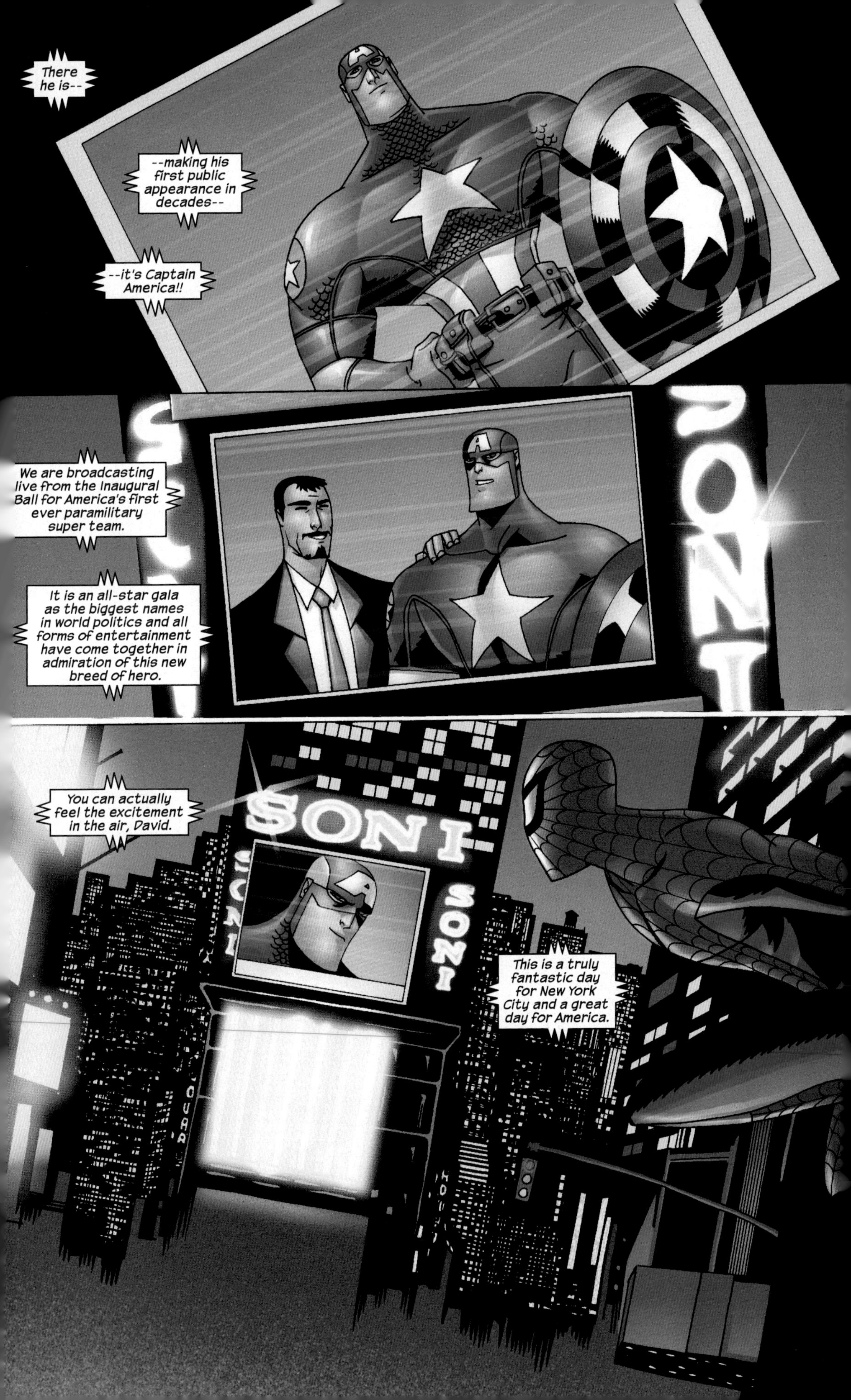
There he is--
--making his first public appearance in decades--
--it's Captain America!!
We are broadcasting live from the Inaugural Ball for America's first ever paramilitary super team.
It is an all-star gala as the biggest names in world politics and all forms of entertainment have come together in admiration of this new breed of hero.
SONI
You can actually feel the excitement in the air, David.
SONI
SONI
SONI
This is a truly fantastic day for New York City and a great day for America.

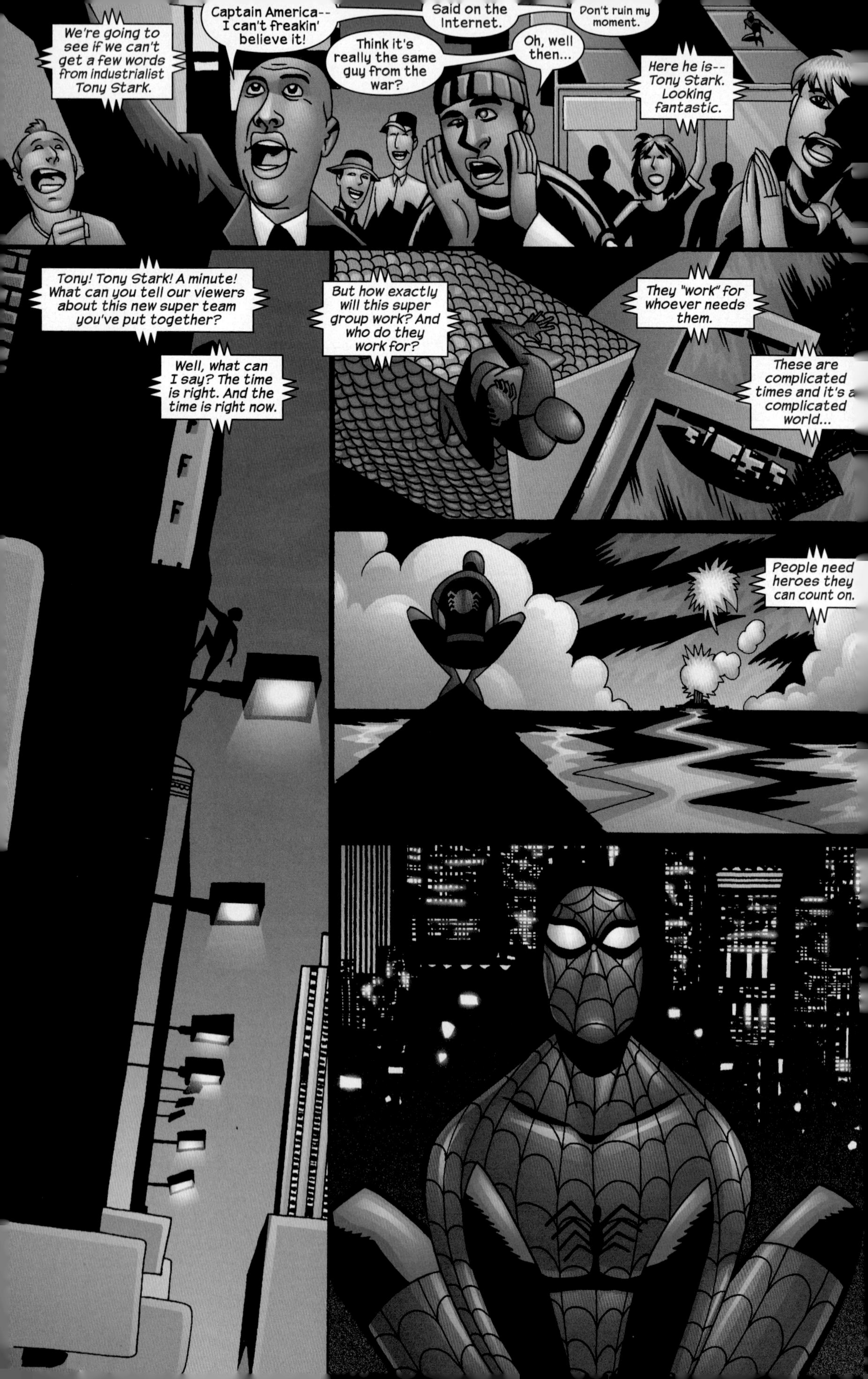
We're going to see if we can't get a few words from industrialist Tony Stark.
Captain America-- I can't freakin' believe it!
Said on the Internet.
Don't ruin my moment.
Think it's really the same guy from the war?
Oh, well then...
Here he is-- Tony Stark. Looking fantastic.
Tony! Tony Stark! A minute! What can you tell our viewers about this new super team you've put together?
Well, what can I say? The time is right. And the time is right now.
But how exactly will this super group work? And who do they work for?
They "work" for whoever needs them.
These are complicated times and it's a complicated world...
People need heroes they can count on.

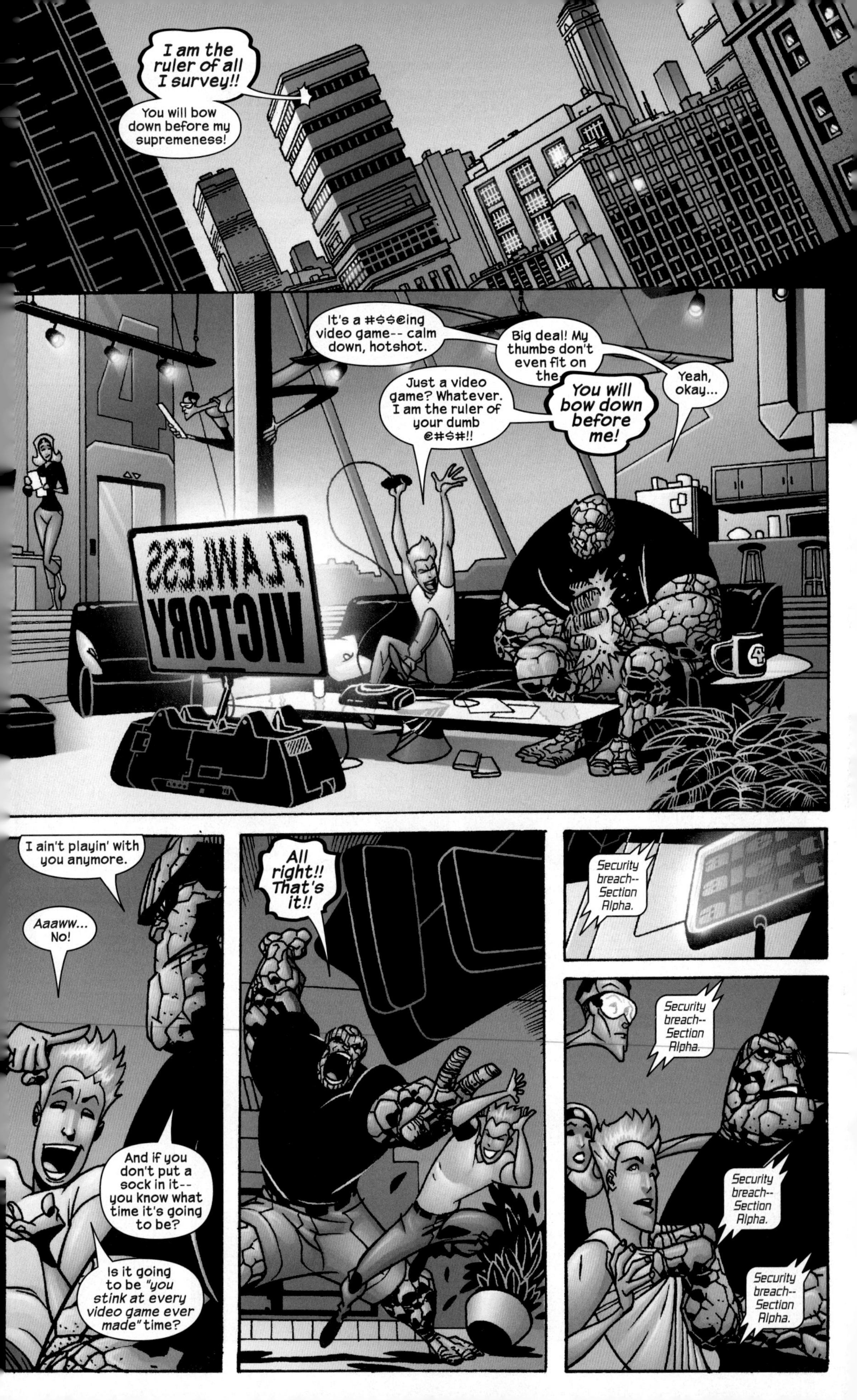

I am the ruler of all I survey!!
You will bow down before my supremeness!
It's a #$$@ing video game-- calm down, hotshot.
Big deal! My thumbs don't even fit on the.
Just a video game? Whatever. I am the ruler of your dumb @#$#!!
You will bow down before me!
Yeah, okay...
FLAWLESS VICTORY
I ain't playin' with you anymore.
Aaaww... No!
And if you don't put a sock in it-- you know what time it's going to be?
Is it going to be "you stink at every video game ever made" time?
All right!! That's it!!
Security breach-- Section Alpha.
Security breach-- Section Alpha.
Security breach-- Section Alpha.
Security breach-- Section Alpha.

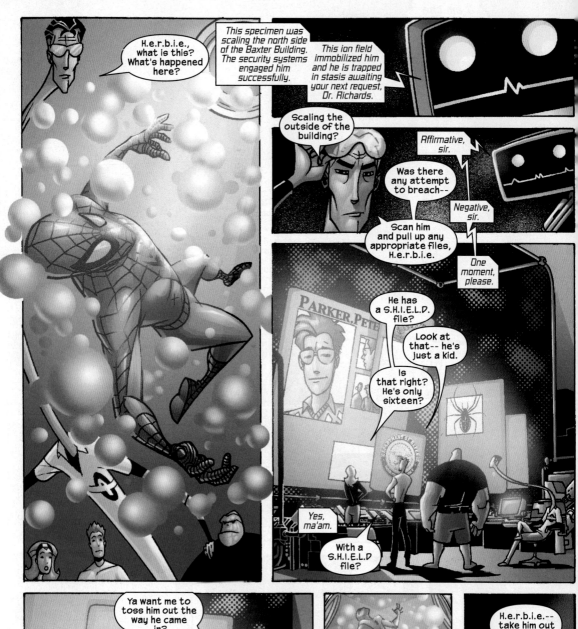

H.e.r.b.i.e., what is this? What's happened here?

This specimen was scaling the north side of the Baxter Building. The security systems engaged him successfully.

This ion field immobilized him and he is trapped in stasis awaiting your next request, Dr. Richards.

Scaling the outside of the building?

Affirmative, sir.

Was there any attempt to breach--

Negative, sir.

Scan him and pull up any appropriate files, H.e.r.b.i.e.

One moment, please.

PARKER, Pete

He has a S.H.I.E.L.D. file?

Look at that-- he's just a kid.

Is that right? He's only sixteen?

Yes, ma'am.

With a S.H.I.E.L.D file?

Ya want me to toss him out the way he came in?

Look at that! Look who his father was.

Hey, I know that name.

H.e.r.b.i.e.-- take him out of stasis.

One moment, please.

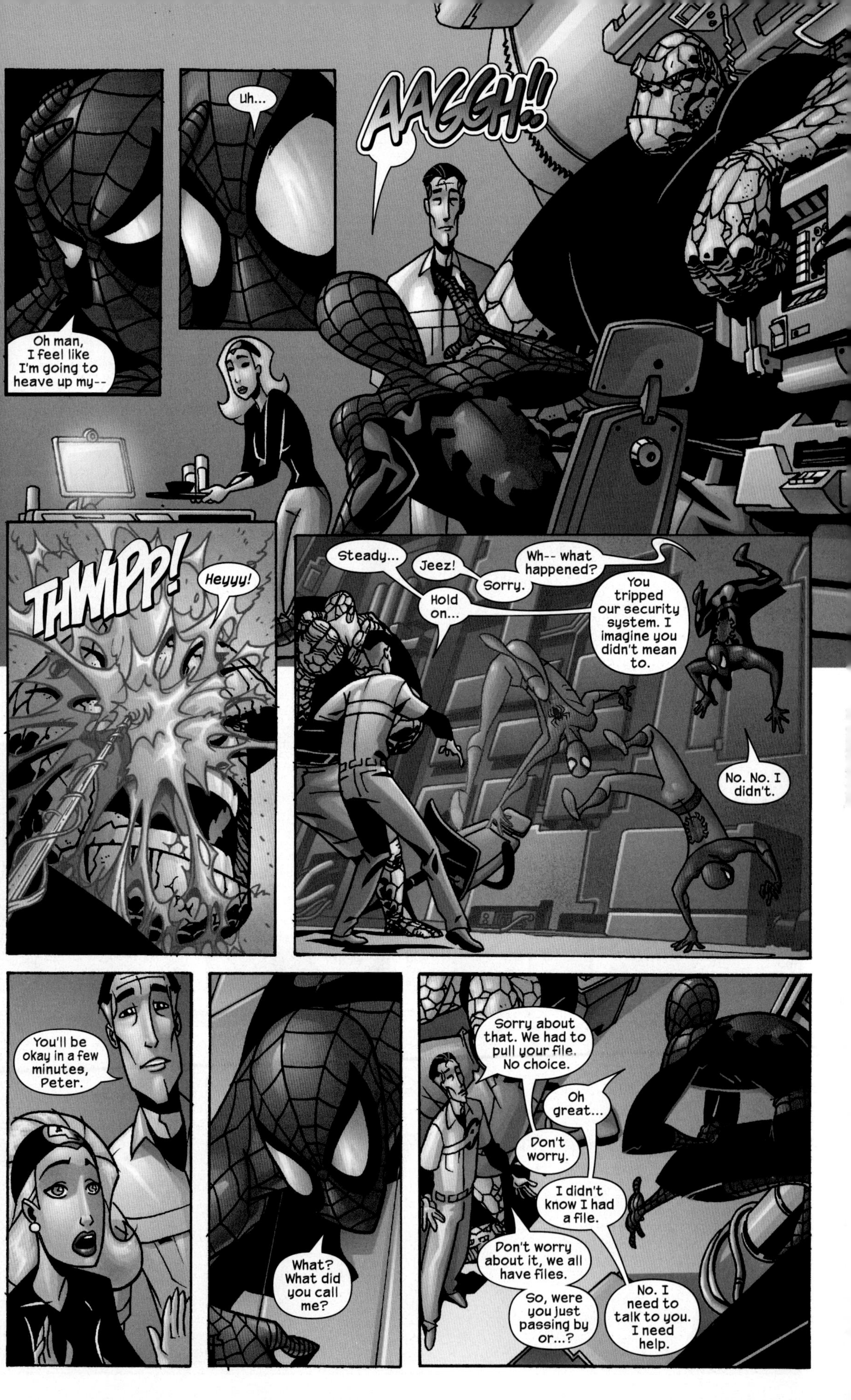

Oh man, I feel like I'm going to heave up my--
Uh...
AAGGH!!
THWIPP!
Heyyy!
Steady...
Jeez!
Sorry.
Wh-- what happened?
Hold on...
You tripped our security system. I imagine you didn't mean to.
No. No. I didn't.
You'll be okay in a few minutes, Peter.
What? What did you call me?
Sorry about that. We had to pull your file. No choice.
Oh great...
Don't worry.
I didn't know I had a file.
Don't worry about it, we all have files.
So, were you just passing by or...?
No. I need to talk to you. I need help.

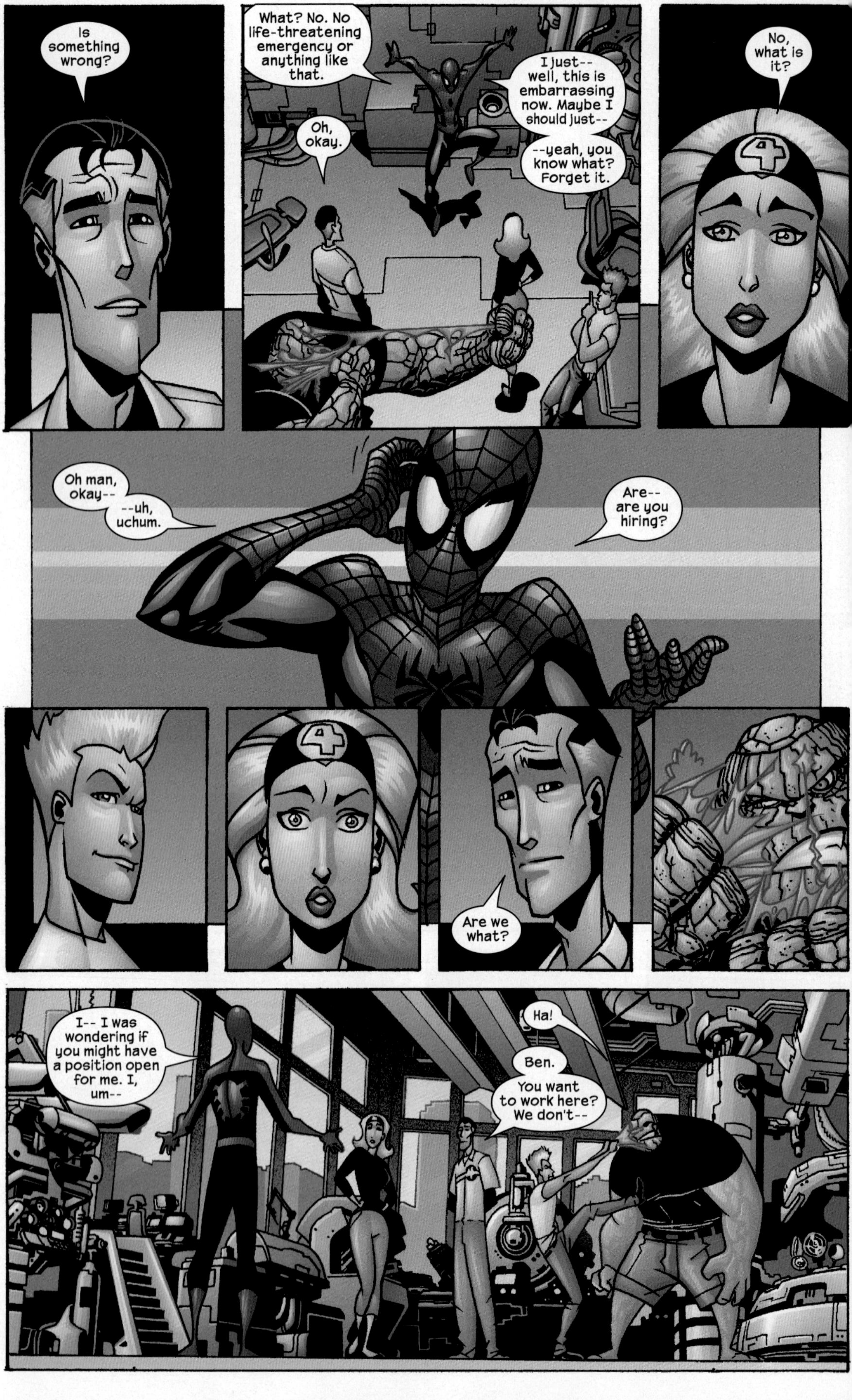
Is something wrong?
What? No. No life-threatening emergency or anything like that.
Oh, okay.
I just-- well, this is embarrassing now. Maybe I should just--
--yeah, you know what? Forget it.
No, what is it?
Oh man, okay--
--uh, uchum.
Are-- are you hiring?
Are we what?
I-- I was wondering if you might have a position open for me. I, um--
Ha!
Ben.
You want to work here? We don't--

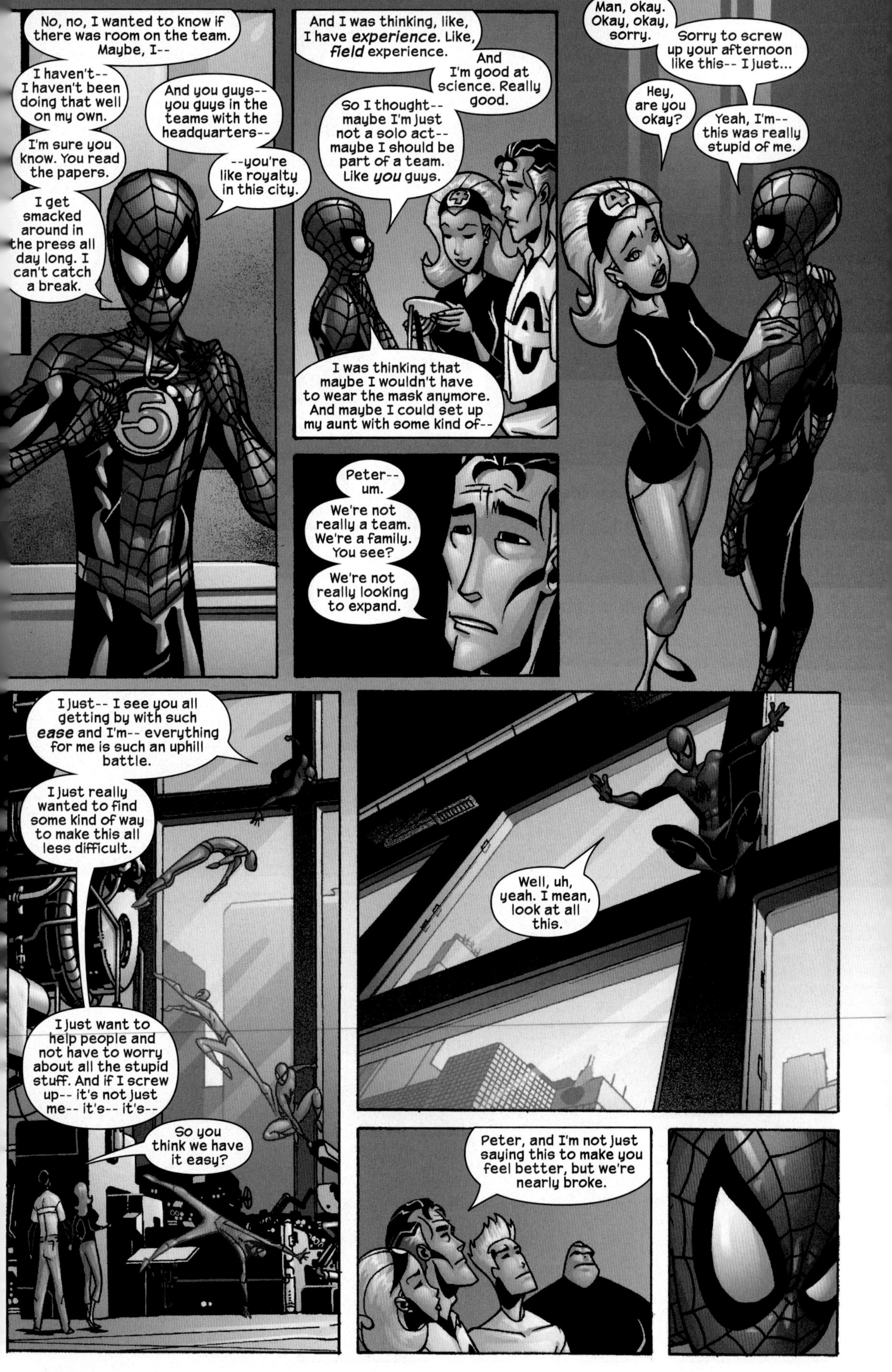

No, no, I wanted to know if there was room on the team. Maybe, I--
I haven't-- I haven't been doing that well on my own.
I'm sure you know. You read the papers.
I get smacked around in the press all day long. I can't catch a break.
And you guys-- you guys in the teams with the headquarters--
--you're like royalty in this city.
And I was thinking, like, I have experience. Like, field experience.
And I'm good at science. Really good.
So I thought-- maybe I'm just not a solo act-- maybe I should be part of a team. Like you guys.
I was thinking that maybe I wouldn't have to wear the mask anymore. And maybe I could set up my aunt with some kind of--
Peter-- um.
We're not really a team. We're a family. You see?
We're not really looking to expand.
Man, okay. Okay, okay, sorry.
Sorry to screw up your afternoon like this-- I just...
Hey, are you okay?
Yeah, I'm-- this was really stupid of me.
I just-- I see you all getting by with such ease and I'm-- everything for me is such an uphill battle.
I just really wanted to find some kind of way to make this all less difficult.
I just want to help people and not have to worry about all the stupid stuff. And if I screw up-- it's not just me-- it's-- it's--
So you think we have it easy?
Well, uh, yeah. I mean, look at all this.
Peter, and I'm not just saying this to make you feel better, but we're nearly broke.

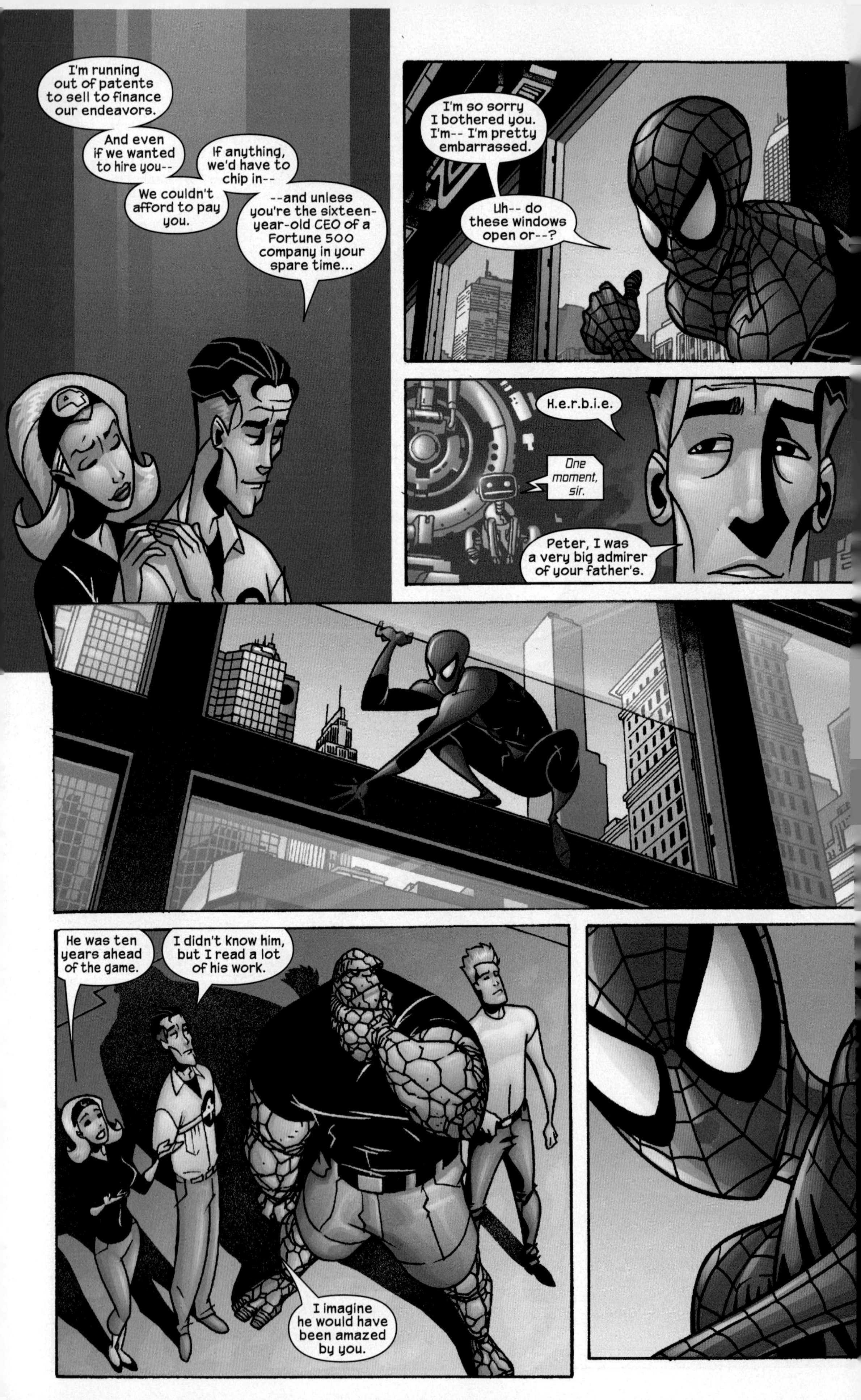
I'm running out of patents to sell to finance our endeavors.
And even if we wanted to hire you--
If anything, we'd have to chip in--
We couldn't afford to pay you.
--and unless you're the sixteen-year-old CEO of a Fortune 500 company in your spare time...
I'm so sorry I bothered you. I'm-- I'm pretty embarrassed.
Uh-- do these windows open or--?
H.e.r.b.i.e.
One moment, sir.
Peter, I was a very big admirer of your father's.
He was ten years ahead of the game.
I didn't know him, but I read a lot of his work.
I imagine he would have been amazed by you.

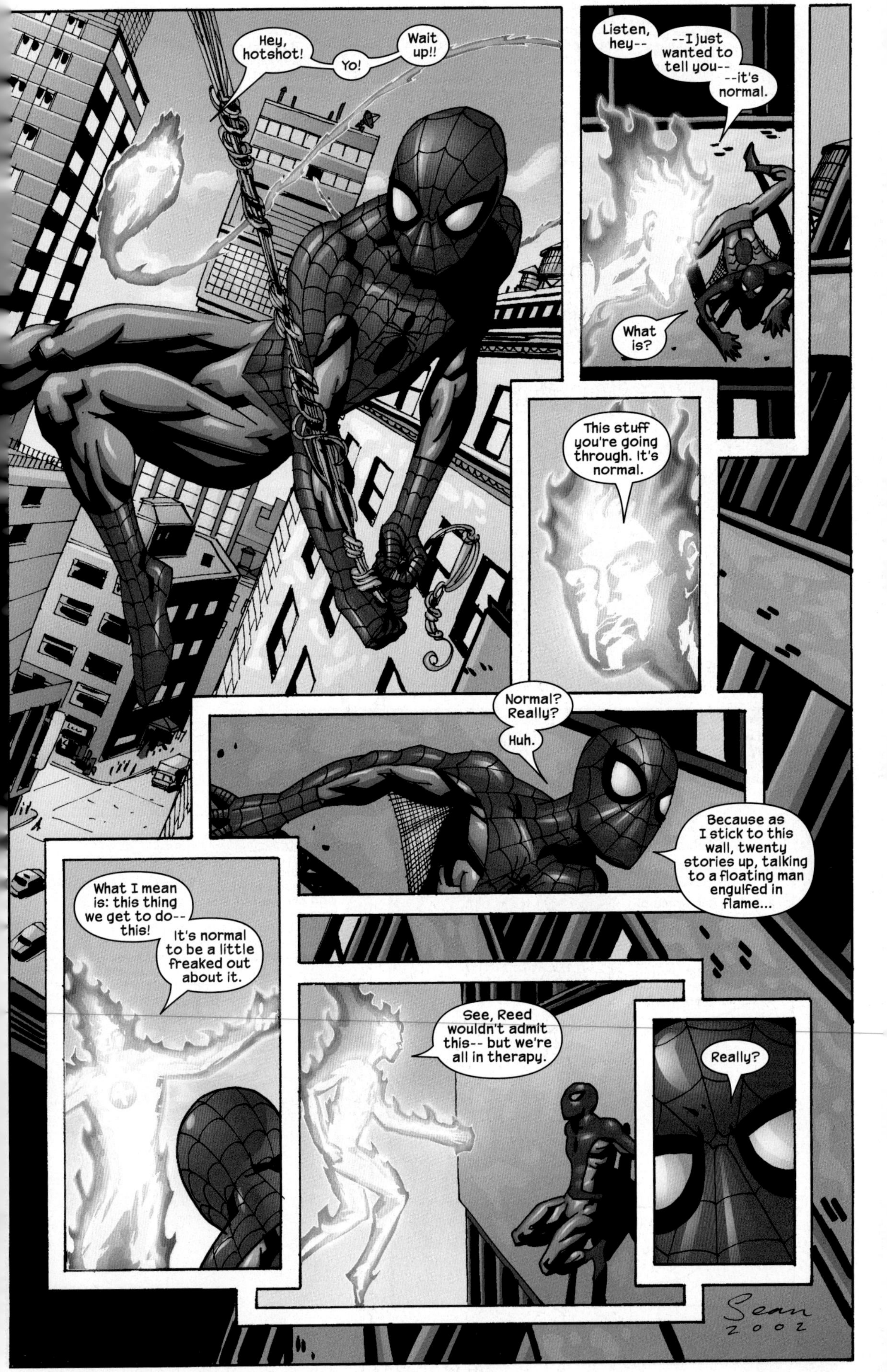
Hey, hotshot!
Yo!
Wait up!!
Listen, hey--
--I just wanted to tell you--
--it's normal.
What is?
This stuff you're going through. It's normal.
Normal? Really?
Huh.
Because as I stick to this wall, twenty stories up, talking to a floating man engulfed in flame...
What I mean is: this thing we get to do--this!
It's normal to be a little freaked out about it.
See, Reed wouldn't admit this-- but we're all in therapy.
Really?
Sean 2002

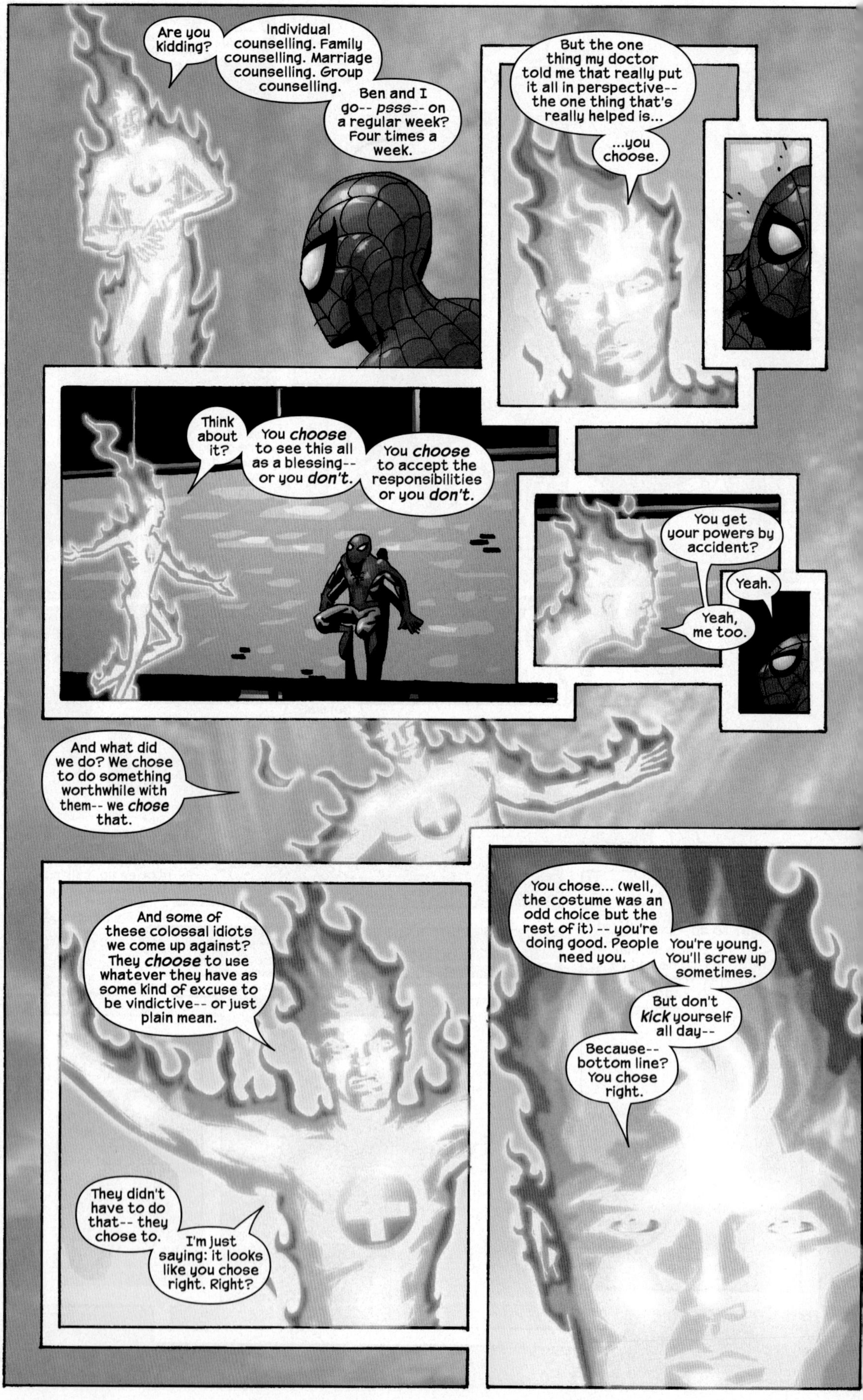
Are you kidding?
Individual counselling. Family counselling. Marriage counselling. Group counselling.
Ben and I go-- *psss*-- on a regular week? Four times a week.
But the one thing my doctor told me that really put it all in perspective-- the one thing that's really helped is...
...you choose.
Think about it?
You *choose* to see this all as a blessing-- or you *don't*.
You *choose* to accept the responsibilities or you *don't*.
You get your powers by accident?
Yeah.
Yeah, me too.
And what did we do? We chose to do something worthwhile with them-- we *chose* that.
And some of these colossal idiots we come up against? They *choose* to use whatever they have as some kind of excuse to be vindictive-- or just plain mean.
They didn't have to do that-- they chose to.
I'm just saying: it looks like you chose right. Right?
You chose... (well, the costume was an odd choice but the rest of it) -- you're doing good. People need you.
You're young. You'll screw up sometimes.
But don't *kick* yourself all day--
Because-- bottom line? You chose right.

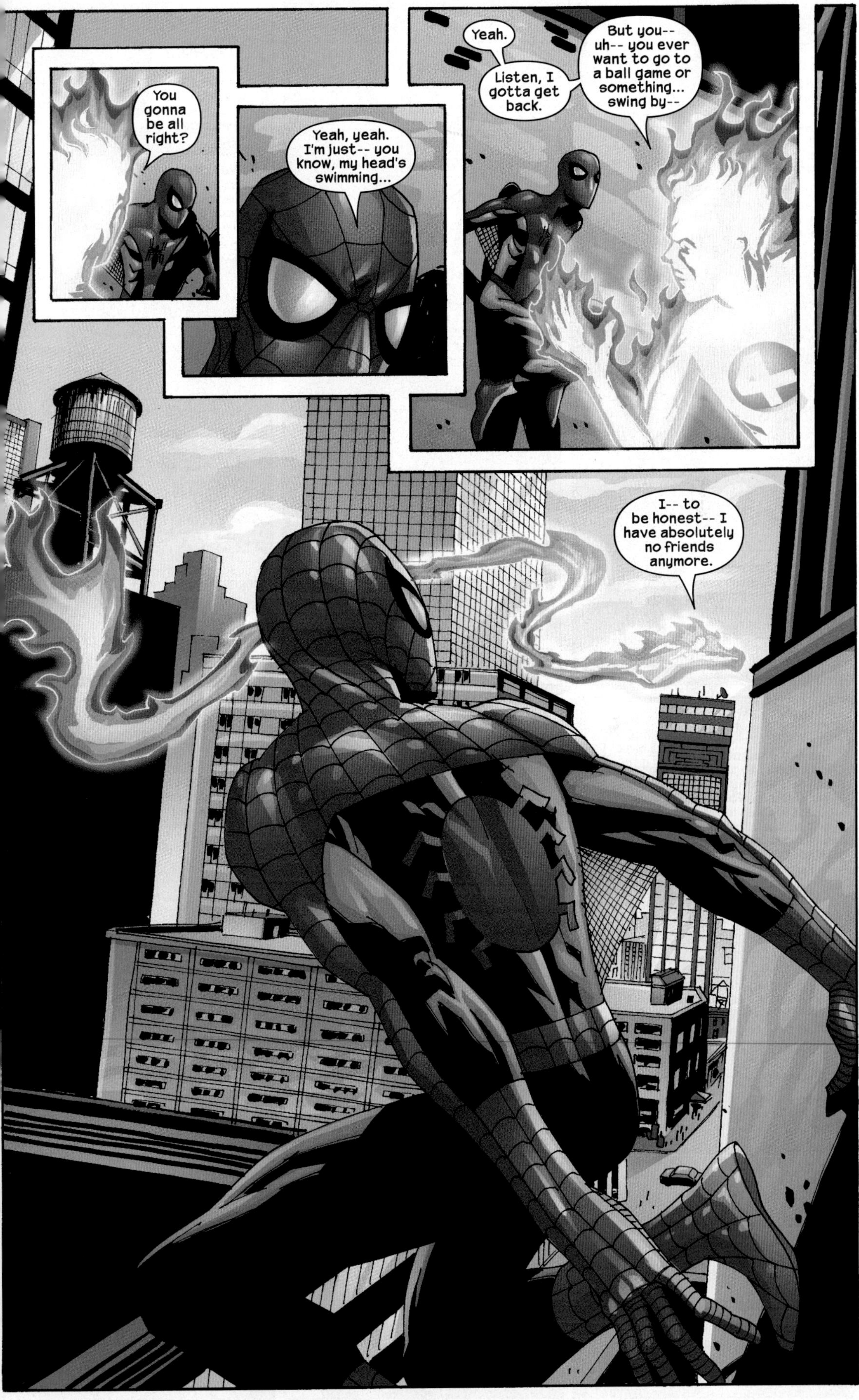
You gonna be all right?
Yeah, yeah. I'm just-- you know, my head's swimming...
Yeah.
Listen, I gotta get back.
But you-- uh-- you ever want to go to a ball game or something... swing by--
I-- to be honest-- I have absolutely no friends anymore.

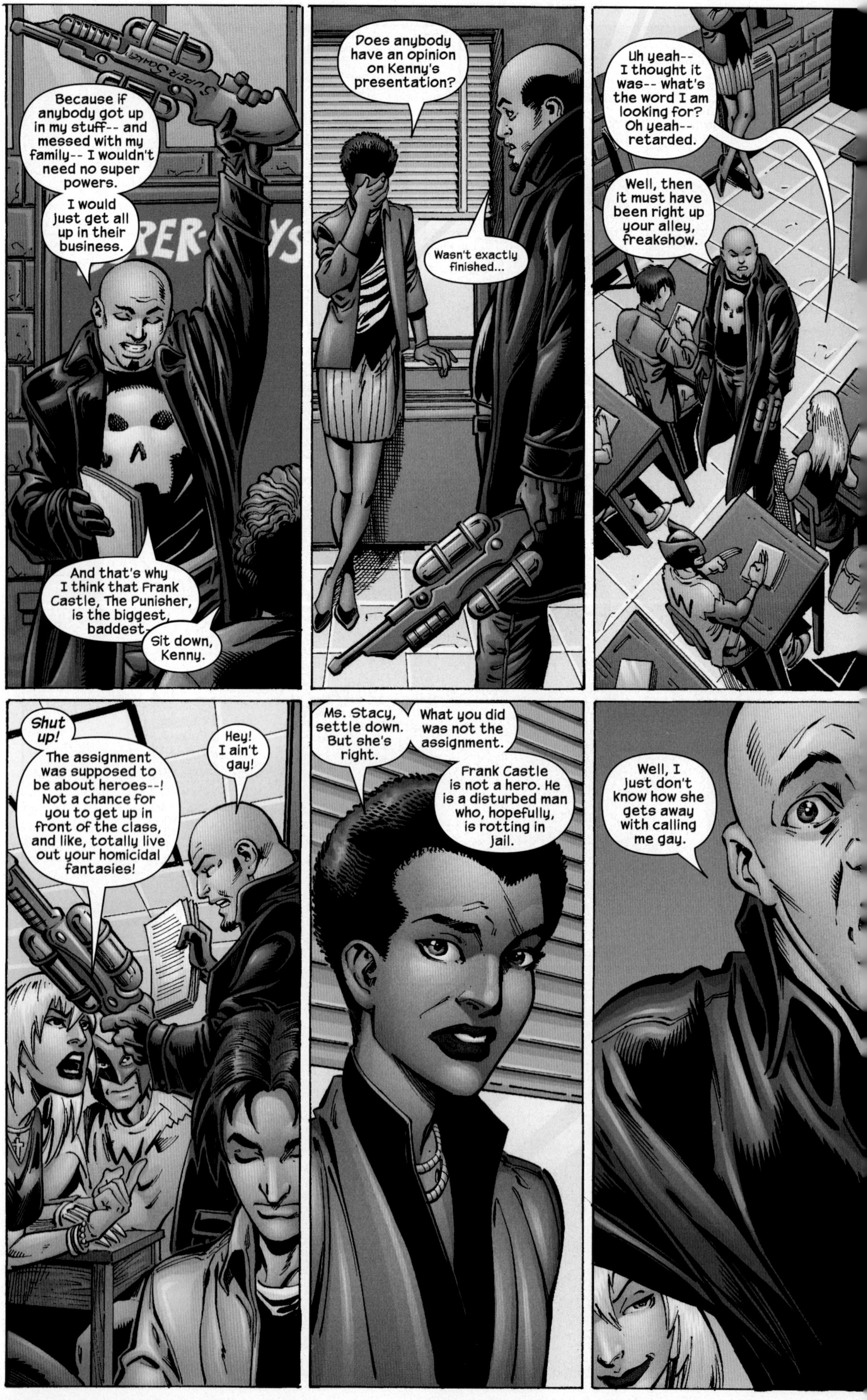

SUPER SOAKER
Because if anybody got up in my stuff-- and messed with my family-- I wouldn't need no super powers.
I would just get all up in their business.
SUPER-TOYS
And that's why I think that Frank Castle, The Punisher, is the biggest, baddest-
Sit down, Kenny.
Does anybody have an opinion on Kenny's presentation?
Wasn't exactly finished...
Uh yeah-- I thought it was-- what's the word I am looking for? Oh yeah-- retarded.
Well, then it must have been right up your alley, freakshow.
Shut up!
The assignment was supposed to be about heroes--! Not a chance for you to get up in front of the class, and like, totally live out your homicidal fantasies!
Hey! I ain't gay!
Ms. Stacy, settle down. But she's right.
What you did was not the assignment.
Frank Castle is not a hero. He is a disturbed man who, hopefully, is rotting in jail.
Well, I just don't know how she gets away with calling me gay.

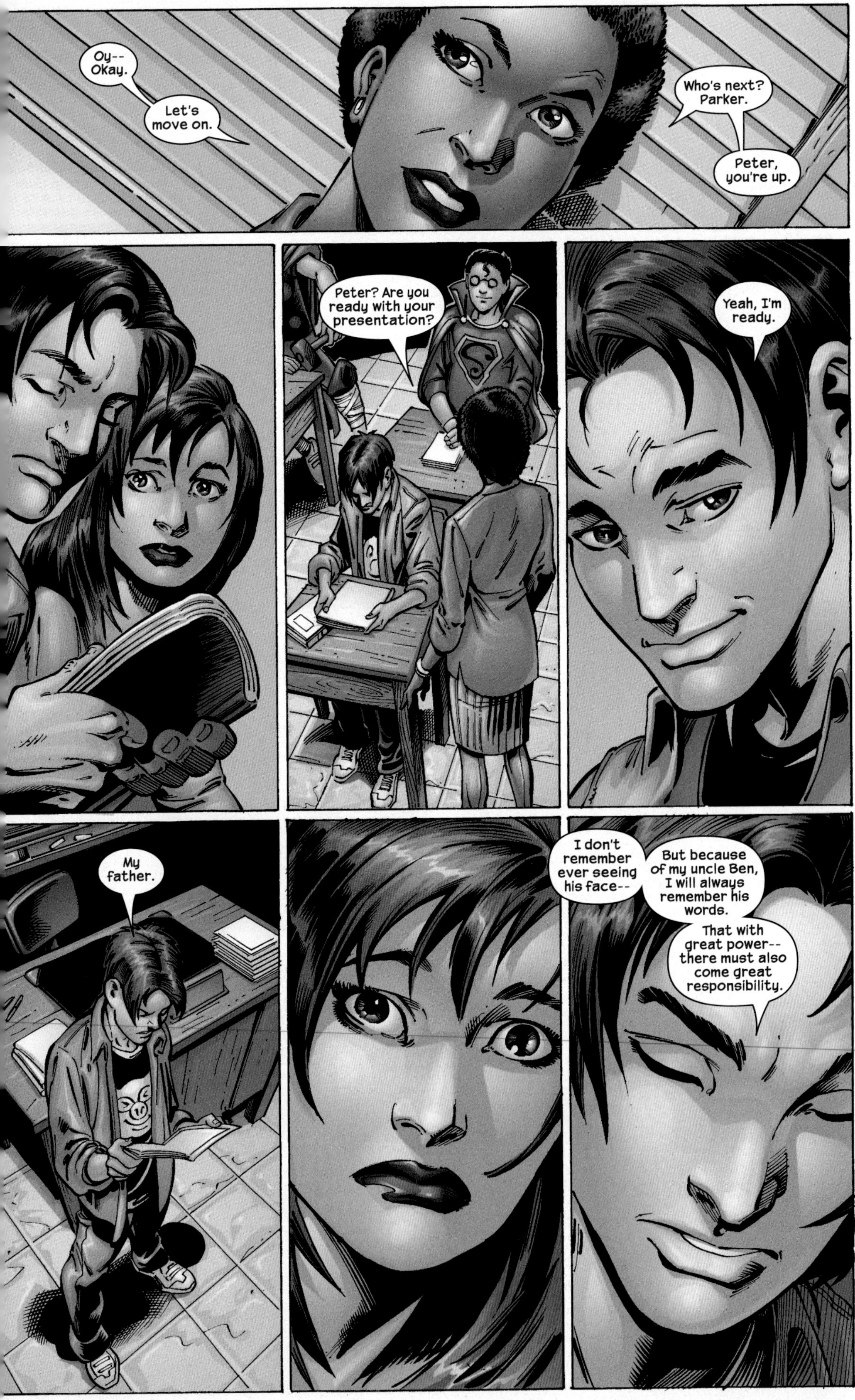
Oy--
Okay.
Let's
move on.
Who's next?
Parker.
Peter,
you're up.
Peter? Are you
ready with your
presentation?
Yeah, I'm
ready.
My
father.
I don't
remember
ever seeing
his face--
But because
of my uncle Ben,
I will always
remember his
words.
That with
great power--
there must also
come great
responsibility.

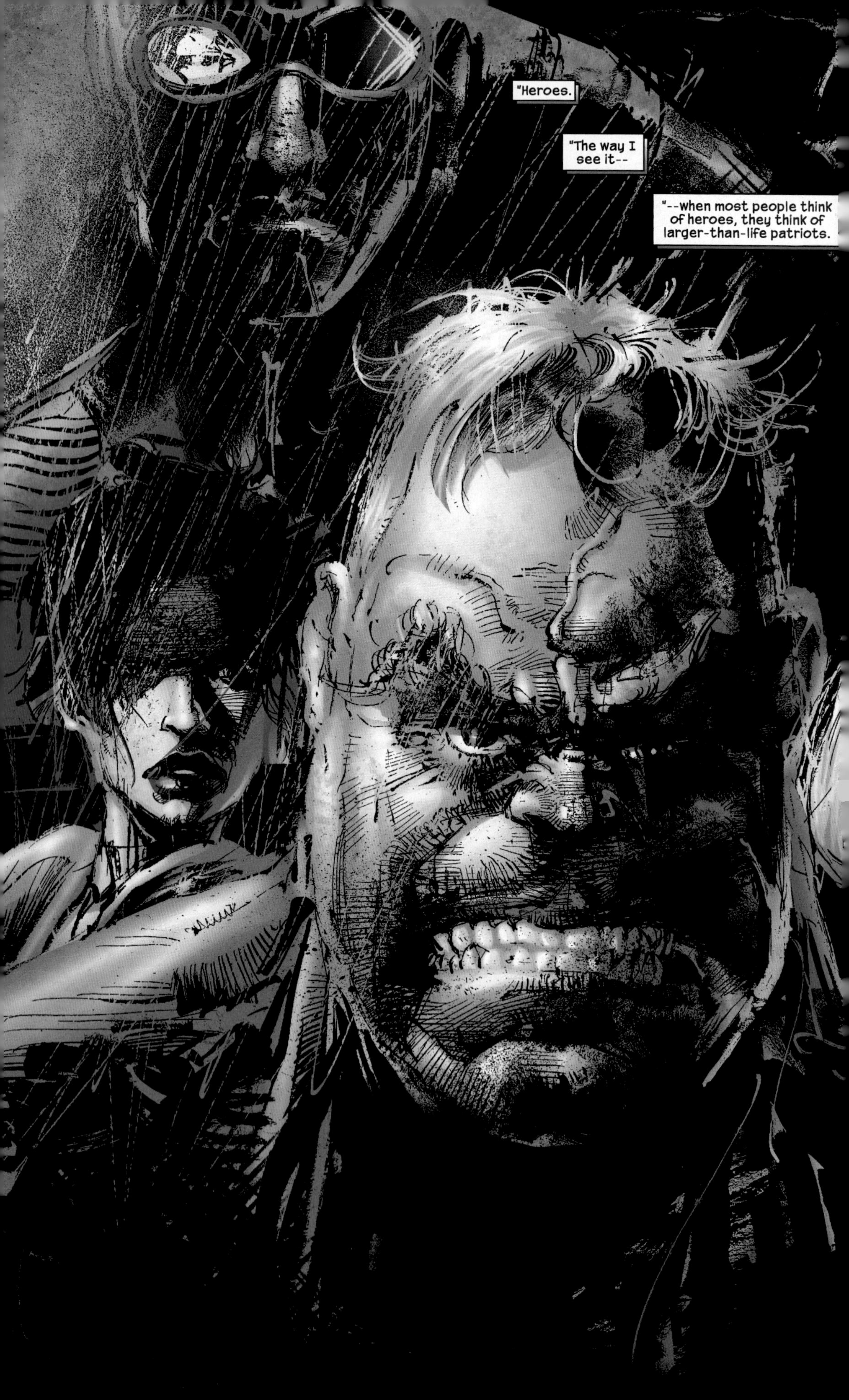
"Heroes.
"The way I see it--
"--when most people think of heroes, they think of larger-than-life patriots.

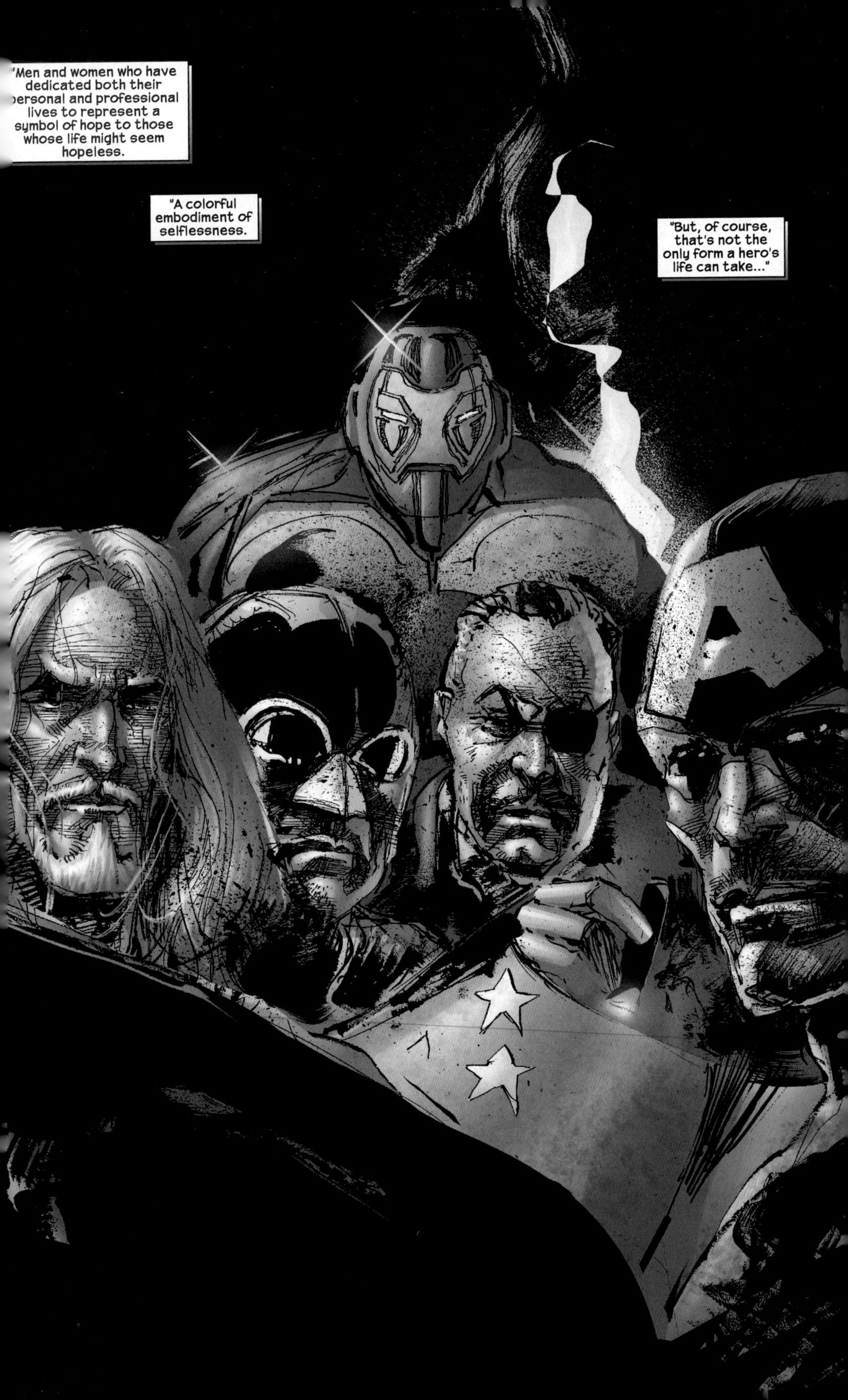
"Men and women who have dedicated both their personal and professional lives to represent a symbol of hope to those whose life might seem hopeless.
"A colorful embodiment of selflessness.
"But, of course, that's not the only form a hero's life can take..."

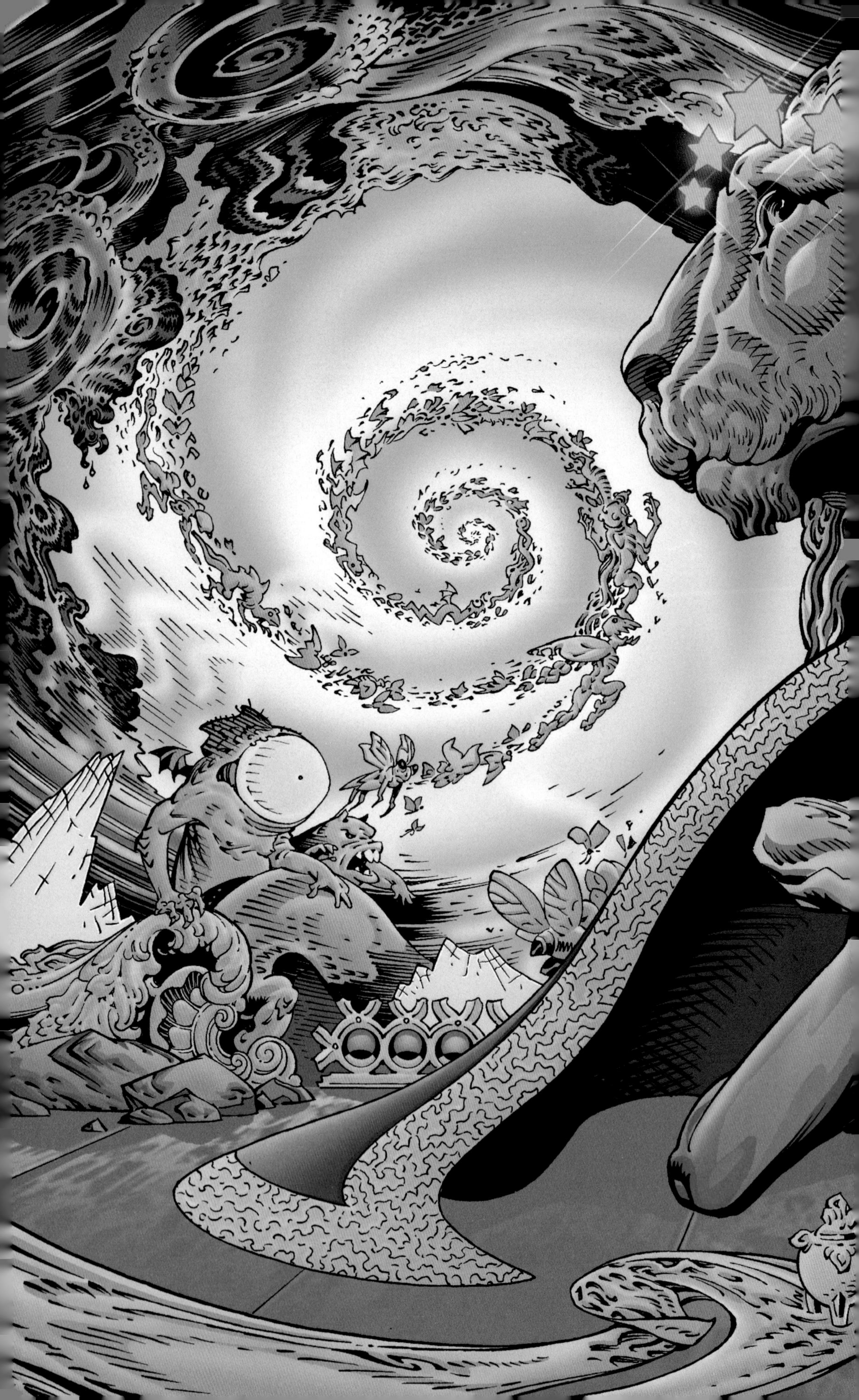

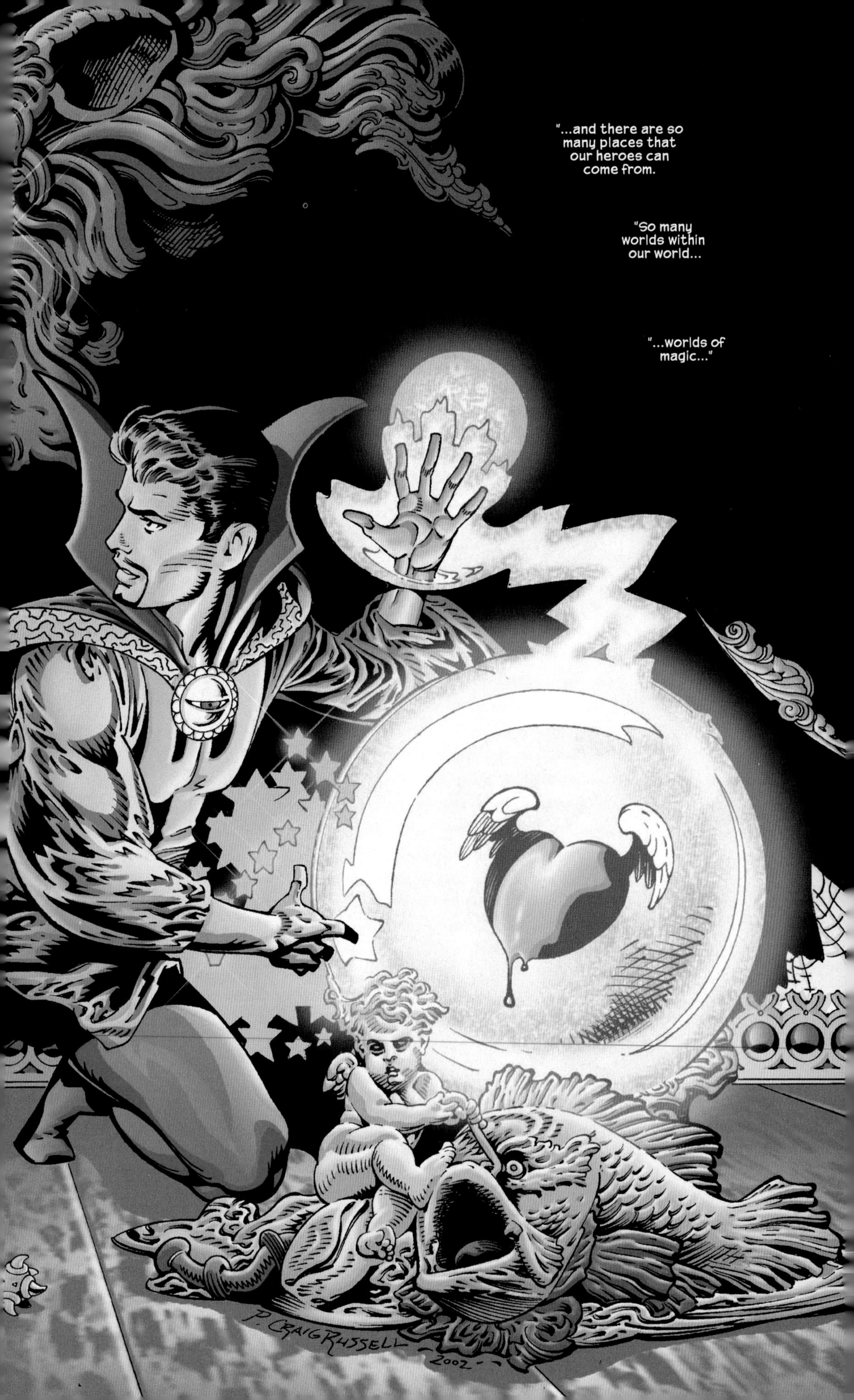
"...and there are so many places that our heroes can come from.
"So many worlds within our world...
"...worlds of magic..."
P. CRAIG RUSSELL 2002

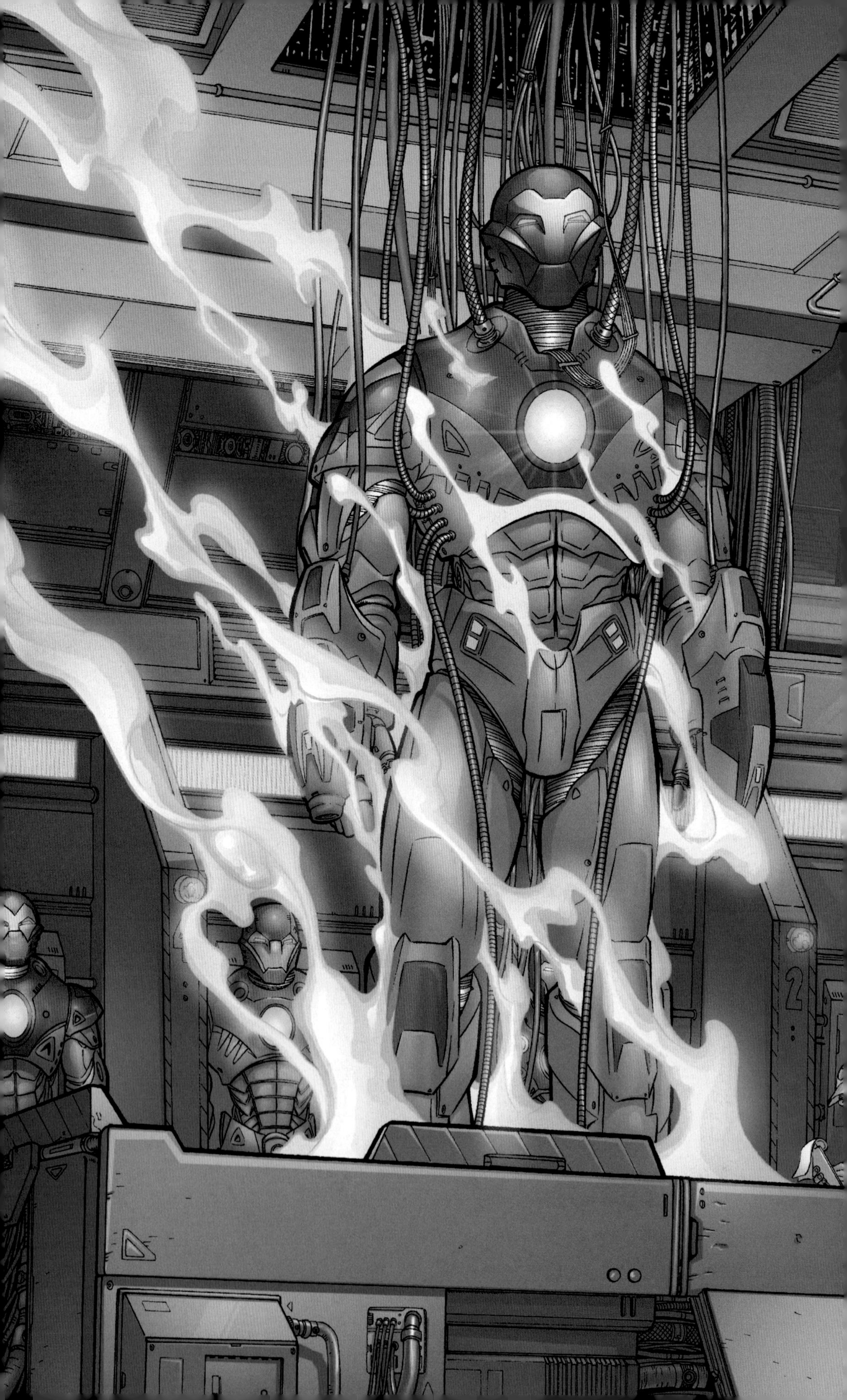
2

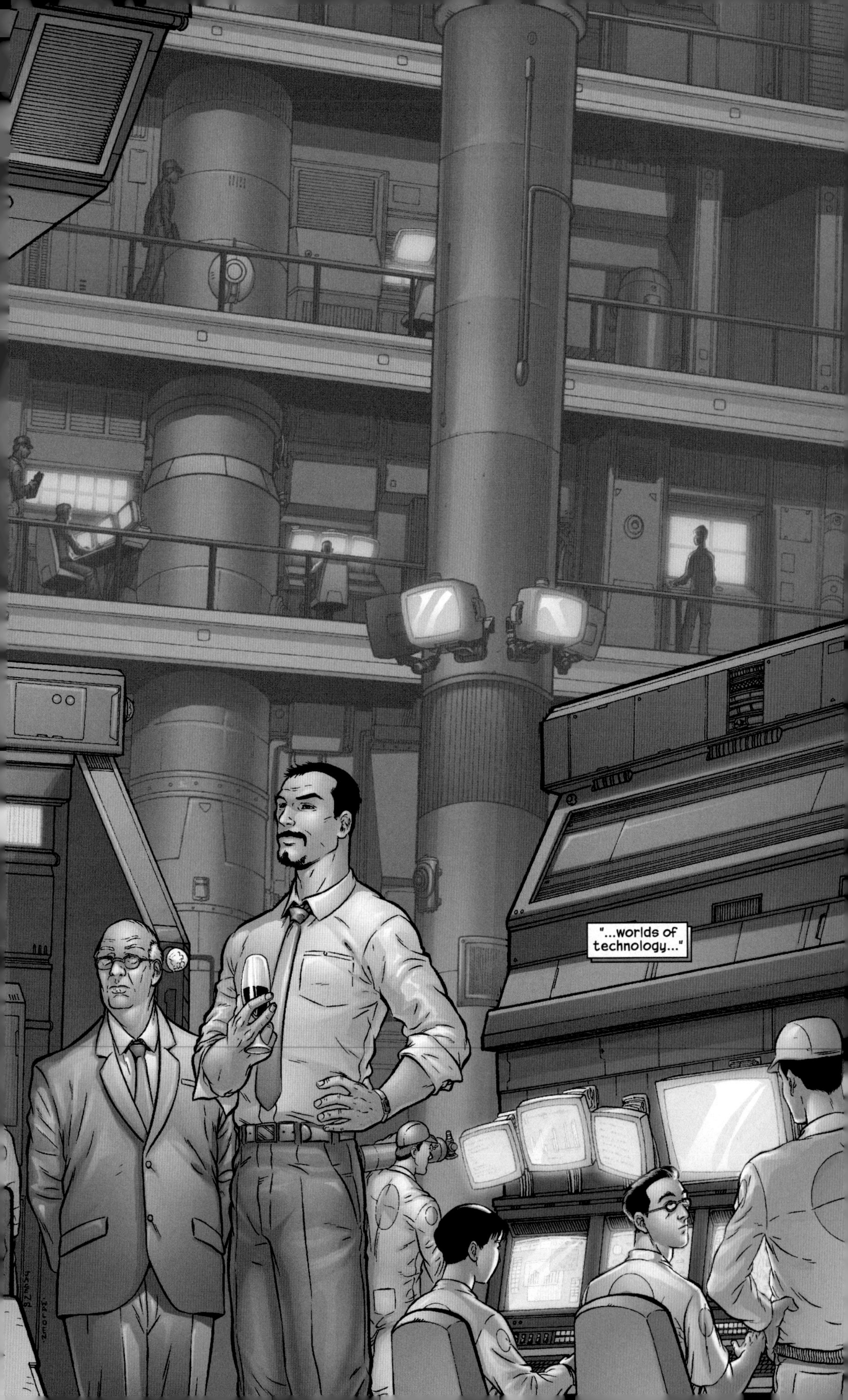
"...worlds of technology..."

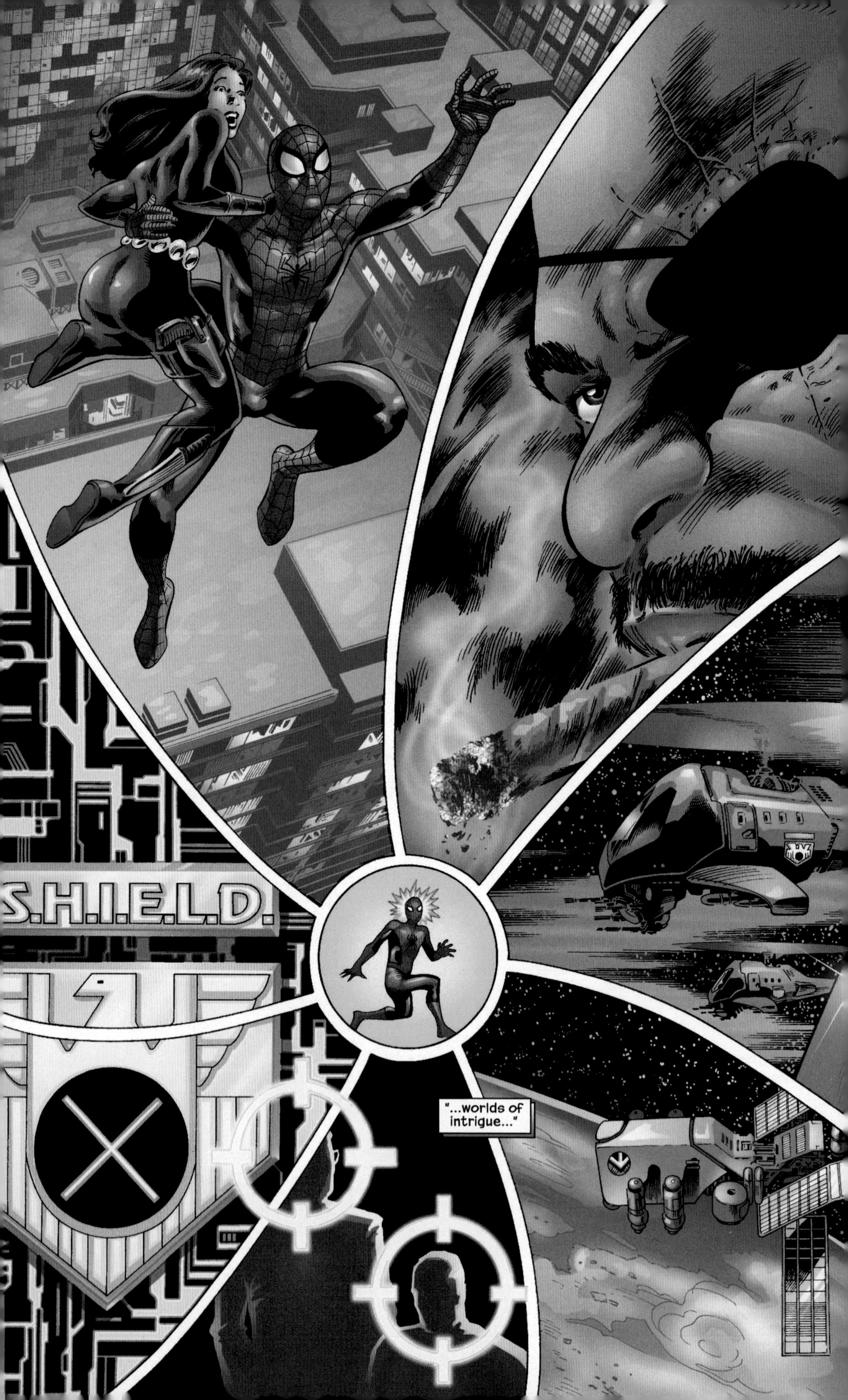
S.H.I.E.L.D.
"...worlds of intrigue..."

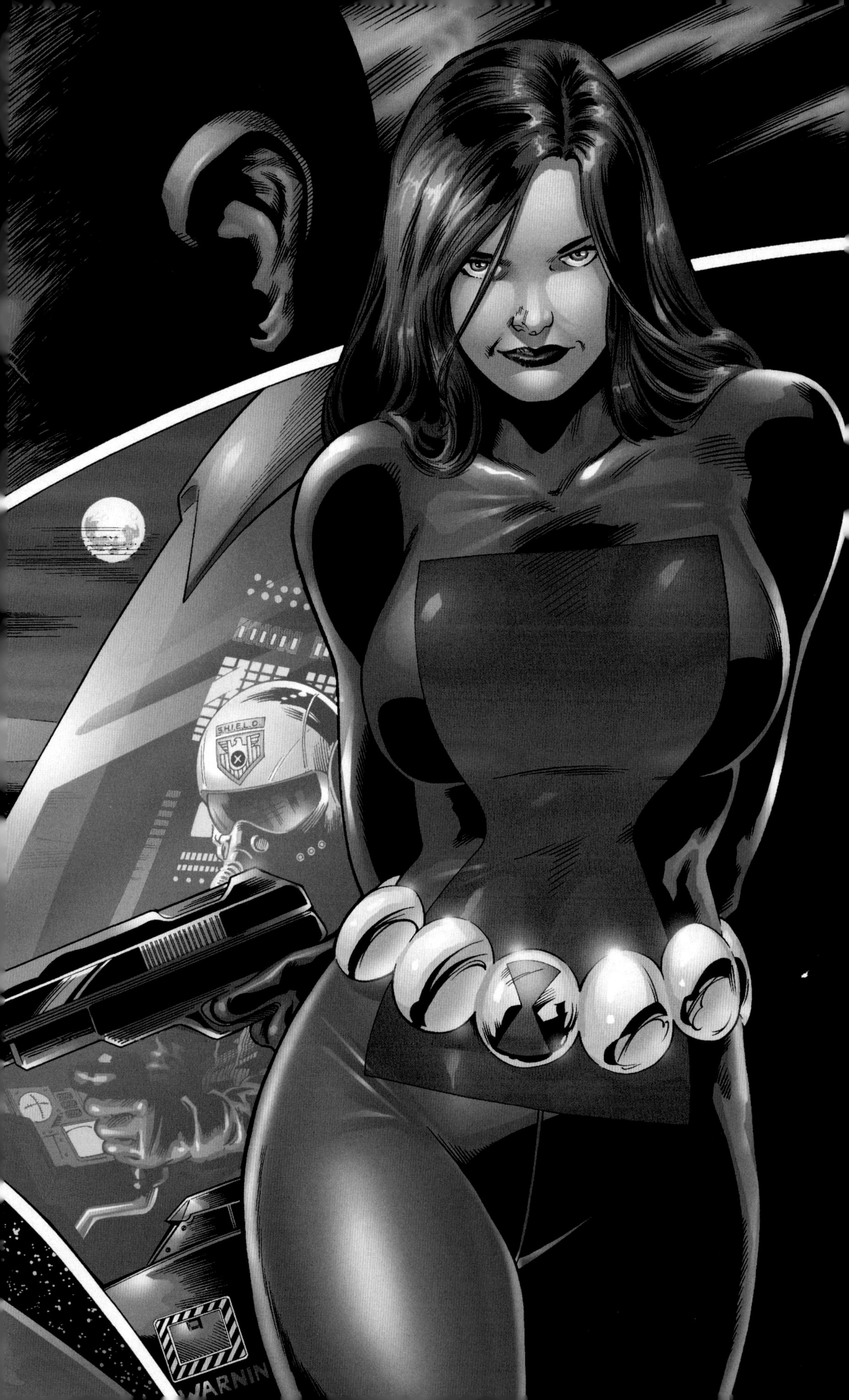
S.H.I.E.L.D.
WARNIN

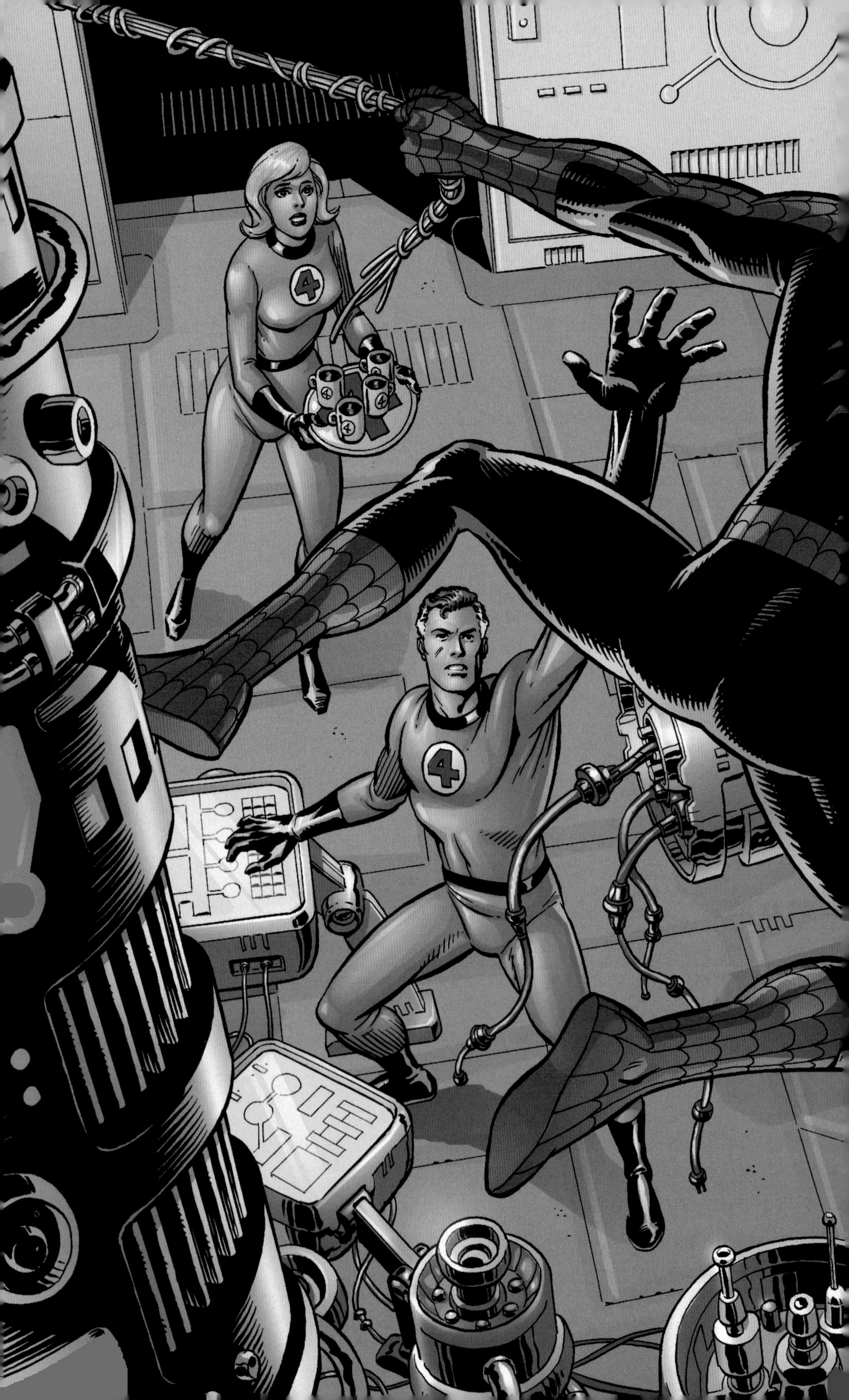

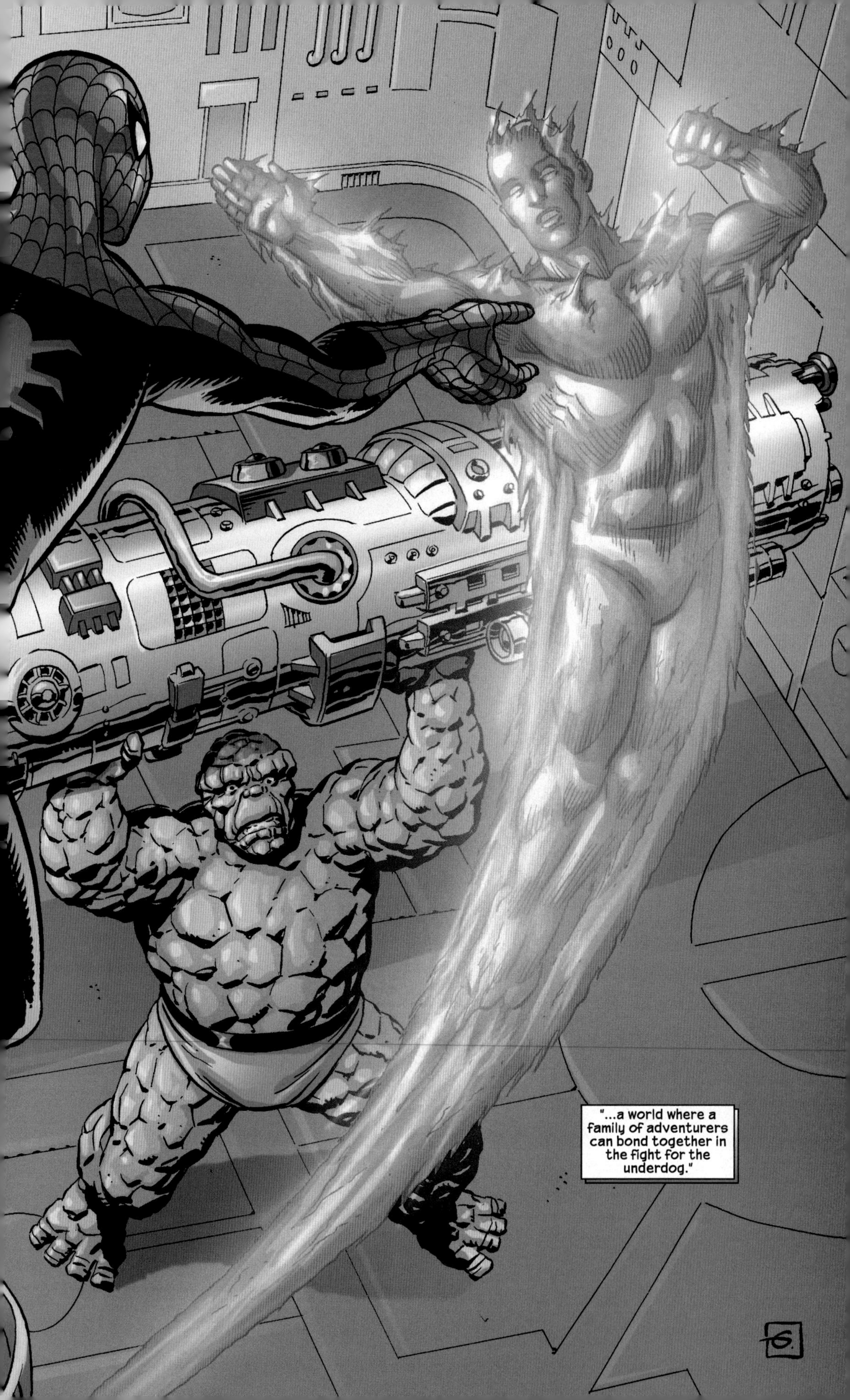
"...a world where a family of adventurers can bond together in the fight for the underdog."

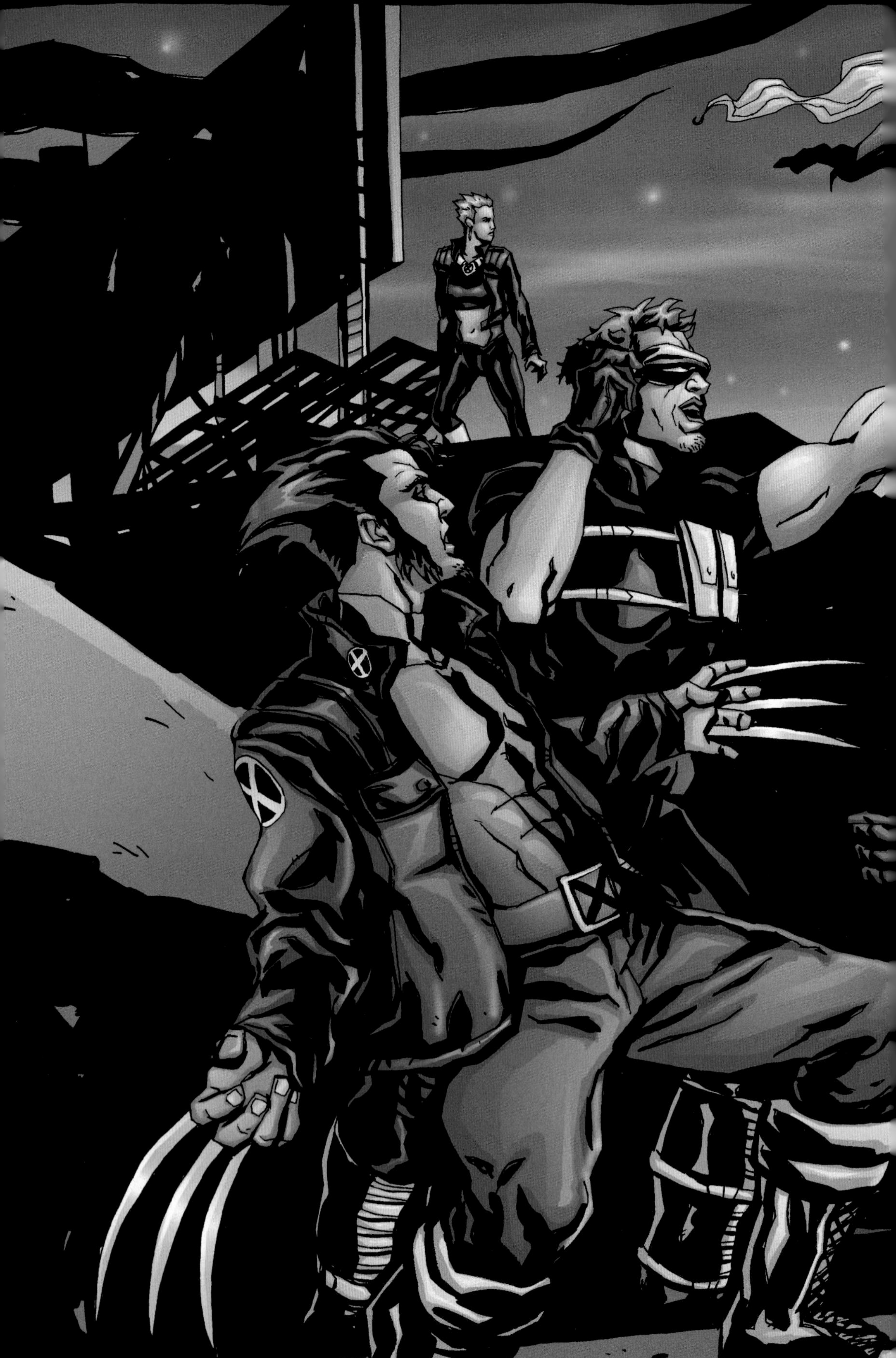

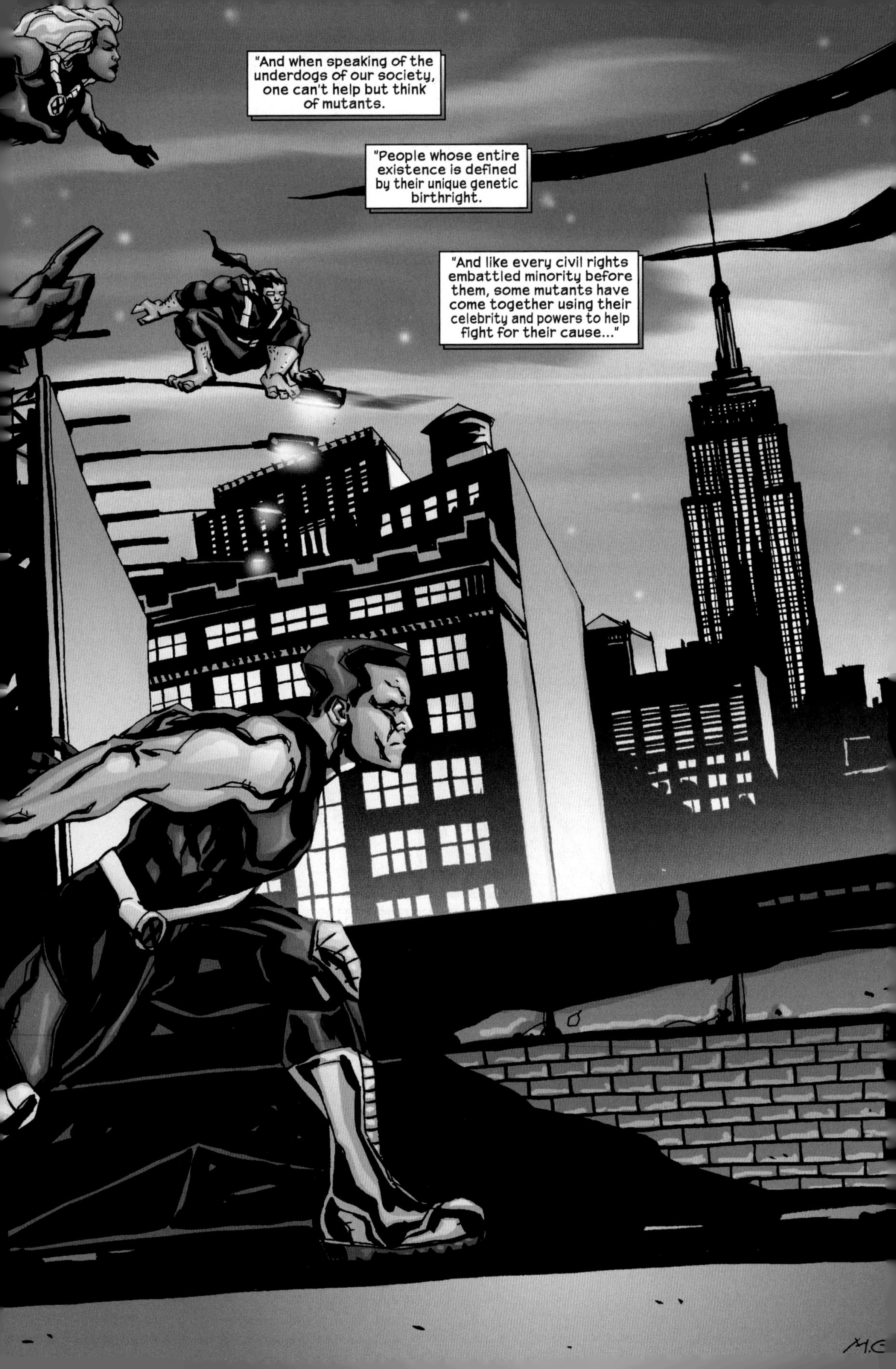
"And when speaking of the underdogs of our society, one can't help but think of mutants.
"People whose entire existence is defined by their unique genetic birthright.
"And like every civil rights embattled minority before them, some mutants have come together using their celebrity and powers to help fight for their cause..."
M.C

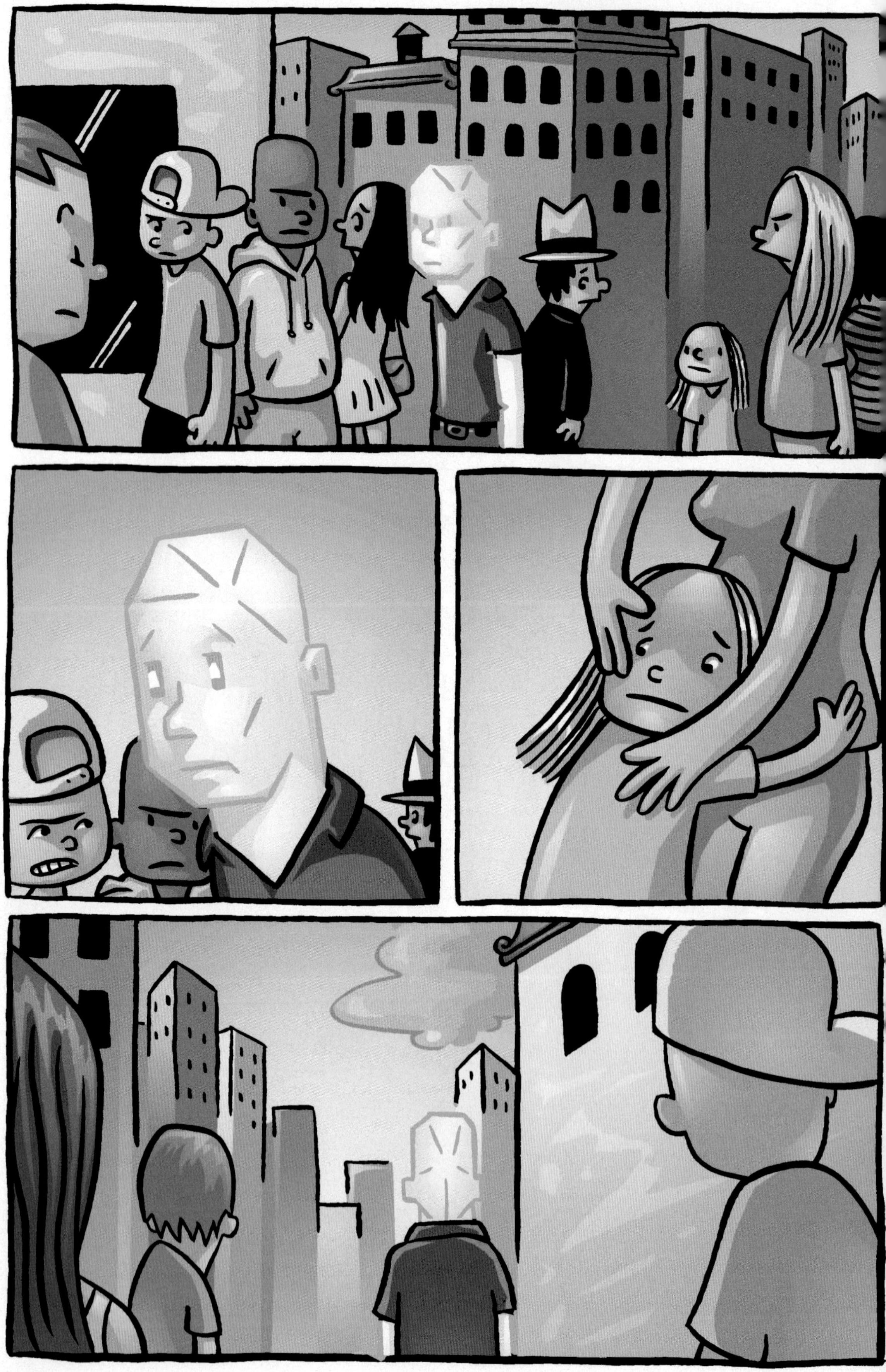

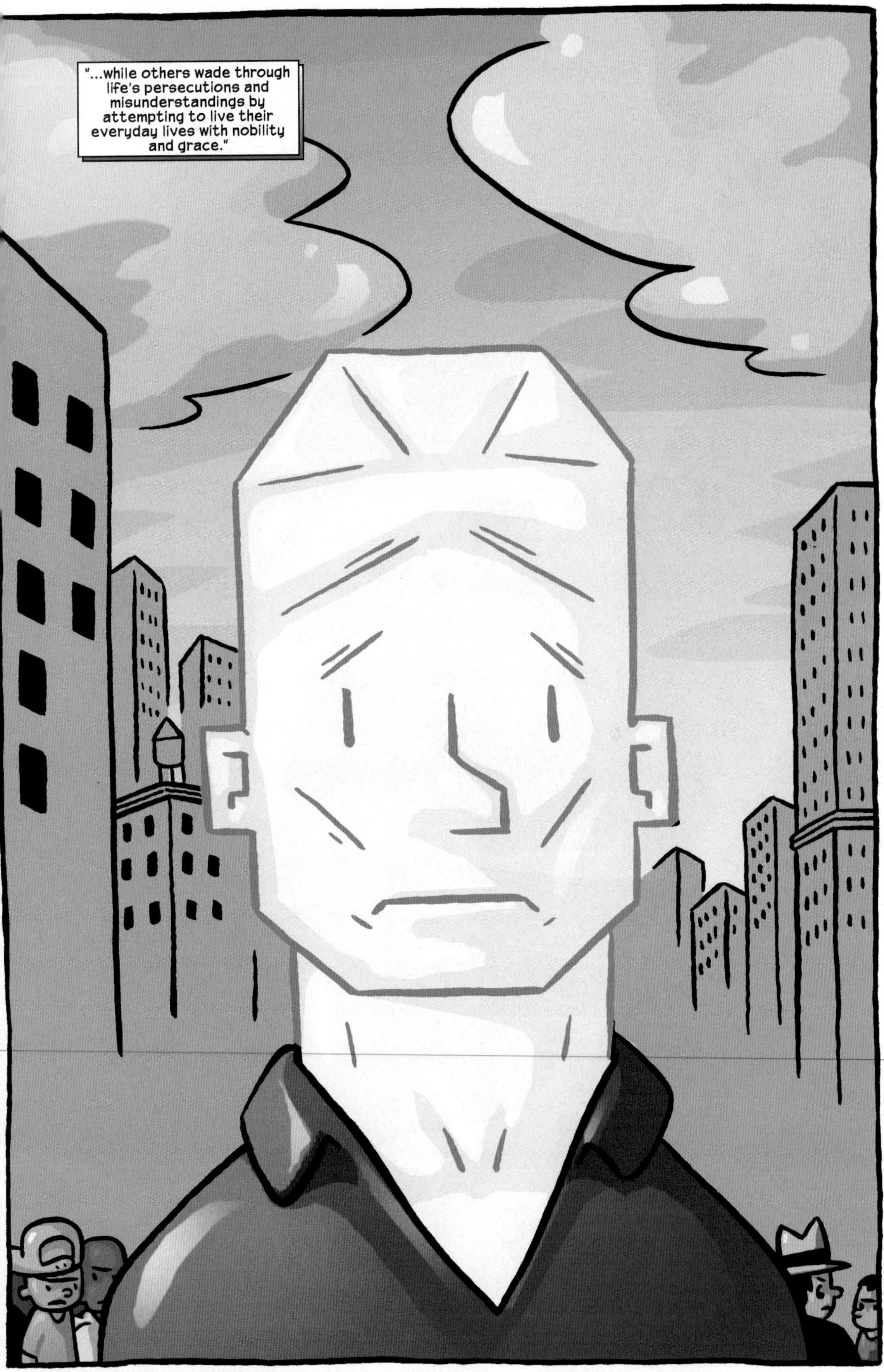
"...while others wade through life's persecutions and misunderstandings by attempting to live their everyday lives with nobility and grace."

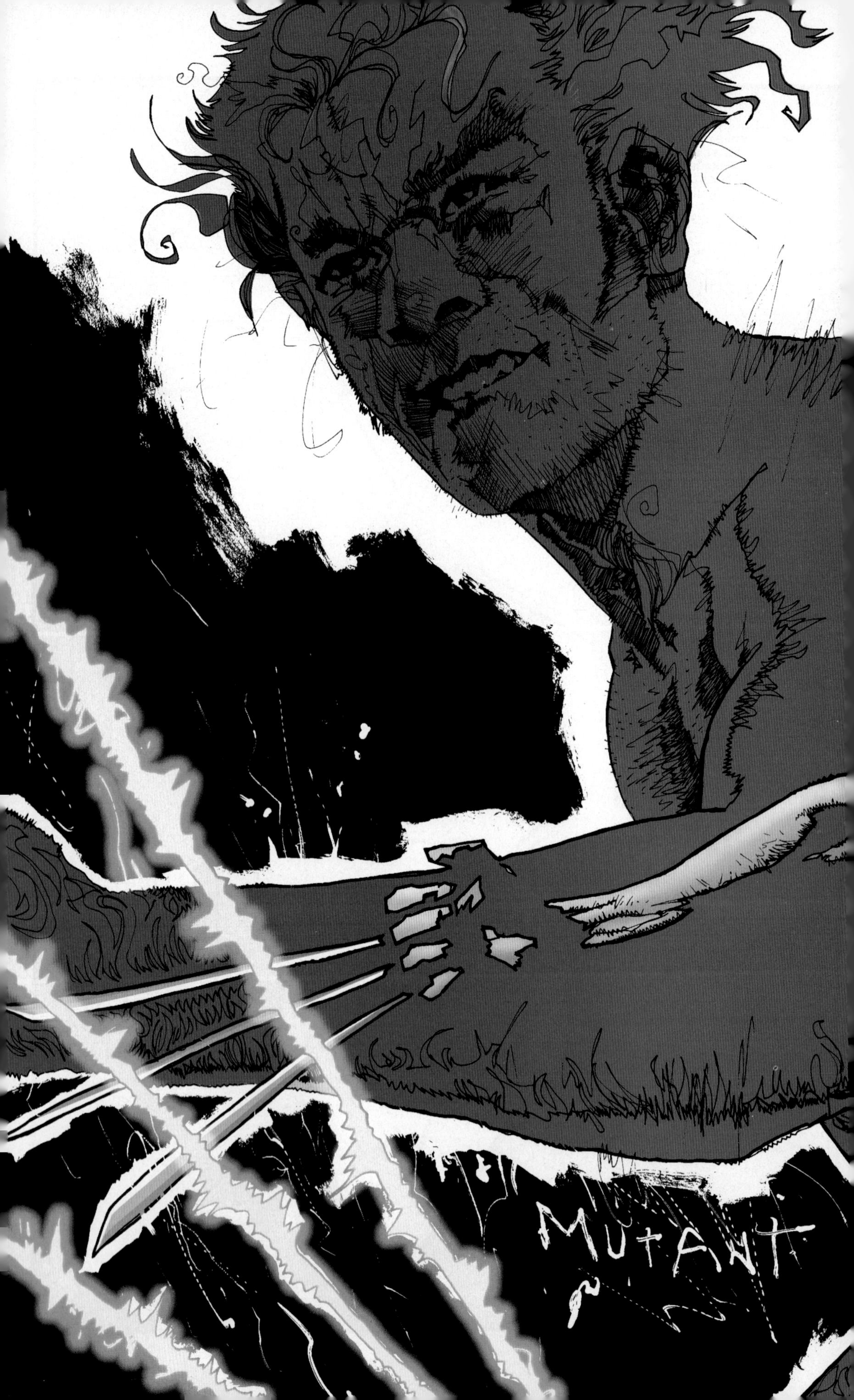
MUTANT

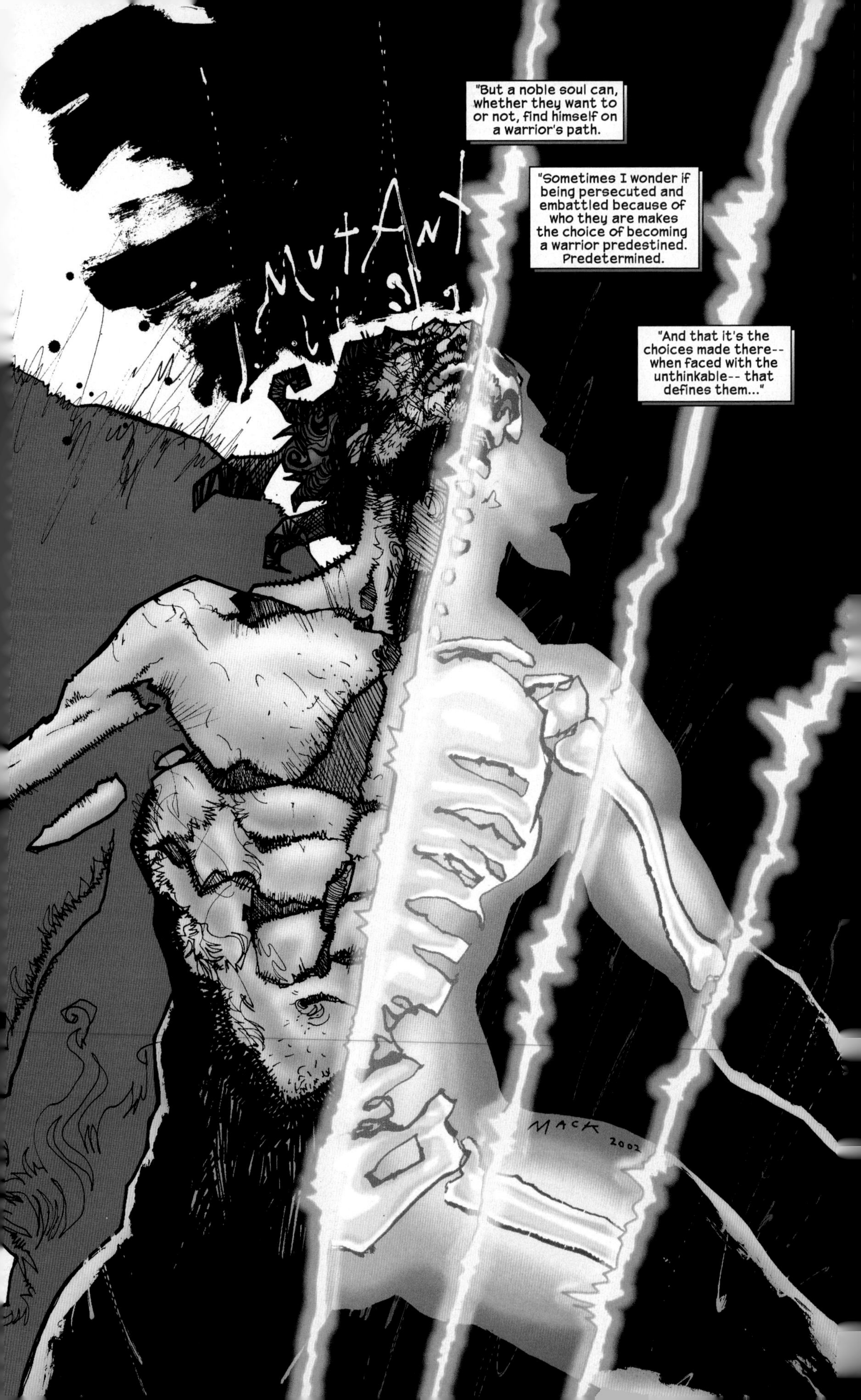
"But a noble soul can, whether they want to or not, find himself on a warrior's path.
"Sometimes I wonder if being persecuted and embattled because of who they are makes the choice of becoming a warrior predestined. Predetermined.
"And that it's the choices made there-- when faced with the unthinkable-- that defines them..."
MUTANT
MACK 2002

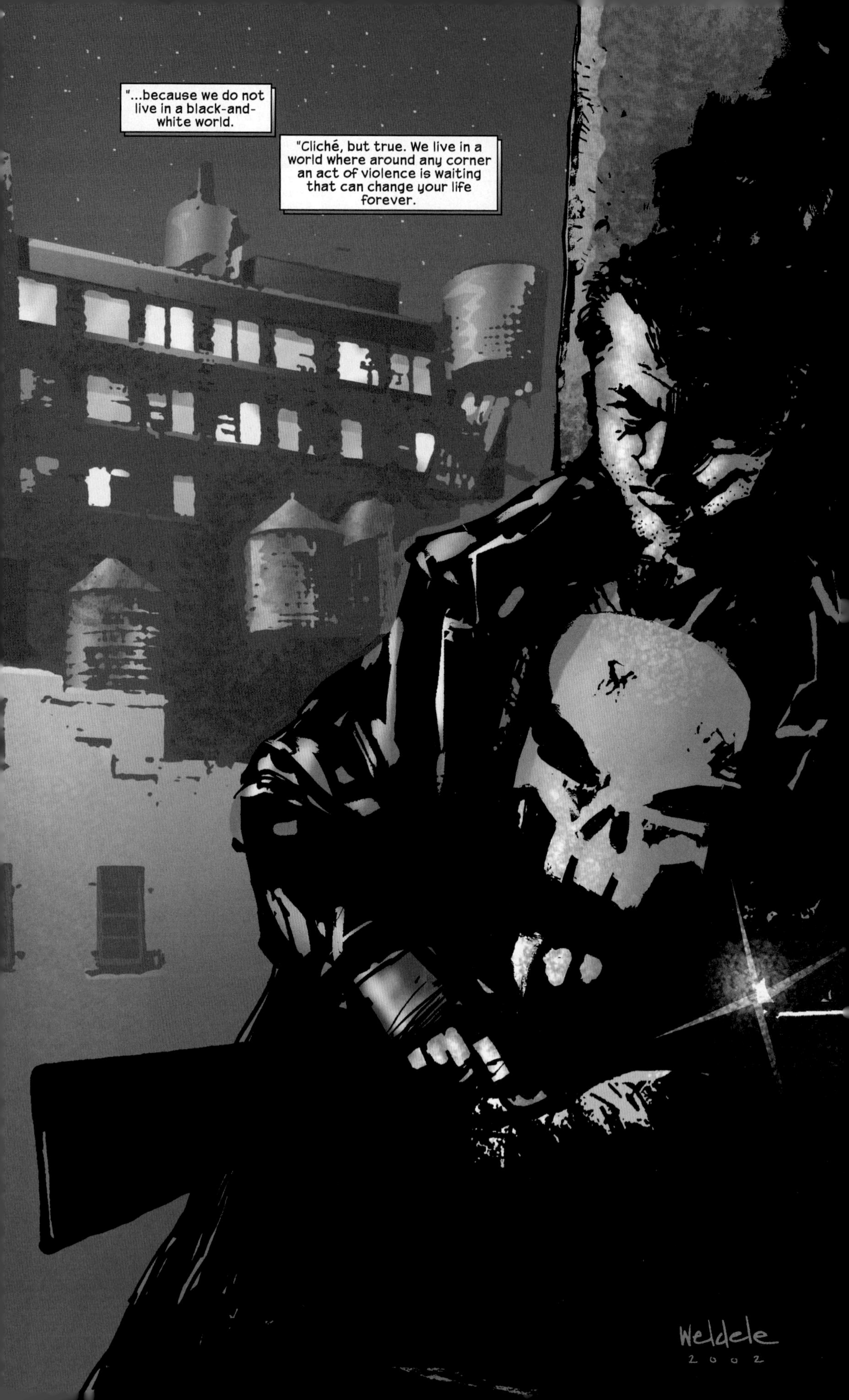
"...because we do not live in a black-and-white world.
"Cliché, but true. We live in a world where around any corner an act of violence is waiting that can change your life forever.
Weldele 2002

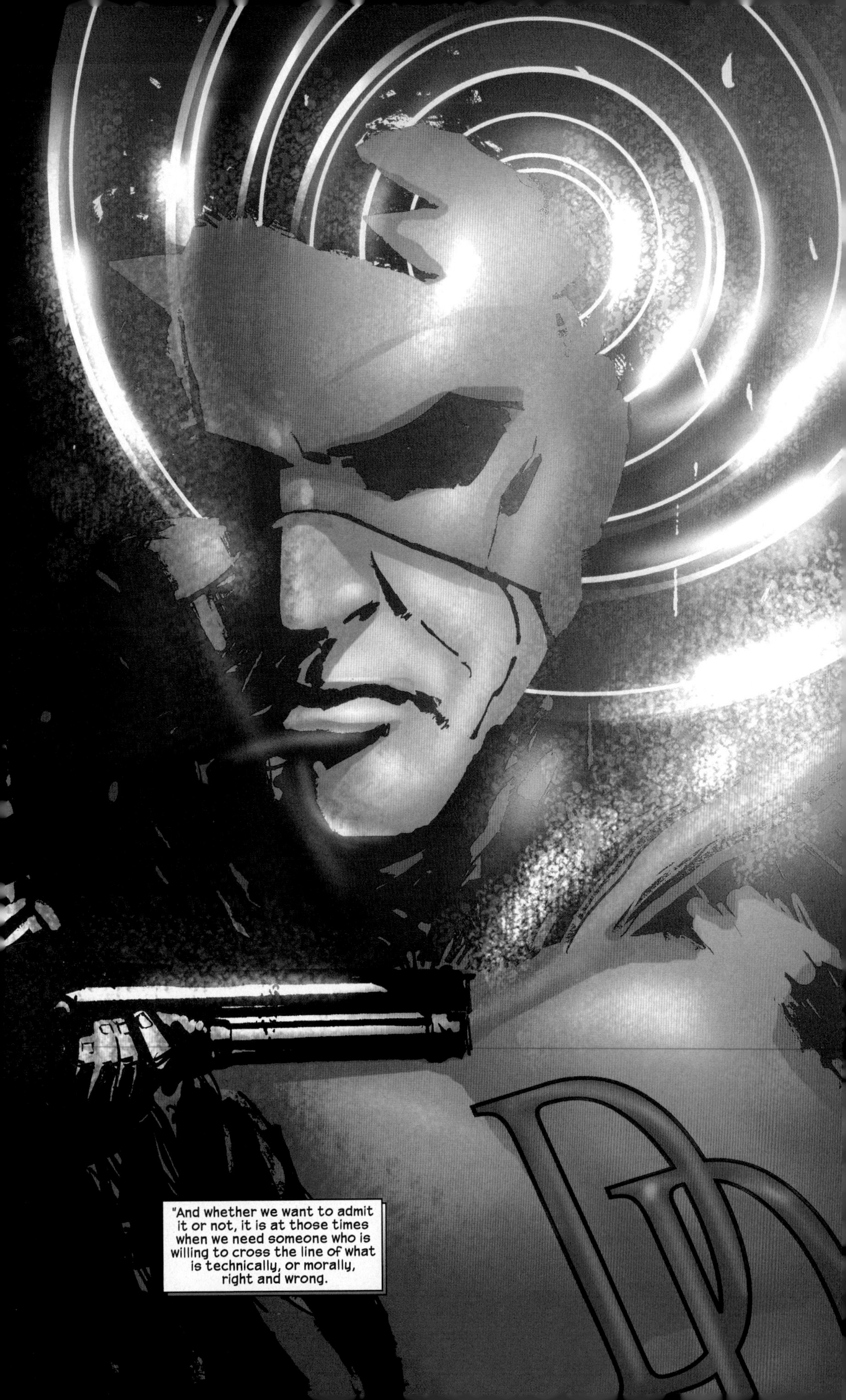
"And whether we want to admit it or not, it is at those times when we need someone who is willing to cross the line of what is technically, or morally, right and wrong.

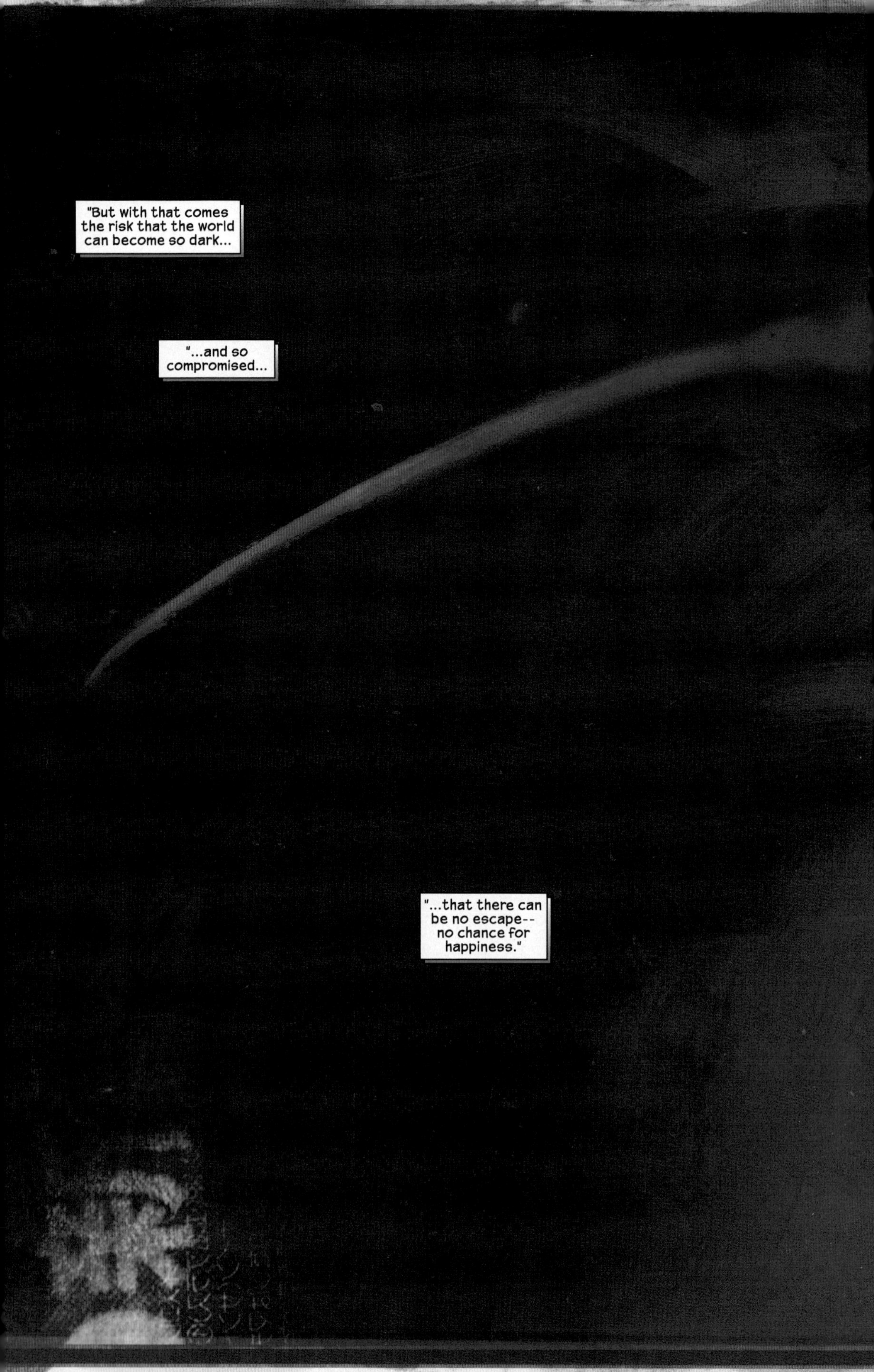
"But with that comes the risk that the world can become so dark...
"...and so compromised...
"...that there can be no escape-- no chance for happiness."

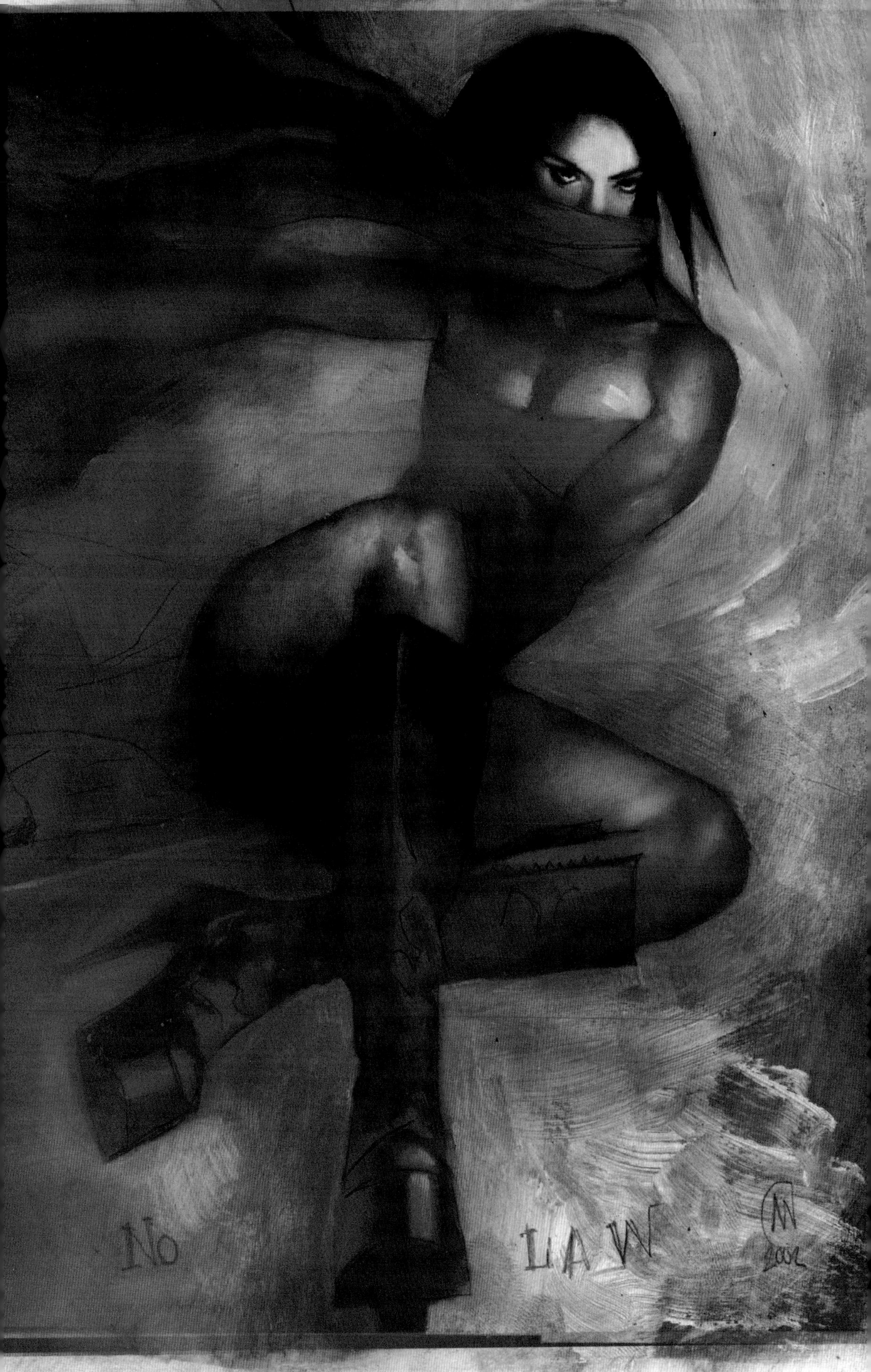
No
LAW

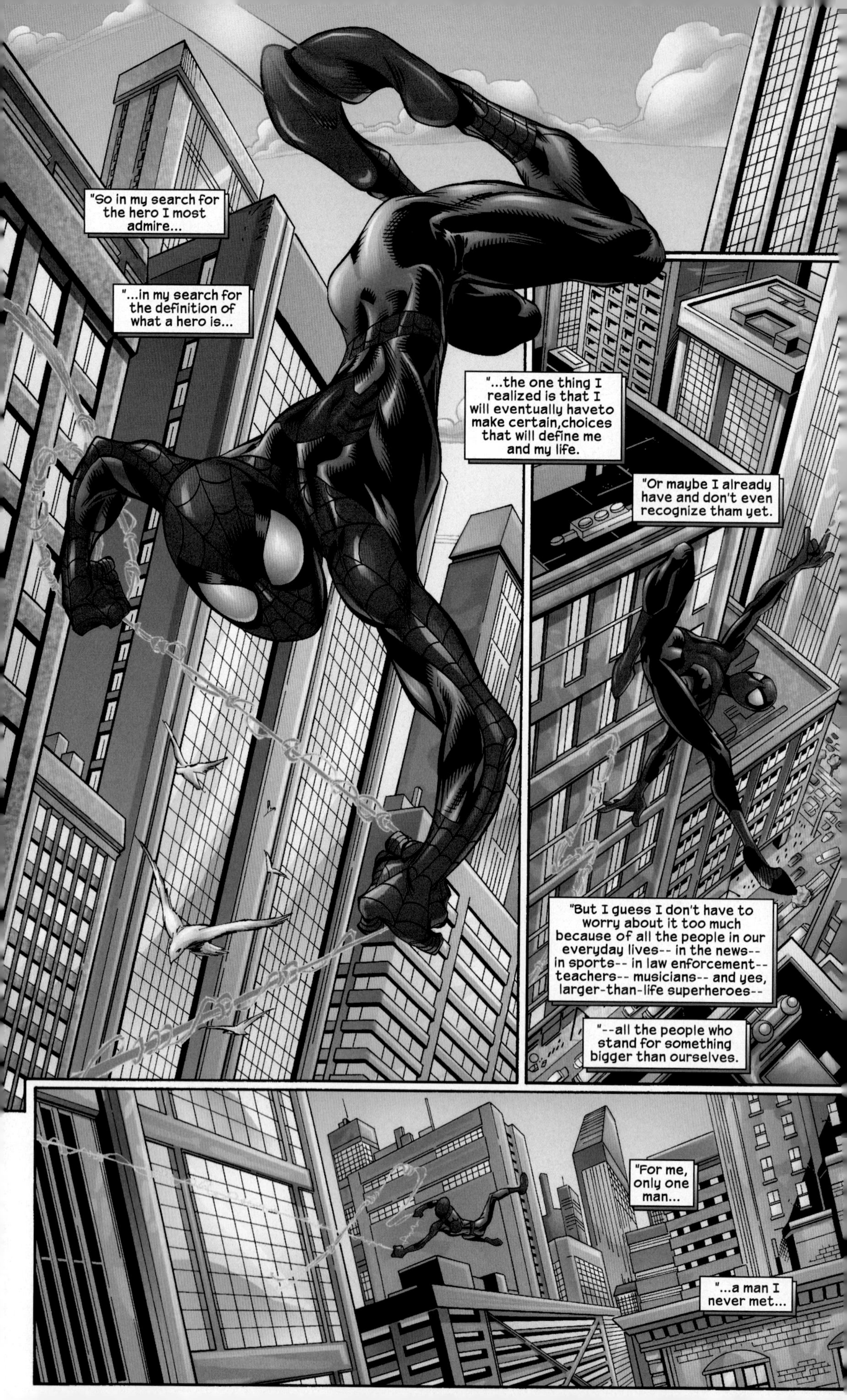
"So in my search for the hero I most admire...
"...in my search for the definition of what a hero is...
"...the one thing I realized is that I will eventually haveto make certain,choices that will define me and my life.
"Or maybe I already have and don't even recognize tham yet.
"But I guess I don't have to worry about it too much because of all the people in our everyday lives-- in the news-- in sports-- in law enforcement-- teachers-- musicians-- and yes, larger-than-life superheroes--
"--all the people who stand for something bigger than ourselves.
"For me, only one man...
"...a man I never met...

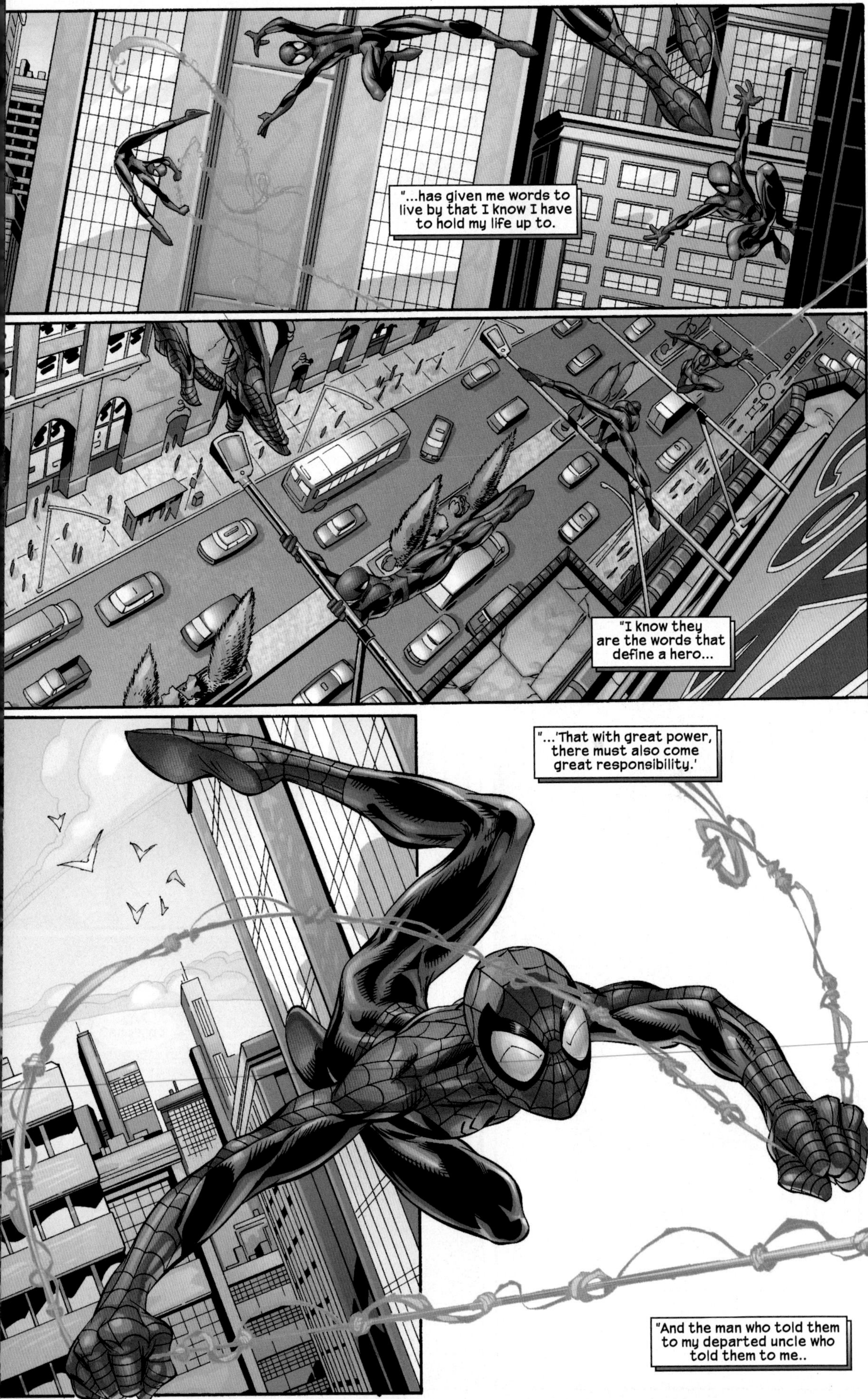
"...has given me words to live by that I know I have to hold my life up to.
"I know they are the words that define a hero...
"...'That with great power, there must also come great responsibility.'
"And the man who told them to my departed uncle who told them to me..

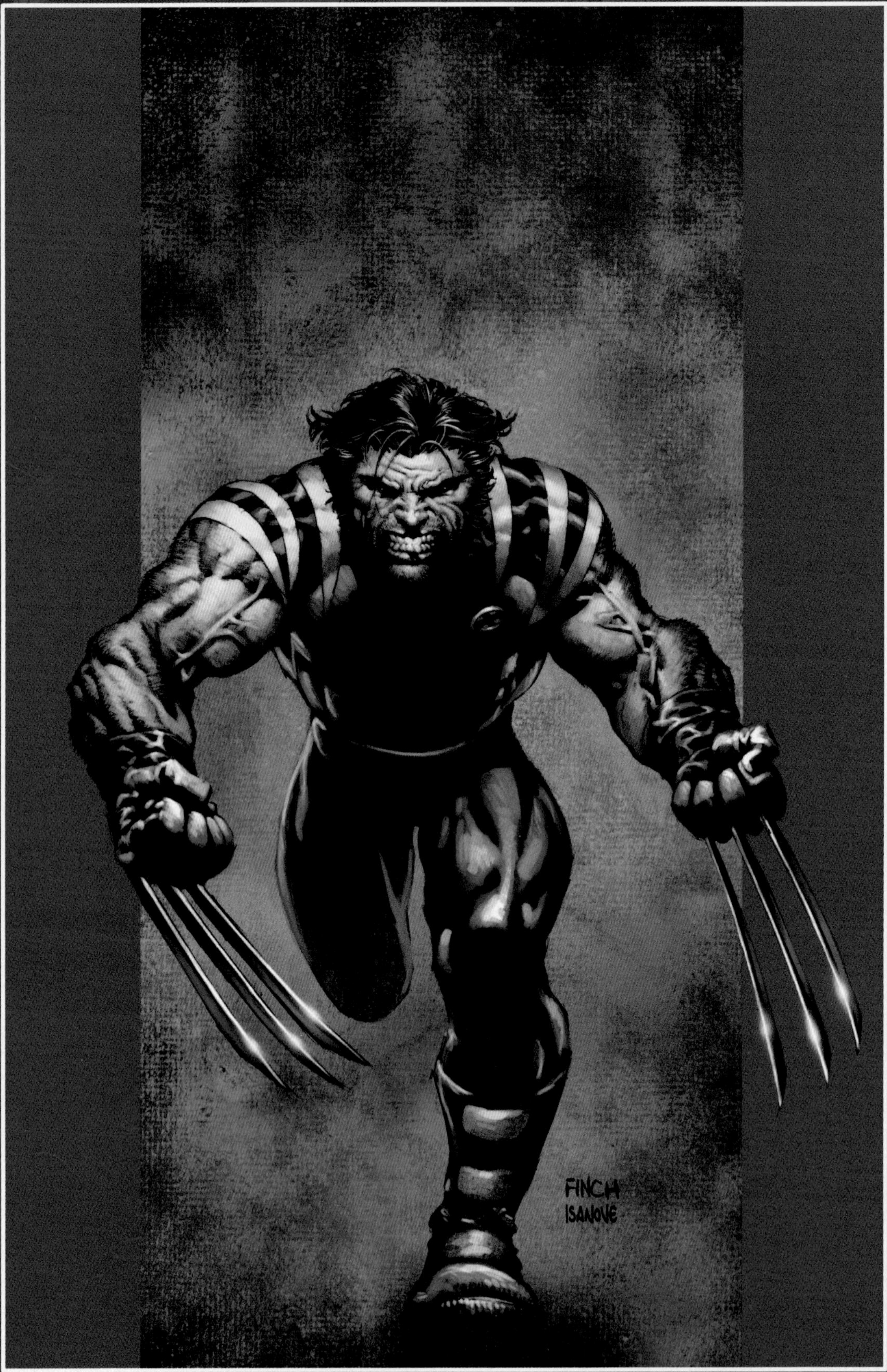
FINCH
ISANOVE

ULTIMATE X-MEN #41

Charles Xavier	Scott Summers	Jean Grey	Ororo Munroe	Logan	Kitty Pryde	Hank McCoy	Peter Rasputin
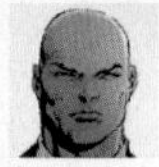	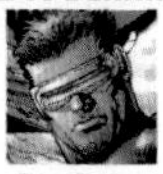	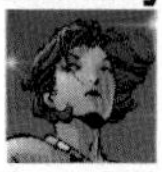	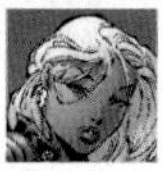	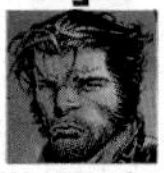	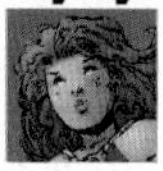	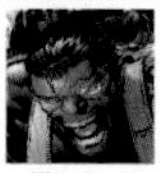	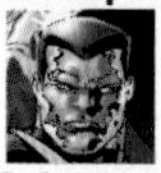
Professor X	Cyclops	Marvel Girl	Storm	Wolverine	Shadowcat	Beast	Colossus

Stan Lee presents:

ULTIMATE X-MEN

Professor Charles Xavier brought them together to bridge the gap between humanity and those born with strange and amazing powers: Cyclops, Marvel Girl, Storm, Iceman, Beast, Colossus and Wolverine. They are the X-Men, soldiers for Xavier's war to bring peace between man and mutant!

PREVIOUSLY IN ULTIMATE X-MEN:

The X-Men have gone public in an attempt to carry their pro mutant/human relations messages forward. The X-Men now fall under the jurisdiction of world security leader Nick Fury with both the government and Xavier trying to figure out exactly how this new relationship will work.

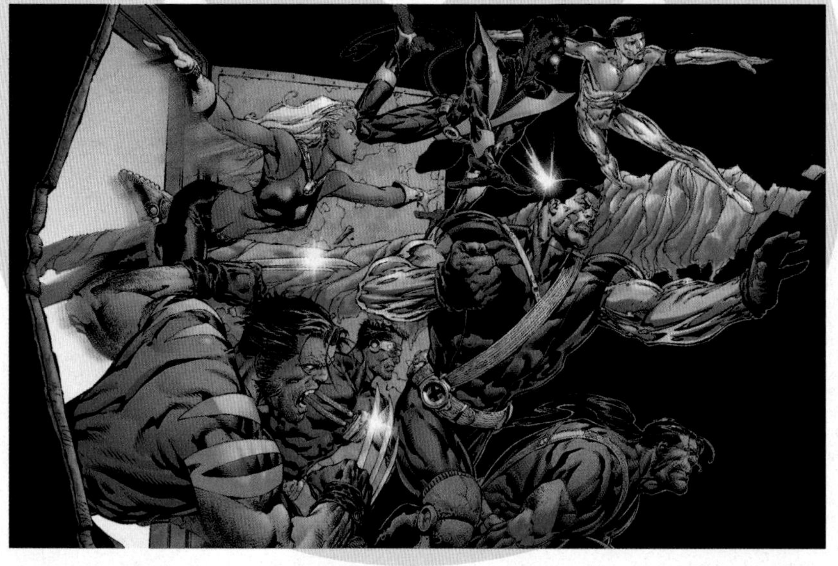

NEW MUTANTS

PART TWO

Brian Michael BENDIS STORY
David FINCH PENCILS
Art THIBERT INKS

Frank D'ARMATA COLORS
Chris ELIOPOULOS LETTERS
MacKenzie CADENHEAD ASSISTANT EDITORS
Nick LOWE EDITORS

C.B. CEBULSKI ASSOCIATE EDITOR
Ralph MACCHIO EDITOR
Joe QUESADA EDITOR IN CHIEF
Dan BUCKLEY PUBLISHER

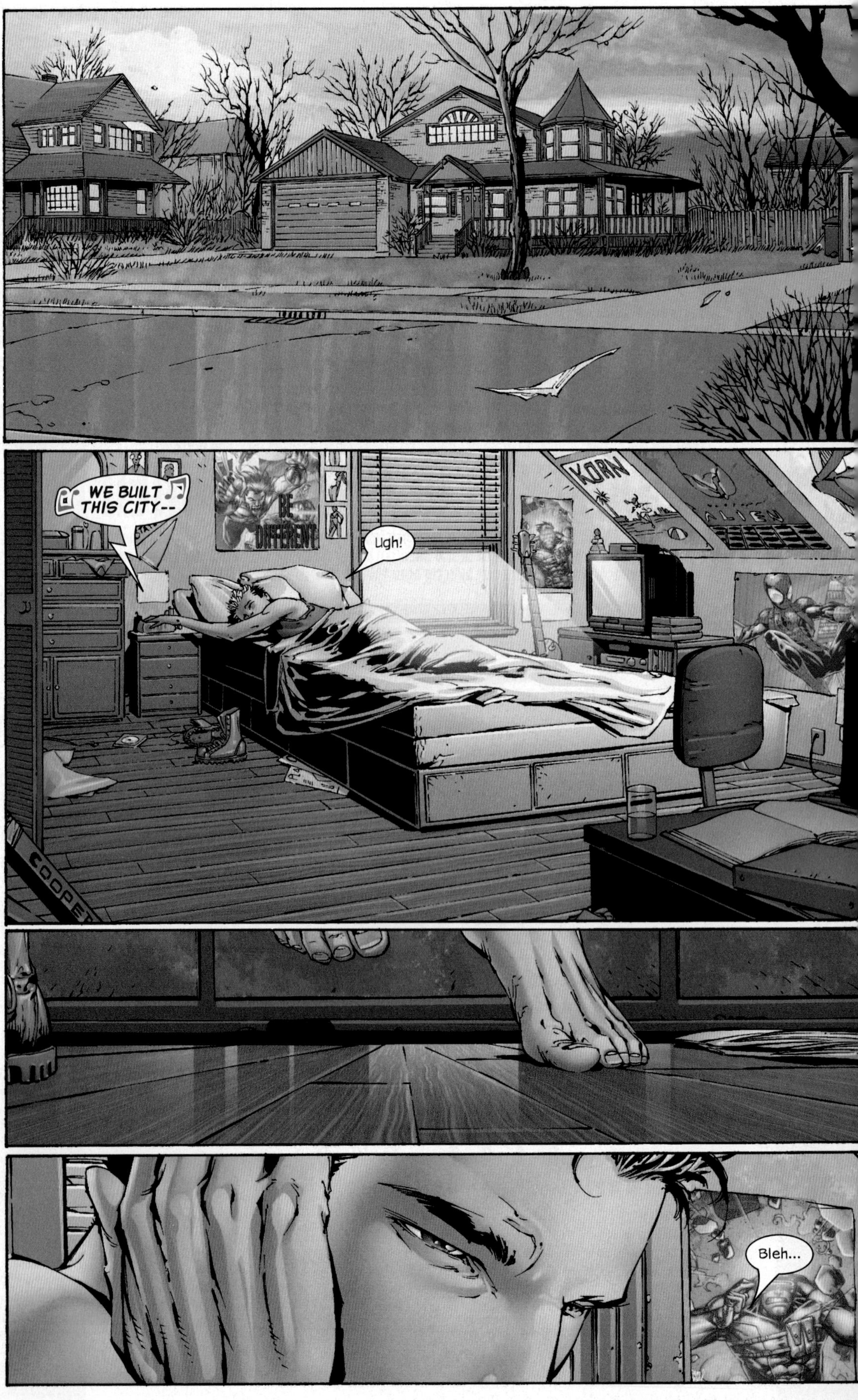
WE BUILT THIS CITY--
BE DIFFERENT
KORN
ALIEN
Ugh!
Bleh...

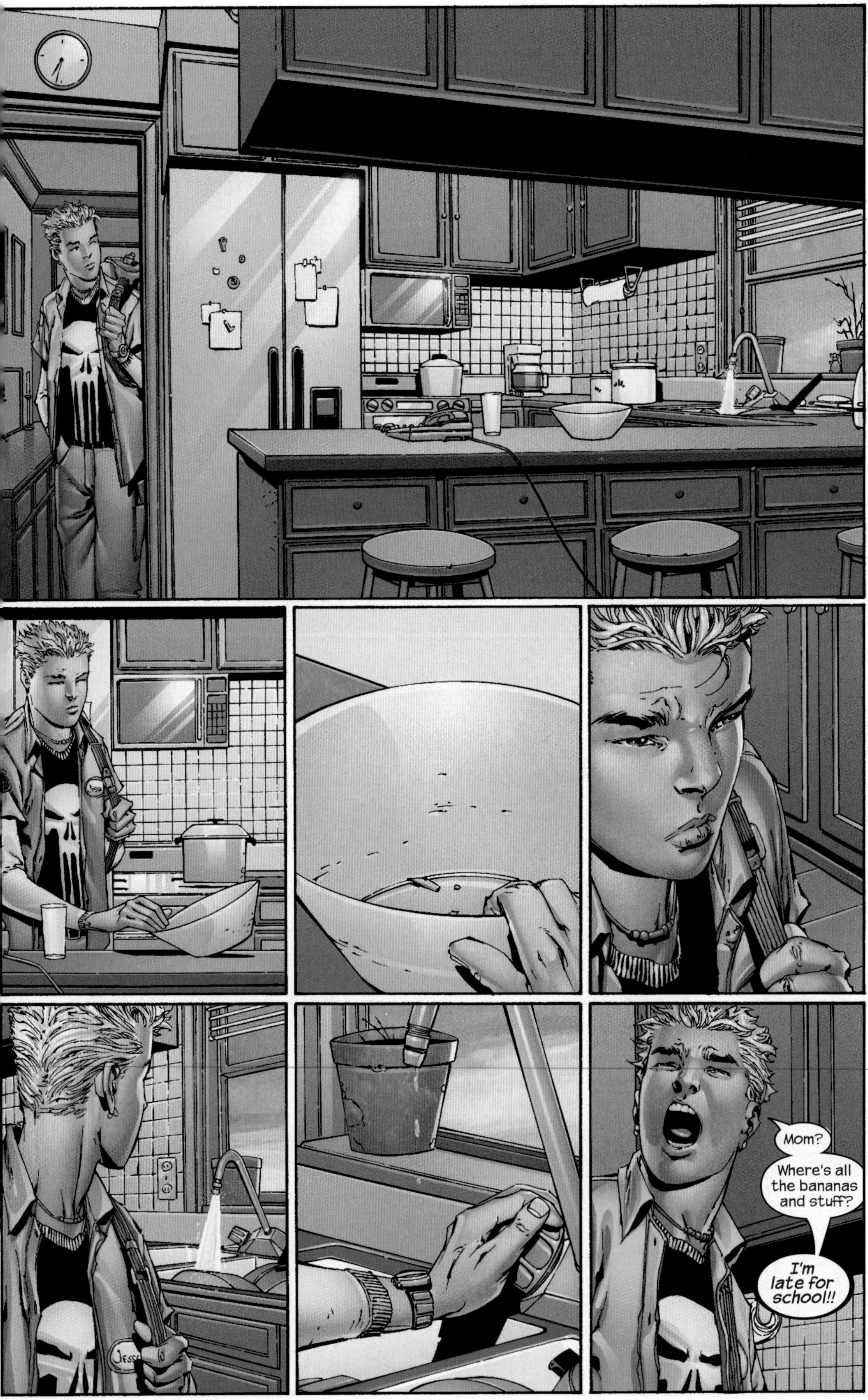
Mom?
Where's all the bananas and stuff?
I'm late for school!!

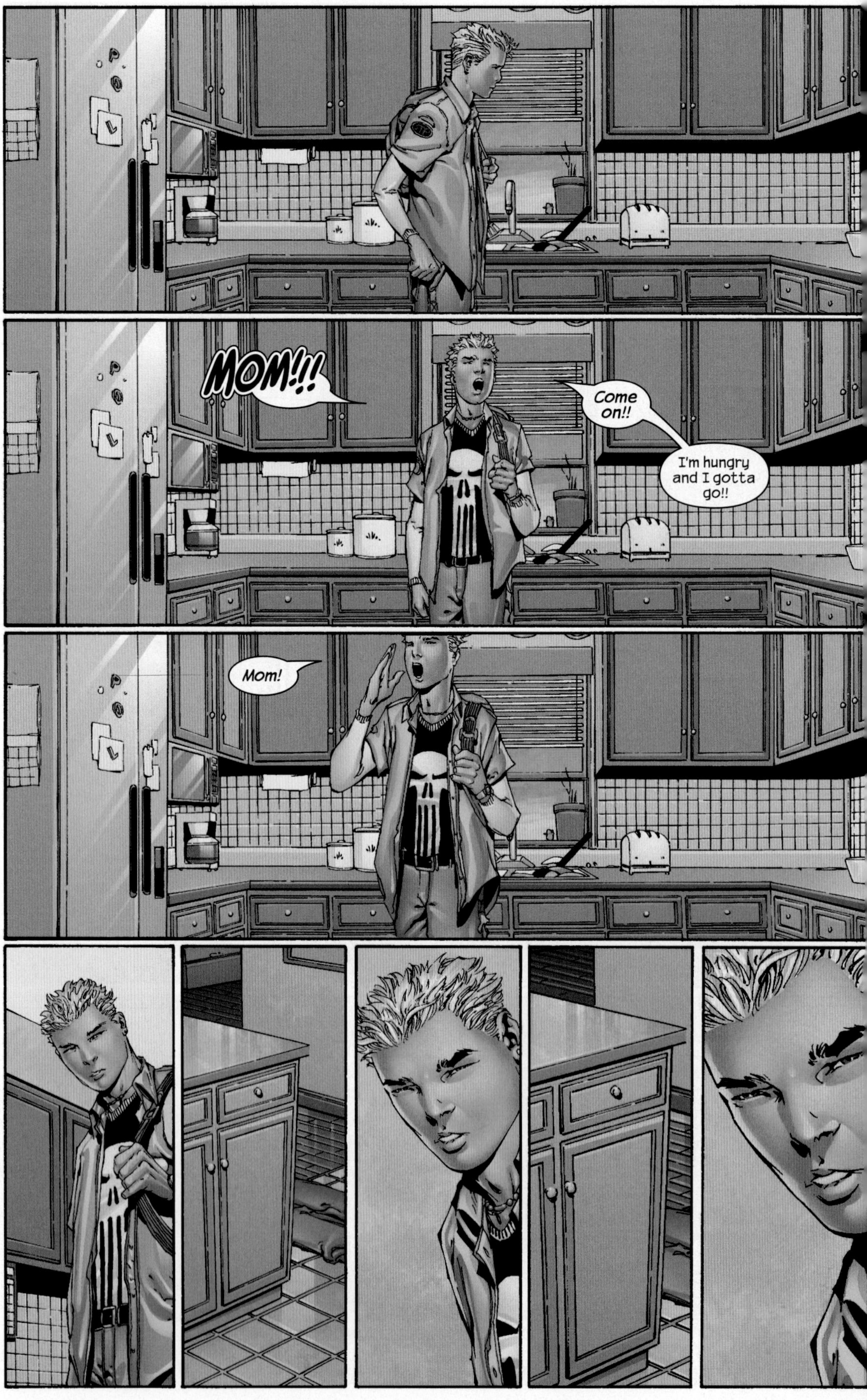
MOM!!!
Come on!!
I'm hungry and I gotta go!!
Mom!

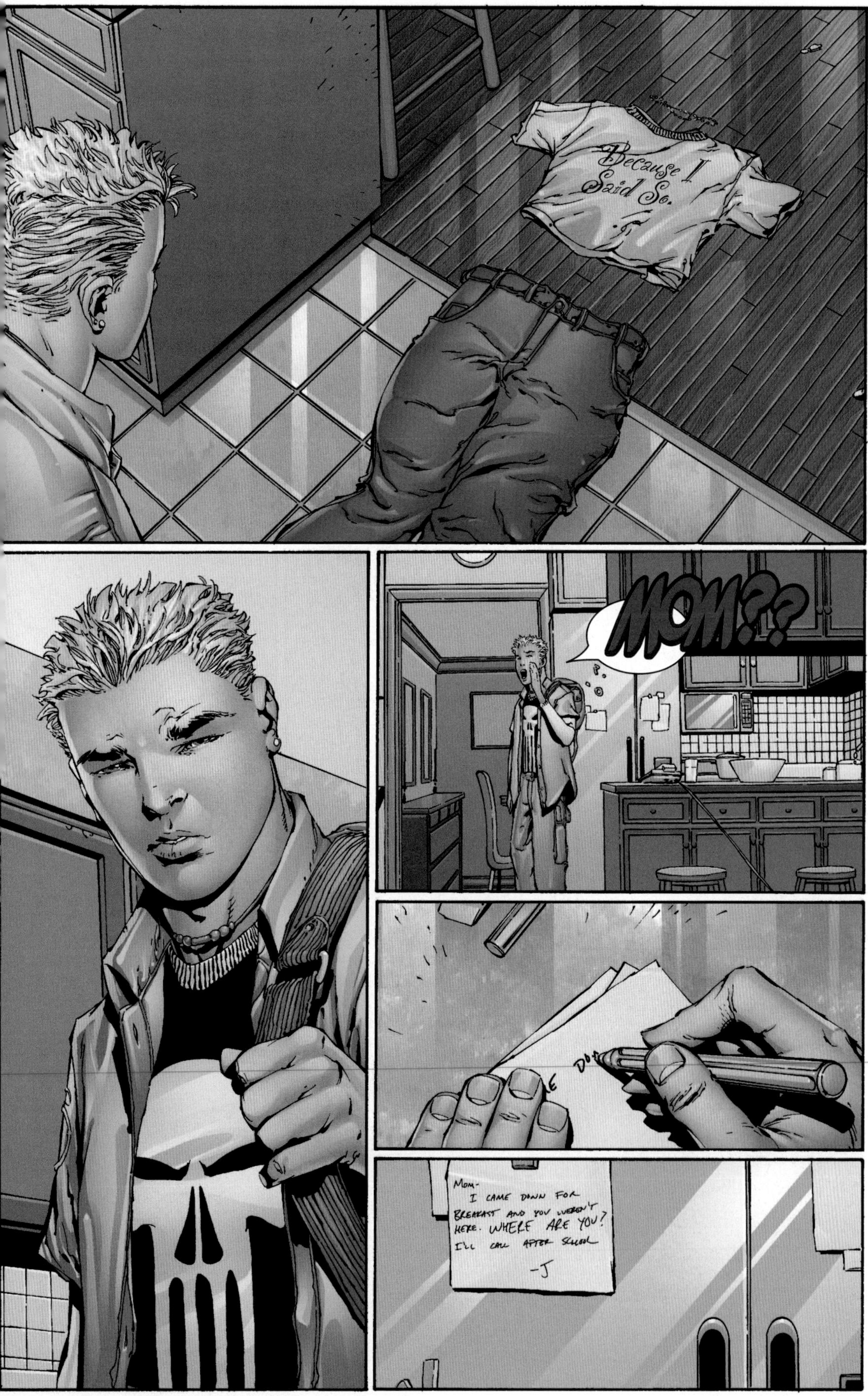
Because I
Said So.
MOM???
Mom-
I CAME DOWN FOR BREAKFAST AND YOU WEREN'T HERE. WHERE ARE YOU?
I'LL CALL AFTER SCHOOL
-J

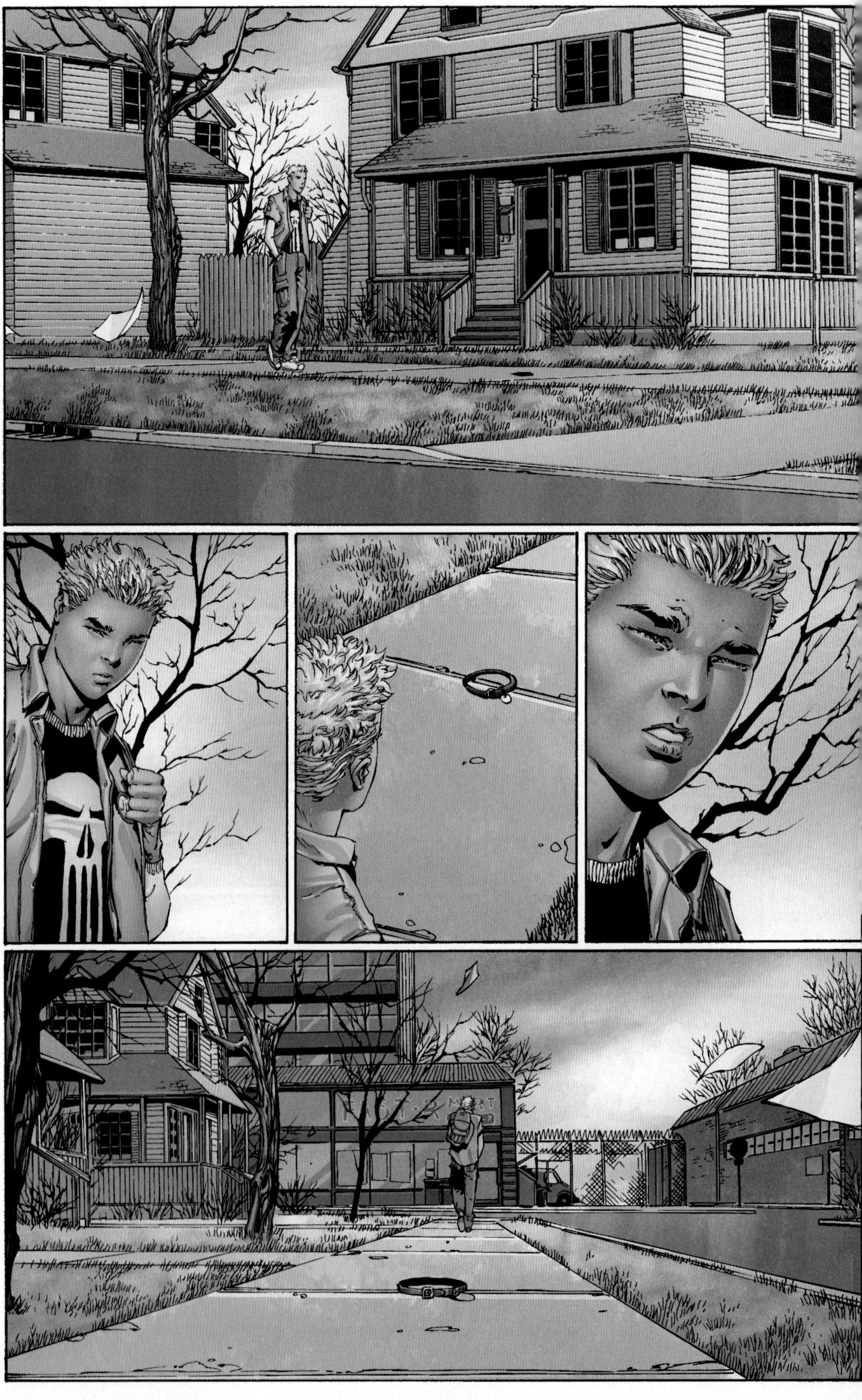

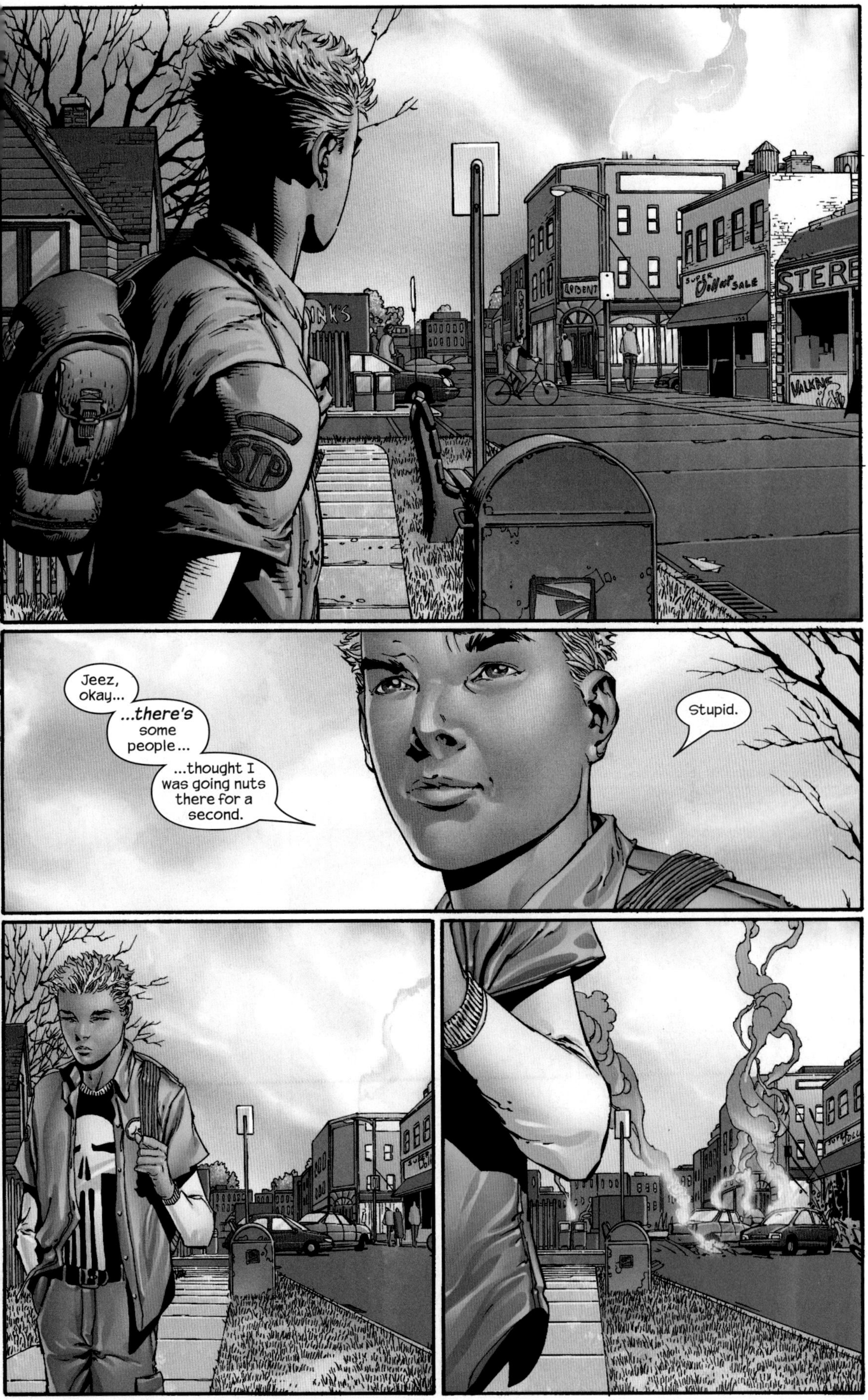
STP
Jeez, okay...
...there's some people...
...thought I was going nuts there for a second.
Stupid.

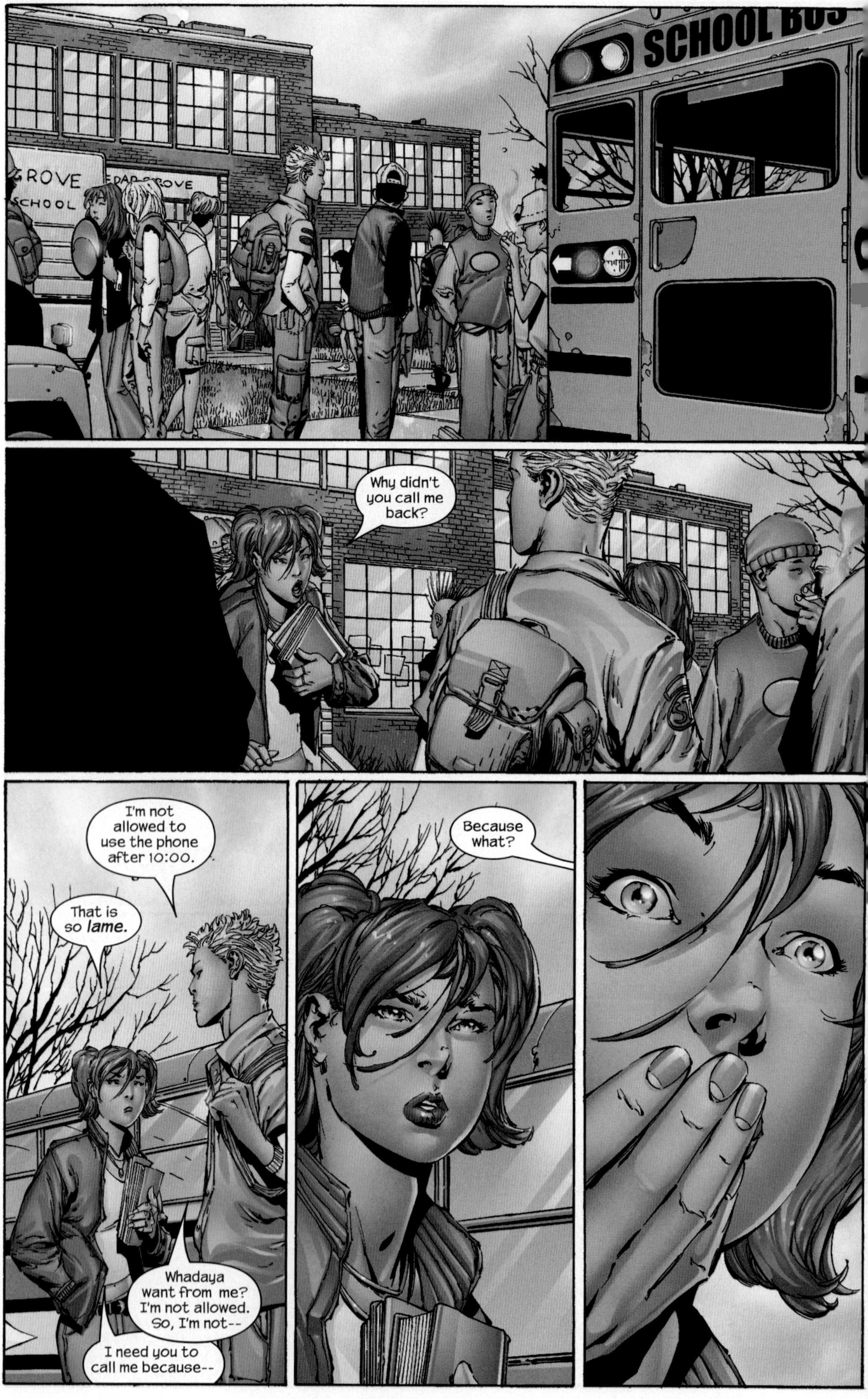

SCHOOL BUS
GROVE SCHOOL
Why didn't you call me back?
I'm not allowed to use the phone after 10:00.
That is so *lame.*
Whadaya want from me? I'm not allowed. So, I'm not--
I need you to call me because--
Because what?

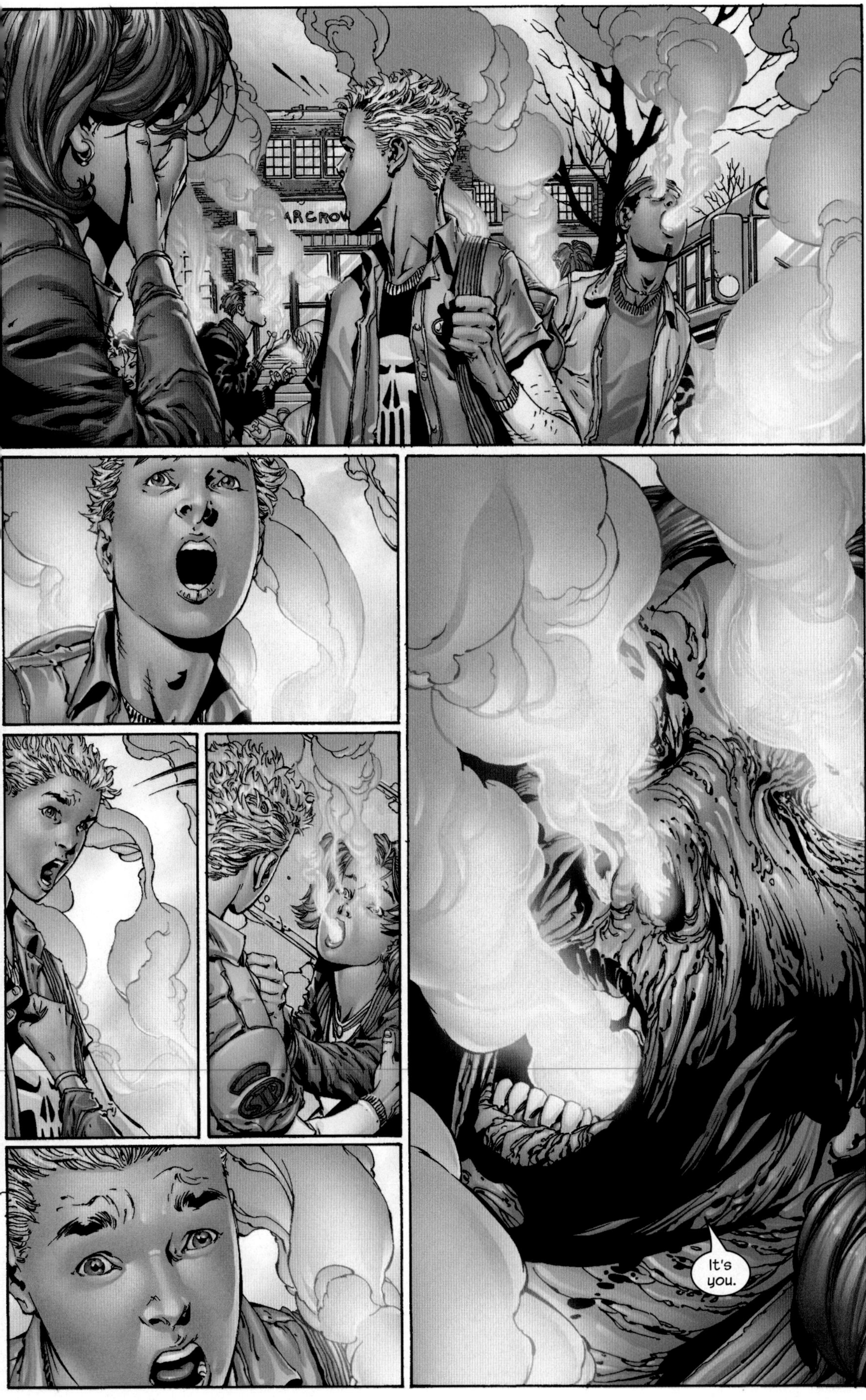
It's you.

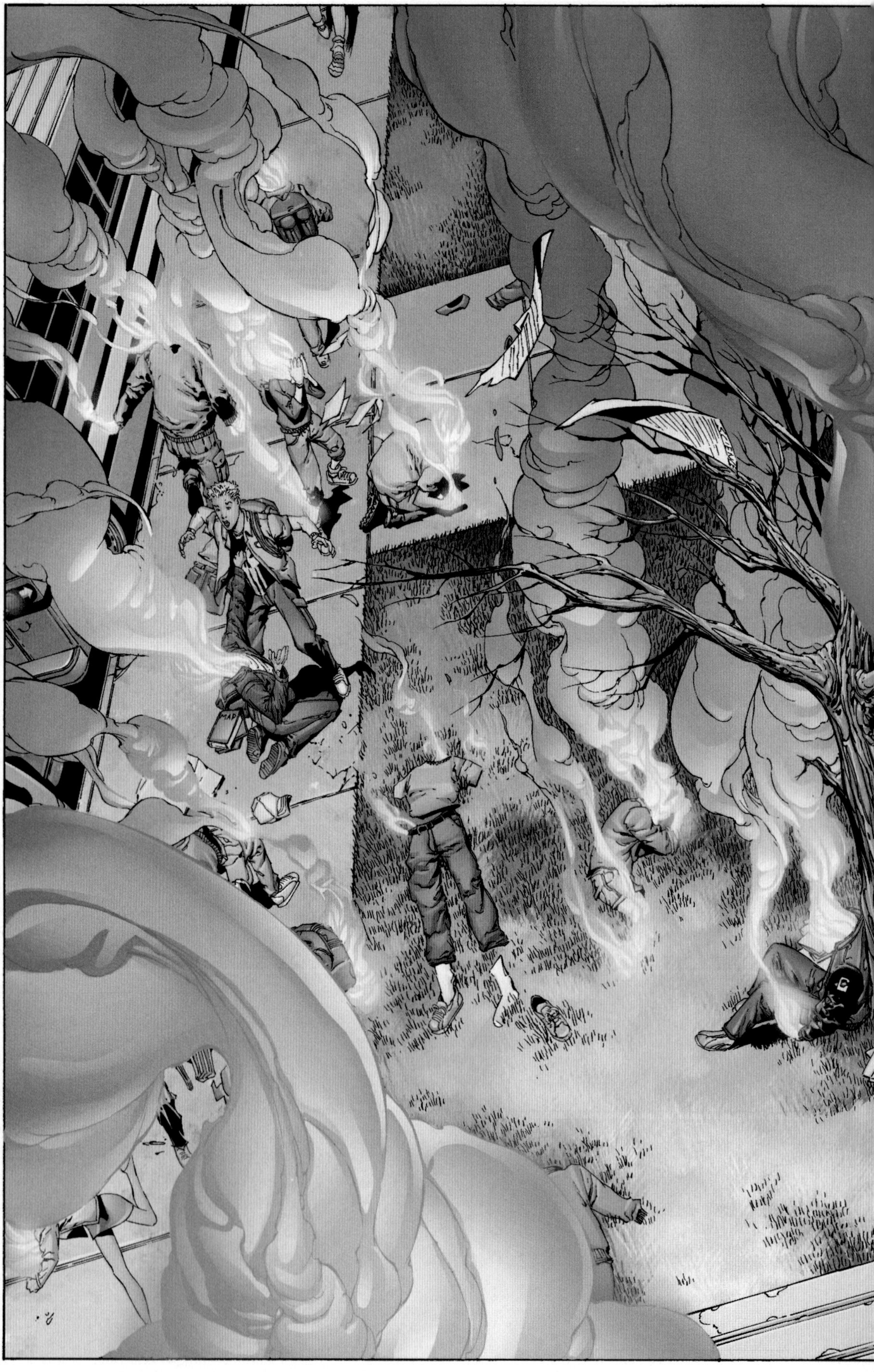

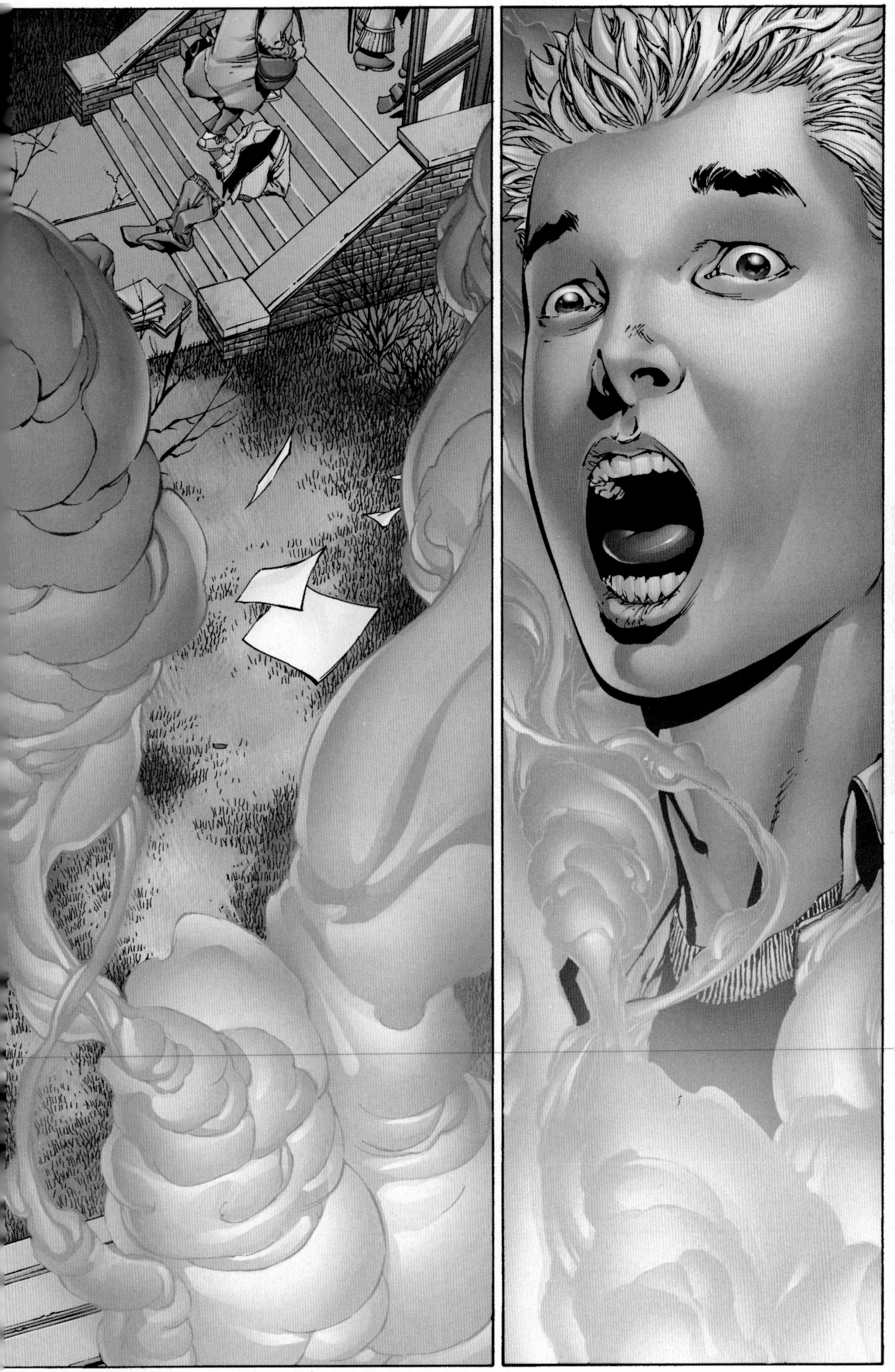

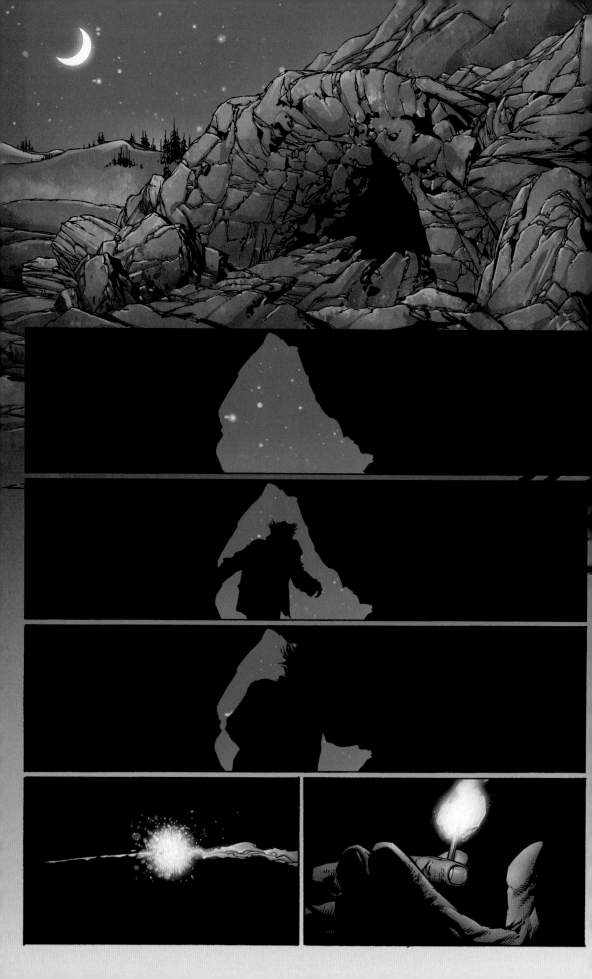

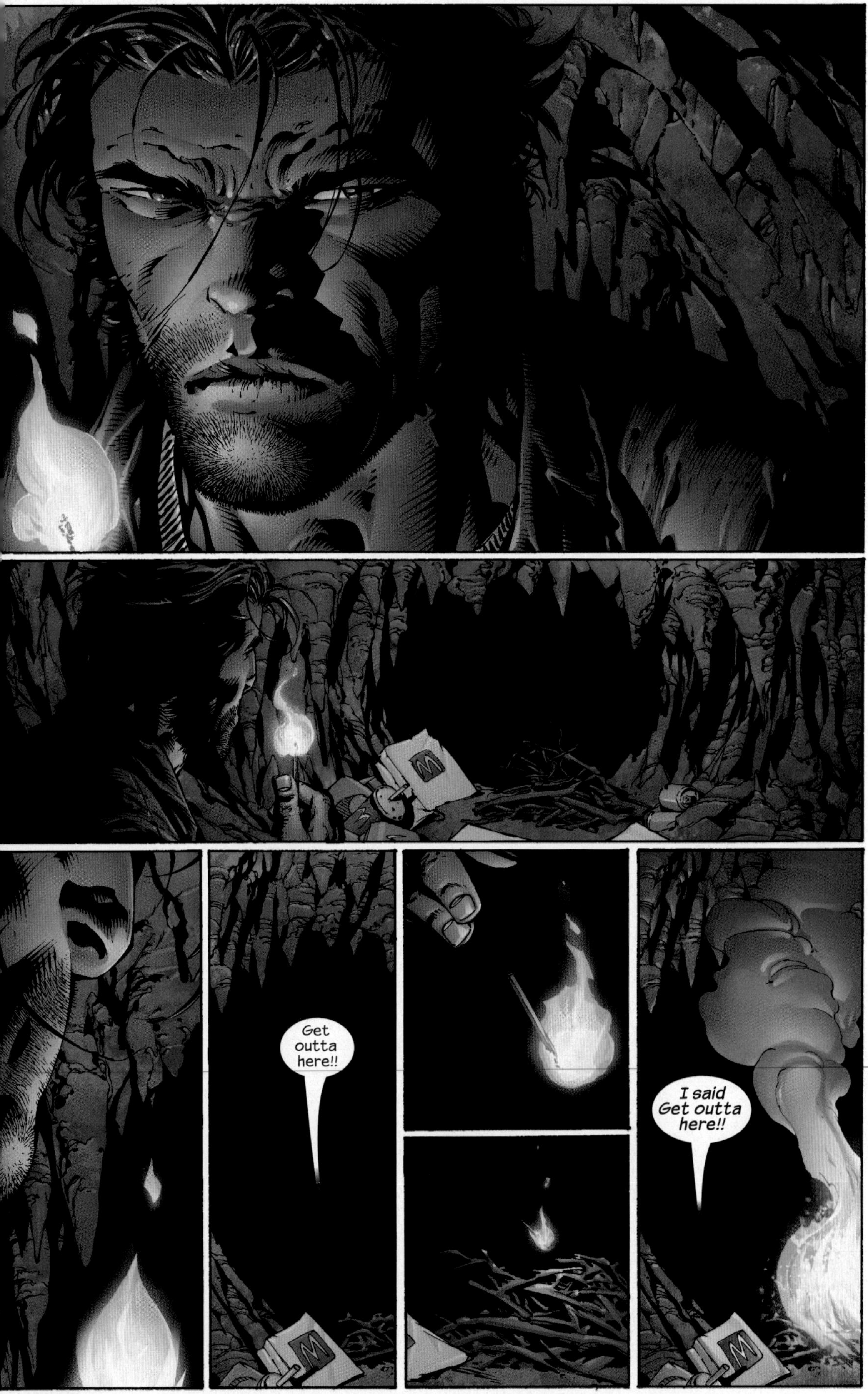
Get outta here!!
I said Get outta here!!

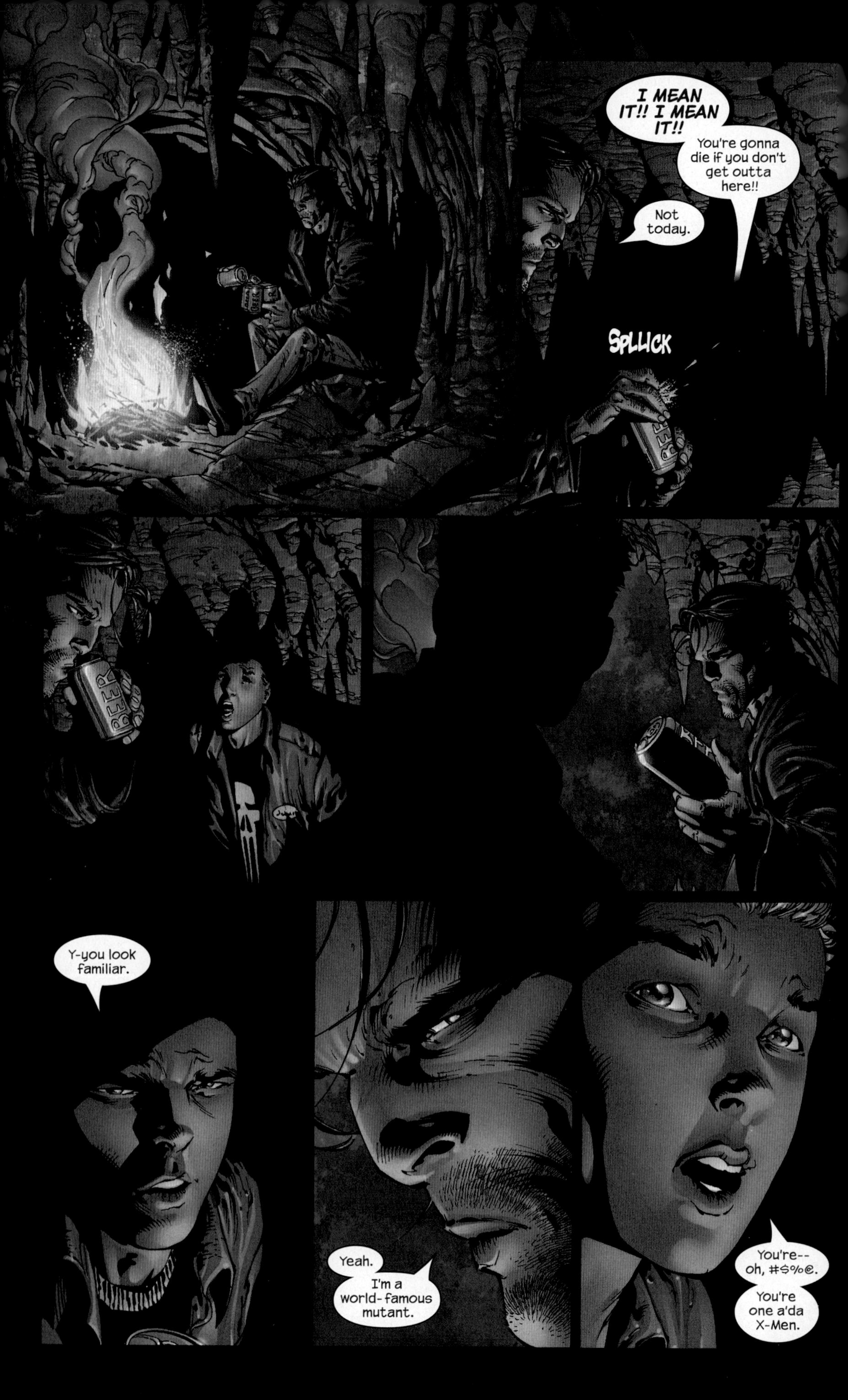
I MEAN IT!! I MEAN IT!!
You're gonna die if you don't get outta here!!
Not today.
SPLLICK
Y-you look familiar.
Yeah.
I'm a world-famous mutant.
You're-- oh, #$%@.
You're one a'da X-Men.

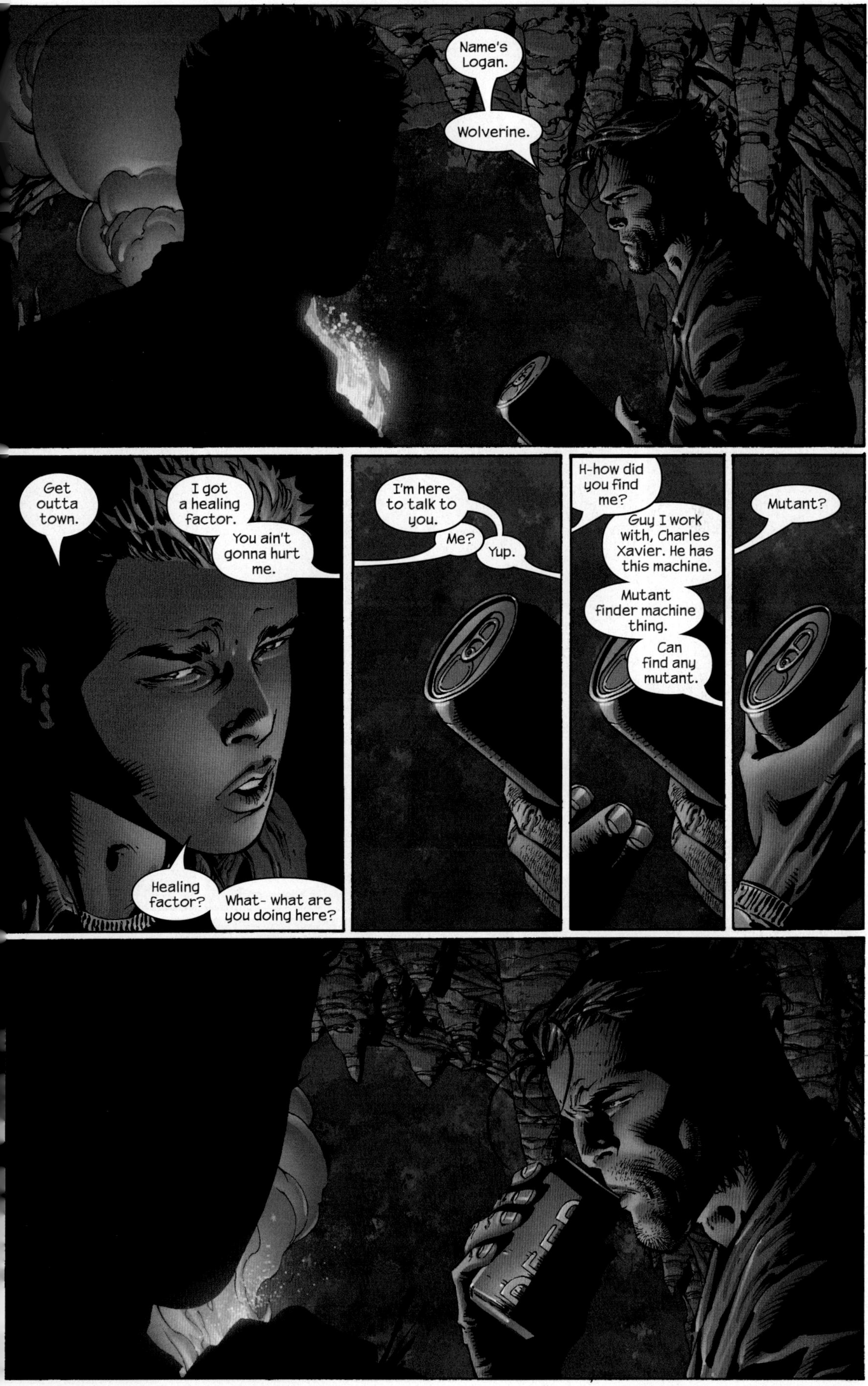
Name's Logan.
Wolverine.
Get outta town.
I got a healing factor.
You ain't gonna hurt me.
Healing factor?
What- what are you doing here?
I'm here to talk to you.
Me?
Yup.
H-how did you find me?
Guy I work with, Charles Xavier. He has this machine.
Mutant finder machine thing.
Can find any mutant.
Mutant?

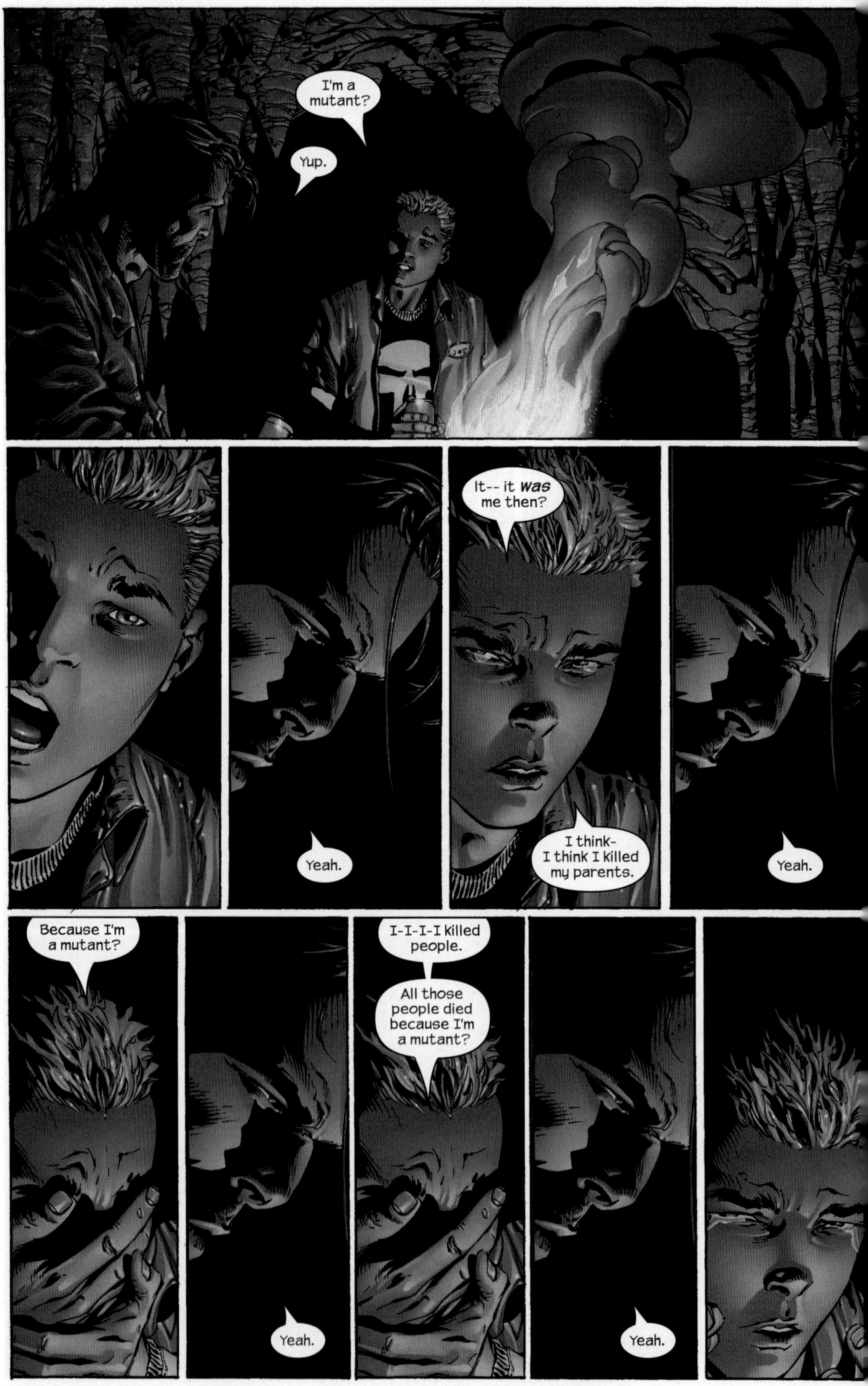
I'm a mutant?
Yup.
Yeah.
It-- it *was* me then?
I think-
I think I killed my parents.
Yeah.
Because I'm a mutant?
Yeah.
I-I-I-I killed people.
All those people died because I'm a mutant?
Yeah.

Sniff...

How many people did I *kill*?

You really don't want to know.

No. Yes.

Please.

They say 265.

Maybe more.

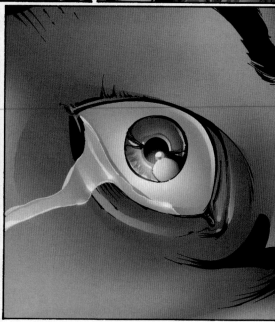

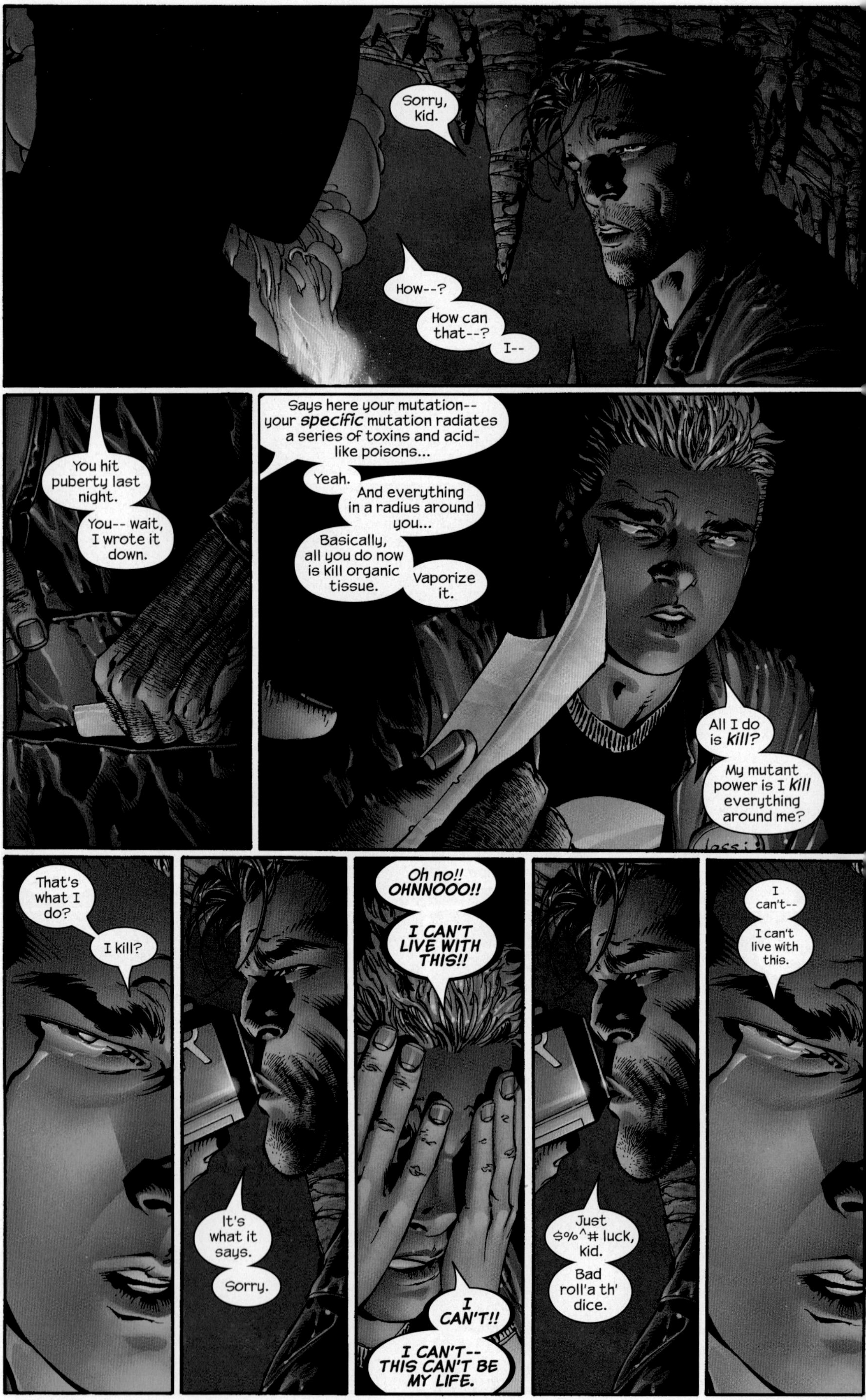
Sorry, kid.
How--?
How can that--?
I--
You hit puberty last night.
You-- wait, I wrote it down.
Says here your mutation-- your *specific* mutation radiates a series of toxins and acid-like poisons...
Yeah.
And everything in a radius around you...
Basically, all you do now is kill organic tissue.
Vaporize it.
All I do is *kill?*
My mutant power is I *kill* everything around me?
That's what I do?
I kill?
It's what it says.
Sorry.
Oh no!! OHNNOOO!!
I CAN'T LIVE WITH THIS!!
I CAN'T!!
I CAN'T-- THIS CAN'T BE MY LIFE.
Just $%^# luck, kid.
Bad roll'a th' dice.
I can't--
I can't live with this.

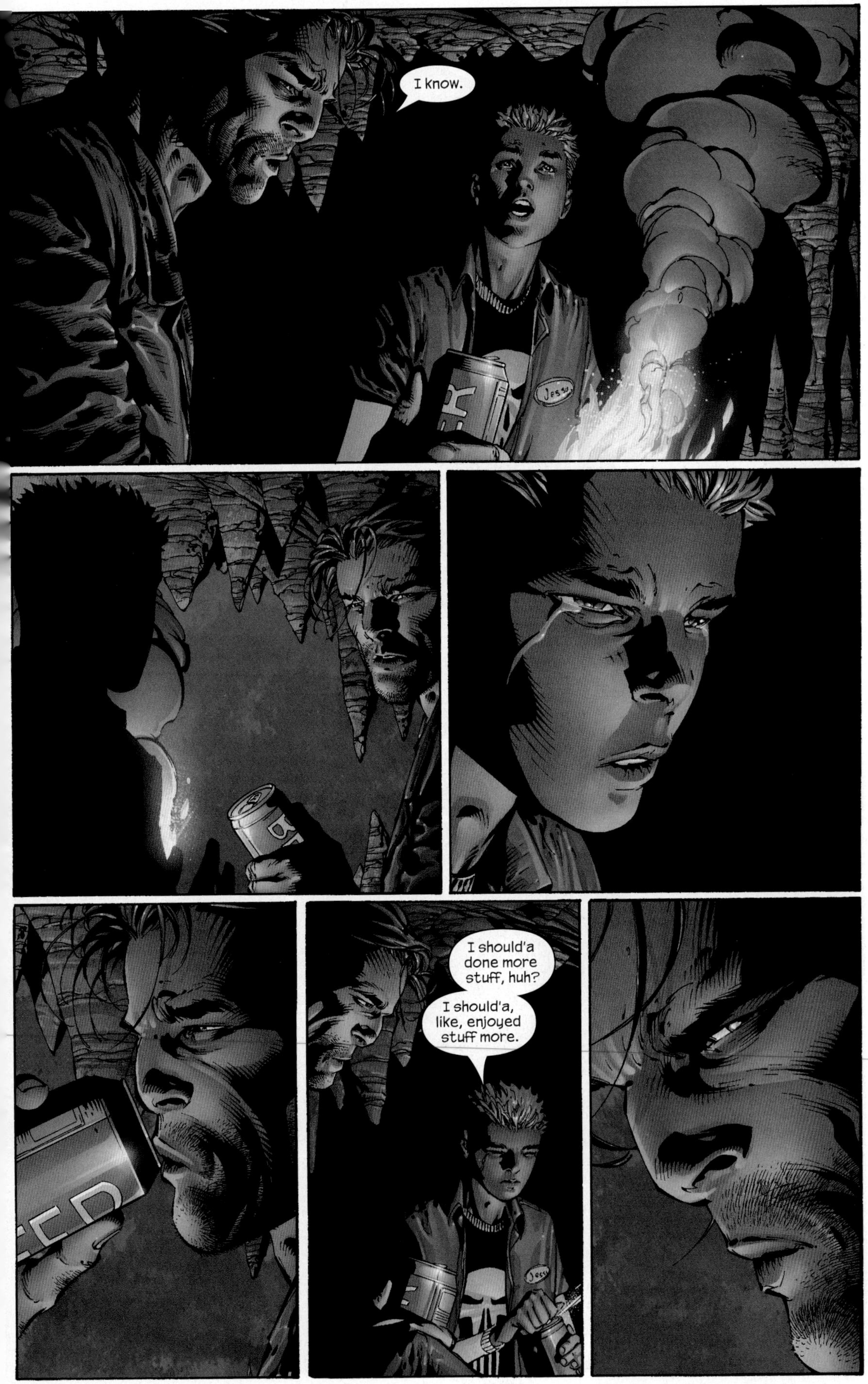
I know.
I should'a done more stuff, huh?
I should'a, like, enjoyed stuff more.

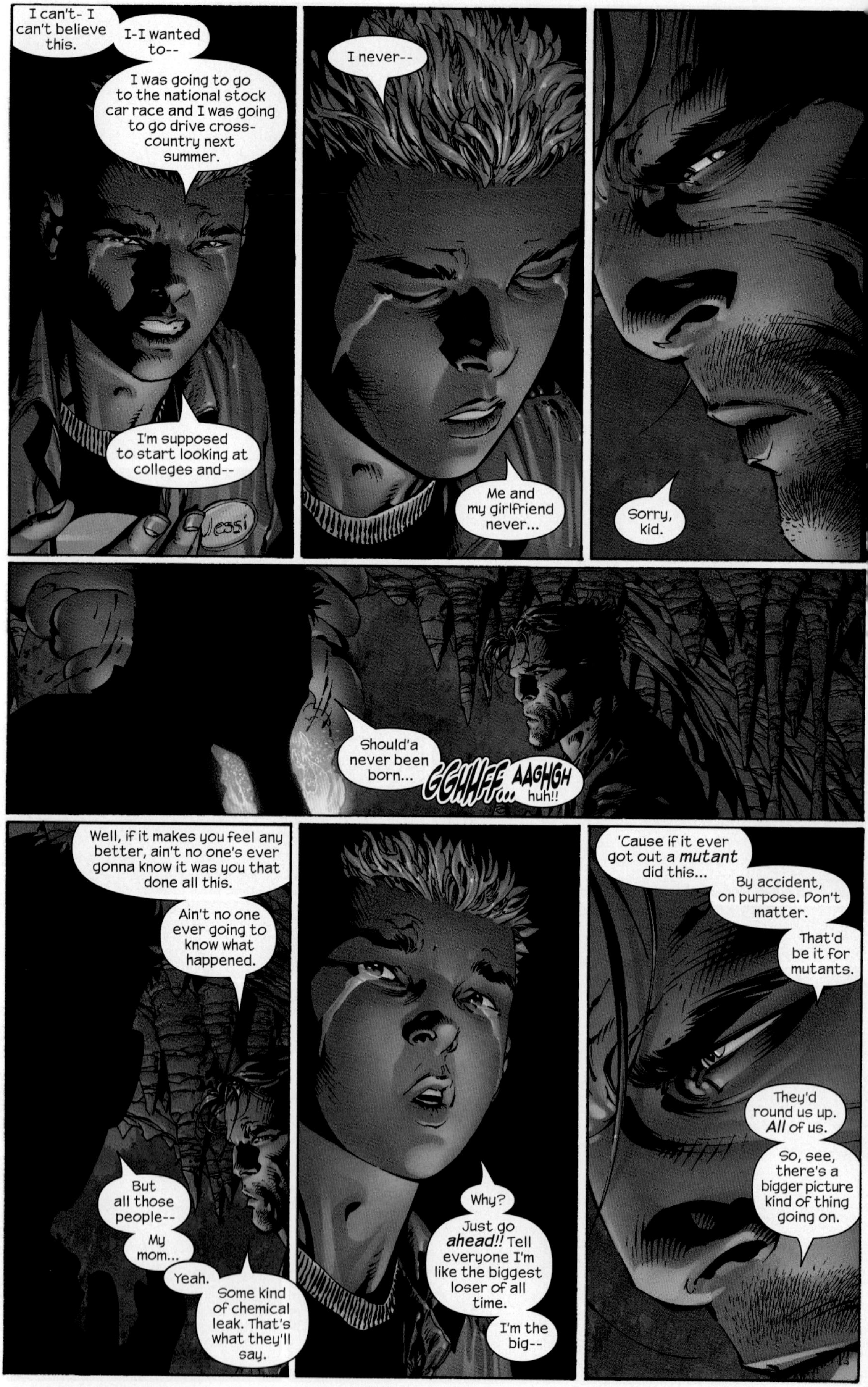
I can't- I can't believe this.
I-I wanted to--
I was going to go to the national stock car race and I was going to go drive cross-country next summer.
I'm supposed to start looking at colleges and--
Jessi
I never--
Me and my girlfriend never...
Sorry, kid.
Should'a never been born...
GGHHFF...
AAGHGH huh!!
Well, if it makes you feel any better, ain't no one's ever gonna know it was you that done all this.
Ain't no one ever going to know what happened.
But all those people--
My mom...
Yeah.
Some kind of chemical leak. That's what they'll say.
Why?
Just go *ahead!!* Tell everyone I'm like the biggest loser of all time.
I'm the big--
'Cause if it ever got out a *mutant* did this...
By accident, on purpose. Don't matter.
That'd be it for mutants.
They'd round us up. *All* of us.
So, see, there's a bigger picture kind of thing going on.

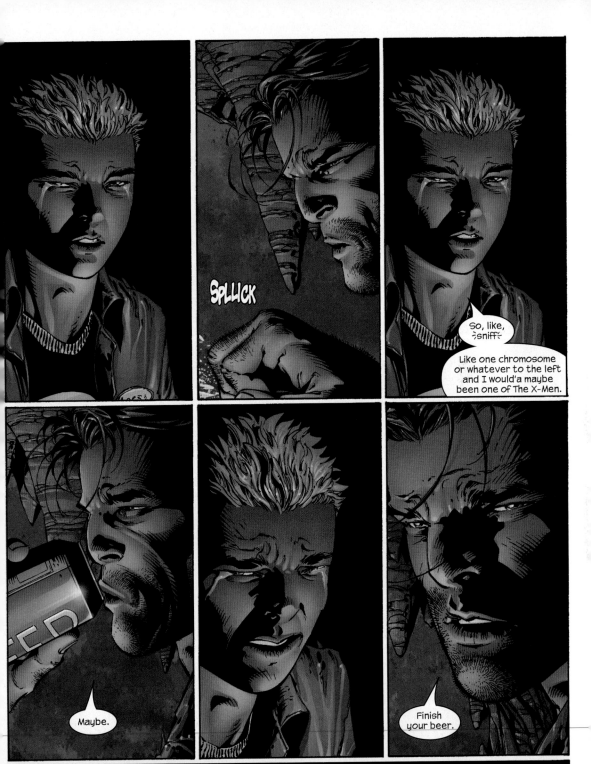

SPLLICK

So, like, ¿sniff¿

Like one chromosome or whatever to the left and I would'a maybe been one of The X-Men.

Maybe.

Finish your beer.

Just do it.

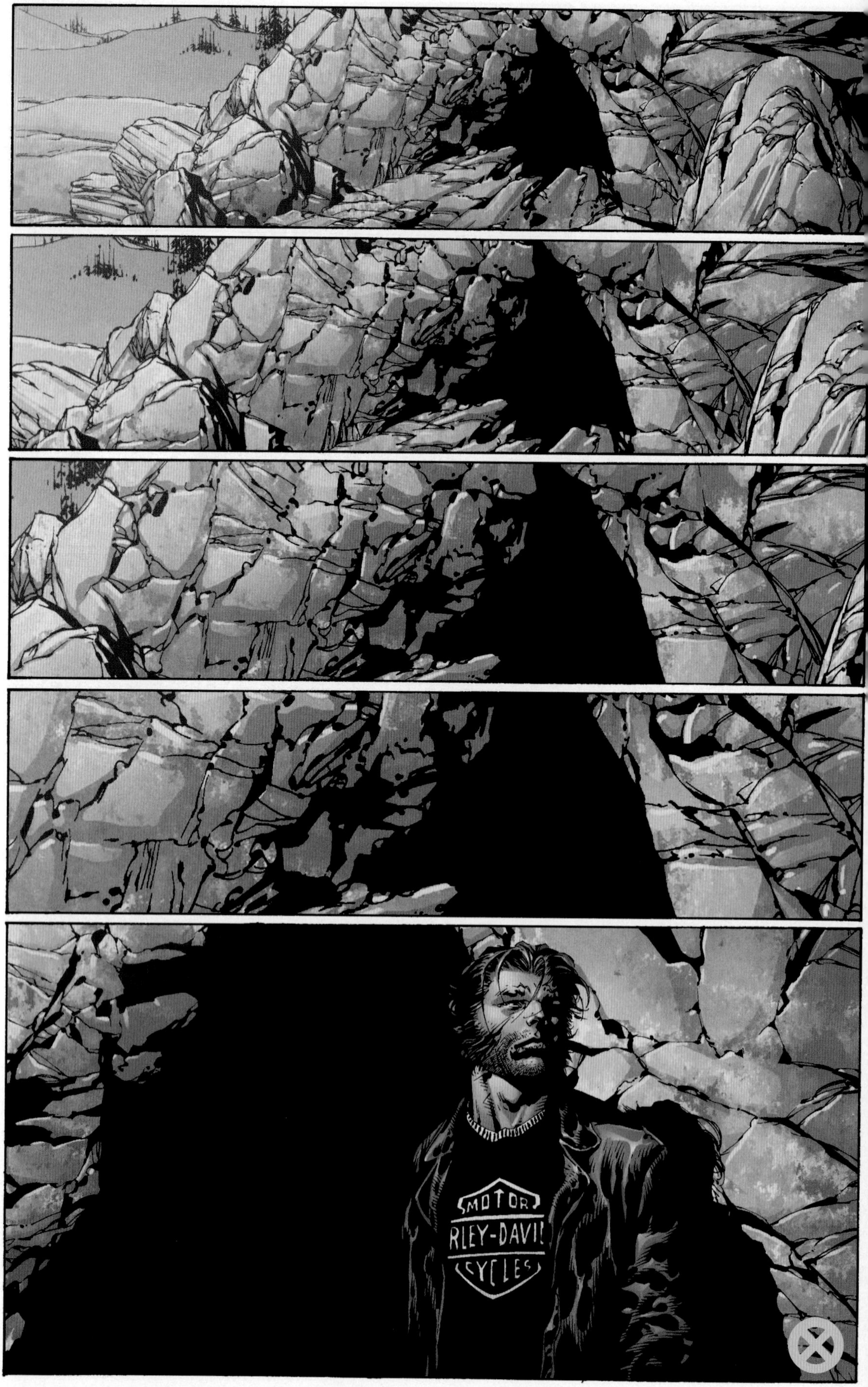
MOTOR
RLEY-DAVI
CYCLES

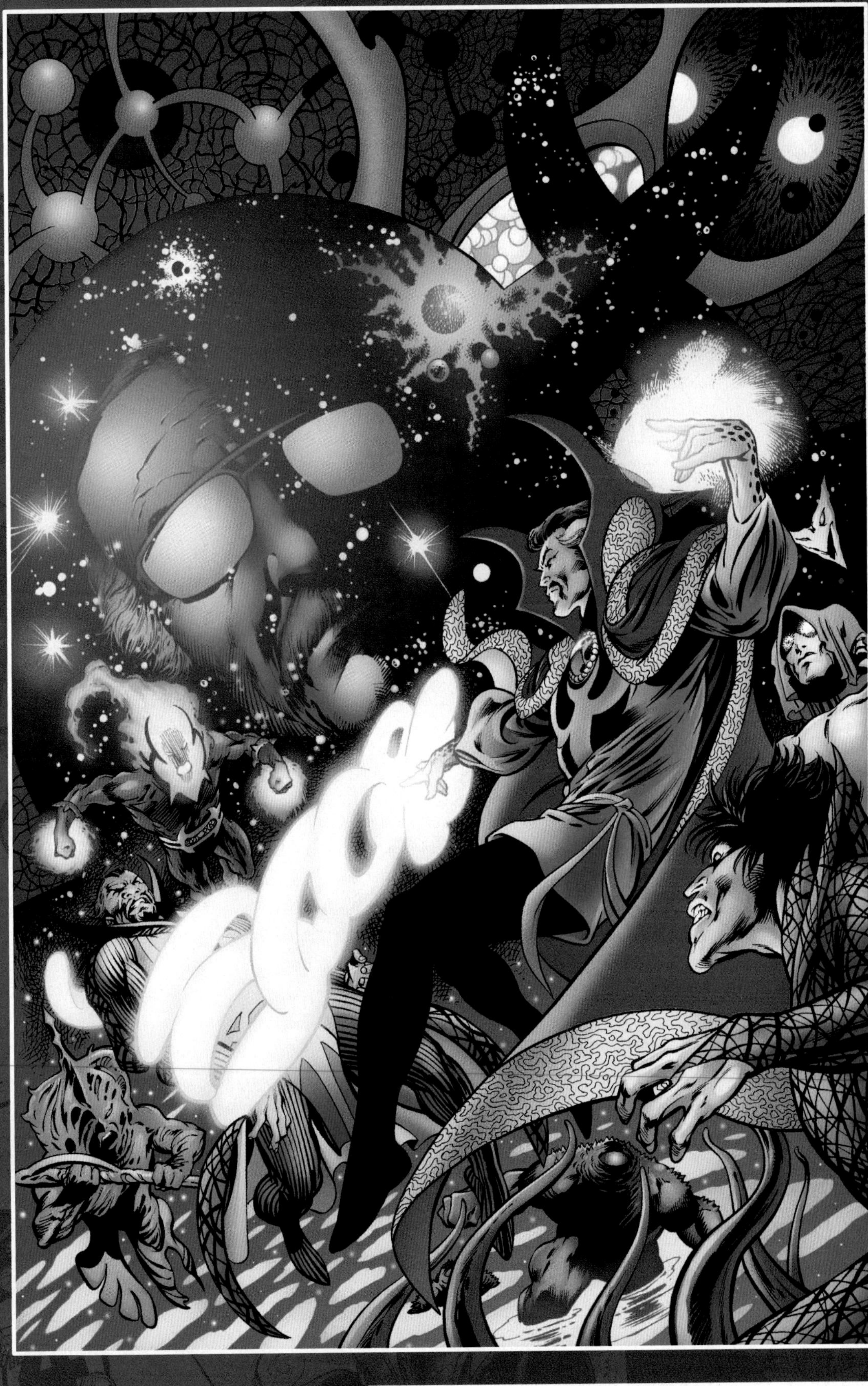

STAN LEE MEETS DR. STRANGE

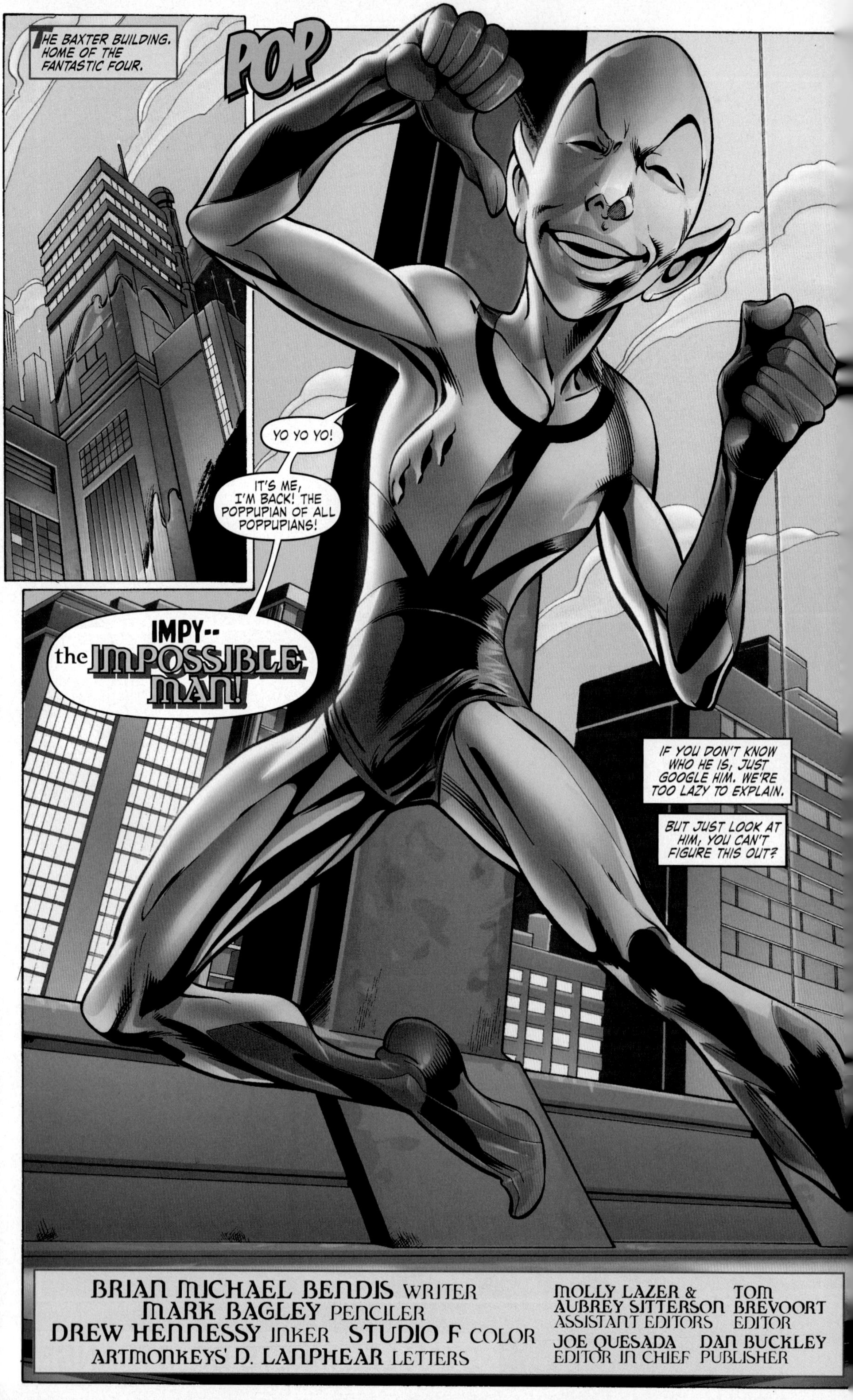
THE BAXTER BUILDING. HOME OF THE FANTASTIC FOUR.
POP
YO YO YO!
IT'S ME, I'M BACK! THE POPPUPIAN OF ALL POPPUPIANS!
IMPY-- the IMPOSSIBLE MAN!
IF YOU DON'T KNOW WHO HE IS, JUST GOOGLE HIM. WE'RE TOO LAZY TO EXPLAIN.
BUT JUST LOOK AT HIM, YOU CAN'T FIGURE THIS OUT?
BRIAN MICHAEL BENDIS WRITER
MARK BAGLEY PENCILER
DREW HENNESSY INKER STUDIO F COLOR
ARTMONKEYS' D. LANPHEAR LETTERS
MOLLY LAZER & AUBREY SITTERSON ASSISTANT EDITORS
TOM BREVOORT EDITOR
JOE QUESADA EDITOR IN CHIEF
DAN BUCKLEY PUBLISHER

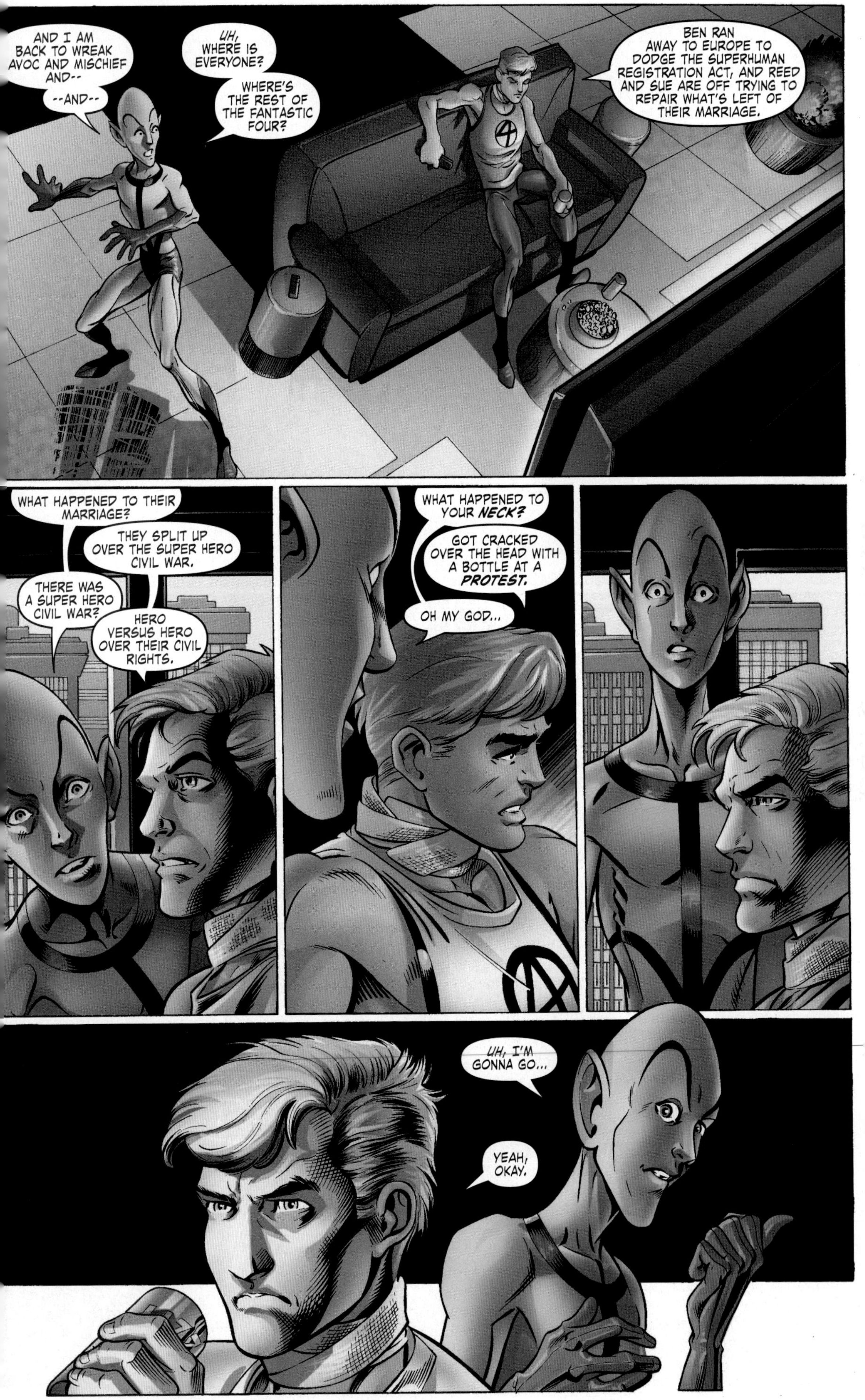
AND I AM BACK TO WREAK AVOC AND MISCHIEF AND--
--AND--
UH, WHERE IS EVERYONE?
WHERE'S THE REST OF THE FANTASTIC FOUR?
BEN RAN AWAY TO EUROPE TO DODGE THE SUPERHUMAN REGISTRATION ACT, AND REED AND SUE ARE OFF TRYING TO REPAIR WHAT'S LEFT OF THEIR MARRIAGE.
WHAT HAPPENED TO THEIR MARRIAGE?
THEY SPLIT UP OVER THE SUPER HERO CIVIL WAR.
THERE WAS A SUPER HERO CIVIL WAR?
HERO VERSUS HERO OVER THEIR CIVIL RIGHTS.
WHAT HAPPENED TO YOUR NECK?
GOT CRACKED OVER THE HEAD WITH A BOTTLE AT A PROTEST.
OH MY GOD...
UH, I'M GONNA GO...
YEAH, OKAY.

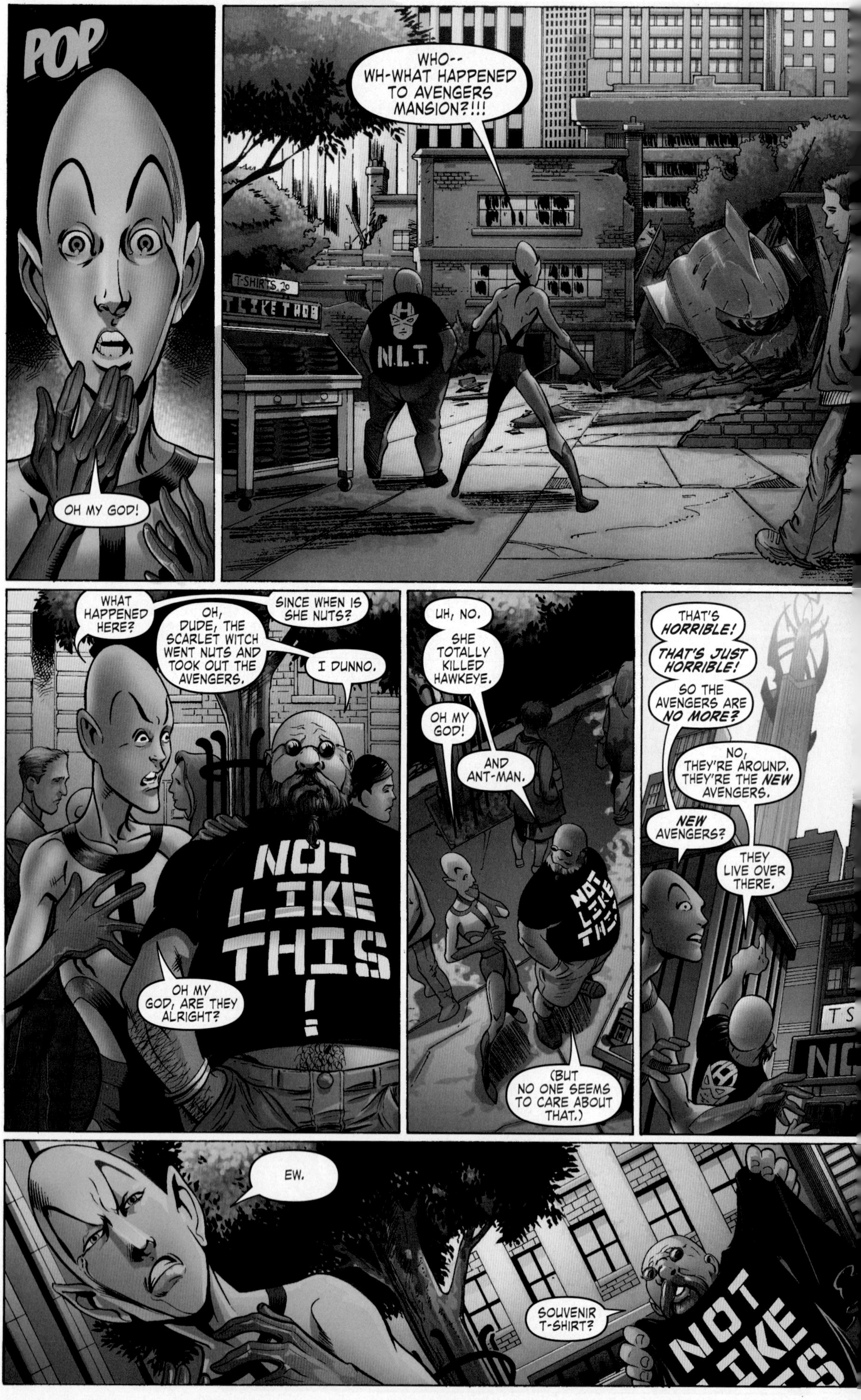
POP
OH MY GOD!
WHO-- WH-WHAT HAPPENED TO AVENGERS MANSION?!!!
T-SHIRTS 20
N.L.T.
WHAT HAPPENED HERE?
OH, DUDE, THE SCARLET WITCH WENT NUTS AND TOOK OUT THE AVENGERS.
SINCE WHEN IS SHE NUTS?
I DUNNO.
NOT LIKE THIS !
OH MY GOD, ARE THEY ALRIGHT?
UH, NO.
SHE TOTALLY KILLED HAWKEYE.
OH MY GOD!
AND ANT-MAN.
(BUT NO ONE SEEMS TO CARE ABOUT THAT.)
THAT'S HORRIBLE!
THAT'S JUST HORRIBLE!
SO THE AVENGERS ARE NO MORE?
NO, THEY'RE AROUND. THEY'RE THE NEW AVENGERS.
NEW AVENGERS?
THEY LIVE OVER THERE.
EW.
SOUVENIR T-SHIRT?

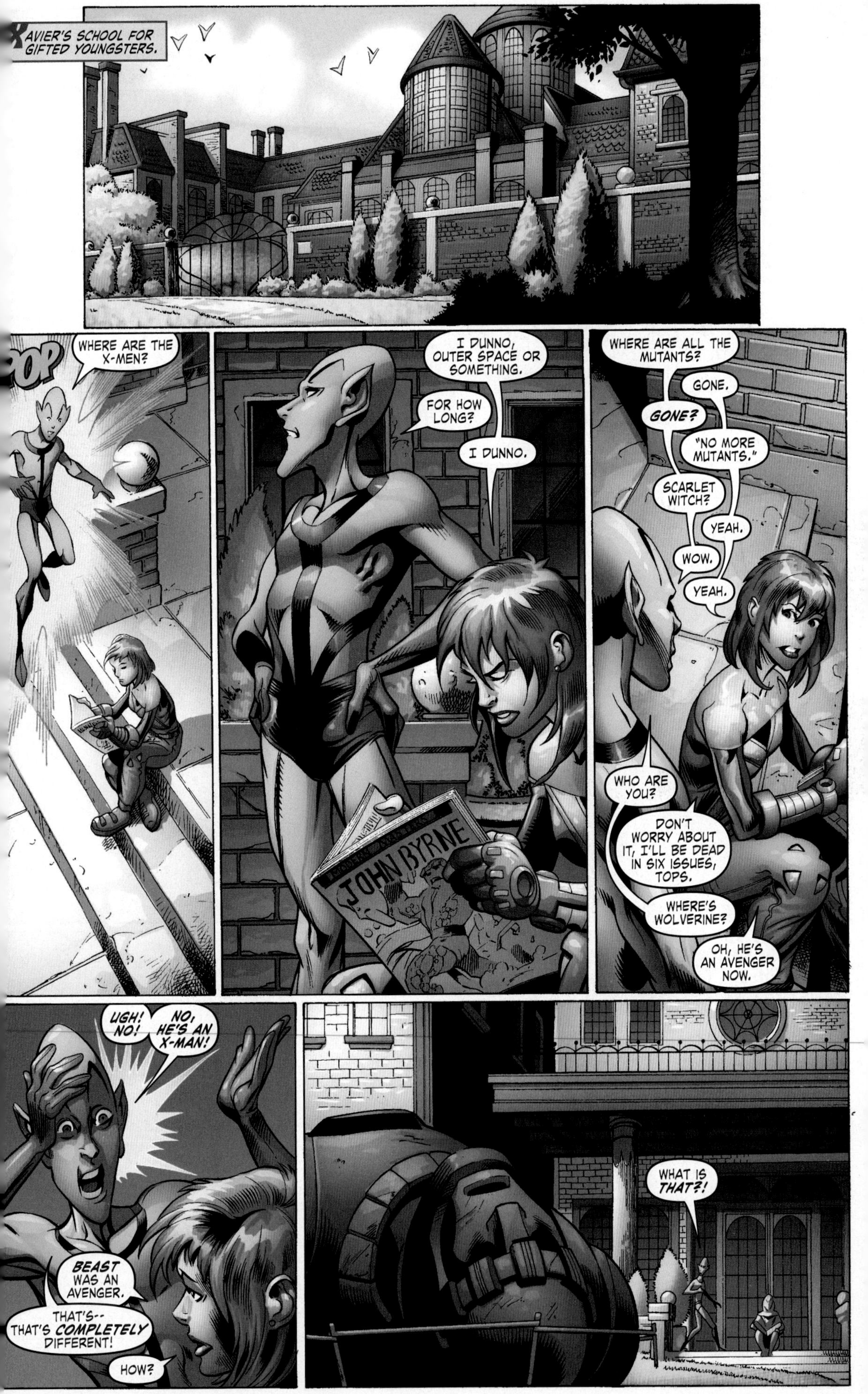
XAVIER'S SCHOOL FOR GIFTED YOUNGSTERS.
POP
WHERE ARE THE X-MEN?
I DUNNO, OUTER SPACE OR SOMETHING.
FOR HOW LONG?
I DUNNO.
JOHN BYRNE
WHERE ARE ALL THE MUTANTS?
GONE.
GONE?
"NO MORE MUTANTS."
SCARLET WITCH?
YEAH.
WOW.
YEAH.
WHO ARE YOU?
DON'T WORRY ABOUT IT, I'LL BE DEAD IN SIX ISSUES, TOPS.
WHERE'S WOLVERINE?
OH, HE'S AN AVENGER NOW.
UGH! NO!
NO, HE'S AN X-MAN!
BEAST WAS AN AVENGER.
THAT'S-- THAT'S COMPLETELY DIFFERENT!
HOW?
WHAT IS THAT?!

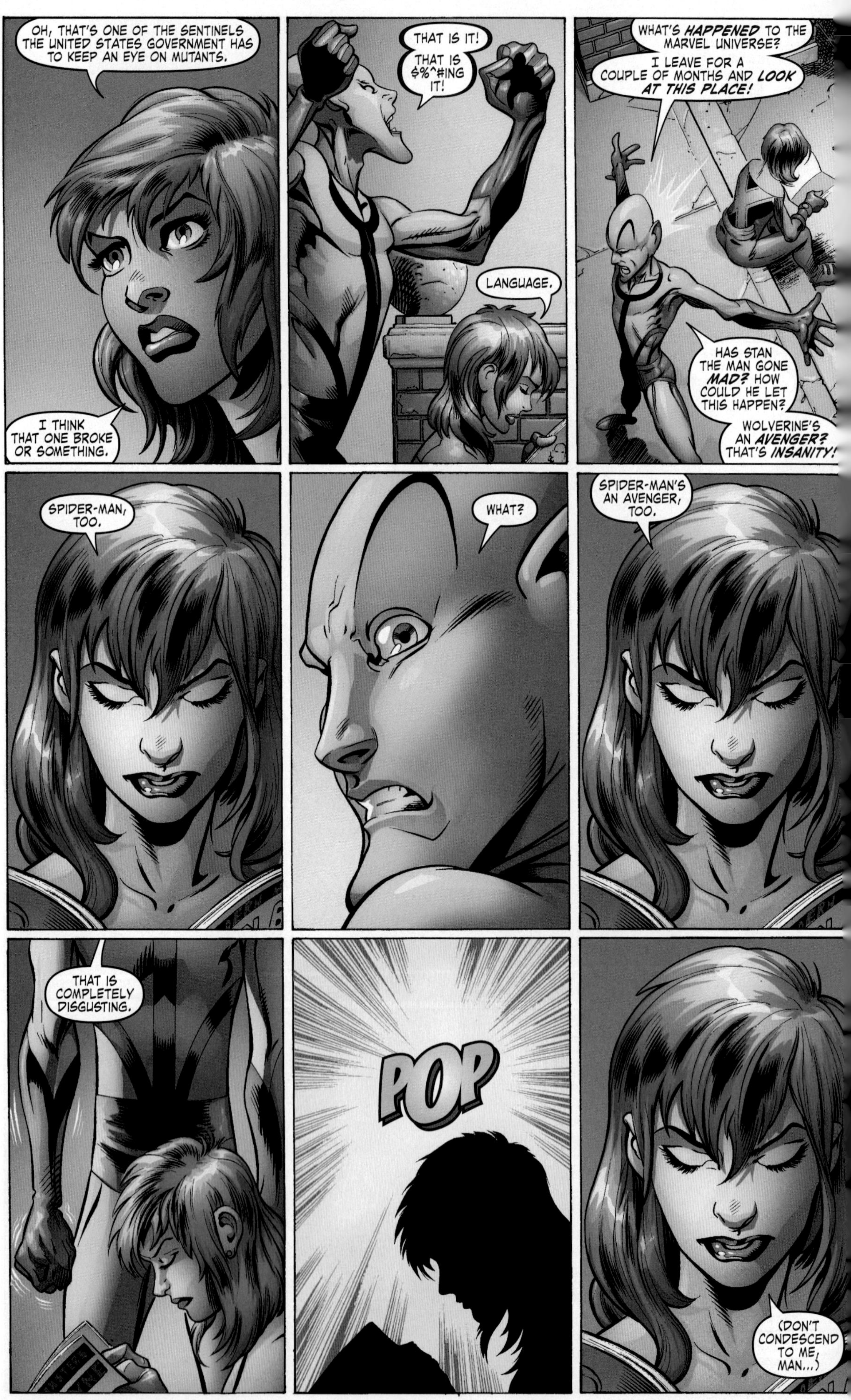

OH, THAT'S ONE OF THE SENTINELS THE UNITED STATES GOVERNMENT HAS TO KEEP AN EYE ON MUTANTS.
I THINK THAT ONE BROKE OR SOMETHING.
THAT IS IT!
THAT IS $%^#ING IT!
LANGUAGE.
WHAT'S HAPPENED TO THE MARVEL UNIVERSE?
I LEAVE FOR A COUPLE OF MONTHS AND LOOK AT THIS PLACE!
HAS STAN THE MAN GONE MAD? HOW COULD HE LET THIS HAPPEN?
WOLVERINE'S AN AVENGER? THAT'S INSANITY!
SPIDER-MAN, TOO.
WHAT?
SPIDER-MAN'S AN AVENGER, TOO.
THAT IS COMPLETELY DISGUSTING.
POP
(DON'T CONDESCEND TO ME, MAN...)

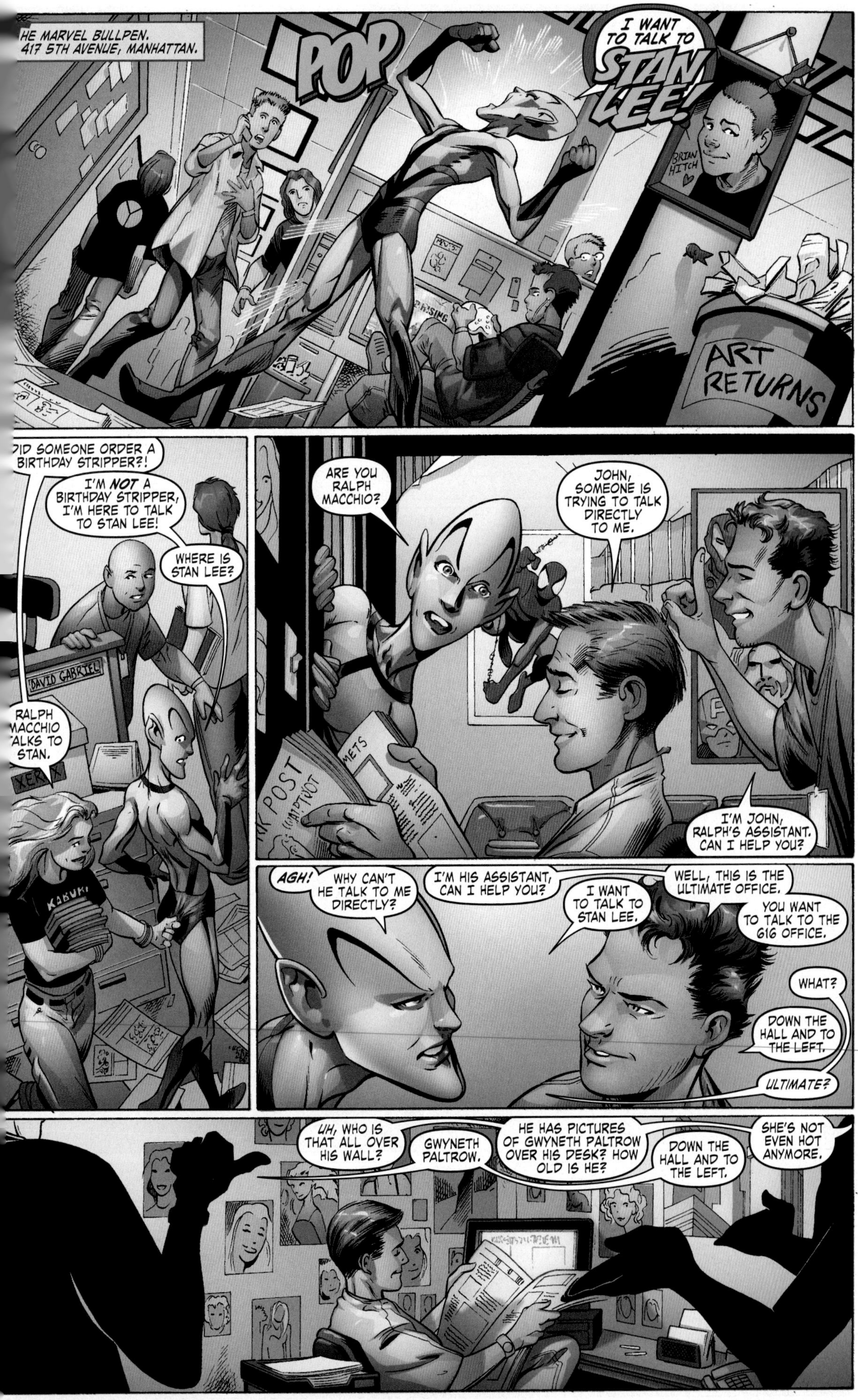
HE MARVEL BULLPEN.
417 5TH AVENUE, MANHATTAN.
POP
I WANT TO TALK TO STAN LEE!
BRIAN HITCH
ART RETURNS
DID SOMEONE ORDER A BIRTHDAY STRIPPER?!
I'M NOT A BIRTHDAY STRIPPER, I'M HERE TO TALK TO STAN LEE!
WHERE IS STAN LEE?
DAVID GARRIEL
RALPH MACCHIO TALKS TO STAN.
KABUKI
ARE YOU RALPH MACCHIO?
JOHN, SOMEONE IS TRYING TO TALK DIRECTLY TO ME.
METS
POST
I'M JOHN, RALPH'S ASSISTANT. CAN I HELP YOU?
AGH!
WHY CAN'T HE TALK TO ME DIRECTLY?
I'M HIS ASSISTANT, CAN I HELP YOU?
I WANT TO TALK TO STAN LEE.
WELL, THIS IS THE ULTIMATE OFFICE.
YOU WANT TO TALK TO THE 616 OFFICE.
WHAT?
DOWN THE HALL AND TO THE LEFT.
ULTIMATE?
UH, WHO IS THAT ALL OVER HIS WALL?
GWYNETH PALTROW.
HE HAS PICTURES OF GWYNETH PALTROW OVER HIS DESK? HOW OLD IS HE?
DOWN THE HALL AND TO THE LEFT.
SHE'S NOT EVEN HOT ANYMORE.

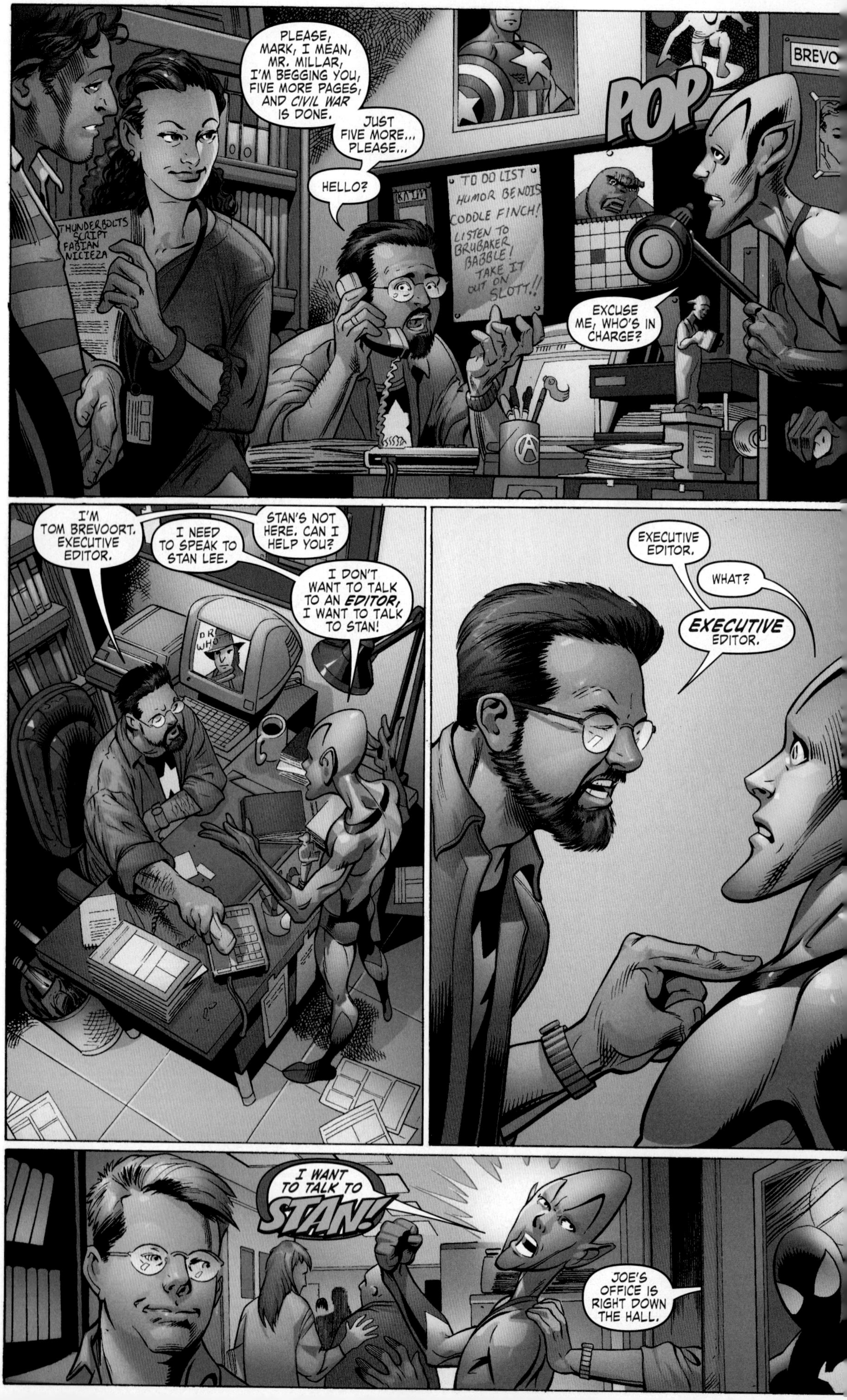
THUNDERBOLTS SCRIPT FABIAN NICIEZA
PLEASE, MARK, I MEAN, MR. MILLAR, I'M BEGGING YOU, FIVE MORE PAGES, AND CIVIL WAR IS DONE.
JUST FIVE MORE... PLEASE...
HELLO?
TO DO LIST HUMOR BENDIS CODDLE FINCH! LISTEN TO BRUBAKER BABBLE! TAKE IT OUT ON SLOTT!!
BREVO
POP
EXCUSE ME, WHO'S IN CHARGE?
I'M TOM BREVOORT. EXECUTIVE EDITOR.
I NEED TO SPEAK TO STAN LEE.
STAN'S NOT HERE. CAN I HELP YOU?
I DON'T WANT TO TALK TO AN EDITOR, I WANT TO TALK TO STAN!
EXECUTIVE EDITOR.
WHAT?
EXECUTIVE EDITOR.
I WANT TO TALK TO STAN!
JOE'S OFFICE IS RIGHT DOWN THE HALL.

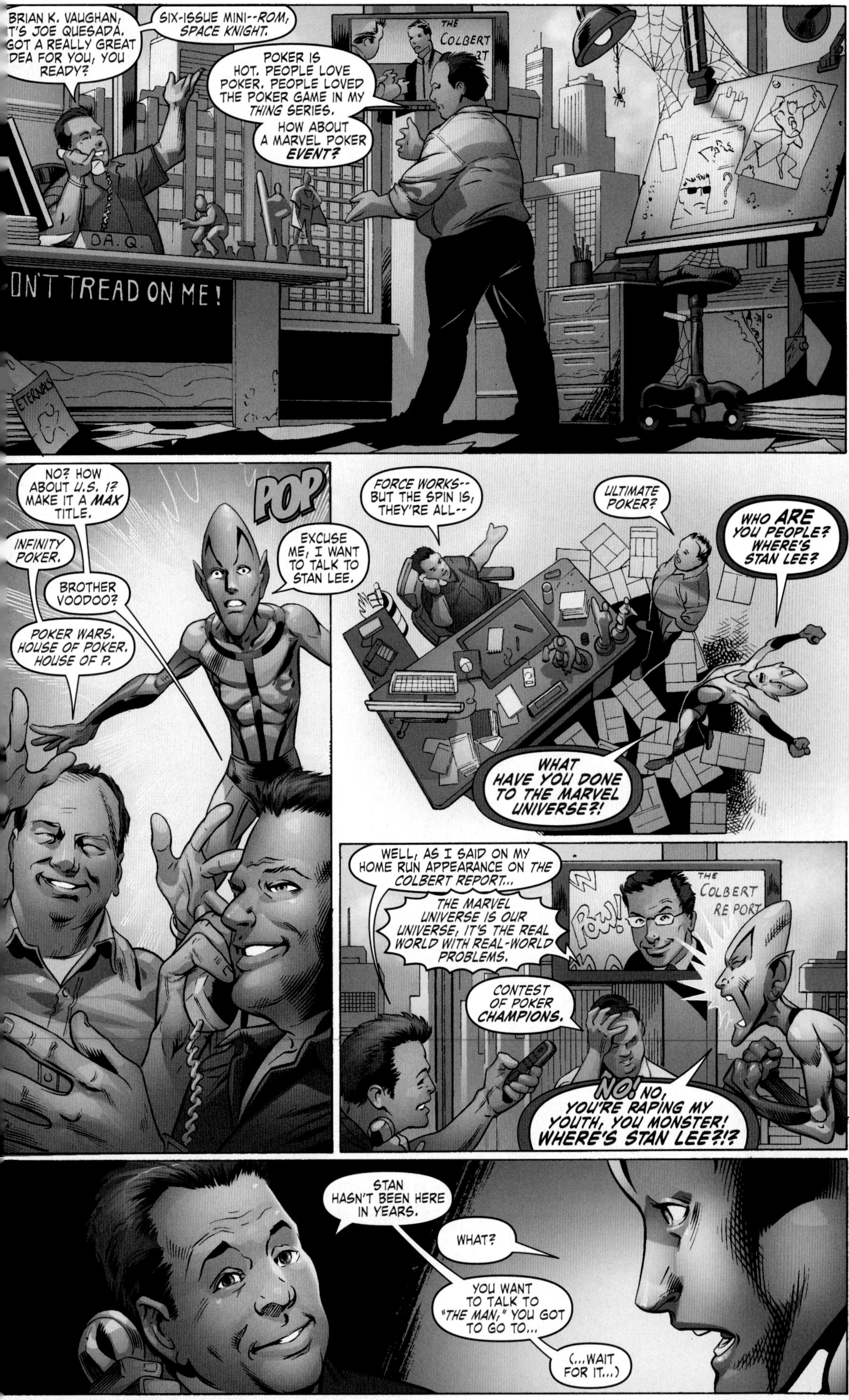
BRIAN K. VAUGHAN, IT'S JOE QUESADA. GOT A REALLY GREAT IDEA FOR YOU, YOU READY?
SIX-ISSUE MINI--ROM, SPACE KNIGHT.
POKER IS HOT. PEOPLE LOVE POKER. PEOPLE LOVED THE POKER GAME IN MY THING SERIES.
HOW ABOUT A MARVEL POKER EVENT?
THE COLBERT
DA. Q.
ON'T TREAD ON ME!
ETERNALS
NO? HOW ABOUT U.S. 1? MAKE IT A MAX TITLE.
INFINITY POKER.
BROTHER VOODOO?
POKER WARS. HOUSE OF POKER. HOUSE OF P.
POP
EXCUSE ME, I WANT TO TALK TO STAN LEE.
FORCE WORKS-- BUT THE SPIN IS, THEY'RE ALL--
ULTIMATE POKER?
WHO ARE YOU PEOPLE? WHERE'S STAN LEE?
WHAT HAVE YOU DONE TO THE MARVEL UNIVERSE?!
WELL, AS I SAID ON MY HOME RUN APPEARANCE ON THE COLBERT REPORT...
THE MARVEL UNIVERSE IS OUR UNIVERSE, IT'S THE REAL WORLD WITH REAL-WORLD PROBLEMS.
THE COLBERT REPORT
POW!
CONTEST OF POKER CHAMPIONS.
NO! NO, YOU'RE RAPING MY YOUTH, YOU MONSTER! WHERE'S STAN LEE?!?
STAN HASN'T BEEN HERE IN YEARS.
WHAT?
YOU WANT TO TALK TO "THE MAN," YOU GOT TO GO TO...
(...WAIT FOR IT...)

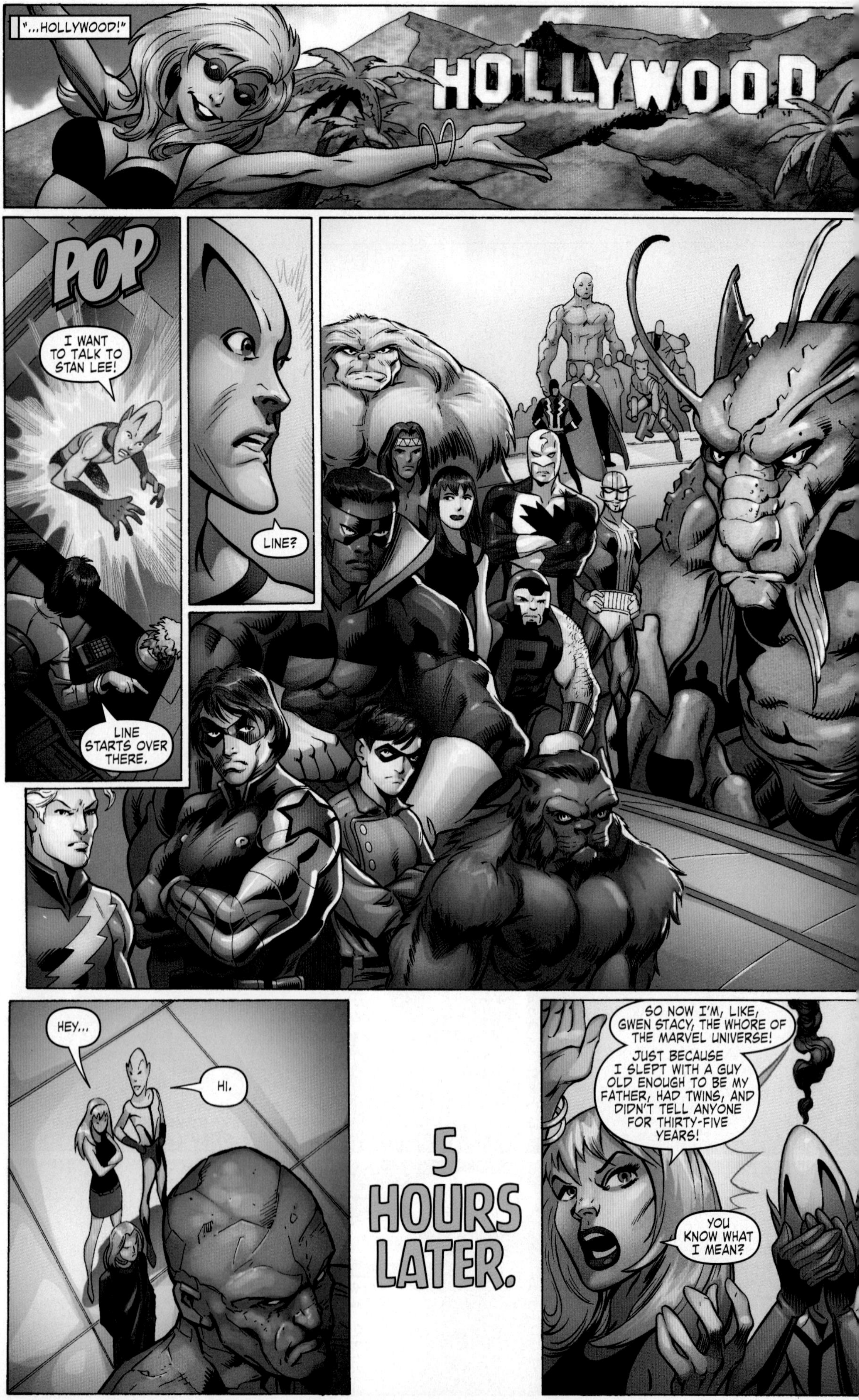
"...HOLLYWOOD!"
HOLLYWOOD
POP
I WANT TO TALK TO STAN LEE!
LINE?
LINE STARTS OVER THERE.
HEY...
HI.
5 HOURS LATER.
SO NOW I'M, LIKE, GWEN STACY, THE WHORE OF THE MARVEL UNIVERSE!
JUST BECAUSE I SLEPT WITH A GUY OLD ENOUGH TO BE MY FATHER, HAD TWINS, AND DIDN'T TELL ANYONE FOR THIRTY-FIVE YEARS!
YOU KNOW WHAT I MEAN?

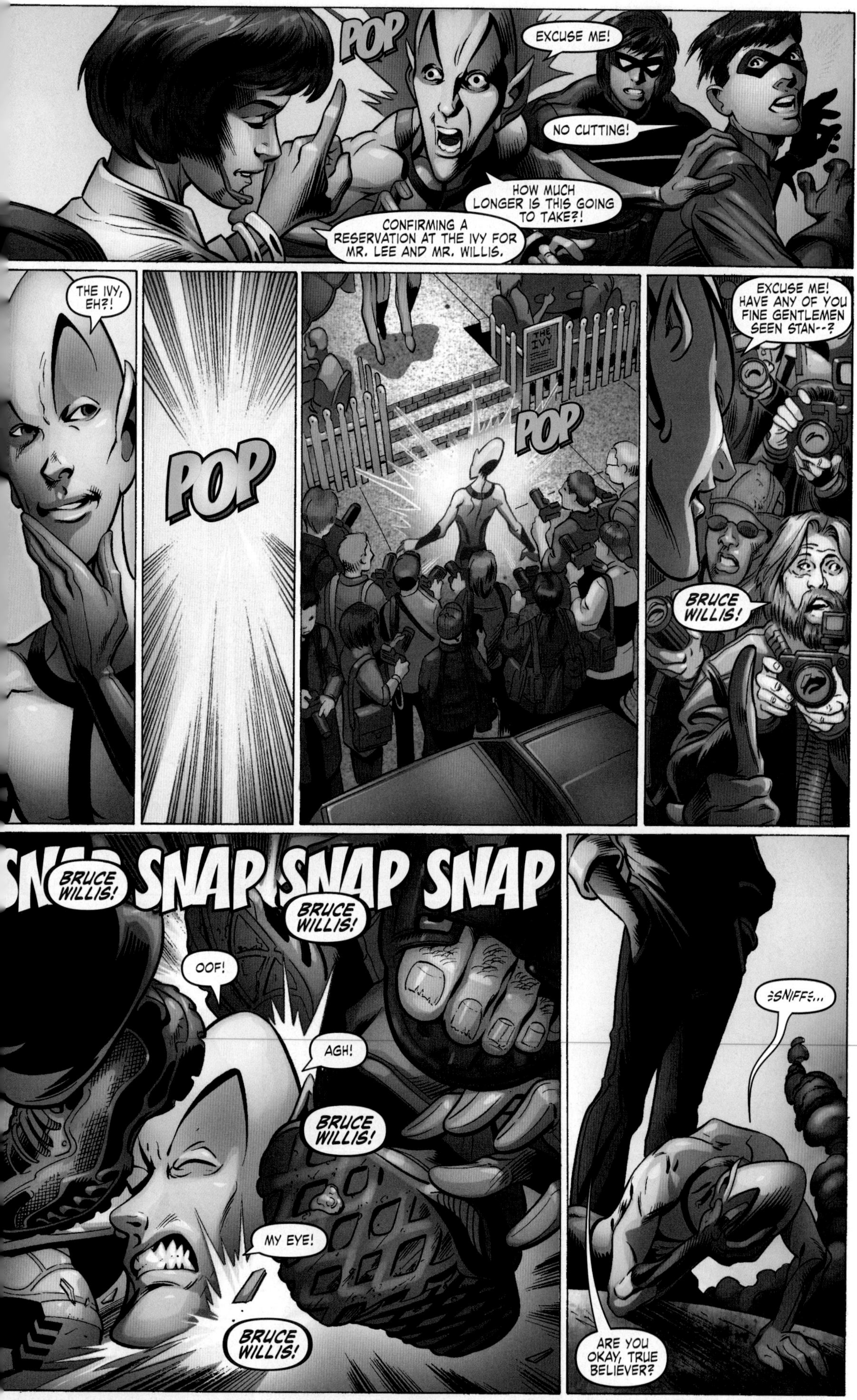
POP
EXCUSE ME!
NO CUTTING!
HOW MUCH LONGER IS THIS GOING TO TAKE?!
CONFIRMING A RESERVATION AT THE IVY FOR MR. LEE AND MR. WILLIS.
THE IVY, EH?!
POP
THE IVY
POP
EXCUSE ME! HAVE ANY OF YOU FINE GENTLEMEN SEEN STAN--?
BRUCE WILLIS!
SNAP SNAP SNAP SNAP
BRUCE WILLIS!
BRUCE WILLIS!
OOF!
AGH!
BRUCE WILLIS!
MY EYE!
BRUCE WILLIS!
=SNIFF=...
ARE YOU OKAY, TRUE BELIEVER?

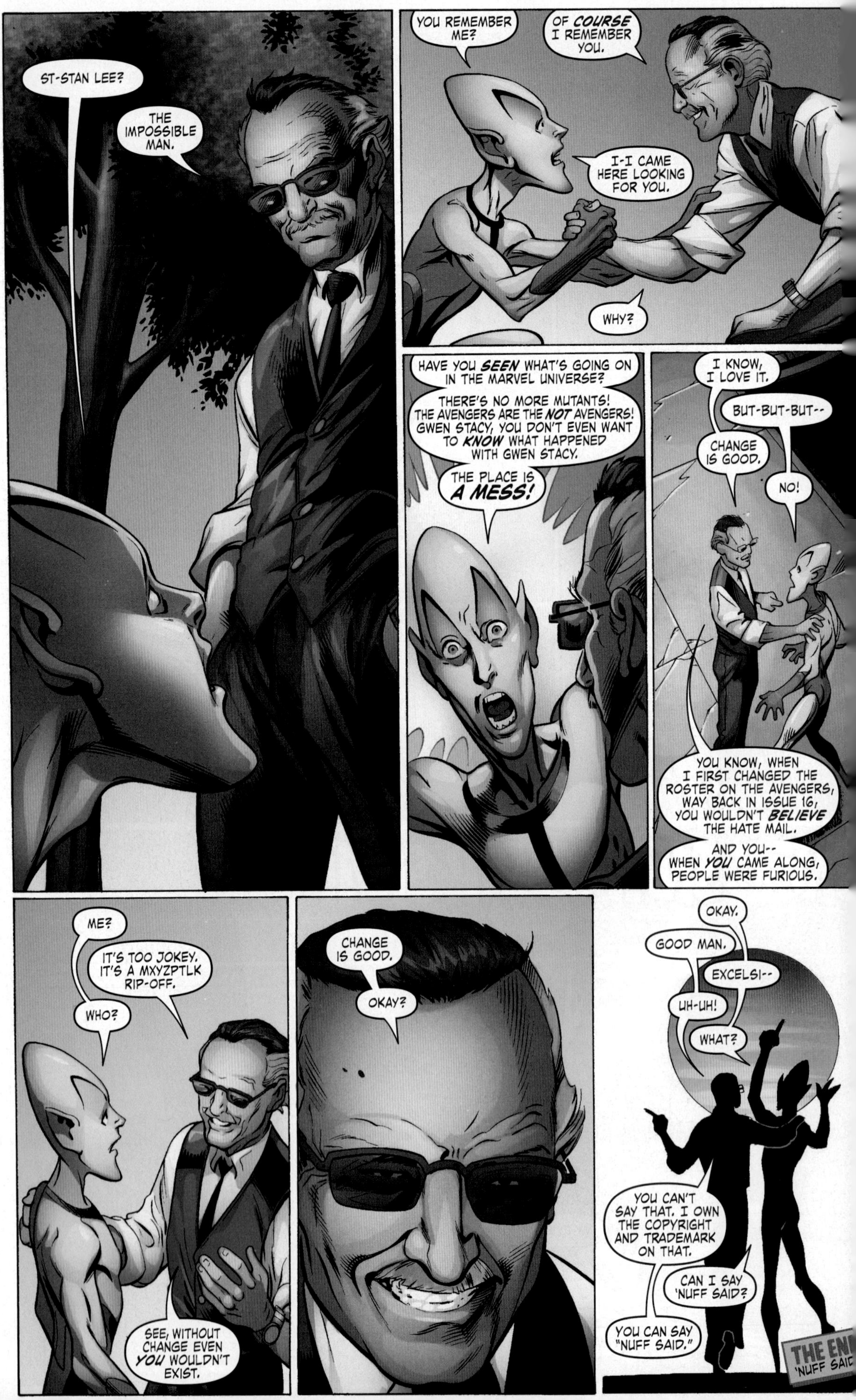
ST-STAN LEE?
THE IMPOSSIBLE MAN.
YOU REMEMBER ME?
OF COURSE I REMEMBER YOU.
I-I CAME HERE LOOKING FOR YOU.
WHY?
HAVE YOU SEEN WHAT'S GOING ON IN THE MARVEL UNIVERSE?
THERE'S NO MORE MUTANTS! THE AVENGERS ARE THE NOT AVENGERS! GWEN STACY, YOU DON'T EVEN WANT TO KNOW WHAT HAPPENED WITH GWEN STACY.
THE PLACE IS A MESS!
I KNOW, I LOVE IT.
BUT-BUT-BUT--
CHANGE IS GOOD.
NO!
YOU KNOW, WHEN I FIRST CHANGED THE ROSTER ON THE AVENGERS, WAY BACK IN ISSUE 16, YOU WOULDN'T BELIEVE THE HATE MAIL.
AND YOU-- WHEN YOU CAME ALONG, PEOPLE WERE FURIOUS.
ME?
IT'S TOO JOKEY. IT'S A MXYZPTLK RIP-OFF.
WHO?
SEE, WITHOUT CHANGE EVEN YOU WOULDN'T EXIST.
CHANGE IS GOOD.
OKAY?
OKAY.
GOOD MAN.
EXCELSI--
UH-UH!
WHAT?
YOU CAN'T SAY THAT. I OWN THE COPYRIGHT AND TRADEMARK ON THAT.
CAN I SAY 'NUFF SAID?
YOU CAN SAY "NUFF SAID."
THE END
'NUFF SAID

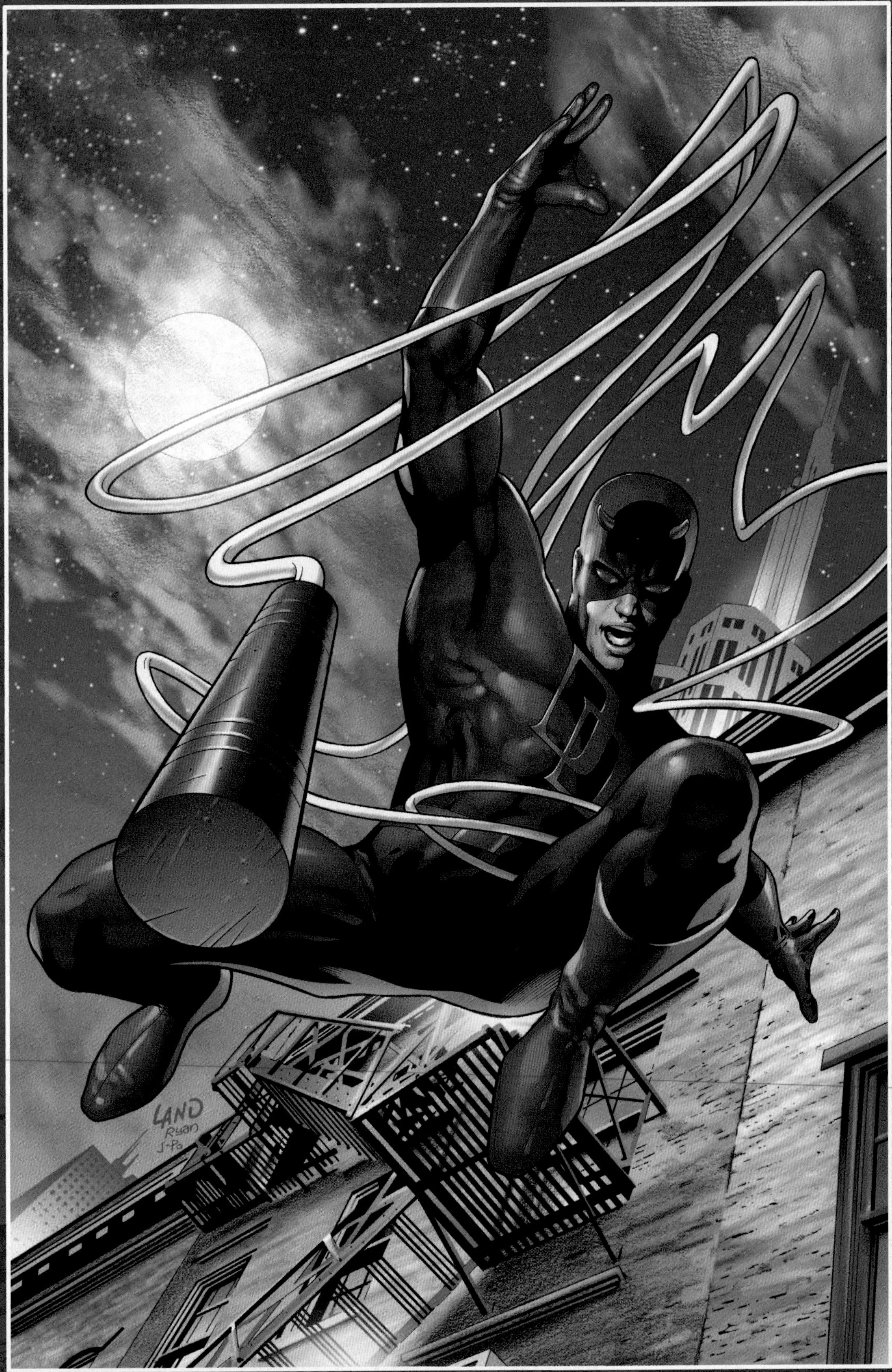
LAND
Ryan
J-Po

DAREDEVIL #65

Attorney Matt Murdock is blind, but his other four senses function with a superhuman sharpness and a radar sense. With amazing fighting skills he stalks the streets at night, a relentless avenger of justice: Daredevil, The Man Without Fear!

PREVIOUSLY

DAREDEVIL
THE MAN WITHOUT FEAR!

"THE UNIVERSE"

#65

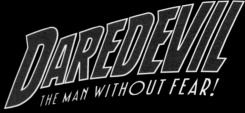

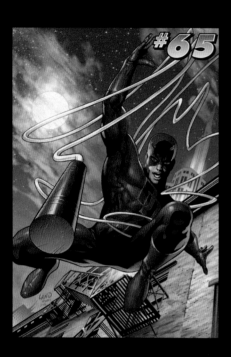

One of the biggest tabloid newspapers in the city outed Matt Murdock: Daredevil's Secret Identity Revealed. The secret is out.

Matt Murdock is now faced with a continuing uphill battle of publicly denying his secret life as Daredevil for fear of disbarment or jail. But Matt's public struggle makes his alter ego more popular with the people than ever before.

One year ago, faced with the growing frustration that his fight with the Kingpin would never end, Daredevil beat him and declared himself the Kingpin. His new rule: Clean up or get out.

During that time, Matt also secretly married his girlfriend, Milla Donovan.

Matt's close friends theorized that his actions might be the result of a nervous breakdown stemming from the death of his first true love, Karen Page.

Horrified that her marriage might be part of Matt's ill mental health, Milla left him and filed for annulment.

The last year of Matt's life has had far-reaching implications beyond just his personal affairs.

A 40th Anniversary Daredevil Super Special brought to you by:

Writer
Brian Michael Bendis

Artists
Michael Golden (p.2-6)
Greg Horn (p.7-12)
P. Craig Russell (p.13-17)
Phil Hester and Ande Parks (p.18-26)
Chris Bachalo and Tim Townsend (p.27-33)
Jae Lee (p.34)
David Finch (p.35)
Frank Quitley (p.36)
Alex Maleev (p.37-38)

Cover
Greg Land and Matt Ryan

Colorists
Justin Ponsor
Greg Horn (p.7-12)
Chris Bachalo (p.27-33)
June Chung (p.34)
Frank Darmata (p.35)

Letterer
Virtual Calligraphy's Randy Gentile

Special Thanks to Jamie Grant

Assistant Editor
Cory Sedlmeier

Editor
Jennifer Lee

Executive Editor
Axel Alonso

Editor in Chief
Joe Quesada

Publisher
Dan Buckley

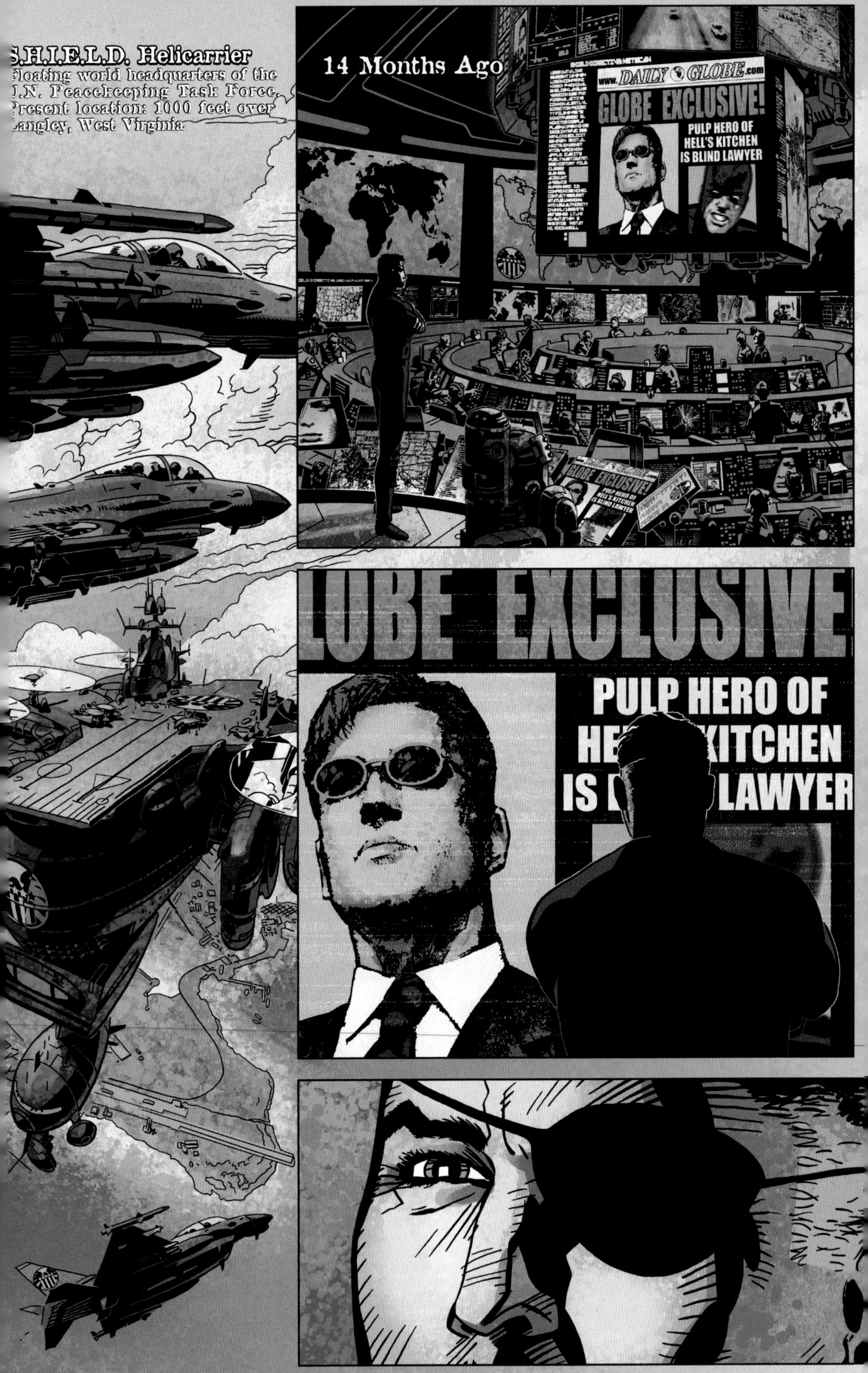

S.H.I.E.L.D. Helicarrier
loating world headquarters of the
.N. Peacekeeping Task Force.
resent location: 1000 feet over
angley, West Virginia
14 Months Ago
www.DAILY GLOBE.com
GLOBE EXCLUSIVE!
PULP HERO OF HELL'S KITCHEN IS BLIND LAWYER
GLOBE EXCLUSIVE!
PULP HERO OF HELL'S KITCHEN IS BLIND LAWYER
LUBE EXCLUSIVE
PULP HERO OF
HE KITCHEN
IS LAWYER

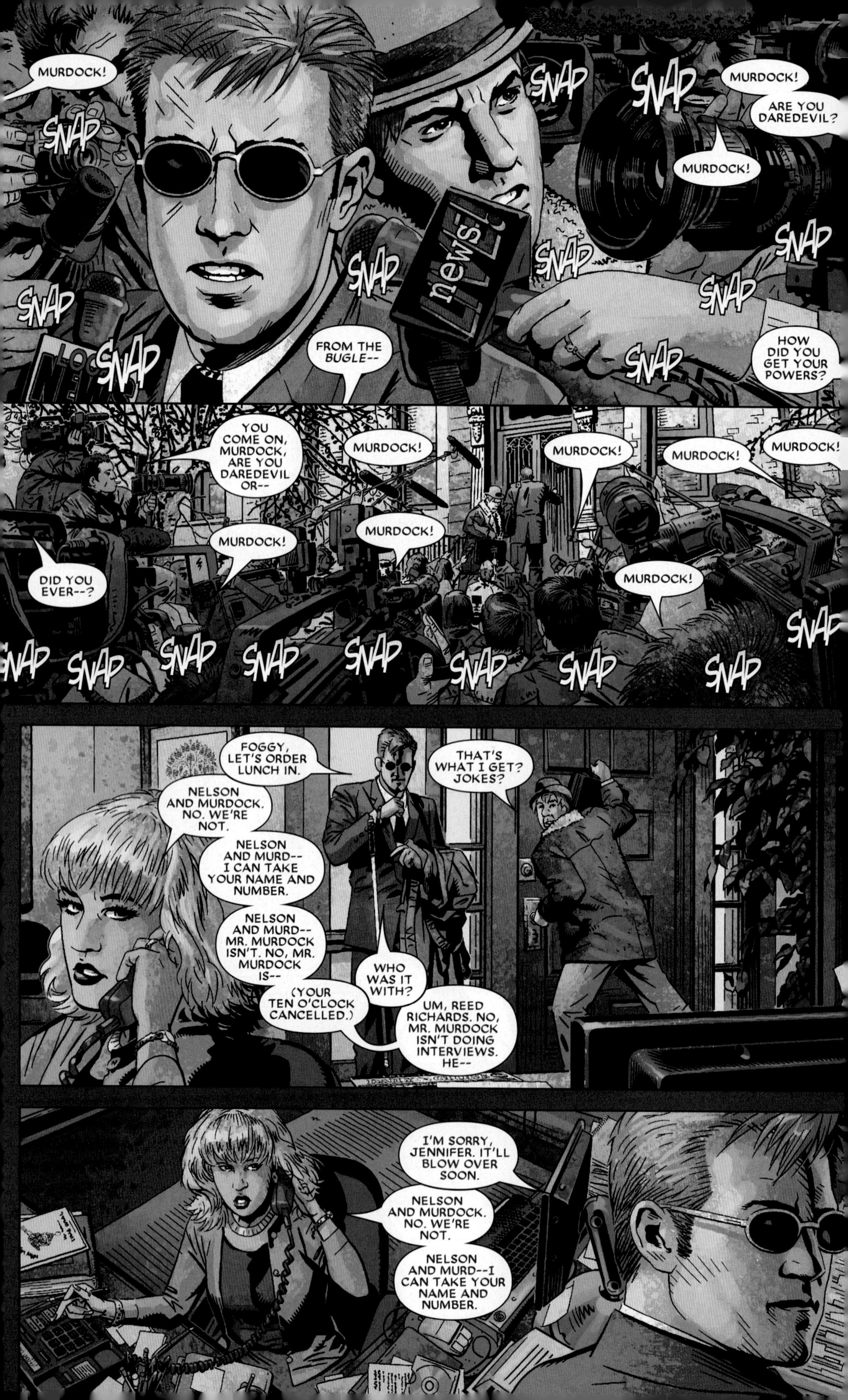
MURDOCK!
SNAP
SNAP
SNAP
SNAP
FROM THE *BUGLE*--
SNAP
SNAP
SNAP
SNAP
MURDOCK!
ARE YOU DAREDEVIL?
MURDOCK!
SNAP
SNAP
SNAP
HOW DID YOU GET YOUR POWERS?
YOU COME ON, MURDOCK, ARE YOU DAREDEVIL OR--
MURDOCK!
MURDOCK!
MURDOCK!
MURDOCK!
MURDOCK!
MURDOCK!
DID YOU EVER--?
MURDOCK!
SNAP
SNAP
SNAP
SNAP
SNAP
SNAP
SNAP
SNAP
SNAP
FOGGY, LET'S ORDER LUNCH IN.
THAT'S WHAT I GET? JOKES?
NELSON AND MURDOCK. NO. WE'RE NOT.
NELSON AND MURD-- I CAN TAKE YOUR NAME AND NUMBER.
NELSON AND MURD-- MR. MURDOCK ISN'T. NO, MR. MURDOCK IS--
WHO WAS IT WITH?
(YOUR TEN O'CLOCK CANCELLED.)
UM, REED RICHARDS. NO, MR. MURDOCK ISN'T DOING INTERVIEWS. HE--
I'M SORRY, JENNIFER. IT'LL BLOW OVER SOON.
NELSON AND MURDOCK. NO. WE'RE NOT.
NELSON AND MURD--I CAN TAKE YOUR NAME AND NUMBER.

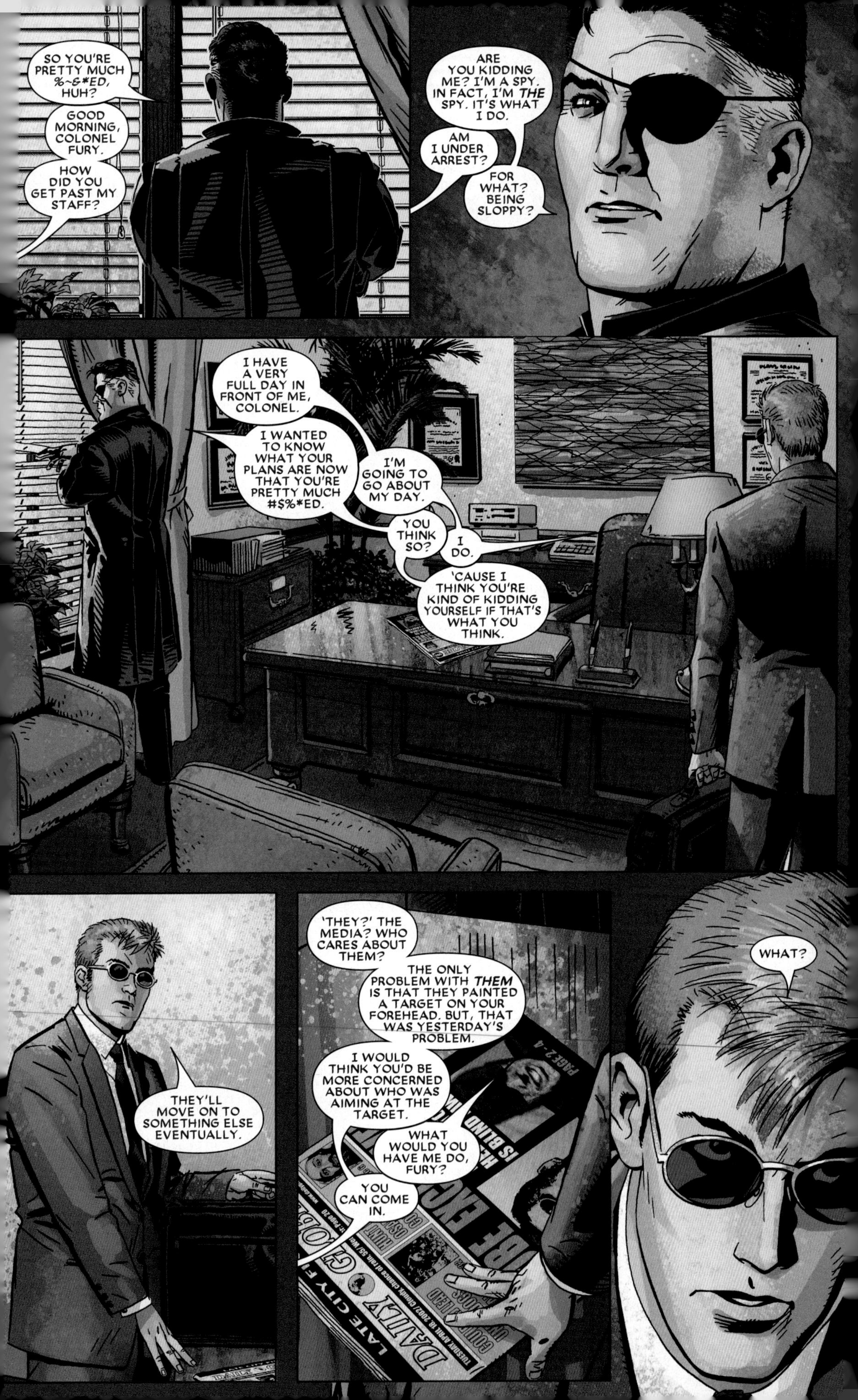
SO YOU'RE PRETTY MUCH %~&*ED, HUH?
GOOD MORNING, COLONEL FURY.
HOW DID YOU GET PAST MY STAFF?
ARE YOU KIDDING ME? I'M A SPY. IN FACT, I'M *THE* SPY. IT'S WHAT I DO.
AM I UNDER ARREST?
FOR WHAT? BEING SLOPPY?
I HAVE A VERY FULL DAY IN FRONT OF ME, COLONEL.
I WANTED TO KNOW WHAT YOUR PLANS ARE NOW THAT YOU'RE PRETTY MUCH #$%*ED.
I'M GOING TO GO ABOUT MY DAY.
YOU THINK SO?
I DO.
'CAUSE I THINK YOU'RE KIND OF KIDDING YOURSELF IF THAT'S WHAT YOU THINK.
THEY'LL MOVE ON TO SOMETHING ELSE EVENTUALLY.
'THEY?' THE MEDIA? WHO CARES ABOUT THEM?
THE ONLY PROBLEM WITH *THEM* IS THAT THEY PAINTED A TARGET ON YOUR FOREHEAD. BUT, THAT WAS YESTERDAY'S PROBLEM.
I WOULD THINK YOU'D BE MORE CONCERNED ABOUT WHO WAS AIMING AT THE TARGET.
WHAT WOULD YOU HAVE ME DO, FURY?
YOU CAN COME IN.
WHAT?

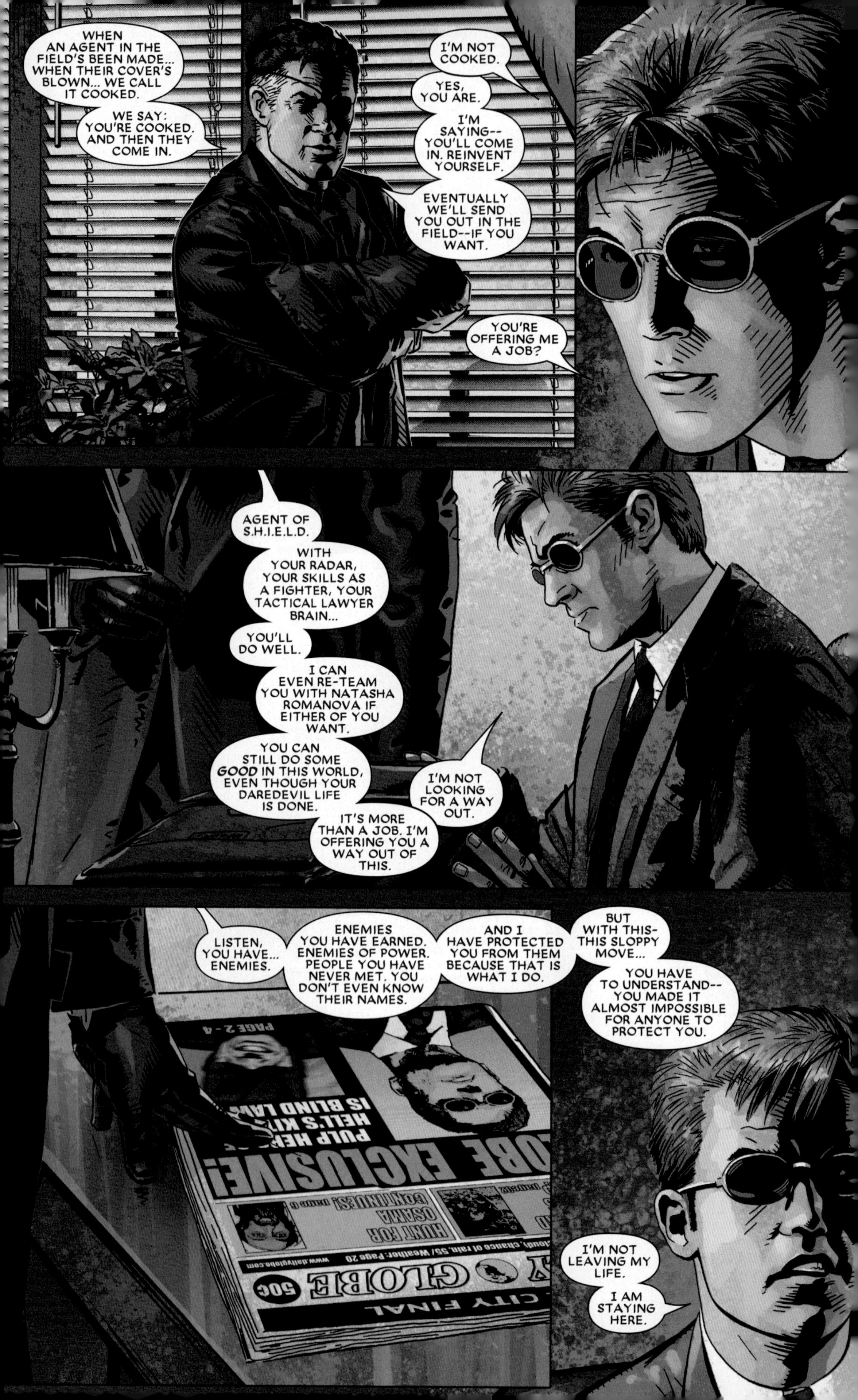
WHEN AN AGENT IN THE FIELD'S BEEN MADE... WHEN THEIR COVER'S BLOWN... WE CALL IT COOKED.
WE SAY: YOU'RE COOKED. AND THEN THEY COME IN.
I'M NOT COOKED.
YES, YOU ARE.
I'M SAYING-- YOU'LL COME IN. REINVENT YOURSELF.
EVENTUALLY WE'LL SEND YOU OUT IN THE FIELD--IF YOU WANT.
YOU'RE OFFERING ME A JOB?
AGENT OF S.H.I.E.L.D.
WITH YOUR RADAR, YOUR SKILLS AS A FIGHTER, YOUR TACTICAL LAWYER BRAIN...
YOU'LL DO WELL.
I CAN EVEN RE-TEAM YOU WITH NATASHA ROMANOVA IF EITHER OF YOU WANT.
YOU CAN STILL DO SOME *GOOD* IN THIS WORLD, EVEN THOUGH YOUR DAREDEVIL LIFE IS DONE.
IT'S MORE THAN A JOB. I'M OFFERING YOU A WAY OUT OF THIS.
I'M NOT LOOKING FOR A WAY OUT.
LISTEN, YOU HAVE... ENEMIES.
ENEMIES YOU HAVE EARNED. ENEMIES OF POWER. PEOPLE YOU HAVE NEVER MET. YOU DON'T EVEN KNOW THEIR NAMES.
AND I HAVE PROTECTED YOU FROM THEM BECAUSE THAT IS WHAT I DO.
BUT WITH THIS-THIS SLOPPY MOVE...
YOU HAVE TO UNDERSTAND-- YOU MADE IT ALMOST IMPOSSIBLE FOR ANYONE TO PROTECT YOU.
I'M NOT LEAVING MY LIFE.
I AM STAYING HERE.

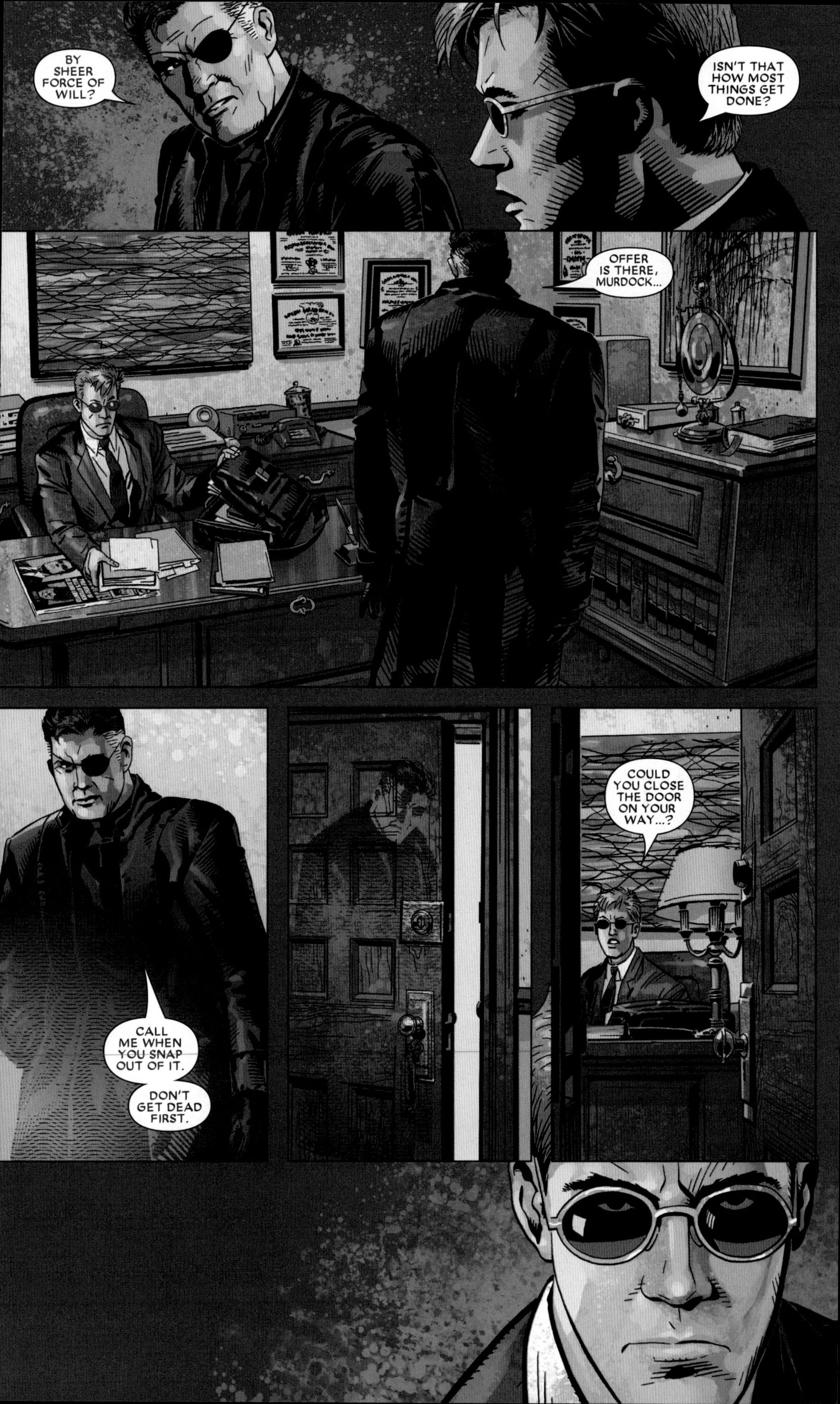

BY SHEER FORCE OF WILL?
ISN'T THAT HOW MOST THINGS GET DONE?
OFFER IS THERE, MURDOCK...
CALL ME WHEN YOU SNAP OUT OF IT.
DON'T GET DEAD FIRST.
COULD YOU CLOSE THE DOOR ON YOUR WAY...?

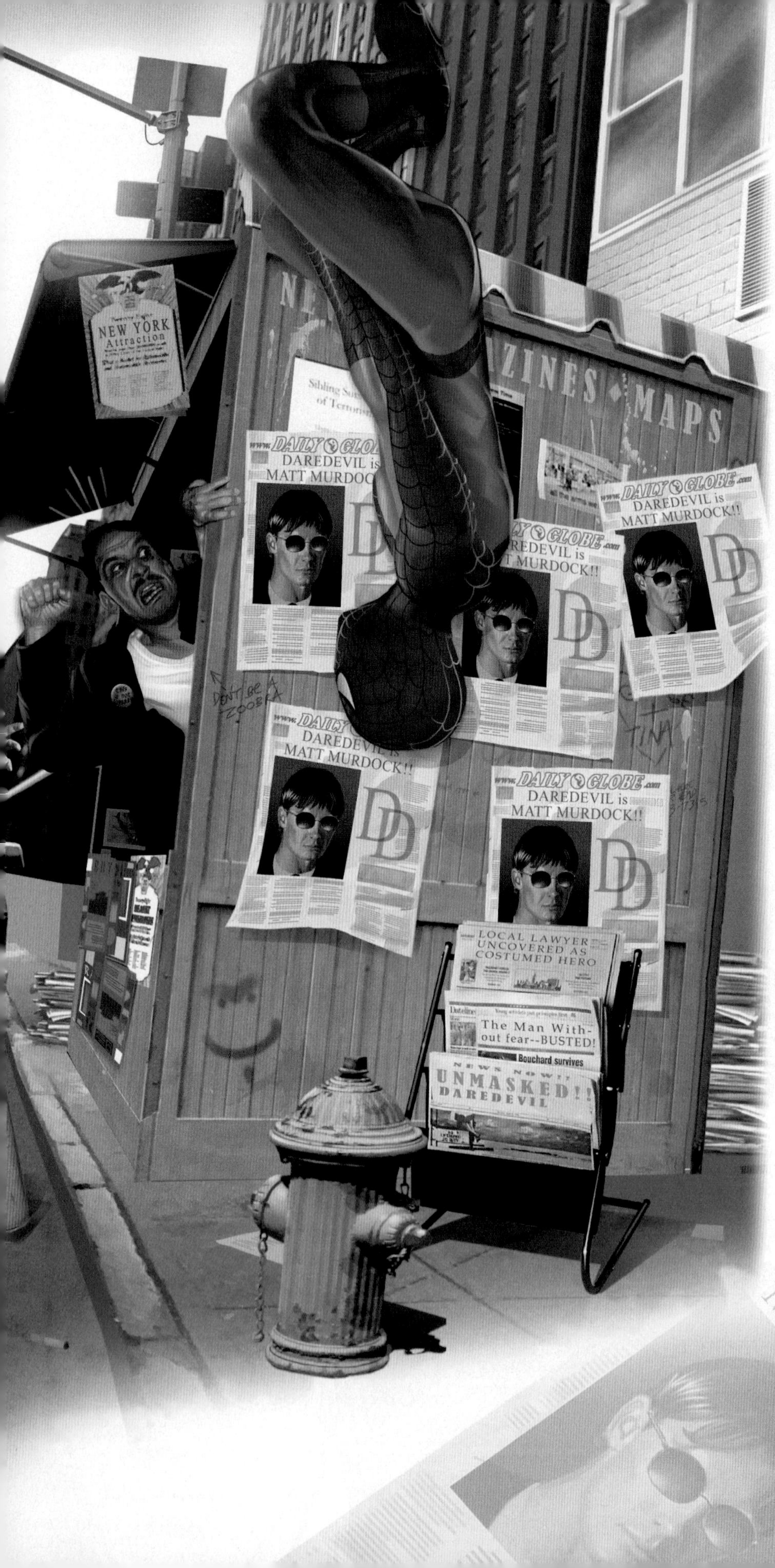
NEW YORK Attraction
MAPS
DAILY GLOBE .com
DAREDEVIL is MATT MURDOCK!!
LOCAL LAWYER UNCOVERED AS COSTUMED HERO
The Man Without fear--BUSTED!
Bouchard survives
NEWS NOW!!
UNMASKED!!
DAREDEVIL

OH MY GOD...

OH MY GOD...
OH MY GOD...
OH MY GOD...
OH MY GOD...

THIS IS A NIGHTMARE!!

THIS-THIS IS-- I'M SHAKING. I'M SHAKING IN MY SPIDER-SOCKS.

I'VE KNOWN MATT MURDOCK FOR YEARS. AND I THOUGHT I WAS LIKE THE ***ONLY*** GUY ON THE PLANET WHO KNEW HE WAS DAREDEVIL.

I FEEL GUILTY BUT THERE'S NO ***WAY*** THIS IS ***MY*** FAULT. IS IT? IS THIS MY-- NO. ***NO.*** I TOLD NO ONE. I NEVER EVEN TOLD MARY JANE.

WE SHARE THIS SECRET, MATT AND I. THIS IS A BOND OF MEN. HE KNOWS I'M PETER PARKER, I KNOW HE'S MATT MURDOCK.

UGH! THIS IS THE ***WORST*** POSSIBLE THING THAT COULD HAPPEN TO SOMEONE IN OUR-OUR--IN THE THING WE DO.

Y'KNOW, I WAS JUST ABOUT TO THINK TO MYSELF THAT BETWEEN THE TWO OF US, MURDOCK AND ME, THAT IF THIS WAS GOING TO HAPPEN TO ONE OF US... I WOULD HAVE BET THE FARMER'S MARKET THAT IT WOULD HAVE BEEN ME!

BUT I DON'T NEED TO FINISH GETTING THE THOUGHT OUT BECAUSE CHEESE BREATH BEHIND THE COUNTER OVER HERE FEELS THE NEED TO YELL THE VERY SAME IDEA RIGHT IN MY ***FACE.***

WELL, THANKS A LOT, MR. NEWS VENDOR.

(EMBARRASS ME LIKE THAT.)

I WANT TO YELL BACK IN ***HIS*** FACE THAT NOW I'M ***NOT*** GOING TO BUY ANYTHING AT HIS RINKY-DINK POPSICLE STAND.

BUT I THINK THE FACT THAT I HAVE NO WALLET, OR MONEY, OR POCKETS, IS GOING TO DAMPEN THE ENTIRE PRESENTATION.

BUT OH MAN...MATT! WHAT ARE YOU GOING TO ***DO?***

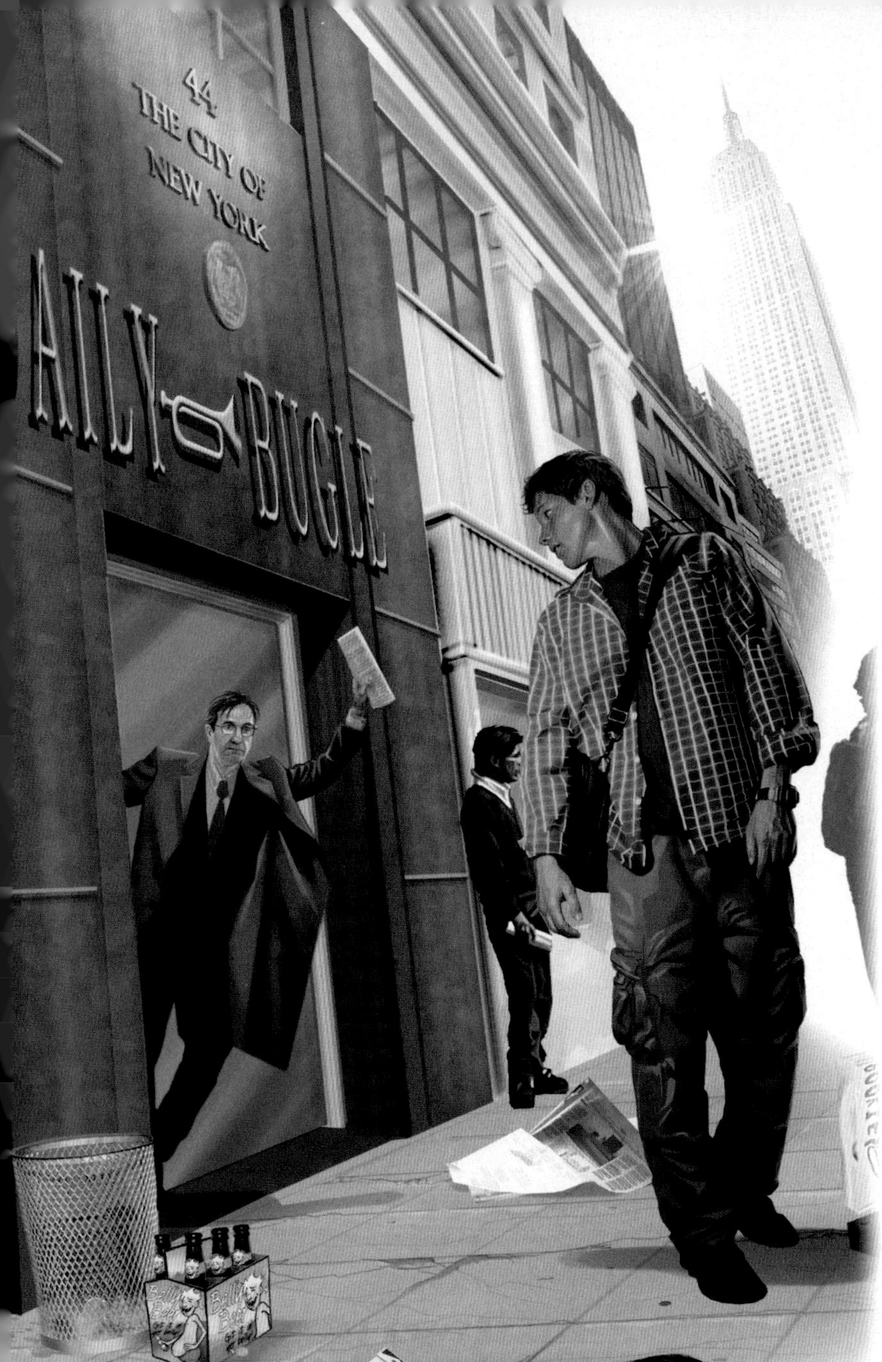
44
THE CITY OF
NEW YORK
AILY BUGLE

I'M ACTUALLY IN SOME SORT OF A PANIC TO FIND A WAY TO HELP. HE ***NEEDS*** MY HELP. I ***HAVE*** TO HELP.

WHY DO I FEEL GUILTY? THERE IS NO ***WAY*** THIS IS MY FAULT.

I SCAMPER OVER TO MY OLD EMPLOYER THE *DAILY BUGLE*, BECAUSE IF I KNOW MY J. JONAH JAMESON (AND I LIKE TO THINK THAT I DO), HE HAS POPPED A CIRCUIT OVER NOT HAVING THIS STORY!

HE ***HATES*** GETTING SCOOPED BY A COMPETING DISHRAG MORE THAN I HATE GETTING BONKED ON THE HEAD BY A MECHANICAL OCTOPUS ARM.

AND I ***REALLY*** HATE GETTING HIT ON THE HEAD BY A MECHANICAL OCTOPUS ARM.

I GO OVER THERE AND I BARGE INTO AN EDITORIAL MEETING, WITH NO IDEA OF WHAT I AM GOING TO SAY OR DO WHEN I GET THERE, AND, LO AND BEHOLD, WHAT DO I SEE...

I SEE REPORTER BEN URICH STANDING RIGHT UP TO JAMESON AND TELLING HIM, BALD FACE, THAT THE STORY ISN'T TRUE. THAT MATT ISN'T DAREDEVIL.

URICH SAYS HE KNOWS WHO DAREDEVIL IS, AND IT ISN'T MATT MURDOCK. WOW. WHAT DOES ***THIS*** MEAN? WHY WOULD HE SAY THAT?

WELL, HE ***MUST*** KNOW MATT IS DAREDEVIL BECAUSE WHY WOULD HE FEEL THE NEED TO LIE AND TELL JONAH HE ***ISN'T?***

I ONCE SAW JONAH FIRE A GUY FOR NOT KNOWING HOW TO SPELL BARBECUE. THIS THING URICH WAS DOING--THIS WAS BRAVE.

THEN, ALL OF A SUDDEN, I HEAR MYSELF BACK UP BEN'S BS LIE. I SAY I, ***TOO,*** KNEW WHO DAREDEVIL IS AND THAT IT ISN'T MATT MURDOCK. AND I WALK OUT.

AND I'M TELLING YOU, I DO NOT NEED SPIDER-SENSE TO KNOW THAT IF JONAH HAD A GUN, HE WOULD HAVE SHOT ME.

AND HE HATES ME ANYHOW.

I RUN OUT OF THE *BUGLE* BEFORE I CAN EVEN CONSIDER HOW FREAKIN' ***SUSPICIOUS*** WHAT I JUST DID WAS. IT WAS ***SO*** RECKLESS.

HERE ON THE DAY WHEN WE HAVE ALL BEEN TAUGHT EXACTLY WHAT WILL HAPPEN TO YOU IF YOU'RE RECKLESS WITH YOUR SECRET IDENTITY.

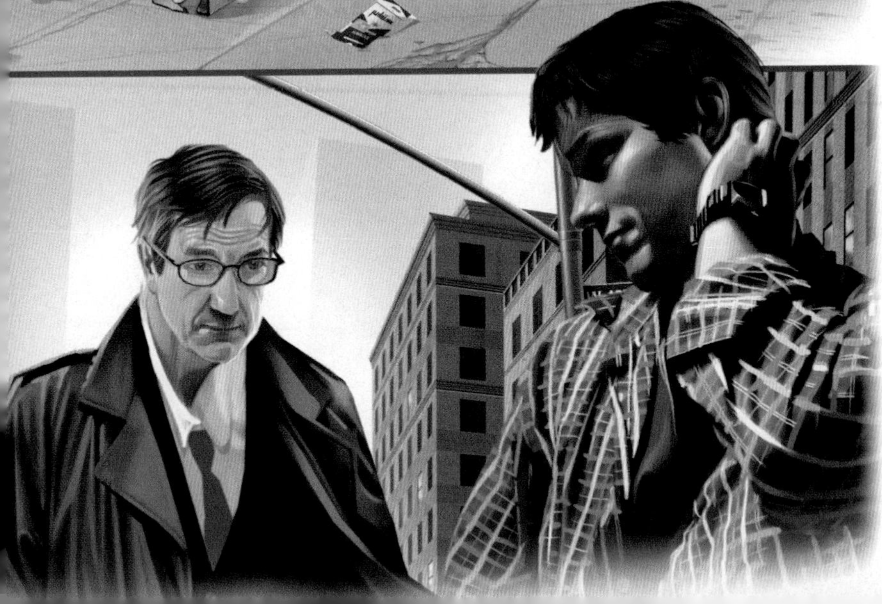

BEN COMES RUNNING AFTER ME. I START SHAKING AGAIN LIKE I'M IN TROUBLE.

AND WE'RE STANDING THERE PRETENDING WE'RE HAVING SMALL TALK, BUT REALLY HE IS GIVING ME THIS LOOK. PROBABLY THE SAME LOOK I'M GIVING HIM.

WE'RE BOTH TRYING TO FIGURE OUT HOW THE OTHER KNOWS MATT IS DAREDEVIL AND WHY WE'RE HELPING HIM BY SCREWING UP OUR OWN CAREERS.

AND HE LOOKS AT ME AND ALL I CAN THINK IS 'OH MY GOD, PLEASE DON'T FIGURE OUT I'M SPIDER-MAN.'

I CAN'T LET THIS HAPPEN TO ME TOO!

STOP LOOKING AT ME.

I GOTTA TALK TO MATT.

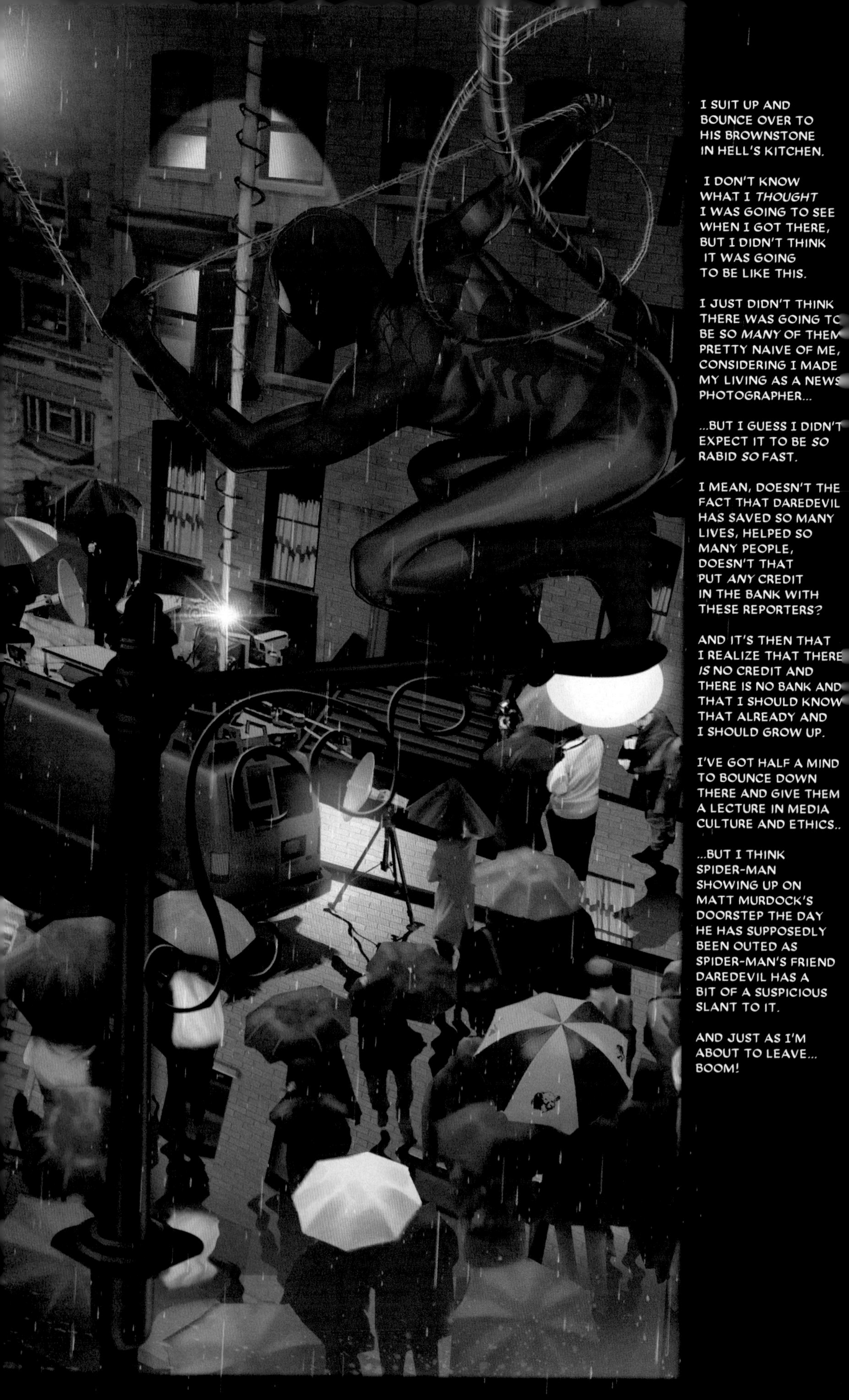
I SUIT UP AND BOUNCE OVER TO HIS BROWNSTONE IN HELL'S KITCHEN.
I DON'T KNOW WHAT I *THOUGHT* I WAS GOING TO SEE WHEN I GOT THERE, BUT I DIDN'T THINK IT WAS GOING TO BE LIKE THIS.
I JUST DIDN'T THINK THERE WAS GOING TO BE SO *MANY* OF THEM. PRETTY NAIVE OF ME, CONSIDERING I MADE MY LIVING AS A NEWS PHOTOGRAPHER...
...BUT I GUESS I DIDN'T EXPECT IT TO BE *SO* RABID *SO* FAST.
I MEAN, DOESN'T THE FACT THAT DAREDEVIL HAS SAVED SO MANY LIVES, HELPED SO MANY PEOPLE, DOESN'T THAT PUT *ANY* CREDIT IN THE BANK WITH THESE REPORTERS?
AND IT'S THEN THAT I REALIZE THAT THERE *IS* NO CREDIT AND THERE IS NO BANK AND THAT I SHOULD KNOW THAT ALREADY AND I SHOULD GROW UP.
I'VE GOT HALF A MIND TO BOUNCE DOWN THERE AND GIVE THEM A LECTURE IN MEDIA CULTURE AND ETHICS..
...BUT I THINK SPIDER-MAN SHOWING UP ON MATT MURDOCK'S DOORSTEP THE DAY HE HAS SUPPOSEDLY BEEN OUTED AS SPIDER-MAN'S FRIEND DAREDEVIL HAS A BIT OF A SUSPICIOUS SLANT TO IT.
AND JUST AS I'M ABOUT TO LEAVE... BOOM!

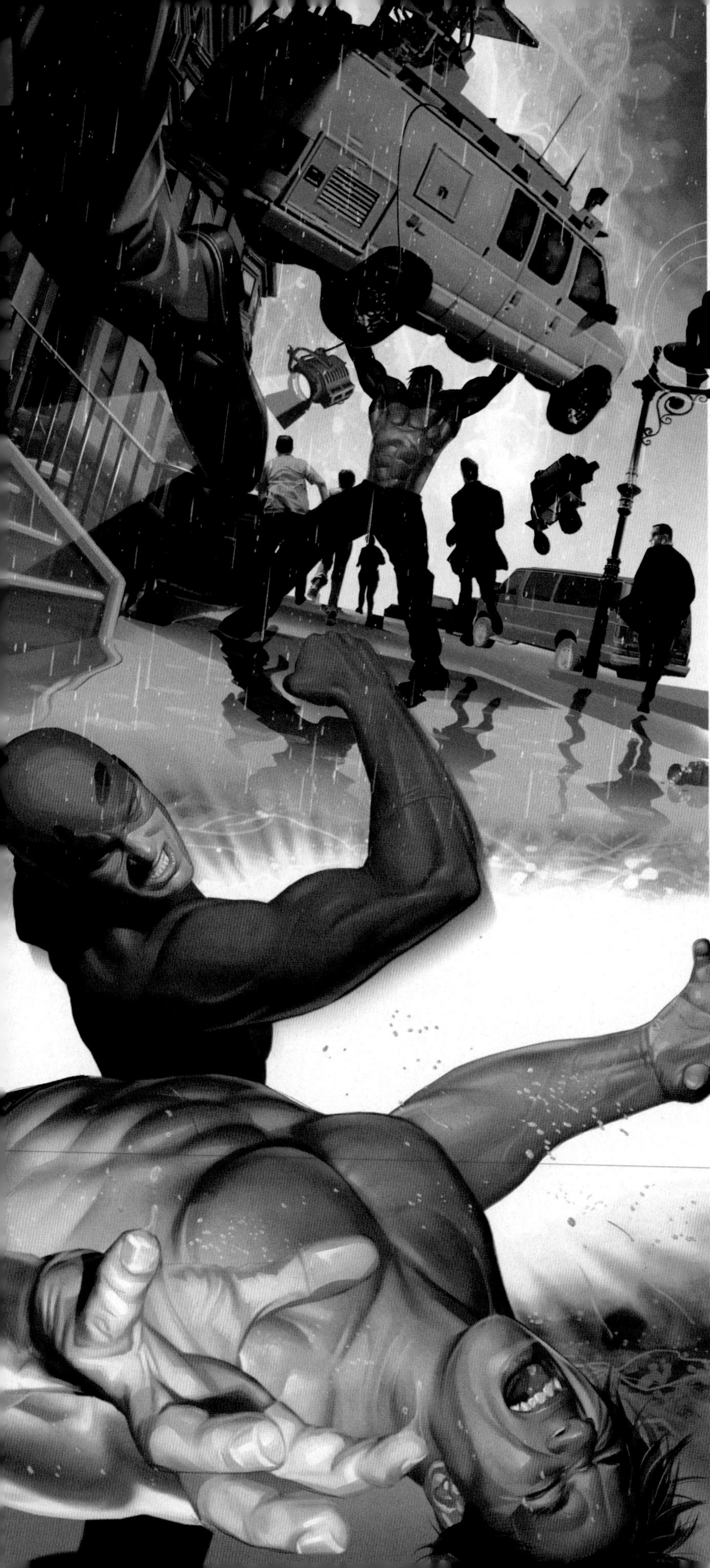

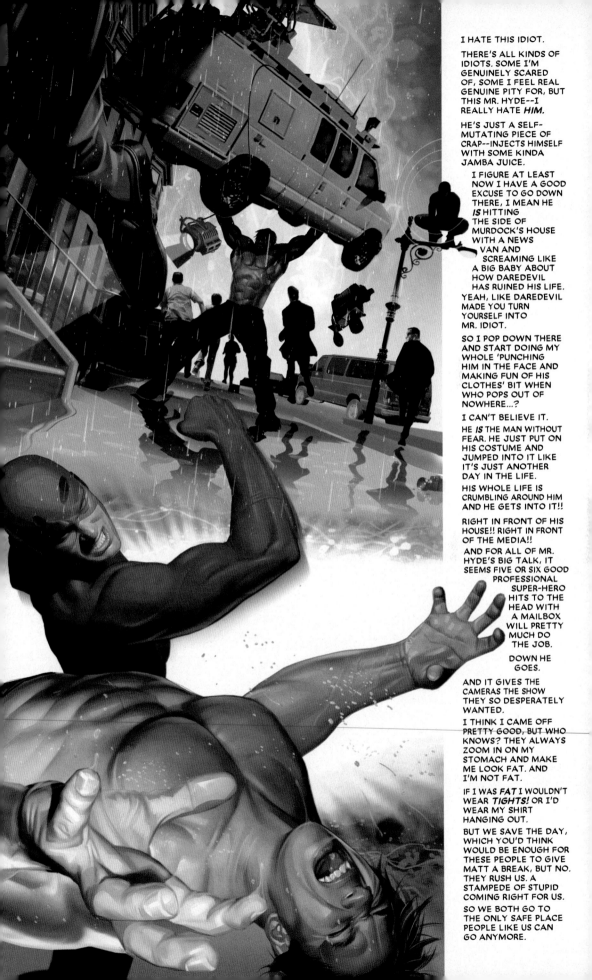

I HATE THIS IDIOT.

THERE'S ALL KINDS OF IDIOTS. SOME I'M GENUINELY SCARED OF, SOME I FEEL REAL GENUINE PITY FOR, BUT THIS MR. HYDE--I REALLY HATE ***HIM.***

HE'S JUST A SELF-MUTATING PIECE OF CRAP--INJECTS HIMSELF WITH SOME KINDA JAMBA JUICE.

I FIGURE AT LEAST NOW I HAVE A GOOD EXCUSE TO GO DOWN THERE, I MEAN HE ***IS*** HITTING THE SIDE OF MURDOCK'S HOUSE WITH A NEWS VAN AND SCREAMING LIKE A BIG BABY ABOUT HOW DAREDEVIL HAS RUINED HIS LIFE.

YEAH, LIKE DAREDEVIL MADE YOU TURN YOURSELF INTO MR. IDIOT.

SO I POP DOWN THERE AND START DOING MY WHOLE 'PUNCHING HIM IN THE FACE AND MAKING FUN OF HIS CLOTHES' BIT WHEN WHO POPS OUT OF NOWHERE...?

I CAN'T BELIEVE IT.

HE ***IS*** THE MAN WITHOUT FEAR. HE JUST PUT ON HIS COSTUME AND JUMPED INTO IT LIKE IT'S JUST ANOTHER DAY IN THE LIFE.

HIS WHOLE LIFE IS CRUMBLING AROUND HIM AND HE GETS INTO IT!!

RIGHT IN FRONT OF HIS HOUSE!! RIGHT IN FRONT OF THE MEDIA!!

AND FOR ALL OF MR. HYDE'S BIG TALK, IT SEEMS FIVE OR SIX GOOD PROFESSIONAL SUPER-HERO HITS TO THE HEAD WITH A MAILBOX WILL PRETTY MUCH DO THE JOB.

DOWN HE GOES.

AND IT GIVES THE CAMERAS THE SHOW THEY SO DESPERATELY WANTED.

I THINK I CAME OFF PRETTY GOOD, BUT WHO KNOWS? THEY ALWAYS ZOOM IN ON MY STOMACH AND MAKE ME LOOK FAT. AND I'M NOT FAT.

IF I WAS ***FAT*** I WOULDN'T WEAR ***TIGHTS!*** OR I'D WEAR MY SHIRT HANGING OUT.

BUT WE SAVE THE DAY, WHICH YOU'D THINK WOULD BE ENOUGH FOR THESE PEOPLE TO GIVE MATT A BREAK, BUT NO. THEY RUSH US. A STAMPEDE OF STUPID COMING RIGHT FOR US.

SO WE BOTH GO TO THE ONLY SAFE PLACE PEOPLE LIKE US CAN GO ANYMORE.

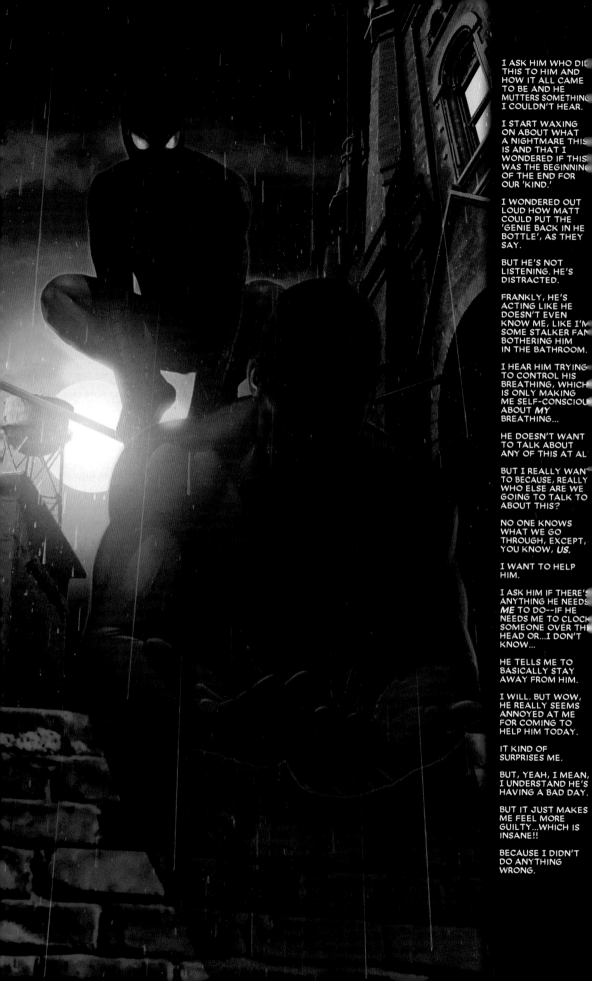

I ASK HIM WHO DID THIS TO HIM AND HOW IT ALL CAME TO BE AND HE MUTTERS SOMETHING I COULDN'T HEAR.

I START WAXING ON ABOUT WHAT A NIGHTMARE THIS IS AND THAT I WONDERED IF THIS WAS THE BEGINNING OF THE END FOR OUR 'KIND.'

I WONDERED OUT LOUD HOW MATT COULD PUT THE 'GENIE BACK IN THE BOTTLE', AS THEY SAY.

BUT HE'S NOT LISTENING. HE'S DISTRACTED.

FRANKLY, HE'S ACTING LIKE HE DOESN'T EVEN KNOW ME, LIKE I'M SOME STALKER FAN BOTHERING HIM IN THE BATHROOM.

I HEAR HIM TRYING TO CONTROL HIS BREATHING, WHICH IS ONLY MAKING ME SELF-CONSCIOUS ABOUT MY BREATHING...

HE DOESN'T WANT TO TALK ABOUT ANY OF THIS AT ALL.

BUT I REALLY WANT TO BECAUSE, REALLY WHO ELSE ARE WE GOING TO TALK TO ABOUT THIS?

NO ONE KNOWS WHAT WE GO THROUGH, EXCEPT, YOU KNOW, US.

I WANT TO HELP HIM.

I ASK HIM IF THERE'S ANYTHING HE NEEDS ME TO DO--IF HE NEEDS ME TO CLOCK SOMEONE OVER THE HEAD OR...I DON'T KNOW...

HE TELLS ME TO BASICALLY STAY AWAY FROM HIM.

I WILL. BUT WOW, HE REALLY SEEMS ANNOYED AT ME FOR COMING TO HELP HIM TODAY.

IT KIND OF SURPRISES ME.

BUT, YEAH, I MEAN, I UNDERSTAND HE'S HAVING A BAD DAY.

BUT IT JUST MAKES ME FEEL MORE GUILTY...WHICH IS INSANE!!

BECAUSE I DIDN'T DO ANYTHING WRONG.

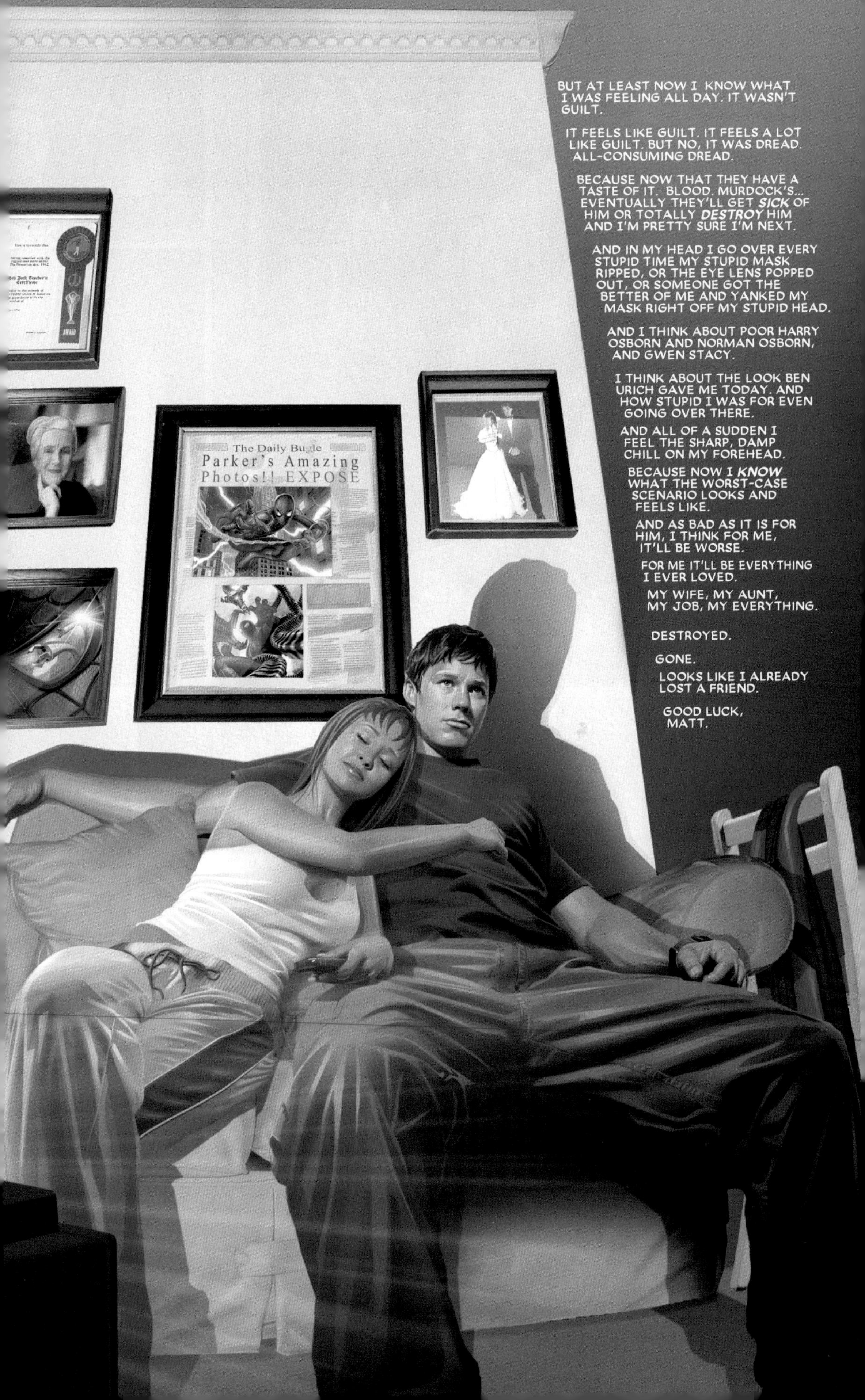
BUT AT LEAST NOW I KNOW WHAT I WAS FEELING ALL DAY. IT WASN'T GUILT.
IT FEELS LIKE GUILT. IT FEELS A LOT LIKE GUILT. BUT NO, IT WAS DREAD. ALL-CONSUMING DREAD.
BECAUSE NOW THAT THEY HAVE A TASTE OF IT. BLOOD. MURDOCK'S... EVENTUALLY THEY'LL GET *SICK* OF HIM OR TOTALLY *DESTROY* HIM AND I'M PRETTY SURE I'M NEXT.
AND IN MY HEAD I GO OVER EVERY STUPID TIME MY STUPID MASK RIPPED, OR THE EYE LENS POPPED OUT, OR SOMEONE GOT THE BETTER OF ME AND YANKED MY MASK RIGHT OFF MY STUPID HEAD.
AND I THINK ABOUT POOR HARRY OSBORN AND NORMAN OSBORN, AND GWEN STACY.
I THINK ABOUT THE LOOK BEN URICH GAVE ME TODAY. AND HOW STUPID I WAS FOR EVEN GOING OVER THERE.
AND ALL OF A SUDDEN I FEEL THE SHARP, DAMP CHILL ON MY FOREHEAD.
BECAUSE NOW I *KNOW* WHAT THE WORST-CASE SCENARIO LOOKS AND FEELS LIKE.
AND AS BAD AS IT IS FOR HIM, I THINK FOR ME, IT'LL BE WORSE.
FOR ME IT'LL BE EVERYTHING I EVER LOVED.
MY WIFE, MY AUNT, MY JOB, MY EVERYTHING.
DESTROYED.
GONE.
LOOKS LIKE I ALREADY LOST A FRIEND.
GOOD LUCK, MATT.
The Daily Bugle
Parker's Amazing Photos!! EXPOSE

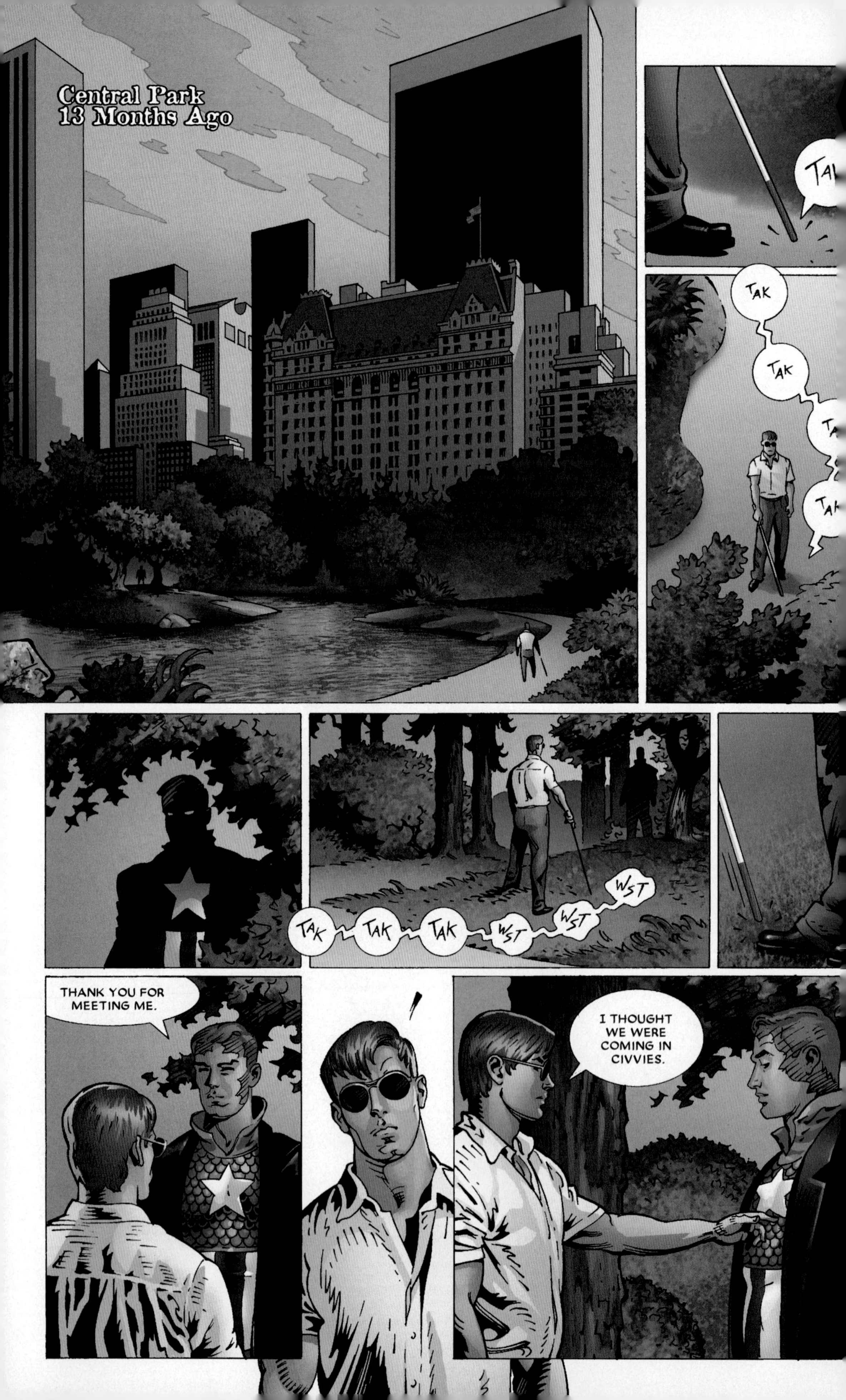

Central Park
13 Months Ago
TAK
TAK
TAK
TAK TAK TAK WST WST WST
THANK YOU FOR MEETING ME.
!
I THOUGHT WE WERE COMING IN CIVVIES.

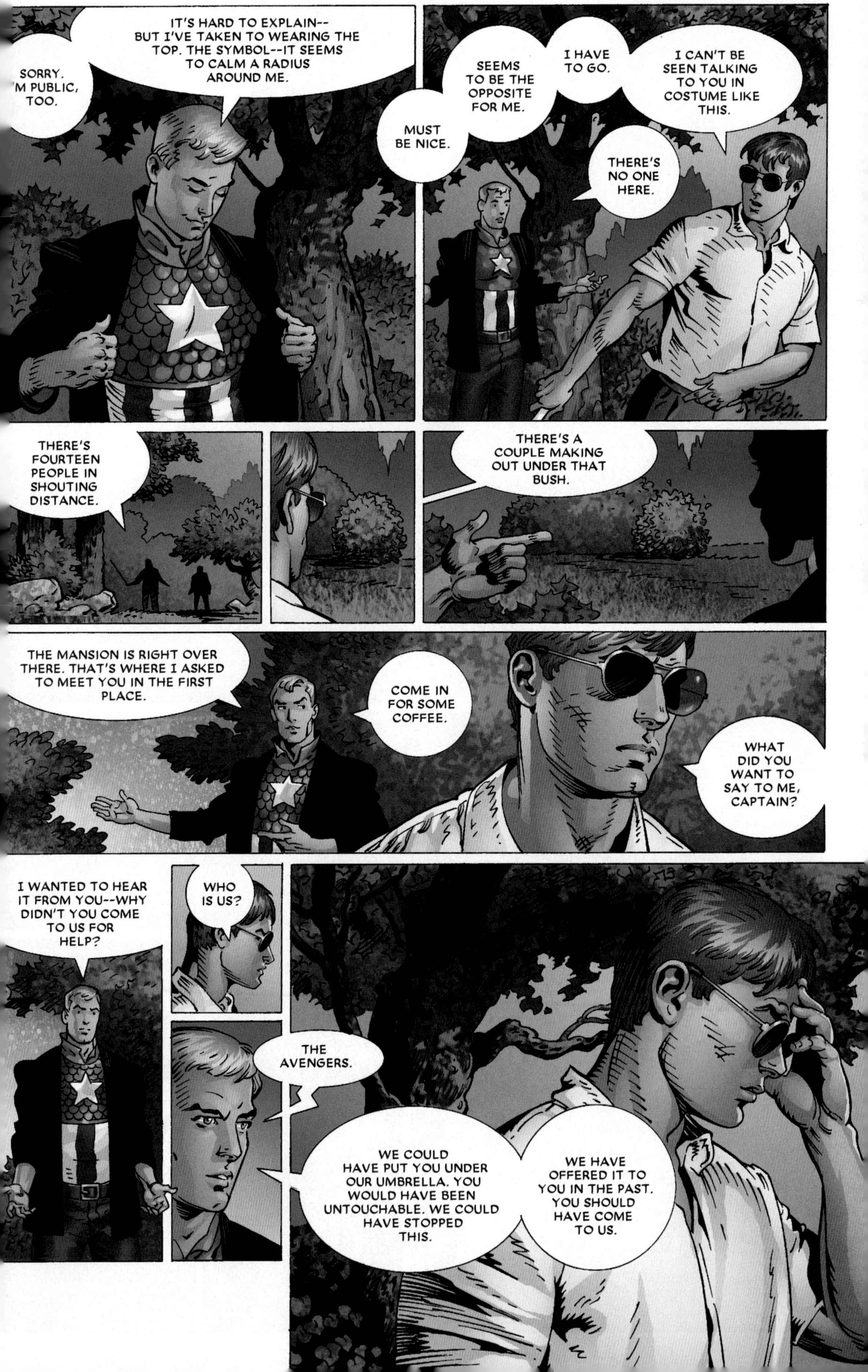

SORRY. 'M PUBLIC, TOO.
IT'S HARD TO EXPLAIN-- BUT I'VE TAKEN TO WEARING THE TOP. THE SYMBOL--IT SEEMS TO CALM A RADIUS AROUND ME.
MUST BE NICE.
SEEMS TO BE THE OPPOSITE FOR ME.
I HAVE TO GO.
I CAN'T BE SEEN TALKING TO YOU IN COSTUME LIKE THIS.
THERE'S NO ONE HERE.
THERE'S FOURTEEN PEOPLE IN SHOUTING DISTANCE.
THERE'S A COUPLE MAKING OUT UNDER THAT BUSH.
THE MANSION IS RIGHT OVER THERE. THAT'S WHERE I ASKED TO MEET YOU IN THE FIRST PLACE.
COME IN FOR SOME COFFEE.
WHAT DID YOU WANT TO SAY TO ME, CAPTAIN?
I WANTED TO HEAR IT FROM YOU--WHY DIDN'T YOU COME TO US FOR HELP?
WHO IS US?
THE AVENGERS.
WE COULD HAVE PUT YOU UNDER OUR UMBRELLA. YOU WOULD HAVE BEEN UNTOUCHABLE. WE COULD HAVE STOPPED THIS.
WE HAVE OFFERED IT TO YOU IN THE PAST. YOU SHOULD HAVE COME TO US.

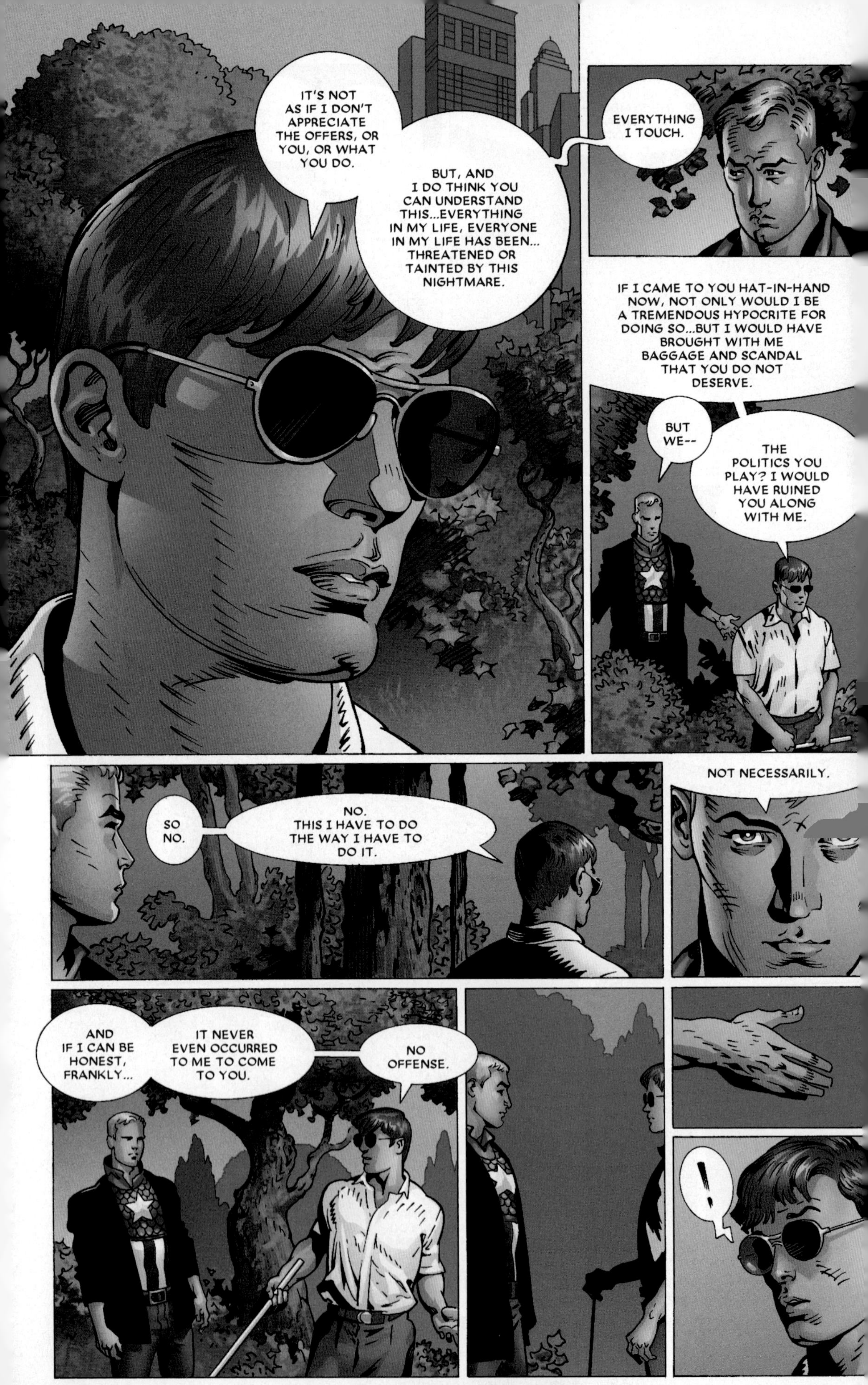
IT'S NOT AS IF I DON'T APPRECIATE THE OFFERS, OR YOU, OR WHAT YOU DO.
BUT, AND I DO THINK YOU CAN UNDERSTAND THIS...EVERYTHING IN MY LIFE, EVERYONE IN MY LIFE HAS BEEN... THREATENED OR TAINTED BY THIS NIGHTMARE.
EVERYTHING I TOUCH.
IF I CAME TO YOU HAT-IN-HAND NOW, NOT ONLY WOULD I BE A TREMENDOUS HYPOCRITE FOR DOING SO...BUT I WOULD HAVE BROUGHT WITH ME BAGGAGE AND SCANDAL THAT YOU DO NOT DESERVE.
BUT WE--
THE POLITICS YOU PLAY? I WOULD HAVE RUINED YOU ALONG WITH ME.
SO NO.
NO. THIS I HAVE TO DO THE WAY I HAVE TO DO IT.
NOT NECESSARILY.
AND IF I CAN BE HONEST, FRANKLY...
IT NEVER EVEN OCCURRED TO ME TO COME TO YOU.
NO OFFENSE.
!

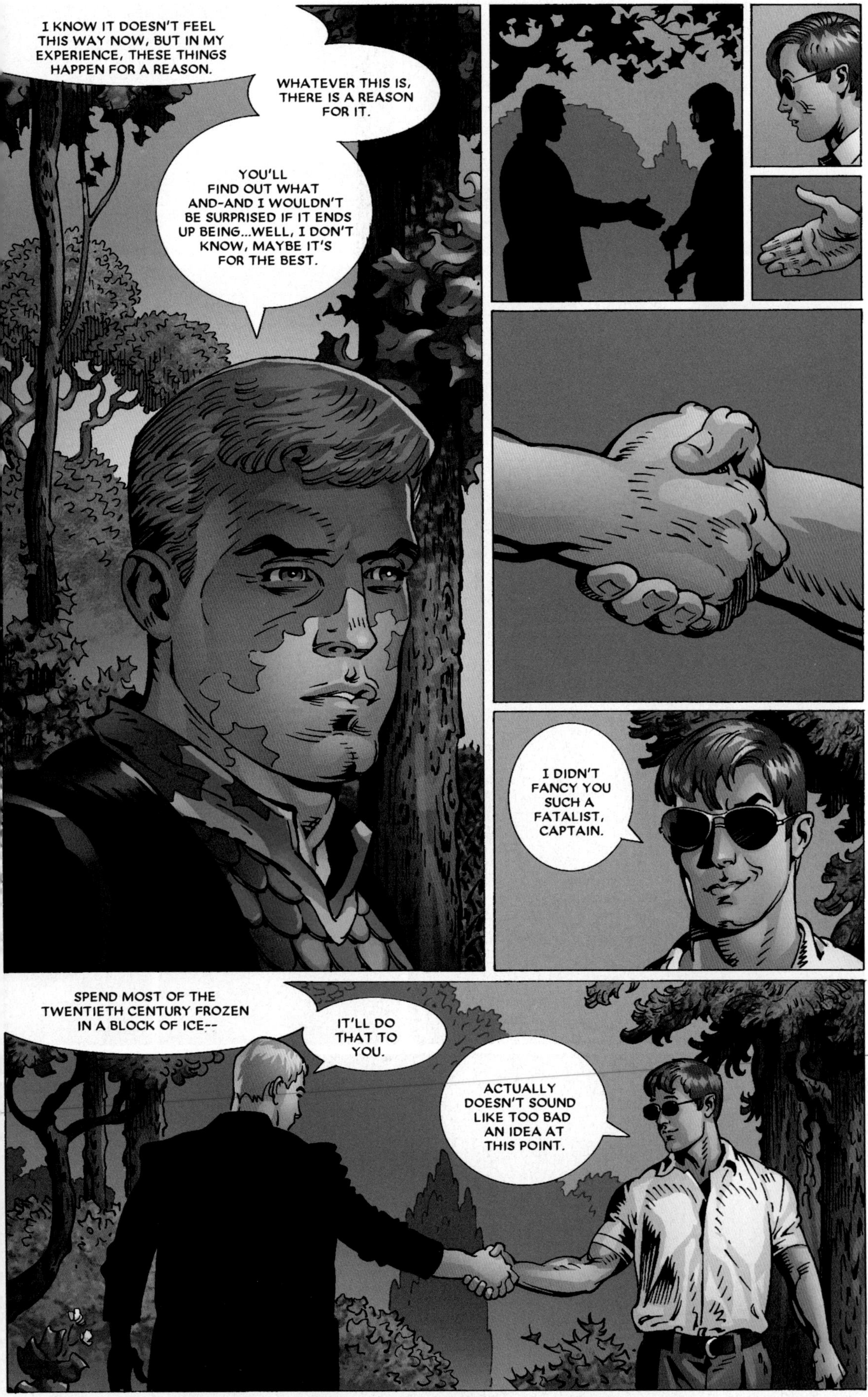
I KNOW IT DOESN'T FEEL THIS WAY NOW, BUT IN MY EXPERIENCE, THESE THINGS HAPPEN FOR A REASON.
WHATEVER THIS IS, THERE IS A REASON FOR IT.
YOU'LL FIND OUT WHAT AND-AND I WOULDN'T BE SURPRISED IF IT ENDS UP BEING...WELL, I DON'T KNOW, MAYBE IT'S FOR THE BEST.
I DIDN'T FANCY YOU SUCH A FATALIST, CAPTAIN.
SPEND MOST OF THE TWENTIETH CENTURY FROZEN IN A BLOCK OF ICE--
IT'LL DO THAT TO YOU.
ACTUALLY DOESN'T SOUND LIKE TOO BAD AN IDEA AT THIS POINT.

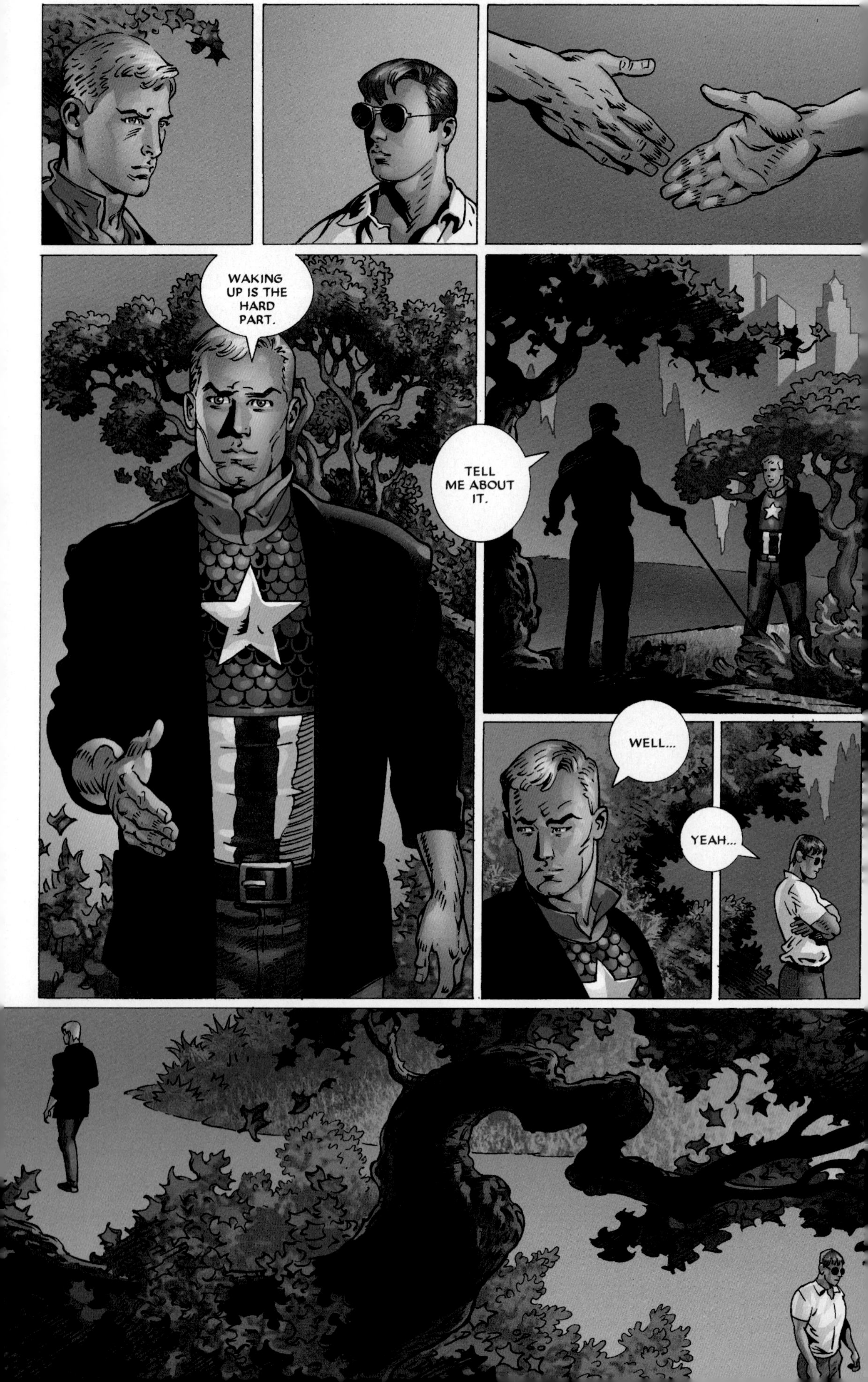
WAKING UP IS THE HARD PART.
TELL ME ABOUT IT.
WELL...
YEAH...

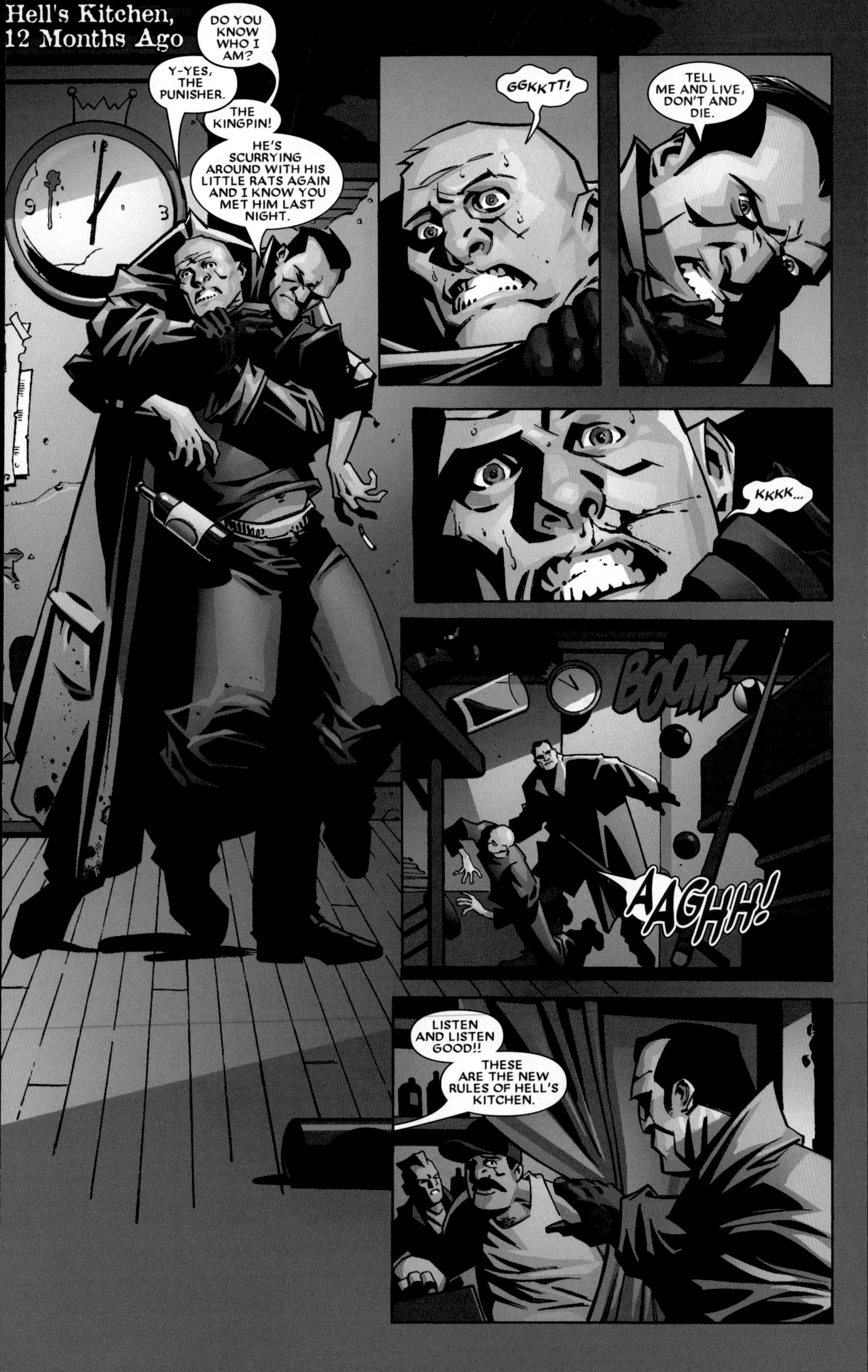
Hell's Kitchen, 12 Months Ago
DO YOU KNOW WHO I AM?
Y-YES, THE PUNISHER.
THE KINGPIN!
HE'S SCURRYING AROUND WITH HIS LITTLE RATS AGAIN AND I KNOW YOU MET HIM LAST NIGHT.
GGKKTT!
TELL ME AND LIVE, DON'T AND DIE.
KKKK...
BOOM!
AAGHH!
LISTEN AND LISTEN GOOD!!
THESE ARE THE NEW RULES OF HELL'S KITCHEN.

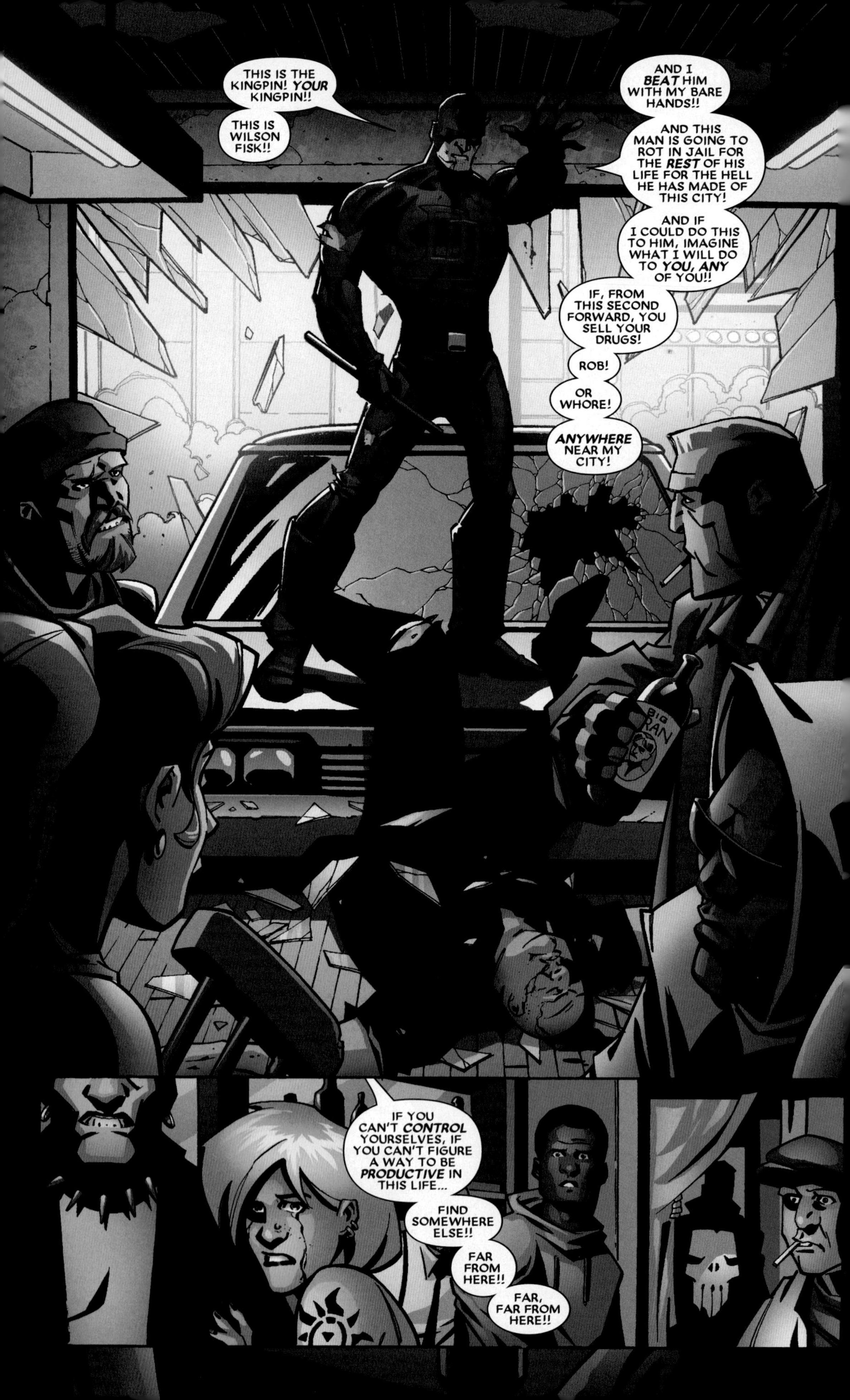
THIS IS THE KINGPIN! *YOUR* KINGPIN!!
THIS IS WILSON FISK!!
AND I *BEAT* HIM WITH MY BARE HANDS!!
AND THIS MAN IS GOING TO ROT IN JAIL FOR THE *REST* OF HIS LIFE FOR THE HELL HE HAS MADE OF THIS CITY!
AND IF I COULD DO THIS TO HIM, IMAGINE WHAT I WILL DO TO *YOU, ANY* OF YOU!!
IF, FROM THIS SECOND FORWARD, YOU SELL YOUR DRUGS!
ROB!
OR WHORE!
ANYWHERE NEAR MY CITY!
IF YOU CAN'T *CONTROL* YOURSELVES, IF YOU CAN'T FIGURE A WAY TO BE *PRODUCTIVE* IN THIS LIFE...
FIND SOMEWHERE ELSE!!
FAR FROM HERE!!
FAR, FAR FROM HERE!!

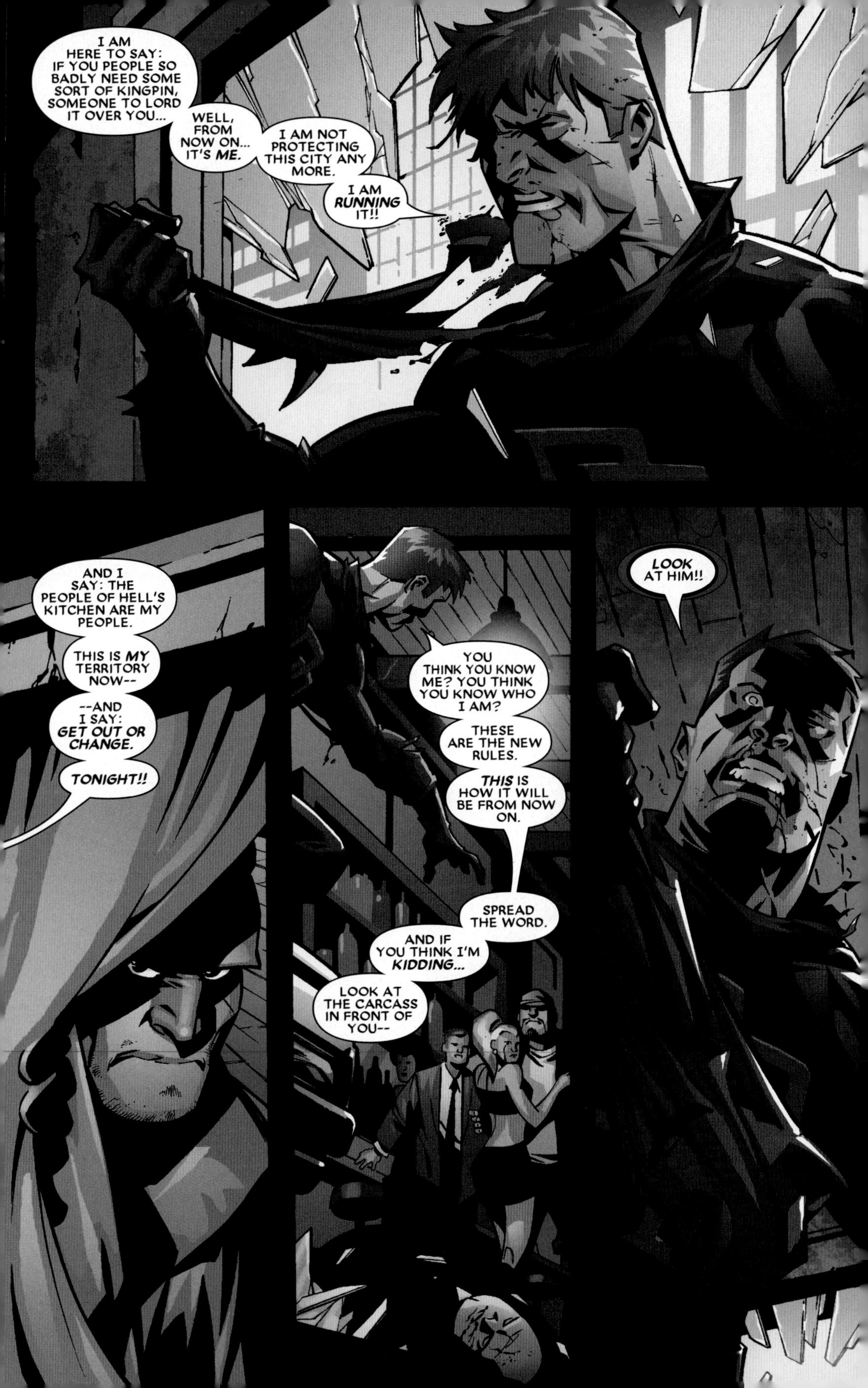
I AM HERE TO SAY: IF YOU PEOPLE SO BADLY NEED SOME SORT OF KINGPIN, SOMEONE TO LORD IT OVER YOU...
WELL, FROM NOW ON... IT'S *ME.*
I AM NOT PROTECTING THIS CITY ANY MORE.
I AM *RUNNING* IT!!
AND I SAY: THE PEOPLE OF HELL'S KITCHEN ARE MY PEOPLE.
THIS IS *MY* TERRITORY NOW--
--AND I SAY: *GET OUT OR CHANGE.*
TONIGHT!!
YOU THINK YOU KNOW ME? YOU THINK YOU KNOW WHO I AM?
THESE ARE THE NEW RULES.
THIS IS HOW IT WILL BE FROM NOW ON.
SPREAD THE WORD.
AND IF YOU THINK I'M *KIDDING...*
LOOK AT THE CARCASS IN FRONT OF YOU--
LOOK AT HIM!!

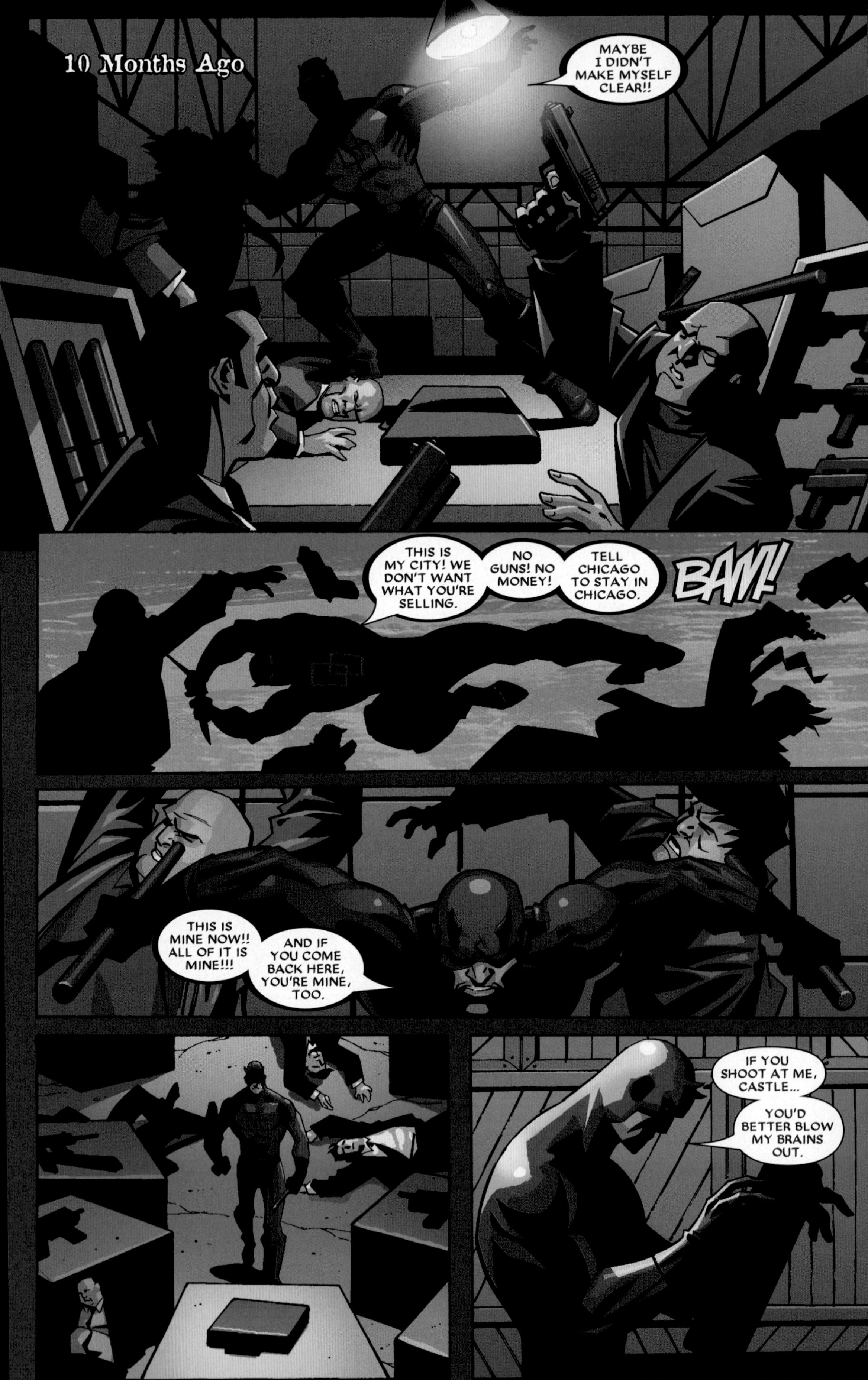
10 Months Ago
MAYBE I DIDN'T MAKE MYSELF CLEAR!!
THIS IS MY CITY! WE DON'T WANT WHAT YOU'RE SELLING.
NO GUNS! NO MONEY!
TELL CHICAGO TO STAY IN CHICAGO.
BAM!
THIS IS MINE NOW!! ALL OF IT IS MINE!!!
AND IF YOU COME BACK HERE, YOU'RE MINE, TOO.
IF YOU SHOOT AT ME, CASTLE...
YOU'D BETTER BLOW MY BRAINS OUT.

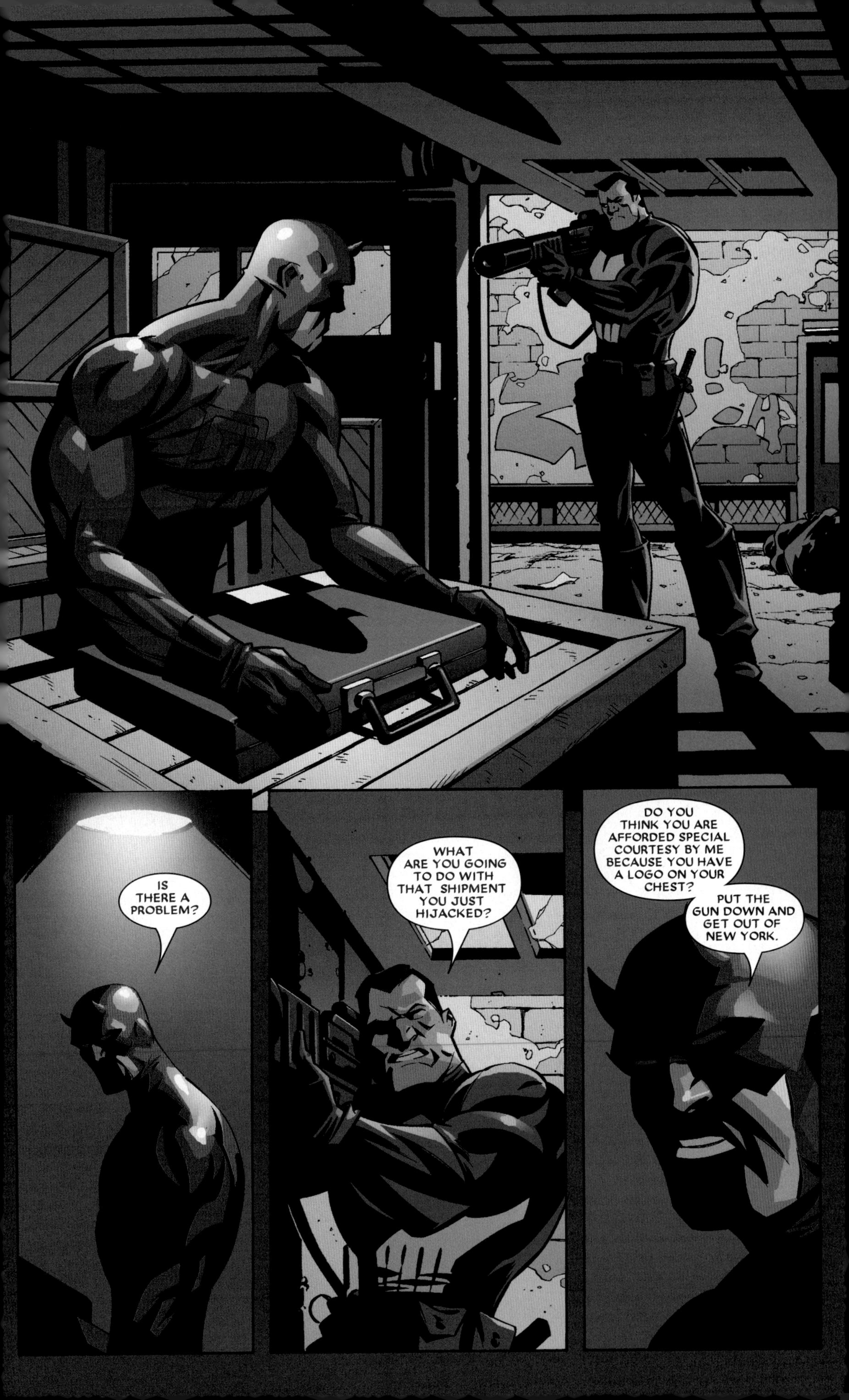
IS THERE A PROBLEM?
WHAT ARE YOU GOING TO DO WITH THAT SHIPMENT YOU JUST HIJACKED?
DO YOU THINK YOU ARE AFFORDED SPECIAL COURTESY BY ME BECAUSE YOU HAVE A LOGO ON YOUR CHEST?
PUT THE GUN DOWN AND GET OUT OF NEW YORK.

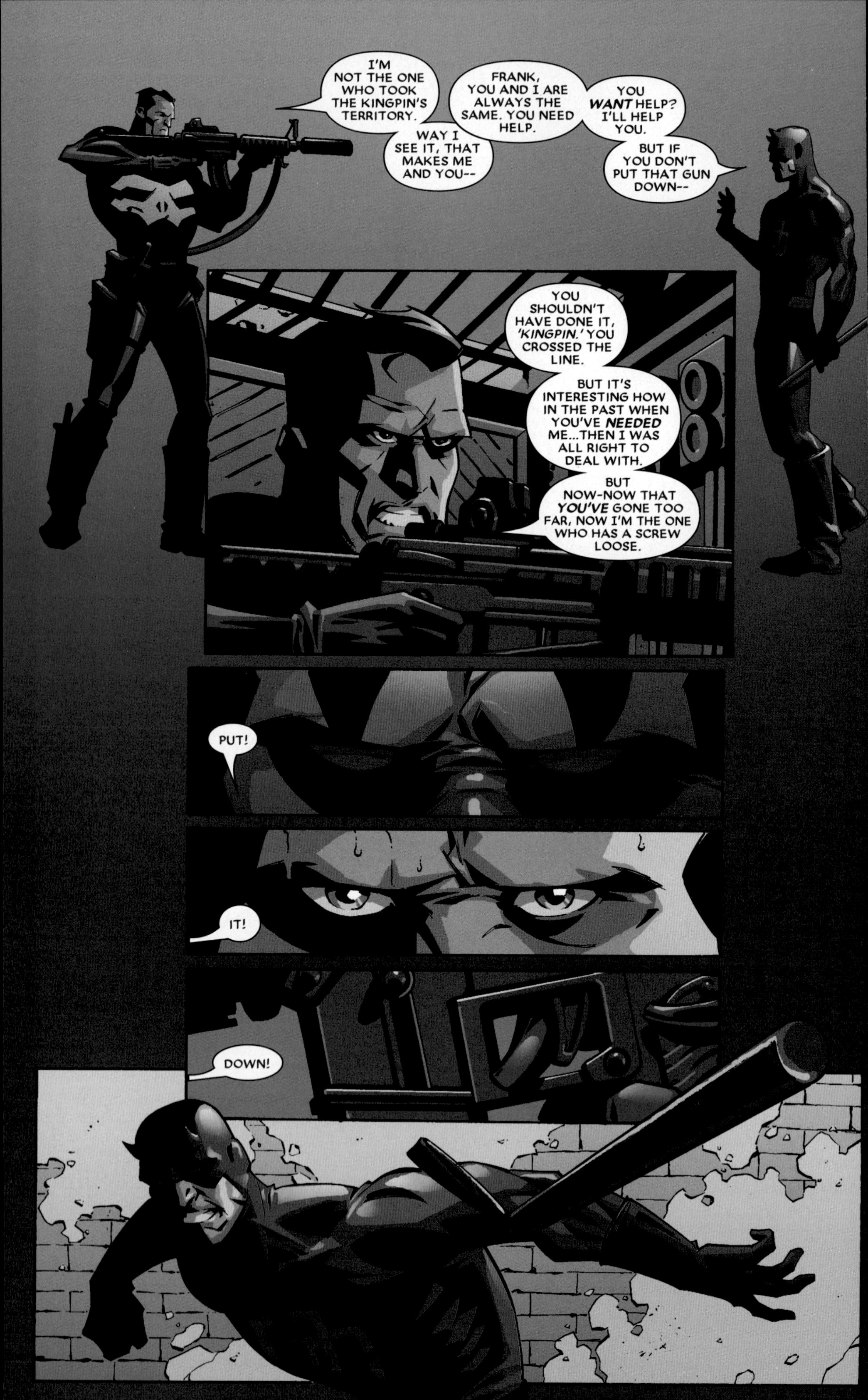
I'M NOT THE ONE WHO TOOK THE KINGPIN'S TERRITORY.
WAY I SEE IT, THAT MAKES ME AND YOU--
FRANK, YOU AND I ARE ALWAYS THE SAME. YOU NEED HELP.
YOU *WANT* HELP? I'LL HELP YOU.
BUT IF YOU DON'T PUT THAT GUN DOWN--
YOU SHOULDN'T HAVE DONE IT, *'KINGPIN.'* YOU CROSSED THE LINE.
BUT IT'S INTERESTING HOW IN THE PAST WHEN YOU'VE *NEEDED* ME...THEN I WAS ALL RIGHT TO DEAL WITH.
BUT NOW-NOW THAT *YOU'VE* GONE TOO FAR, NOW I'M THE ONE WHO HAS A SCREW LOOSE.
PUT!
IT!
DOWN!

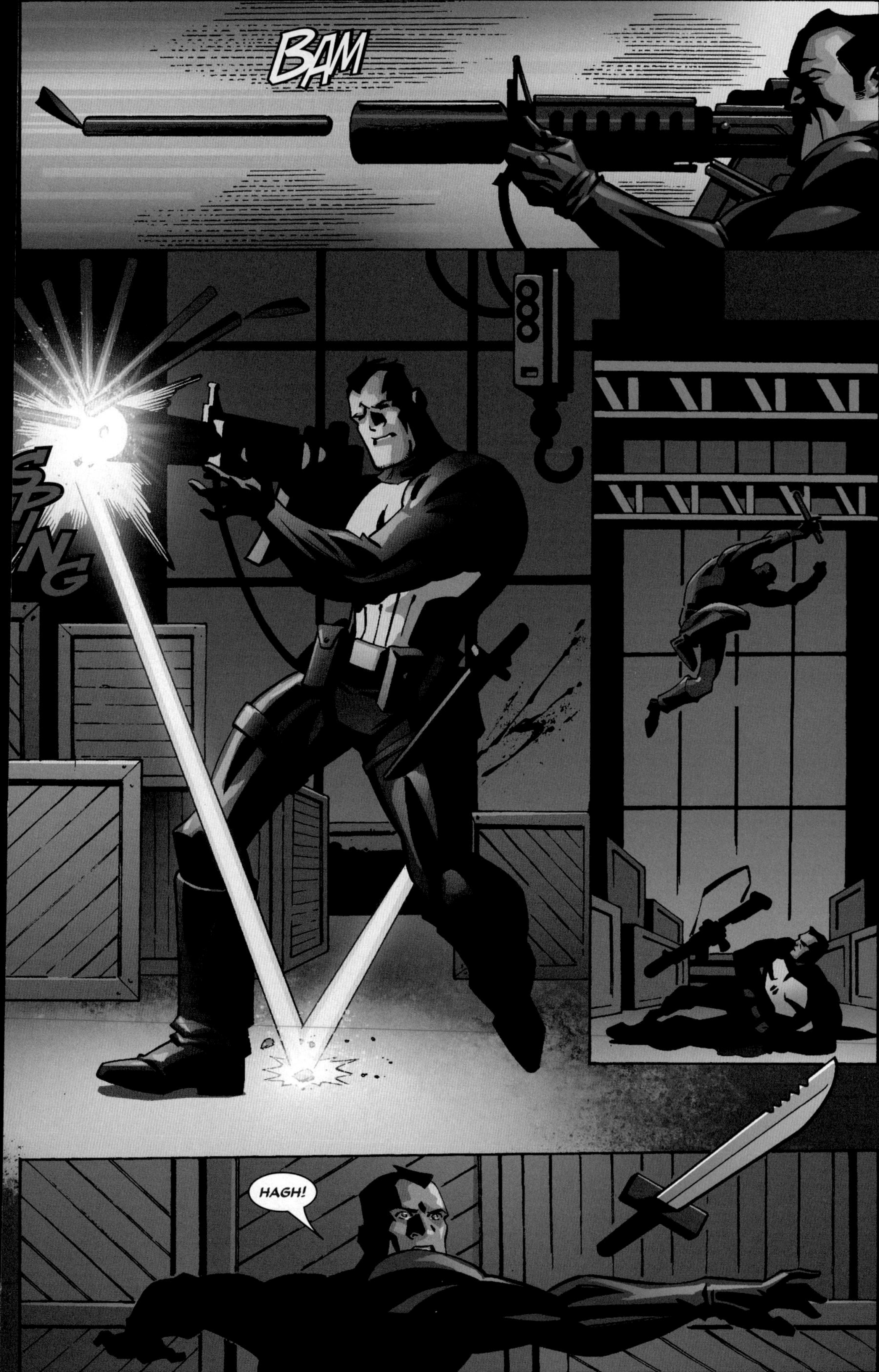
BAM
SPING
HAGH!

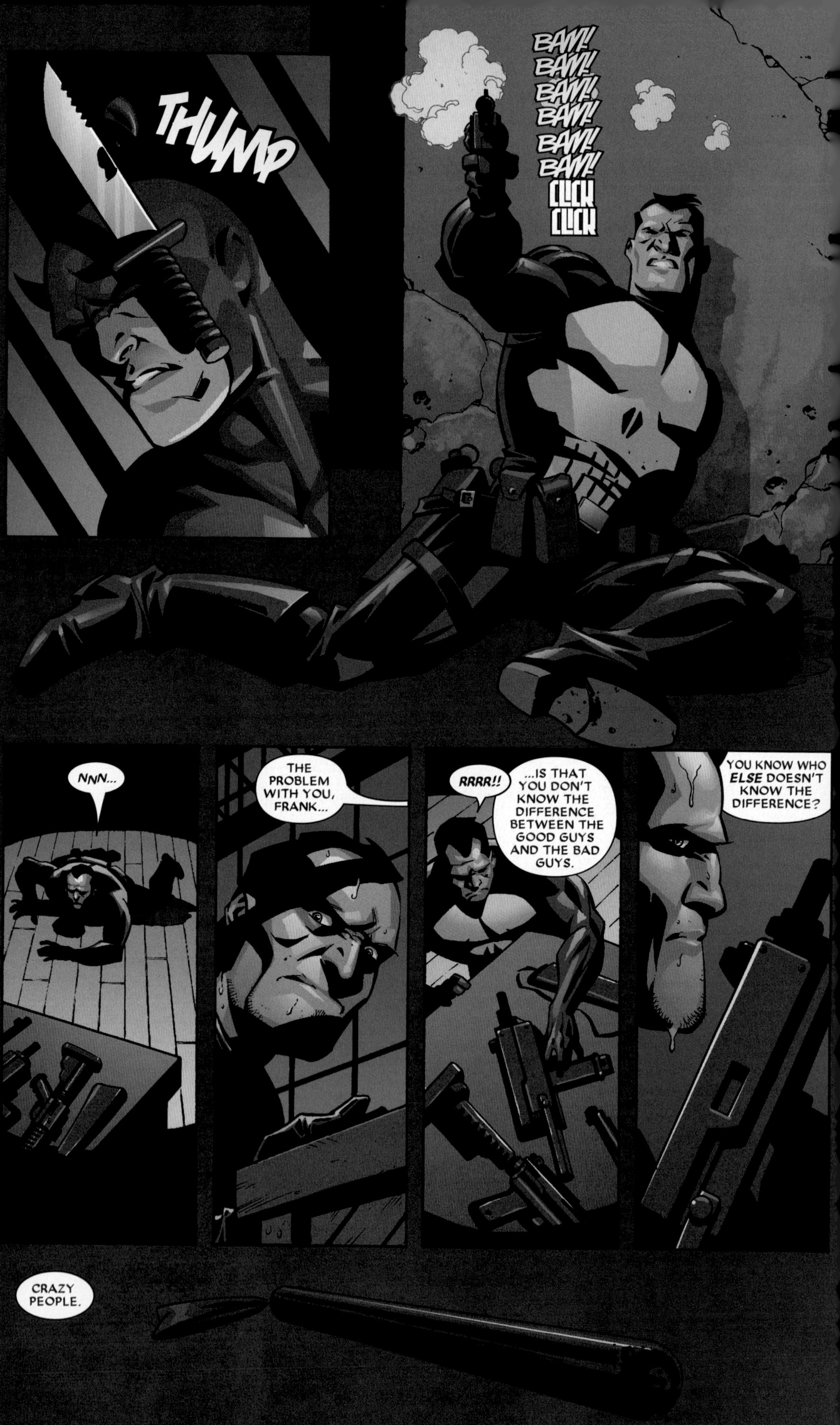
THUMP
BAM! BAM! BAM! BAM! BAM! BAM!
CLICK CLICK
NNN...
THE PROBLEM WITH YOU, FRANK...
RRRR!!
...IS THAT YOU DON'T KNOW THE DIFFERENCE BETWEEN THE GOOD GUYS AND THE BAD GUYS.
YOU KNOW WHO ELSE DOESN'T KNOW THE DIFFERENCE?
CRAZY PEOPLE.

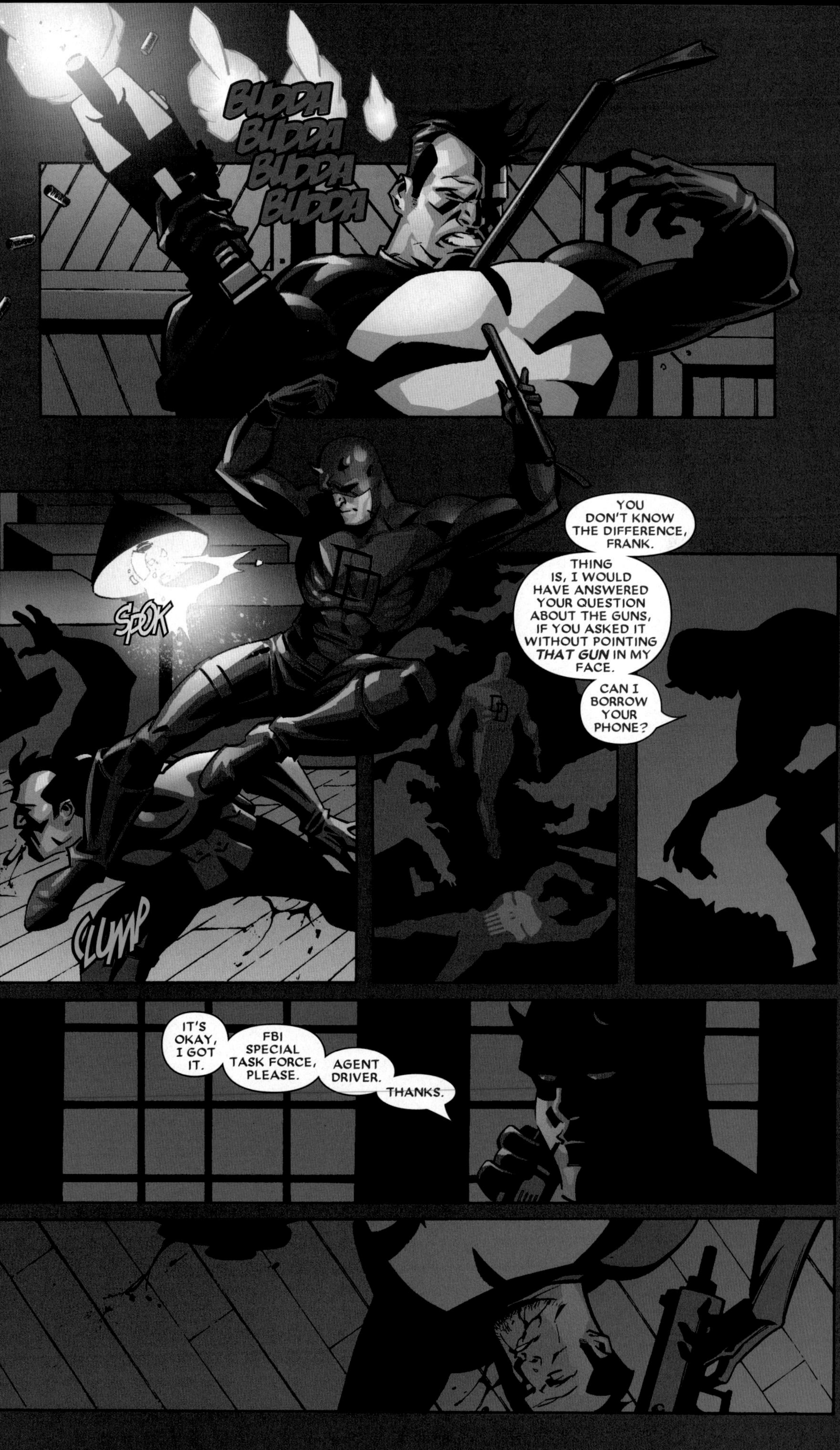
BUDDA BUDDA BUDDA BUDDA
YOU DON'T KNOW THE DIFFERENCE, FRANK.
THING IS, I WOULD HAVE ANSWERED YOUR QUESTION ABOUT THE GUNS, IF YOU ASKED IT WITHOUT POINTING *THAT GUN* IN MY FACE.
SPOK
CLUMP
CAN I BORROW YOUR PHONE?
IT'S OKAY, I GOT IT.
FBI SPECIAL TASK FORCE, PLEASE.
AGENT DRIVER.
THANKS.

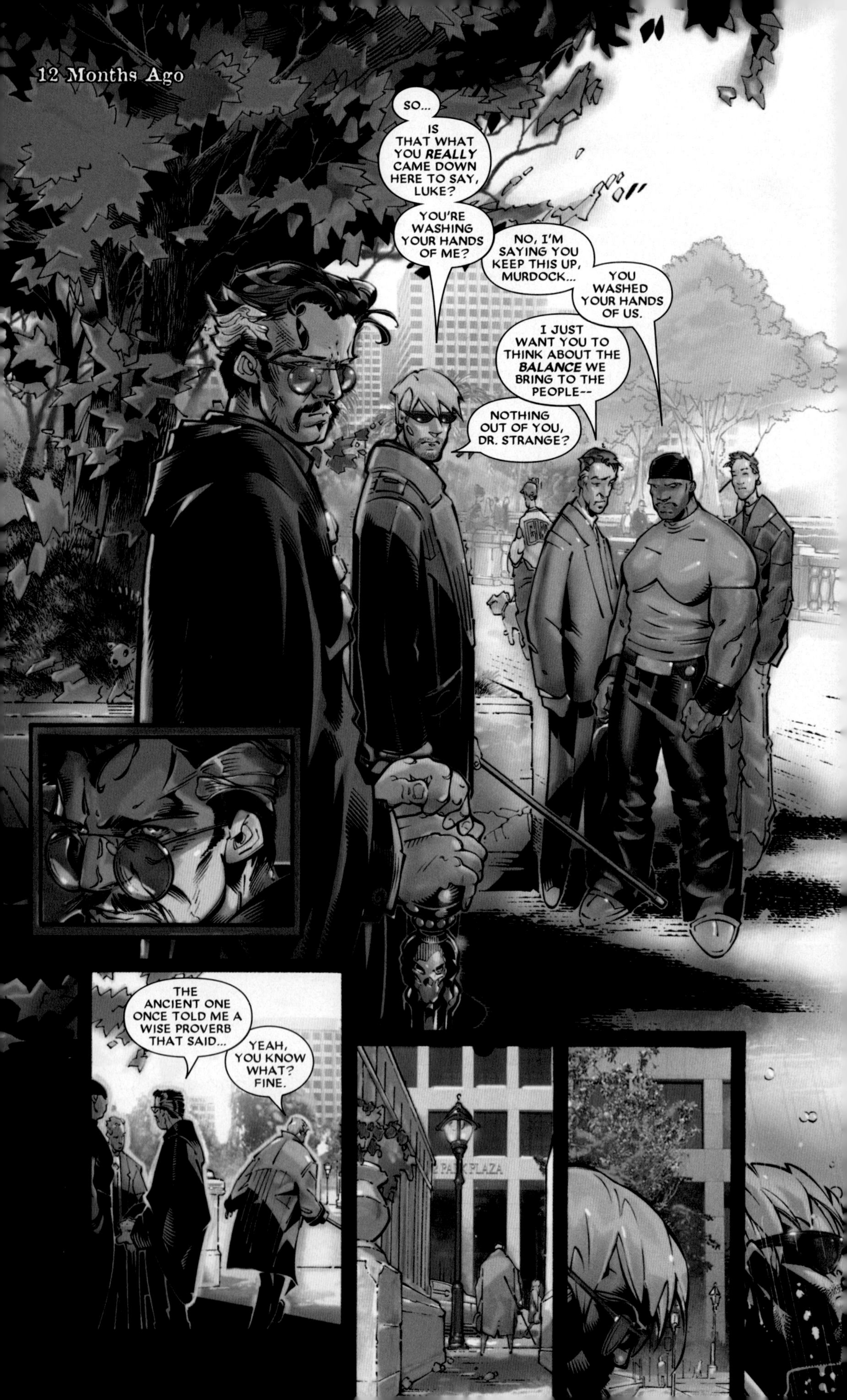
12 Months Ago
SO...
IS THAT WHAT YOU REALLY CAME DOWN HERE TO SAY, LUKE?
YOU'RE WASHING YOUR HANDS OF ME?
NO, I'M SAYING YOU KEEP THIS UP, MURDOCK...
YOU WASHED YOUR HANDS OF US.
I JUST WANT YOU TO THINK ABOUT THE BALANCE WE BRING TO THE PEOPLE--
NOTHING OUT OF YOU, DR. STRANGE?
THE ANCIENT ONE ONCE TOLD ME A WISE PROVERB THAT SAID...
YEAH, YOU KNOW WHAT? FINE.

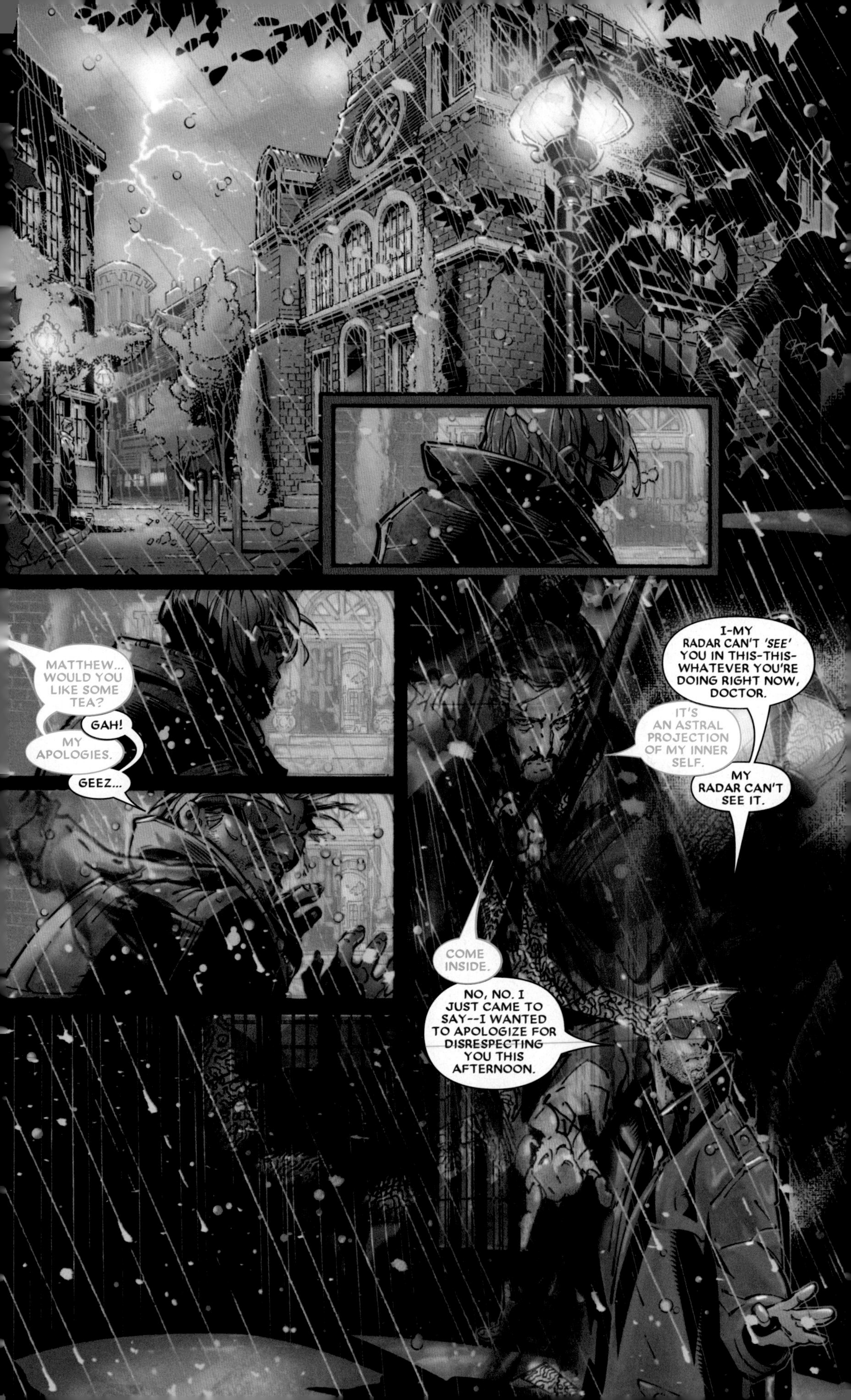
MATTHEW... WOULD YOU LIKE SOME TEA?
GAH!
MY APOLOGIES.
GEEZ...
I-MY RADAR CAN'T 'SEE' YOU IN THIS-THIS-WHATEVER YOU'RE DOING RIGHT NOW, DOCTOR.
IT'S AN ASTRAL PROJECTION OF MY INNER SELF.
MY RADAR CAN'T SEE IT.
COME INSIDE.
NO, NO. I JUST CAME TO SAY--I WANTED TO APOLOGIZE FOR DISRESPECTING YOU THIS AFTERNOON.

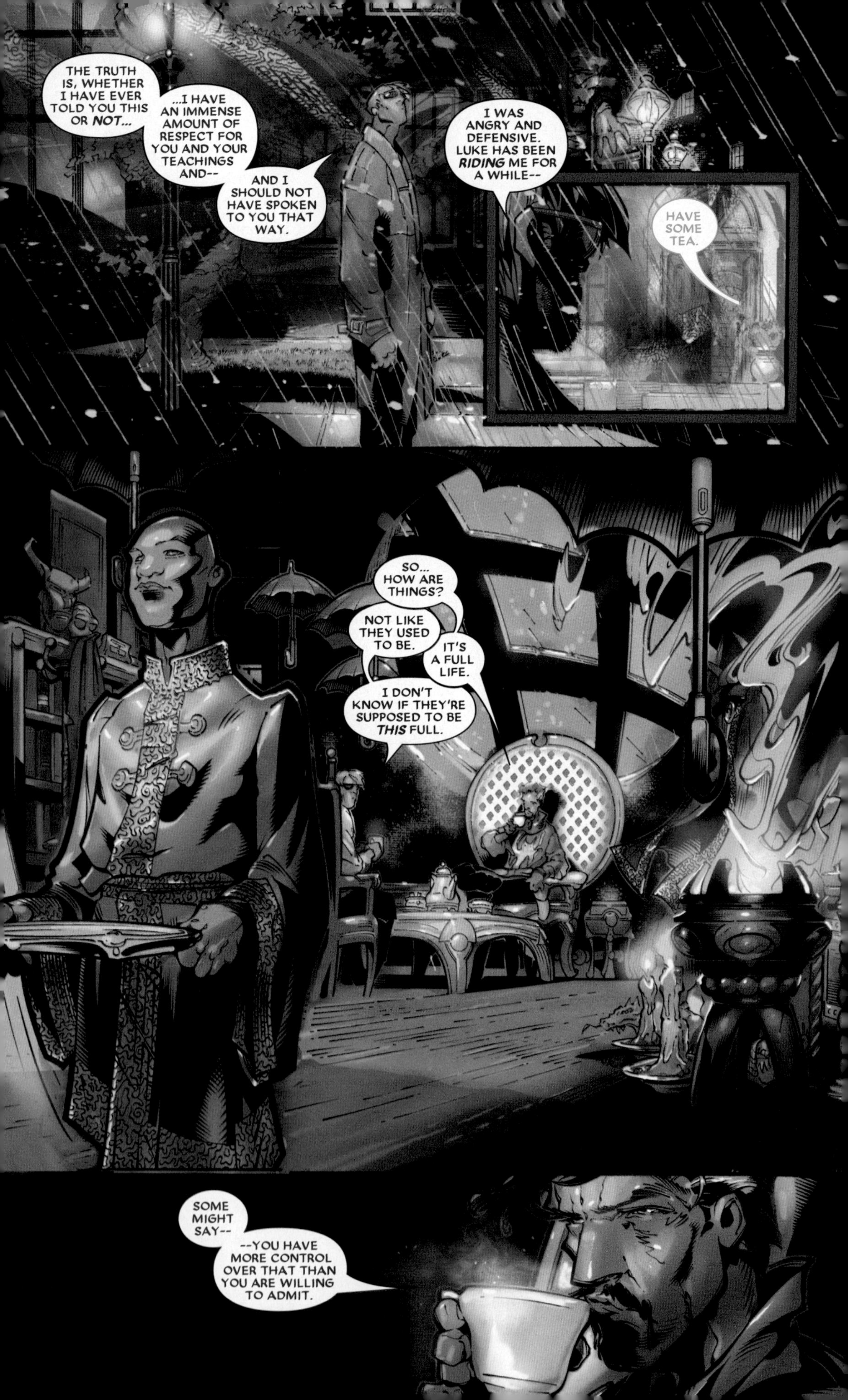
THE TRUTH IS, WHETHER I HAVE EVER TOLD YOU THIS OR *NOT*...
...I HAVE AN IMMENSE AMOUNT OF RESPECT FOR YOU AND YOUR TEACHINGS AND--
AND I SHOULD NOT HAVE SPOKEN TO YOU THAT WAY.
I WAS ANGRY AND DEFENSIVE. LUKE HAS BEEN *RIDING* ME FOR A WHILE--
HAVE SOME TEA.
SO... HOW ARE THINGS?
NOT LIKE THEY USED TO BE.
IT'S A FULL LIFE.
I DON'T KNOW IF THEY'RE SUPPOSED TO BE *THIS* FULL.
SOME MIGHT SAY--
--YOU HAVE MORE CONTROL OVER THAT THAN YOU ARE WILLING TO ADMIT.

YOU'VE MADE SOME INTERESTING LIFE CHOICES OF LATE...

KINGPIN?

I'VE MADE A MESS. I KNOW.

BUT I THINK ABOUT WHAT MY LIFE WAS LIKE BEFORE ALL OF THIS...

AND I WOULD BE KIDDING MYSELF IF I DIDN'T ADMIT...THAT IT WAS A MESS THEN, TOO.

BUT IT SEEMS THAT I SOMEWHAT PREFERRED THE OLD MESS TO THIS ONE.

WHY HAVE YOU COME HERE, REALLY?

TO APOLOGIZE, YES.

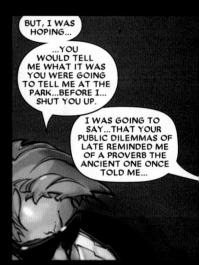

BUT, I WAS HOPING...

...YOU WOULD TELL ME WHAT IT WAS YOU WERE GOING TO TELL ME AT THE PARK...BEFORE I... SHUT YOU UP.

I WAS GOING TO SAY...THAT YOUR PUBLIC DILEMMAS OF LATE REMINDED ME OF A PROVERB THE ANCIENT ONE ONCE TOLD ME...

THE PROVERB GOES:

"THE NAIL WHICH STICKS OUT WILL GET HAMMERED DOWN."

UM, HOW ABOUT..."EVEN AN EXCELLENT SWIMMER CAN GET CARRIED AWAY BY THE RIVER"?

I HAVE 1,309 MORE, BUT I'M THINKING NOW...

...THAT YOU MAY NOT BE THE PROVERB TYPE.

GUESS NOT.

BUT I APPRECIATE THAT YOU ARE LOOKING FOR SPIRITUAL GUIDANCE...

WHEN WAS THE LAST TIME YOU WENT TO YOUR CHURCH?

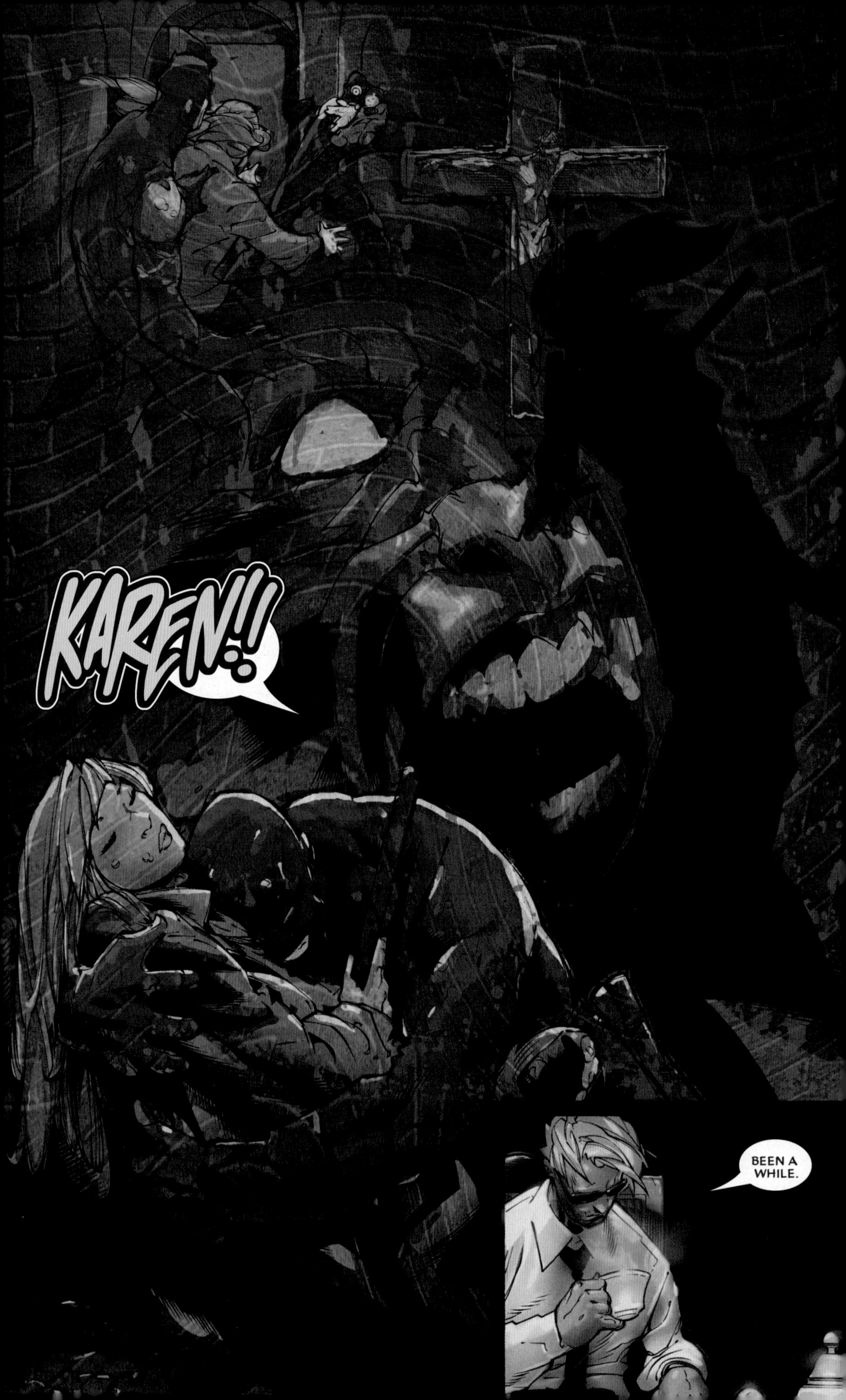
KAREN!!
BEEN A WHILE.

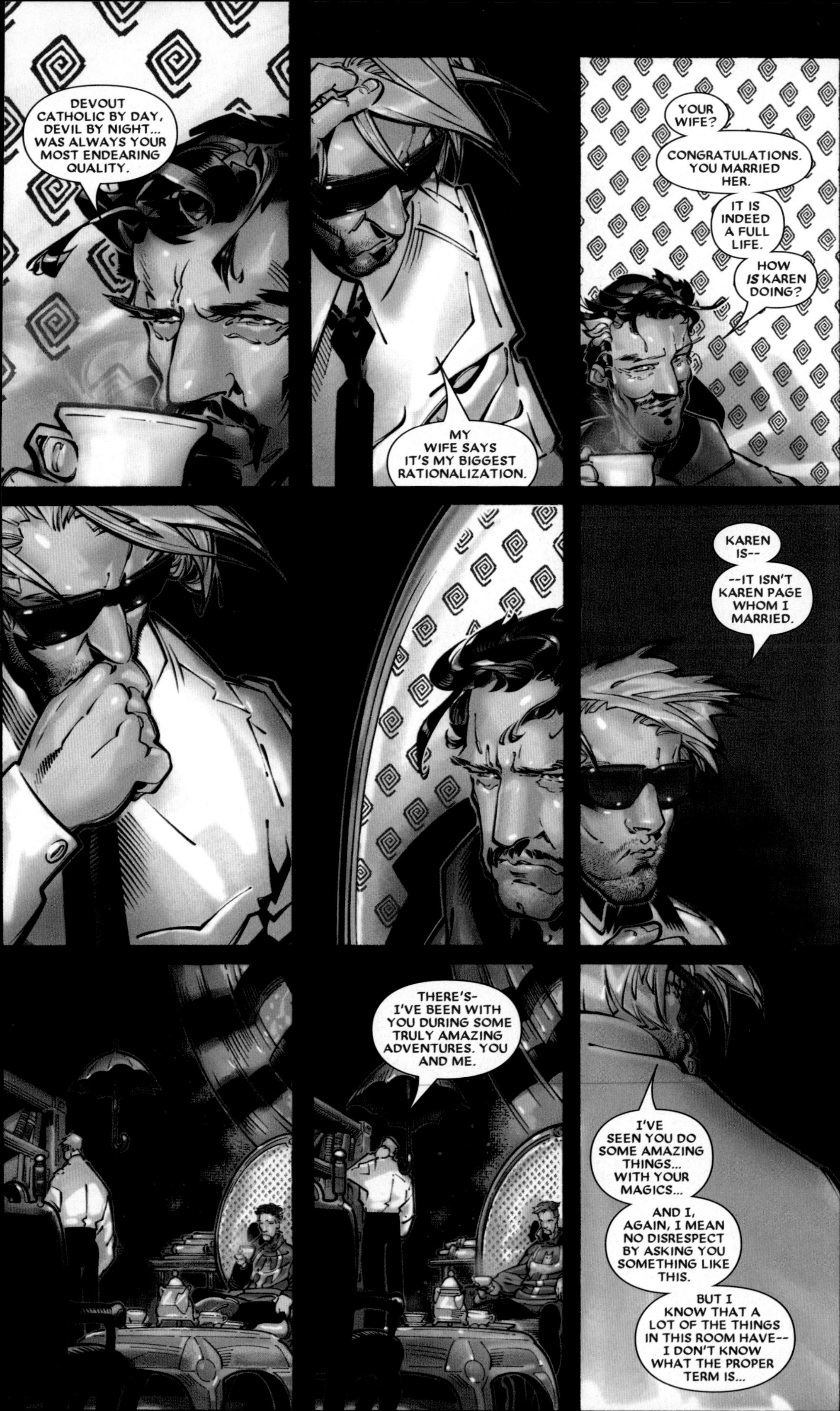

DEVOUT CATHOLIC BY DAY, DEVIL BY NIGHT... WAS ALWAYS YOUR MOST ENDEARING QUALITY.
MY WIFE SAYS IT'S MY BIGGEST RATIONALIZATION.
YOUR WIFE?
CONGRATULATIONS. YOU MARRIED HER.
IT IS INDEED A FULL LIFE.
HOW *IS* KAREN DOING?
KAREN IS--
--IT ISN'T KAREN PAGE WHOM I MARRIED.
THERE'S- I'VE BEEN WITH YOU DURING SOME TRULY AMAZING ADVENTURES. YOU AND ME.
I'VE SEEN YOU DO SOME AMAZING THINGS... WITH YOUR MAGICS...
AND I, AGAIN, I MEAN NO DISRESPECT BY ASKING YOU SOMETHING LIKE THIS.
BUT I KNOW THAT A LOT OF THE THINGS IN THIS ROOM HAVE-- I DON'T KNOW WHAT THE PROPER TERM IS...

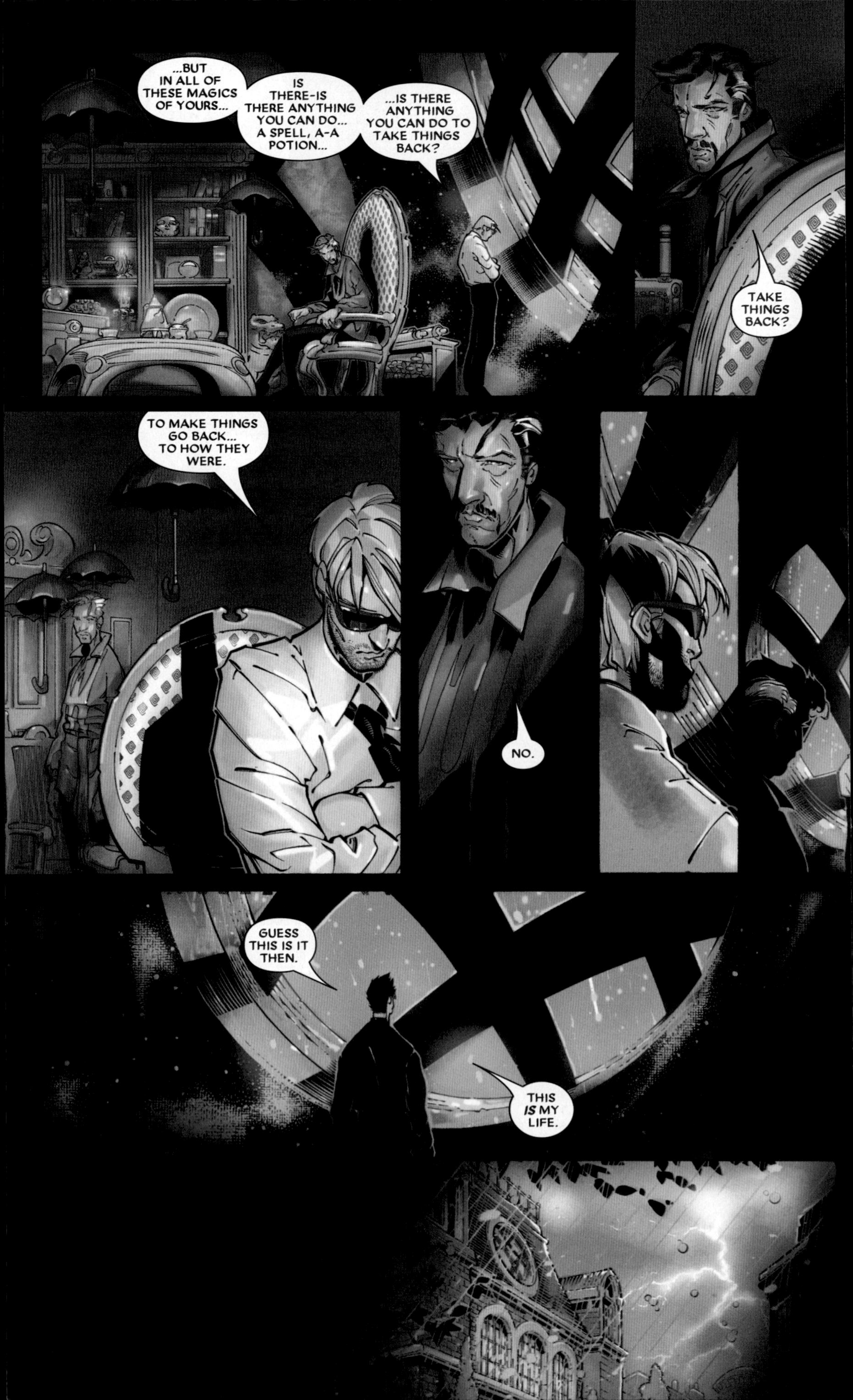
...BUT IN ALL OF THESE MAGICS OF YOURS...
IS THERE-IS THERE ANYTHING YOU CAN DO... A SPELL, A-A POTION...
...IS THERE ANYTHING YOU CAN DO TO TAKE THINGS BACK?
TAKE THINGS BACK?
TO MAKE THINGS GO BACK... TO HOW THEY WERE.
NO.
GUESS THIS IS IT THEN.
THIS *IS* MY LIFE.

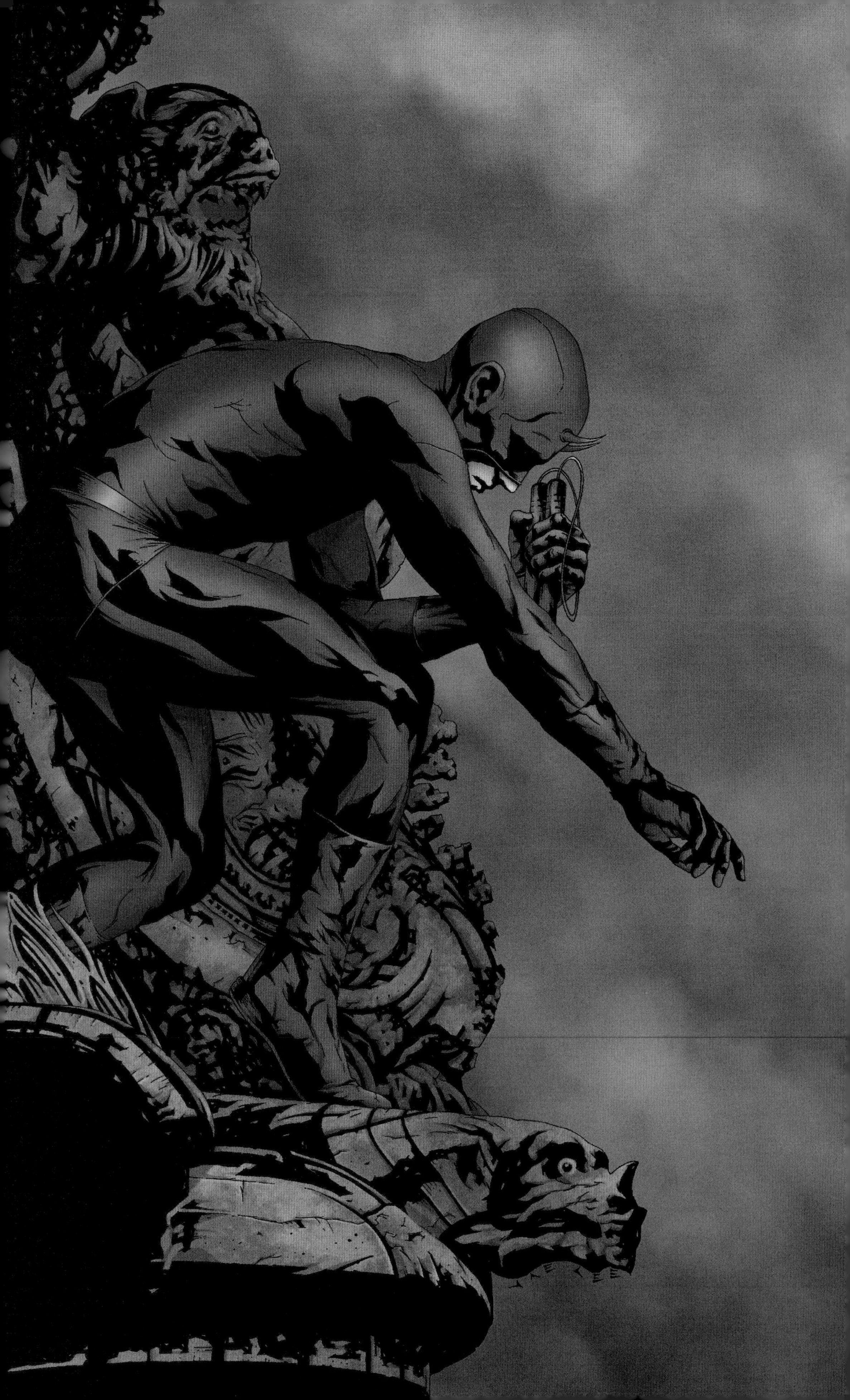

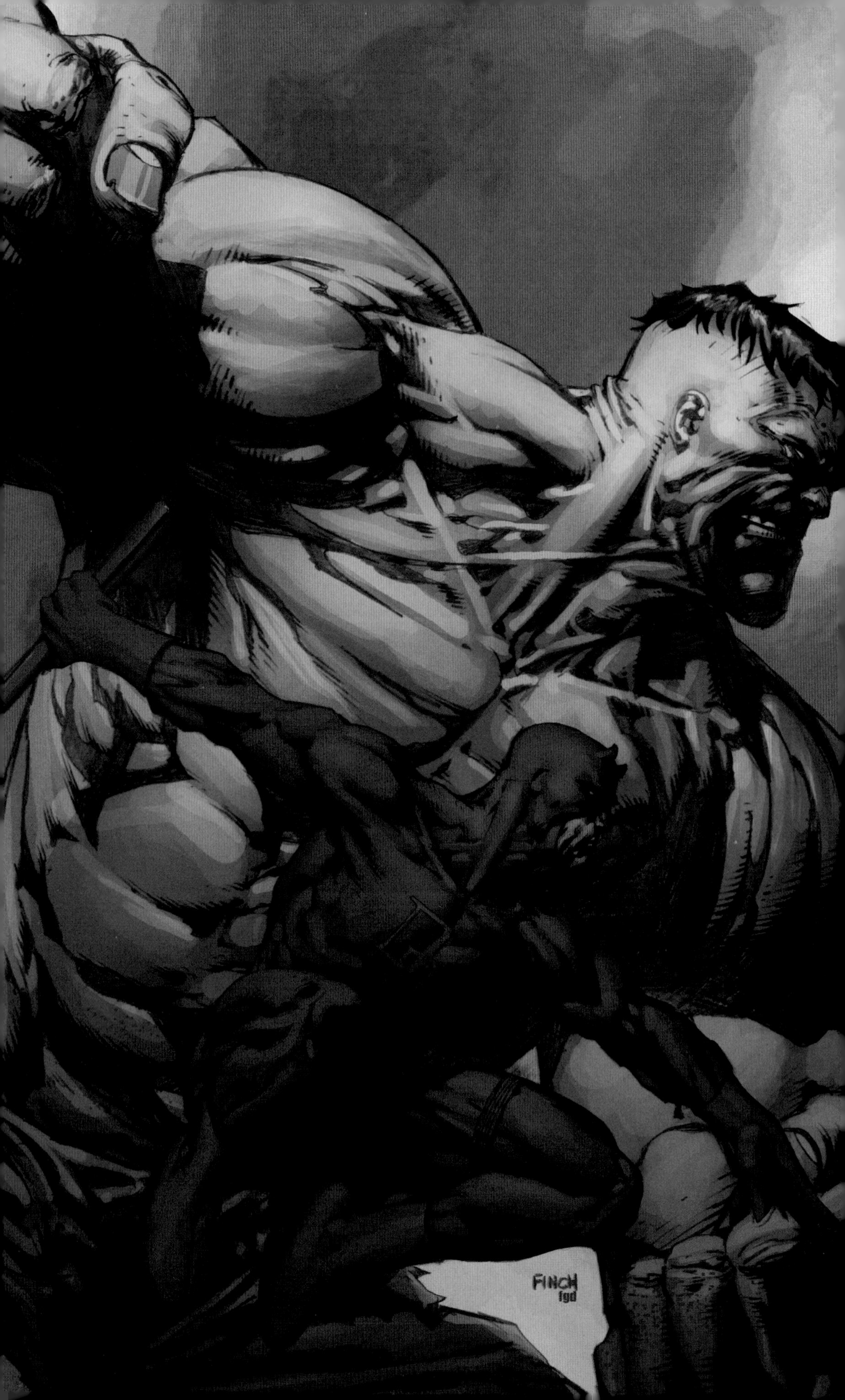
FINCH
fgd

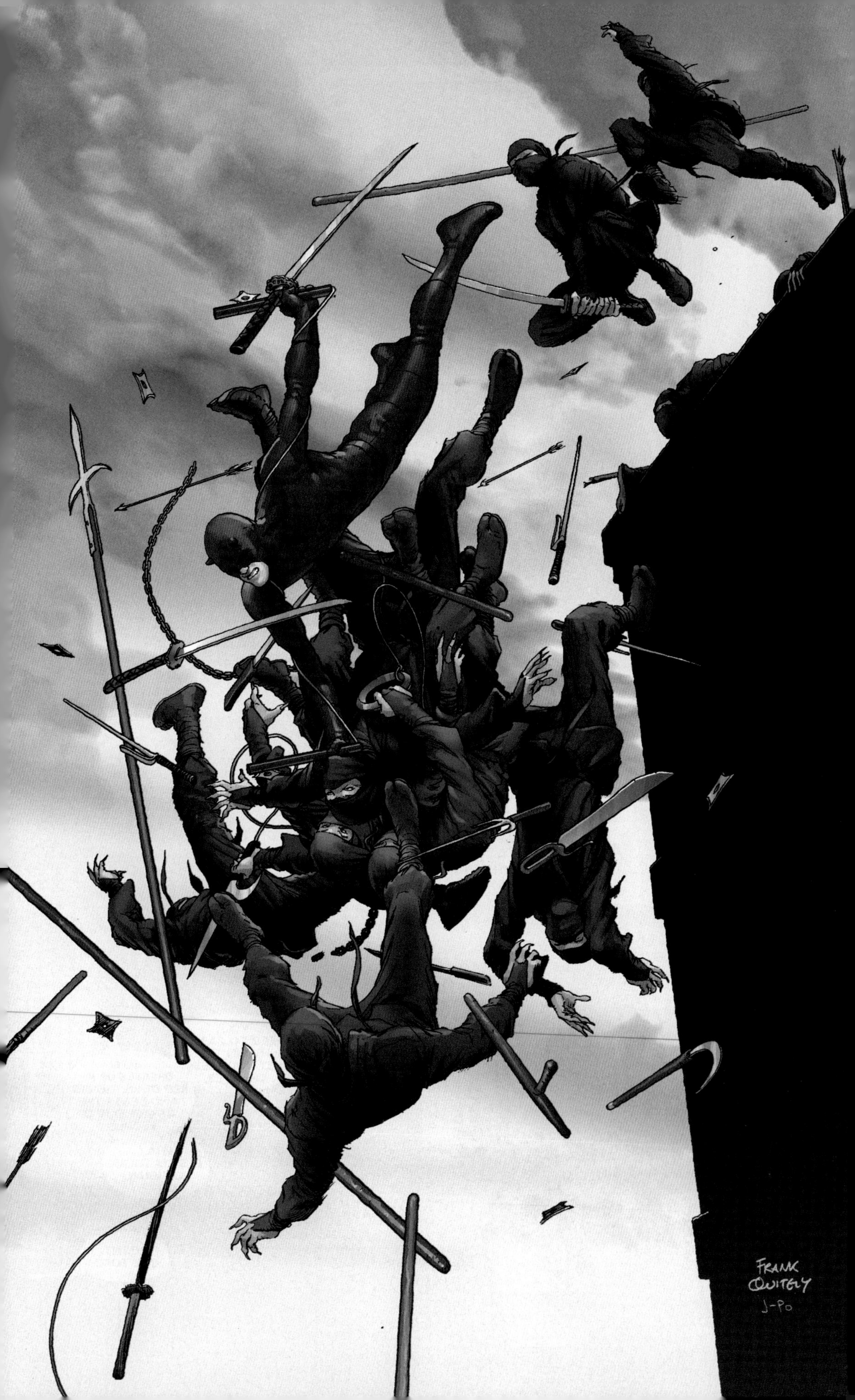
FRANK
QUITELY
J-PO

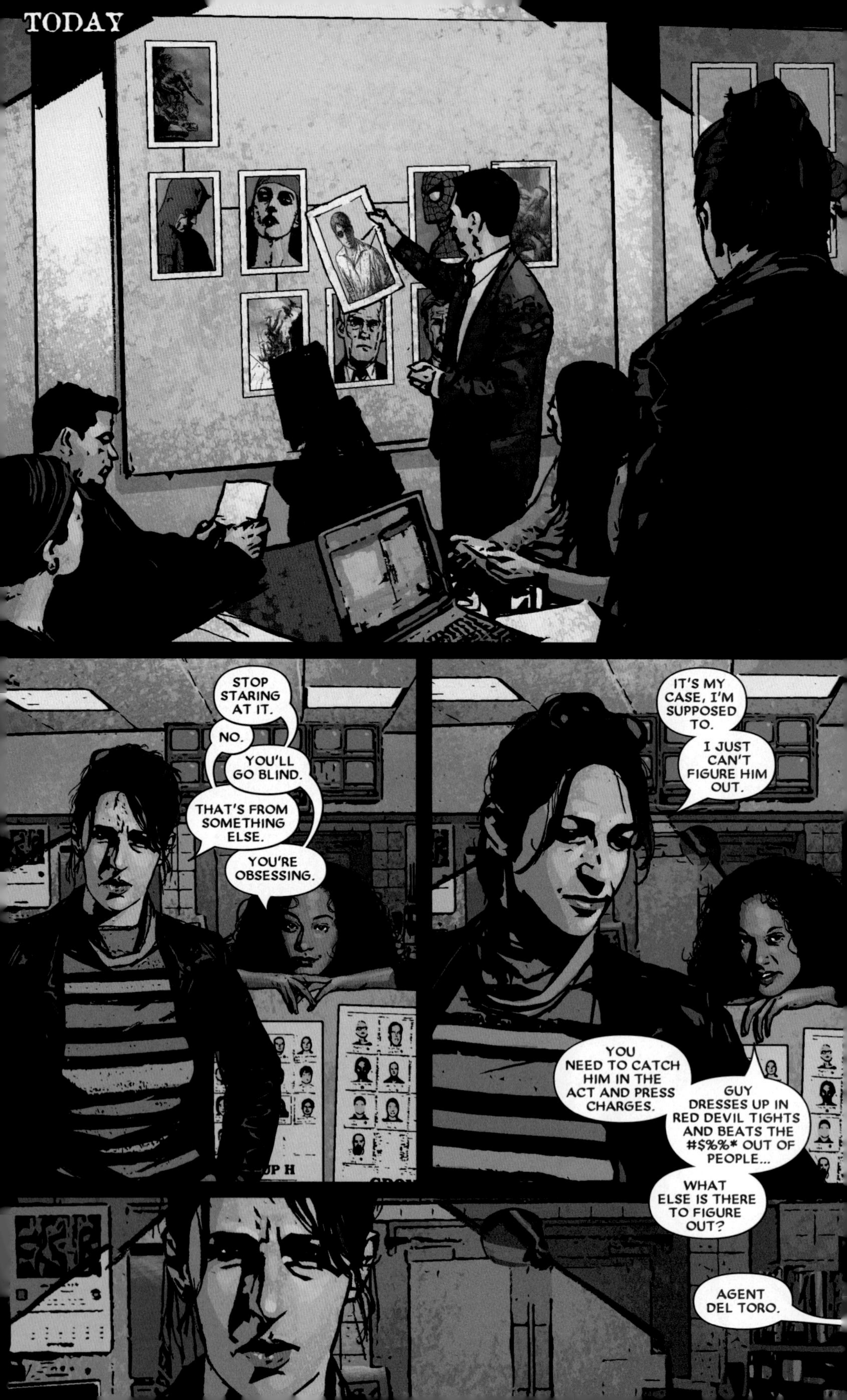
TODAY
STOP STARING AT IT.
NO.
YOU'LL GO BLIND.
THAT'S FROM SOMETHING ELSE.
YOU'RE OBSESSING.
IT'S MY CASE, I'M SUPPOSED TO.
I JUST CAN'T FIGURE HIM OUT.
YOU NEED TO CATCH HIM IN THE ACT AND PRESS CHARGES.
GUY DRESSES UP IN RED DEVIL TIGHTS AND BEATS THE #$%%* OUT OF PEOPLE...
WHAT ELSE IS THERE TO FIGURE OUT?
AGENT DEL TORO.

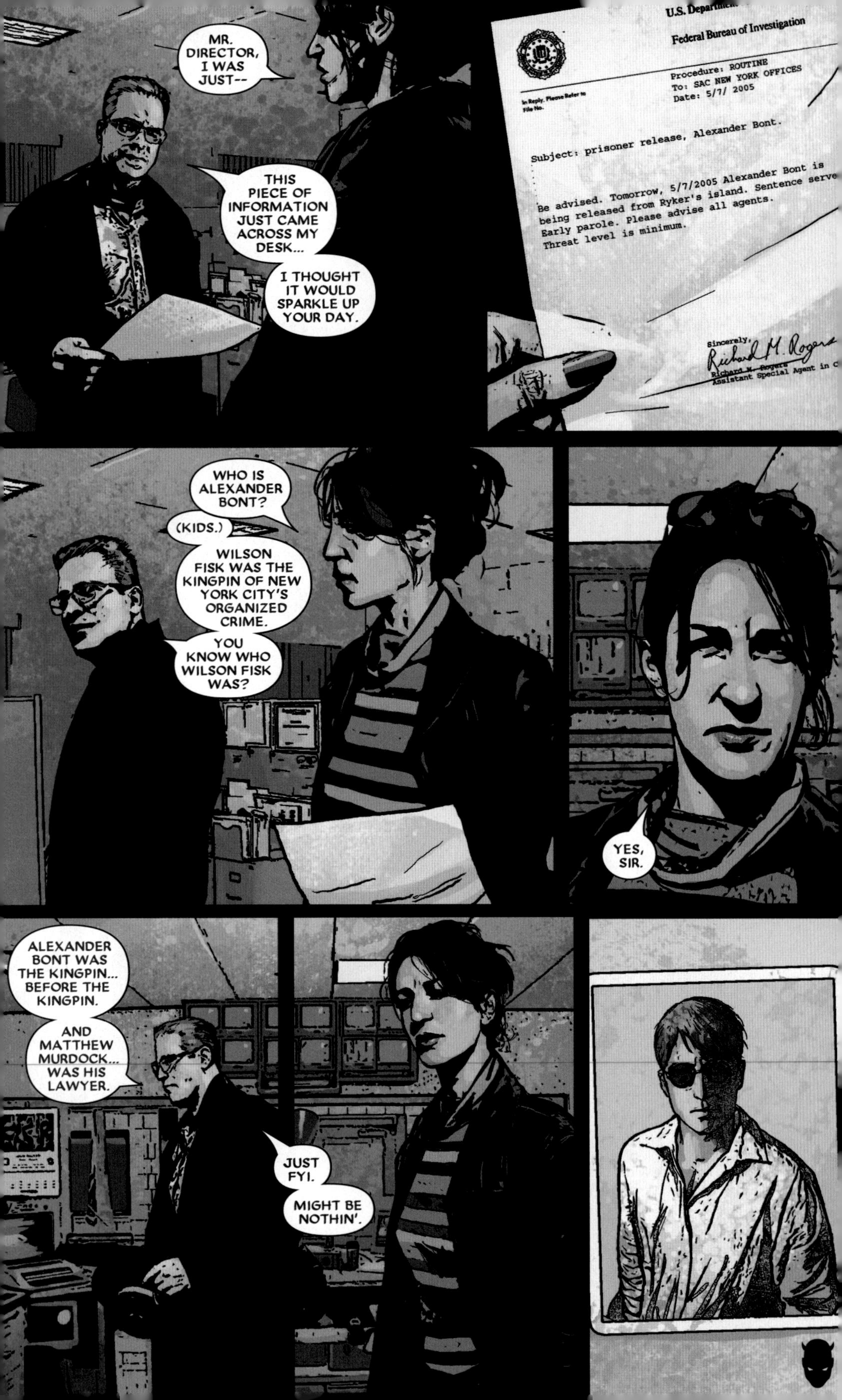
MR. DIRECTOR, I WAS JUST--
U.S. Departm
Federal Bureau of Investigation
In Reply, Please Refer to File No.
Procedure: ROUTINE
To: SAC NEW YORK OFFICES
Date: 5/7/ 2005
Subject: prisoner release, Alexander Bont.
Be advised. Tomorrow, 5/7/2005 Alexander Bont is being released from Ryker's island. Sentence serve
Early parole. Please advise all agents.
Threat level is minimum.
Sincerely,
Richard M. Rogers
Richard M. Rogers
Assistant Special Agent in C
THIS PIECE OF INFORMATION JUST CAME ACROSS MY DESK...
I THOUGHT IT WOULD SPARKLE UP YOUR DAY.
WHO IS ALEXANDER BONT?
(KIDS.)
WILSON FISK WAS THE KINGPIN OF NEW YORK CITY'S ORGANIZED CRIME.
YOU KNOW WHO WILSON FISK WAS?
YES, SIR.
ALEXANDER BONT WAS THE KINGPIN... BEFORE THE KINGPIN.
AND MATTHEW MURDOCK... WAS HIS LAWYER.
JUST FYI.
MIGHT BE NOTHIN'.

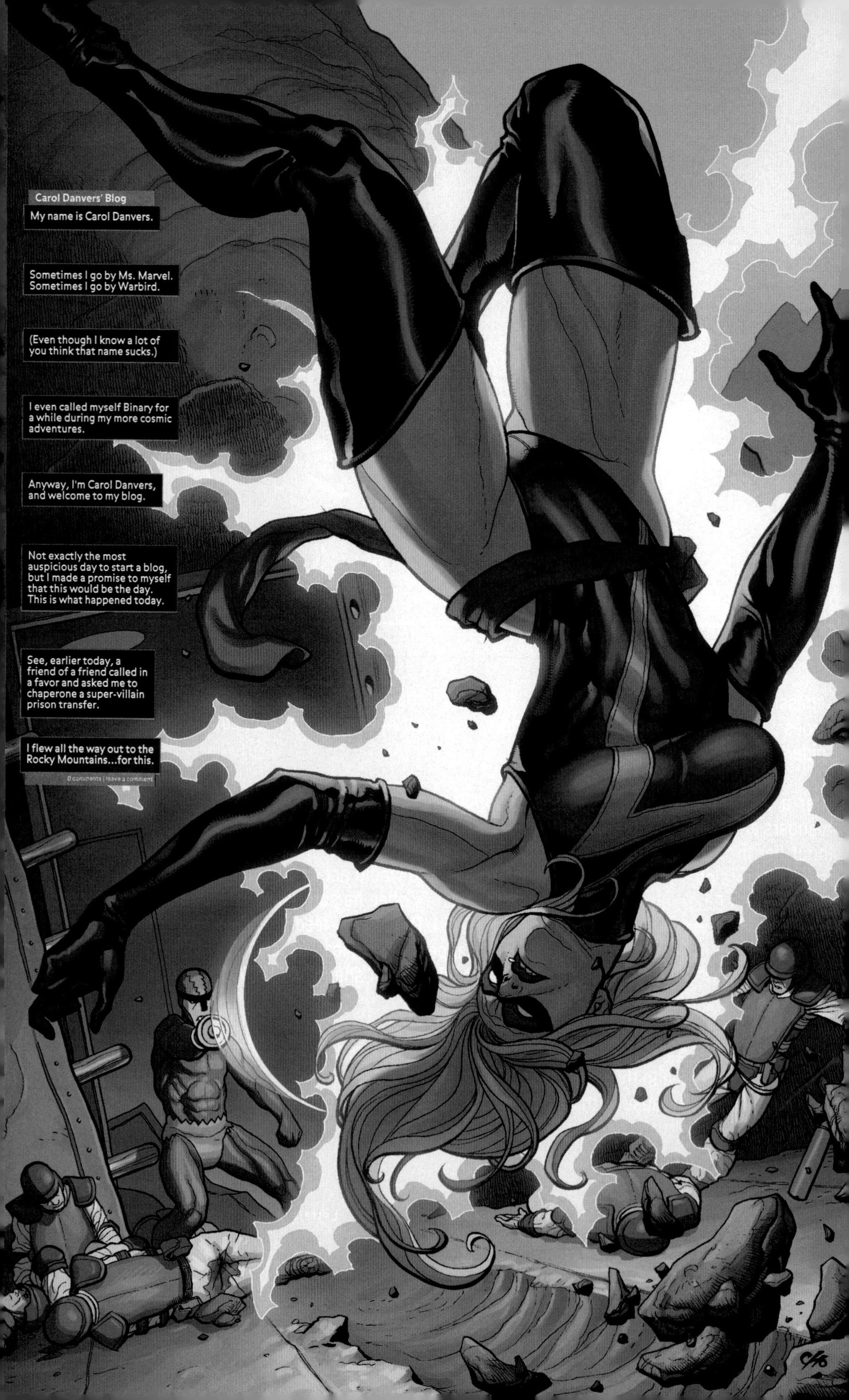
Carol Danvers' Blog
My name is Carol Danvers.
Sometimes I go by Ms. Marvel. Sometimes I go by Warbird.
(Even though I know a lot of you think that name sucks.)
I even called myself Binary for a while during my more cosmic adventures.
Anyway, I'm Carol Danvers, and welcome to my blog.
Not exactly the most auspicious day to start a blog, but I made a promise to myself that this would be the day. This is what happened today.
See, earlier today, a friend of a friend called in a favor and asked me to chaperone a super-villain prison transfer.
I flew all the way out to the Rocky Mountains...for this.
0 comments | leave a comment

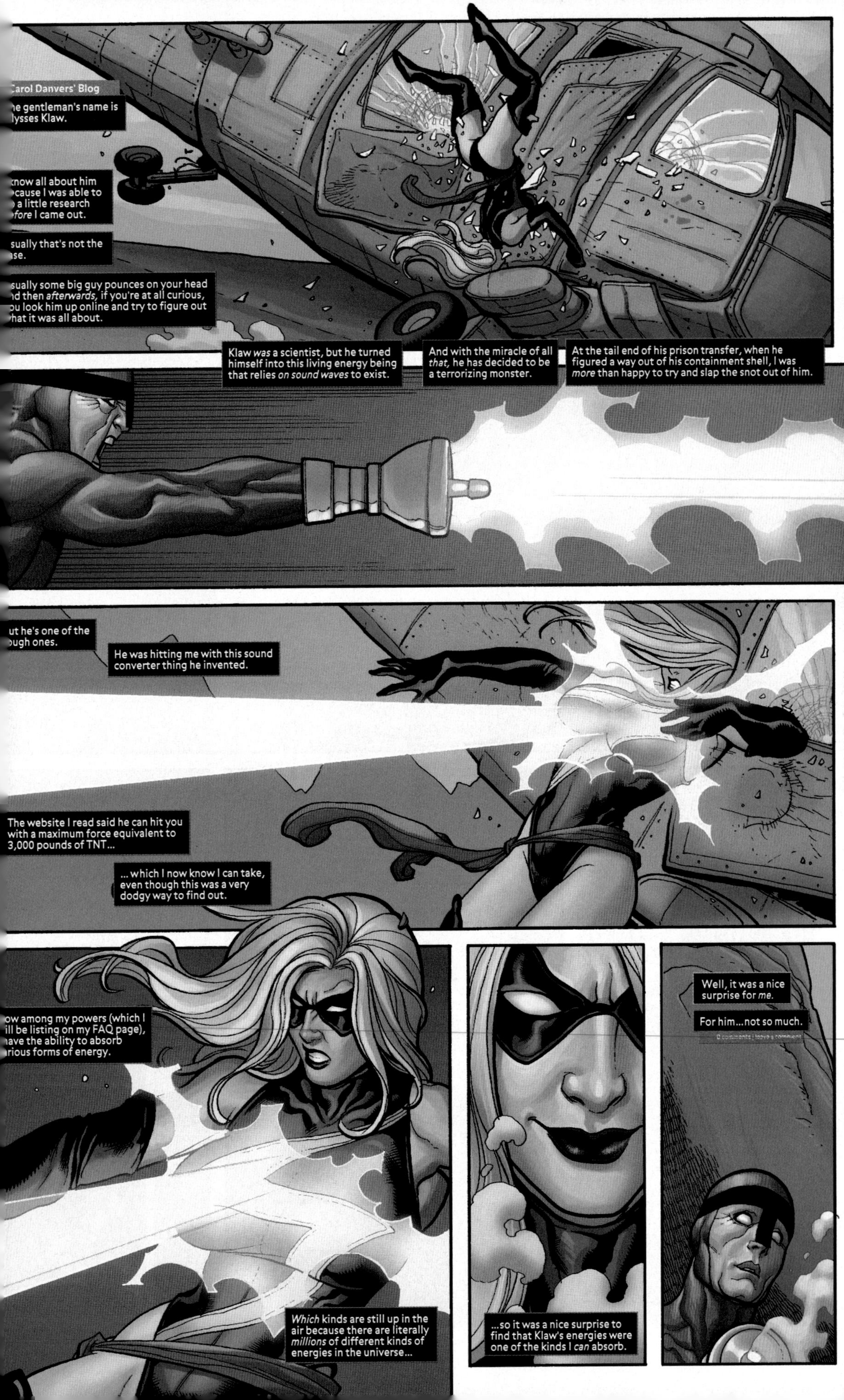

Carol Danvers' Blog
he gentleman's name is
lysses Klaw.
know all about him
cause I was able to
a little research
fore I came out.
sually that's not the
ase.
sually some big guy pounces on your head
d then *afterwards,* if you're at all curious,
ou look him up online and try to figure out
hat it was all about.
Klaw *was* a scientist, but he turned himself into this living energy being that relies *on sound waves* to exist.
And with the miracle of all *that,* he has decided to be a terrorizing monster.
At the tail end of his prison transfer, when he figured a way out of his containment shell, I was *more* than happy to try and slap the snot out of him.
ut he's one of the
ough ones.
He was hitting me with this sound converter thing he invented.
The website I read said he can hit you with a maximum force equivalent to 3,000 pounds of TNT...
...which I now know I can take, even though this was a very dodgy way to find out.
ow among my powers (which I
ill be listing on my FAQ page),
ave the ability to absorb
rious forms of energy.
Which kinds are still up in the air because there are literally *millions* of different kinds of energies in the universe...
...so it was a nice surprise to find that Klaw's energies were one of the kinds I *can* absorb.
Well, it was a nice surprise for *me.*
For him...not so much.
0 comments | leave a comment

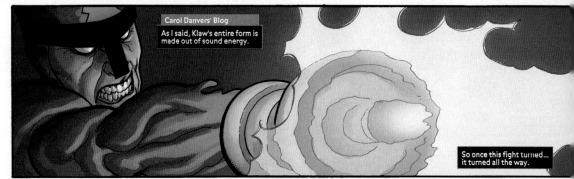

As I said, Klaw's entire form is made out of sound energy.

So once this fight turned... it turned all the way.

Without control of his sound energies, he was losing control of his entire self.

And without control of his body it sucked itself right into his own energy transfer invention.

It was a loud ending.

But it was an ending.

0 comments | leave a comment

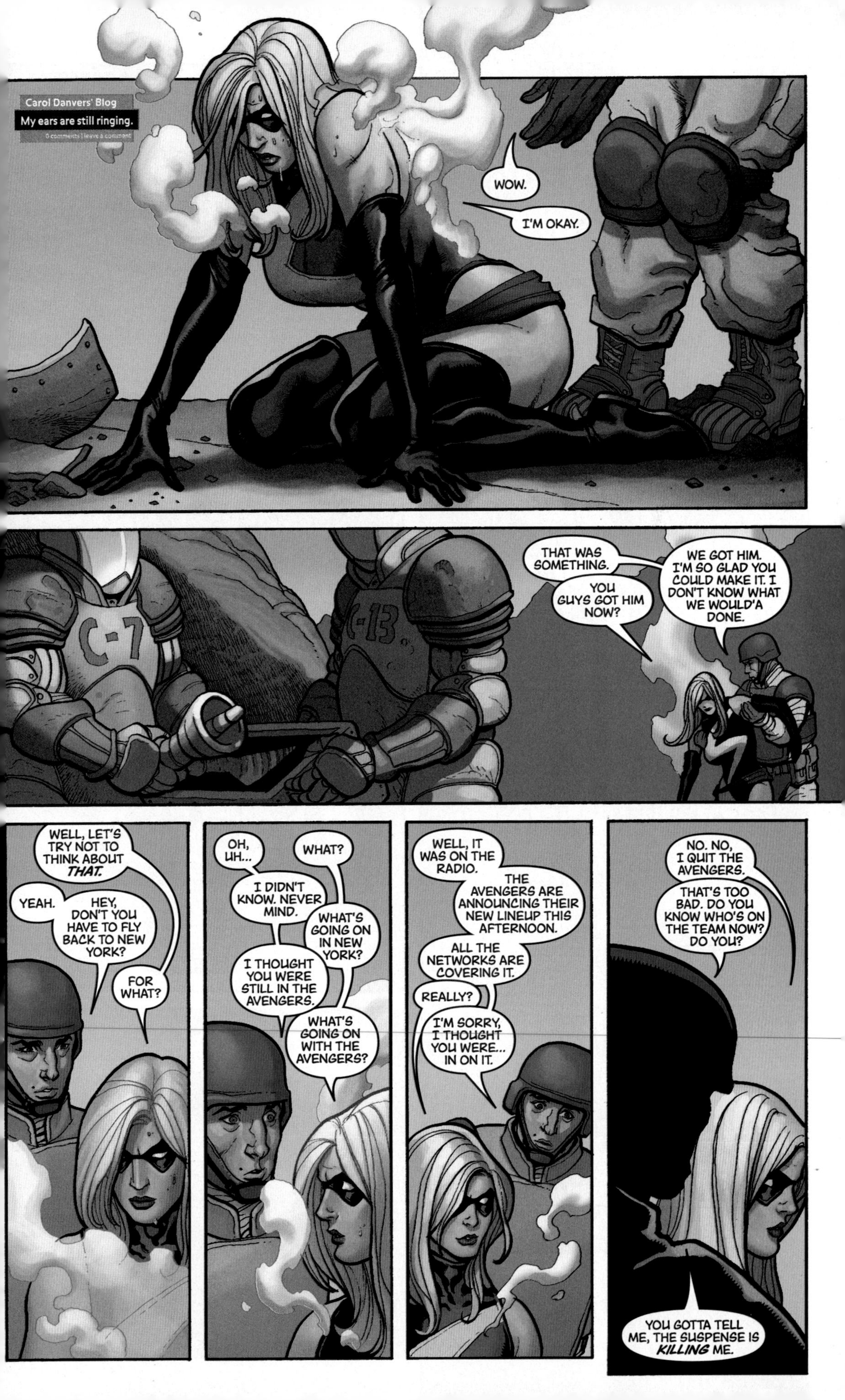
Carol Danvers' Blog
My ears are still ringing.
0 comments | leave a comment
WOW.
I'M OKAY.
THAT WAS SOMETHING.
YOU GUYS GOT HIM NOW?
WE GOT HIM. I'M SO GLAD YOU COULD MAKE IT. I DON'T KNOW WHAT WE WOULD'A DONE.
WELL, LET'S TRY NOT TO THINK ABOUT *THAT.*
YEAH.
HEY, DON'T YOU HAVE TO FLY BACK TO NEW YORK?
FOR WHAT?
OH, UH...
WHAT?
I DIDN'T KNOW. NEVER MIND.
WHAT'S GOING ON IN NEW YORK?
I THOUGHT YOU WERE STILL IN THE AVENGERS.
WHAT'S GOING ON WITH THE AVENGERS?
WELL, IT WAS ON THE RADIO.
THE AVENGERS ARE ANNOUNCING THEIR NEW LINEUP THIS AFTERNOON.
ALL THE NETWORKS ARE COVERING IT.
REALLY?
I'M SORRY, I THOUGHT YOU WERE... IN ON IT.
NO. NO, I QUIT THE AVENGERS.
THAT'S TOO BAD. DO YOU KNOW WHO'S ON THE TEAM NOW? DO YOU?
YOU GOTTA TELL ME, THE SUSPENSE IS *KILLING* ME.

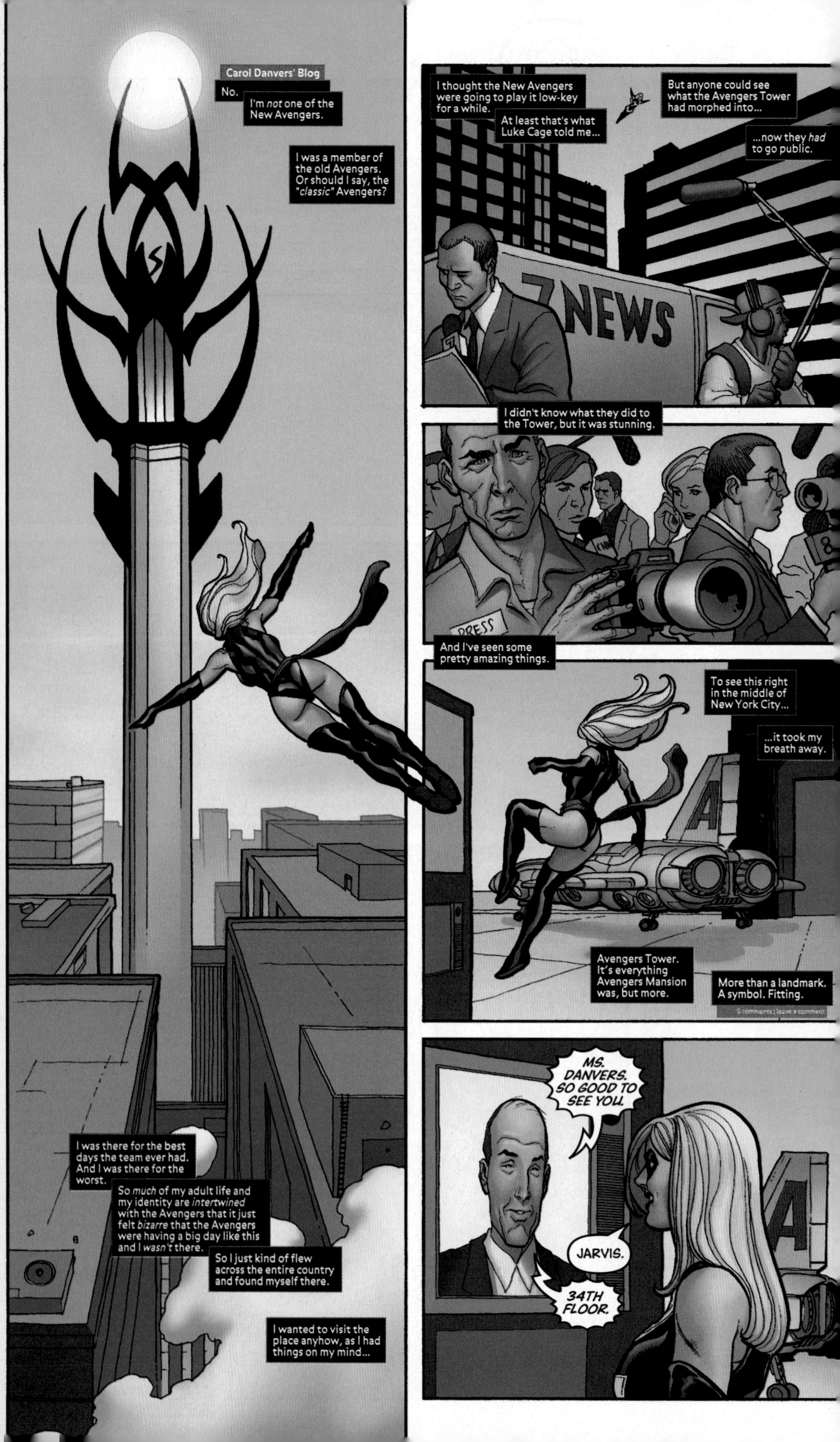
Carol Danvers' Blog
No.
I'm *not* one of the New Avengers.
I was a member of the old Avengers. Or should I say, the "*classic*" Avengers?
I was there for the best days the team ever had. And I was there for the worst.
So *much* of my adult life and my identity are *intertwined* with the Avengers that it just felt *bizarre* that the Avengers were having a big day like this and I *wasn't* there.
So I just kind of flew across the entire country and found myself there.
I wanted to visit the place anyhow, as I had things on my mind...
I thought the New Avengers were going to play it low-key for a while.
At least that's what Luke Cage told me...
But anyone could see what the Avengers Tower had morphed into...
...now they *had* to go public.
7 NEWS
I didn't know what they did to the Tower, but it was stunning.
PRESS
And I've seen some pretty amazing things.
To see this right in the middle of New York City...
...it took my breath away.
Avengers Tower. It's everything Avengers Mansion was, but more.
More than a landmark. A symbol. Fitting.
0 comments | leave a comment
MS. DANVERS. SO GOOD TO SEE YOU.
JARVIS.
34TH FLOOR.

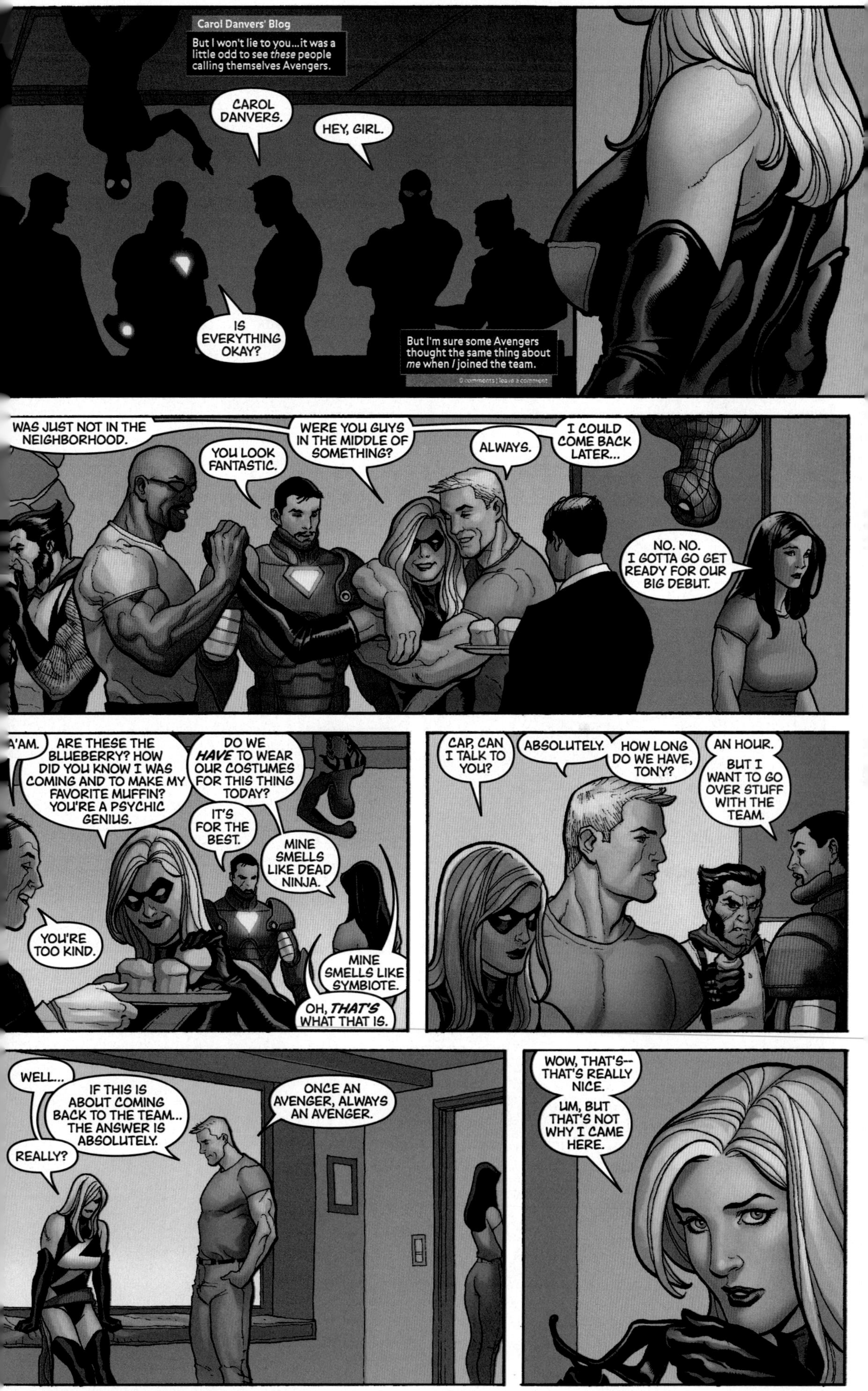

Carol Danvers' Blog
But I won't lie to you...it was a little odd to see *these* people calling themselves Avengers.
CAROL DANVERS.
HEY, GIRL.
IS EVERYTHING OKAY?
But I'm sure some Avengers thought the same thing about *me* when *I* joined the team.
0 comments | leave a comment
WAS JUST NOT IN THE NEIGHBORHOOD.
YOU LOOK FANTASTIC.
WERE YOU GUYS IN THE MIDDLE OF SOMETHING?
ALWAYS.
I COULD COME BACK LATER...
NO. NO. I GOTTA GO GET READY FOR OUR BIG DEBUT.
'AM.
ARE THESE THE BLUEBERRY? HOW DID YOU KNOW I WAS COMING AND TO MAKE MY FAVORITE MUFFIN? YOU'RE A PSYCHIC GENIUS.
YOU'RE TOO KIND.
DO WE *HAVE* TO WEAR OUR COSTUMES FOR THIS THING TODAY?
IT'S FOR THE BEST.
MINE SMELLS LIKE DEAD NINJA.
MINE SMELLS LIKE SYMBIOTE.
OH, *THAT'S* WHAT THAT IS.
CAP, CAN I TALK TO YOU?
ABSOLUTELY.
HOW LONG DO WE HAVE, TONY?
AN HOUR.
BUT I WANT TO GO OVER STUFF WITH THE TEAM.
WELL...
IF THIS IS ABOUT COMING BACK TO THE TEAM... THE ANSWER IS ABSOLUTELY.
REALLY?
ONCE AN AVENGER, ALWAYS AN AVENGER.
WOW, THAT'S-- THAT'S REALLY NICE.
UM, BUT THAT'S NOT WHY I CAME HERE.

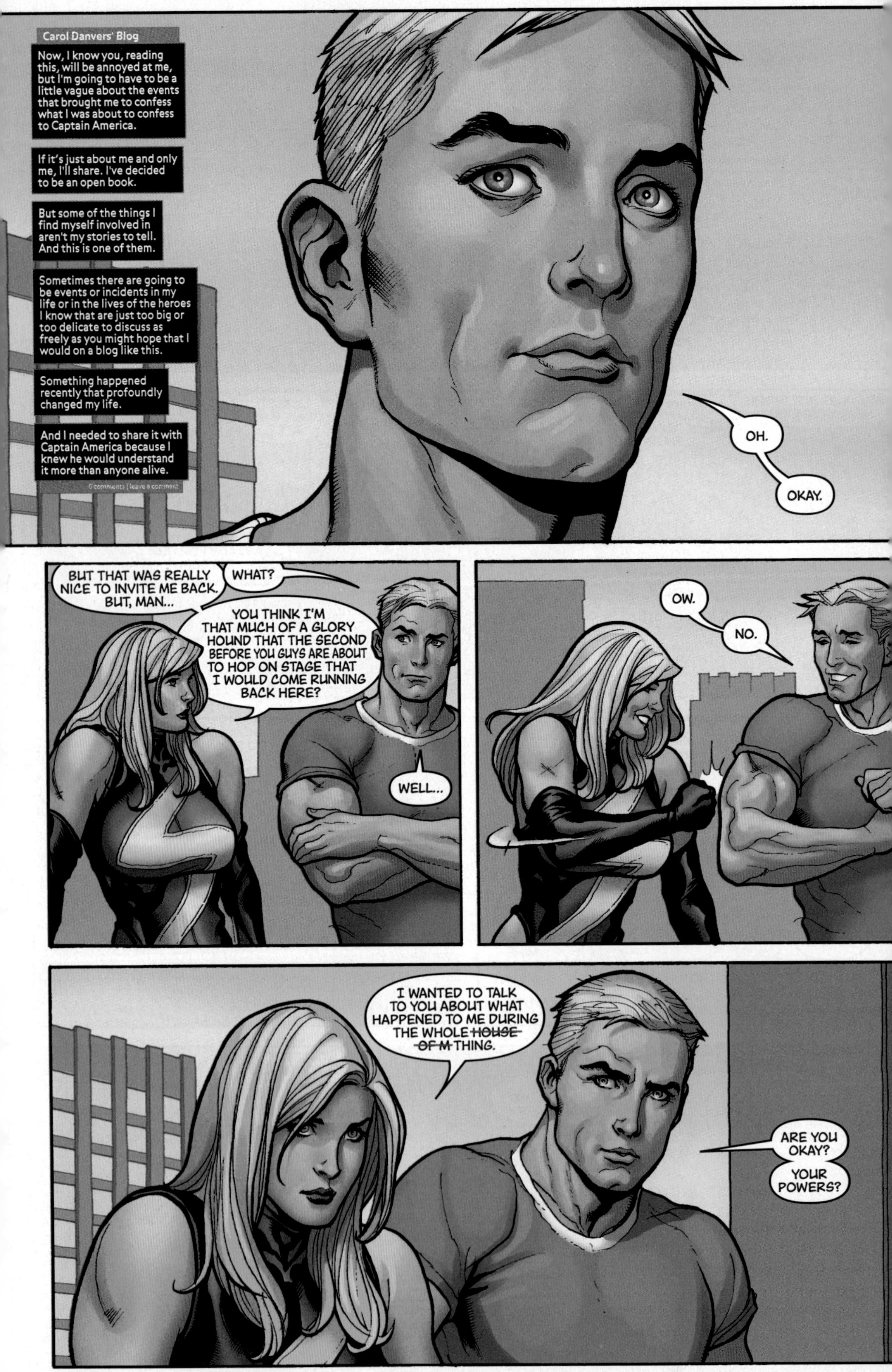
Carol Danvers' Blog
Now, I know you, reading this, will be annoyed at me, but I'm going to have to be a little vague about the events that brought me to confess what I was about to confess to Captain America.
If it's just about me and only me, I'll share. I've decided to be an open book.
But some of the things I find myself involved in aren't my stories to tell. And this is one of them.
Sometimes there are going to be events or incidents in my life or in the lives of the heroes I know that are just too big or too delicate to discuss as freely as you might hope that I would on a blog like this.
Something happened recently that profoundly changed my life.
And I needed to share it with Captain America because I knew he would understand it more than anyone alive.
0 comments | leave a comment
OH.
OKAY.
BUT THAT WAS REALLY NICE TO INVITE ME BACK. BUT, MAN...
WHAT?
YOU THINK I'M THAT MUCH OF A GLORY HOUND THAT THE SECOND BEFORE YOU GUYS ARE ABOUT TO HOP ON STAGE THAT I WOULD COME RUNNING BACK HERE?
WELL...
OW.
NO.
I WANTED TO TALK TO YOU ABOUT WHAT HAPPENED TO ME DURING THE WHOLE ~~HOUSE OF M~~ THING.
ARE YOU OKAY?
YOUR POWERS?

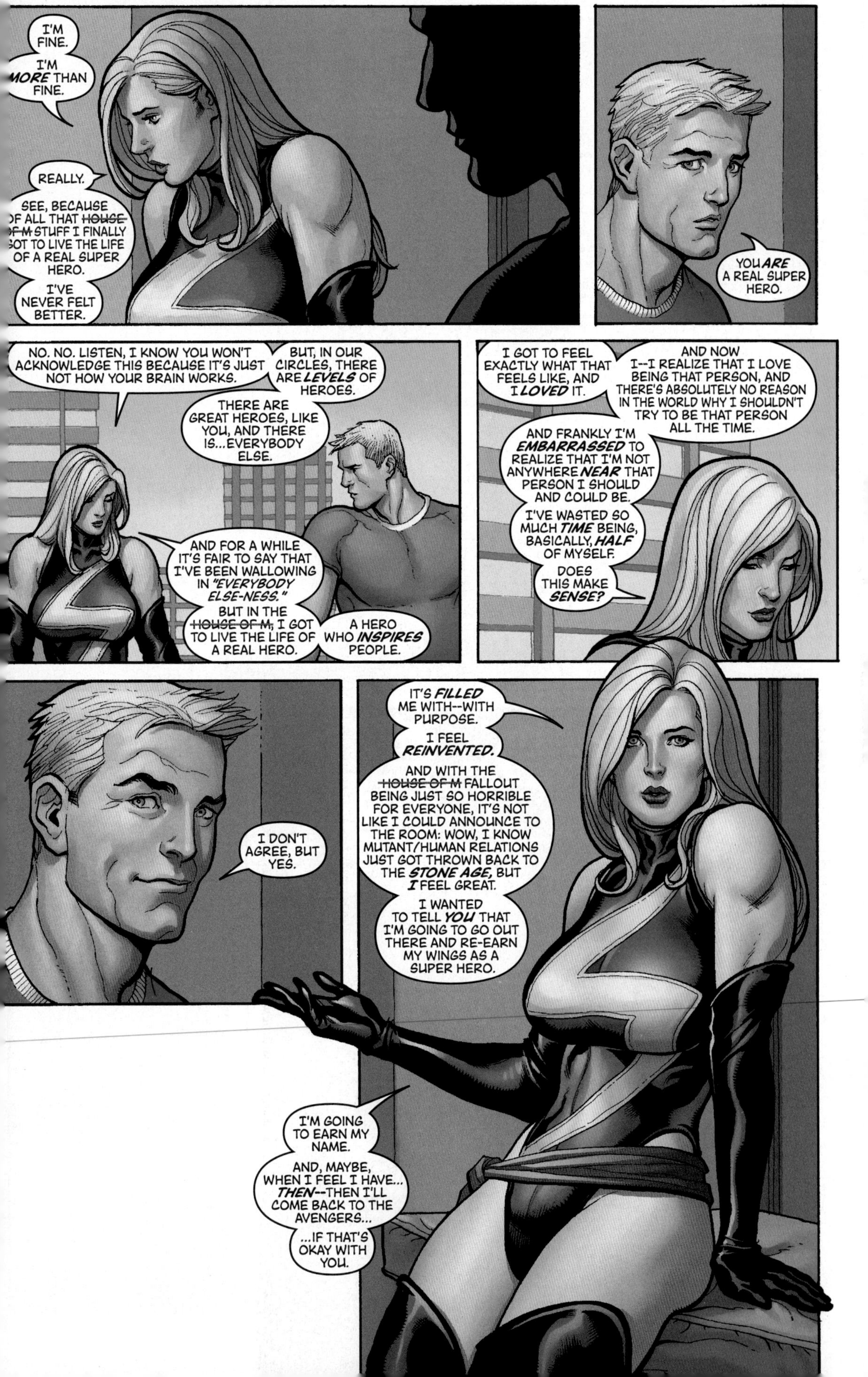

I'M FINE.
I'M MORE THAN FINE.
REALLY.
SEE, BECAUSE OF ALL THAT HOUSE OF M STUFF I FINALLY GOT TO LIVE THE LIFE OF A REAL SUPER HERO.
I'VE NEVER FELT BETTER.
YOU ARE A REAL SUPER HERO.
NO. NO. LISTEN, I KNOW YOU WON'T ACKNOWLEDGE THIS BECAUSE IT'S JUST NOT HOW YOUR BRAIN WORKS.
BUT, IN OUR CIRCLES, THERE ARE LEVELS OF HEROES.
THERE ARE GREAT HEROES, LIKE YOU, AND THERE IS...EVERYBODY ELSE.
AND FOR A WHILE IT'S FAIR TO SAY THAT I'VE BEEN WALLOWING IN "EVERYBODY ELSE-NESS."
BUT IN THE HOUSE OF M, I GOT TO LIVE THE LIFE OF A REAL HERO.
A HERO WHO INSPIRES PEOPLE.
I GOT TO FEEL EXACTLY WHAT THAT FEELS LIKE, AND I LOVED IT.
AND NOW I--I REALIZE THAT I LOVE BEING THAT PERSON, AND THERE'S ABSOLUTELY NO REASON IN THE WORLD WHY I SHOULDN'T TRY TO BE THAT PERSON ALL THE TIME.
AND FRANKLY I'M EMBARRASSED TO REALIZE THAT I'M NOT ANYWHERE NEAR THAT PERSON I SHOULD AND COULD BE.
I'VE WASTED SO MUCH TIME BEING, BASICALLY, HALF OF MYSELF.
DOES THIS MAKE SENSE?
I DON'T AGREE, BUT YES.
IT'S FILLED ME WITH--WITH PURPOSE.
I FEEL REINVENTED.
AND WITH THE HOUSE OF M FALLOUT BEING JUST SO HORRIBLE FOR EVERYONE, IT'S NOT LIKE I COULD ANNOUNCE TO THE ROOM: WOW, I KNOW MUTANT/HUMAN RELATIONS JUST GOT THROWN BACK TO THE STONE AGE, BUT I FEEL GREAT.
I WANTED TO TELL YOU THAT I'M GOING TO GO OUT THERE AND RE-EARN MY WINGS AS A SUPER HERO.
I'M GOING TO EARN MY NAME.
AND, MAYBE, WHEN I FEEL I HAVE... THEN--THEN I'LL COME BACK TO THE AVENGERS...
...IF THAT'S OKAY WITH YOU.

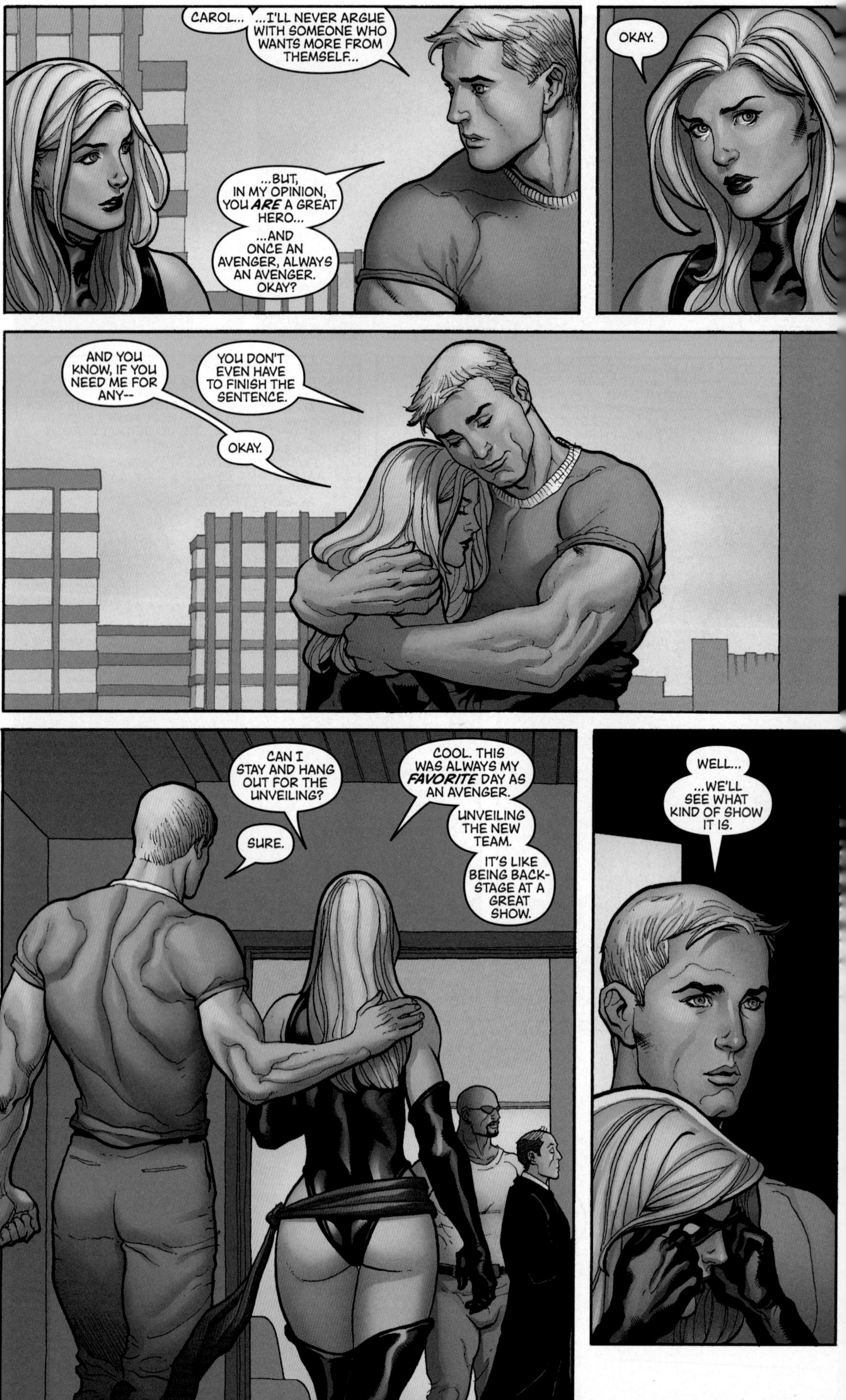

CAROL...
...I'LL NEVER ARGUE WITH SOMEONE WHO WANTS MORE FROM THEMSELF...
...BUT, IN MY OPINION, YOU ARE A GREAT HERO...
...AND ONCE AN AVENGER, ALWAYS AN AVENGER. OKAY?
OKAY.
AND YOU KNOW, IF YOU NEED ME FOR ANY--
YOU DON'T EVEN HAVE TO FINISH THE SENTENCE.
OKAY.
CAN I STAY AND HANG OUT FOR THE UNVEILING?
SURE.
COOL. THIS WAS ALWAYS MY FAVORITE DAY AS AN AVENGER.
UNVEILING THE NEW TEAM.
IT'S LIKE BEING BACK-STAGE AT A GREAT SHOW.
WELL...
...WE'LL SEE WHAT KIND OF SHOW IT IS.

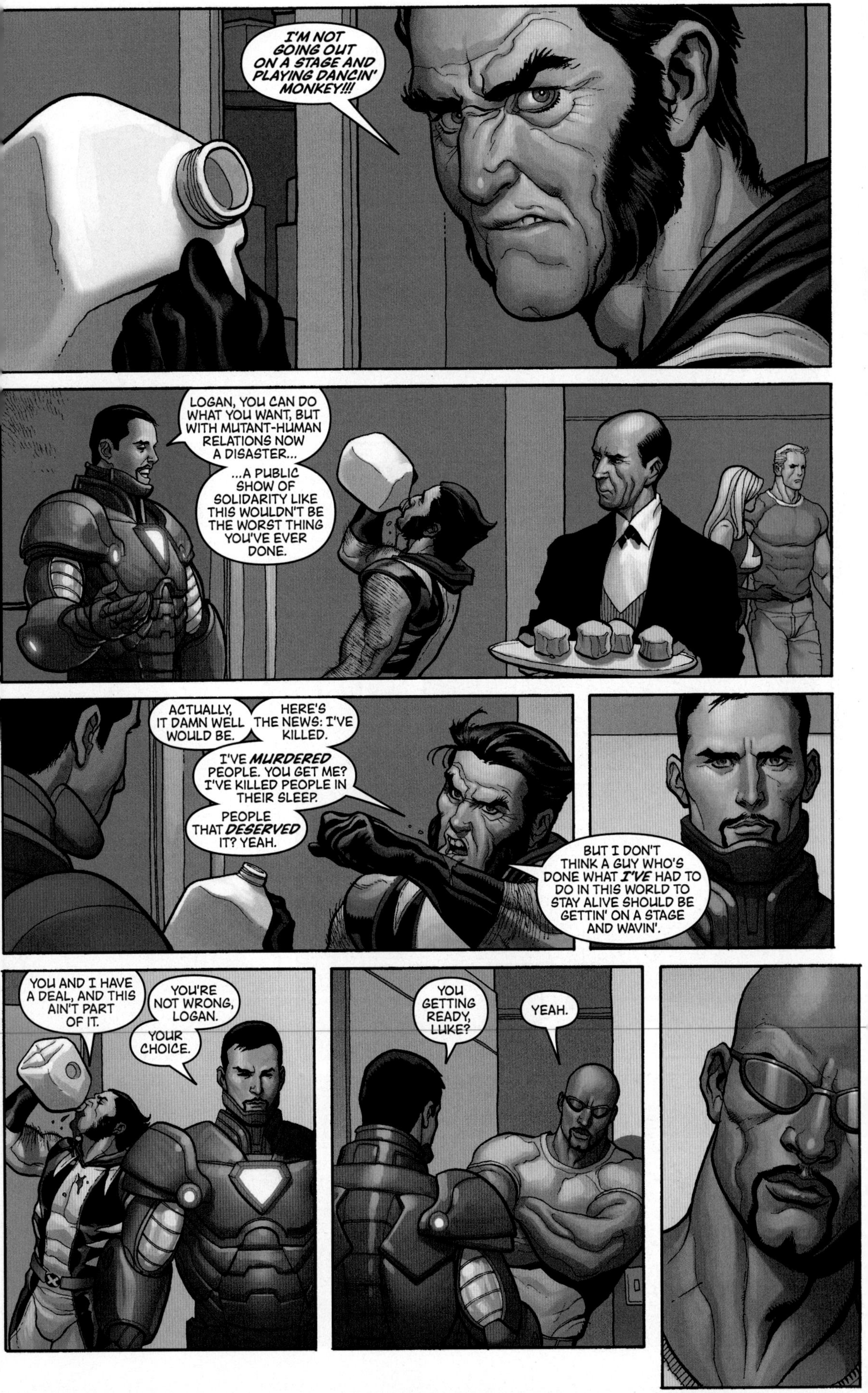

I'M NOT GOING OUT ON A STAGE AND PLAYING DANCIN' MONKEY!!!
LOGAN, YOU CAN DO WHAT YOU WANT, BUT WITH MUTANT-HUMAN RELATIONS NOW A DISASTER...
...A PUBLIC SHOW OF SOLIDARITY LIKE THIS WOULDN'T BE THE WORST THING YOU'VE EVER DONE.
ACTUALLY, IT DAMN WELL WOULD BE.
HERE'S THE NEWS: I'VE KILLED.
I'VE *MURDERED* PEOPLE. YOU GET ME? I'VE KILLED PEOPLE IN THEIR SLEEP.
PEOPLE THAT *DESERVED* IT? YEAH.
BUT I DON'T THINK A GUY WHO'S DONE WHAT *I'VE* HAD TO DO IN THIS WORLD TO STAY ALIVE SHOULD BE GETTIN' ON A STAGE AND WAVIN'.
YOU AND I HAVE A DEAL, AND THIS AIN'T PART OF IT.
YOU'RE NOT WRONG, LOGAN.
YOUR CHOICE.
YOU GETTING READY, LUKE?
YEAH.

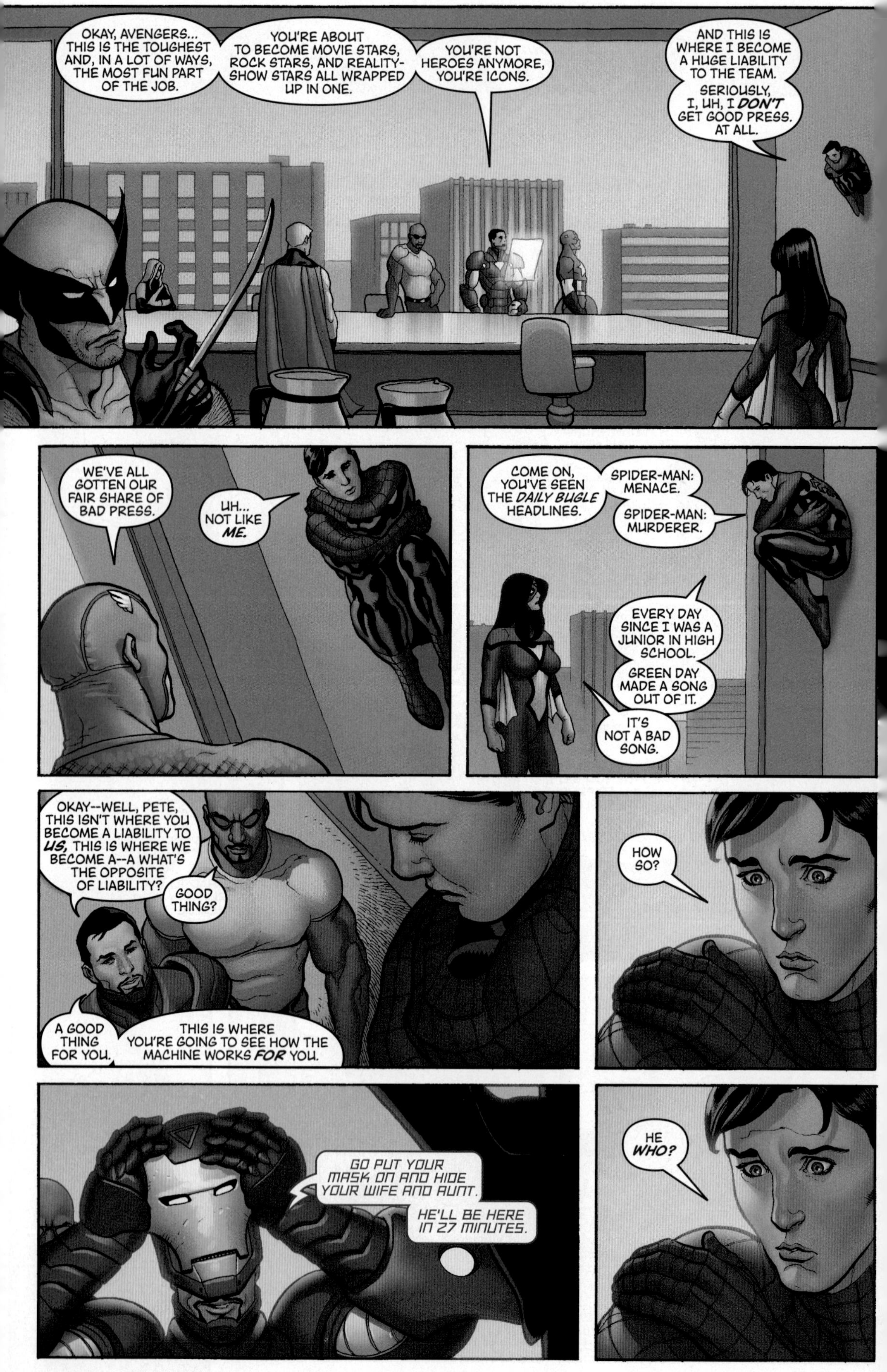

OKAY, AVENGERS... THIS IS THE TOUGHEST AND, IN A LOT OF WAYS, THE MOST FUN PART OF THE JOB.
YOU'RE ABOUT TO BECOME MOVIE STARS, ROCK STARS, AND REALITY-SHOW STARS ALL WRAPPED UP IN ONE.
YOU'RE NOT HEROES ANYMORE, YOU'RE ICONS.
AND THIS IS WHERE I BECOME A HUGE LIABILITY TO THE TEAM.
SERIOUSLY, I, UH, I DON'T GET GOOD PRESS. AT ALL.
WE'VE ALL GOTTEN OUR FAIR SHARE OF BAD PRESS.
UH... NOT LIKE ME.
COME ON, YOU'VE SEEN THE DAILY BUGLE HEADLINES.
SPIDER-MAN: MENACE.
SPIDER-MAN: MURDERER.
EVERY DAY SINCE I WAS A JUNIOR IN HIGH SCHOOL.
GREEN DAY MADE A SONG OUT OF IT.
IT'S NOT A BAD SONG.
OKAY--WELL, PETE, THIS ISN'T WHERE YOU BECOME A LIABILITY TO US, THIS IS WHERE WE BECOME A--A WHAT'S THE OPPOSITE OF LIABILITY?
GOOD THING?
A GOOD THING FOR YOU.
THIS IS WHERE YOU'RE GOING TO SEE HOW THE MACHINE WORKS FOR YOU.
HOW SO?
GO PUT YOUR MASK ON AND HIDE YOUR WIFE AND AUNT.
HE'LL BE HERE IN 27 MINUTES.
HE WHO?

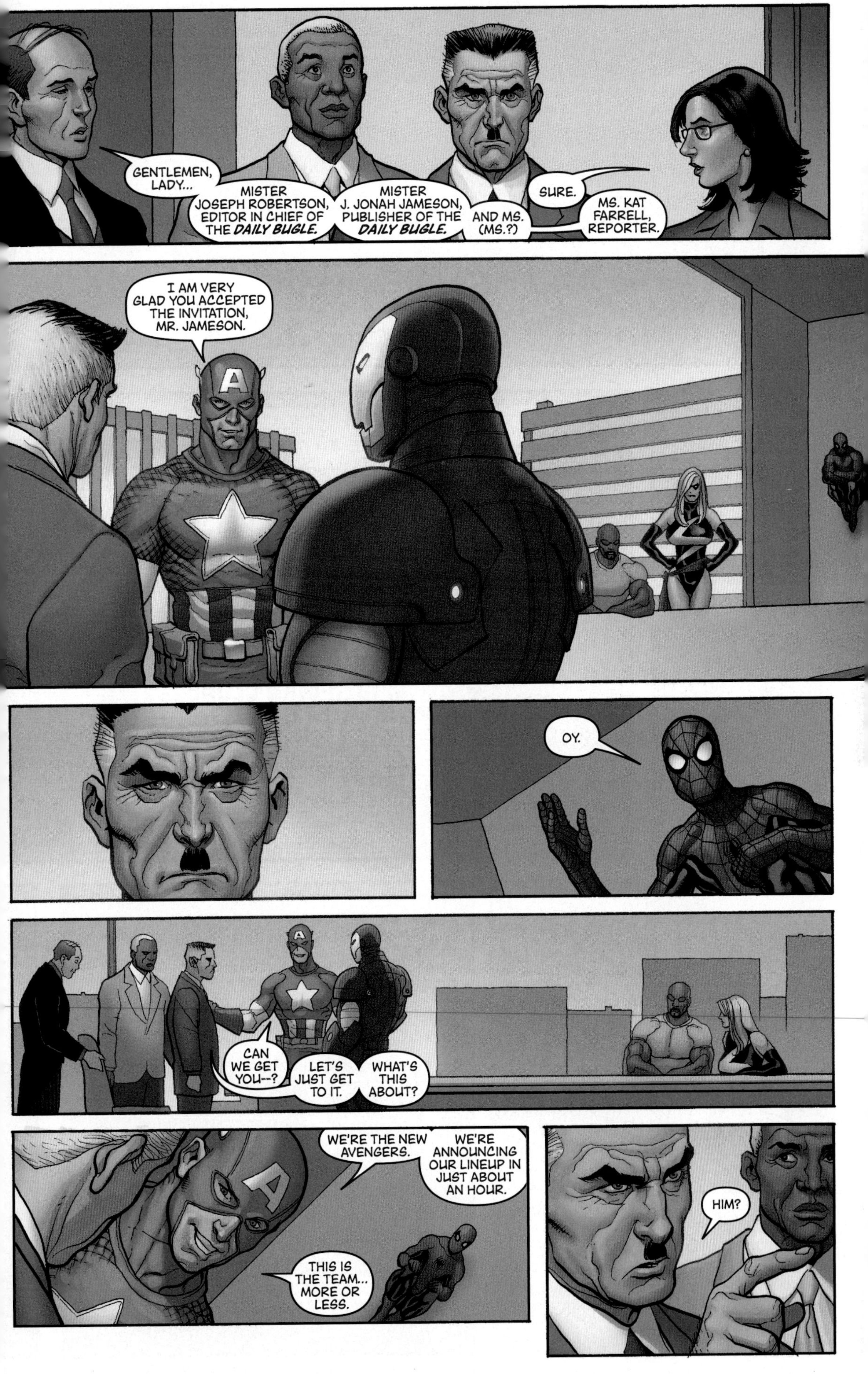
GENTLEMEN, LADY...
MISTER JOSEPH ROBERTSON, EDITOR IN CHIEF OF THE *DAILY BUGLE.*
MISTER J. JONAH JAMESON, PUBLISHER OF THE *DAILY BUGLE.*
AND MS. (MS.?)
SURE.
MS. KAT FARRELL, REPORTER.
I AM VERY GLAD YOU ACCEPTED THE INVITATION, MR. JAMESON.
OY.
CAN WE GET YOU--?
LET'S JUST GET TO IT.
WHAT'S THIS ABOUT?
WE'RE THE NEW AVENGERS.
WE'RE ANNOUNCING OUR LINEUP IN JUST ABOUT AN HOUR.
THIS IS THE TEAM... MORE OR LESS.
HIM?

YES. AND WE KNOW YOU AND HE HAVE A HISTORY.

I KNOW YOU HAVE YOUR OPINIONS ABOUT HIM, BUT I WANTED TO TELL YOU, FROM *ME*, THAT THE MAN IN THAT UNIFORM IS A TRUE AMERICAN HERO.

THIS IS A FACT. I'VE SEEN HIM IN ACTION WITH MY OWN EYES.

HE'S BEEN THROUGH MORE THAN ALL OF US PUT TOGETHER, AND STILL HE PERSEVERES.

I REPORT THE *NEWS*.

AND YOU EDITORIALIZE.

AND THAT'S YOUR RIGHT.

IT'S YOUR PAPER AND IT'S YOUR POINT OF VIEW.

AND YOU HAVE TO FILL THOSE PAGES.

DAILY BUGLE — NEW YORK'S FINEST DAILY NEWSPAPER
SPIDER-MAN: MURDERER

DAILY BUGLE — NEW YORK'S FINEST DAILY NEWSPAPER
SPIDER-MAN: MENACE

DAILY BUGLE — NEW YORK'S FINEST DAILY NEWSPAPER
SPIDER-MAN CLONE IS A MENACE

DAILY BUGLE — NEW YORK'S FINEST DAILY NEWSPAPER
WEBBED WOND[E]
TERRORIZES CI[TY]

EXCLUSIVE COVERAGE.

EXCLUSIVE ACCESS.

IF I LAY OFF HIM....

SAY YES OR I QUIT.

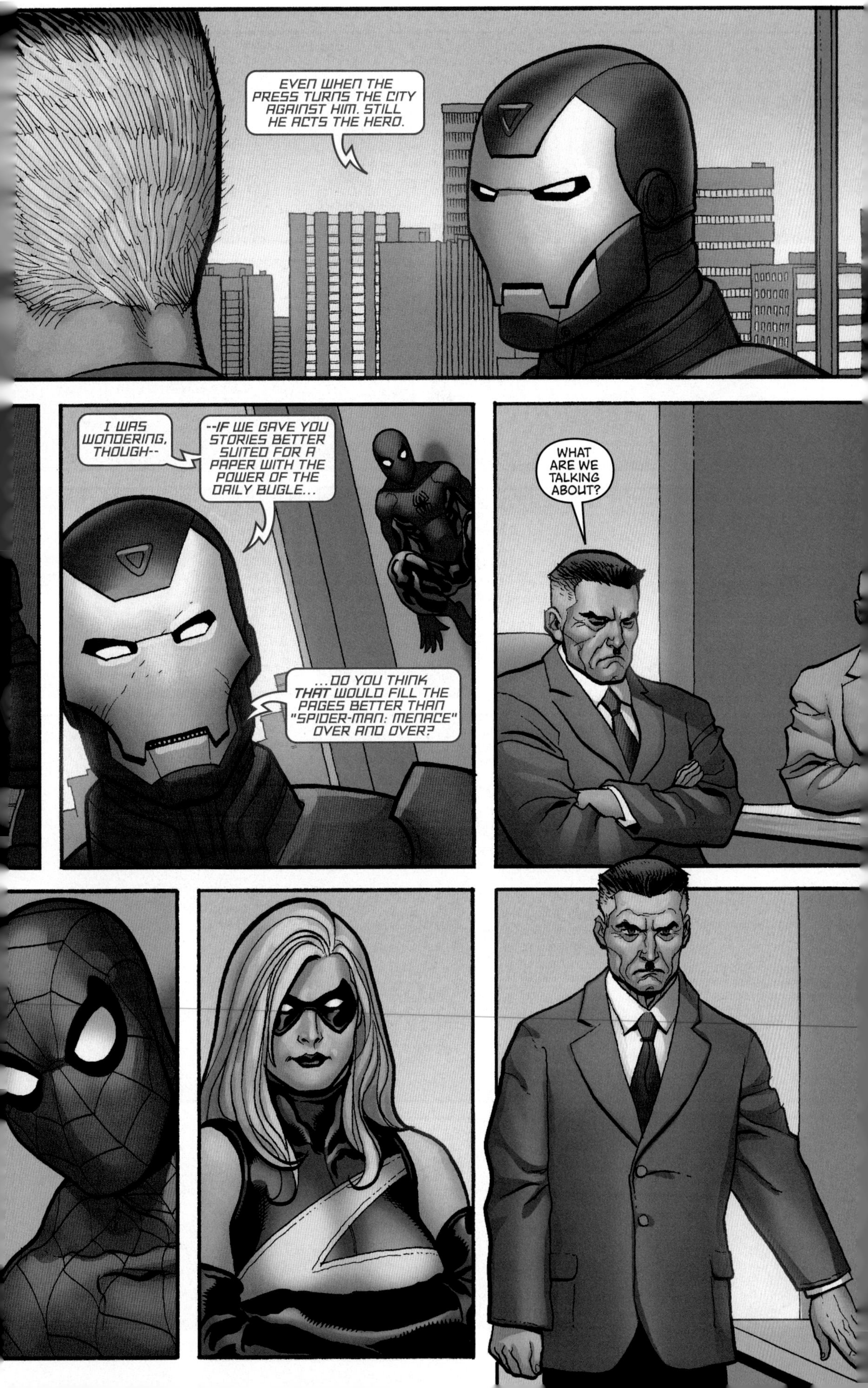
EVEN WHEN THE PRESS TURNS THE CITY AGAINST HIM. STILL HE ACTS THE HERO.
I WAS WONDERING, THOUGH--
--IF WE GAVE YOU STORIES BETTER SUITED FOR A PAPER WITH THE POWER OF THE DAILY BUGLE...
...DO YOU THINK THAT WOULD FILL THE PAGES BETTER THAN "SPIDER-MAN: MENACE" OVER AND OVER?
WHAT ARE WE TALKING ABOUT?

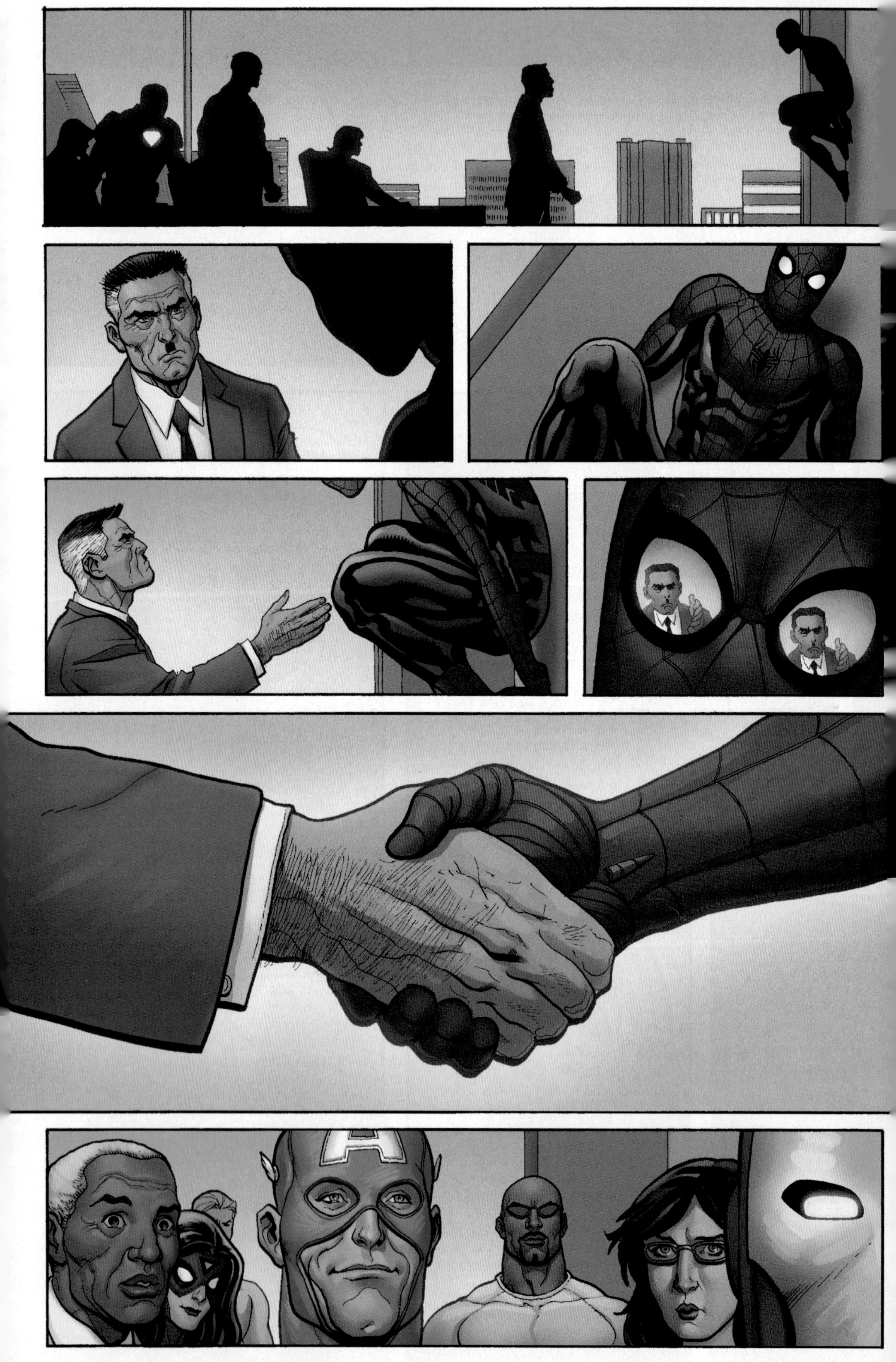

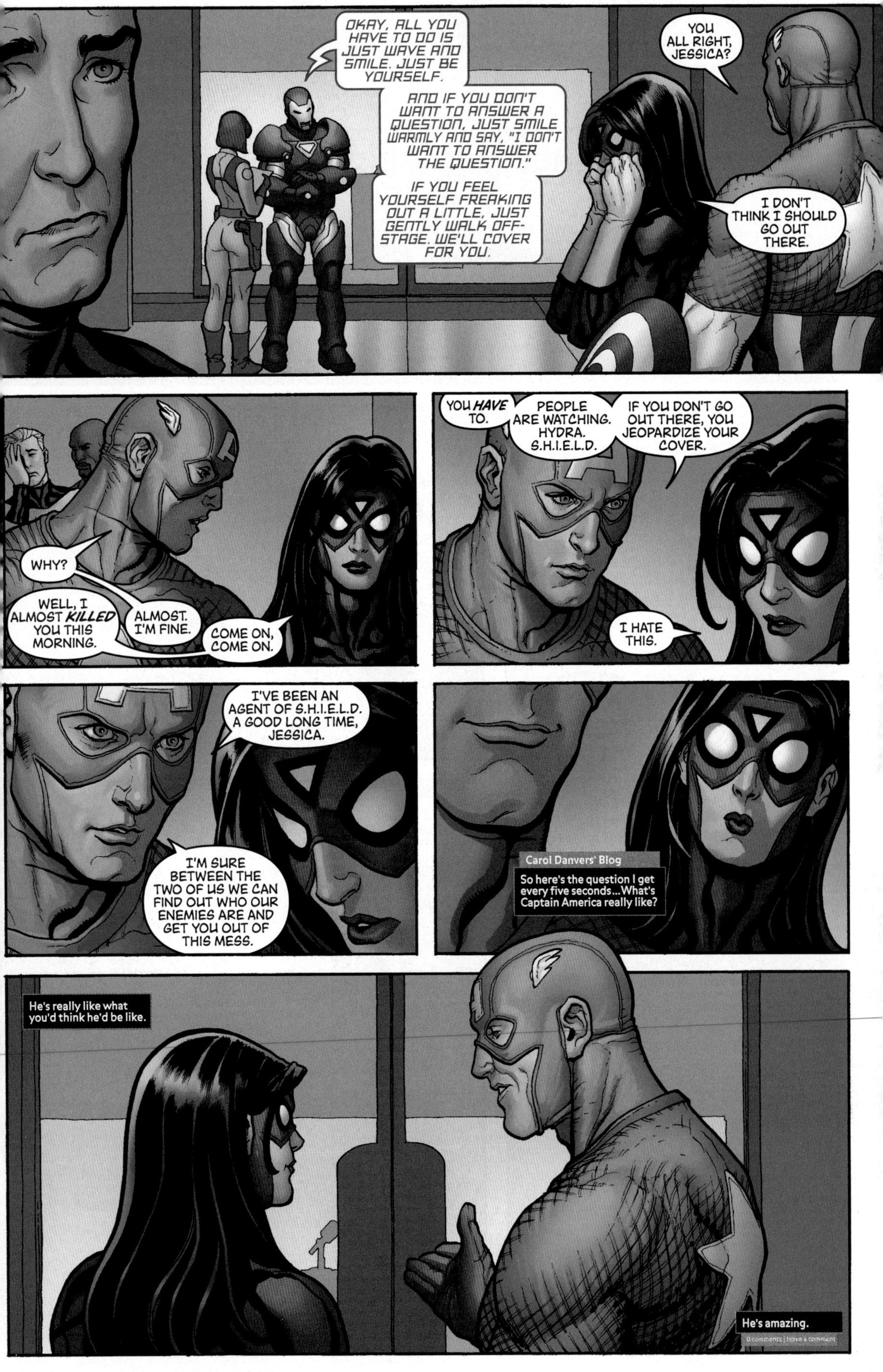
OKAY, ALL YOU HAVE TO DO IS JUST WAVE AND SMILE. JUST BE YOURSELF.
AND IF YOU DON'T WANT TO ANSWER A QUESTION, JUST SMILE WARMLY AND SAY, "I DON'T WANT TO ANSWER THE QUESTION."
IF YOU FEEL YOURSELF FREAKING OUT A LITTLE, JUST GENTLY WALK OFF-STAGE. WE'LL COVER FOR YOU.
YOU ALL RIGHT, JESSICA?
I DON'T THINK I SHOULD GO OUT THERE.
WHY?
WELL, I ALMOST KILLED YOU THIS MORNING.
ALMOST. I'M FINE.
COME ON, COME ON.
YOU HAVE TO.
PEOPLE ARE WATCHING. HYDRA. S.H.I.E.L.D.
IF YOU DON'T GO OUT THERE, YOU JEOPARDIZE YOUR COVER.
I HATE THIS.
I'VE BEEN AN AGENT OF S.H.I.E.L.D. A GOOD LONG TIME, JESSICA.
I'M SURE BETWEEN THE TWO OF US WE CAN FIND OUT WHO OUR ENEMIES ARE AND GET YOU OUT OF THIS MESS.
Carol Danvers' Blog
So here's the question I get every five seconds...What's Captain America really like?
He's really like what you'd think he'd be like.
He's amazing.
0 comments | leave a comment

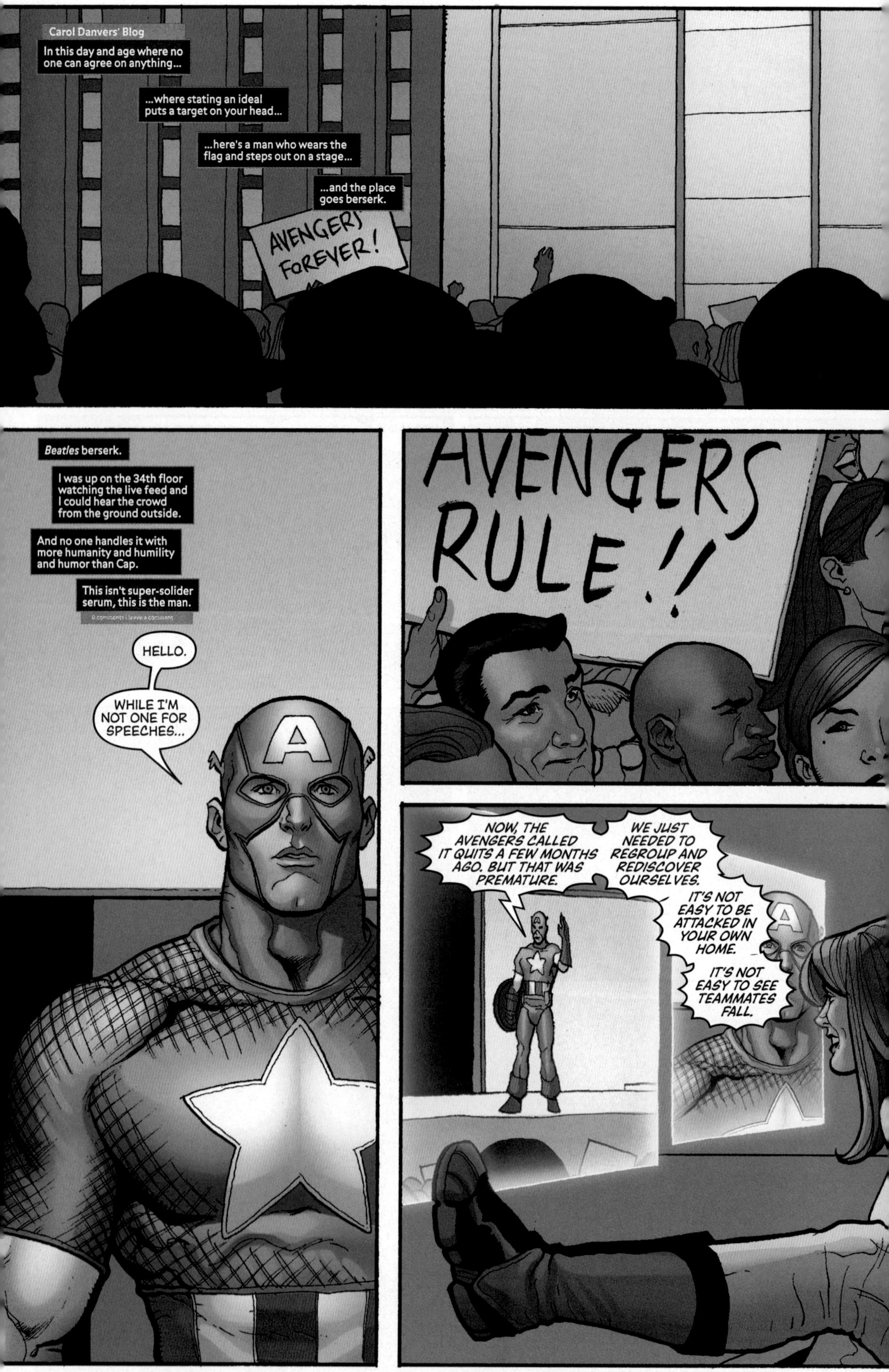
Carol Danvers' Blog
In this day and age where no one can agree on anything...
...where stating an ideal puts a target on your head...
...here's a man who wears the flag and steps out on a stage...
...and the place goes berserk.
AVENGERS FOREVER!
Beatles berserk.
I was up on the 34th floor watching the live feed and I could hear the crowd from the ground outside.
And no one handles it with more humanity and humility and humor than Cap.
This isn't super-solider serum, this is the man.
0 comments | leave a comment
HELLO.
WHILE I'M NOT ONE FOR SPEECHES...
AVENGERS RULE!!
NOW, THE AVENGERS CALLED IT QUITS A FEW MONTHS AGO. BUT THAT WAS PREMATURE.
WE JUST NEEDED TO REGROUP AND REDISCOVER OURSELVES.
IT'S NOT EASY TO BE ATTACKED IN YOUR OWN HOME.
IT'S NOT EASY TO SEE TEAMMATES FALL.

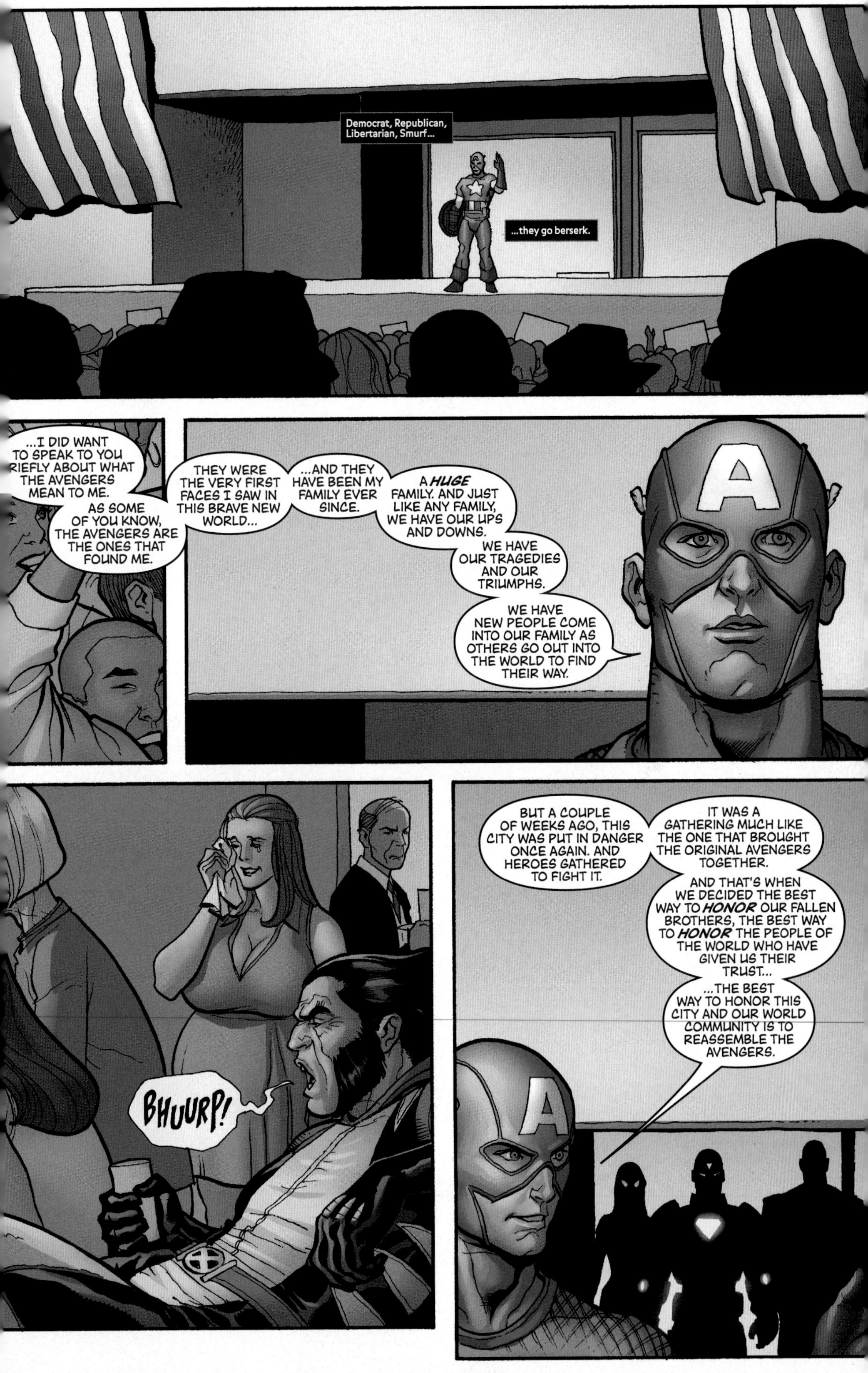
Democrat, Republican, Libertarian, Smurf...
...they go berserk.
...I DID WANT TO SPEAK TO YOU RIEFLY ABOUT WHAT THE AVENGERS MEAN TO ME.
AS SOME OF YOU KNOW, THE AVENGERS ARE THE ONES THAT FOUND ME.
THEY WERE THE VERY FIRST FACES I SAW IN THIS BRAVE NEW WORLD...
...AND THEY HAVE BEEN MY FAMILY EVER SINCE.
A *HUGE* FAMILY. AND JUST LIKE ANY FAMILY, WE HAVE OUR UPS AND DOWNS.
WE HAVE OUR TRAGEDIES AND OUR TRIUMPHS.
WE HAVE NEW PEOPLE COME INTO OUR FAMILY AS OTHERS GO OUT INTO THE WORLD TO FIND THEIR WAY.
BHUURP!
BUT A COUPLE OF WEEKS AGO, THIS CITY WAS PUT IN DANGER ONCE AGAIN. AND HEROES GATHERED TO FIGHT IT.
IT WAS A GATHERING MUCH LIKE THE ONE THAT BROUGHT THE ORIGINAL AVENGERS TOGETHER.
AND THAT'S WHEN WE DECIDED THE BEST WAY TO *HONOR* OUR FALLEN BROTHERS, THE BEST WAY TO *HONOR* THE PEOPLE OF THE WORLD WHO HAVE GIVEN US THEIR TRUST...
...THE BEST WAY TO HONOR THIS CITY AND OUR WORLD COMMUNITY IS TO REASSEMBLE THE AVENGERS.

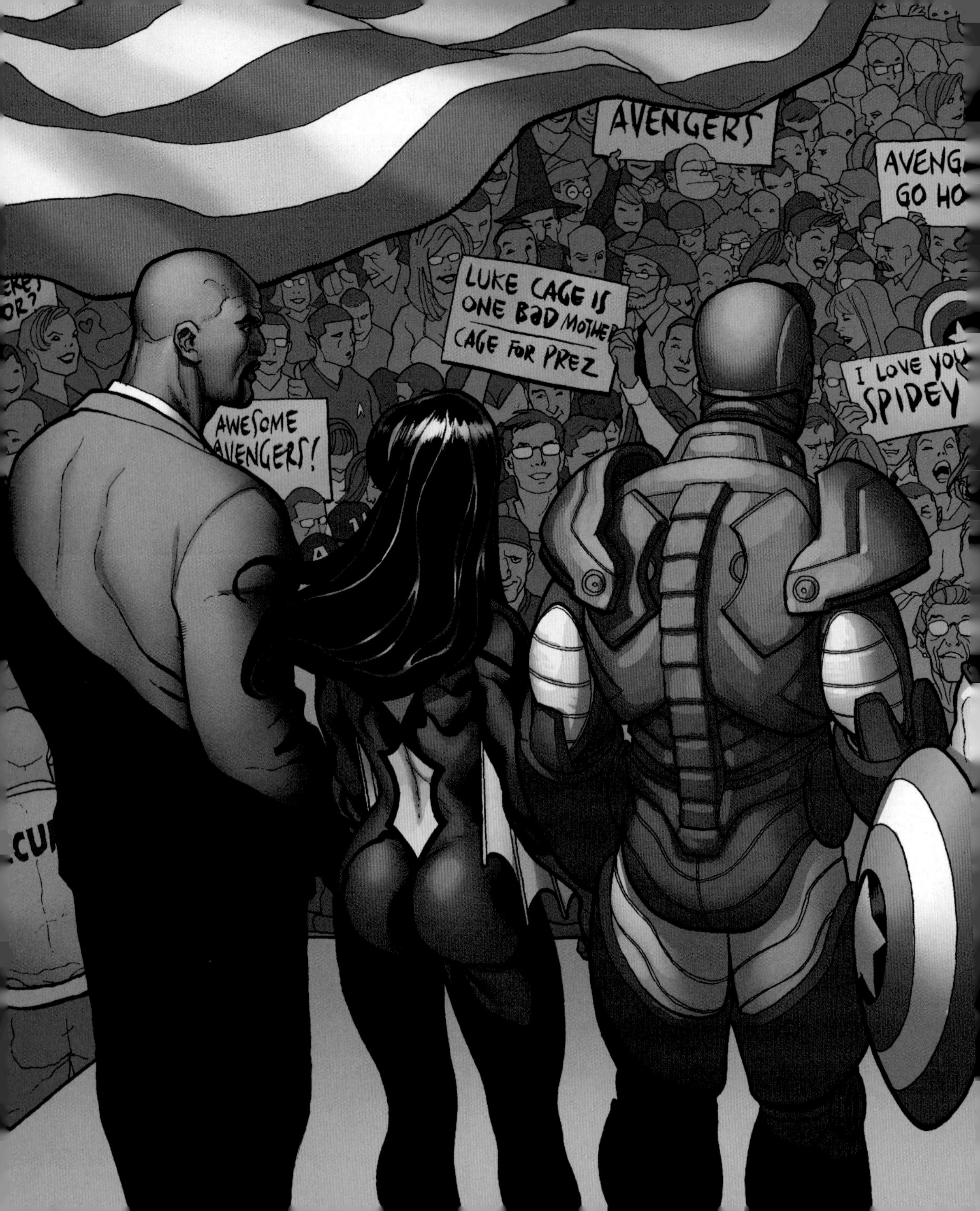
AVENGERS
LUKE CAGE IS ONE BAD MOTHE
CAGE FOR PREZ
AWESOME AVENGERS!
I LOVE YO
SPIDEY
AVENG
GO HO

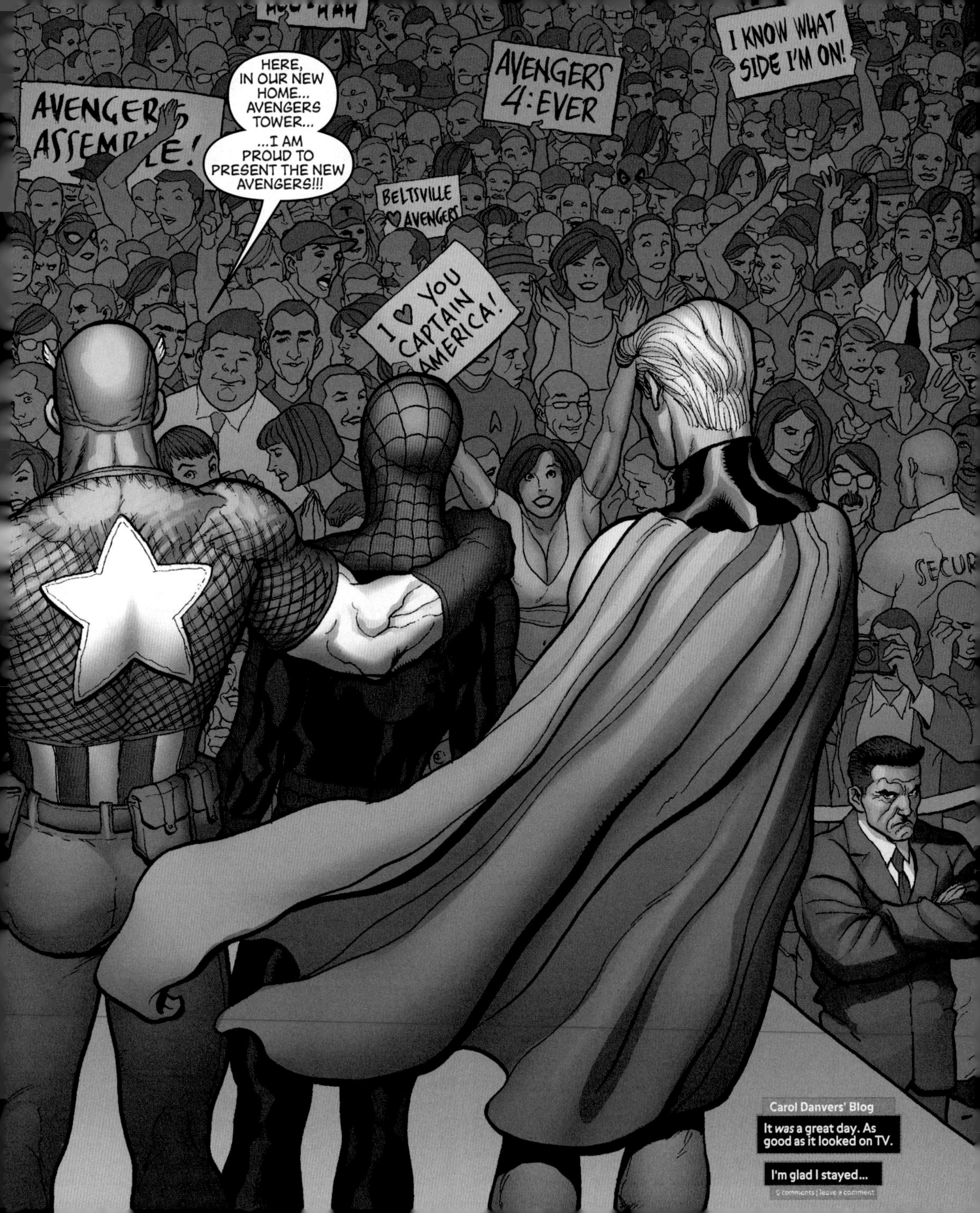

HERE, IN OUR NEW HOME... AVENGERS TOWER...
...I AM PROUD TO PRESENT THE NEW AVENGERS!!!
AVENGERS 4:EVER
I KNOW WHAT SIDE I'M ON!
BELTSVILLE ♥ AVENGERS
I ♥ YOU CAPTAIN AMERICA!
Carol Danvers' Blog
It *was* a great day. As good as it looked on TV.
I'm glad I stayed...
0 comments | leave a comment

Carol Danvers' Blog
...I should have left before it got ugly.
0 comments | leave a comment

NO!

"A WANTED MURDERER, AN ALLEGED EX-MEMBER OF A GLOBAL TERRORIST ORGANIZATION, AND A CONVICTED HEROIN DEALER ARE JUST A FEW OF THE NEW RECRUITS WHO ARE POSED TO BURY THE ONCE GOOD NAME OF THE AVENGERS ONCE AND FOR ALL."

WHO'S A TERRORIST?

ME.

WHO'S A CONVICTED HEROIN--?

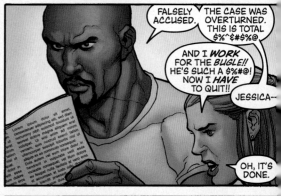

FALSELY ACCUSED.

THE CASE WAS OVERTURNED. THIS IS TOTAL $%^¢#$%@

AND I **WORK** FOR THE **BUGLE!!** HE'S SUCH A $%#@! NOW I **HAVE** TO QUIT!!

JESSICA--

OH, IT'S DONE.

I CAN'T **BELIEVE** JAMESON WALKED RIGHT INTO MY HOME, LOOKED ME RIGHT IN THE EYE AND TOLD ME WE HAD A DEAL, AND THEN WENT AND **DID** THIS. I CAN'T BELIEVE IT.

"AND TO IMAGINE THAT THESE MASKED VIGILANTES HAD THE GALL TO INVITE ME...

SEE... I CAN.

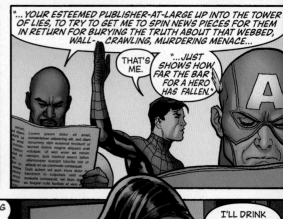

"... YOUR ESTEEMED PUBLISHER-AT-LARGE UP INTO THE TOWER OF LIES, TO TRY TO GET ME TO SPIN NEWS PIECES FOR THEM IN RETURN FOR BURYING THE TRUTH ABOUT THAT WEBBED, WALL-- CRAWLING, MURDERING MENACE...

THAT'S ME.

"...JUST SHOWS HOW FAR THE BAR FOR A HERO HAS FALLEN."

I'M GOING OUT.

I'LL COME WITH.

NAH, I'VE HAD A DAY OF IT. I NEED ALONE TIME.

I'LL DRINK YOU UNDER THE TABLE SOME OTHER TIME.

BELTSVILLE

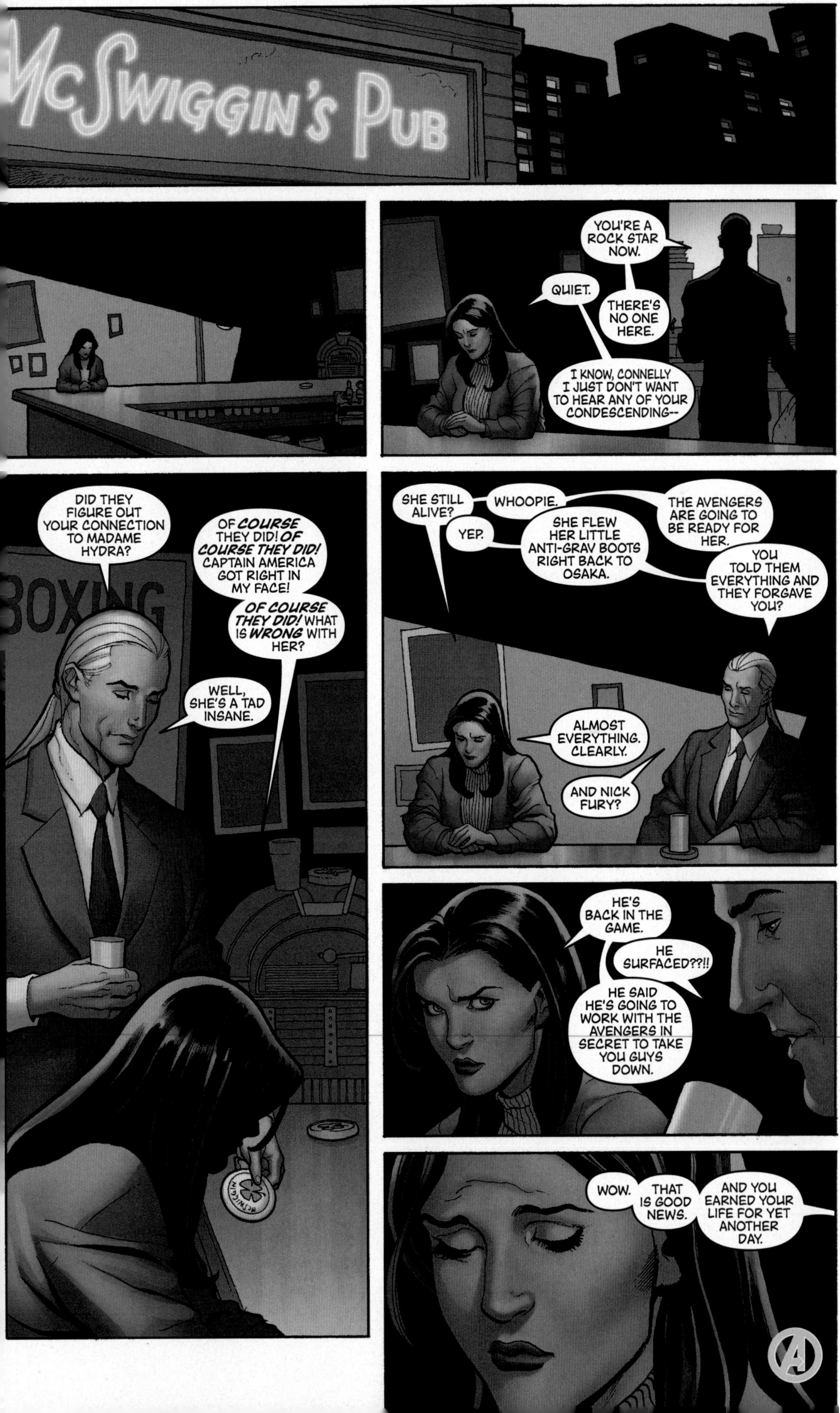
McSWIGGIN'S PUB
YOU'RE A ROCK STAR NOW.
QUIET.
THERE'S NO ONE HERE.
I KNOW, CONNELLY I JUST DON'T WANT TO HEAR ANY OF YOUR CONDESCENDING--
DID THEY FIGURE OUT YOUR CONNECTION TO MADAME HYDRA?
BOXING
OF COURSE THEY DID! OF COURSE THEY DID! CAPTAIN AMERICA GOT RIGHT IN MY FACE!
OF COURSE THEY DID! WHAT IS WRONG WITH HER?
WELL, SHE'S A TAD INSANE.
McSWIGGIN
SHE STILL ALIVE?
YEP.
WHOOPIE.
SHE FLEW HER LITTLE ANTI-GRAV BOOTS RIGHT BACK TO OSAKA.
THE AVENGERS ARE GOING TO BE READY FOR HER.
YOU TOLD THEM EVERYTHING AND THEY FORGAVE YOU?
ALMOST EVERYTHING. CLEARLY.
AND NICK FURY?
HE'S BACK IN THE GAME.
HE SURFACED??!!
HE SAID HE'S GOING TO WORK WITH THE AVENGERS IN SECRET TO TAKE YOU GUYS DOWN.
WOW.
THAT IS GOOD NEWS.
AND YOU EARNED YOUR LIFE FOR YET ANOTHER DAY.

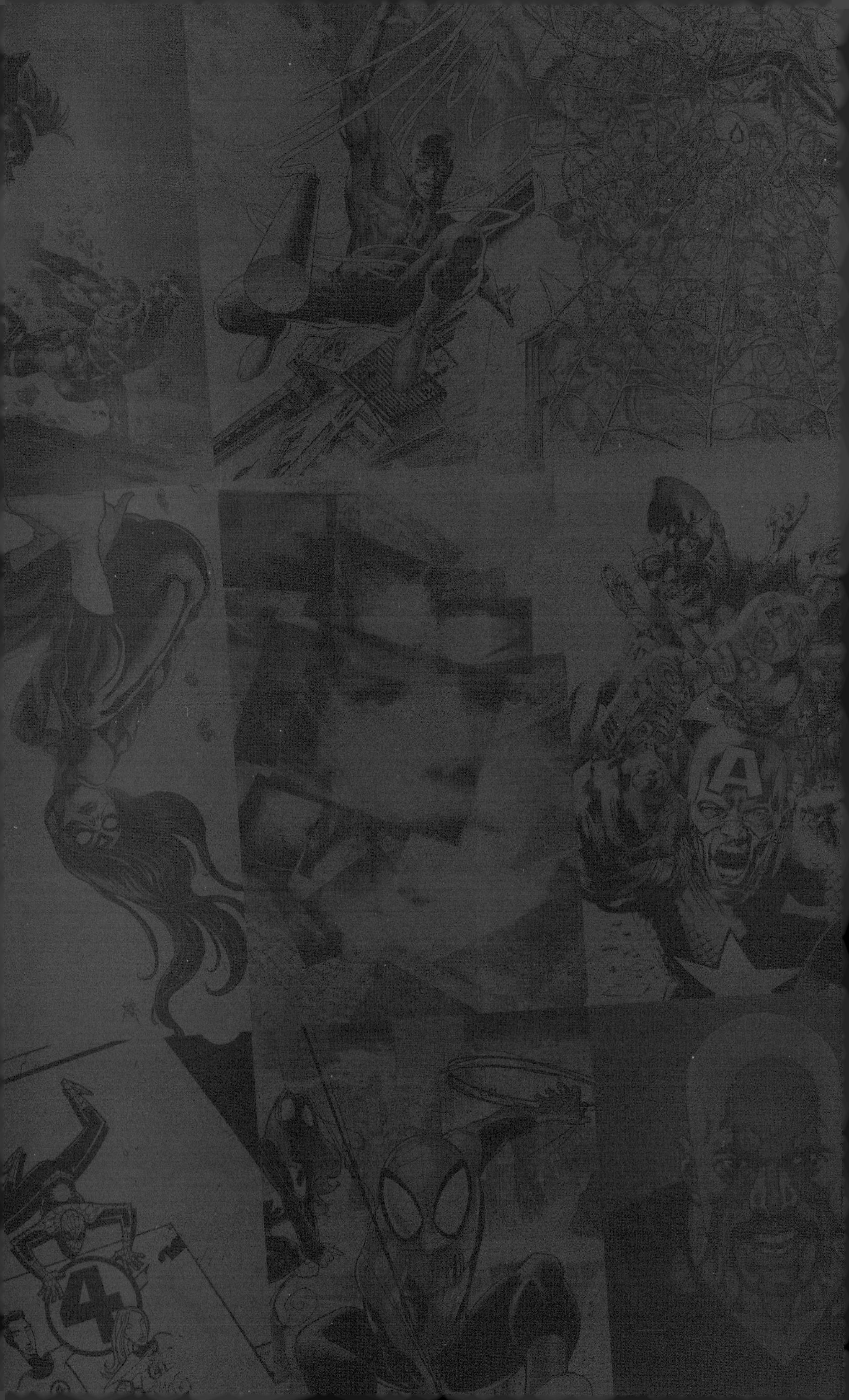

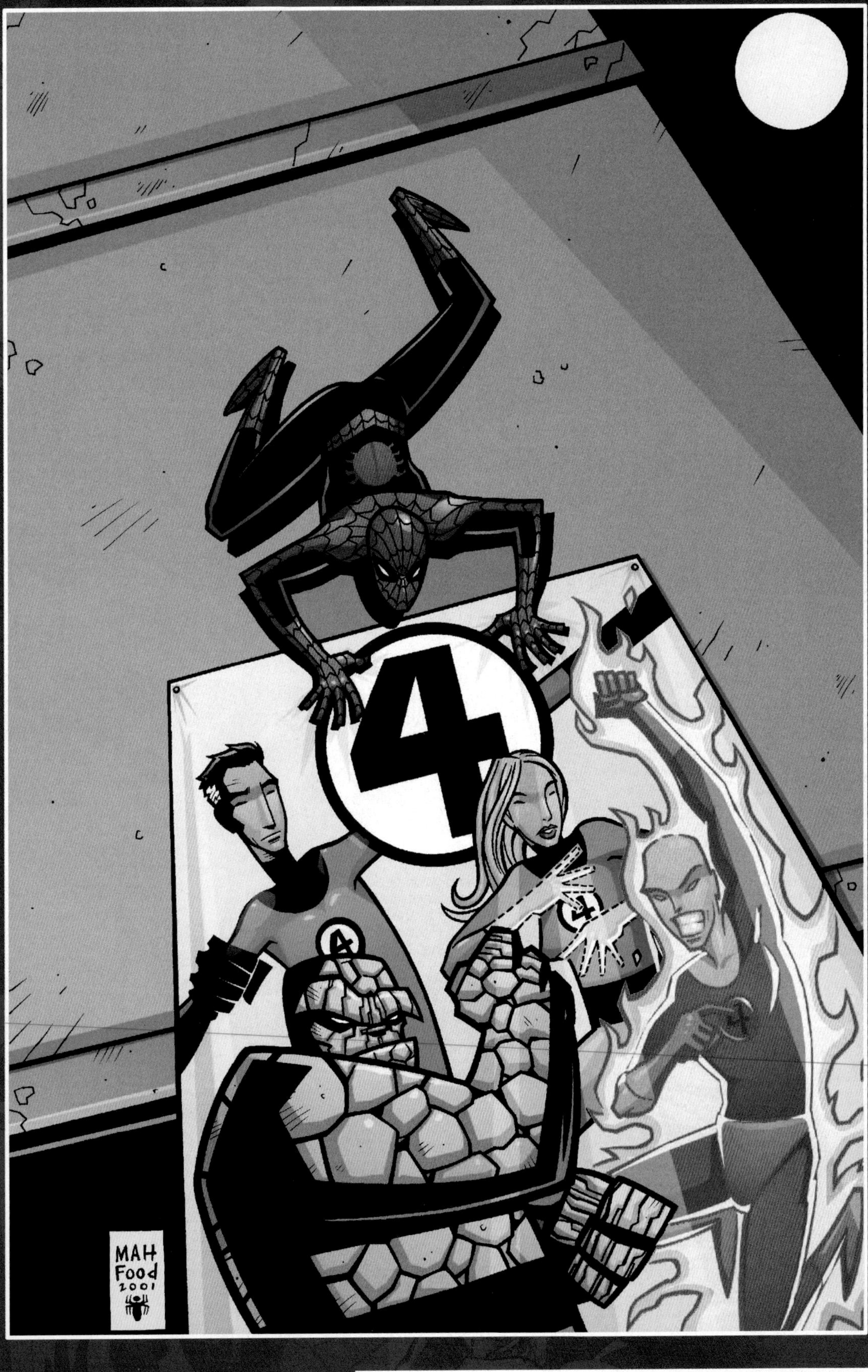
4
MAH
Food
2001

ULTIMATE MARVEL TEAM-UP #9

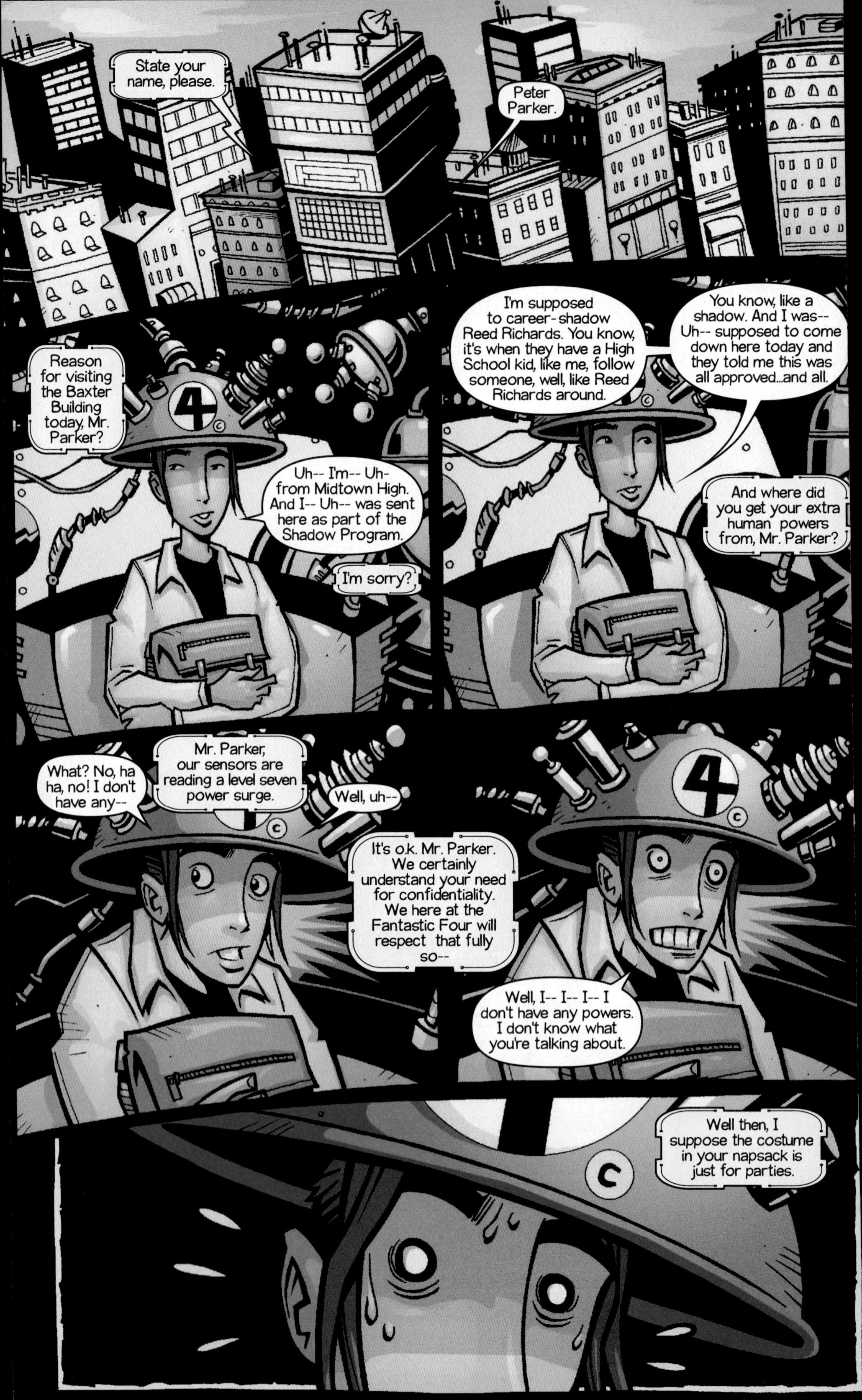
State your name, please.
Peter Parker.
Reason for visiting the Baxter Building today, Mr. Parker?
Uh-- I'm-- Uh- from Midtown High. And I-- Uh-- was sent here as part of the Shadow Program.
I'm sorry?
I'm supposed to career-shadow Reed Richards. You know, it's when they have a High School kid, like me, follow someone, well, like Reed Richards around.
You know, like a shadow. And I was-- Uh-- supposed to come down here today and they told me this was all approved...and all.
And where did you get your extra human powers from, Mr. Parker?
What? No, ha ha, no! I don't have any--
Mr. Parker, our sensors are reading a level seven power surge.
Well, uh--
It's o.k. Mr. Parker. We certainly understand your need for confidentiality. We here at the Fantastic Four will respect that fully so--
Well, I-- I-- I-- I don't have any powers. I don't know what you're talking about.
Well then, I suppose the costume in your napsack is just for parties.

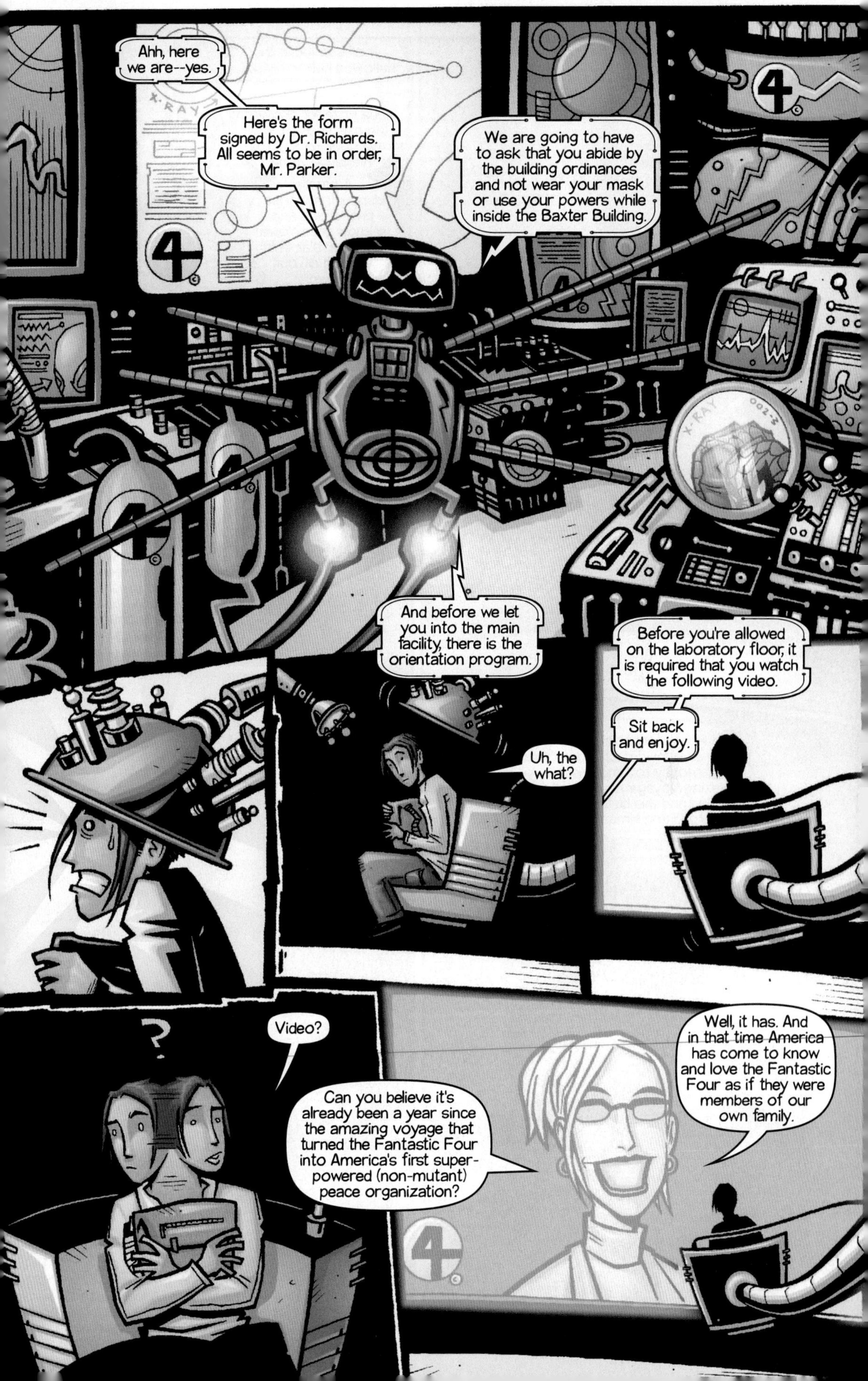

Ahh, here we are--yes.
Here's the form signed by Dr. Richards. All seems to be in order, Mr. Parker.
We are going to have to ask that you abide by the building ordinances and not wear your mask or use your powers while inside the Baxter Building.
And before we let you into the main facility, there is the orientation program.
Uh, the what?
Before you're allowed on the laboratory floor, it is required that you watch the following video.
Sit back and enjoy.
Video?
Can you believe it's already been a year since the amazing voyage that turned the Fantastic Four into America's first super-powered (non-mutant) peace organization?
Well, it has. And in that time America has come to know and love the Fantastic Four as if they were members of our own family.

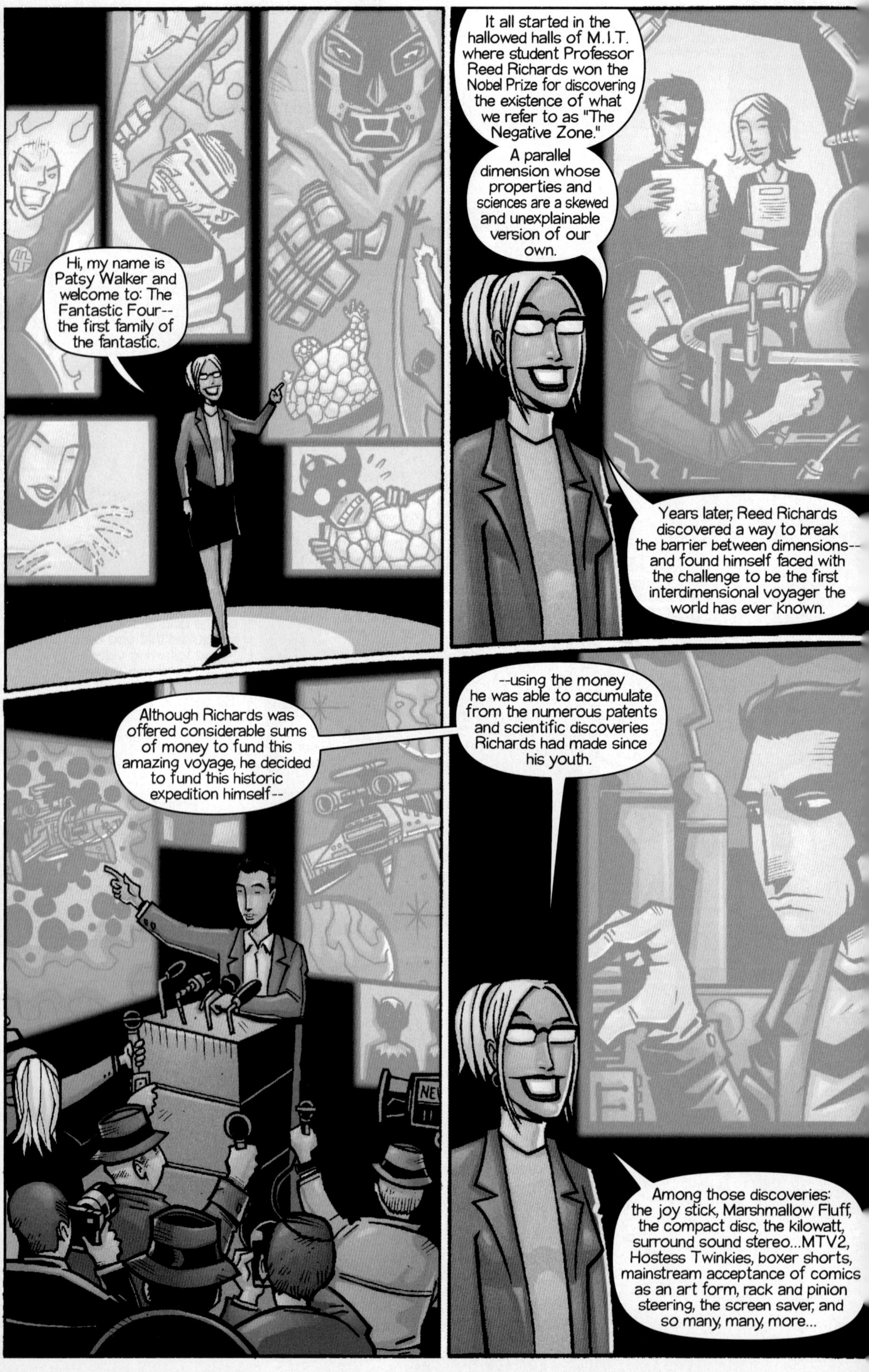

Hi, my name is Patsy Walker and welcome to: The Fantastic Four-- the first family of the fantastic.
It all started in the hallowed halls of M.I.T. where student Professor Reed Richards won the Nobel Prize for discovering the existence of what we refer to as "The Negative Zone."
A parallel dimension whose properties and sciences are a skewed and unexplainable version of our own.
Years later, Reed Richards discovered a way to break the barrier between dimensions-- and found himself faced with the challenge to be the first interdimensional voyager the world has ever known.
Although Richards was offered considerable sums of money to fund this amazing voyage, he decided to fund this historic expedition himself--
--using the money he was able to accumulate from the numerous patents and scientific discoveries Richards had made since his youth.
Among those discoveries: the joy stick, Marshmallow Fluff, the compact disc, the kilowatt, surround sound stereo...MTV2, Hostess Twinkies, boxer shorts, mainstream acceptance of comics as an art form, rack and pinion steering, the screen saver, and so many, many, more...

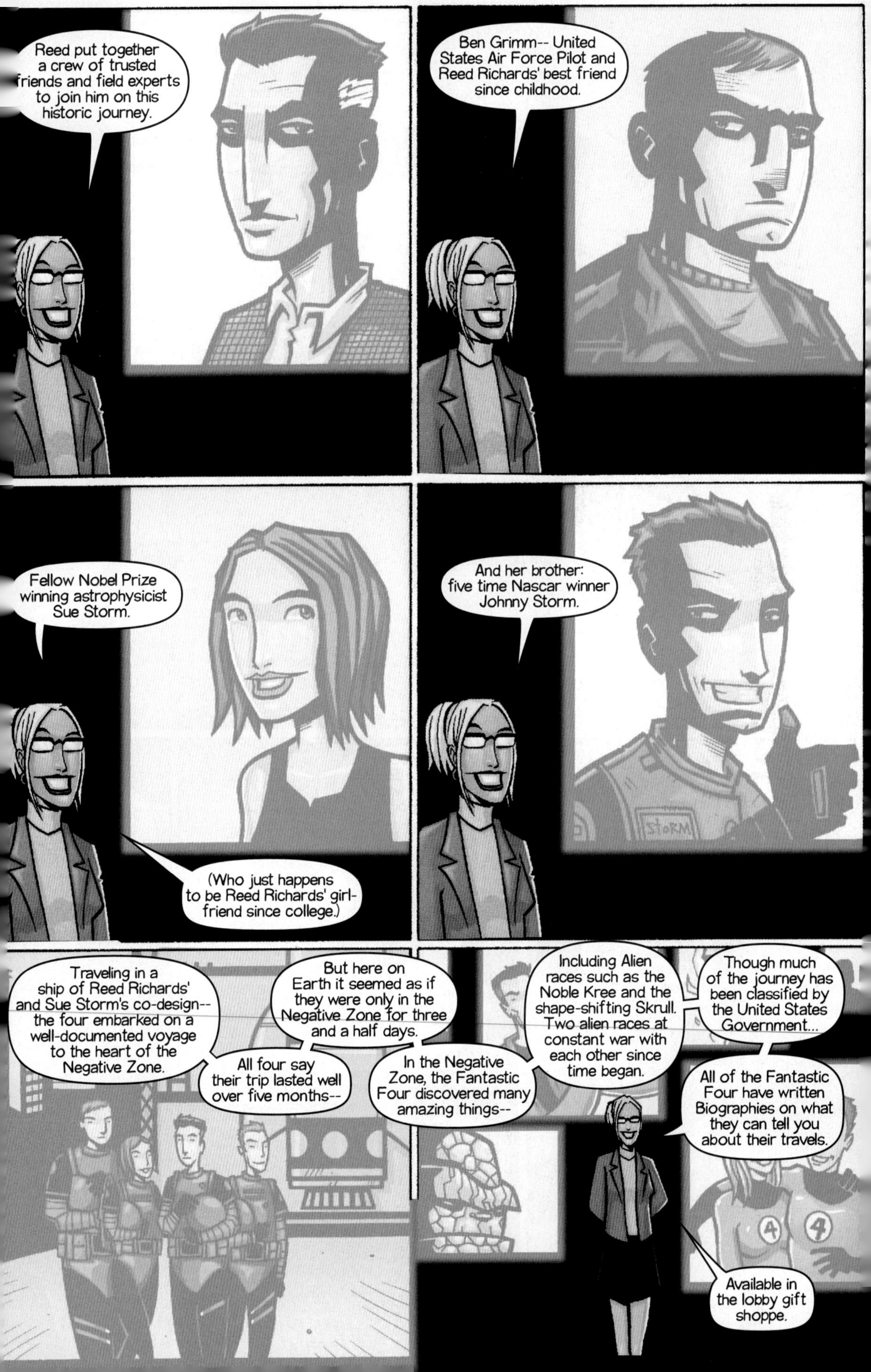
Reed put together a crew of trusted friends and field experts to join him on this historic journey.
Ben Grimm-- United States Air Force Pilot and Reed Richards' best friend since childhood.
Fellow Nobel Prize winning astrophysicist Sue Storm.
(Who just happens to be Reed Richards' girl-friend since college.)
And her brother: five time Nascar winner Johnny Storm.
STORM
Traveling in a ship of Reed Richards' and Sue Storm's co-design-- the four embarked on a well-documented voyage to the heart of the Negative Zone.
All four say their trip lasted well over five months--
But here on Earth it seemed as if they were only in the Negative Zone for three and a half days.
In the Negative Zone, the Fantastic Four discovered many amazing things--
Including Alien races such as the Noble Kree and the shape-shifting Skrull. Two alien races at constant war with each other since time began.
Though much of the journey has been classified by the United States Government...
All of the Fantastic Four have written Biographies on what they can tell you about their travels.
Available in the lobby gift shoppe.

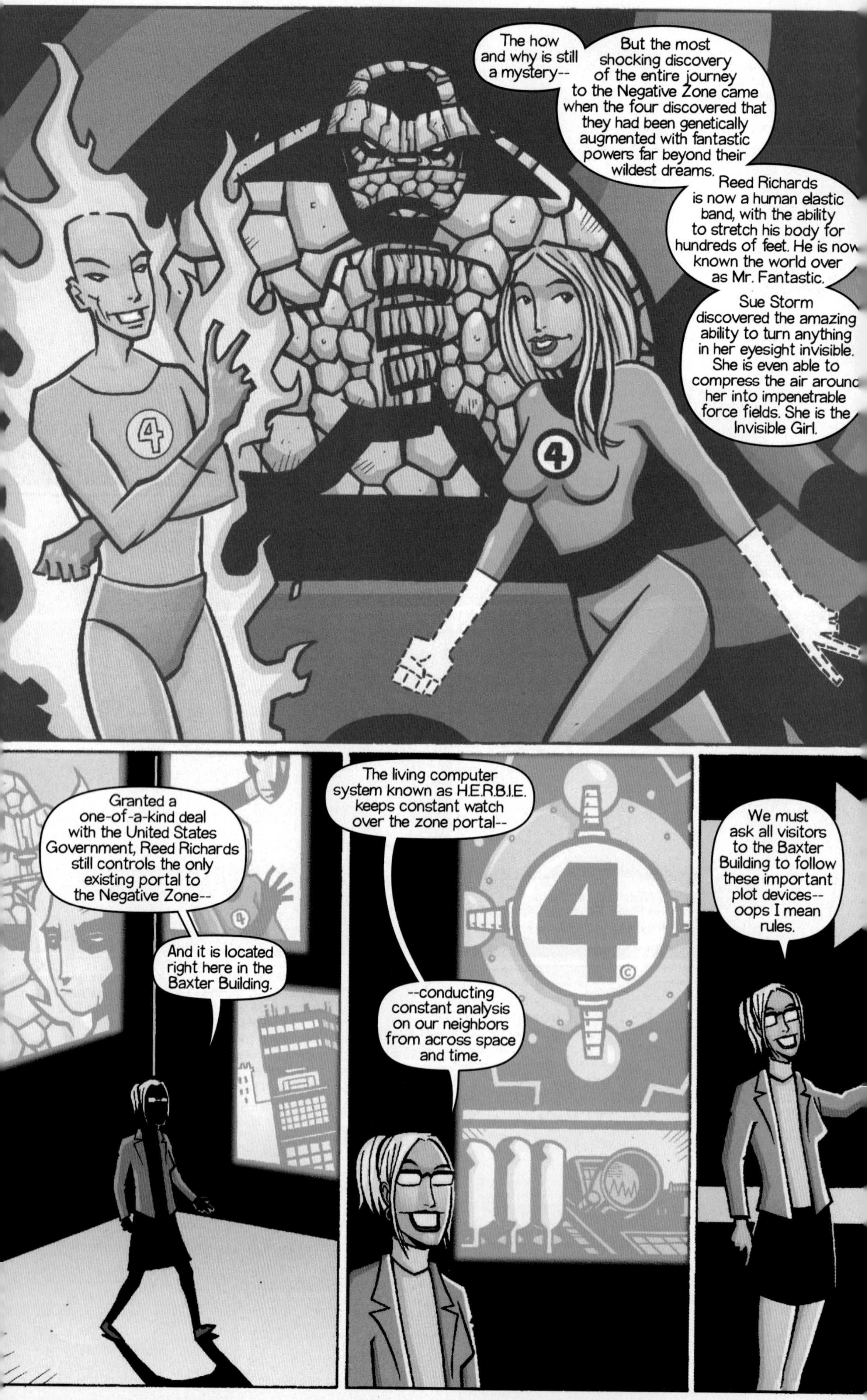
The how and why is still a mystery--
But the most shocking discovery of the entire journey to the Negative Zone came when the four discovered that they had been genetically augmented with fantastic powers far beyond their wildest dreams.
Reed Richards is now a human elastic band, with the ability to stretch his body for hundreds of feet. He is now known the world over as Mr. Fantastic.
Sue Storm discovered the amazing ability to turn anything in her eyesight invisible. She is even able to compress the air around her into impenetrable force fields. She is the Invisible Girl.
Granted a one-of-a-kind deal with the United States Government, Reed Richards still controls the only existing portal to the Negative Zone--
And it is located right here in the Baxter Building.
The living computer system known as H.E.R.B.I.E. keeps constant watch over the zone portal--
--conducting constant analysis on our neighbors from across space and time.
We must ask all visitors to the Baxter Building to follow these important plot devices-- oops I mean rules.

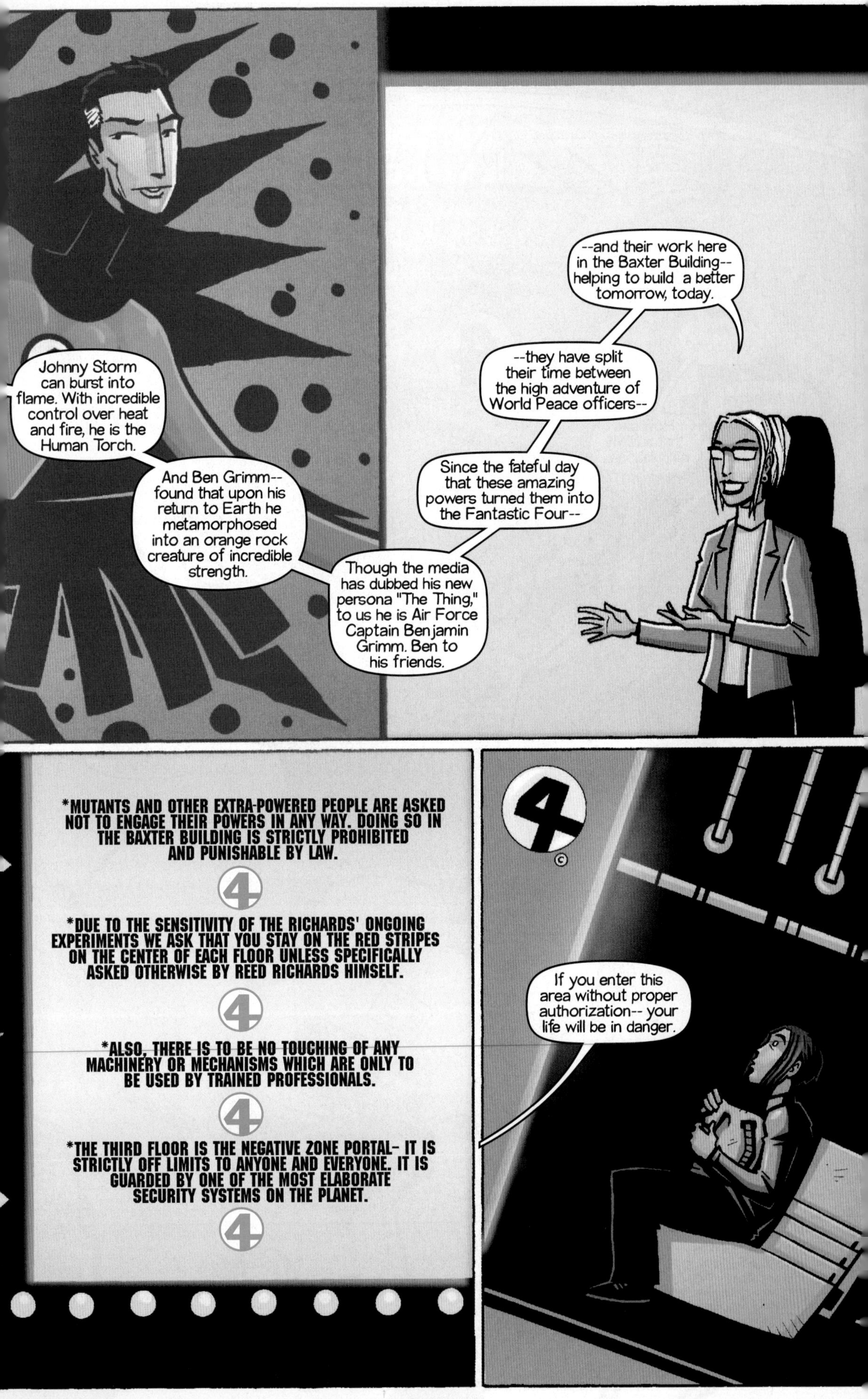
Johnny Storm can burst into flame. With incredible control over heat and fire, he is the Human Torch.
And Ben Grimm-- found that upon his return to Earth he metamorphosed into an orange rock creature of incredible strength.
Though the media has dubbed his new persona "The Thing," to us he is Air Force Captain Benjamin Grimm. Ben to his friends.
Since the fateful day that these amazing powers turned them into the Fantastic Four--
--they have split their time between the high adventure of World Peace officers--
--and their work here in the Baxter Building-- helping to build a better tomorrow, today.
*MUTANTS AND OTHER EXTRA-POWERED PEOPLE ARE ASKED NOT TO ENGAGE THEIR POWERS IN ANY WAY. DOING SO IN THE BAXTER BUILDING IS STRICTLY PROHIBITED AND PUNISHABLE BY LAW.
*DUE TO THE SENSITIVITY OF THE RICHARDS' ONGOING EXPERIMENTS WE ASK THAT YOU STAY ON THE RED STRIPES ON THE CENTER OF EACH FLOOR UNLESS SPECIFICALLY ASKED OTHERWISE BY REED RICHARDS HIMSELF.
*ALSO, THERE IS TO BE NO TOUCHING OF ANY MACHINERY OR MECHANISMS WHICH ARE ONLY TO BE USED BY TRAINED PROFESSIONALS.
*THE THIRD FLOOR IS THE NEGATIVE ZONE PORTAL- IT IS STRICTLY OFF LIMITS TO ANYONE AND EVERYONE. IT IS GUARDED BY ONE OF THE MOST ELABORATE SECURITY SYSTEMS ON THE PLANET.
If you enter this area without proper authorization-- your life will be in danger.

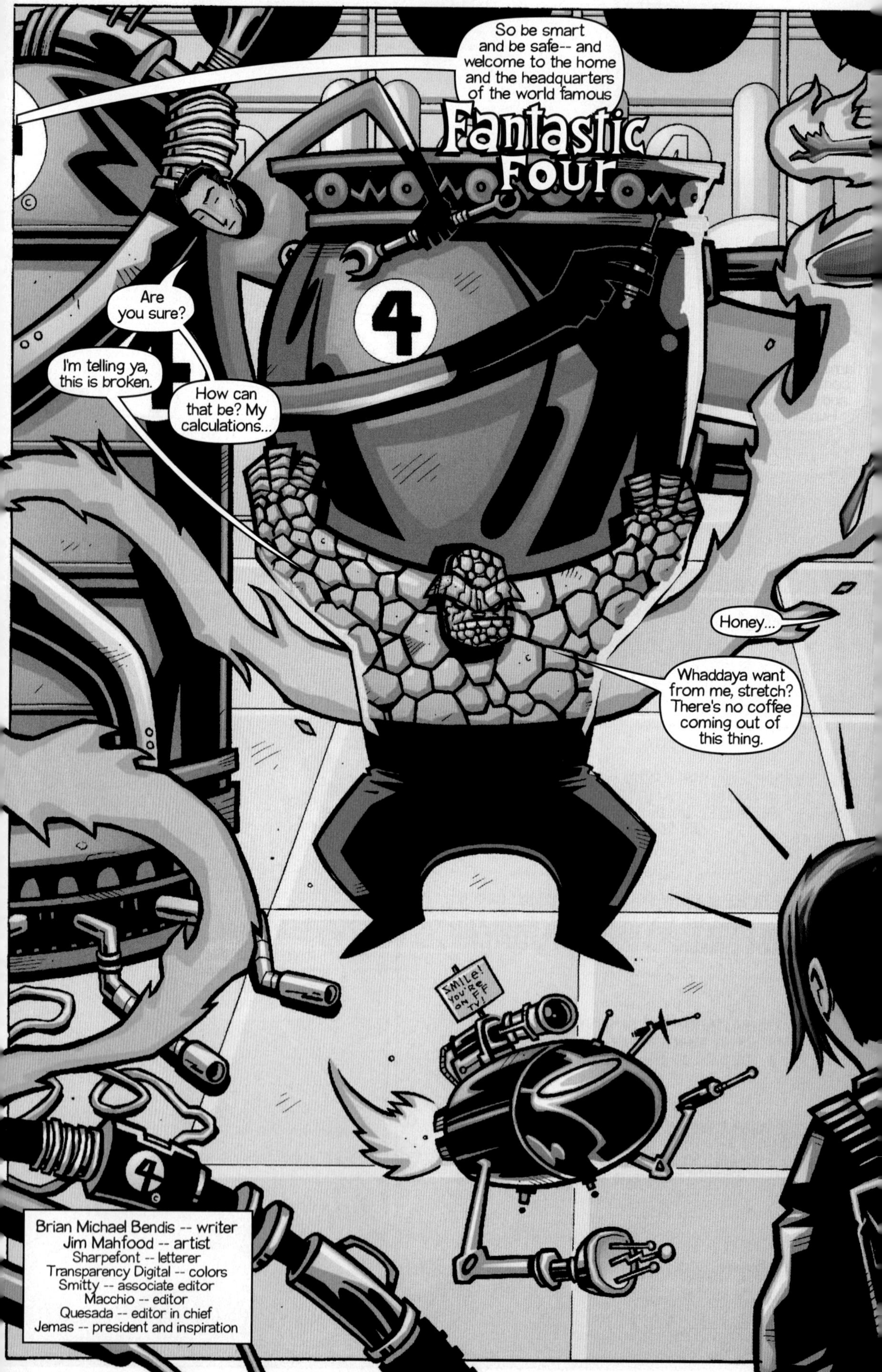

So be smart and be safe-- and welcome to the home and the headquarters of the world famous
Fantastic Four
Are you sure?
I'm telling ya, this is broken.
How can that be? My calculations...
Honey...
Whaddaya want from me, stretch? There's no coffee coming out of this thing.
SMILE! YOU'RE ON TV!

Brian Michael Bendis -- writer
Jim Mahfood -- artist
Sharpefont -- letterer
Transparency Digital -- colors
Smitty -- associate editor
Macchio -- editor
Quesada -- editor in chief
Jemas -- president and inspiration

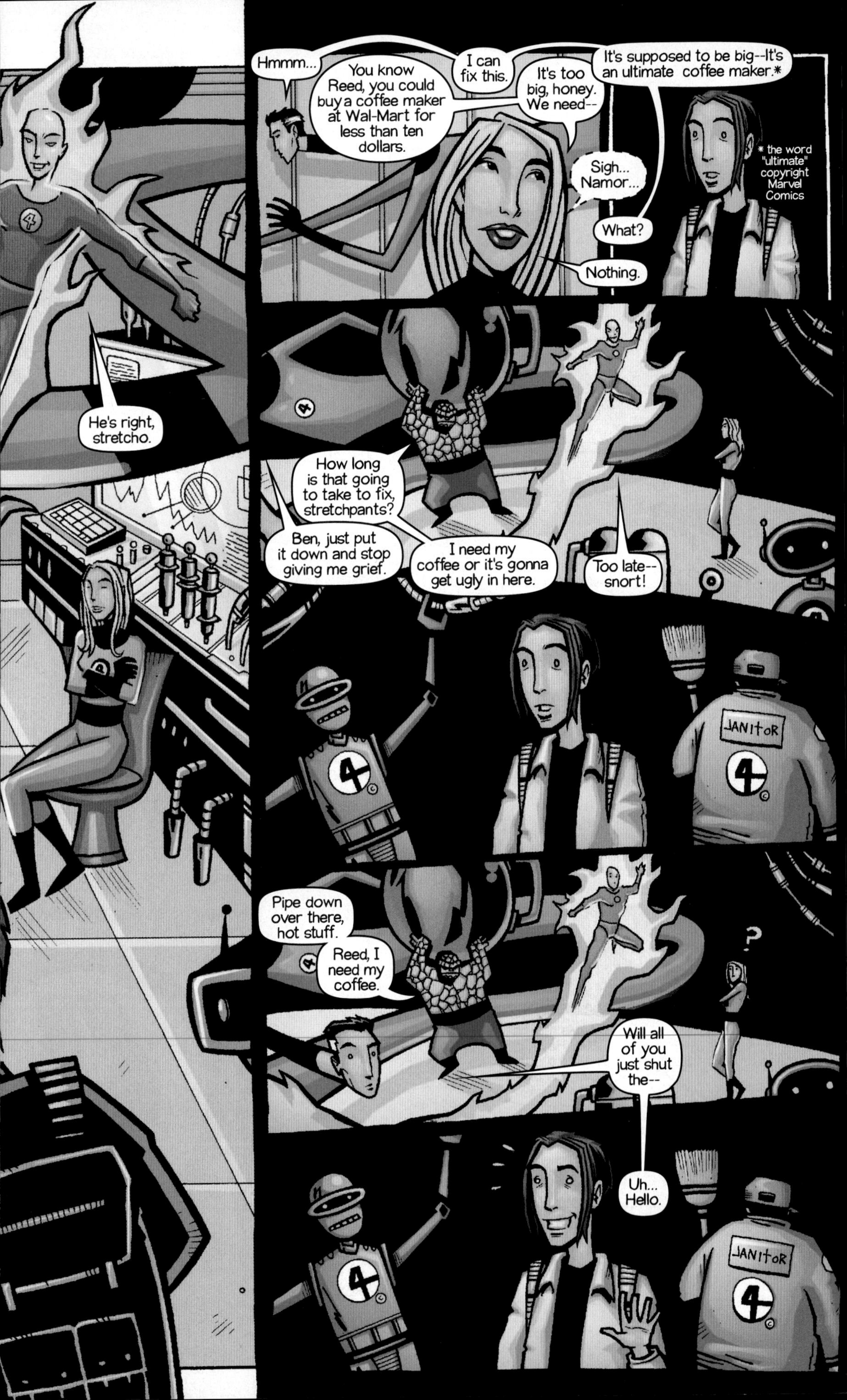
He's right, stretcho.
Hmmm...
You know Reed, you could buy a coffee maker at Wal-Mart for less than ten dollars.
I can fix this.
It's too big, honey. We need--
It's supposed to be big--It's an ultimate coffee maker.*
Sigh... Namor...
What?
Nothing.
* the word "ultimate" copyright Marvel Comics
How long is that going to take to fix, stretchpants?
Ben, just put it down and stop giving me grief.
I need my coffee or it's gonna get ugly in here.
Too late-- snort!
JANITOR
Pipe down over there, hot stuff.
Reed, I need my coffee.
?
Will all of you just shut the--
Uh... Hello.
JANITOR

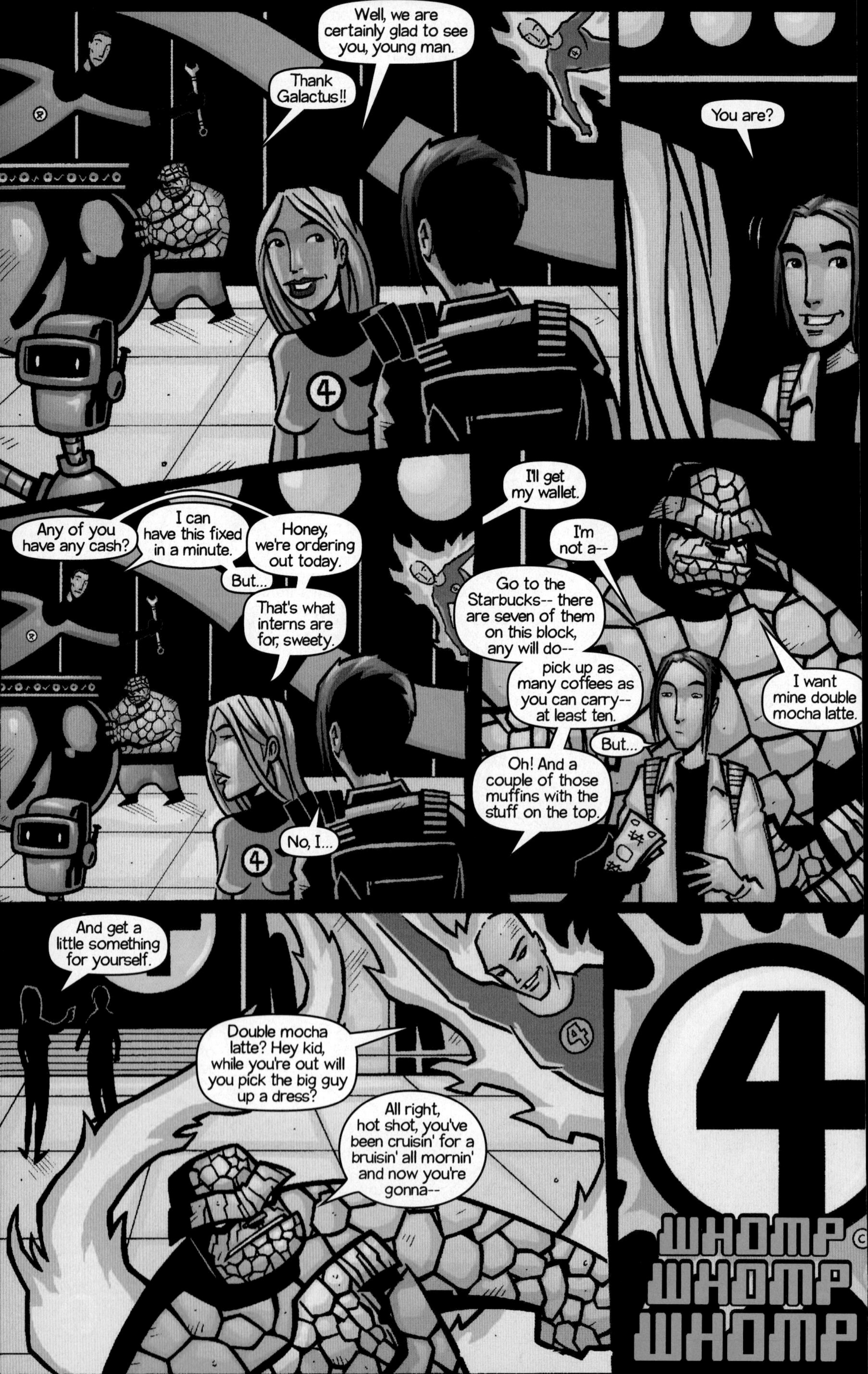

Thank Galactus!!
Well, we are certainly glad to see you, young man.
You are?
Any of you have any cash?
I can have this fixed in a minute.
Honey, we're ordering out today.
But...
That's what interns are for, sweety.
No, I...
I'll get my wallet.
I'm not a--
Go to the Starbucks-- there are seven of them on this block, any will do--
pick up as many coffees as you can carry-- at least ten.
I want mine double mocha latte.
But...
Oh! And a couple of those muffins with the stuff on the top.
And get a little something for yourself.
Double mocha latte? Hey kid, while you're out will you pick the big guy up a dress?
All right, hot shot, you've been cruisin' for a bruisin' all mornin' and now you're gonna--
WHOMP WHOMP WHOMP

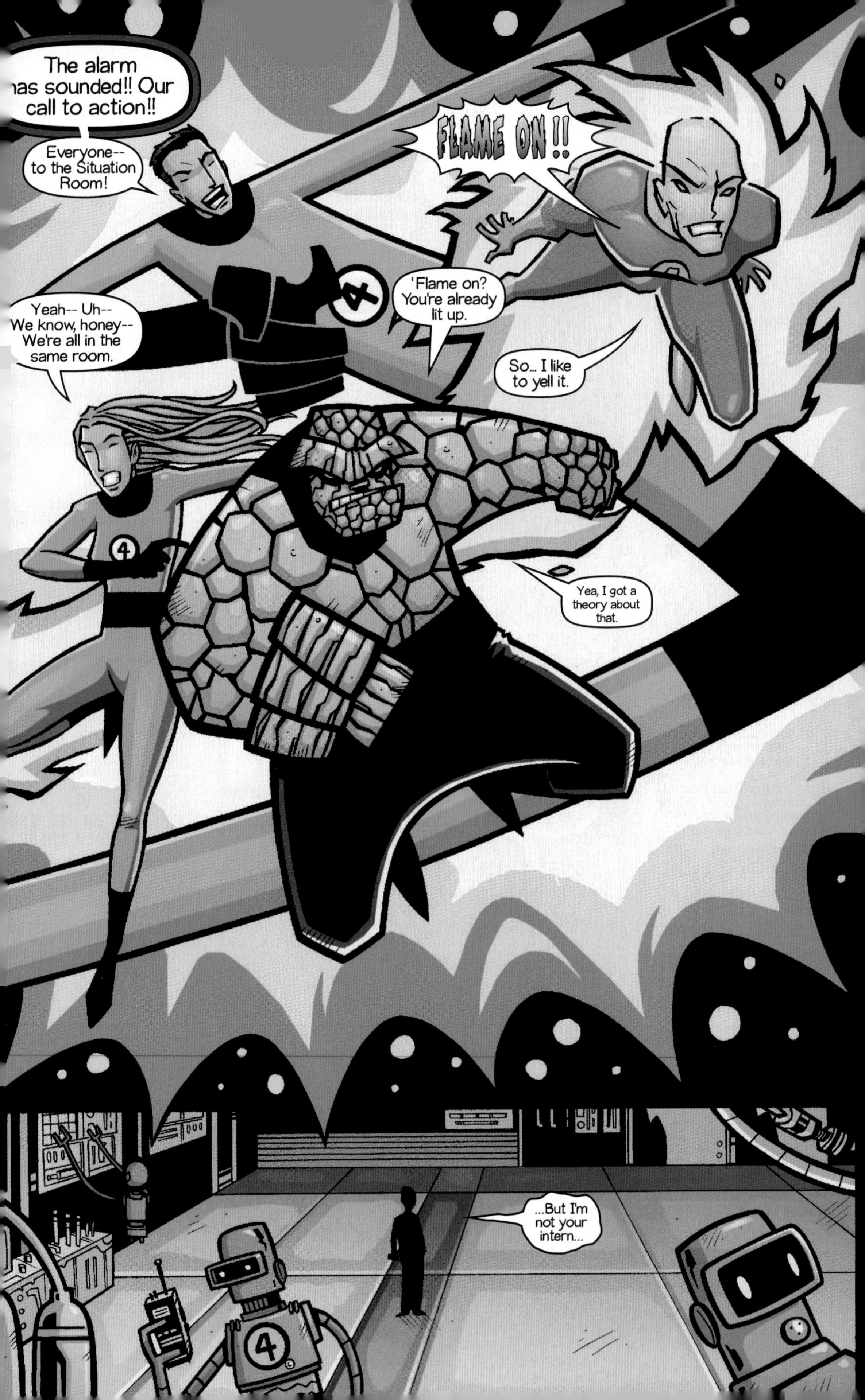
The alarm has sounded!! Our call to action!!
Everyone-- to the Situation Room!
FLAME ON!!
'Flame on? You're already lit up.
Yeah-- Uh-- We know, honey-- We're all in the same room.
So... I like to yell it.
Yea, I got a theory about that.
...But I'm not your intern...

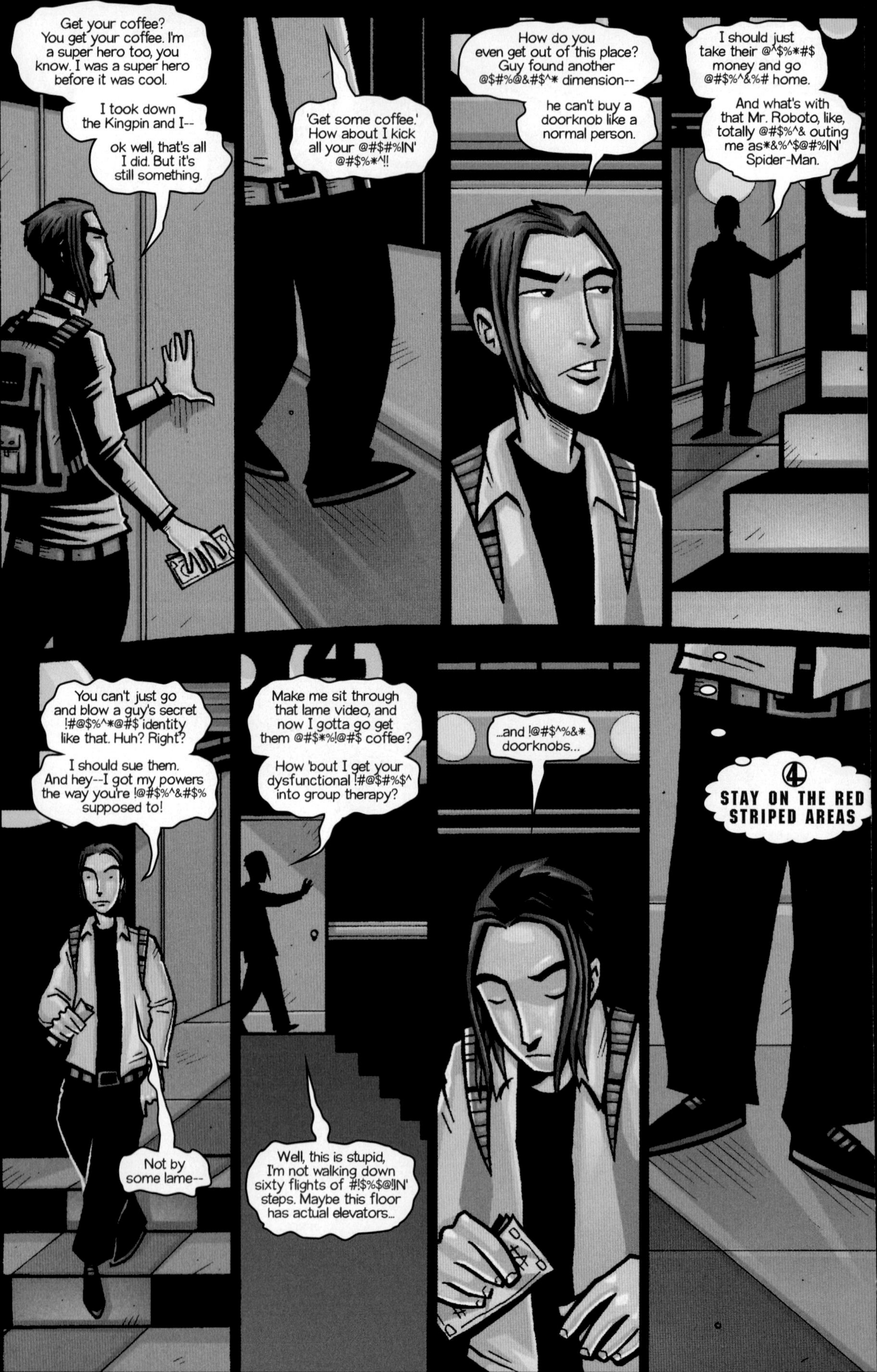
Get your coffee? You get your coffee. I'm a super hero too, you know. I was a super hero before it was cool.
I took down the Kingpin and I--
ok well, that's all I did. But it's still something.
'Get some coffee.' How about I kick all your @#$#%IN' @#$%*^!!
How do you even get out of this place? Guy found another @$#%@&#$^* dimension--
he can't buy a doorknob like a normal person.
I should just take their @^$%*#$ money and go @#$%^&%# home.
And what's with that Mr. Roboto, like, totally @#$%^& outing me as*&%^$@#%IN' Spider-Man.
You can't just go and blow a guy's secret !#@$%^*@#$ identity like that. Huh? Right?
I should sue them. And hey--I got my powers the way you're !@#$%^&#$% supposed to!
Not by some lame--
Make me sit through that lame video, and now I gotta go get them @#$*%!@#$ coffee?
How 'bout I get your dysfunctional !#@$#%$^ into group therapy?
Well, this is stupid, I'm not walking down sixty flights of #!$%$@!IN' steps. Maybe this floor has actual elevators...
...and !@#$^%&* doorknobs...
STAY ON THE RED STRIPED AREAS

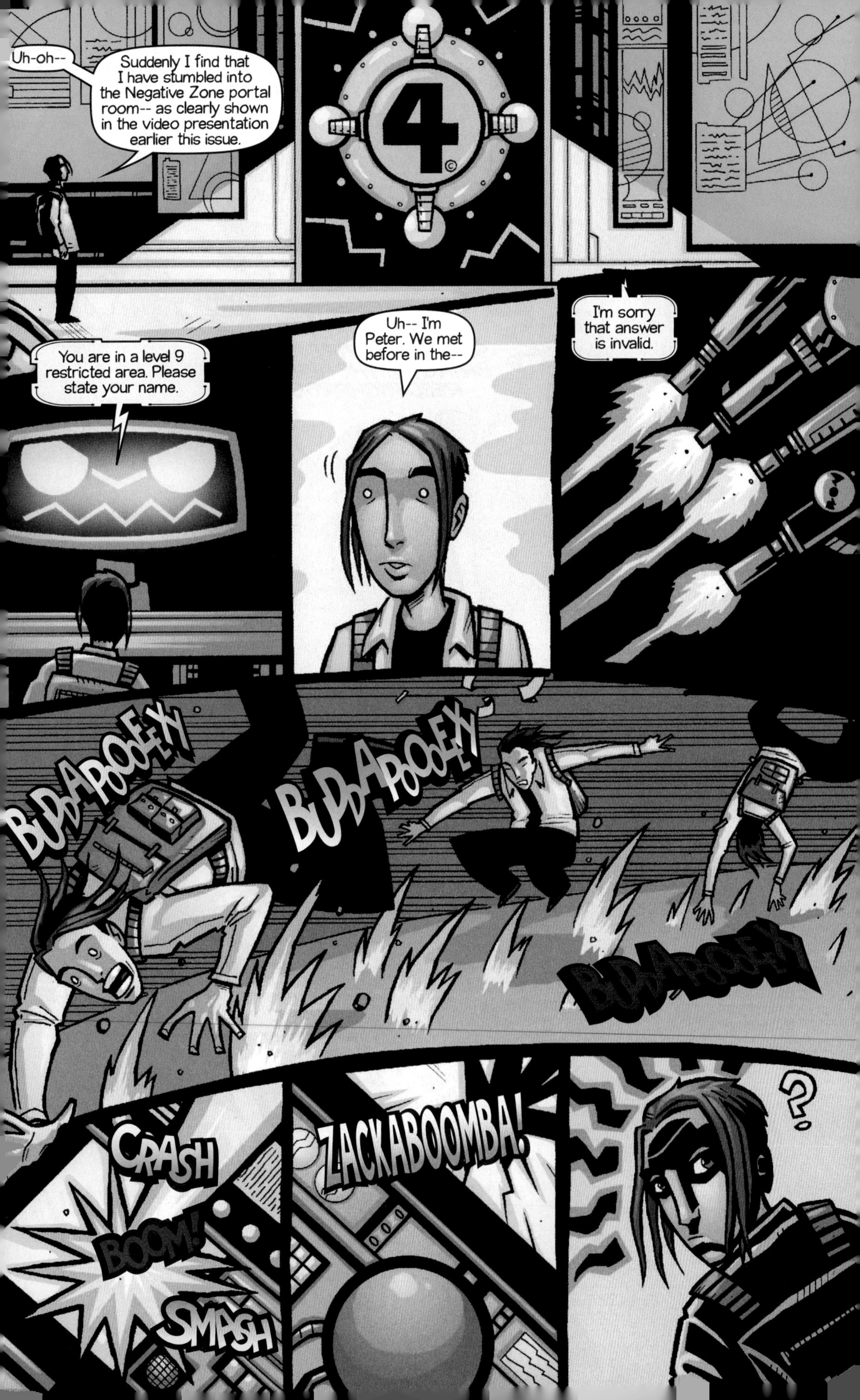
Uh-oh--
Suddenly I find that I have stumbled into the Negative Zone portal room-- as clearly shown in the video presentation earlier this issue.
You are in a level 9 restricted area. Please state your name.
Uh-- I'm Peter. We met before in the--
I'm sorry that answer is invalid.
BUDDAPOOOEY
BUDDAPOOOEY
BUDDAPOOOEY
CRASH
BOOM!
SMASH
ZACKABOOMBA!
?

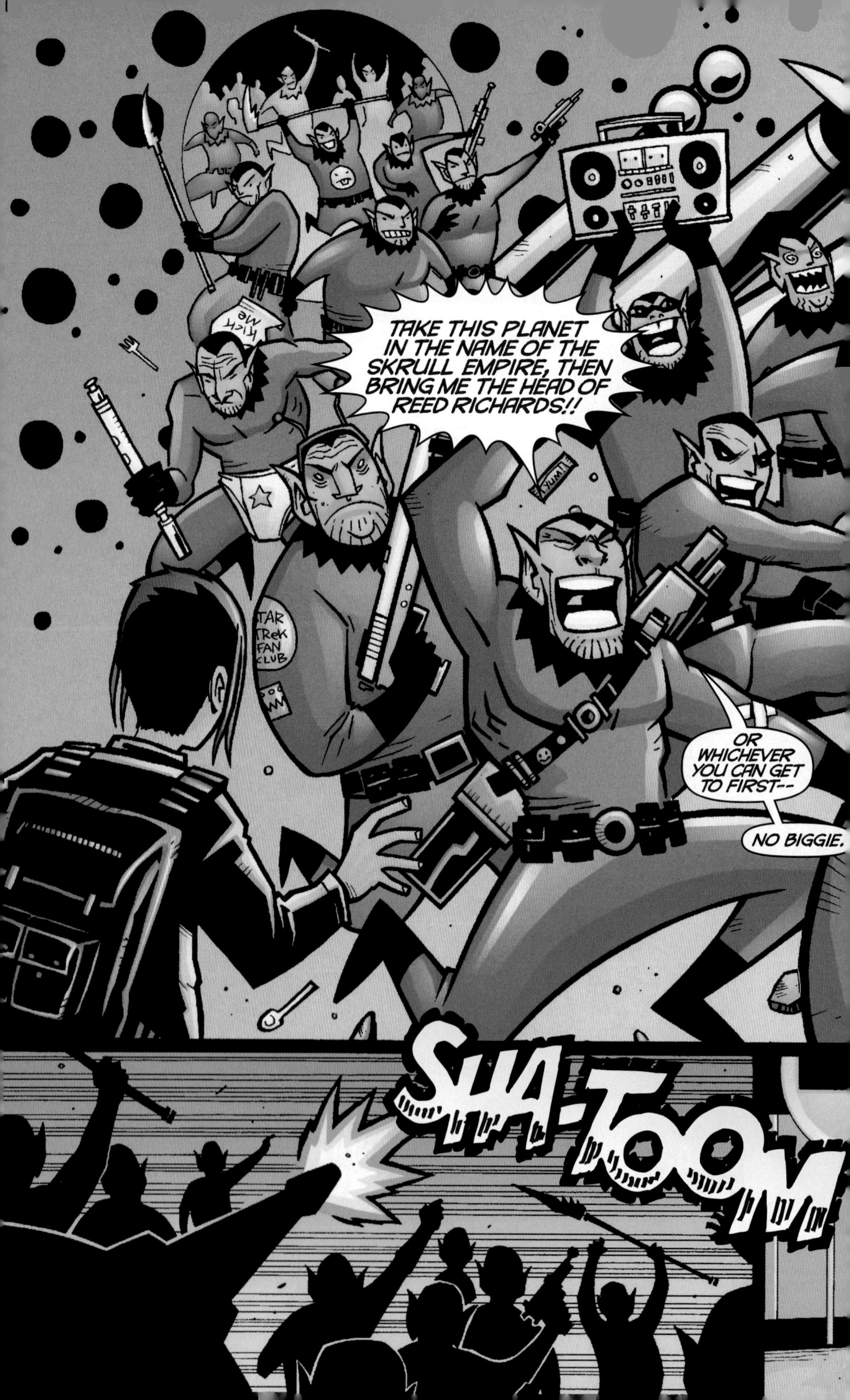
kick me
TAKE THIS PLANET IN THE NAME OF THE SKRULL EMPIRE, THEN BRING ME THE HEAD OF REED RICHARDS!!
YUM!
STAR TREK FAN CLUB
OR WHICHEVER YOU CAN GET TO FIRST--
NO BIGGIE.
SHA-TOOM

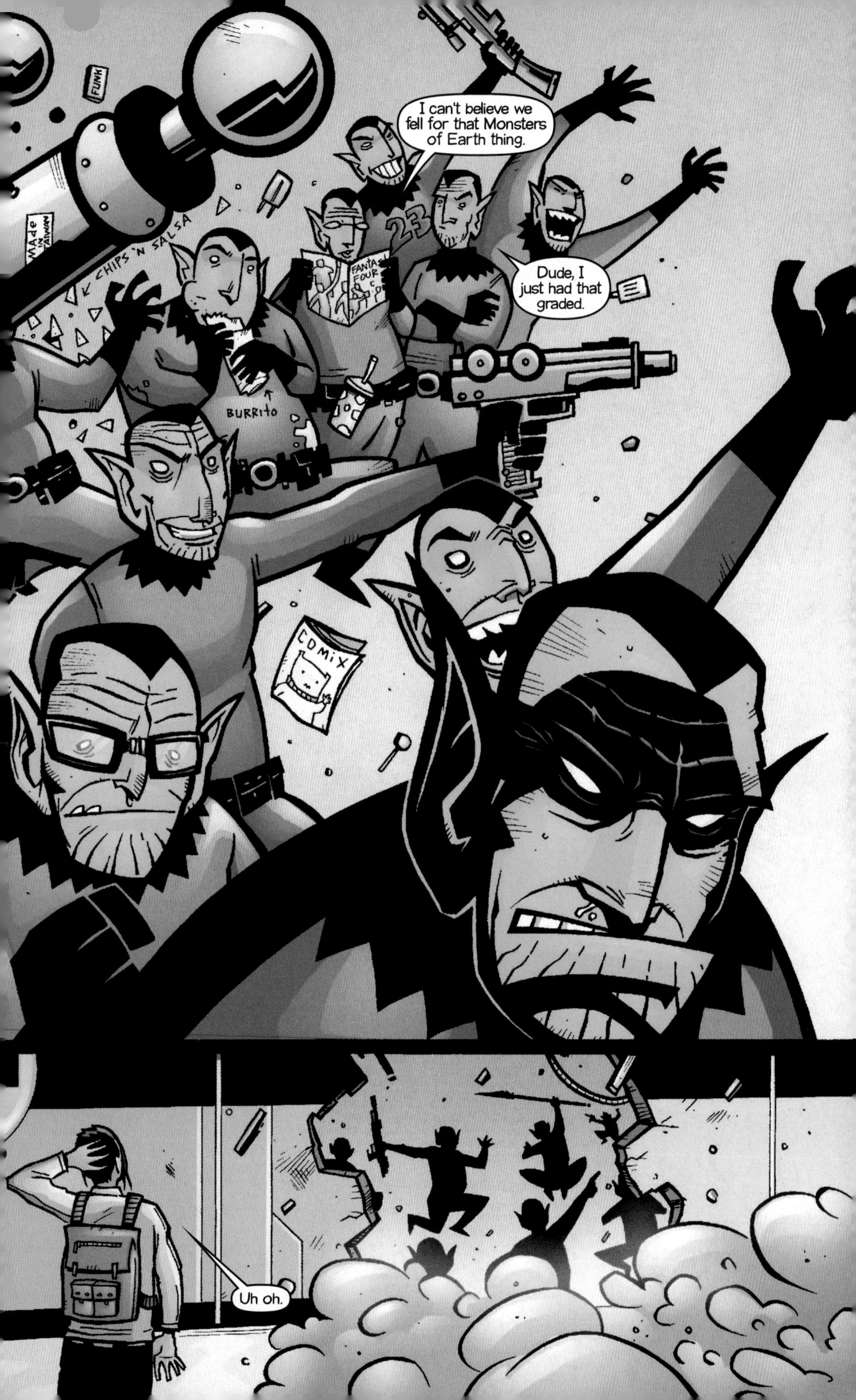
FUNK
MADE IN TAIWAN
CHIPS 'N SALSA
I can't believe we fell for that Monsters of Earth thing.
FANTA FOUR
Dude, I just had that graded.
BURRITO
COMIX
Uh oh.

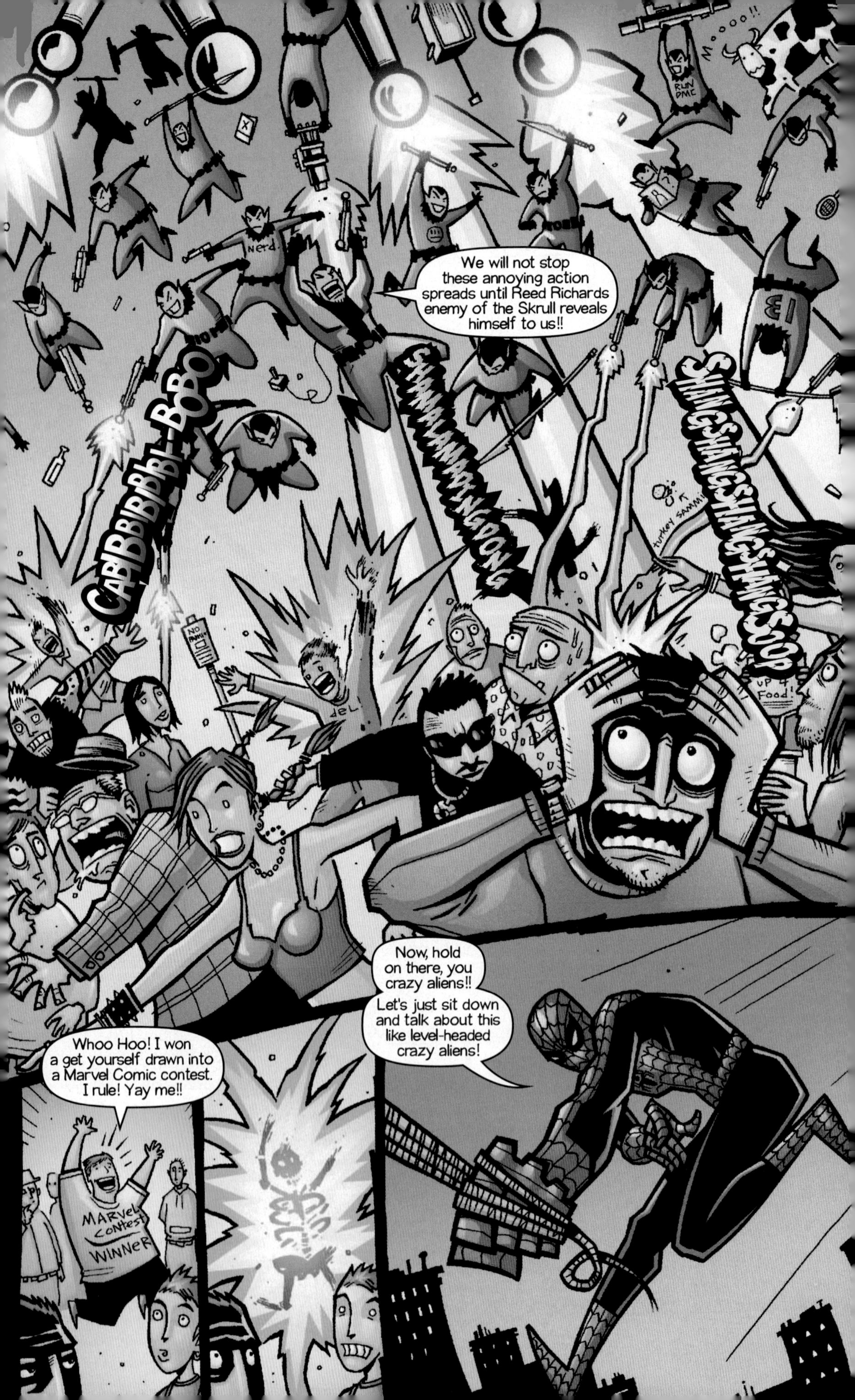
Moooo!!
RUN DMC
Nerd
We will not stop these annoying action spreads until Reed Richards enemy of the Skrull reveals himself to us!!
up 4 Food!
Whoo Hoo! I won a get yourself drawn into a Marvel Comic contest. I rule! Yay me!!
MARVEL CONTEST WINNER
Now, hold on there, you crazy aliens!!
Let's just sit down and talk about this like level-headed crazy aliens!

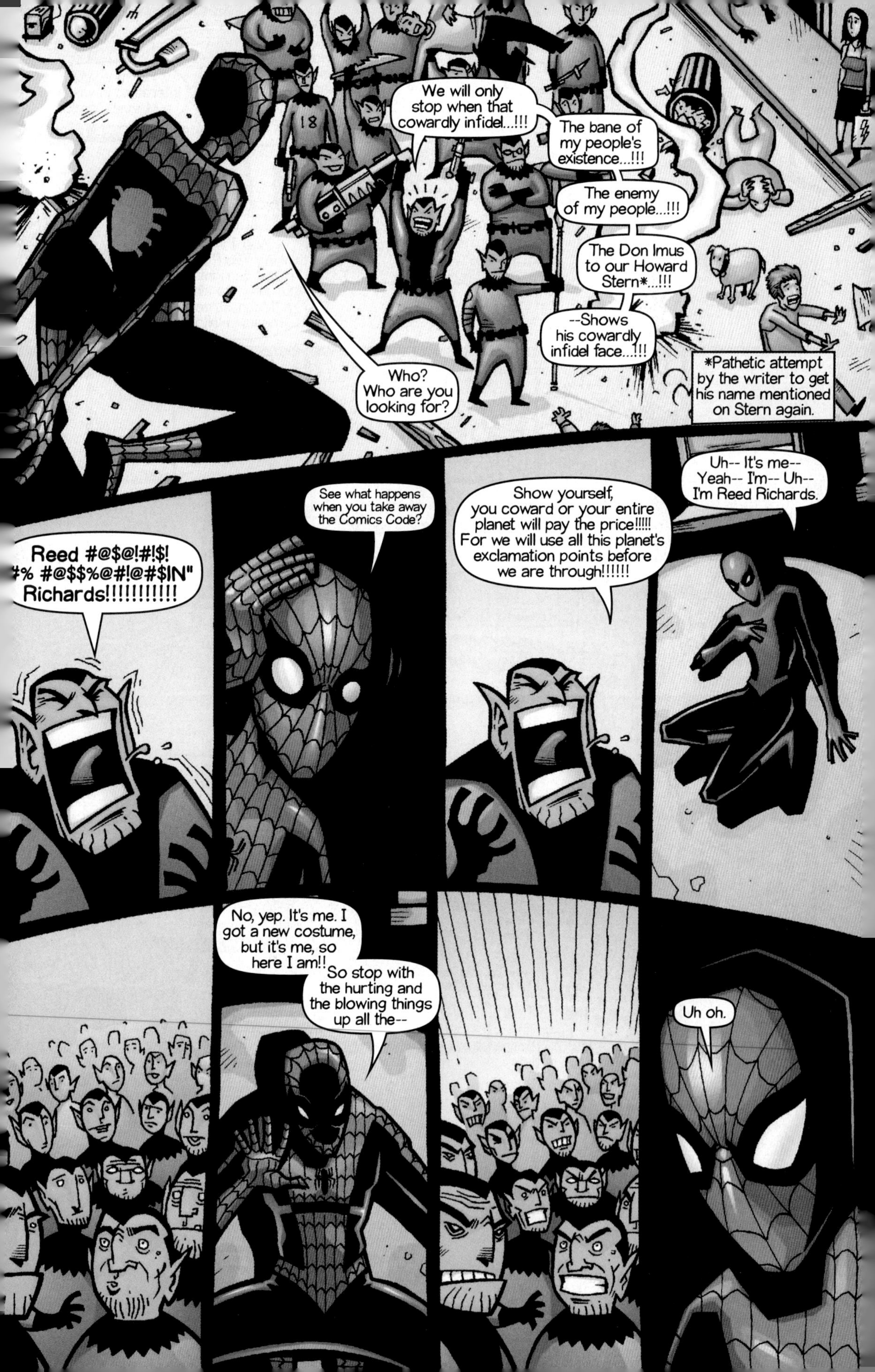
We will only stop when that cowardly infidel...!!!
The bane of my people's existence...!!!
The enemy of my people...!!!
The Don Imus to our Howard Stern*...!!!
--Shows his cowardly infidel face...!!!
Who? Who are you looking for?
*Pathetic attempt by the writer to get his name mentioned on Stern again.
Reed #@$@!#!$! #% #@$$%@#!@#$IN" Richards!!!!!!!!!!!
See what happens when you take away the Comics Code?
Show yourself, you coward or your entire planet will pay the price!!!!! For we will use all this planet's exclamation points before we are through!!!!!!
Uh-- It's me-- Yeah-- I'm-- Uh-- I'm Reed Richards.
No, yep. It's me. I got a new costume, but it's me, so here I am!!
So stop with the hurting and the blowing things up all the--
Uh oh.

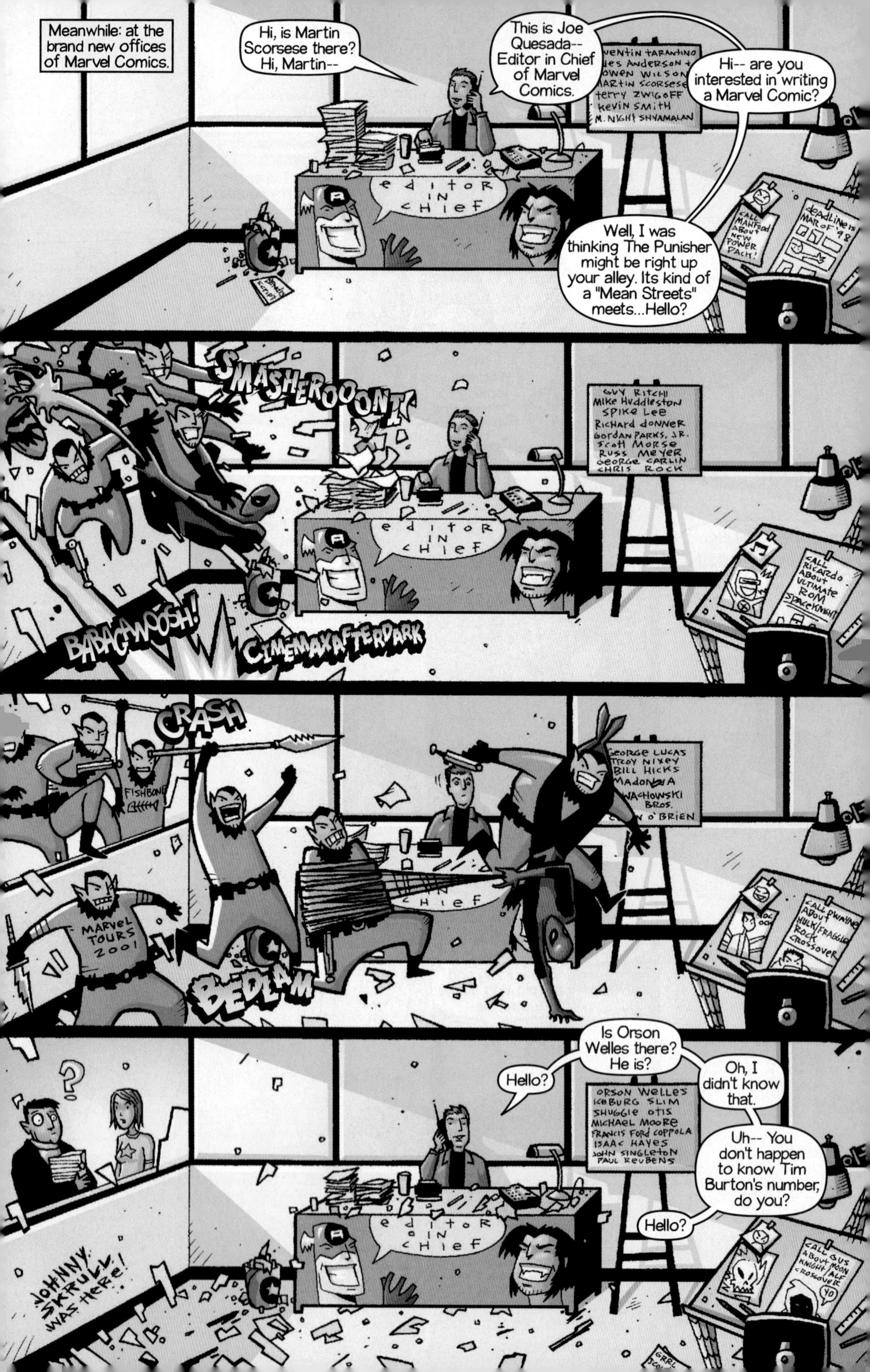

Meanwhile: at the brand new offices of Marvel Comics.
Hi, is Martin Scorsese there? Hi, Martin--
This is Joe Quesada-- Editor in Chief of Marvel Comics.
Hi-- are you interested in writing a Marvel Comic?
QUENTIN TARANTINO
WES ANDERSON + OWEN WILSON
MARTIN SCORSESE
TERRY ZWIGOFF
KEVIN SMITH
M. NIGHT SHYAMALAN
EDITOR IN CHIEF
CALL MAHFOOD ABOUT NEW POWER PACK!
DEADLINE IS MAR OF '98
Well, I was thinking The Punisher might be right up your alley. Its kind of a "Mean Streets" meets...Hello?
SMASHEROOOONI
GUY RITCHI
MIKE HUDDLESTON
SPIKE LEE
RICHARD DONNER
GORDAN PARKS, JR.
SCOTT MORSE
RUSS MEYER
GEORGE CARLIN
CHRIS ROCK
EDITOR IN CHIEF
CALL RICARDO ABOUT ULTIMATE ROM SPACEKNIGHT
BABACHWOOSH!
CINEMAXAFTERDARK
CRASH
GEORGE LUCAS
TROY NIXEY
BILL HICKS
MADONNA
WACHOWSKI BROS.
FISHBONE
MARVEL TOURS 2001
CHIEF
CALL DWAYNE ABOUT HULK/FRAGGLE ROCK CROSSOVER
BEDLAM
Hello?
Is Orson Welles there? He is?
Oh, I didn't know that.
ORSON WELLES
ICEBURG SLIM
SHUGGIE OTIS
MICHAEL MOORE
FRANCIS FORD COPPOLA
ISAAC HAYES
JOHN SINGLETON
PAUL REUBENS
Uh-- You don't happen to know Tim Burton's number, do you?
Hello?
EDITOR IN CHIEF
CALL GUS ABOUT MOON KNIGHT/ALF CROSSOVER
YO
JOHNNY SKRULL WAS HERE!

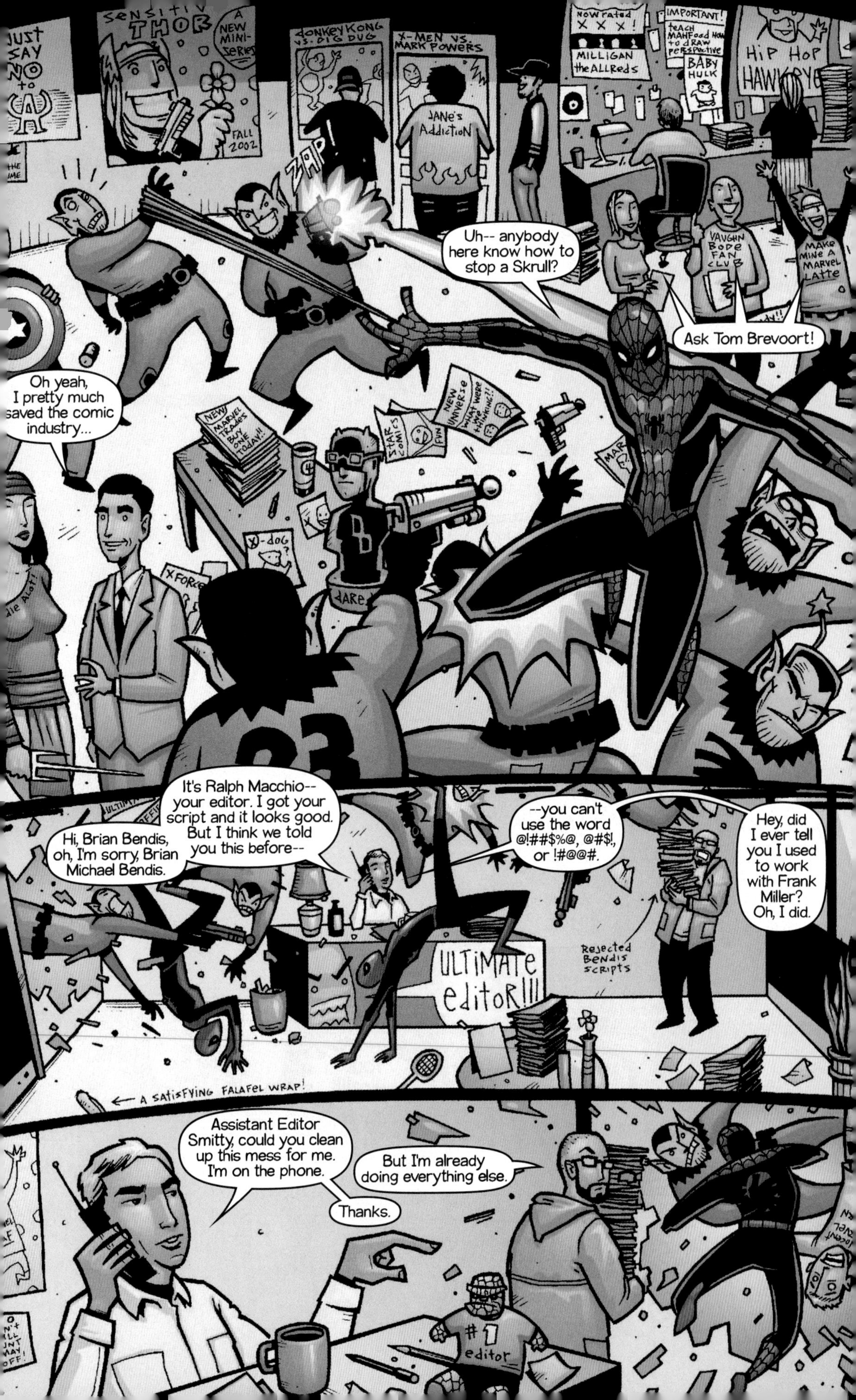
JUST SAY NO to
SENSITIV THOR
A NEW MINI-SERIES
FALL 2002
DONKEY KONG VS. DIG DUG
X-MEN VS. MARK POWERS
JANE'S Addiction
ZAP!
NOW rated XXX!
MILLIGAN the ALLREDS
IMPORTANT! teach MAHFood how to draw perspective
BABY HULK
HIP HOP HAWKEYE
Uh-- anybody here know how to stop a Skrull?
VAUGHN BODE FAN CLUB
MAKE MINE A MARVEL LATTE
Ask Tom Brevoort!
Oh yeah, I pretty much saved the comic industry...
NEW MARVEL TRADES BUY ONE TODAY!!
STAR COMICS
NEW UNIVERSE WHAT WERE WE THINKING?!
X-FORCE
X-DOG?
It's Ralph Macchio-- your editor. I got your script and it looks good. But I think we told you this before--
Hi, Brian Bendis, oh, I'm sorry, Brian Michael Bendis.
--you can't use the word @!##$%@, @#$!, or !#@@#.
Hey, did I ever tell you I used to work with Frank Miller? Oh, I did.
ULTIMATE editor!!!
Rejected Bendis scripts
A SATISFYING FALAFEL WRAP!
Assistant Editor Smitty, could you clean up this mess for me. I'm on the phone.
But I'm already doing everything else.
Thanks.
#1 editor

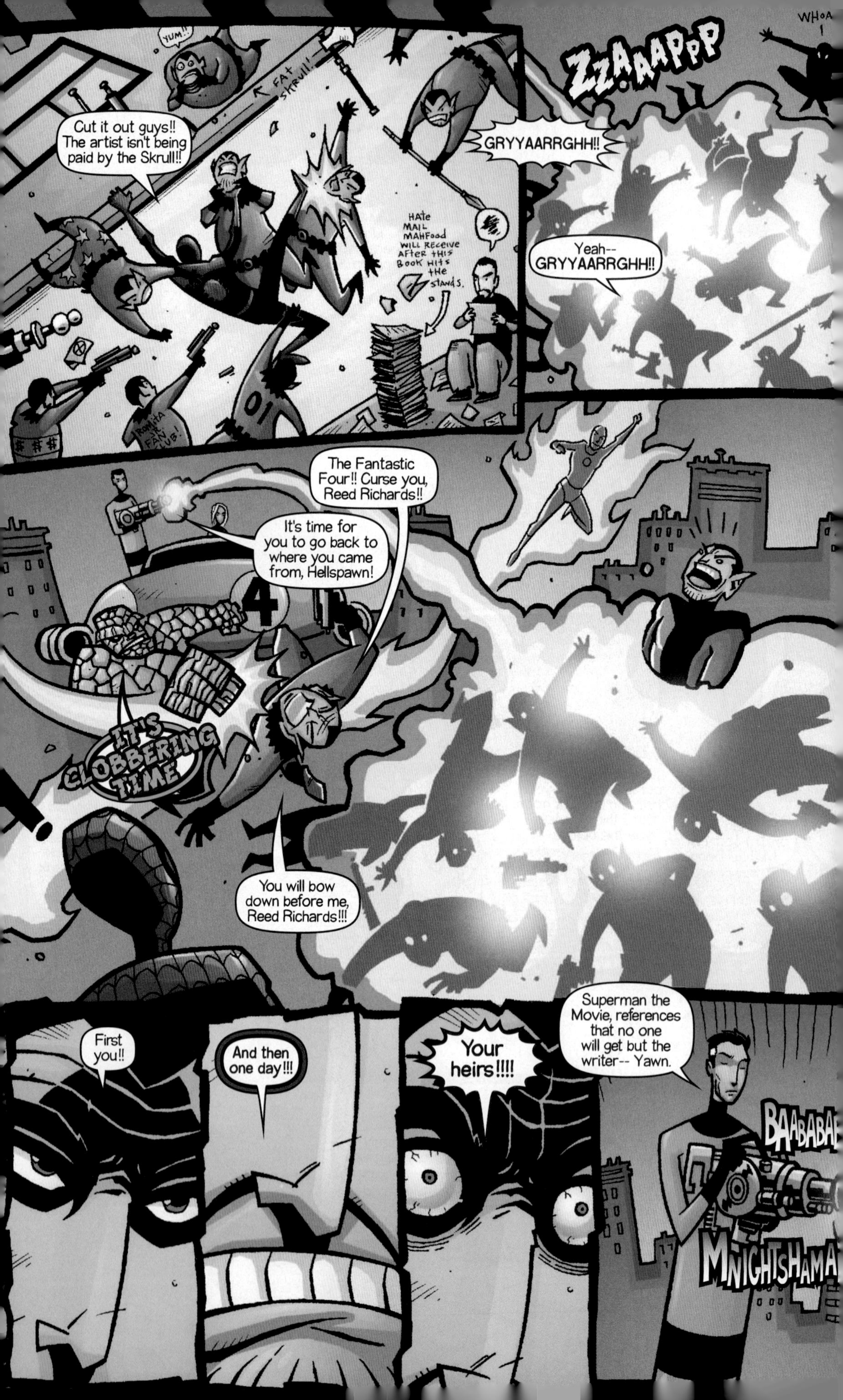

YUM!!
FAT SKRULL!
Cut it out guys!! The artist isn't being paid by the Skrull!!
GRYYAARRGHH!!
HATE MAIL MAHFood WILL RECEIVE AFTER THIS BOOK HITS THE STANDS.
ZZAAAPPP
WHOA!
Yeah-- GRYYAARRGHH!!
The Fantastic Four!! Curse you, Reed Richards!!
It's time for you to go back to where you came from, Hellspawn!
IT'S CLOBBERING TIME
You will bow down before me, Reed Richards!!!
First you!!
And then one day!!!
Your heirs!!!!
Superman the Movie, references that no one will get but the writer-- Yawn.
BAABABAB
MNIGHTSHAMA

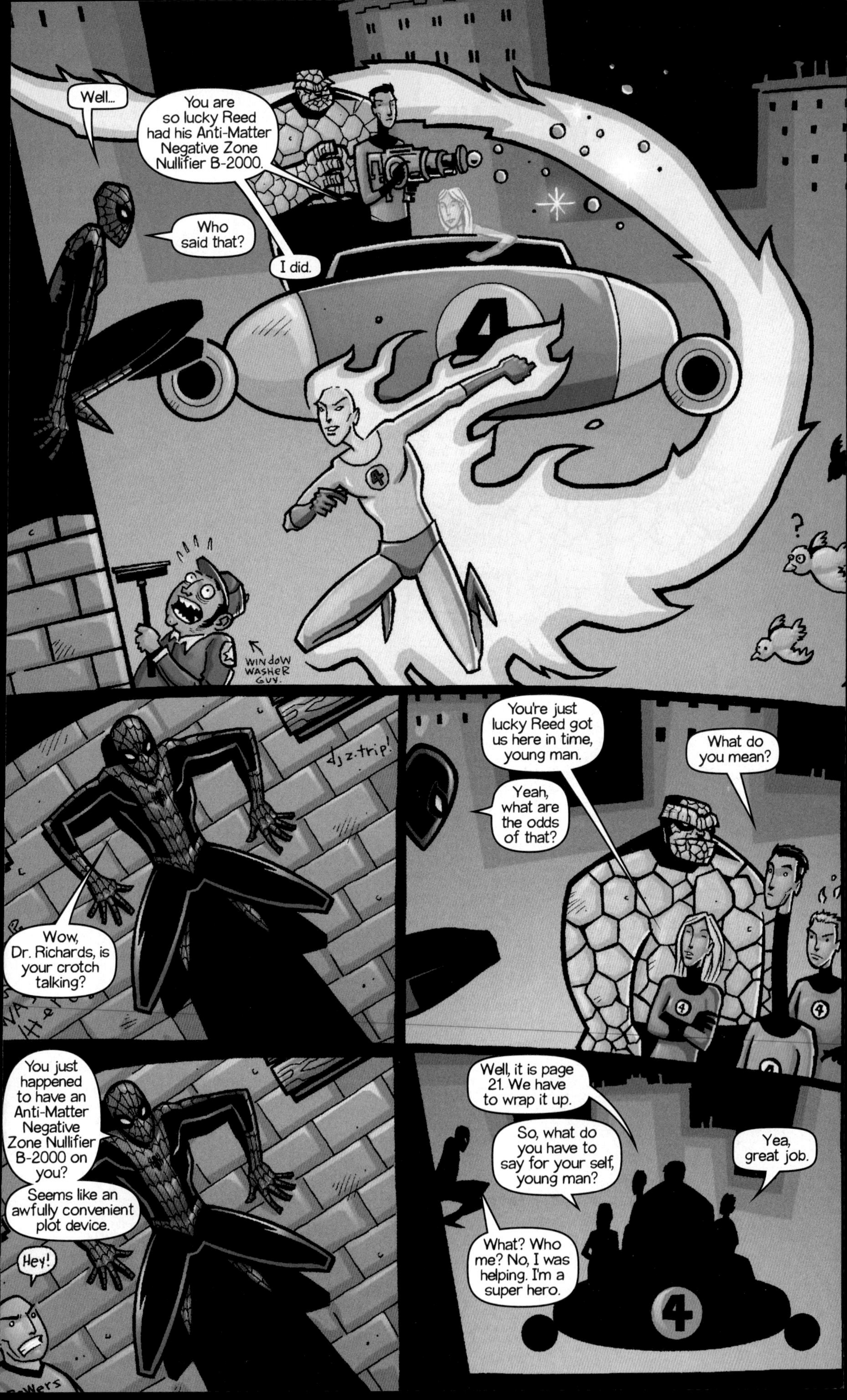
Well...
You are so lucky Reed had his Anti-Matter Negative Zone Nullifier B-2000.
Who said that?
I did.
WINDOW WASHER GUY.
Wow, Dr. Richards, is your crotch talking?
djz.trip!
You're just lucky Reed got us here in time, young man.
Yeah, what are the odds of that?
What do you mean?
You just happened to have an Anti-Matter Negative Zone Nullifier B-2000 on you?
Seems like an awfully convenient plot device.
Hey!
Well, it is page 21. We have to wrap it up.
So, what do you have to say for your self, young man?
Yea, great job.
What? Who me? No, I was helping. I'm a super hero.

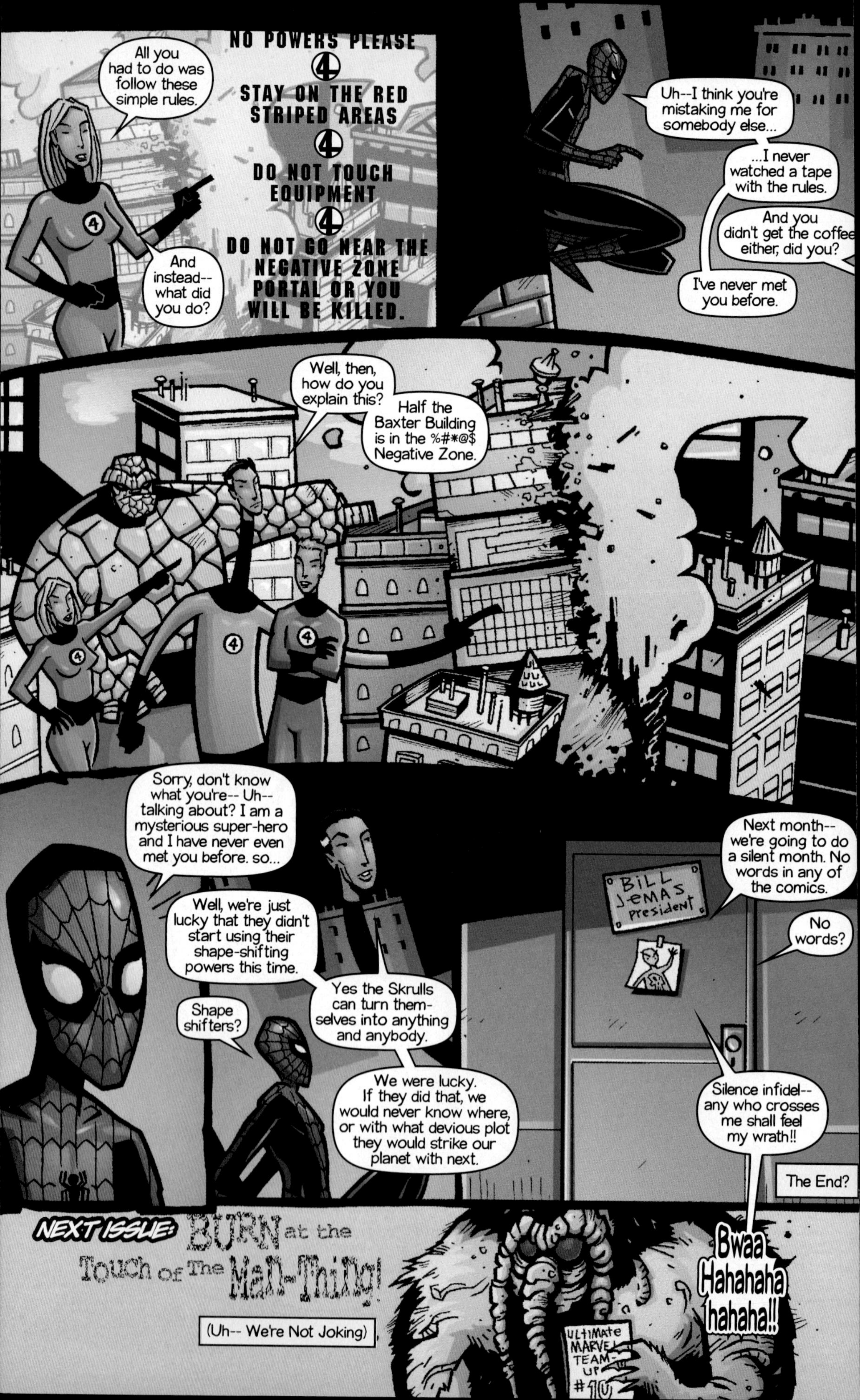
NO POWERS PLEASE
STAY ON THE RED STRIPED AREAS
DO NOT TOUCH EQUIPMENT
DO NOT GO NEAR THE NEGATIVE ZONE PORTAL OR YOU WILL BE KILLED.
All you had to do was follow these simple rules.
And instead-- what did you do?
Uh--I think you're mistaking me for somebody else...
...I never watched a tape with the rules.
And you didn't get the coffee either, did you?
I've never met you before.
Well, then, how do you explain this?
Half the Baxter Building is in the %#*@$ Negative Zone.
Sorry, don't know what you're-- Uh-- talking about? I am a mysterious super-hero and I have never even met you before. so...
Well, we're just lucky that they didn't start using their shape-shifting powers this time.
Shape shifters?
Yes the Skrulls can turn themselves into anything and anybody.
We were lucky. If they did that, we would never know where, or with what devious plot they would strike our planet with next.
BILL JEMAS President
Next month-- we're going to do a silent month. No words in any of the comics.
No words?
Silence infidel-- any who crosses me shall feel my wrath!!
The End?
Bwaa Hahahaha hahaha!!
NEXT ISSUE: BURN at the Touch of The Man-Thing!
(Uh-- We're Not Joking)
ULTIMATE MARVEL TEAM-UP #10

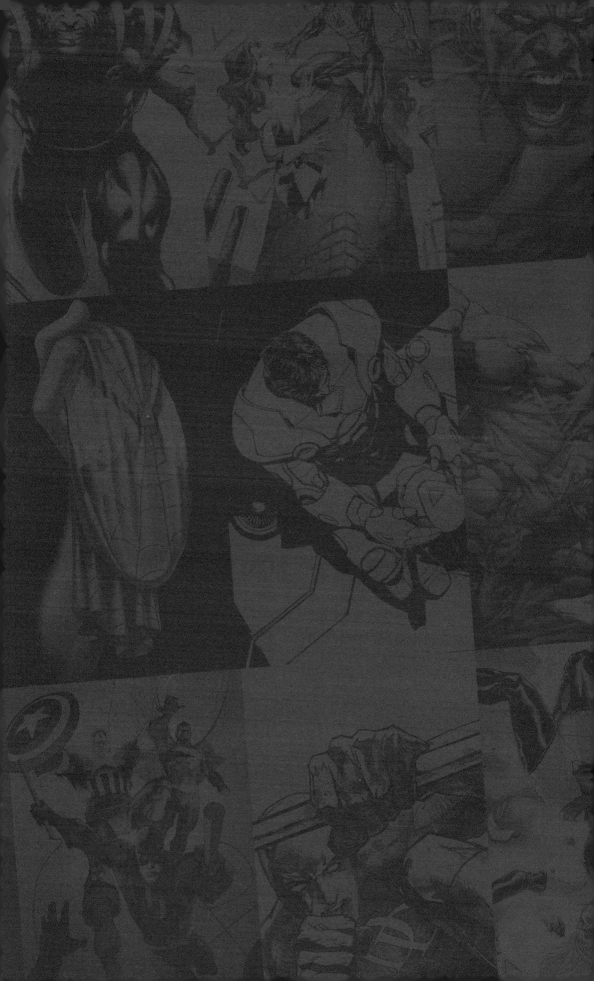

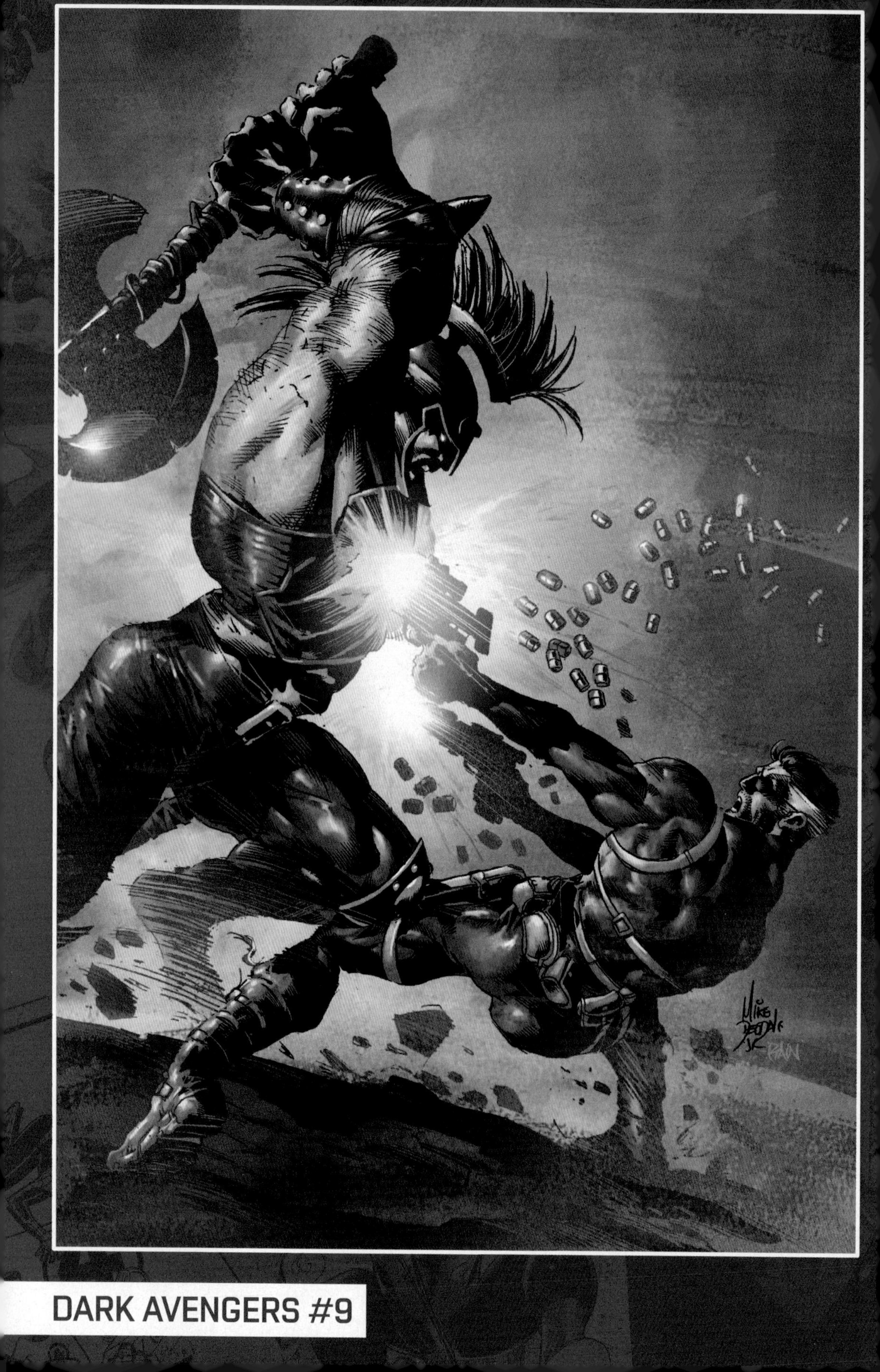

DARK AVENGERS #9

DARK AVENGERS

NORMAN OSBORN, FORMER THUNDERBOLTS LEADER, HAS RISEN TO POWER AND WAS APPOINTED TO REPLACE TONY STARK AS HEAD OF THE NATIONAL PEACEKEEPING TASK FORCE, H.A.M.M.E.R., WHICH INCLUDES HIS OWN TEAM OF AVENGERS.

THEY'RE A GATHERING OF CONTROVERSIAL FIGURES THAT NORMAN HAS GIVEN THE ICONIC LIKENESSES OF MANY OF THE FAMOUS AVENGERS, AS WELL AS THE SECRET IDENTITIES THAT GO WITH THEM. JOINING FORMER MIGHTY AVENGERS ARES AND SENTRY ARE THE ASSASSIN BULLSEYE, NOW HAWKEYE; REFORMED CRIMINAL MOONSTONE, NOW MS. MARVEL; WOLVERINE'S DISTURBED SON DAKEN, NOW WOLVERINE; VENOM HAS BEEN TRANSFORMED INTO A NEW SPIDER-MAN; KREE WARRIOR MARVEL BOY TOOK ON THE MANTLE OF CAPTAIN MARVEL; AND NORMAN UNVEILED HIS NEW IDENTITY...
THE IRON PATRIOT.

NORMAN IS ALSO TRYING TO HELP THE POWERFUL SENTRY DEAL WITH HIS DEMONS
WHILE HE CONTINUES TO DEAL WITH HIS OWN.

WITH NICK FURY OUT OF POWER, NORMAN HAS TAKEN OVER AS TOP COP OF THE WORLD. FURY HAS GONE UNDERGROUND AND ASSEMBLED A GROUP OF TEENAGE SECRET WARRIORS INCLUDING ARES' SON ALEX AKA PHOBOS THE GOD OF FEAR.

BRIAN MICHAEL BENDIS – WRITER   MIKE DEODATO – ART
RAIN BEREDO – COLOR ART   VC'S CORY PETIT – LETTERER
DEODATO AND BEREDO – COVER ART   LAUREN SANKOVITCH – ASSOCIATE EDITOR
TOM BREVOORT – EDITOR   JOE QUESADA – EDITOR IN CHIEF
DAN BUCKLEY – PUBLISHER   ALAN FINE – EXECUTIVE PRODUCER

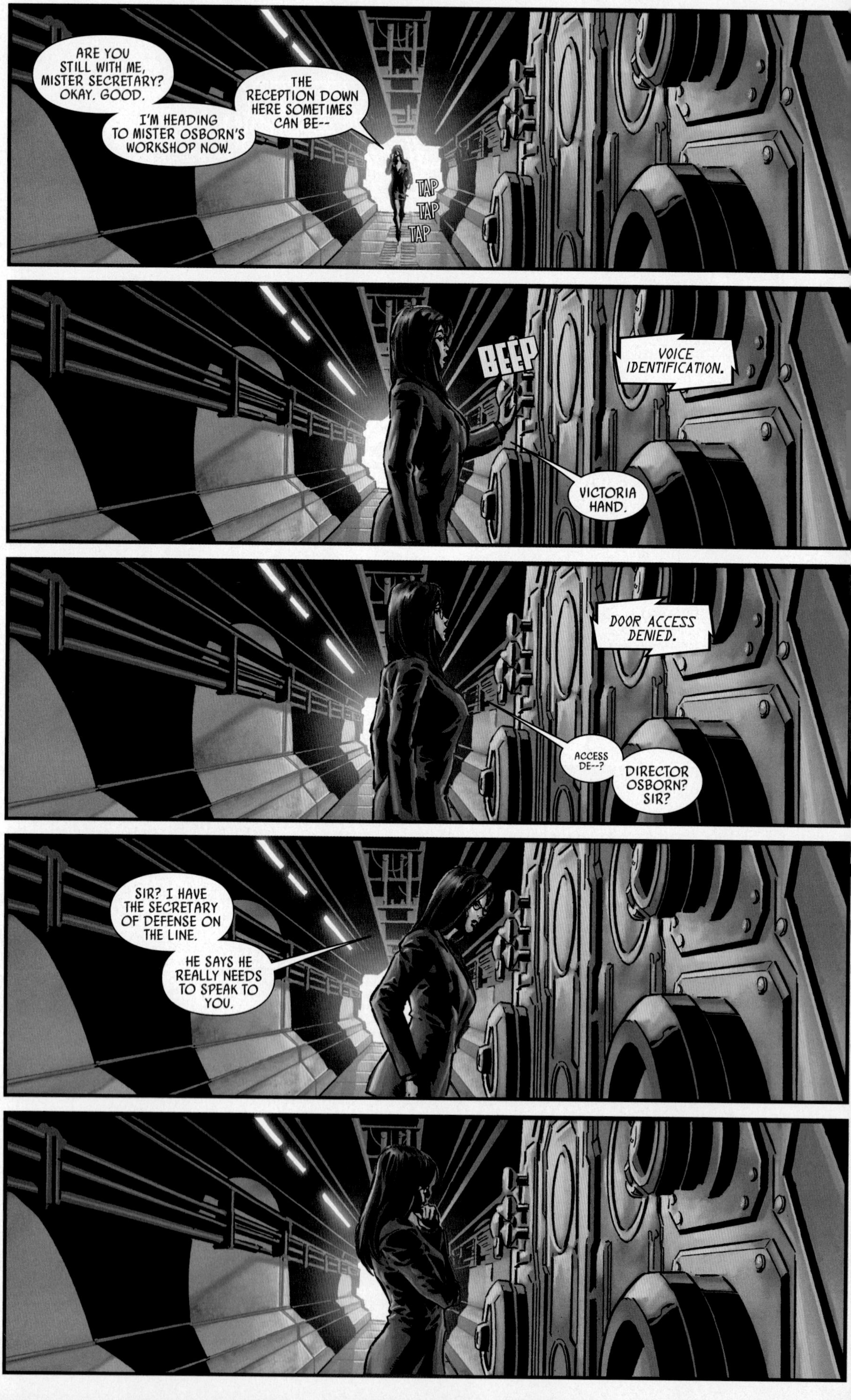
ARE YOU STILL WITH ME, MISTER SECRETARY? OKAY. GOOD.
I'M HEADING TO MISTER OSBORN'S WORKSHOP NOW.
THE RECEPTION DOWN HERE SOMETIMES CAN BE--
TAP
TAP
TAP
BEEP
VOICE IDENTIFICATION.
VICTORIA HAND.
DOOR ACCESS DENIED.
ACCESS DE--?
DIRECTOR OSBORN? SIR?
SIR? I HAVE THE SECRETARY OF DEFENSE ON THE LINE.
HE SAYS HE REALLY NEEDS TO SPEAK TO YOU.

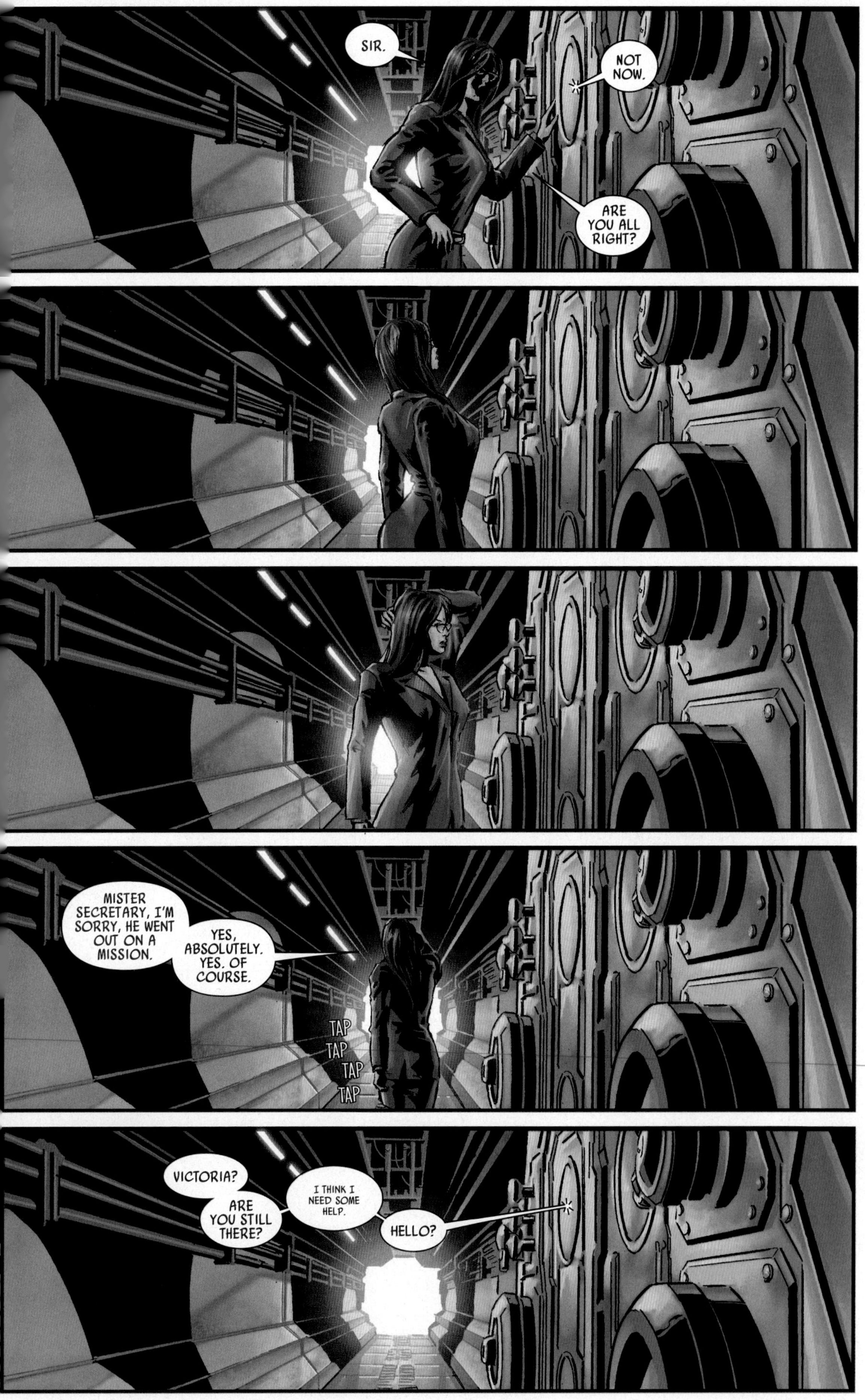
SIR.
NOT NOW.
ARE YOU ALL RIGHT?
MISTER SECRETARY, I'M SORRY, HE WENT OUT ON A MISSION.
YES, ABSOLUTELY. YES. OF COURSE.
TAP
TAP
TAP
TAP
VICTORIA?
ARE YOU STILL THERE?
I THINK I NEED SOME HELP.
HELLO?

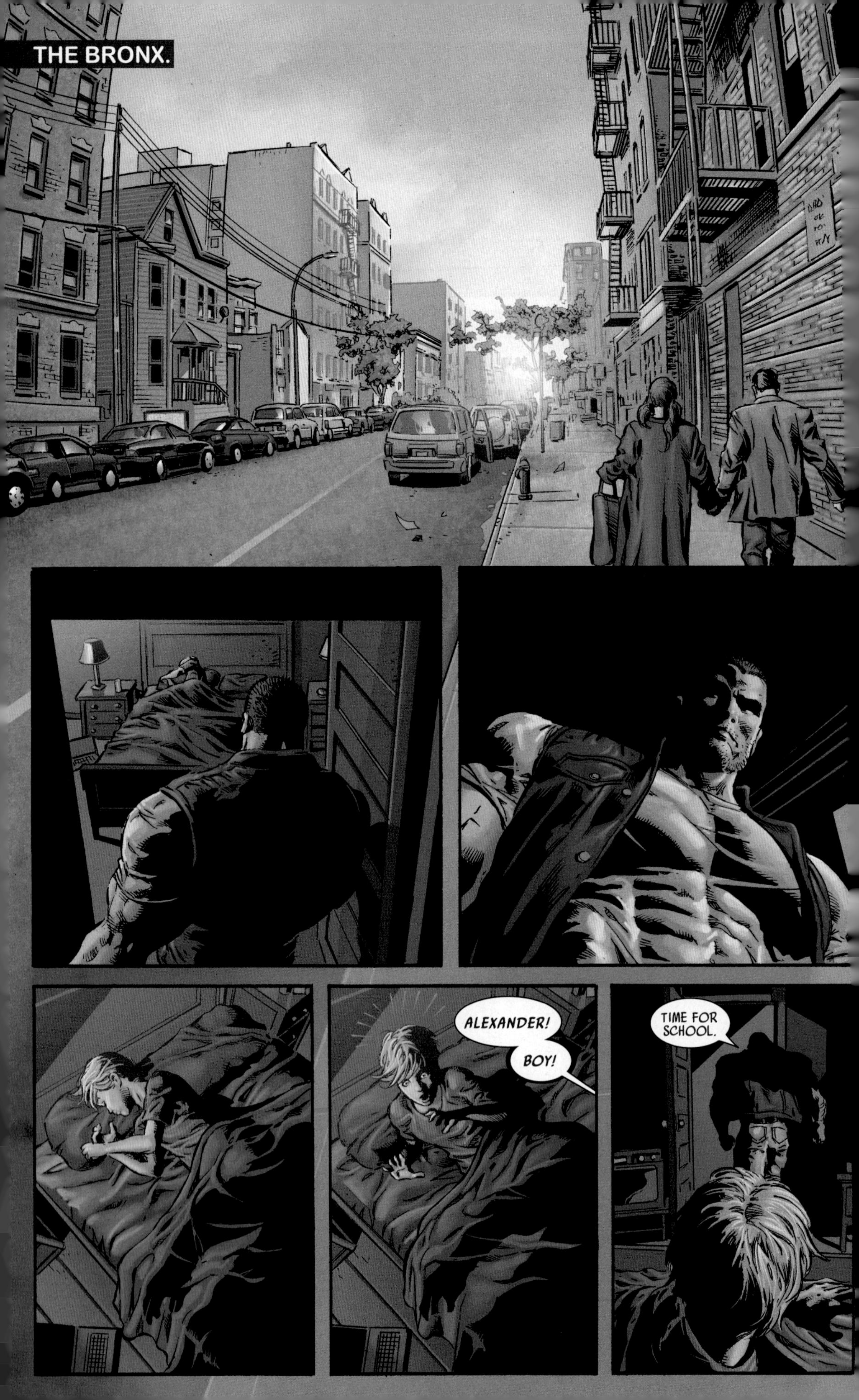
THE BRONX.
ALEXANDER!
BOY!
TIME FOR SCHOOL.

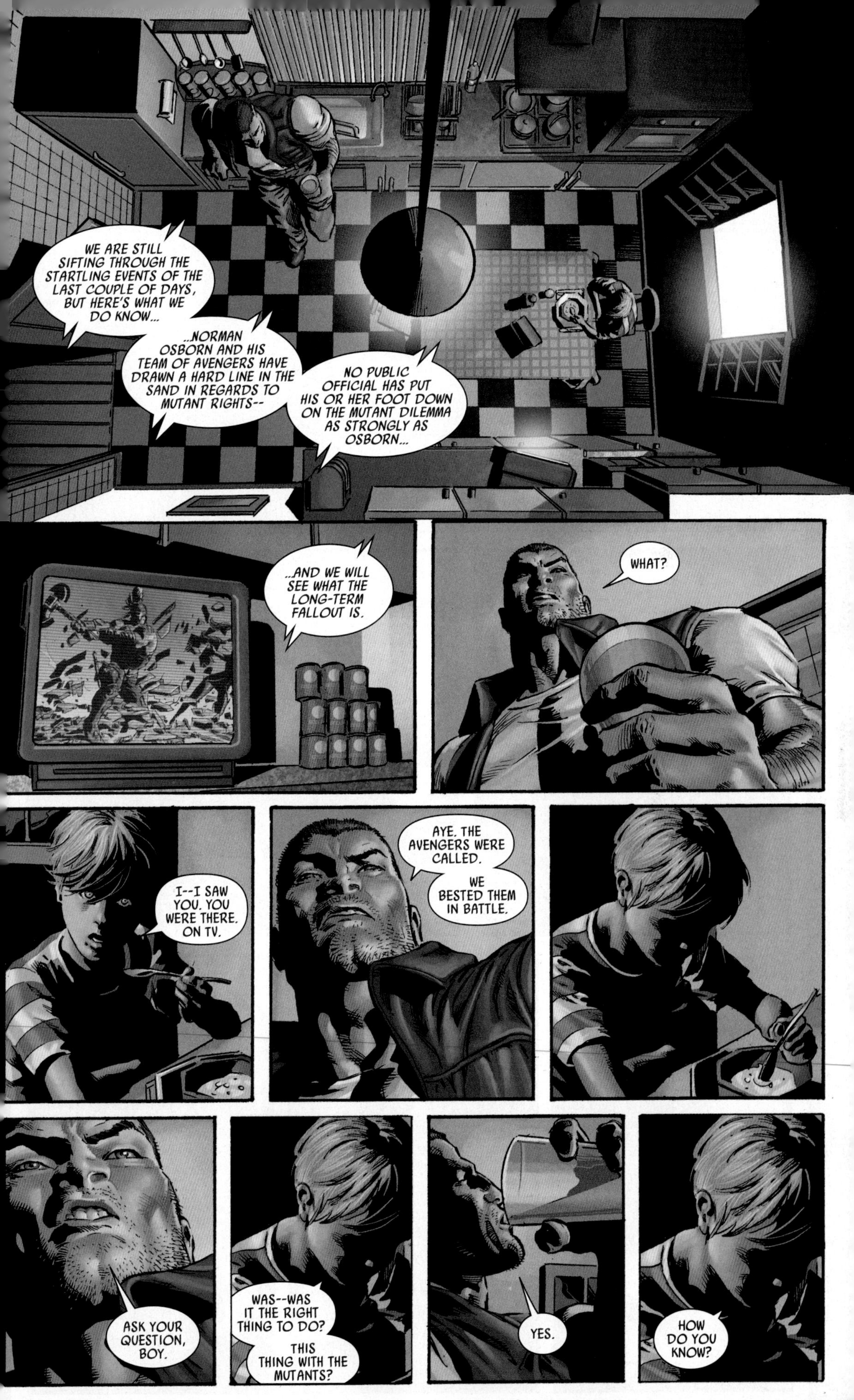
WE ARE STILL SIFTING THROUGH THE STARTLING EVENTS OF THE LAST COUPLE OF DAYS, BUT HERE'S WHAT WE DO KNOW...
...NORMAN OSBORN AND HIS TEAM OF AVENGERS HAVE DRAWN A HARD LINE IN THE SAND IN REGARDS TO MUTANT RIGHTS--
NO PUBLIC OFFICIAL HAS PUT HIS OR HER FOOT DOWN ON THE MUTANT DILEMMA AS STRONGLY AS OSBORN...
...AND WE WILL SEE WHAT THE LONG-TERM FALLOUT IS.
WHAT?
I--I SAW YOU. YOU WERE THERE. ON TV.
AYE. THE AVENGERS WERE CALLED.
WE BESTED THEM IN BATTLE.
ASK YOUR QUESTION, BOY.
WAS--WAS IT THE RIGHT THING TO DO?
THIS THING WITH THE MUTANTS?
YES.
HOW DO YOU KNOW?

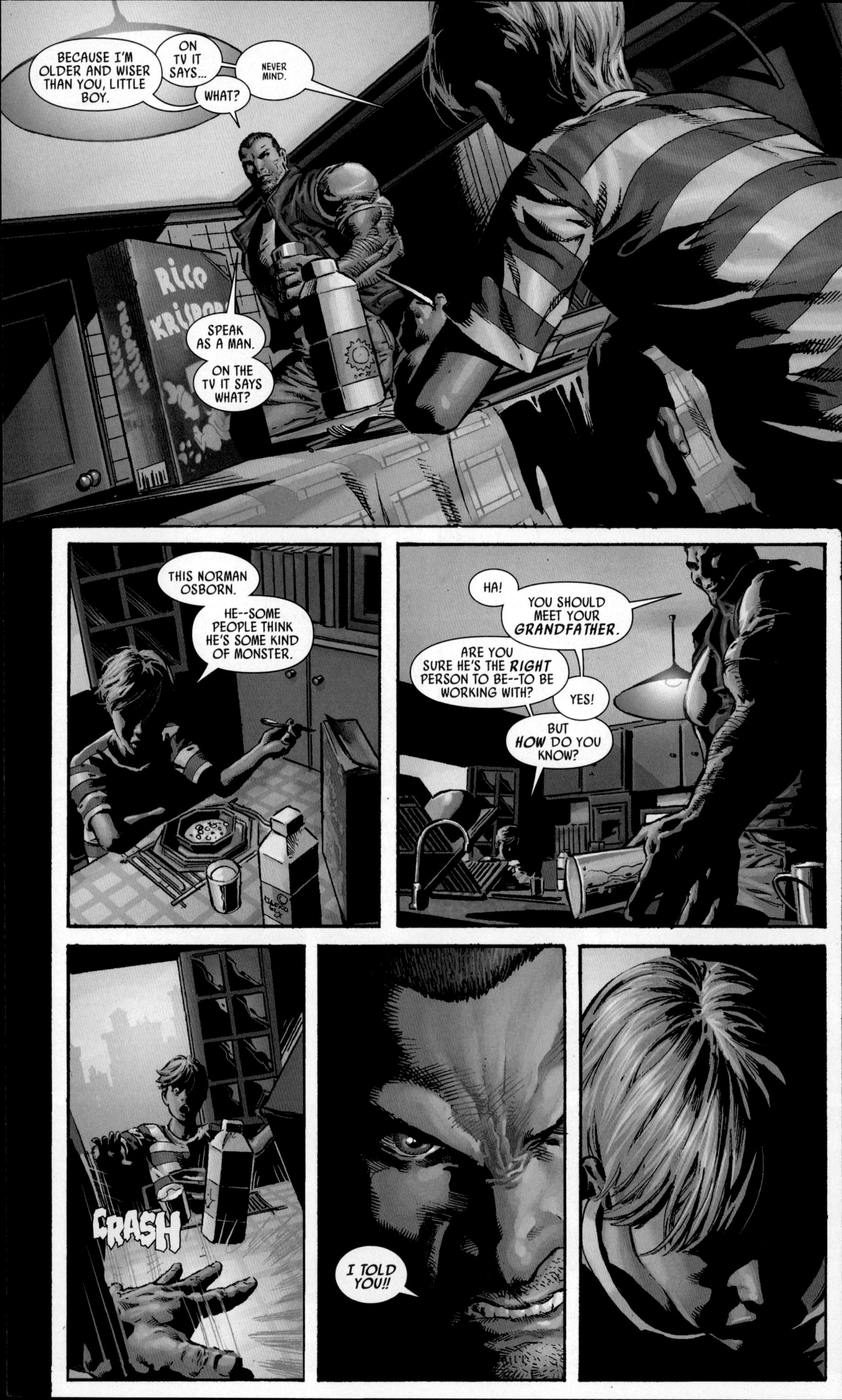
BECAUSE I'M OLDER AND WISER THAN YOU, LITTLE BOY.
ON TV IT SAYS...
WHAT?
NEVER MIND.
SPEAK AS A MAN.
ON THE TV IT SAYS WHAT?
THIS NORMAN OSBORN.
HE--SOME PEOPLE THINK HE'S SOME KIND OF MONSTER.
HA!
YOU SHOULD MEET YOUR GRANDFATHER.
ARE YOU SURE HE'S THE RIGHT PERSON TO BE--TO BE WORKING WITH?
YES!
BUT HOW DO YOU KNOW?
CRASH
I TOLD YOU!!

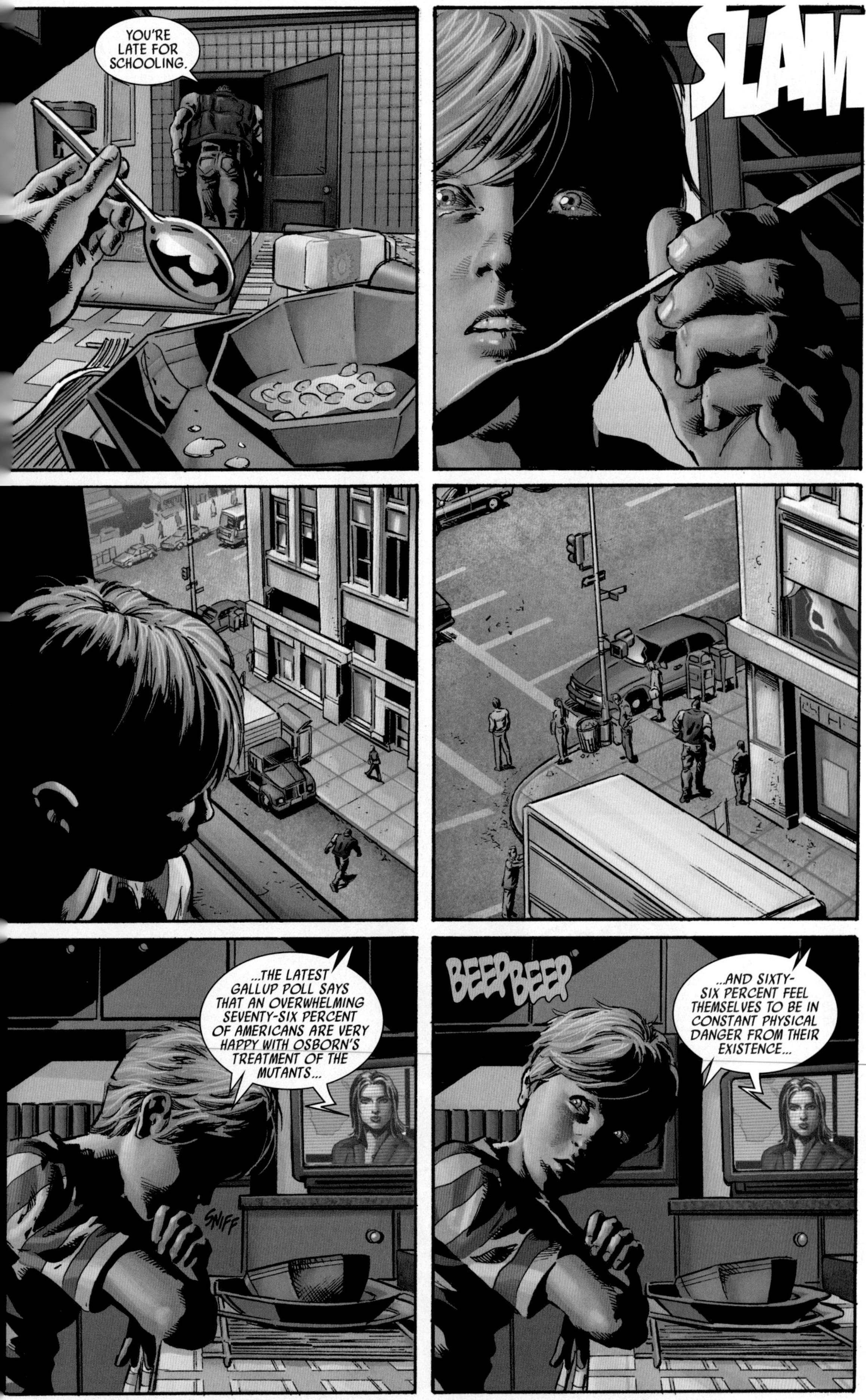
YOU'RE LATE FOR SCHOOLING.
SLAM
...THE LATEST GALLUP POLL SAYS THAT AN OVERWHELMING SEVENTY-SIX PERCENT OF AMERICANS ARE VERY HAPPY WITH OSBORN'S TREATMENT OF THE MUTANTS...
SNIFF
BEEPBEEP
...AND SIXTY-SIX PERCENT FEEL THEMSELVES TO BE IN CONSTANT PHYSICAL DANGER FROM THEIR EXISTENCE...

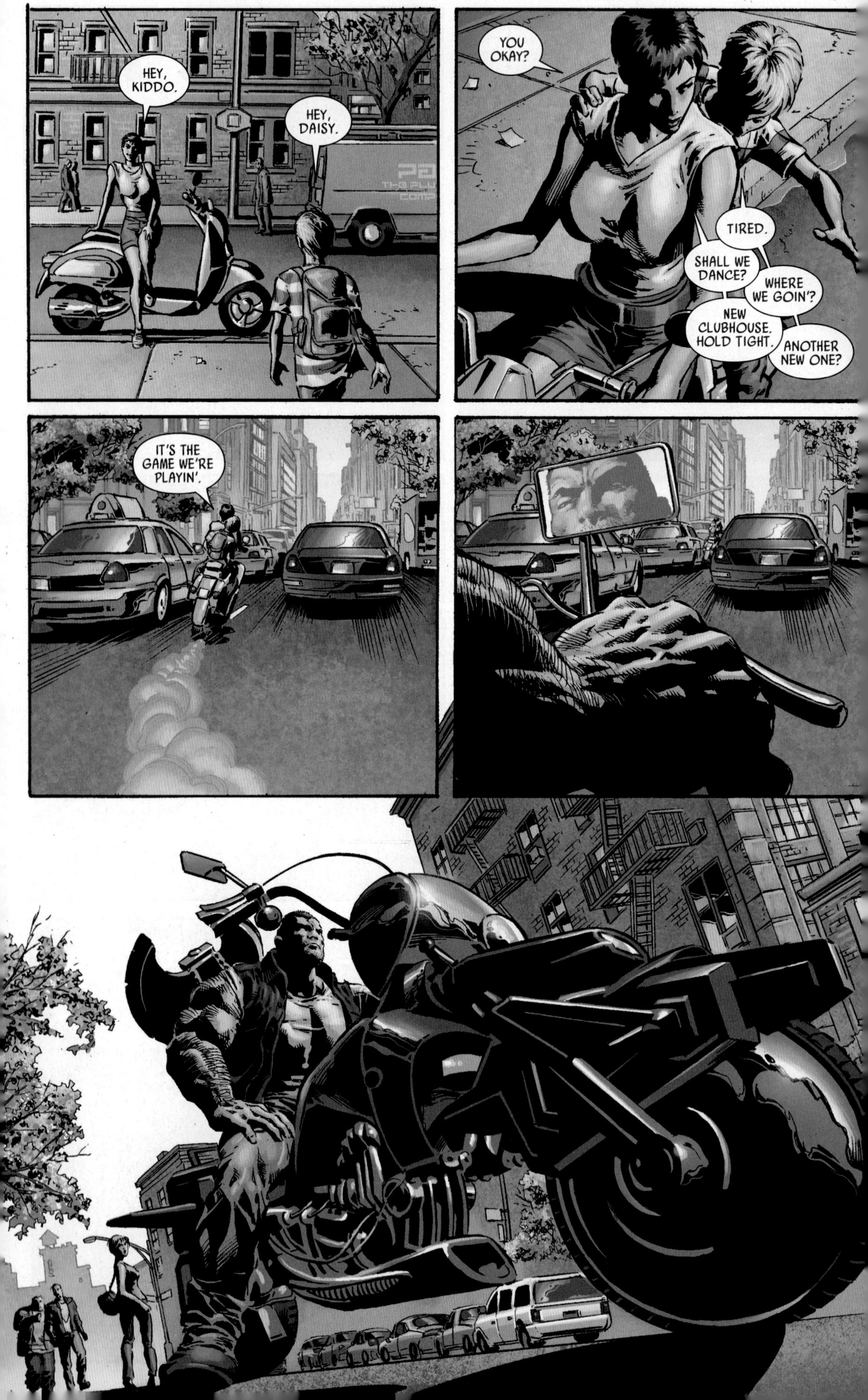
HEY, KIDDO.
HEY, DAISY.
YOU OKAY?
TIRED.
SHALL WE DANCE?
WHERE WE GOIN'?
NEW CLUBHOUSE. HOLD TIGHT.
ANOTHER NEW ONE?
IT'S THE GAME WE'RE PLAYIN'.

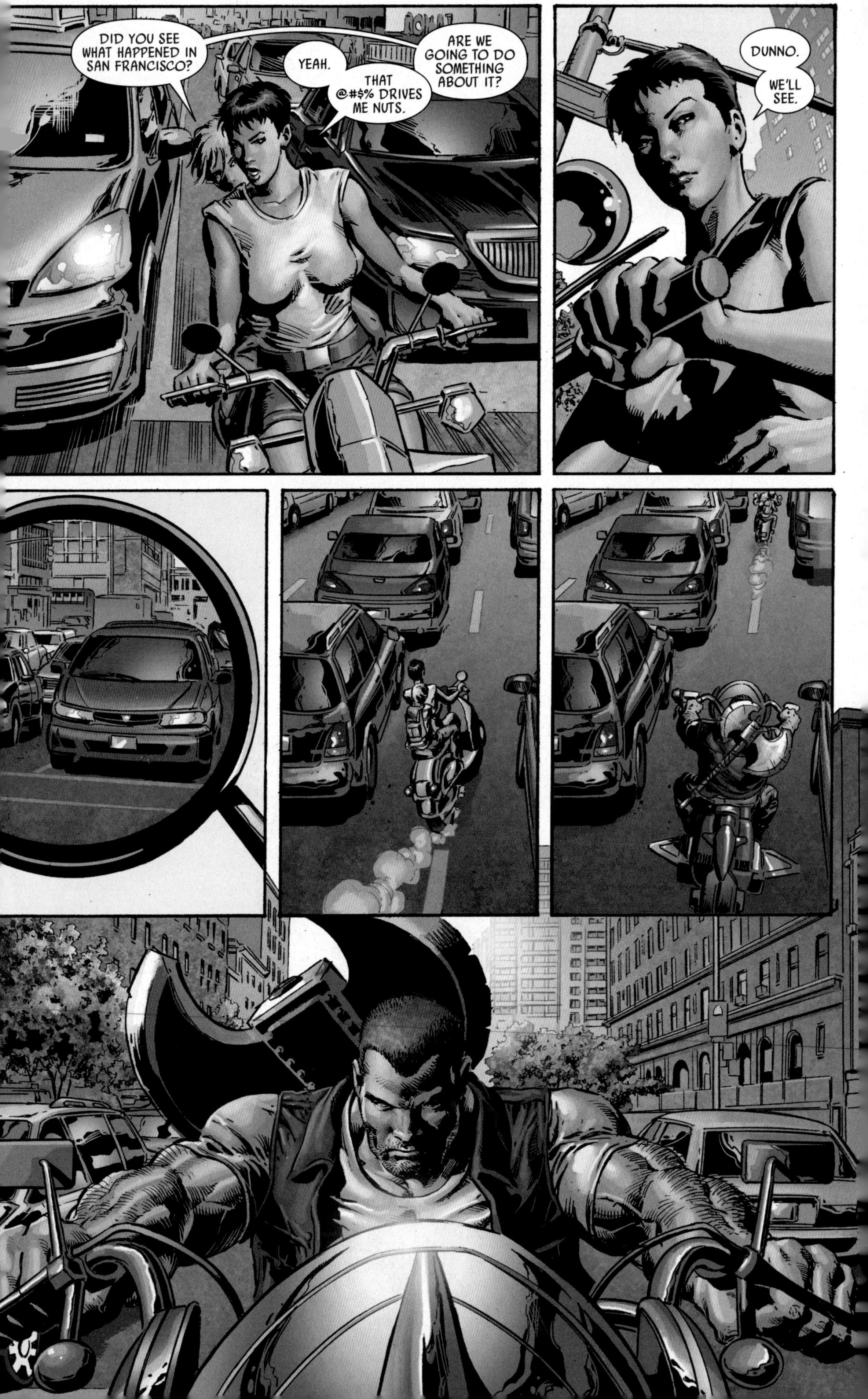
DID YOU SEE WHAT HAPPENED IN SAN FRANCISCO?
YEAH.
THAT @#$% DRIVES ME NUTS.
ARE WE GOING TO DO SOMETHING ABOUT IT?
DUNNO.
WE'LL SEE.

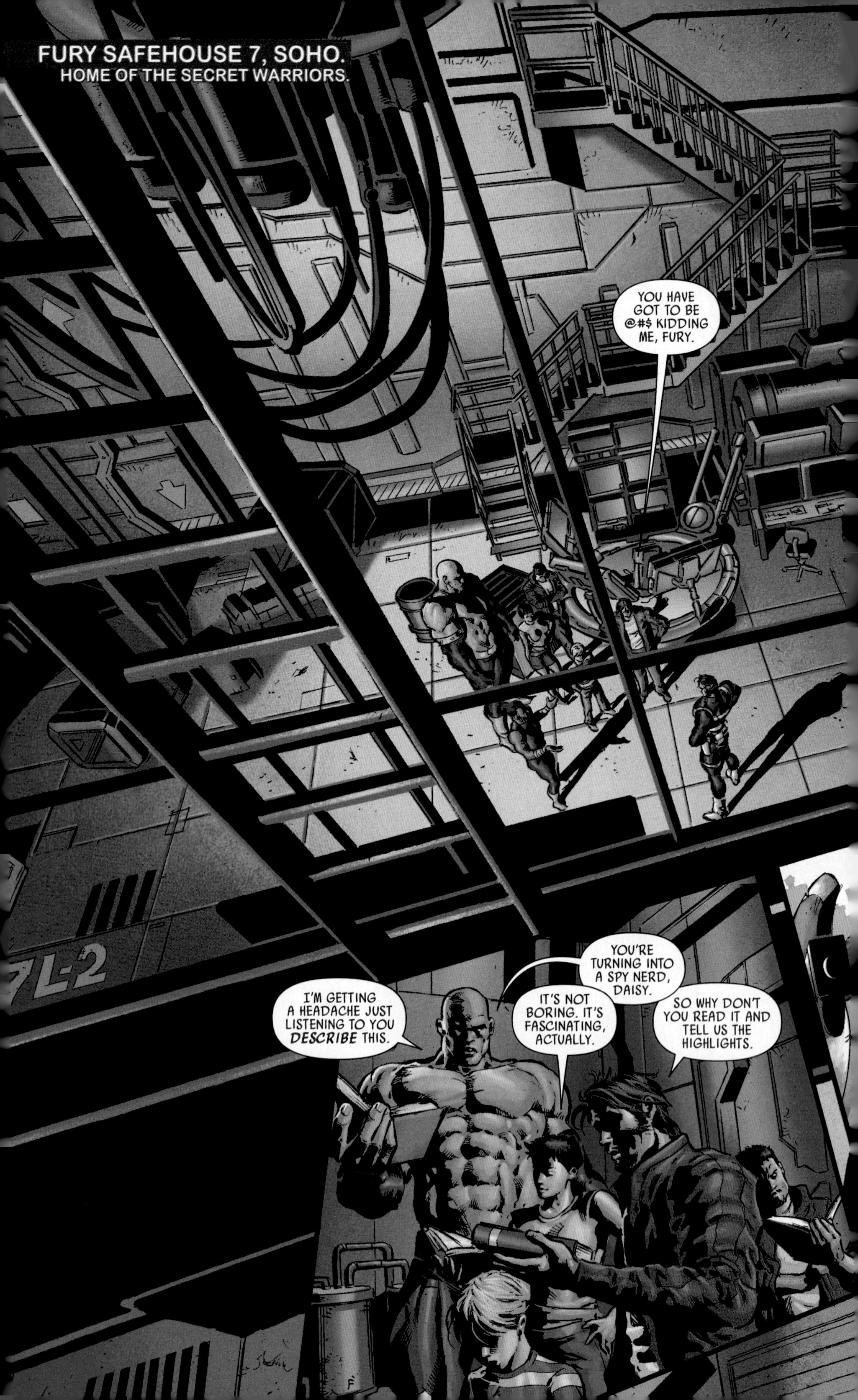
FURY SAFEHOUSE 7, SOHO.
HOME OF THE SECRET WARRIORS.
YOU HAVE GOT TO BE @#$ KIDDING ME, FURY.
7L-2
I'M GETTING A HEADACHE JUST LISTENING TO YOU *DESCRIBE* THIS.
IT'S NOT BORING. IT'S FASCINATING, ACTUALLY.
YOU'RE TURNING INTO A SPY NERD, DAISY.
SO WHY DON'T YOU READ IT AND TELL US THE HIGHLIGHTS.

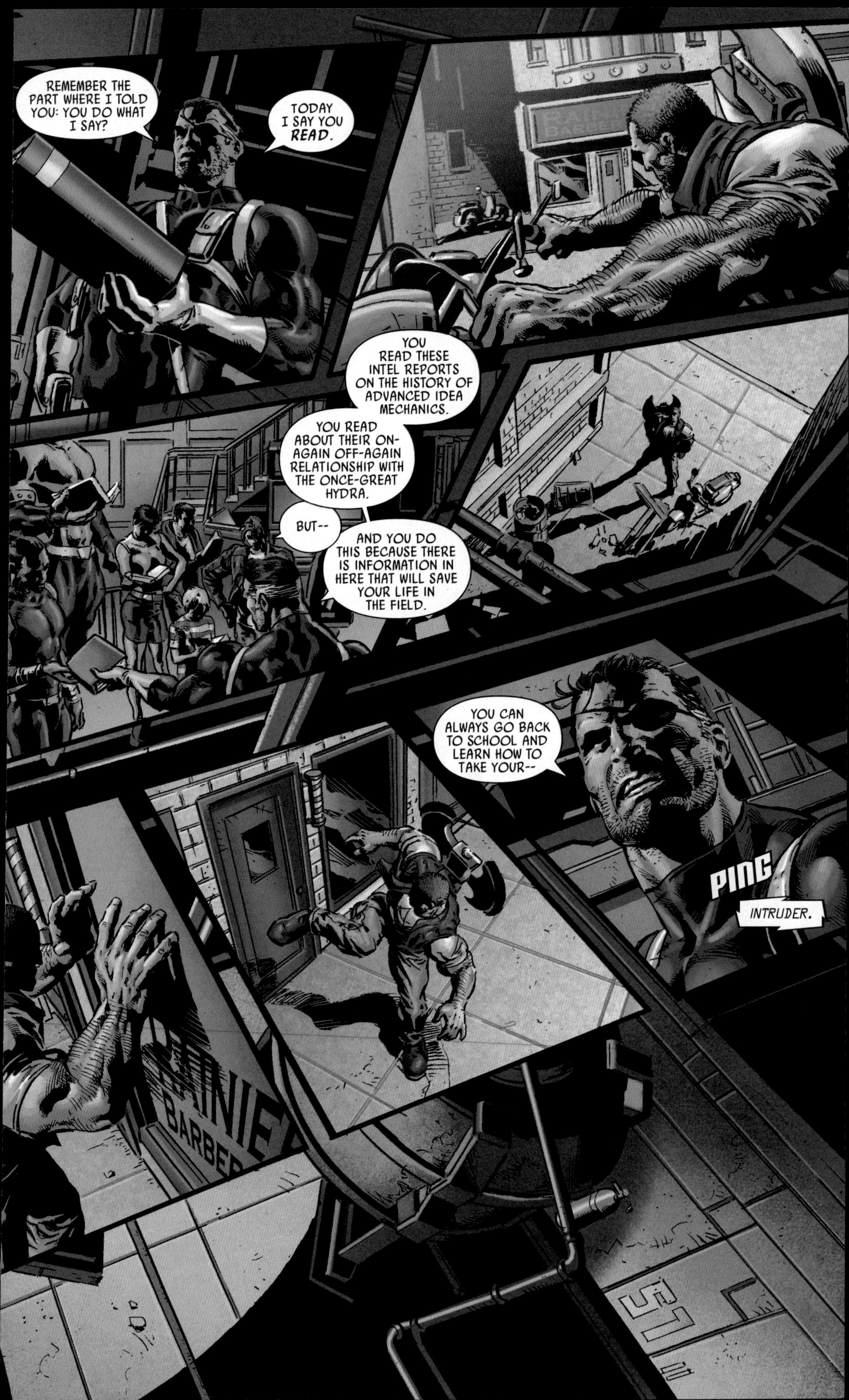
REMEMBER THE PART WHERE I TOLD YOU: YOU DO WHAT I SAY?
TODAY I SAY YOU READ.
YOU READ THESE INTEL REPORTS ON THE HISTORY OF ADVANCED IDEA MECHANICS.
YOU READ ABOUT THEIR ON-AGAIN OFF-AGAIN RELATIONSHIP WITH THE ONCE-GREAT HYDRA.
BUT--
AND YOU DO THIS BECAUSE THERE IS INFORMATION IN HERE THAT WILL SAVE YOUR LIFE IN THE FIELD.
YOU CAN ALWAYS GO BACK TO SCHOOL AND LEARN HOW TO TAKE YOUR--
PING
INTRUDER.

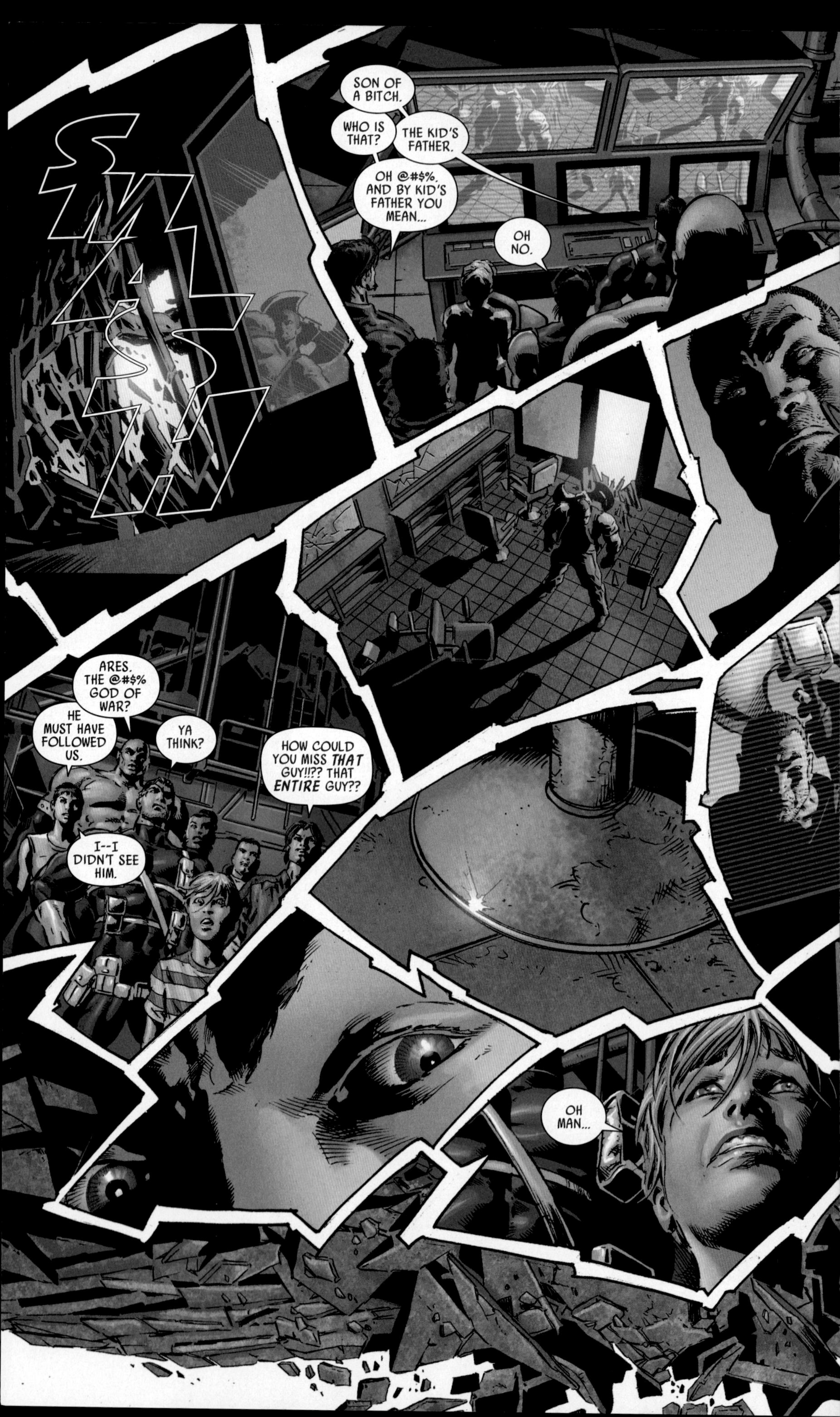
SON OF A BITCH.
WHO IS THAT?
THE KID'S FATHER.
OH @#$%. AND BY KID'S FATHER YOU MEAN...
OH NO.
ARES. THE @#$% GOD OF WAR?
HE MUST HAVE FOLLOWED US.
YA THINK?
HOW COULD YOU MISS *THAT* GUY!!?? THAT *ENTIRE* GUY??
I--I DIDN'T SEE HIM.
OH MAN...

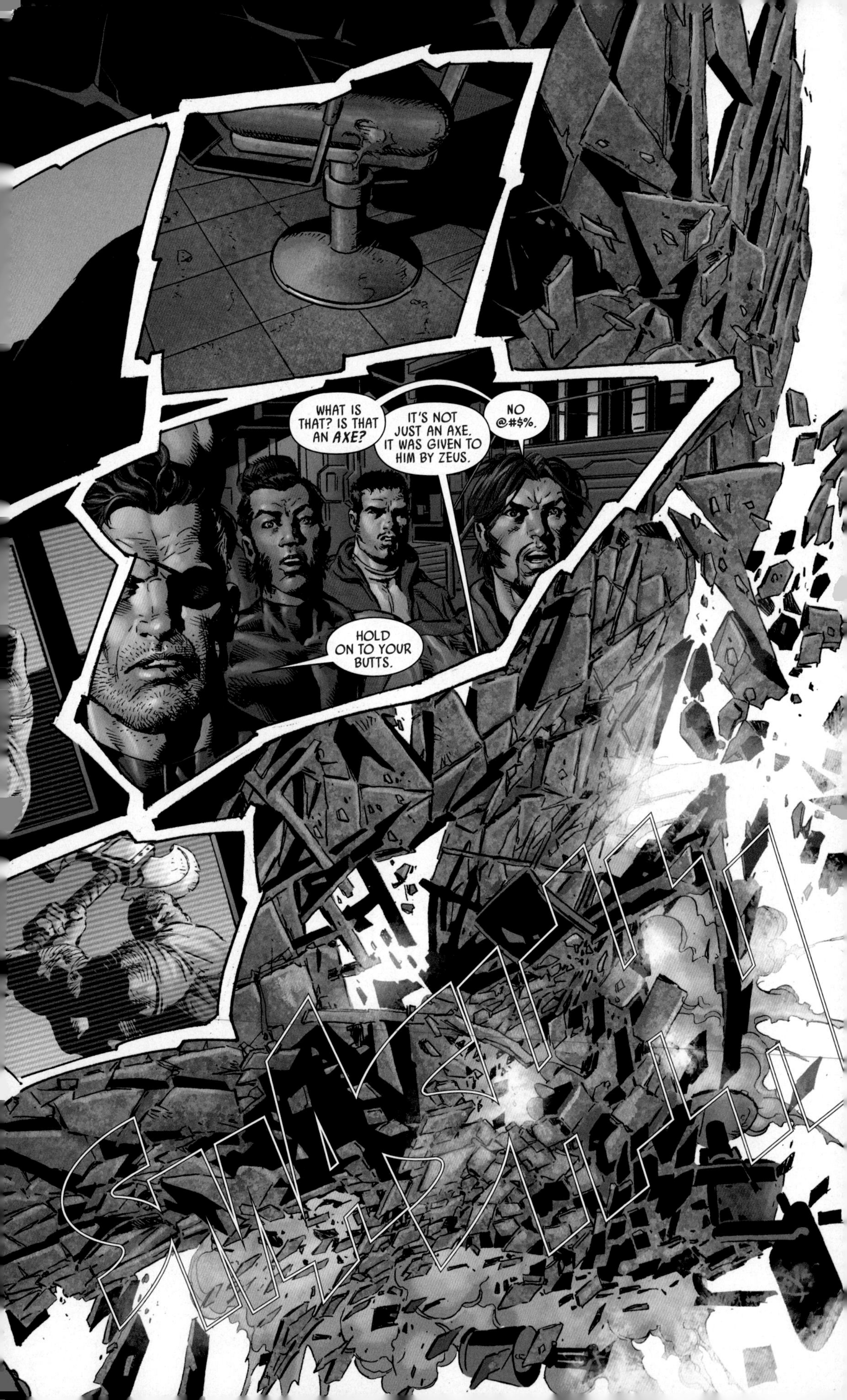
WHAT IS THAT? IS THAT AN AXE?
IT'S NOT JUST AN AXE. IT WAS GIVEN TO HIM BY ZEUS.
NO @#$%.
HOLD ON TO YOUR BUTTS.

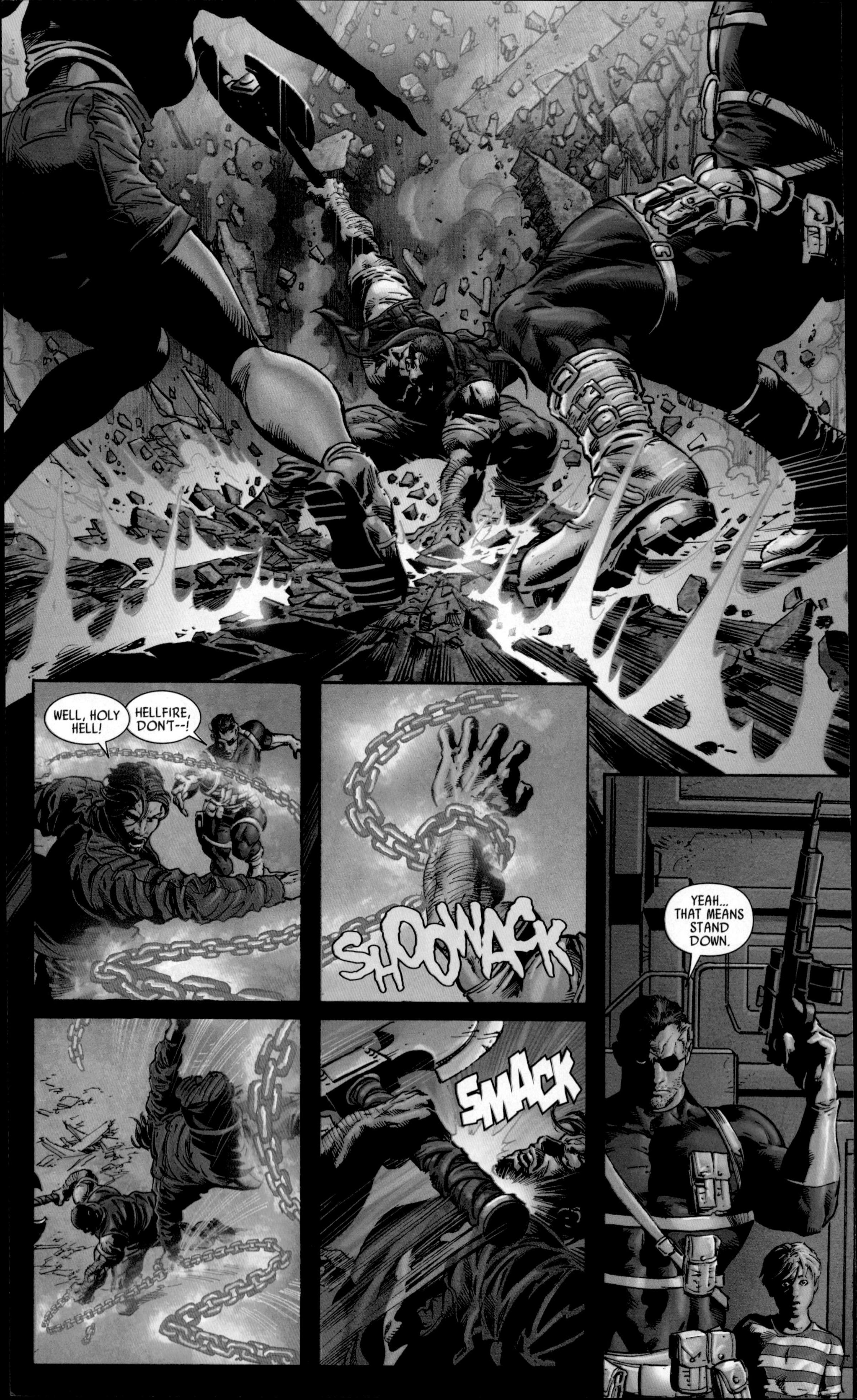
WELL, HOLY HELL!
HELLFIRE, DON'T--!
SHOOWACK
SMACK
YEAH... THAT MEANS STAND DOWN.

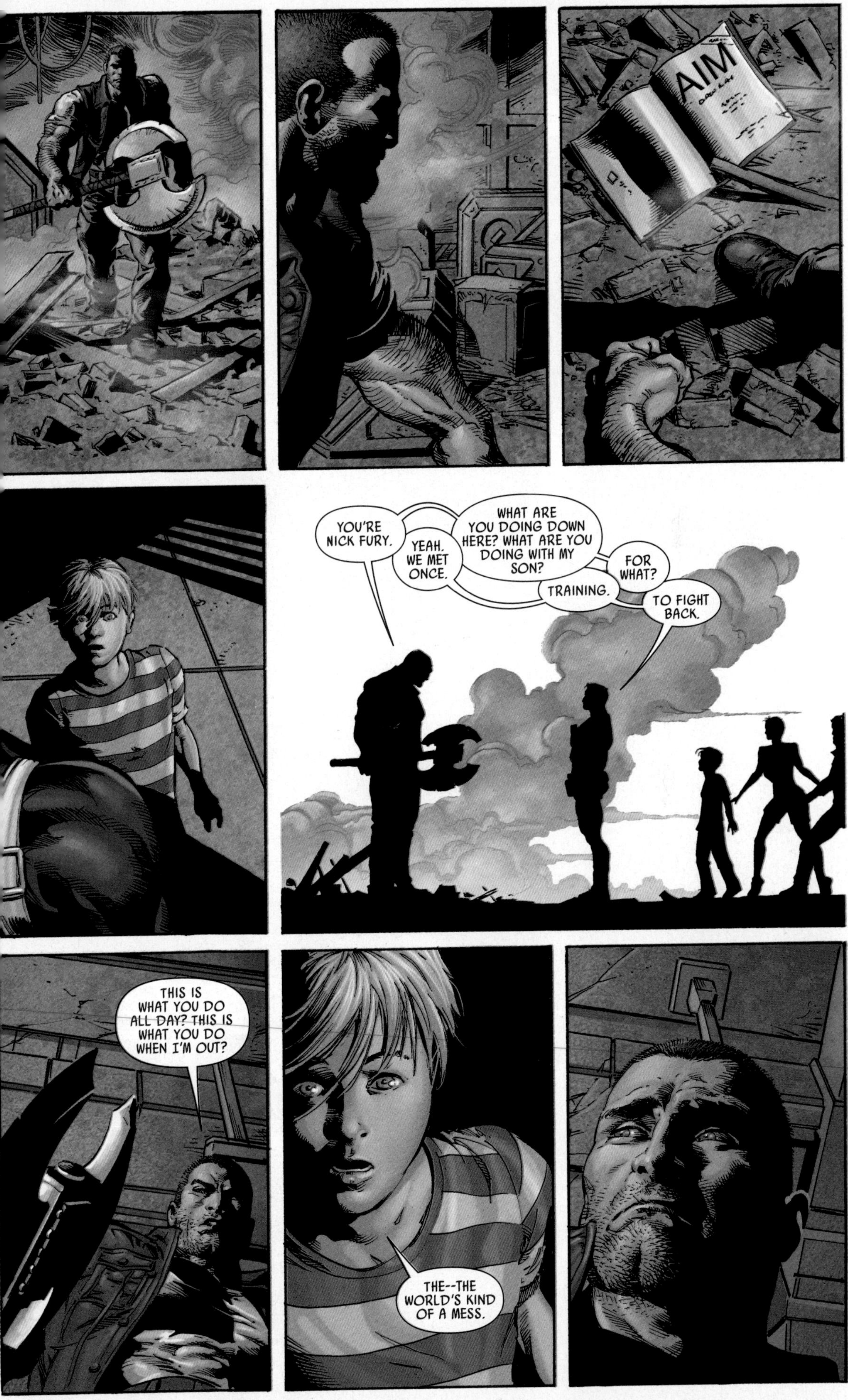
YOU'RE NICK FURY.
YEAH. WE MET ONCE.
WHAT ARE YOU DOING DOWN HERE? WHAT ARE YOU DOING WITH MY SON?
TRAINING.
FOR WHAT?
TO FIGHT BACK.
THIS IS WHAT YOU DO ALL DAY? THIS IS WHAT YOU DO WHEN I'M OUT?
THE--THE WORLD'S KIND OF A MESS.

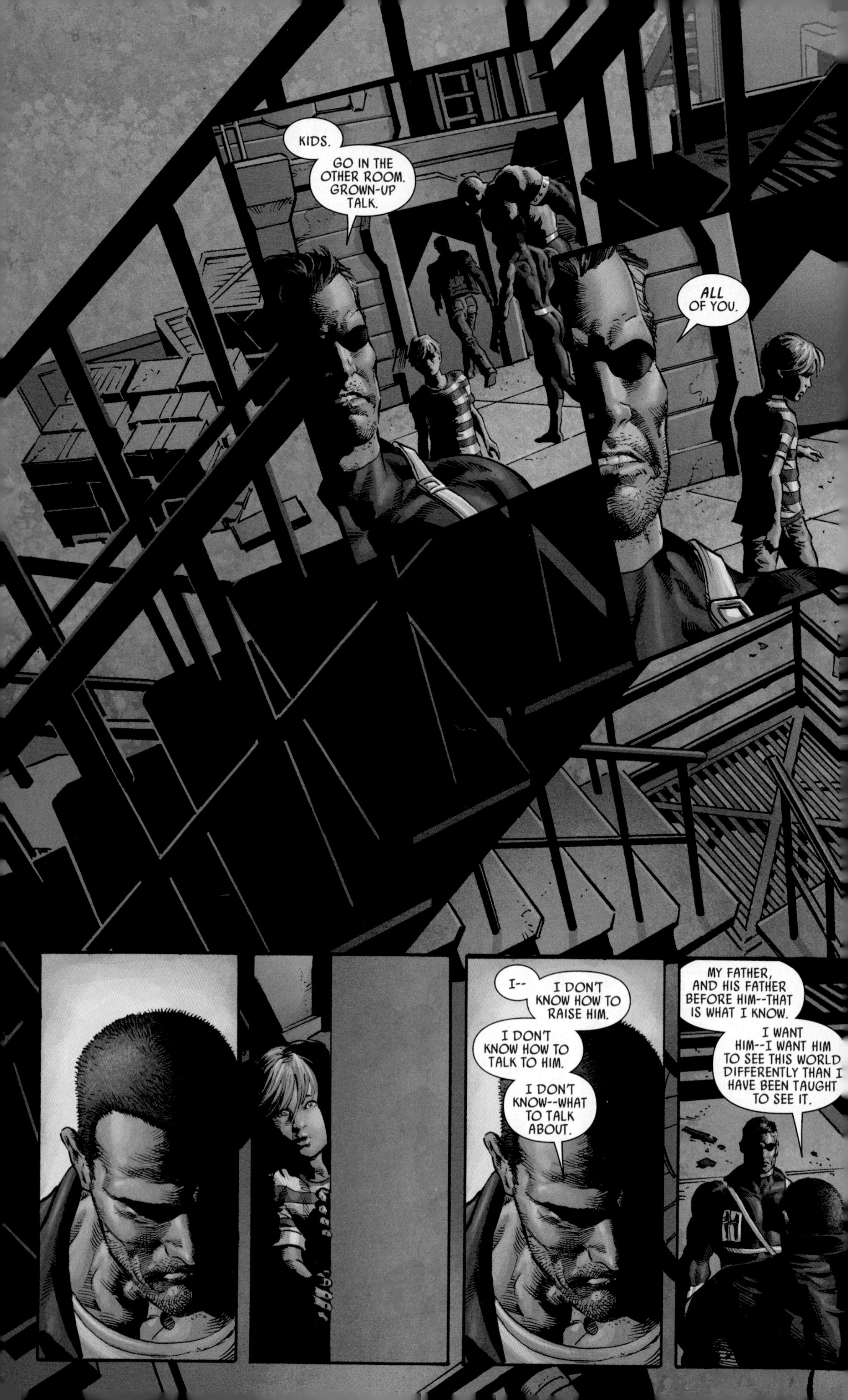
KIDS.
GO IN THE OTHER ROOM. GROWN-UP TALK.
ALL OF YOU.
I--
I DON'T KNOW HOW TO RAISE HIM.
I DON'T KNOW HOW TO TALK TO HIM.
I DON'T KNOW--WHAT TO TALK ABOUT.
MY FATHER, AND HIS FATHER BEFORE HIM--THAT IS WHAT I KNOW.
I WANT HIM--I WANT HIM TO SEE THIS WORLD DIFFERENTLY THAN I HAVE BEEN TAUGHT TO SEE IT.

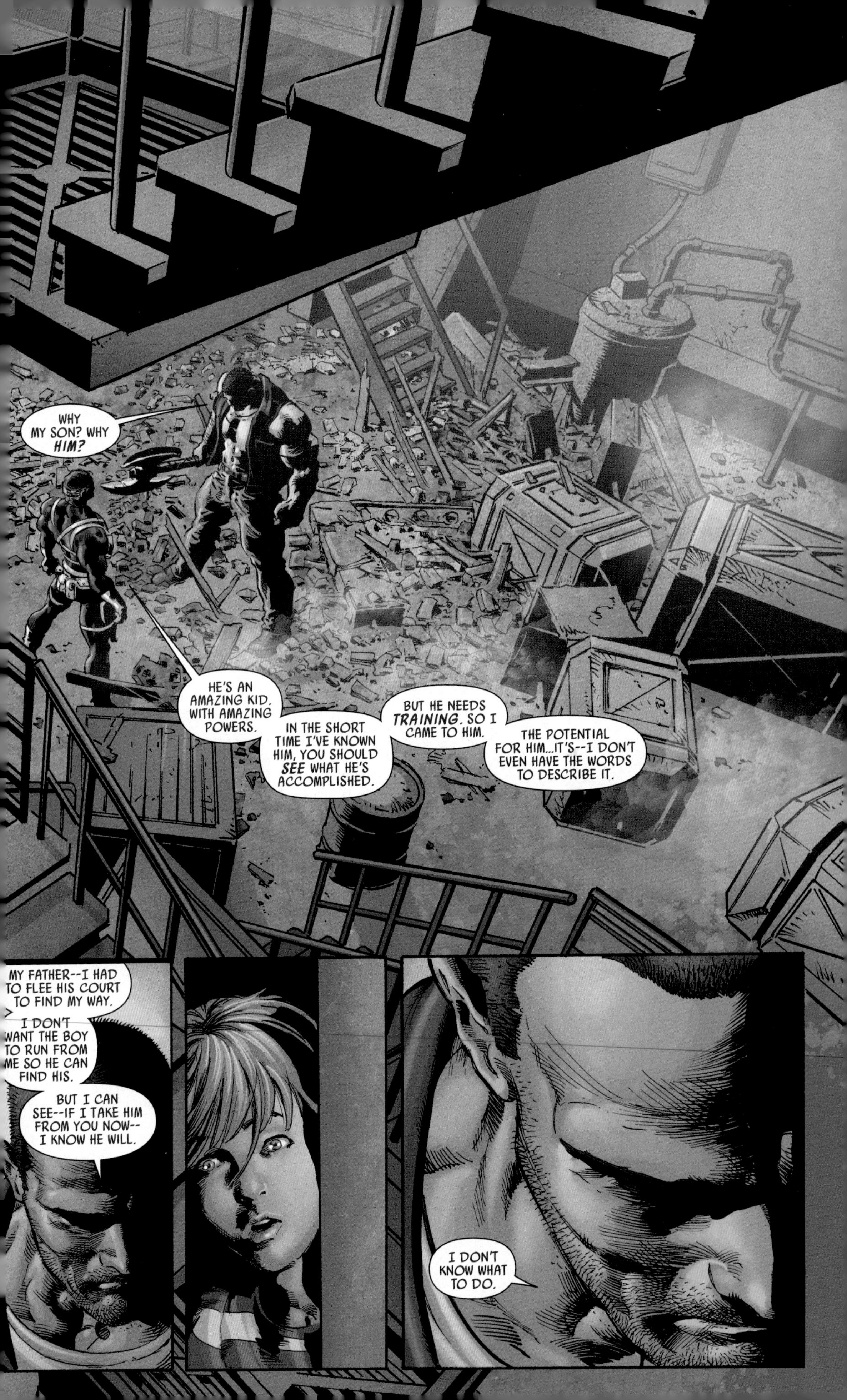
WHY MY SON? WHY *HIM?*
HE'S AN AMAZING KID. WITH AMAZING POWERS.
IN THE SHORT TIME I'VE KNOWN HIM, YOU SHOULD *SEE* WHAT HE'S ACCOMPLISHED.
BUT HE NEEDS *TRAINING*. SO I CAME TO HIM.
THE POTENTIAL FOR HIM...IT'S--I DON'T EVEN HAVE THE WORDS TO DESCRIBE IT.
MY FATHER--I HAD TO FLEE HIS COURT TO FIND MY WAY.
I DON'T WANT THE BOY TO RUN FROM ME SO HE CAN FIND HIS.
BUT I CAN SEE--IF I TAKE HIM FROM YOU NOW--I KNOW HE WILL.
I DON'T KNOW WHAT TO DO.

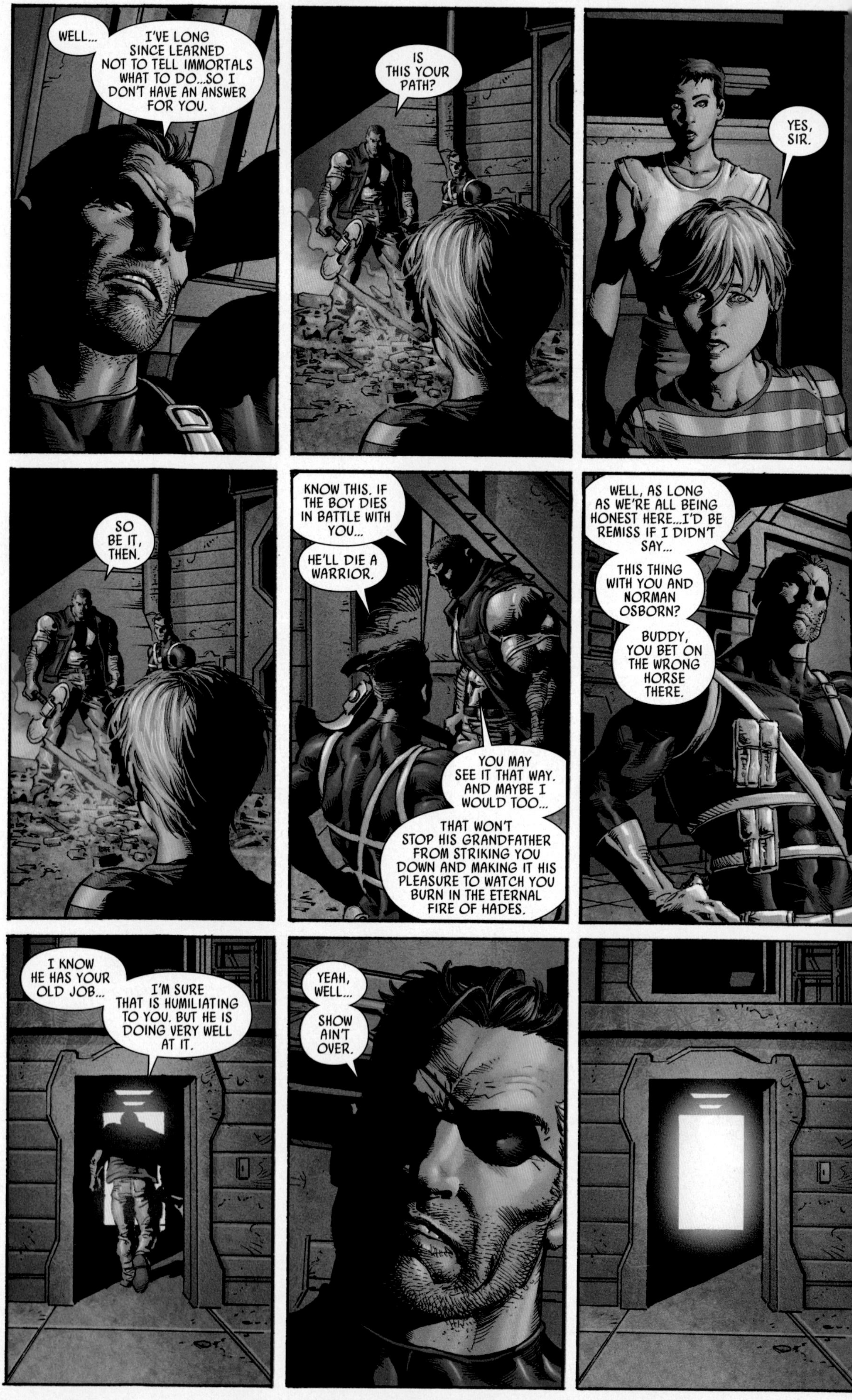
WELL...
I'VE LONG SINCE LEARNED NOT TO TELL IMMORTALS WHAT TO DO...SO I DON'T HAVE AN ANSWER FOR YOU.
IS THIS YOUR PATH?
YES, SIR.
SO BE IT, THEN.
KNOW THIS. IF THE BOY DIES IN BATTLE WITH YOU...
HE'LL DIE A WARRIOR.
YOU MAY SEE IT THAT WAY. AND MAYBE I WOULD TOO...
THAT WON'T STOP HIS GRANDFATHER FROM STRIKING YOU DOWN AND MAKING IT HIS PLEASURE TO WATCH YOU BURN IN THE ETERNAL FIRE OF HADES.
WELL, AS LONG AS WE'RE ALL BEING HONEST HERE...I'D BE REMISS IF I DIDN'T SAY...
THIS THING WITH YOU AND NORMAN OSBORN?
BUDDY, YOU BET ON THE WRONG HORSE THERE.
I KNOW HE HAS YOUR OLD JOB...
I'M SURE THAT IS HUMILIATING TO YOU. BUT HE IS DOING VERY WELL AT IT.
YEAH, WELL...
SHOW AIN'T OVER.

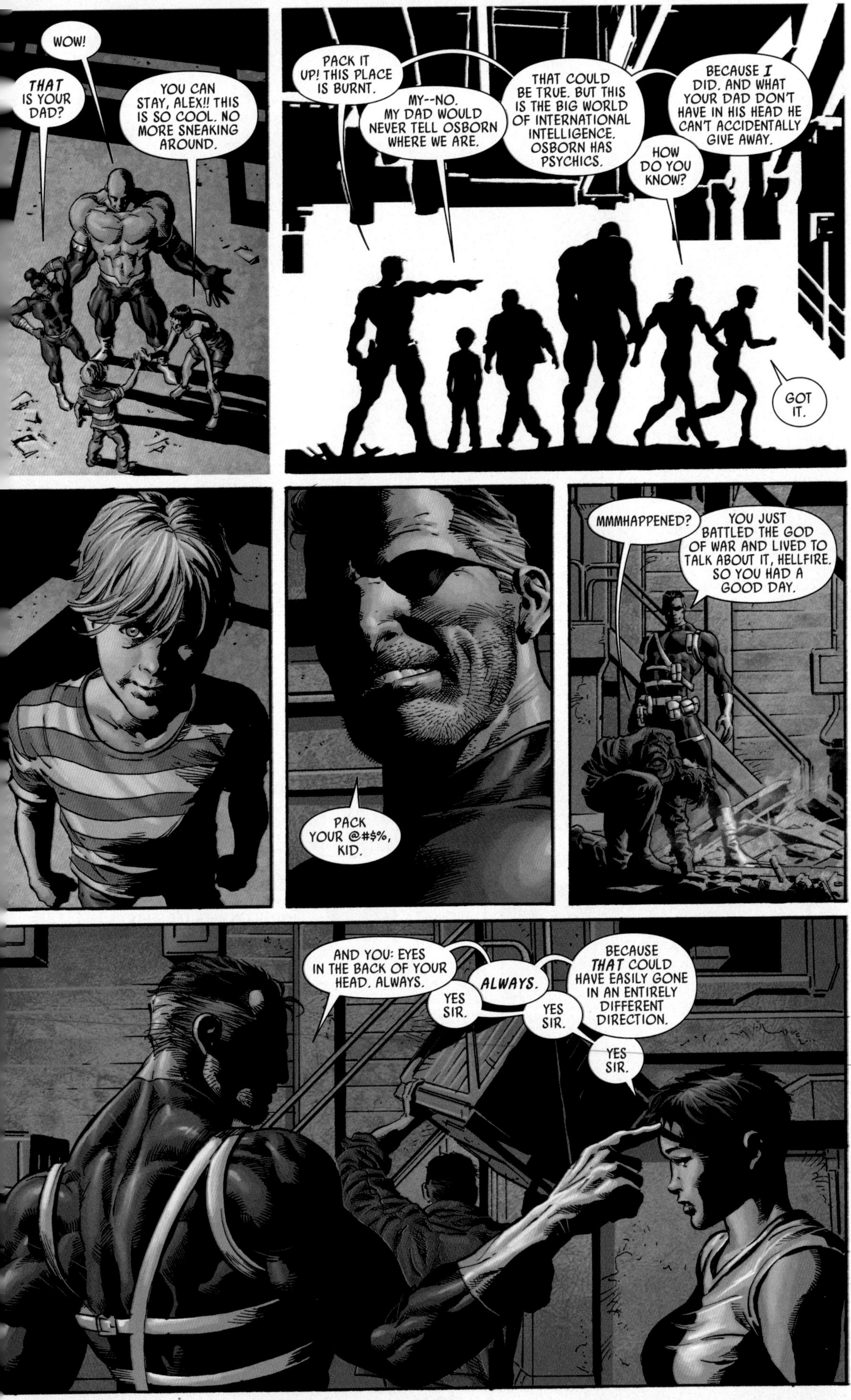
WOW!
THAT IS YOUR DAD?
YOU CAN STAY, ALEX!! THIS IS SO COOL. NO MORE SNEAKING AROUND.
PACK IT UP! THIS PLACE IS BURNT.
MY--NO. MY DAD WOULD NEVER TELL OSBORN WHERE WE ARE.
THAT COULD BE TRUE. BUT THIS IS THE BIG WORLD OF INTERNATIONAL INTELLIGENCE. OSBORN HAS PSYCHICS.
HOW DO YOU KNOW?
BECAUSE I DID. AND WHAT YOUR DAD DON'T HAVE IN HIS HEAD HE CAN'T ACCIDENTALLY GIVE AWAY.
GOT IT.
PACK YOUR @#$%, KID.
MMMHAPPENED?
YOU JUST BATTLED THE GOD OF WAR AND LIVED TO TALK ABOUT IT, HELLFIRE. SO YOU HAD A GOOD DAY.
AND YOU: EYES IN THE BACK OF YOUR HEAD. ALWAYS.
YES SIR.
ALWAYS.
YES SIR.
BECAUSE THAT COULD HAVE EASILY GONE IN AN ENTIRELY DIFFERENT DIRECTION.
YES SIR.

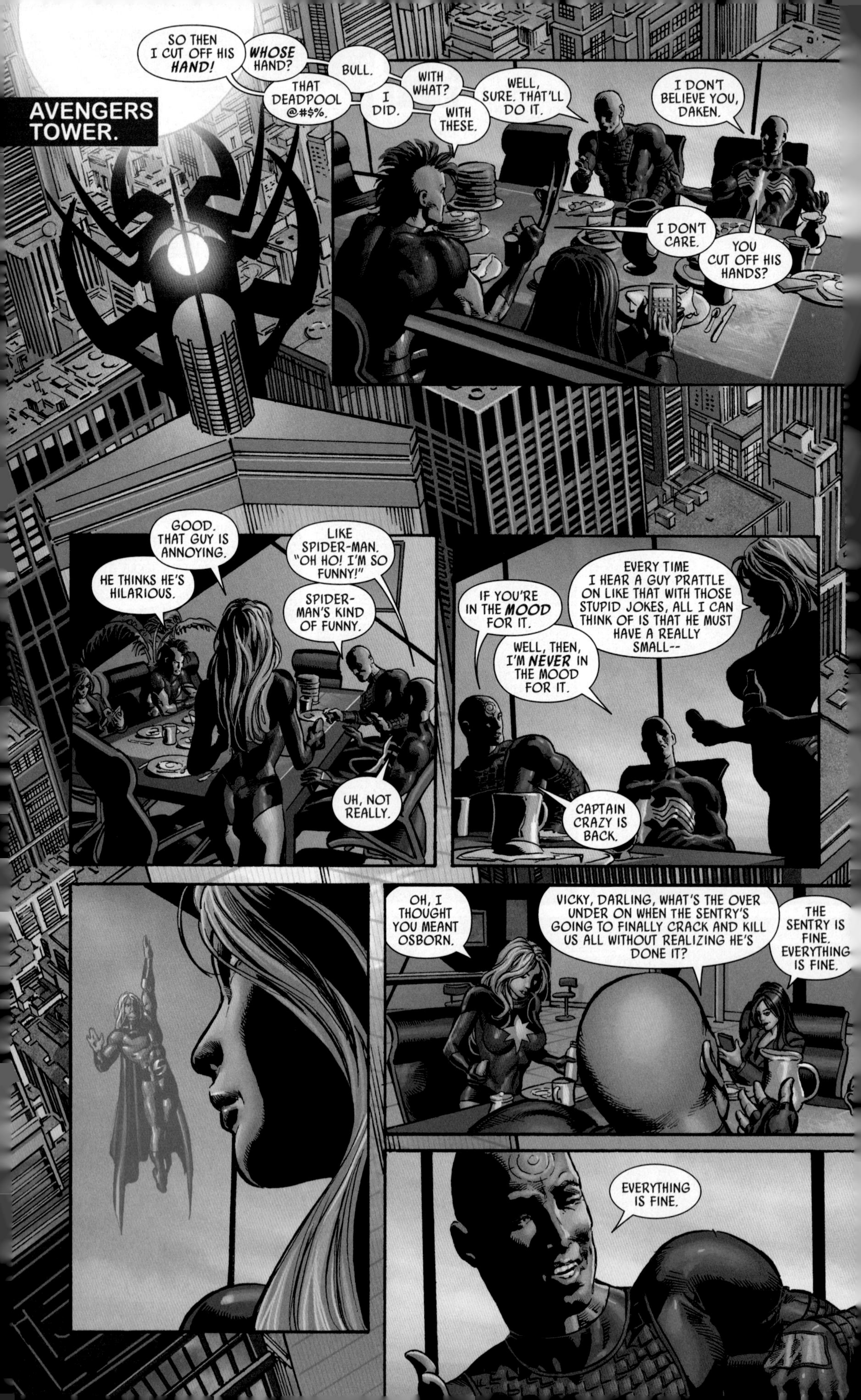
AVENGERS TOWER.
SO THEN I CUT OFF HIS HAND!
WHOSE HAND?
THAT DEADPOOL @#$%.
BULL.
I DID.
WITH WHAT?
WITH THESE.
WELL, SURE. THAT'LL DO IT.
I DON'T BELIEVE YOU, DAKEN.
I DON'T CARE.
YOU CUT OFF HIS HANDS?
GOOD. THAT GUY IS ANNOYING.
HE THINKS HE'S HILARIOUS.
LIKE SPIDER-MAN. "OH HO! I'M SO FUNNY!"
SPIDER-MAN'S KIND OF FUNNY.
UH, NOT REALLY.
EVERY TIME I HEAR A GUY PRATTLE ON LIKE THAT WITH THOSE STUPID JOKES, ALL I CAN THINK OF IS THAT HE MUST HAVE A REALLY SMALL--
IF YOU'RE IN THE MOOD FOR IT.
WELL, THEN, I'M NEVER IN THE MOOD FOR IT.
CAPTAIN CRAZY IS BACK.
OH, I THOUGHT YOU MEANT OSBORN.
VICKY, DARLING, WHAT'S THE OVER UNDER ON WHEN THE SENTRY'S GOING TO FINALLY CRACK AND KILL US ALL WITHOUT REALIZING HE'S DONE IT?
THE SENTRY IS FINE. EVERYTHING IS FINE.
EVERYTHING IS FINE.

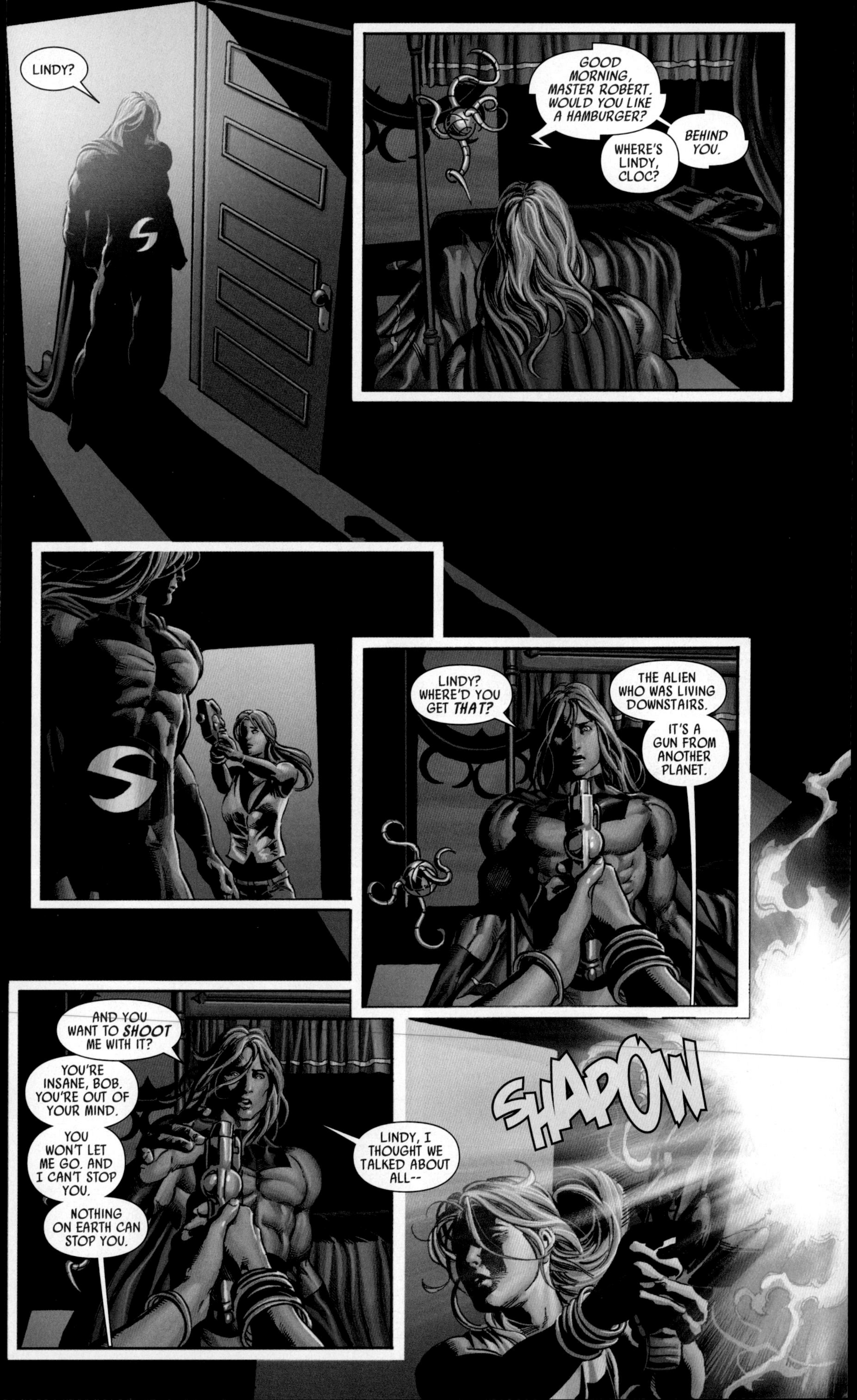
LINDY?
GOOD MORNING, MASTER ROBERT. WOULD YOU LIKE A HAMBURGER?
WHERE'S LINDY, CLOC?
BEHIND YOU.
LINDY? WHERE'D YOU GET THAT?
THE ALIEN WHO WAS LIVING DOWNSTAIRS.
IT'S A GUN FROM ANOTHER PLANET.
AND YOU WANT TO SHOOT ME WITH IT?
YOU'RE INSANE, BOB. YOU'RE OUT OF YOUR MIND.
YOU WON'T LET ME GO. AND I CAN'T STOP YOU.
NOTHING ON EARTH CAN STOP YOU.
LINDY, I THOUGHT WE TALKED ABOUT ALL--
SHAPOW

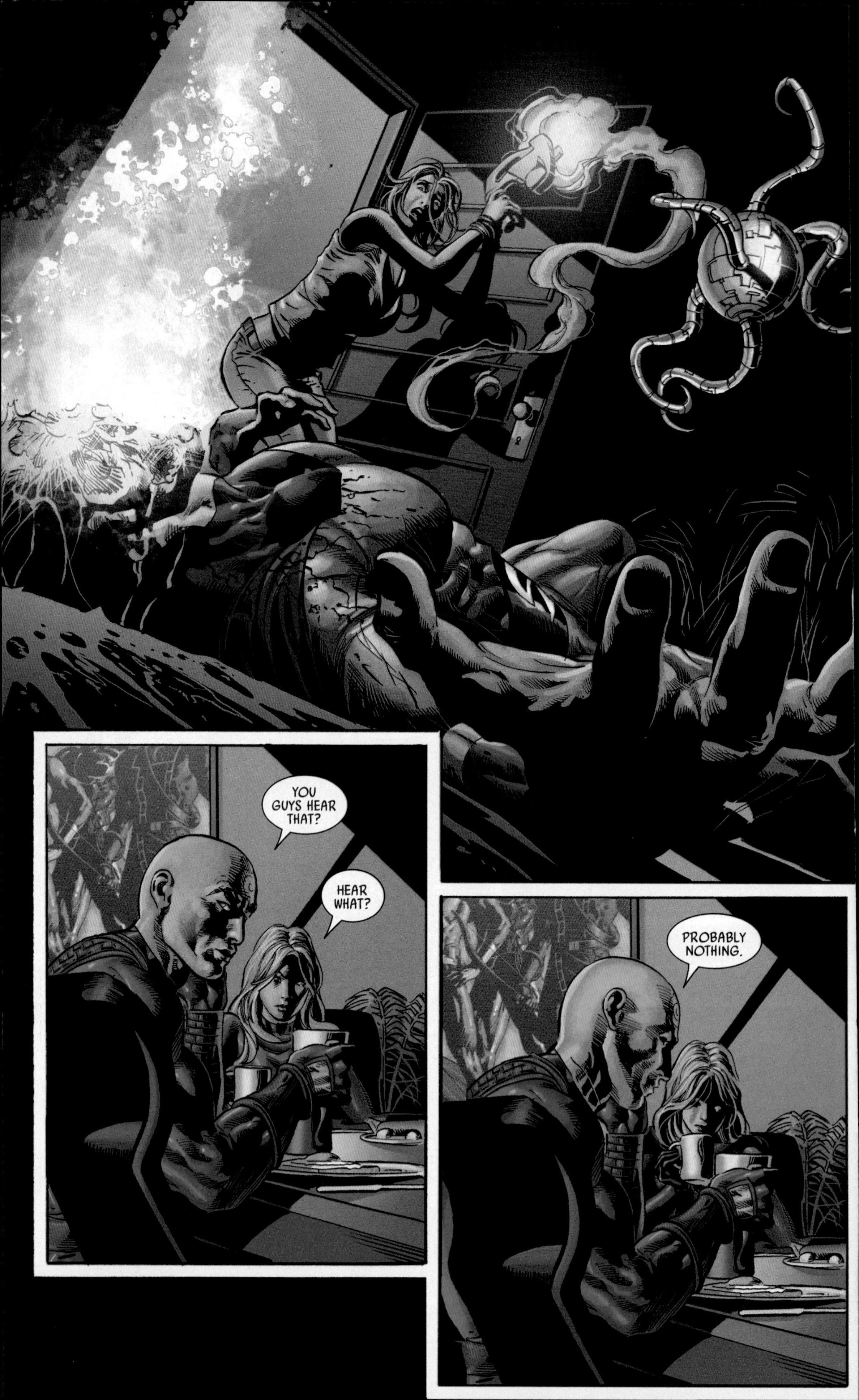
YOU GUYS HEAR THAT?
HEAR WHAT?
PROBABLY NOTHING.

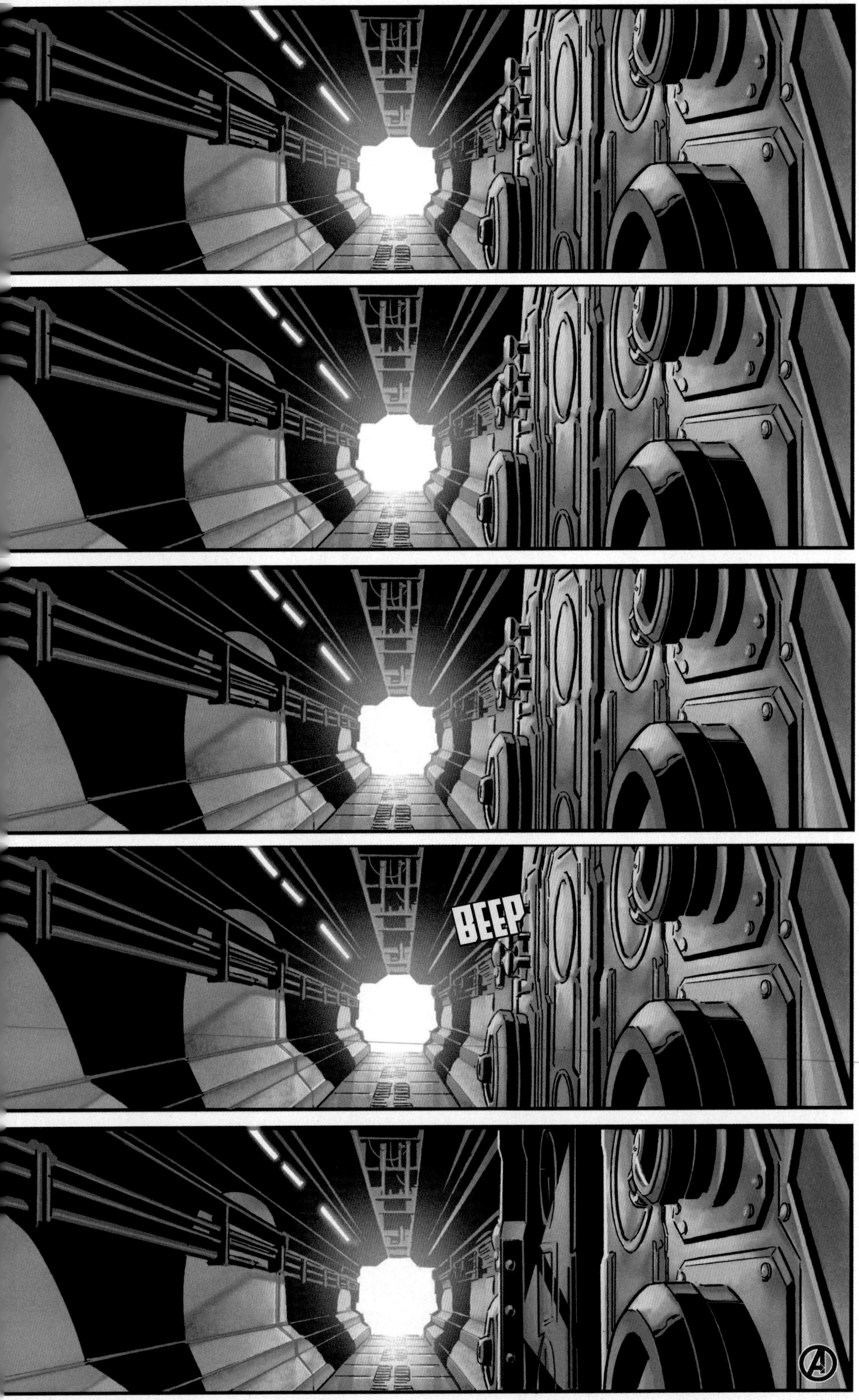
BEEP

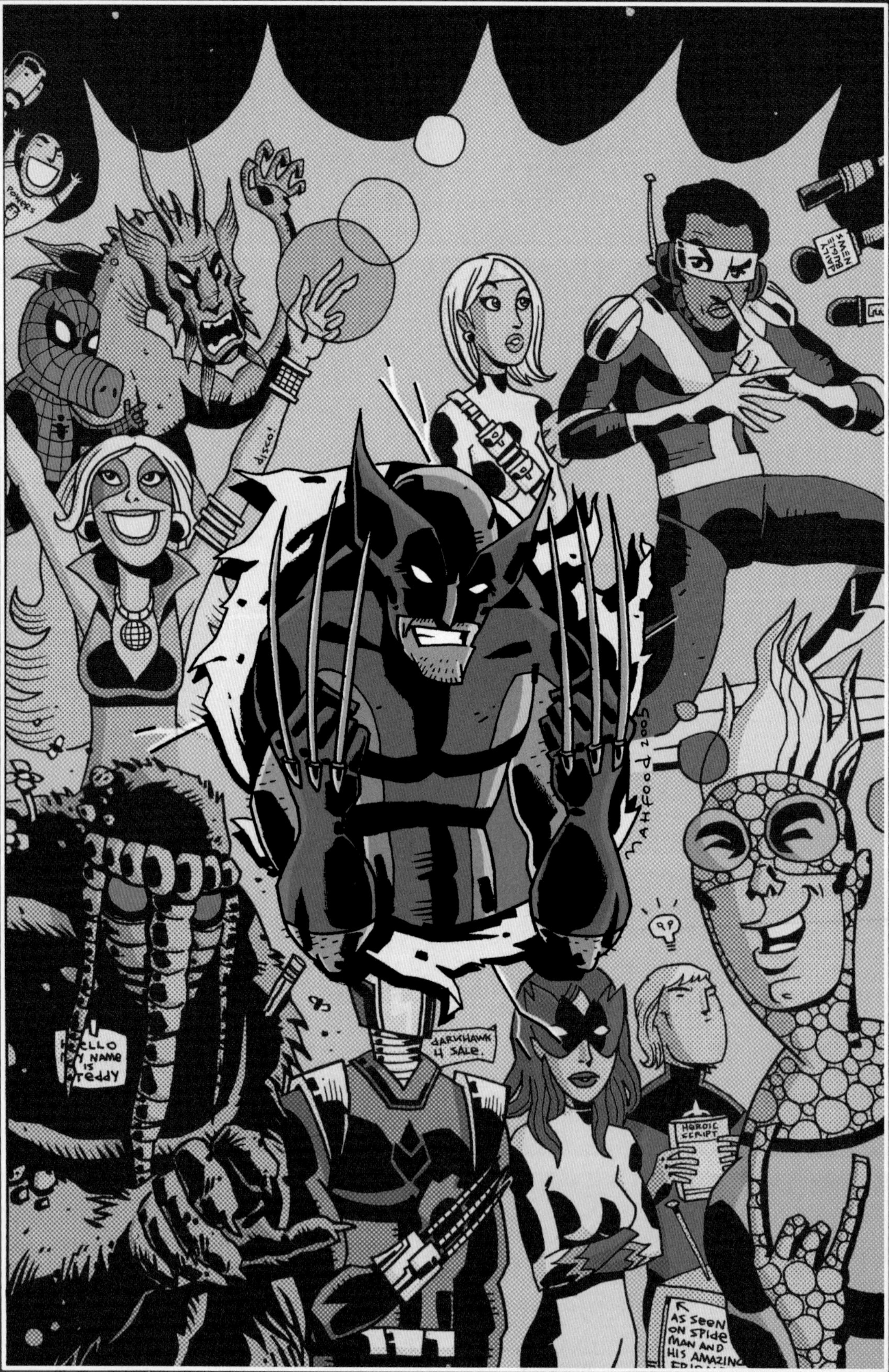
POWERS
disco!
DAILY BUGLE NEWS
MAHFOOD 2005
HELLO MY NAME IS Teddy
DARKHAWK 4 SALE.
HEROIC SCRIPT
AS SEEN ON SPIDE MAN AND HIS AMAZING

WHA...HUH? #1

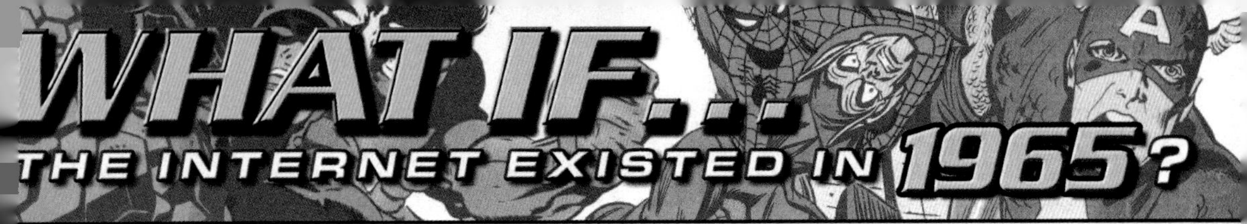

WHAT IF... THE INTERNET EXISTED IN 1965?

THWiP!
Joined: 12 Dec 1962
Posted: Wed Jul 28, 1965 6:19 am
Post subject: KIRBY OVERLOAD

Who the hell does Jack Kirby think he is? Why can't he let someone else draw a damn comic book? Who died and made him king?

MASTER OF Mystic DARTS
Joined: 10 Oct 1964
Posted: Wed Jul 28, 1965 6:22 am
Post subject: AVENGERS OUTRAGE

Um, I just read the latest Avengers and I could not believe my eyes. The Avengers now consist of two Brotherhood of Evil Mutants and some dude in purple with a bow and arrow? No more Iron Man? No more Thor?!

No more Avengers as far as I am concerned!

If you think this is such a great idea, why don't you call this new team something else and leave THE AVENGERS ALONE?! Stan really jumped the shark on this one and that saying won't even mean anything until the mid 1990's.

RANGER CHIC!
Joined: 02 Dec 1965
Posted: Wed Jul 28, 1955 6:26 am
Post subject: YOU PEOPLE SUCK!

Spoilers, damn it! How hard can it be?

Denny_H
Joined: 05 Aug 1963
Posted: Wed Jul 28, 1965 6:28 am
Post subject: DISGUSTING

In the latest Amazing Spider-Man, J. Jonah Jameson uttered a series of exclamation symbols in reference to something Spider-Man did. There was a @ then a $ then a % then a #. I just don't understand how such an obvious typo could have occurred.

RED SKULL!
Joined: 28 Jul 1965
Posted: Wed Jul 28, 1965 6:29 am
Post subject: MARVEL CRASH AND BURN

I bought the latest issue of FANTASTIC FOUR, and when I got to the counter, the guy told me I needed two extra cents! Twelve cents for a comic book?! That's just too much to pay! I used to be able to follow the entire Marvel line for $1.70, but now it costs over two bucks! This sort of price-gouging is the reason why comic book sales have been falling all these years!

How do you people sleep at night? Make mine ATLAS! Hippies!!

ImprovingGODDARD
Joined: 12 Aug 1963
Posted: Wed Jul 28, 1965 9:19 am
Post subject: ANOTHER NEW TITLE?!

They're bringing back that weird Spider-Man character, but rather than picking up with AMAZING FANTASY #16, they're going with an all-new #1! Don't they understand the storied history of AMAZING FANTASY? I've been following it since it was AMAZING ADVENTURES, and then AMAZING ADULT FANTASY— and now, they're throwing my loyalty away in a transparent bid for new readers! But will those new readers still be around when AMAZING SPIDER-MAN becomes AMAZING ADULT SPIDER-MAN? I don't think so!

THWiP!
Joined: 12 Dec 1962
Posted: Wed Jul 28, 1965 11:33 am
Post subject: Re: AVENGERS OUTRAGE

What's a spoiler?

Diana
Joined: 05 Feb 1964
Posted: Wed Jul 28, 1965 1:53 pm
Post subject: DAREDEVIL'S COSTUME!

Have you seen Daredevil's new costume? Yuck!! What were they thinking? It's so drab and dull, all that same color red! I refuse to buy another issue until they restore DD's classic and proper yellow attire!

DUM DUM DUFAN
Joined: 28 Jun 1965
Posts: 597
Posted: Wed Jul 28, 2004 3:40 pm
Post subject: THE SENTRY RULES!!

That is all.

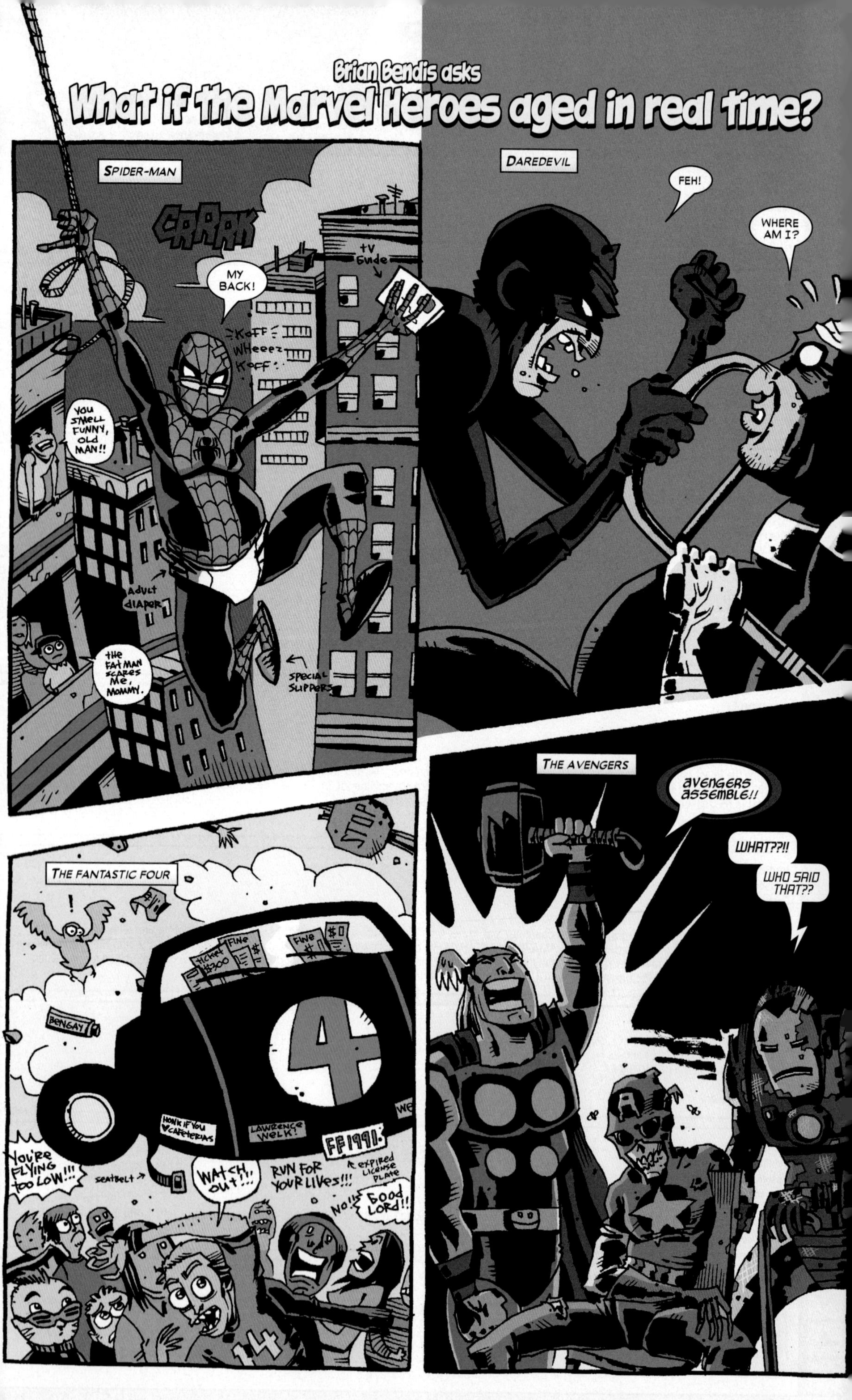
Brian Bendis asks
What if the Marvel Heroes aged in real time?
SPIDER-MAN
CRRRK
MY BACK!
KOFF WHEEEZ KOFF
TV GUIDE
YOU SMELL FUNNY, OLD MAN!!
ADULT DIAPER
THE FAT MAN SCARES ME, MOMMY.
SPECIAL SLIPPERS
DAREDEVIL
FEH!
WHERE AM I?
THE FANTASTIC FOUR
!
TICKET $300
FINE
FINE
$0
BENGAY
HONK IF YOU ♥ CAFETERIAS
LAWRENCE WELK!
FF1991
YOU'RE FLYING TOO LOW!!!
SEATBELT
WATCH OUT!!!
RUN FOR YOUR LIVES!!!
EXPIRED LICENSE PLATE
NO!!
GOOD LORD!!
THE AVENGERS
AVENGERS ASSEMBLE!!
WHAT??!!
WHO SAID THAT??

WHAT IF... THE INTERNET EXISTED IN 1975?

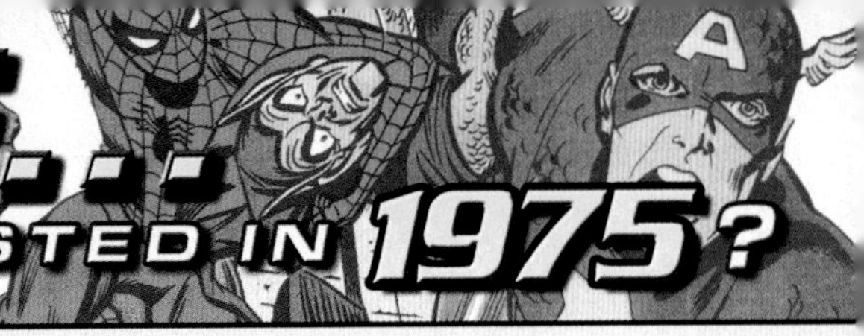

Johnny38
Joined: 23 Aug 1973
Posted: Wed Jul 28, 1975 7:38 am
Post subject: HOWARD THE DUCK – COMIC GENIUS!

Do what I tell you Marvel and stop with all the Spider-Man! Howard the Duck is the best comic ever published and you should stop publishing everything else but that. If I was publisher, I would fire all your asses and just put out Howard all day long. Enough with Spider-Man already.already.

blackcatbooyah
Joined: 11 Aug 1974
Posted: Tues Sept 19, 1975 9:09 am
Post subject: YOU IDIOTS SUCK!

Huge continuity snafu, you jerks. Nick Fury was around in World War II, so that would make him at least a billion years old. Don't you people know how to count or are you too busy reading Lord of the Rings and burning incense all day?!

Cyclopsian
Joined: 06 Sep 1972
Posted: Tues Sept 19, 1975 10:15 am
Post subject: X-Losers!

This new X-Men team sucks! Why are they coming up with "great" new characters like Storm (a white-haired black woman--give me a break) and Colossus (like the Thing, but Russian) when we all know they're all going to fail. The only cool one was Thunderbird, so of course they killed him off! It's an insult to fans of the real X-Men, Stan Lee's X-Men, that we're forced to endure these pretenders!

Webhead101
Joined: 08 June 1973
Posted: Tues Sept 19, 1975 11:05 am
Post subject: Slow Down Already

MARVEL IS GOUGING ME!

...with all of these new Spider-Man books! First AMAZING SPIDER-MAN, then MARVEL-TEAM UP and then GIANT-SIZE SPIDER-MAN! And now I hear they're going to be doing PETER PARKER, THE SPECTACULAR SPIDER-MAN! Nobody can afford to keep up with Spidey's adventures at thirty cents a pop!

Rifleman
Joined: 12 May 1972
Posted: Tues Sept 19, 1975 12:22 pm
Post subject: That's What I'm Talking About

The Punisher is the coolest! Marvel should give all its heroes guns!

RobotLove
Joined: 29 Dec 1974
Posted: Tues Sept 19, 1975 2:22 pm
Post subject: Honker

THE WORLD IS ENDING...

Iron Man has a nose on his armor now?

HeroWorship
Joined: 19 April 1973
Posted: Tues Sept 19, 1975 4:19 pm
Post subject: Kill Me Now!

What's with all of these damn monster comics, like TOMB OF DRACULA or WEREWOLF BY NIGHT! Doesn't Marvel realize that people only like super hero comics--we don't want this junk!

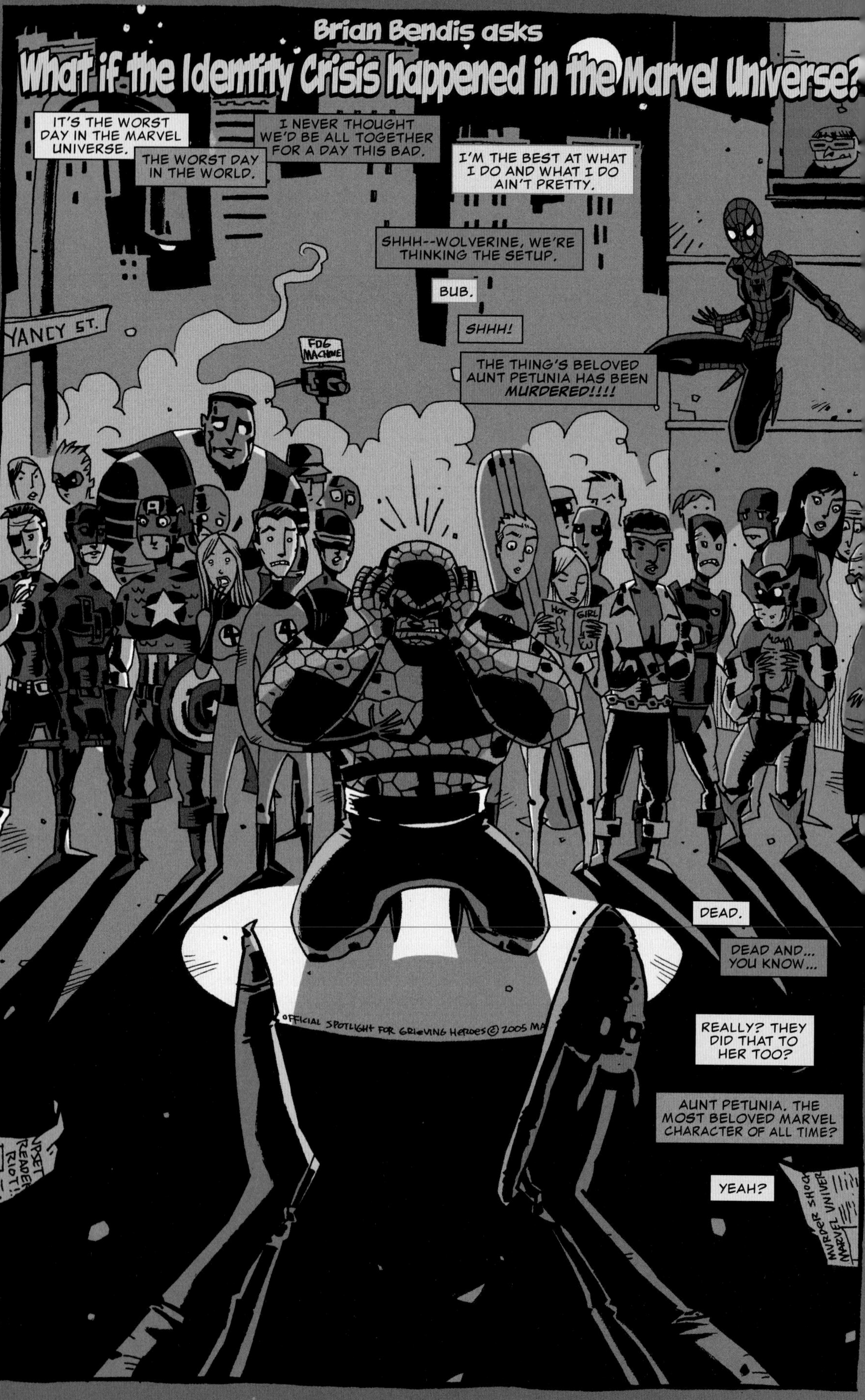
Brian Bendis asks
What if the Identity Crisis happened in the Marvel Universe?
IT'S THE WORST DAY IN THE MARVEL UNIVERSE.
THE WORST DAY IN THE WORLD.
I NEVER THOUGHT WE'D BE ALL TOGETHER FOR A DAY THIS BAD.
I'M THE BEST AT WHAT I DO AND WHAT I DO AIN'T PRETTY.
SHHH--WOLVERINE, WE'RE THINKING THE SETUP.
BUB.
SHHH!
THE THING'S BELOVED AUNT PETUNIA HAS BEEN MURDERED!!!!
YANCY ST.
FOG MACHINE
HOT GIRL
DEAD.
DEAD AND... YOU KNOW...
REALLY? THEY DID THAT TO HER TOO?
AUNT PETUNIA. THE MOST BELOVED MARVEL CHARACTER OF ALL TIME?
YEAH?
OFFICIAL SPOTLIGHT FOR GRIEVING HEROES © 2005 MA
UPSET READER RIOT!!
MURDER SHOCK MARVEL UNIVER

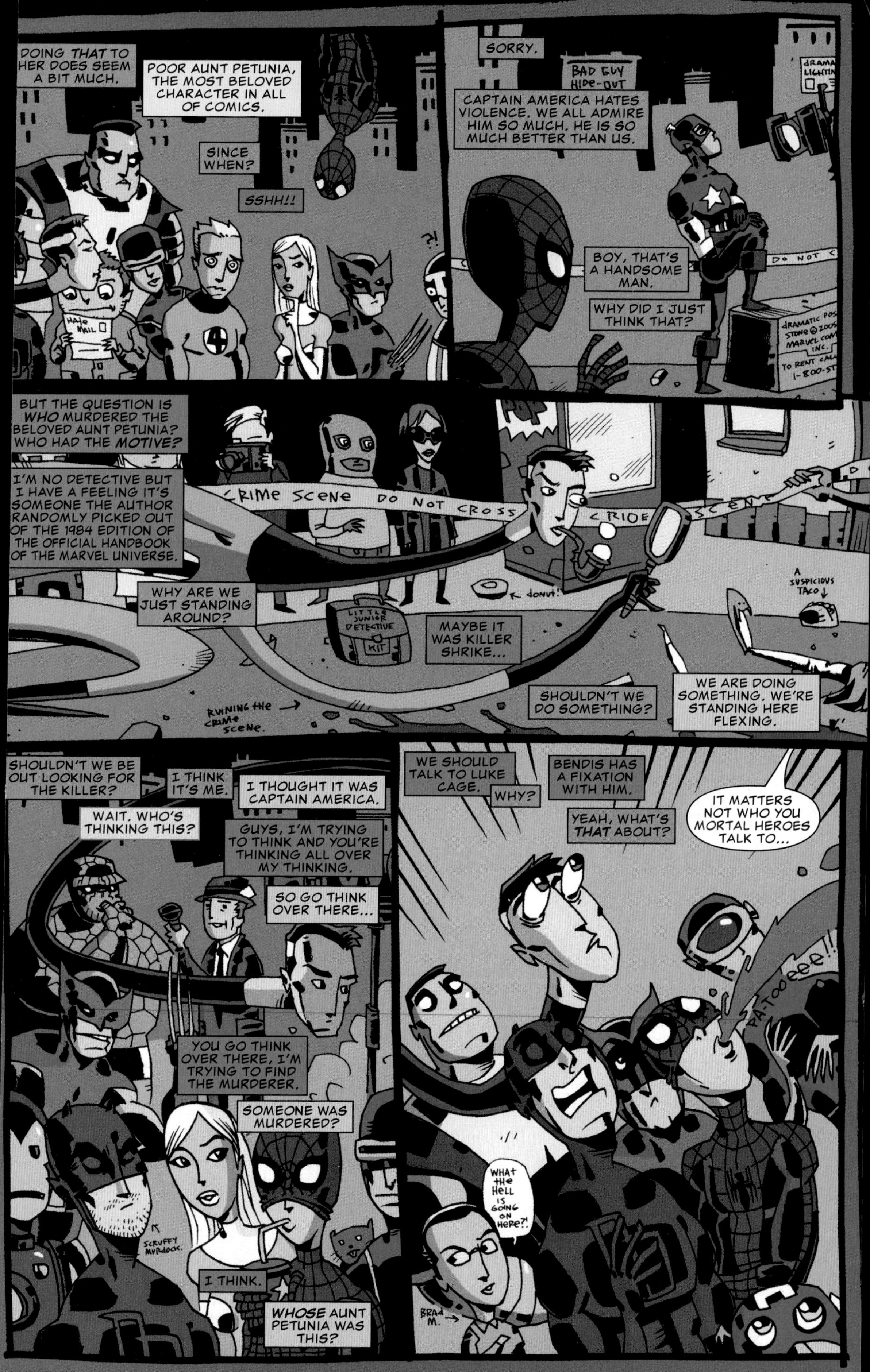
DOING *THAT* TO HER DOES SEEM A BIT MUCH.
POOR AUNT PETUNIA, THE MOST BELOVED CHARACTER IN ALL OF COMICS.
SINCE WHEN?
SSHH!!
HATE MAIL
?!
SORRY.
BAD GUY HIDE-OUT
dramatic LIGHTING
CAPTAIN AMERICA HATES VIOLENCE. WE ALL ADMIRE HIM SO MUCH. HE IS SO MUCH BETTER THAN US.
BOY, THAT'S A HANDSOME MAN.
WHY DID I JUST THINK THAT?
BUT THE QUESTION IS *WHO* MURDERED THE BELOVED AUNT PETUNIA? WHO HAD THE *MOTIVE?*
I'M NO DETECTIVE BUT I HAVE A FEELING IT'S SOMEONE THE AUTHOR RANDOMLY PICKED OUT OF THE 1984 EDITION OF THE OFFICIAL HANDBOOK OF THE MARVEL UNIVERSE.
CRIME SCENE DO NOT CROSS
WHY ARE WE JUST STANDING AROUND?
LITTLE JUNIOR DETECTIVE KIT
donut!
A SUSPICIOUS TACO
MAYBE IT WAS KILLER SHRIKE...
RUINING THE CRIME SCENE.
SHOULDN'T WE DO SOMETHING?
WE ARE DOING SOMETHING. WE'RE STANDING HERE FLEXING.
SHOULDN'T WE BE OUT LOOKING FOR THE KILLER?
I THINK IT'S ME.
I THOUGHT IT WAS CAPTAIN AMERICA.
WAIT. WHO'S THINKING THIS?
GUYS, I'M TRYING TO THINK AND YOU'RE THINKING ALL OVER MY THINKING.
SO GO THINK OVER THERE...
YOU GO THINK OVER THERE, I'M TRYING TO FIND THE MURDERER.
SOMEONE WAS MURDERED?
SCRUFFY MURDOCK.
I THINK.
WHOSE AUNT PETUNIA WAS THIS?
WE SHOULD TALK TO LUKE CAGE.
WHY?
BENDIS HAS A FIXATION WITH HIM.
YEAH, WHAT'S *THAT* ABOUT?
IT MATTERS NOT WHO YOU MORTAL HEROES TALK TO...
PA-TOOEEE!!
What the Hell is going on here?!
BRAD M.

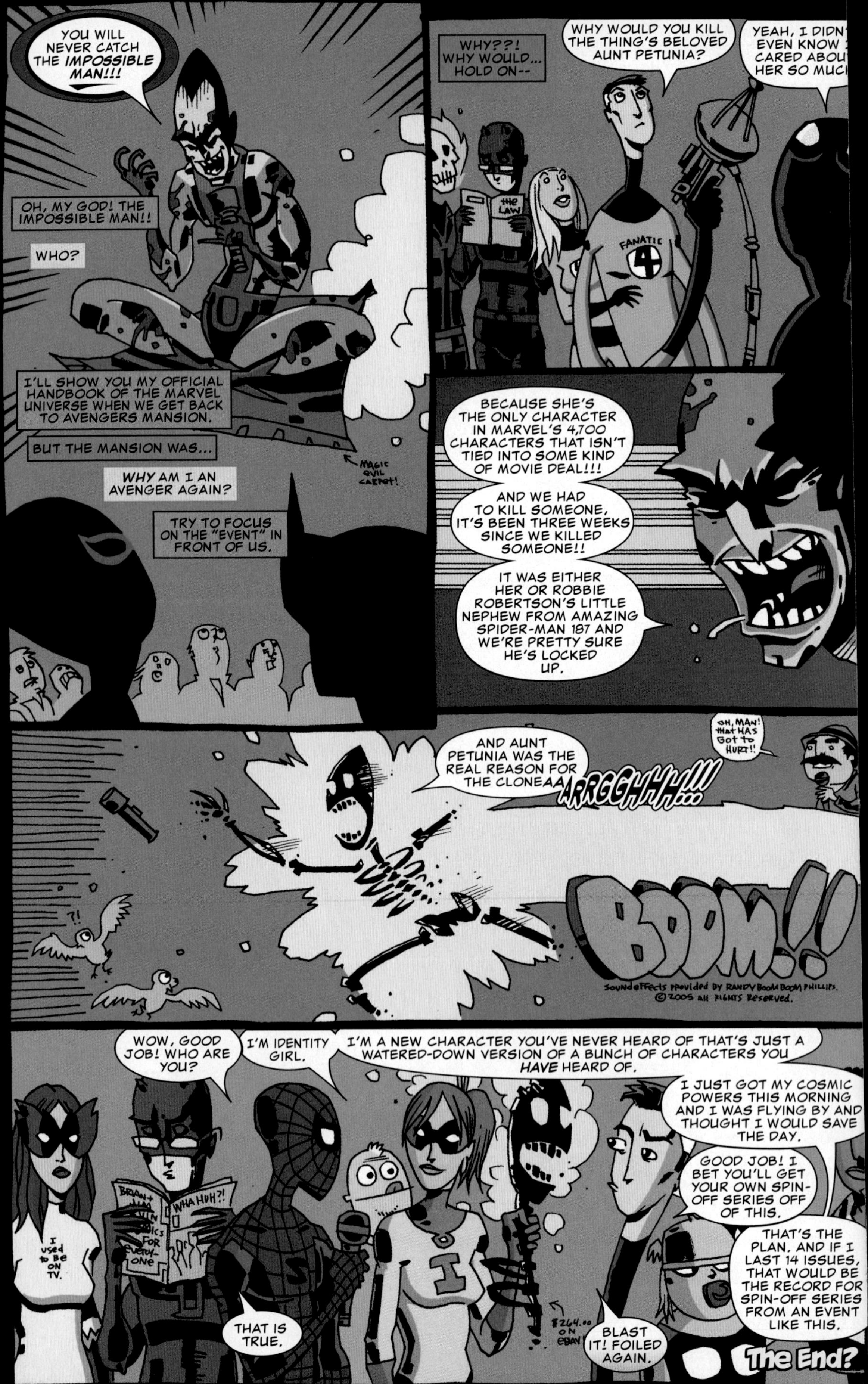
YOU WILL NEVER CATCH THE IMPOSSIBLE MAN!!!
OH, MY GOD! THE IMPOSSIBLE MAN!!
WHO?
I'LL SHOW YOU MY OFFICIAL HANDBOOK OF THE MARVEL UNIVERSE WHEN WE GET BACK TO AVENGERS MANSION.
BUT THE MANSION WAS...
WHY AM I AN AVENGER AGAIN?
TRY TO FOCUS ON THE "EVENT" IN FRONT OF US.
MAGIC EVIL CARPET!
WHY??! WHY WOULD... HOLD ON--
WHY WOULD YOU KILL THE THING'S BELOVED AUNT PETUNIA?
YEAH, I DIDN'T EVEN KNOW I CARED ABOUT HER SO MUCH
THE LAW
FANATIC 4
BECAUSE SHE'S THE ONLY CHARACTER IN MARVEL'S 4,700 CHARACTERS THAT ISN'T TIED INTO SOME KIND OF MOVIE DEAL!!!
AND WE HAD TO KILL SOMEONE, IT'S BEEN THREE WEEKS SINCE WE KILLED SOMEONE!!
IT WAS EITHER HER OR ROBBIE ROBERTSON'S LITTLE NEPHEW FROM AMAZING SPIDER-MAN 187 AND WE'RE PRETTY SURE HE'S LOCKED UP.
AND AUNT PETUNIA WAS THE REAL REASON FOR THE CLONEAA
ARRGGHHH!!!...
OH, MAN! THAT HAS GOT TO HURT!!
?!
BOOM!!
SOUND EFFECTS PROVIDED BY RANDY BOOM BOOM PHILLIPS. ©2005 ALL RIGHTS RESERVED.
WOW, GOOD JOB! WHO ARE YOU?
I'M IDENTITY GIRL.
I'M A NEW CHARACTER YOU'VE NEVER HEARD OF THAT'S JUST A WATERED-DOWN VERSION OF A BUNCH OF CHARACTERS YOU HAVE HEARD OF.
I JUST GOT MY COSMIC POWERS THIS MORNING AND I WAS FLYING BY AND THOUGHT I WOULD SAVE THE DAY.
GOOD JOB! I BET YOU'LL GET YOUR OWN SPIN-OFF SERIES OFF OF THIS.
THAT'S THE PLAN. AND IF I LAST 14 ISSUES, THAT WOULD BE THE RECORD FOR SPIN-OFF SERIES FROM AN EVENT LIKE THIS.
WHA HUH?!
BRIAN + MAX FUN COMICS FOR EVERYONE
I USED TO BE ON TV.
THAT IS TRUE.
$264.00 ON EBAY!
BLAST IT! FOILED AGAIN.
The End?

WHAT IF. . . THE INTERNET EXISTED IN 1985?

Raven_G
Joined: 06 Sep 1982
Posted: Wed Jul 28, 1985 6:19 am
Post subject: DAREDEVIL??

All of a sudden Matt Murdock is a ninja?? You gotta be kidding me?! Bring back Gene Colan and stop giving your books to these crazy people who clearly have never read a comic book before.

STEVE_Z
Joined: 02 Sep 1983
Posted: Wed Jul 28, 1985 6:21 am
Post subject: WHO WATCHES THE HYPE?

Just read the latest issue of Watchmen. What a load of crap! If I wanted to read a pirate comic I would buy a #$%in' pirate comic! Stop stretching out the story and get to the point!!

ZEPPE
Joined: 11 Sep 1980
Posted: Wed Jul 28, 1985 6:22 am
Post subject: CLAREWHO?

Chris Claremont should be ashamed of himself! Killing Dark Phoenix was lame! Desperate and lame! I predict he will be out of comics in a year and back working at the donut shoppe from whence he came!

auron
Member Joined: 29 Jul 1984
Posted: Wed Jul 28, 1985 6:25 am
Post subject: TIIIGGRRAAAA!!!!

Tigra?! Tigra is an Avenger?! You people are clearly trying to end my life. I am having a stroke every ten minutes! Stop doing this to me! Tigra! Who's next, Jessica Drew?!

BLOODYheck
Joined: 24 Nov 1984
Posted: Wed Jul 28, 1985 8:53 am
Post subject: WHO IS IN CHARGE OVER THERE??!!

Are these MARVEL FANFARE stories in continuity? What about that Silver Surfer story in EPIC MAGAZINE? (Not to mention that strange graphic novel by Stan and Jack, the one without the FF. Where does THAT fit in?!) I can't make heads or tails of what's in continuity and what isn't anymore--they should label it all clearly on the cover!

ALYSA McK
Joined: 26 Jan 1985
Posted: Wed Jul 28, 1985 9:27 am
Post subject: ARGH!

Phoenix is dead?? Thanks a lot for ruining it!! I don't get my comics till Thursday because I'm a Canadian who loves to go online and complain about when my comics ship and how much they cost in Canada, even though clearly it's my fault for living here.

AgentDESMOND
Joined: 11 Aug 1983
Posted: Wed Jul 28, 1985 6:27 am
Post subject: I HAVE SPOKEN!

Marvel should can that waste Ralph Macchio! He'll never last!

DUM DUM DUFAN
Joined: 28 Jun 1984 Posts: 597
Posted: Wed Jul 28, 1985 3:40 PM
Post subject: THE SENTRY RULES!!

That is all.

BEHIND THE PAGE: BRIAN MICHAEL BENDIS

By Vaneta Rogers,
Courtesy of *Newsarama.com*

Ten years ago, an independent comics writer named Brian Michael Bendis got a phone call from Marvel Comics. Would he be interested in writing for the publisher?

A decade later, Bendis has been a driving force behind the direction of Marvel Comics ever since. As Marvel was climbing out of the bankruptcy that plagued the company in the late '90s, Bendis helped shape efforts to diversify and update the publisher's super heroes, launching comics that defined the new Ultimate line, the new MAX imprint and even the Marvel Universe itself.

As Marvel makes plans for a 10-year retrospective collection of the writer's work to be released in December, Newsarama talked to Bendis about his 10th anniversary. In this two-part special edition of Behind the Page, we find out more about how the last decade at Marvel has affected the writer, both professionally and personally.

Newsarama: You mentioned recently that it was 10 years ago that you first got a call from Joe Quesada?

Brian Michael Bendis: It was! It's weird, too, because it didn't feel like 10 years. Ultimate Spider-Man debuted in 2000, and I'd already done Daredevil and Daredevil: Ninja. By the time Ultimate Spider-Man came out, I'd already, as they say, banged a few issues in the fear of being fired, as was the case prior to that job — I would be fired quickly. So I was writing a lot before it shipped. So I've been there since 1999.

NRAMA: Now, everyone sees you as a Marvel guy. But before you got the call from Joe, was Marvel a goal? Were you a Marvel guy even then?

BMB: I definitely was a Marvel kid, and as I grew older and more fascinated by the art form, I became much more aware of the voices of comics — the storytelling art form. And I became much more obsessed in following creators, whoever they were. And a lot of them were at Marvel when I found them, went to DC, and started bouncing back and forth. Guys like John Byrne or George Perez. You know what I mean? I only bought Wonder Woman when George Perez did Wonder Woman. And when John Byrne left Fantastic Four to Superman, I left Fantastic Four to go read Superman.

But I was a Marvel kid, and digging through the archives, as one does when one moves, I found graphic novels that I had written and drawn in my youth. My young, young youth. And there was this Captain America vs.

Thunderstrike graphic novel — four or five times I'd done it. When I went to high school, I just kept doing that over and over again. The joke in high school was you knew what books were mine because I was drawing Namor in every single textbook I had on every single page. All I did was draw Namor all day. I don't know why that is, but most people thought it was Mr. Spock that I was drawing, which has either something to do with my artistic ability or no one knows who Namor is outside us nerds on Nerdarama.

NRAMA: Let's set the stage for this phone call. You were still living in Cleveland when you got the call, right?

BMB: Yeah, I didn't move to Portland until 2001, so yeah, I was in Cleveland a couple years after getting that call.

NRAMA: And didn't you get an Eisner in 1999 as a talent deserving more recognition?

BMB: Yeah, I had. I was struggling. I was grateful to have any audience I had. And I had a couple thousand people who would buy the issues, which is just enough to make another issue. So it was just enough and Image was cool. As long as I wasn't costing anybody money, Image and Caliber before them were like, yeah, go ahead. And I would barrel ahead.

But you have it in your head that if you win an Eisner, someone will call you and save you from this. Someone will call! Somebody has to call! And I did, I won an Eisner. And I shook Will Eisner's hand. And the night after next, I was back at a Bat Mitzvah doing caricatures. That's how I made money. It's a good living because they pay a lot of money per hour, so you do two or three gigs and you were good for the week. So I could spend a whole week working on my graphic novel, saving enough money to pay my bills and eke by.

But drawing caricatures is a nightmare. Some people are drunk or they're mean to each other, and some people don't even understand the concept of the character, so you draw the character and they get offended. It was just mortifying.

And I was just sitting there doing this gig going, "but... I won an Eisner!"

NRAMA: What prefaced the call? Wasn't it David Mack who was working at Marvel first?

BMB: Yeah, my dear, dear friend David Mack had gotten a call from Joe. And Joe was quite enamored with Kabuki. And David and Joe were working on Daredevil together, and I was like, [whispering] "show him my stuff, man!" 'Cause I was really digging what Joe was doing. I wasn't digging mainstream comics in general, just because of where they were at the time. They were kind of squeezing the Heroes Reborn juice out of life or whatever. But Joe seemed to have something going on. He seemed to be putting the right people on the right books, and it was cool. Like Paul Jenkins on Inhumans — that stuff was cool. So I was like, "hey man! Show him my stuff!" And eventually Joe did get to my stuff and he gave me a call.

NRAMA: See? The Eisner did make the call happen.

BMB: I did get the call! But you know, it's fine to say that a few months later, but I didn't know it was coming. And no one ever said to me that once you win an Eisner, something will happen. But I had this in my head. If you've won something and Will Eisner shook your hand, something must change! There will be a difference! But in those months, I was just rubbing my head and going, "oh my God!"

NRAMA: Was the first thing you were offered Daredevil? Was that their idea or yours?

BMB: Joe called, and what he does is he feels you out for what you want to do. Like, what are you thinking? And I pitched what I've now found out is what everybody pitches when they get the call, which is your Daredevil story, your Nick Fury story and your Dr. Strange story. That's what everybody pitches. And everyone has a great take on Dr. Strange, yet nobody ever buys a Dr. Strange book, no matter what happens.

The shock of the call was I thought I was being asked what I wanted to draw. I thought it was for artwork. When I had solicited for jobs at DC and Marvel and Vertigo, it was always for penciling. And he was startled by my asking, well what do you need an artist for? And he said, "Artist??! Your art's not that good!" And I was like, awww, this is mean. And he said, "You know you're a very good writer." And I was like, what? The conversation I had imagined in my head wasn't happening. But I did appreciate the honesty. I've since figured out that's a good friend. And he's been that over the last 10 years. I can always count on him to not bullshit me.

And he said, "You're a great writer, and I bet if you stop drawing, your whole career will change." And he was right.

NRAMA: So what was your Dr. Strange story?

BMB: You know, I keep shoehorning it in and I'm almost there. I did things like Dr. Strange had walked the earth like Caine in Kung Fu and figured out what it means to be the Sorcerer Supreme.

NRAMA: Yeah, you're kind of doing that.

BMB: I just keep slowly whittling it away. So we're almost there, if people are reading New Avengers. But I literally had that story in my head since I was seven.

And no one wants it but me. I know this. It's OK.

NRAMA: Now on Daredevil, you started out with David Mack as your artist, right?

BMB: Yeah, what happened was I pitched a couple things to Joe. Daredevil: Ninja got greenlit, and that was intended to be a sort of swashbuckling Jackie Chan movie. And he liked the script, and Joe said, "You know what we really need? Daredevil is our signature book, and its schedule is a mess. Kevin [Smith], for reasons, is behind and I'm behind. It's behind. So could you come on the book and take it over until Kevin comes back? Kevin's coming back. But could you just do the book until he comes back?"

And I thought, "Oh my God I'm on Daredevil!" I didn't even hear "Kevin's coming back" or whatever. But I figure, I'm on Daredevil! So I was on Daredevil five and a half years. He never came back.

NRAMA: That first break at Marvel was a pretty big deal?

BMB: Well, I can't even reiterate to people how many starts and stops there were for me in mainstream comics in the '90s. There were a lot of almosts and maybes and bad auditions and me just f__king it up completely. A lot of false starts. So this thing with Joe was literally almost 10 years of hundreds of submissions and what-have-you.

And now I'm on Daredevil with my best friend. And I said, "Let's just go nuts. Let's just do it." And I knew David's work better than I know my own work. We had literally lived together and traveled together all through the '90s. We were at Caliper together and at Image together. He was like my brother. We're just very, very, very close. And to do Daredevil together, and we're both Frank Miller kids, was insane! So we got to do Daredevil.

I handed in the first couple scripts of Daredevil and thought,

Art by Alex Maleev

oh man, I'm just going to write the shit out of this. And if it works, it works; if it doesn't, it doesn't. I'm just going to give it my all. And you always wait for what do you hear back — "good job?" or "this sucks?" or "here are your notes." You don't know what you're going to hear back.

And I heard, "Hey, listen. Do you know who Bill Jemas is?" And I said, "No." And he said, "Well, he's the guy who's running Marvel now. And he's got this idea about starting Spider-Man over from scratch. Is that something you'd be interested in doing?" And I'm like, you know, now you're like, "OK, What???"

And literally, three days later I talked to Bill Jemas and we had a long conversation. And he'd been working on Ultimate Spider-Man — or it was called, "Ground Zero Comics" at the time, which would have been a disaster, for numerous reasons. And they had tried it with another writer and it just didn't work. And that other writer had done what I probably would have done if I didn't have the benefit of getting to read his version.

NRAMA: What was that?

BMB: He was faithful to Amazing Fantasy #15. And I probably would have done that too if I hadn't seen that it's not the right thing to do.

So I got to sit with it and really think about it. And that was greenlit as a mini-series. That was a six-issue mini-series. And I did this thing where I ignored them. I just pretended I didn't know it was a six-issue miniseries. I kept writing. And I did this with [Image founder] Todd [McFarlane] when I was on Sam and Twitch. That was also a miniseries, and I just pretended I didn't hear it and I kept going for 19 issues. 'Cause my feeling is, if it works, why stop? If everyone's feeling good about it, and at the time everyone was, let's just keep it going. If it tanks, it tanks. But it will be more than we thought.

And with Ultimate Spider-Man, I just said, "Well, we put all this effort into it. Why don't we just keep going?" And he's like, "O...K..." But I just barreled ahead.

NRAMA: Compared to your other work before that, Ultimate Spider-Man seems to have a completely different feel to it. Why do you think they chose you to write this kind of updated, youthful Spider-Man story?

BMB: I only know 'cause they flat-out told me. If you asked me that question when I didn't know the answer, I wouldn't be able to tell you. But what they were very focused on was that there wasn't a lot of character-driven drama going on in comics. There weren't a lot of characters talking to each other. There was a lot of heavy exposition going on in the late '90s. And it was just heavy. You know what I mean? It was time to grow up and there were more interesting writing styles going on in other places. And I think Joe saw people like me and Paul Jenkins and Mark Millar as people who were doing something else. And he said, "We need character stuff. This has to be about Peter Parker, not about Spider-Man." So that's where my interest was. It was because my voice is in characters. So that's why they thought of me.

'Cause you even read those first Daredevil comics I wrote with David and, you know, it's nothing like what's in Spider-Man.

NRAMA: Was that a challenge? I've read before that you identify with Peter Parker, so was it easier to write a character you feel like you know?

BMB: You know, it's funny, I go on long bike rides and think about this stuff, and I realized that I'd been writing for years, but I'd never picked at the wounds of high school. Like those high school wounds that we have? That stuff where, even at our age, you remember every awful thing that you said or did or thought or that was done to you. It comes back very quickly, 'cause it's never going to be resolved. And I realized that I'd never opened that box and used it for my writing. So it was very, very easy to put myself in the place of Peter Parker and use my own wounds.

By the way, that box is still half full. [laughs] That's the sad part. I haven't even gotten to the good stuff yet.

NRAMA: At what point did your life change because of all this? I assume you weren't doing the bat mitzvahs anymore.

BMB: You know, I was about 10 issues into writing it. I really hated doing the caricatures. I know I sound like a baby, because the money was great. But I didn't want to do it. I was literally sitting at a table and drawing this woman, and her husband says, "Hey, don't forget her mustache! Heh heh heh." And it was awful. I just hated it. And everything I was going to learn about myself doing it, I had learned, and yet I was still there, you know?

But the world of freelance, which is the world I had been living in, is so touchy. And I'd had so many false starts that I stayed with the caricatures, I think, through Issue #6. And I mean, by the time it shipped. You know, it's money on the table and it's hard to walk away from it. But after Issue #6 came out, I turned to my wife and I said, "I've got to stop." And she said, "I wasn't sure why you hadn't before."

At the time it felt like Ultimate Spider-Man wasn't going to go away unless I just completely screwed it up.

NRAMA: Were you surprised by how big of a hit it was?

BMB: I remember having no comprehension of numbers. Like the initial order for the first issue was 55,000. I wasn't sure if that was good. I kept going, "Is that good?" That's all I'd say to Joe or whoever. "Is 55 good?" And I remember Joe saying, "What did Torso sell?" And I said, "2." And he said, "Well, this is 53 more!"

And my dear friend Jonathan Hickman, he's just recently gone through this. The numbers for Secret Warriors had just come through, and he wasn't sure if they were good or not. And I said, "How much did Nightly News sell?" And it was pretty much the same. And I said, "Well, this is that much more." And he said, "Yeah, that's a good point." And I was like, yeah, I stole that from Joe.

So we all go through it. Even Elektra debuted really high and it was a top 10 book, and I wasn't sure if it was satisfactory. And I wasn't sure what I was supposed to do. And the level kept changing every month because things were so in the toilet at Marvel.

In comic book distribution, like, 55,000 wouldn't get you anywhere near the top 20 now. But at the time, that was

Art by Michael Gaydos

But that was my first taste of it. And in retrospect, I'm glad it happened because I had to learn that stuff. But some people don't survive that. They kind of let themselves get sucked under the bus a little bit or they let themselves get sucked under. And I tried to understand it. And I do understand it now.

NRAMA: You do?

BMB: Well, I've got to tell you, it took me well into my Avengers run.

NRAMA: Oh, wait, is this the sports fan analogy?

BMB: Yeah!

NRAMA: I love that analogy! People follow Spider-Man or Batman or whatever like a sports fan follows a certain team, whether they like what they're doing or not.

BMB: Exactly. But I didn't understand that. I was like, "Why are you yelling at me? Just don't buy it!"

NRAMA: And people were like, "But it's my team!"

BMB: And once I understood that, no problem. I totally get it! I absolutely understand it. But it was years before I got it, because I was the guy following the creators, not the team.

NRAMA: These early years with Ultimate Spider-Man, isn't that around the time you launched Alias?

BMB: Yeah, Ultimate Spider-Man launched well. And we were actually selling more every issue. We were on that weird thing where it was doing better and better every issue. But at the same time, I was still going Sam and Twitch over at Todd's company. Todd was not happy that I was doing Spider-Man and let me go.

I didn't understand it, because up until that moment, we had nary a bad moment together. Like, I don't think I had an awkward moment with him. But it was going back to stuff that was way before me and didn't have anything to do with me in particular. But he was steamed about it because I had asked to be let go of Hellspawn. I was having trouble writing it. It was just darker than I... I didn't feel comfortable with it. And all he heard was that I'd chosen Spider-Man over Spawn, which wasn't what I'd done. But that's what he heard. And that had to be explained to me by somebody else. And that was that.

considered a massive success. And the reorders and stuff were good for Ultimate Spider-Man. And it was weird because when the Ultimate line was announced, there was a lot of bile on the internet. Not just from the normal places — not just the message boards. People just didn't like the idea of it. And I'm just not used to people shitting on me for no reason — or at least, they hadn't read it or seen any of it. But just the idea of it was making them say, "F__k you! This is terrible!" And I wasn't aware there had been other attempts at it. I just wasn't in that circle, you know?

NRAMA: You probably weren't used to people even talking much about your comics on the internet.

BMB: Yeah! In independent comics, nobody knows who you are, and I was wearing it like a warm blanket. I was like, oh look, I can sit at a con and no one will bother me. This is lovely. So any other reaction, I was like, "What??"

But anybody who reads your stuff when you have this independent audience are just thrilled with the experience. That's all I had before this. So when Ultimate Spider-Man debuted, the reaction was like a slingshot. I thought I was going to be digging out of this hole forever. And then it just all went away like it never happened. And that was one of the many, many lessons I had to learn as I went along.

NRAMA: Are you a counselor for the guys at Amazing Spider-Man now?

BMB: [laughs] No, but you know, it's funny, I do have people coming to me like I have some wisdom. Not just Spider-Man guys, but every once in awhile I see guys coming to me looking for something, and all I can offer them is, I don't know when to quit. I just don't stop. And sometimes that's what you have to do.

And I called Joe. He and I had now developed a creative friendship. And I said, "Todd just fired me off Sam and Twitch," because I knew that was a book Joe had been enjoying. He said, "What??" And I was like, yeah, I don't know what happened. And he said, "Well, you know, we've been wanting you to do a crime book over here. We were going to talk to you about this. So just shake it off and let us know when you're ready to do a crime book."

At the time, I thought me and Alex [Maleev] would do this crime comic. But Joe said we should do Daredevil, which obviously worked out. But I pitched it as Marvel Inc. or something. Every pitch, the first name is always stupid. For a second it was Jessica Drew. But it became Jessica Jones, because it wasn't Jessica Drew I was writing.

NRAMA: I was wondering how Alias went through, because it was such a different concept for a super-hero publisher. So they asked for a crime comic? Did they know it would be something so different?

BMB: Well, I had the concept. And I sat with it for awhile. And I remember that I talked to Bill and said, "I have this concept, and it's kind of like an R-rated movie. The theme is adult. And I can't imagine it without the language. And you guys just don't publish that." And Bill goes, "Why don't we publish that?" And I said, "I don't know. You're the publisher."

And then instead of writing it as a pitch, I wrote it as a script — just the first 11 pages, so they could see the flavor and see what it is. And he called me two hours later and said, "No, we're doing this. We're starting an adult line and this is the first book and that's it!" And I was like, OK.

It was pretty cool, actually. That was even cooler, really, than getting Daredevil because I wasn't even trying to push it that hard. I was just trying to find where the levels were. And I found out I was with someone who hadn't set the level yet.

NRAMA: That's pretty unique for someone fairly new into the system at Marvel, isn't it?

BMB: You know, it's more than just me strolling along at this time. Mark was coming in and doing great. And Paul was doing really great. There were just a lot of guys who were hitting all their cylinders. And the feeling was that this was just the way to go. I was part of a wave that was thinking this is better than what was going on before.

But at the same time, keep in mind that the company was bankrupt. And when things are that bad, this stuff happens. I even joke that that's why we were hired in the

first place, because they were that far down the list. And when you're that desperate, you make bolder choices. And that's cool. They were like, yeah, let's go for the Vertigo audience. Let's go for this audience. What we're doing now isn't working.

So I was glad that I had a creative solution to the problem. And that went well too.

NRAMA: Was that atmosphere at Marvel of "let's try all this new stuff" a unique time in your career?

BMB: It's still the atmosphere that I'm in. That's the shocker. And I'm not kissing their ass. I have the full ability to choose to go away if it wasn't like that. I have found over the years that I can trust Joe creatively just as much as when I first met him. So it's a relief, actually. And it's saved me a lot of embarrassment. [laughs]

NRAMA: At what point did you think, "Wow, I've really made it at Marvel." Was it Alias and the fact they made this whole new line based on that comic, taking that risk for your creation?

BMB: Alias was a big one. When they asked for the exclusive contract, that's a big one. And when you start getting calls from, like, I got a call from John Romita Sr. saying that he liked Ultimate Spider-Man. Then I heard from Stan Lee. That's when you get a little glassy-eyed over it, you know? This is working out alright.

But there are little milestones that probably don't mean much to anyone else, that nobody saw but me, like the email from Stan and stuff, that help a great deal.

Yet over the years, things keep happening like that. Like even my last contract when they asked me to be part of the movie stuff, and they've never gone that route with a freelance creator before. There's usually this point where the creator gets mad and leaves or they get mad at a creator and they're gone. And instead we went this other way where things are great. And you're like, Oh this is so nice. Everyone's learning from the past, like I think I do. But you need to be surrounded by people who learn the same way for it to work.

So there have been a lot of things over the years like that. And sometimes it's as simple as looking at the shelf and going, "Oooo! I made a lot of comics! Cool! Alright!"

Newsarama: We talked about your first writing gigs at Marvel, like Ultimate Spider-Man and Daredevil and Alias. What do you think was your next milestone at Marvel? Was it the Avengers?

Brian Michael Bendis: To me, honestly, and this is one not everyone would think of, but the one that made me think, wow, everything's going to work, is Ultimate Marvel Team-Up, and I'll tell you why. They called me up and said, "We want more. We want the Ultimate line to be four. If you have a second title you want to do, you're our first choice." And I said, "Wow, I want to do Marvel Fanfare. And I want to do Marvel Team-up. And I want to squish them into one book. And I want to call creators. We've got every base covered as far as what the Ultimate line means for new readers. But there should be a title that's about the art of comic books. It should be about, 'Look what we have in comics that you can't get anywhere else. We have Bill Sienkiewicz, and Matt Wagner and John Totleben

Art by Ted McKeever

and Jim Mahfood and Chynna Clugston-Major. Look what we have.'"

And by this time, I'm so obsessed with the act of collaboration with artists. Like, I learned the lessons of collaborations so that I'm obsessed with the high of it, that I want that high every month. I want to find an artist, I want them to tell me what they want to draw, and I want to write it for them. Matt Wagner, what do you want to draw? And I said, I bet I'll get awesome issues. So that entire series was me calling my heroes and my peers, and writing for them.

When Marvel was allowing this to go on, I was like, "holy shit." That's when I thought, wow, they're really behind me. And I felt like we did do a little Marvel Fanfare in there.

NRAMA: After that, would your work on the Avengers be the next big milestone?

BMB: Yeah, I guess Avengers was the big one.

NRAMA: I'm not forcing you there. If there was something else...

BMB: Nah, it was a big one. It was a big deal. 'Cause it meant more than just getting the gig. There was a lot more to it behind the scenes, because now things had escalated to the point where Bill Jemas started doing these retreats, and they were flying us to New York, and we were sitting in a big room together. And me and Mark and other creators are pontificating and arguing. So that took it to the next level. We were really part of the team. And things were cooking. Now Marvel was asking us to help with their video games and cartoons. You know? It was like all this other stuff to do, you know?

And the Avengers retreat itself said so much. Because that retreat was where he wrote every character on the wall. And, using Iron Man as an example, he'd go, what is Iron Man about? Not just that we publish it because we own it. What is it supposed to be about and does it do that? Is that the story being told? And we'd come up with, at its core, Iron Man is a boy and his toy. Right? And from there comes Warren Ellis' Extremis story.

So we get to the Avengers, and Mark and I start babbling. And Mark tells a story about how, he lives in Scotland, and if he only had 10 cents, he'd buy the Justice League because you get 10 heroes for the price of one. And that's what cheap Scottish people do. And I said, "Hey, yeah, why aren't Spider-Man and Wolverine on the Avengers?" And Tom Brevoort turned purple and almost killed me. And Bill said, "That's it! They're on the Avengers!" And then it turned into this big fight in the room about, "No, they're not Avengers!" And people started yelling. And when everyone starts yelling at each other, all Bill sees is dollar signs. Usually when we fight in the room, about six months from now, that fight will be happening on the internet. And that means it's a story worth telling.

And there was a question of who would do the Avengers book, between me and Mark. And I did not come there looking for a job. I felt I was good with what I was doing. But this seemed like a story I could tell. Both of us wanted to do it. But Mark was already kind of doing the Avengers, by doing the Ultimates. And doing both was weird. And I was like, "I want to do it." And there you go.

NRAMA: Was that something you always wanted to do? Even before this retreat?

BMB: Oh, I loved the Avengers. I was still trying to figure out the language of team books. Team books have their own language. And a very specific language. And I was still trying to figure out what my version of it is. Because the nature of it is that there is a lot of exposition in the dialogue, just by the nature of it, because everyone's trying to tell everyone who everyone else is. And that kind of offends me as a writer. It didn't bother me as a reader as much. But as a writer, I didn't think I could do it. Then I started saying, well, that's not good enough. As a writer, what would you do? And I thought, this sub-genre of comics needs to take a giant leap forward in its storytelling, but still be fun and exciting and bombastic and stuff. And that's what I've tried to do. I just thought, if this is supposed to be Earth's Mightiest Heroes, it should be Earth's Mightiest Heroes.

NRAMA: It's interesting to hear you talk about retreats taking place during this time, because it's also about the time that all these big "event" comics started happening. Much of what you're writing now, Brian, touches so many other parts of the Marvel Universe and has to be coordinated and planned out with a lot of other people. Do you ever long for the days when you could just write your Daredevil or Alias book and not have to deal with all these big events?

BMB: Well, we can. And we do. A great deal of time is spent doing stuff like that. It's just the louder noise is what people hear. There's all kinds of cool little books being produced. I mean, Spider-Woman, definitely, is well within that description.

NRAMA: Yeah, what's up with Spider-Woman?

BMB: Oh, it's coming. It just took a little more time to produce the motion comic, because we're trying to do something where we're in new water. And it took a little more time to produce it because everyone agrees that it has to be OK. There's a lot riding on it, not just the book itself, but this idea of doing motion comics at all.

NRAMA: We've talked a lot about your work on this and how it's somewhere between comic writing and scripting for animation. How are you feeling about the product?

BMB: Oh, it's fantastic. Holy crap. It's so good. But we needed that to ship a little bit before the comic. I'm literally 10 months ahead. I stopped writing it because I don't know what the Marvel Universe will look like in 10 months. I've got to stop writing.

So it's coming.

NRAMA: I'm going to go off on a tangent here a little bit because you're talking about a book you're doing with Alex Maleev. And your Daredevil run was so defined by his art and your collaboration with him. I remember you talking at a recent con about how attached you get to your artists, and you mentioned earlier how you love the feeling of collaboration and tailoring stories to your artists. Do you still do that kind of thing now? Do you think that's one of your strengths as a writer? Or are you tied down by the event stuff?

BMB: Oh, I definitely still do it. I'm not sure what I do right and wrong. But I absolutely know I do this right. I'm afforded this luxury, and not all my peers are, so I don't want to sound like I do something special. I don't start writing until I know exactly who's drawing it. And I write it imagining the world according to them. Not that I always get what I imagine. But consciously and even subconsciously, an artist knows this, that it's being written for them or to their strengths, which is sometimes something they haven't made the most of yet. Sometimes I'll see a little panel in someone's work and I'll go, see what they're doing there? That's their future.

Even with [Olivier] Coipel, I'm doing something new with him now, and we've been talking since House of M about his page layouts and breakdowns and things he wants to attempt. A very European panel design and I'm eager for him to approach his pages that way. I want him to do what he wants to do.

But most of the time it's not like I come up with a story and say, gee, I wish Jack Kirby was drawing this. I end up writing it, imagining that world. Like now that Stuart Immonen is drawing Avengers, I can't imagine the books but what I imagine Stuart will do with it.

NRAMA: You had said, at the time you came into comics that you thought you, Mark and Paul [Jenkins] were offering a new voice for the industry.

BMB: And other people too. Those names just came to mind.

NRAMA: But do you think that is going to happen again? Or is Marvel looking to change the voice of comics again? Or have you adjusted to the new direction?

BMB: Well, nothing's broken. I think everything's doing alright. But I always have high hopes for people. And sometimes they really pan out, and sometimes they don't. It's more than just writing. Even like we talked about the internet relationship, for some writers — some have a great mystique that pulls them along while some can't handle that. People choose to handle that differently. I choose to be very much there. Some people choose not to be anywhere near it. But that's part of it. And a writer having the right book. Finding the book that's perfect for them. It's career management as well. One bad choice and you can really knock yourself down the stairs again. So there have been a lot of people over the last 10 years that we had a lot of hopes for, but they didn't quite make it. Or they just did good on their independent books, but mainstream wasn't really for them, even though we thought it would be.

But right now there are three or four guys that we're all hugely rooting for. And I really want them to have all that I've experienced. I'm a huge fan of comics. I just want as many good comics a month as I can get. So yeah, there are a couple good guys that are coming up. I don't know if there's a movement as such. There are a few guys that Marvel's already labeled. These "Write Stuff" guys. They're pals of ours. Those guys particularly, we're really rooting for them. Jason [Aaron] and Jon Hickman and [Rick] Remender and [Andy] Diggle. Not that those are the only guys, but those are the ones with that "young guns" writer label, even though I think half of them are older than me. But we want good comics.

NRAMA: What's your next challenge at Marvel?

BMB: I don't want to say yet because I already have it approved. We just came back from a retreat where we had a lot of homework to do. It wasn't just a retreat where you come in and see what happens. Joe gave us an assignment, which is about where he feels comics will be in the next two years. You know how you were asking about, do you wish things were different than they were with the events? Well, something may happen that will be different. So we came up with all our pitches. And mine were all approved, which was pretty cool. And almost everyone came out of there richer when they left. So I do have some challenges coming up.

Plus working on all the movie stuff with Kevin [Feige of Marvel Studios] and the creative committees on the movies. That's a lot of fun. I've got to tell ya. That is a lot of fun. The Iron Man 2 script is so good. I've had to read it 30 times now.

NRAMA: I don't think most people are aware of your movie work. Do you spend a lot of time doing that part of your job?

BMB: It's kind of like everything in Hollywood. There are giant spurts where there are a ton of things to do, and a ton of things to read, but then there will be nothing for a few weeks. And everything in Hollywood is like that. Everything I do in L.A., they're like, "do it right now! We need it right now!" We'll be working and working and then just all of a sudden, it's not there anymore.

Like the Iron Man, Cap and Thor outlines all came in in a day. And they all had to be read by Friday. You know? But this week, all the writers are writing and there's nothing to do.

NRAMA: So what exactly is your job here, Brian? Are you just reviewing outlines?

BMB: No, this is a little different than how Hollywood usually does it, which is a compliment to Kevin. Usually, Hollywood just does what it does. I know there are some comic book movies I hear that the people never even read a comic book based on the thing they're working on.

They've asked me to be part of this team of guys who they pick their brains and take their advice. And for me it's great to watch these writers deal with it and handle it. Watching them is a lot of fun.

And they fly us out. Like, when Kenneth Branagh was hired for Thor, they flew us out and we got to spend the day listening to a seven-hour performance of what he imagines the Thor movie would be.

NRAMA: Seven hours?

BMB: No, but it was Shakespearean, with flourishes. It was cool. It was a lot of fun. My wife goes, OK, that one I'm jealous of. She's got a crush on him. And honestly, he's not a let-down. I can see it. I can understand it. You're spending enough time with someone that you know if they're cool. And he's cool.

But one thing I'm thinking of and I want to say before anything else. There was something else that was unbelievable to me throughout these 10 years, and this

Art by David Lafuente

is something I should say: the Icon line. I didn't know Dan Buckley that well. He's the reason I'm on the creative committee for the movies. And he's also the one who started the Icon line and gave Powers a home. If you think back, that was insane and seemed like it would never happen. And it's been years now and they've been unbelievably generous with us in giving us a home to tell our stories on our book. I know some people say, "Yeah, but it's not for everybody." But every comic company, it's not for everybody. But this was one of the times I went, wow, I backed the right pony.

NRAMA: Can you explain what you mean by "it's not for everybody?"

BMB: Oh, yeah, when I say Icon gives you a place for your creator-owned books, some people get sore that it's only for certain creators. Because it's not for everybody, and you have to be making Marvel money for it to be offered to you. Dan has said that in interviews. But the existence of it is great.

I mean, I look back, and I got to do the Ultimate line when there was no Ultimate line; I got to do the Max line before there was a Max line; and I got to do the Icon line when there wasn't an Icon line. And now we're doing the digital comics. I love that they keep entrusting me with these firsts. And I haven't done anything horribly embarrassing yet.

NRAMA: When we talked about the next stage of the Ultimate Universe, we talked about how it's no longer going to focus on "new twists" of existing Marvel characters, but will instead have a lot of new characters and new villains. Newsarama has spoken recently with a couple people at DC about this effort to "recharge" with new characters,

and now you're saying that the Ultimate Universe is concentrating on that same thing. It's certainly a hallmark of the current Green Lantern run, and a lot of these "Write Stuff" guys you've talked about are doing it. Is this a new trend in the industry? To create new characters?

BMB: There are two things at work here as to why this is happening. Number one, there's so many characters in both companies, and you can include other publishers' characters too. But if you're working at Marvel and you come up with someone who's a lot like the Wasp, then don't do that character. Just do the Wasp. Don't do a shittier version of it. But at the same time, our generation is very aware that anyone can create the new Joker or Lobo or whatever. Even the third lead in the Omega Men could end up being Lobo. And you don't want to create a situation for yourself where you create Deadpool and he's in a movie and you're pissed off. You want to create a situation where you're like Rob [Liefeld] and you're excited about it. So you want to make sure you've created something you're proud of.

NRAMA: Wait, can you explain that point about Deadpool?

BMB: You see Rob on Twitter and he's very happy. I actually don't know Rob. I'm just saying that I follow him on Twitter, and I see how he reacts to this character he created, and I'm saying I'd rather be that guy than Alan Moore who's all pissed about the contracts he signed. That's all I'm saying.

And we're all aware of that now. We're all grown-ups. We're not just all gung-ho and putting on a show. We're aware that any one of these creations could be a huge movie franchise.

NRAMA: And your point is that, therefore, the industry is more concentrated on creating new, quality characters?

BMB: I feel comfortable for myself to do so. I created the Secret Warriors and other characters that are coming up through the pipeline that I feel that way about. I think Dan Buckley has created a situation for me and other people where it's encouraging us to create. And I think people are feeling that.

And also, it feels like the master class of comic book stuff once you've written the super heroes and kind of analyzed the icons and judged them. So creating things that aren't just like Batman is something you just have to do. It's like, what do I have to offer? And what is the modern version of it?

Also, when enough time goes by. The world's different than it was even when I started at Marvel. The whole world is different. Information is different. So what would the super heroes of this world be? You have to remember, even in the '70s, they were creating super heroes that were whatever was popular in movies that week. "Oh, here's our Bruce Lee. Here's our surfer." You really couldn't do that today. It's hilarious. Despite how much we love those characters, that wouldn't work today. "Oh, what's popular at the box office? Hangover? I made Hangover Man!" You can't do it.

NRAMA: I never really thought of it that way, but you look at a lot of the villains of the '60s and '70s and they're based on what we feared at the time.

BMB: When Mark and I first met each other and we were flown up to New York and were sitting in Joe's office, we were talking about the Ultimate Universe, right when it was starting. And we were talking about, what does the Ultimate Universe mean? What did the Marvel Universe mean? And the entire Marvel Universe was born out of nuclear paranoia and the Cold War. Every single character is an irradiated version of something. This is what will happen if I get irradiated. And all of it was born out of that. And today, we're not fearful of that. We're fearful of other things. We have more of a genetic fear than a radiation fear. We don't live in a Cold War; we think we're being poisoned.

NRAMA: It's a "new science" kind of fear.

BMB: Yeah. So you think about it, and that's part of why there's this feeling that we've got something new with these new characters. But it's just reflecting the world we're living in. And you don't even realize it. Even Stan and those guys didn't realize they were doing it until afterward. It's a writer thing. I've done that. I've written whole stories of stuff, even in mainstream comics, where I didn't realize what I had done.

NRAMA: So you get this reviewer saying, "He was clearly making a comment on this aspect of modern society," and you realize you were?

BMB: Yeah, but even sometimes it's personal. Like, even the stuff about Jessica and Luke's baby. I wasn't even aware until I thought about it later, and I thought, wow, thank God I have an outlet for this fatherly neurosis.

And not to be too dramatic, but my wife had had an allergic reaction to a medication she had never taken before, and she went into a coma. And they told me that was it. She was never coming out. Her brain tissue had swelled. And that's brain damage. And that's it.

And I literally had a six-month-old baby. And they told me, here's a beeper. We'll let you know if anything has changed. Just go take care of the baby. And literally just four days later, everything was fine. It's been six years and she's fine.

I wrote, over the course of that year, at least 11 coma scenes. There's the Kingpin looking at his wife, there's Jessica looking at Luke. Everyone's in a coma. And I didn't even realize I was doing it. The artwork would come back and I would say, "What the f__k am I doing?" I mean, I had to be the strong guy, but it's amazing how these fictional characters can take on the role filling therapeutic needs.

NRAMA: That begs the question, as we finish up this interview, how has this affected you over the last 10 years? Is your neurosis gone now that you're the Kingpin at Marvel?

BMB: [laughs] I've always been a perfect stew of arrogance and self-loathing. Like, I have all the arrogance to push forward and write my comics and make my comics and do my thing, but at the same time I'm going, "Why? why? why?!!" So yeah, I'm able to balance that very nicely. I try not to pick at that scab too much, because it seems to have worked out.

NRAMA: And there are probably some stories that come out of that.

BMB: Yeah. I'd be a fool not to be aware of it. But yeah, when I first got to Marvel I was newly married, living in Cleveland. Now I have two children and I'm in Portland. And this job has given me the chance to travel all over the world and meet people and hear hundreds of stories about how much these characters mean personally to people, in every language you can imagine. I remember when Issue #50 came out of Ultimate Spider-Man, these soldiers in Afghanistan had flown an issue of Ultimate Spider-Man over the country and then framed it with a patch that it had flown over Afghanistan as a thank you to me. It's all they had for fun, you know? They had one movie and some TV and this comic. And they wrote this whole letter.

And not to get all weird about it, but the responsibility of it never leaves me, that someone really needs to relax and this is how they're going to relax. And this is how they're having fun. And I've had that feeling where I've had a really bad day and I think, please, I hope this cheers me up. This comic excites me or does something cool.

NRAMA: But that's affected you personally?

BMB: Absolutely. Every single thing that has happened, all of these things, have affected me dramatically. I take the fun aspect of comics very seriously. Not to sound like a dork. That was very "Inside the Actors Studio" of me. But literally every day I get mail from people that are just having a great time and are really relying on me for it, and have been very, very loyal to me and my work. And every whacked out thing I've done. I mean, I've not delivered the same product every year. I try something new every year. And I thank God I have enough people into that. People who are into me trying all these different things enough that I've been able to do it. So I take their loyalty very seriously. •